Homilies on the
Gospel of John 1-40

Augustinian Heritage Institute, Inc.

www.augustinianheritage.org

Board of Directors

+ John E. Rotelle, O.S.A. (1939-2002), founding director

Michael T. Dolan
Joseph T. Kelley
Thomas Martin, O.S.A.

Daniel E. Doyle, O.S.A.
Patricia H. Lo
Jane E. Merdinger

Boniface Ramsey

Translation Advisory Board

Gerald Bonner
Allan D. Fitzgerald, O.S.A.
Joseph McGowan

+Maria Boulding, O.S.B.
Edmund Hill, O.P.
Boniface Ramsey

Roland J. Teske, S.J.

THE WORKS OF SAINT AUGUSTINE
A Translation for the 21st Century

Part III – Homilies

Volume 12:

Homilies on the Gospel of John 1-40

THE WORKS OF SAINT AUGUSTINE
A Translation for the 21st Century

Homilies on the Gospel of John 1-40

I/12

translation and notes by
Edmund Hill, O.P.

*edited and with an
introduction and notes by*
Alan Fitzgerald, O.S.A.

series editor
Boniface Ramsey

New City Press
Hyde Park, New York

Published in the United States by New City Press
202 Comforter Blvd., Hyde Park, New York 12538
©2009 Augustinian Heritage Institute

Cover design by Leandro De Leon
Cover picture: Artwork located in the Augustinian monastery in Würzburg (Germany)

Library of Congress Cataloging-in-Publication Data:

Augustine, Saint, Bishop of Hippo.
    The works of Saint Augustine.
    "Augustinian Heritage Institute"
    Includes bibliographical references and indexes.
    Contents: — pt. 3, v .15. Expositions of the Psalms, 1-32
—pt. 3, v. 1. Sermons on the Old Testament, 1-19.
— pt. 3, v. 2. Sermons on the Old Testament, 20-50 — [et al.] — pt. 3,
v. 10 Sermons on various subjects, 341-400.
    1.   Theology — Early church, ca. 30-600.   I. Hill,
Edmund.   II. Rotelle, John E.   III. Augustinian
Heritage Institute.   IV. Title.
BR65.A5E53   1990   270.2   89-28878

ISBN 978-1-56548-055-1 (series)
ISBN 978-1-56548-319-4 (cloth)
ISBN 978-1-56548-318-7 (paperb.)

Printed in the United States of America

Contents

Introduction · · · · · · · · · · · · · · · · · · · 9
Some Technical Matters · · · · · · · · · · · · · 25
Dates · 27
Bibliography · · · · · · · · · · · · · · · · · · · 35
Editor's Notes · · · · · · · · · · · · · · · · · · 38
Homily 1 · 39
Homily 2 · 55
Homily 3 · 68
Homily 4 · 86
Homily 5 · 101
Homily 6 · 121
Homily 7 · 145
Homily 8 · 168
Homily 9 · 183
Homily 10 · 197
Homily 11 · 210
Homily 12 · 228
Homily 13 · 242
Homily 14 · 260
Homily 15 · 275
Homily 16 · 297
Homily 17 · 305
Homily 18 · 320

Homily 19 · 334
Homily 20 · 357
Homily 21 · 371
Homily 22 · 389
Homily 23 · 405
Homily 24 · 423
Homily 25 · 430
Homily 26 · 449
Homily 27 · 466
Homily 28 · 477
Homily 29 · 489
Homily 30 · 496
Homily 31 · 504
Homily 32 · 515
Homily 33 · 524
Homily 34 · 532
Homily 35 · 542
Homily 36 · 557
Homily 37 · 565
Homily 38 · 575
Homily 39 · 586
Homily 40 · 594

Introduction

An introduction to a fifth-century book can safely presume that the reader wants something more than an invitation to begin to read. And yet introducing a reader into Augustine's *Homilies on the Gospel of John* requires something other than a summary of its contents—even if such a feat were possible. As the first and only commentary dedicated to the Gospel of John in ancient Latin literature, something significant and quite unique is found here.[1] More than a general theological treatise on Christ or on the Church, more than an example of Augustine's many exegetical skills, these homilies are part of the bond that tied him to his people—and he is quite explicit about wanting to make his understandings and the results of his searchings theirs: "That I should be nourished by it according to my capacity, and that I should serve to you what has nourished me."[2]

The commentary on the Gospel of John—a set of 124 homilies on John's gospel—is part of the history of that interaction, combining a certain concreteness with its universal (and universally applicable) perspectives. By participating in the interchange between Augustine and his listeners, this commentary also asks today's reader to relate to the gospel as they did,[3] to appreciate who Jesus Christ was for them and for their Church, and to understand—both for that time and for today—how all this attention to the Gospel of John gives rise to new insights and renewed insight. These introductory pages thus seek to provide a limited historical context, to suggest why Augustine chose to undertake a commentary on this gospel, and to show what it means to say that this work was—from beginning to end—a theology in the making, a work-in-progress.

---

1. Some attention has been given to the relationship of this commentary to those found in Greek literature; D.J. Milewski, *"Nec locus Dei sumus.* Augustine's Exegesis and the Theology of John 17 in the light of *In Evangelium Iohannis Tractatus CIV-CXI*" (Doctoral dissertation, Augustinian Patristic Institute, 2000) 59 describes the influence of previous Greek commentaries on this one as the "subtle persuasiveness of the ancient Christian heritage"—but he indicates no dependence on previous commentaries.
2. Homily 2,1: *Et pro nostra capacitate pascamur, et ministremus uobis unde et nos pascimur.* Henceforth the *Homilies on the Gospel of John* will be referred to in the notes simply as Homilies (or, individually, as Homily.)
3. Homily 3,18 says, *evangelium interroga*, i.e.,"interrogate the Gospel," suggesting a strong, interactive process.

Returning regularly to the tight connection that he establishes between Christ who already was *in the beginning* (Jn 1:1) and Christ who *took up residence among us* (Jn 1:14), Augustine repeatedly asks his listeners to pay attention to that framework so that they might grow in knowledge and in understanding. Rather than asking his listeners to learn what their bishop thinks,[4] Augustine tries to place them—and us—at the feet of the one who alone teaches (Mt 23:10); for his love has been poured into our hearts (Rom 5:5) so that we might all be one in him. The reader of this commentary is thus invited to journey through the gospel with Augustine and his community and to be fellow seekers with them.

What is a tractatus*? a homily, a sermon, a tractate?*[5]

In early Christian Latin, *tractatus* could be a technical word, i.e., preaching that was "exegetical in nature, didactic in purpose, and geared toward a deeper, more sophisticated understanding of the Bible and its doctrines than the usual liturgical homily."[6] Augustine speaks of "popular tractates" (*tractatus populares*) as well as of "sermons," which the Greeks call "homilies."[7] Augustine's language was once described as "fluctuating,"[8] a characterization which can also be applied to his use of *tractatus*, *sermo* and *homilia*. Something similar could be said about his works on the psalms and on the First Epistle of John.

But, no matter how they are called, the *Homilies on the Gospel of John* are instruction based on and rooted in the scriptures: "We are called interpreters (*tractatores*) of the scriptures, not those who assert their own

---

4. *The Teacher* 14,45: "Do teachers claim that their own thoughts and not the disciplines about which they speak are what pupils perceive and retain? Who, indeed, is so silly as to send a child to school to learn what the teacher thinks?" (*Num hoc magistri profitentur, ut cogitata eorum ac non ipsae disciplinae, quas loquendo se tradere putant, percipiantur atque teneantur? nam quis tam stulte curiosus est, qui filium suum mittat ad scholam, ut quid magister cogitet discat?*)
5. See Milewski 62-65. Those pages are briefly summarized here.
6. Ibid. 63. See Augustine's description in *Teaching Christianity* IV,4,6.
7. See Letter 224, 2: "sermons to the people which the Greeks call homilies" (*tractatus populares quos Graece homilias vocant*). For Augustine's use of "sermon," see Homilies 105, 8; 108, 5; 120, 9.
8. That is, *flottant*. See H.-I. Marrou, *Saint Augustin et la fin de la culture antique* (Paris: É. de Boccard, 1949) 245.

opinions."⁹ The authority of Christian preaching is found in its fidelity to the scriptures, not in the education, the logic or the persuasiveness of the preacher, and preaching is the encounter of the community with Christ, not just something that the speaker does.

The homilies on John "combine a high level of exegetical skill and sophisticated doctrinal content within the unpredictable, popular setting of a diversified and boisterous Christian community,"¹⁰ and Augustine saw himself as Christ's minister, seeking to "instruct, correct, and deepen the awareness of the Bible's implications for all aspects of life, no matter how spiritually mature or immature the listeners were."¹¹

D. J. Milewski aptly summarizes:

> [T]he tractates attempt to achieve a seemingly impossible goal: the delivery of a detailed, intricate exegetical and theological discourse to a frequently unpredictable general audience.... [Augustine] walks a tightrope between the restrictions of a formal commentary on the one hand and the greater textual liberty of a popular sermon on the other, and, in so doing, the bishop gives these tractates a certain universal accessibility based upon their doctrinal content and not dependent upon any historically specific occasion or audience.¹²

Initial perspectives

The Gospel of John had singular significance in Augustine's life—at least from the time of his stay in Milan. In his description of the final stages of his conversion, the prologue of that gospel helped him to appreciate the value of the Christian scriptures as different and far superior to the doctrines of the neo-Platonists.¹³ John's words also explained and enhanced what he once felt about the name of Christ, which he drank in with his mother milk, and what he found when he read the *Hortensius*, which had inflamed him with a desire to find a wisdom that did not exclude that name.¹⁴ His spiritual yearnings thus

---

9. Sermon 270, 3: *Scripturarum tractatores dicimur, non nostrarum opinionum affirmatores.*
10. Milewski 65.
11. Ibid. 64-65.
12. Ibid. 70-71.
13. See *Confessions* VII,9,13-14.
14. See ibid. III,4,7-8.

engaged both heart and mind.[15] But, while his spiritual journey had found its biblical base, it accentuated his need to grapple with its mystery and to become stretched by it. After many years he would remember and record the words of Simplician about the prologue of John: "This passage should be inscribed in letters of gold and set up in the most prominent place in every church."[16]

In all of Augustine's preaching, that prologue would be a mainstay,[17] a text that was ever more fully intertwined with his experience and with his understanding of other biblical texts, and especially with those in the epistles of Saint Paul.[18] But, early in the fifth century, when he spoke of his desire to comment on the whole Gospel of John "without skipping any passage,"[19] that was more than a personal challenge. From the beginning of his priesthood he had recognized his need to examine the scriptures closely so as to discover how to exercise his ministry for the salvation of others.[20] Jesus' actions in the Gospel of John "not only stir up our hearts by their wondrous quality, but build them up in the teachings of the faith as well."[21] The programmatic dimension of that observation is only reinforced: "Please give the undivided attention of your heart to the gospel."[22]

Fuller appreciation of how the words of John's gospel would be part of his response to a certain way of understanding Jesus Christ and the Church will be one of the benefits of a thoughtful reading of his commentary. John's words challenge "grown-up minds, who have reached an inner maturity," giving them something to exercise and nourish them.[23] Again and again he will note how that challenge was not the same for everyone,

---

15. See, e.g., T. Martin, *Our Restless Heart: The Augustinian Tradition* (London: Darton, Longman and Todd, 2003) 15-16 on Augustinian spirituality as thoughtful.
16. *The City of God* X, 29.
17. Jn 1:1 is cited at least 250 times and the first 8 verses of the prologue are cited more than 1000 times. See H. I. Marrou, *St. Augustine and His Influence through the Ages* (New York: Harper, 1957) 83.
18. G. Madec, *La Patrie et La Voie* (Paris: Desclée, 1989) 35-50; E. Cassidy, *"Per Christum hominem ad Christum Deum*: Augustine's Homilies on John's Gospel," in T. Finan and V. Twomey, eds., *Studies in Patristic Christology* (Dublin: Four Courts Press, 1998) 122-143.
19. Homily 2, 1: *nullum locum praetermittens*.
20. See Letter 21, 4 to Valerius, his bishop, where, shortly after being ordained a priest (391), Augustine asked for some "time off" so as to learn what the scriptures would tell him about how to care for the needs of others—that they might be saved (see 1 Cor 10,33).
21. Homily 9, 1: *Non solum ualent ad excitanda corda nostra miraculis, sed etiam ad aedificanda in doctrina fidei*.
22. Homily 12, 1: *Tota intentio cordis ad euangelium feratur*.
23. Homily 18, 1: *Grandiusculis autem quibusque mentibus et ad aetatem quamdam interius uirilem peruenientibus, dat aliquid uerbis his, quo et exerceantur, et pascantur*.

and we can appreciate how he adapted his words to the needs, the capacity, and the experience of the people of Hippo. But, even there, his effort to "exercise" their minds and hearts is fully grounded in the words of the gospel—challenging old habits of thinking and acting and providing food for thoughtful growth. We may never fully know why Augustine decided to begin this commentary, but what he said about the progress he recognized in his listeners may provide a glimpse into what made him persevere:

> When we exercise ourselves in these things, and then return again, as it were by our own weight, to that which is habitual, we are like bleary-eyed people who . . , when brought into the daylight, also begin to recover some of their sight, thanks to the doctor's treatment. . . . So then, brothers and sisters, if by any chance something like that has happened in your hearts, if you have lifted up your heart to see the Word, and, stunned by his light, have fallen back into your old habits, ask the doctor to apply some stinging eye-salve—the precepts of justice. There is something to see, but you do not succeed in seeing it. Earlier, you were not believing me that there was something for you to see, but you were led forward with some reasoning as a guide; you drew near, you took a good look, your heart beat faster—you took to flight.[24] You certainly now know that there is something for you to see, but that you are not fit to see it. So then, carry on with the cure.[25]

Thus does he often "stand on the cusp" of human experience: having sight and yet not seeing; believing and yet needing increase. Such is the dynamic of his thinking, of his preaching, of his hope for his listeners: by recognizing what already is, he constantly invites his listeners to grow (*crescere, dilatare, augmentare*), by clinging (*adhaerere*) to God, and by forward-reaching faith. Thus are they called to turn away from unworthy habits, temptation and sin[26] toward forgiveness[27] and toward an understanding of God's design of salvation in Christ.[28] What has nourished Augustine in this gospel becomes nourishment for his listeners.[29]

---

24. See Sermon 52, 16; *The Trinity* XII, 24, 23; XV, 6, 10; *Exposition of Psalm* 41, 10.
25. Homily 18, 11.
26. See Homily 49, 3, 14.
27. See Homilies 31, 9; 33, 7-8; 45, 12.
28. Homilies 9, 9-10; 17, 1.
29. Homily 2, 1.

A neglected work

Given all the richness that Augustine found in John's gospel, one may rightly wonder why, over the years, this commentary has failed to hold the interest of scholars. Except for the studies on technical matters, such as its dating, composition, transmission and provenance,[30] the commentary on John's gospel has received too little attention.[31] One explanation for that neglect can be found in the tendency of scholars to study those works which were most well-known or most readily available, for example, the *Confessions* and *The City of God*. In other cases, however, the tendency was to focus on those works which were seen as useful in the conduct of doctrinal disputes. Since the sixteenth century, in fact, the polemical works of Augustine which dealt with such issues as the sacraments, grace and freedom have been claimed by each "side" to support sometimes opposing positions.[32] That interest in doctrinal—rather than in historical or pastoral—issues was dominant for much of the twentieth century. The writings of the early Church Fathers were often treated as proof-texts, thus failing to give them their own value.

Along with that rather general explanation, however, another can be suggested. In his commentary, Augustine is always—in more or less subtle ways —connecting the Gospel of John to the experience of the local community. Such theology-in-context thus asks the reader to appreciate more than the interpretation of the gospel text itself, since Augustine interprets it according to the socio-cultural experiences and the thought-patterns of his people. That can be a source of discouragement or of confusion to a modern reader—whether that reader is looking for spiritual nourishment, exegetical insight or theological clarity. Since the historical circumstances of a given homily are part of the message, an unsuspecting reader can be put off and fail to be "on the same page" as Augustine. Hence, the fact that this is a fifth-century book could mean that a reader who is not well-versed in the life and history of those for whom it was first intended

---

30. D.J. Milewski, "Augustine's 124 Tractates on the Gospel of John: *The Status Quaestionis* and the State of Neglect," *Augustinian Studies* 33/1 (2002) 61-77.
31. See ibid. 61.
32. See A. Fitzgerald, "Tracing the passage from a doctrinal to an historical approach to the study of Augustine," *Revue des Études Augustiniennes et Patristiques* 50/2 (2004) 295-310.

might set it aside. It is, after all, a series of sermons rather than a book that neatly connects all of its homilies to one another. Hence, it may be helpful to think about reading it in the way one thinks about a conversation with a friend. Whether we are renewing an old friendship or developing a new one, each conversation involves a kind of soul-stretching: a friend, no matter how well known, will never be fully known; thus is a friend a constant invitation into something more, into mystery.

Hence, although it may not be surprising that this commentary has been given limited attention, the renewed interest in educating in the faith that is evident today may help us—like the Christians of Hippo before us—to come to these sermons with patient longing, persevering at least because Augustine asks us (with them) to do so. For this gospel has again today found a central place in the liturgical year and in baptismal catechesis. That may make it easier for us to ask *how* Augustine drew his listeners into the Johannine text.

Questioning[33]

From the first accounts that he gives us of his youth, Augustine was always asking questions. Later, as bishop, he would question creation about God and affirm, "My questioning was my attentive spirit, and their reply was their beauty."[34] The interplay between someone who seeks and the created world illustrates one aspect of the process whereby questioning creation leads to a fuller understanding of the creator. But his questioning also had a specifically human dimension—most evident perhaps in his self-questioning and in the questions asked of others.

Augustine's self-questioning was not psychological introspection or mere general curiosity. See, for example, how he characterizes his searching in his words to Honoratus in *The Advantage of Believing*: "I felt that I should not keep from you my thoughts about finding and holding to the truth. This, as you know, has been my burning passion since early

---

33. See the reflections of J.-L. Chrétien, *Saint Augustin et les actes de parole* (Paris: Presses Universitaires de France, 2002) 13-23 for a more extended reflection on questioning in Augustine.
34. *Confessions* X, 6, 9: *Interrogatio mea intentio mea, et responsio eorum species eorum.* See too *Exposition of Psalm* 144, 13: "As you reflect on these things you long to question the earth; your searching is an asking of questions" (*Vides, et consideratione tua tamquam interrogas eam; et ipsa inquisitio interrogatio est*); Sermon 241, 2: *pulchritudo eorum, confessio eorum.*

youth."[35] By probing his spirit again and again, he came to discover his heart—and to listen to the truth that had been placed there.[36] That process appears to have become a model for the way he interacted with others as well. How often, after all, does Augustine interject a phrase which invites his listeners to search *with* him, to listen *with* him, to ask for insight *with* him![37] He clearly trusts them—and, again and again, entrusts himself to their ability to question with him, to search with him. Hence, the recommendation to "ask your heart"[38] is something more than a rhetorical device; it is situated within a process which passes from words to practical experience.[39] The request that he makes in one of his homilies, "Let us knock together" (see Mt 7:8), shows that Augustine was creating the homily on the spot, i.e., his searching did not finish with the preparation for speaking; new insights could come from the very process of communicating with his listeners: "I think that I can either grasp them when I ponder them, or that they can be grasped when I am speaking!"[40] For even if he knew within what he wanted to say, bringing one's thoughts to expression was not simply a matter of speaking; it engaged speaker and listeners in a new effort, in a renewed search for shared understanding,[41] for a fuller participation in that same mystery.

At the end of the fourth homily on the Gospel of John, there is more than a hint of how important it had become for Augustine to raise questions. Knowing how difficult it was for his people to deal with the Catholic-Donatist division of Christianity, he asks them to continue to reflect on the question he had asked about John the Baptist's knowledge of Christ. He

---

35. *The Advantage of Believing* 1, 1: *Dum haec ergo ita sint, non putaui apud te silendum esse, quid mihi de inuenienda ac retinenda ueritate uideatur, cuius, ut scis, ab ineunte adulescentia magno amore flagrauimus.*
36. See Rom 5, 5; *Homily on the First Epistle of John* 6, 10.
37. Homily 20, 6: "So return with me to what I was saying, and perhaps the question may be understood in such a way that we can both get beyond it" (*Redi ergo me cum ad id quod dicebam, ne forte sic intellegendum sit, ut de quaestione ambo exeamus*).
38. *Exposition of Psalm* 98, 3: *Interroga cor tuum*; *Homily on the First Epistle of John* 6, 10: *Interroget cor suum.*
39. *City of God* XVI, 32: *Non verbo, sed experimento temptatione quodam modo interrogante.*
40. Homily 36, 5. In many places Augustine also speaks about knocking at the door of truth so as to come to understanding (see Mt 7:7), e.g., Homily 15, 6: "May he open the door both to me and to you." See too Homilies 8, 3; 18, 1; 32, 6; 40, 10; 45, 7; 57, 4; *Teaching Christianity* IV, 15, 32.
41. See Augustine's words to Deogratias about the difference between words in the mind and words that are spoken, *Instructing Beginners in Faith* 2,3-2,4.

asks them to think about it between then and the next occasion he will talk with them: "Until the matter is solved, ask questions about it peaceably, without wrangling, without raising voices, without in-fighting, without mutual hostility; look for answers together and question other people, and say, 'This is the problem our bishop put to us today; if the Lord will allow it, he will soon resolve it. But whether it is solved or not, believe me that I have set you a problem that bothers me. Yes, it bothers me a lot.'"[42]

But the questions are not merely from Augustine's lips. He asks his listeners to let the text of the gospel question them, exercising their minds and hearts when the text is obscure: "They are tested by obscure passages of scripture ... prompting them to ask questions." But, he continues, Christians are not worn out by the difficulty but "exercised by the obscurity of such things; when they discover the meaning, they are not puffed up but strengthened."[43] Thus do questions give Augustine a way to continue to grow along with his listeners:[44] "If we are forging ahead in the charity by which we love things known and desire things still to be known, the Holy Spirit is both teaching the faithful now—insofar as each of us is capable of grasping spiritual things—and kindling a greater desire in our hearts as well."[45]

---

42. Homily 4,16: *Donec soluatur; interrogate pacifice, sine rixa, sine contentione, sine altercationibus, sine inimicitiis; et uobiscum quaerite, et alios interrogate, et dicite: hanc quaestionem proposuit nobis hodie episcopus noster, aliquando si dominus concesserit, soluturus eam. sed siue soluatur siue non soluatur, putate me proposuisse quid me mouet: moueor enim multum.*
43. *Exposition of Psalm* 10, 8: *Hi quippe quibusdam scripturarum locis obscuris ... exercentur ut quaerant ... qui neque fatigantur rerum obscuritate, sed exercentur, neque inflantur cognitione, sed confirmantur.* See too *Teaching Christianity* 2, 6, 8.
44. Homily 38, 9: Augustine asks his listeners to think about Christ's words, *Unless you believe that I am* [Jn 8:24], saying: "Will I dare question the Lord? Listen to me questioning, not arguing, seeking more than assuming I know the answer, learning rather than teaching; and, in fact, in me or through me, you too should be raising questions. The Lord, who is everywhere, is also close by; may he listen to the affection of his questioners and give them understanding." (*Debo ipsum dominum interrogare? audite me interrogantem potius quam disputantem, magis quaerentem quam praesumentem, potius discentem quam docentem, et certe in me uel per me etiam uos interrogate. praesto est etiam ipse dominus qui ubique est, audiat interrogandi affectum, et intellegendi praestet effectum.*) Note the next section of the homily, where Augustine appeals to the inner Teacher.
45. Homily 38, 10: *Ipse ergo spiritus sanctus et nunc docet fideles, quanta quisque potest capere spiritalia, et eorum pectora desiderio maiore succendit, si quisque in ea caritate proficiat, qua et diligat cognita, et cognoscenda desideret.* See too *Homily on the First Epistle of John* 3, 13; Sermon 340A, 4.

John the Evangelist

Who was John the Evangelist?[46] Augustine believed that John, the disciple whom Jesus loved,[47] was the author of this gospel,[48] and he calls John a mountain,[49] an eagle,[50] the evangelist who rose above all of creation.[51] But, most significantly, he stresses that what John knew, what John wrote about the Word of God—especially about the eternal origins of the Word (*In the beginning was the Word*)—was something that he had received. He learned it at the Last Supper when "he laid his head on the Lord's breast and from the Lord's breast drank in what he would give us to drink."[52] Throughout his writings, the episode in the life of John the Evangelist when he drank from the Lord's breast (Jn. 13:23-26) is the one that Augustine recalls frequently and insistently.[53] "Notice, John poured himself out for us like a running brook, he brought us the Word from on high, humbled him and, in a way, lowered him to ground level, so that we might not dread the exalted one, but might approach the humble one."[54]

Why does Augustine cite that event so often? What does that repetition tell us about Augustine's motivation for commenting on the Gospel of John? In fact, existing scholarship does not seem to have given much attention to the concrete social circumstances that may have motivated Augustine. M. Pontet once suggested that Augustine chose to explain this gospel

---

46. See M.-F. Berrouard, Bibliotheque Augustinienne [henceforth BA] 71, 55-63 for a more complete exposition of Augustine's interest in John the Evangelist.
47. Homilies 16, 2; 113, 2; *Homily on the First Epistle of John* 5, 1; Sermons 120, 1; 244, 1; 245, 1; 253, 3-4. Even though Jesus loved all of the apostles, he loved John "more closely, in a more familiar way than the rest; for, at the supper he had him recline against his breast. That, I like to think, was to commend more profoundly the divine superiority of this gospel." (Homily 119, 2)
48. See BA 71, 39-40. Augustine believed that this John was also the author of the Johannine epistles and of the Book of Revelation.
49. Homilies 1, 5.6; 2, 5.
50. Homilies 15, 1; 36, 1.5; 40, 1; 48, 6.
51. Homily 48, 6; see too Homilies 1, 5; 15, 1; 20, 13; 36, 1.5.
52. Homily 1, 7: *Inde qui haec dixit, accepit Iohannes ille, fratres, qui discumbebat super pectus domini, et de pectore domini bibebat quod propinaret nobis.* See Berrouard's discussion of this oft-cited episode (BA 71, 57-60): Homilies 61, 4; 1, 7; 16, 2; 18, 1; 20,1; 36, 1; 119, 2; 124, 7; *Homilies on the First Epistle of John* 1, 8; 5, 1; *Exposition of Psalm* 144, 9; *The Harmony of the Gospels* 1, 4, 7; 4, 10, 19-20; Sermons 34, 1, 2; 119, 1; 120, 1; 305A, 9; *The Gift of Perseverance* 9, 21.
53. See BA 71, 40.
54. Homily 21, 12: *Ecce ipse Iohannes nobis tamquam riuulus emanauit, perduxit ad nos de alto uerbum, humiliauit, et quodammodo strauit, ut non horreamus altum, sed accedamus ad humilem.*

because of "a deep affinity between his temperament and that of the spiritual gospel." M.-F. Berrouard says that the teaching on Christ that is found in John's gospel was an important motivating factor.[55] Agostino Vita highlights the pastoral quality of this work, emphasizing Augustine's passion for Christ as the dominant factor in his choice to explain this "Gospel of the Trinity".[56] Each of those explanations has some value. Taken together, they help to appreciate the love for Christ that Augustine expresses in this commentary.

However, the immediate motivation for undertaking this commentary is most likely found in social and not merely doctrinal realities. In the first set of homilies, the Catholic-Donatist division[57] is a significant presence. Hence, it is at least reasonable to ask whether Augustine—even if only intuitively—recognized that this preaching would help him respond to the Donatists in a more effective way than was previously possible. Was there something about the Gospel of John that would give him a way to address the division between Catholics and Donatists?

Donatism—an intractable schism

The Donatist community was significantly more important than the Catholic community when Augustine's ministry as a priest began in 390/391.[58] Some of the tension that he experienced at that time is evident in his letter to his bishop Valerius. Writing shortly after his ordination to the priesthood, Augustine says that his priestly ministry "now torments and crushes me."[59] He asks for time to study the scriptures, so that he can learn

---

55. See M. Pontet, *L'exégèse de saint Augustin prédicateur* (Marseille: Aubier, 1944) 558 (cited in BA 71, 44).
56. Agostino Vita, "Introduzione," *Commento al Vangelo e alla Prima Epistola di San Giovanni* (Rome, Città Nuova, 1968) xi-lix.
57. See Homily 13, 10-11. Berrouard, BA 71, 55-78, discusses Donatism at some length; he writes: "Il paraît hors de doute que les malheurs de la division ont profondément influencé Augustin quand il choisit de commenter durant la semaine de Pâques la première Epître de Jean" (p. 55). Those same words apply equally to the initial motivation for the commentary on the gospel.
58. For pertinent details about Donatism and about the early years of Augustine's ministry, see Allan Fitzgerald, "When Augustine was a priest: pride, common good and Donatism," *Augustinian Studies* 40/1 (2009) forthcoming.
59. Augustine, Letter 21, 3: *Quale me nunc torquet et conterit*.

how to exercise his ministry for the salvation of others.[60] By the time Augustine finally began to preach on the Gospel of John (winter 406-407), his major works against the Donatists had been written.[61] Imperial legislation against heretics with its heavy penalties had begun to be applied to the Donatists—especially because of their practice of re-baptizing Catholics.[62] In his preaching on the Gospel of John (Homilies 1-16), on the Psalms of Ascent (Psalms 119-133) and on John's first epistle (Easter week of 407),[63] Augustine appears to have sensed that preaching on the centrality of Jesus Christ would be an effective way to counter Donatist influence. As M.-F. Berrouard notes, such an idea can be found in previous writings, but it never had the force or the coherence that one finds in the commentary on John. In the early homilies, in fact, Christ—whose mediation and honor are diminished by the Donatists—becomes the center of Augustine's refutation of Donatism.[64]

That such an emphasis in Augustine's preaching may have motivated his project to begin a commentary on the Gospel of John is important for several reasons.[65]

1. Instead of merely reacting to Donatist writings, Augustine could take a positive approach toward the development of a coherent position *about Jesus Christ* in everyday Catholic life.

---

60. Augustine, Letter 21, 4: *Sed hoc ipsum quomodo ministrem ad salutem aliorum.* See Fitzgerald, "When Augustine was priest: Pride, common good and Donatism"; L. Verheijen, "Eléments d'un commentaire de la Règle de saint Augustin. La charité ne cherche pas ses propres intérêts," *Augustiniana* 34 (1984) 75-144.
61. *Against the Letter of Parmenian, Against the Letters of Petillian, About Baptism, On the Unity of the Church*, and the work addressed *To Cresconius*.
62. See BA 71, 57.
63. See the paragraphs which address Donatism, e.g., 1, 8.12-13; 2, 2-4; 3, 5-10.
64. See BA 71, 61-70, and 78: "Augustin a l'intuition qu'en prêchant le Christ et son amour il démasque le schisme, détruit ses arguments et avance sa ruine." See too Augustine's *Homilies on the First Epistle of John* 3, 7-10; 6, 13-14. Augustine had already recognized the problem in the years of his priesthood: see the *Psalm against the Donatists* v. 295: *Quia quod debetis pro Christo, pro Donato uultis ferre ; Exposition of Psalm* 10, 5: *Itaque isti cogunt eos qui accipiunt sacramenta, spem suam in homine ponere, cuius cor uidere non possunt.* See too Sermon 26*, 45.52, probably preached in 404.
65. In the light of Augustine's experience of Donatists, Berrouard's comments on Donatism (BA 71, 55-78) become more than a description of historical facts about them. See G. Madec, *Introduction aux Révisions et à la Lecture des Œuvres de Saint Augustin* (Paris: Institut d'Études Augustiniennes, 1996) 64: "C'est un commentaire lié à l'actualité par ses nombreuses allusions anti-donatistes, surtout dans les premières homélies."

2. Turning to the scriptures for answers to the Donatist-Catholic stand-off may be the clearest indication that his own episcopal interventions and writings against Donatist texts—as well as the enforcement of imperial legislation—did not have the intended results.

3. The Donatists emphasized the "pure" quality of their Church, their ministers and their sacraments. That emphasis shifted the focus to Donatist ministers who then saw themselves in the role of mediator, thus taking Christ's place or diminishing his importance. Hence, the controversy is not just about sacramental practice or a mere difference of opinion about baptism or about the Church, but about Jesus Christ as the only one in whom salvation can be obtained. In that context, John's gospel would have been singularly appropriate. Christ alone bridges the gap between God and man; Christ's words and deeds counter the pride of Donatist leaders.

What was it about the Gospel of John which provided Augustine with a way to respond to that strongly-felt and deeply-entrenched division? In a word, John presented the mystery of Christ more fully than any of the other evangelists, showing how Church and sacrament were integral parts of that mystery.[66] When John said that Christ is *the one who baptizes* (Jn 1:33), for example, Augustine showed how the understanding of that phrase could defeat "the party of Donatus completely," such that they "will have nothing further to say about the grace of baptism."[67] For Christ—not Donatus or his followers—is the one who saves.

In the first sixteen homilies, Augustine commented on the first four chapters of the Gospel of John. Then there was a pause of about seven years before he resumed the effort. By that time the Conference of Carthage (411) had taken place and the broad lines of a return to unity between Catholics and Donatists had been agreed upon.[68] Subsequent homilies have very little to say about Donatism. The significant difference in the place given to Donatism in the rest of this commentary highlights its importance when he began it. Nevertheless, changed social circumstances

---

66. See Homily 36, 1.
67. Homily 4, 16.
68. Homilies 23, 5; 27, 11; 28, 12; see BA 72, 833: "Progrès du christianisme au début du ve siècle."

did not diminish Augustine's desire to continue to sound the depths of John's words about Christ.

From the point of view of the full commentary, the mystery of Christ is primary, as Augustine sought to raise up the hearts and minds of his listeners to the Lord's divinity. For John proclaimed[69] what he had drunk in and spoke of Christ as did no other: "From that breast he drank in secret; but what he drank in secret, he proclaimed openly, so that all nations might learn not only about the incarnation, the passion, death and resurrection of the Son of God, but also about that which was before the incarnation: that he was the only Son of the Father, the Word of the Father, co-eternal with the one who begot him and equal to him by whom he was sent."[70]

Augustine's listeners

The Basilica Pacis, which was Augustine's cathedral church in Hippo, measured 123 by 60 feet (37.5 by 18.5 meters); hence, the number of those who could have fit into that space—since there were no seats, his listeners stood—may have been as many as 600, at least for occasions that the people regarded as special. Augustine's voice, which was sometimes weak, was more fully tested when the church was full—a reality that led him to shorten his sermon, for example, on the wedding at Cana.[71]

Augustine's dedication to the task of preaching confronted many diverse challenges. Yet a single motivating force underlies his work: love for those who had been redeemed by the blood of Christ. From his first letter as a priest, his dedication to the health of others was explicitly rooted in the example of Christ. He asked Valerius, "How am I to exercise this ministry for the salvation of others, *not seeking what is beneficial for me, but for many, that they may be saved* (1 Cor 10:33)?"[72] Years later, he will acknowledge his joy: "I rejoice with you,[73] because you are many and you have come together eagerly, quite beyond my expecta-

---

69. Literally, belched (*ructabat*); see Homily 20, 1; Sermons 34, 2; 119, 1-2; 120, 1; 133, 6; 313A, 2.
70. Homily 36, 1.
71. Homily 8, 13.
72. Letter 21, 4. See M.-F. Berrouard, "Saint Augustin et le ministère de la prédication," *Recherches Augustiniennes* 2 (1962) 447-501, esp. 475-481.
73. Homily 7, 1: "I rejoice with *frequentiae vestrae*," literally, "at your presence in greater numbers."

tions. This is what delights and consoles me in the midst of the toils and dangers of this life: your love for God, loyal efforts, constant hope and fervor of spirit."[74]

Who were Augustine's listeners?[75] The community at Hippo was, in general, a diverse[76] group of Catholics who came to church more or less faithfully—which meant that the number of those who were present on any given occasion varied considerably.[77] Hence, they were young and old, culturally diverse,[78] those who could read and those who could not,[79] poor and well-off,[80] married, single and widowed,[81] ascetics and consecrated virgins,[82] and so forth. Augustine's images suggest that many were artisans.[83] But when he was preaching on the Gospel of John, there is no indication that anyone other than catechumens or faithful[84] was present.[85]

The problems that Augustine faced were familiar ones: his listeners were easily distracted, found spiritual reflection difficult,[86] and may have left church on any given day without having learned anything.[87] Hence, these homilies are sprinkled throughout with words that seek to revive the attention of his listeners; he will not treat them as beginners or as ignorant.[88] Augustine addressed bad habits in his community,[89] such as

---

74. Homily 7, 1. See Homilies 6, 2; 11, 12; 3, 21; *Exposition of Psalms* 119, 3; 126, 1; *Homilies on the First Epistle of John* 7, 4-6; 9, 10-11.
75. See BA 71, 27-38; 103-109; F. Van Der Meer, *Augustine the Bishop* (New York: Sheed and Ward, 1961) 169-177.
76. See Homily 51, 13.
77. Once they are called a "multitude" (Homily 40, 7), but their number varied (Homilies 35, 1; 37, 1; 54, 5.7), e.g., depending on the feast or when he said that he would speak about division among Christians, i.e., about Donatism (Homily 12, 1).
78. See Homily 51, 13.
79. See Homilies 12, 11; 10, 2. 4.
80. See Homily 50, 6; *Exposition of Psalm* 51, 14.
81. See Homily 13, 11.
82. See Homily 13, 11-12.
83. See Homilies 24, 5; 27, 11; 34, 3.
84. See Homily 44, 3.
85. In spite of the conjecture of M.-F. Berrouard, BA 71, 28, n. 152.
86. See Homily on *the First Epistle of John* 6, 14: *tardiores fratres*.
87. See *Exposition of Psalm* 128, 1; *Homilies on the First Epistle of John* 3, 13; 4, 1.
88. See Homily 17, 4.
89. Homilies 6, 2.12; 11, 8. 10; *Exposition of Psalm* 128, 2.8; *Homilies on the First Epistle of John* 3, 9.

adultery, greed and drunkenness,[90] as frequently as in any other Catholic community.

While Augustine did speak about the fervor[91] of his people and about the desire of some for spiritual growth,[92] some less positive themes appear often: he recognized in his listeners an attachment to superstitious practices, pagan feasts and worship, and recourse to astrologers,[93] as well as a way of loving or of thinking that was carnal, not spiritual,[94] that is, which was concerned primarily with one's own needs.[95]

---

90. See a fuller list in Homily 6, 17.
91. See, e.g., Homilies 6, 1. 3. 4.13; 9, 9; 40, 8; 96, 4.
92. See Homily 8, 13; 9, 9; 13, 1.
93. See BA 71, 32-33.
94. Hence, Augustine contrasts *secundum carnem* and *secundum spiritum*, e.g., in Homilies 1, 1; 18, 7.11; 27, 1, 37, 1; 94, 4; he warns against merely carnal love, e.g., in Homilies 11; 12; 65, 1; 123, 4.
95. See Homilies 6, 18; 10, 6; 12, 4; 25, 17; 46, 5-7. See L. Verheijen ("La charité ne cherche pas ses propres intérêts," *Nouvelle approche de la Règle de saint Augustin* 2 [Bégrolles-en-Mauges: Abbaye Bellefontaine, 1988] 220-289), who collected Augustine's commentaries on the scriptural texts that refer to this theme: Ps 21:30; Rom 15:3; 1 Cor 10:24.33; 13:5; 2 Cor 5:15.

Some Technical Matters

Dating the homilies: historical dimensions[1]

Much effort has been expended in attempting to date these homilies. In 1680, the Maurist editors dated all of them to the year 416. Early in the eighteenth century, the great Church scholar Le Nain de Tillemont proposed the date 412.[2] In 1930, Marie Comeau argued in favor of the Maurists' chronology, noting that Homily 99, 8-9 was cited in *The Trinity* XV,27,48.[3] In 1933, S. Zarb divided the homilies into two distinct groups, 1-54 and 55-124,[4] the first of which was assigned to 413 and the second to 418, when Augustine was absent from Hippo for several months.[5] Zarb argued that the second group of homilies was dictated and served as sermon-outlines that could be used by others.

M. Le Landais revived the discussion in 1953 by noting that Homilies 1-12 were intertwined with the *Exposition of Psalms* 119-133. He held that the ten *Homilies on the First Epistle of John* were preached shortly after the first twelve homilies on the Gospel of John and dated Homilies 1-27 to the period from December 414 to August 415. He also concluded that Augustine preached all 124 homilies in person.[6]

Further precision was proposed in 1965 by Anne-Marie La Bonnardière, who divided the first group of homilies into four further groups:

1. Homilies 1-12 were assigned to 406-407, along with the *Homilies on the First Epistle of John* and the *Exposition of Psalms* 95, 119-133.[7]

---

1. See Maurist edition, *Opera Omnia S. Augustini* (Paris: 1680) III. 2, 285-286. This account of the historical background depends on Milewski, art. cit. 61-77 and on J.W. Rettig, *Saint Augustine, Tractates on the Gospel of John* (1-10) (Washington, D.C.: Fathers of the Church, 1988).
2. Le Nain de Tillemont, cited by Seraphinus M. Zarb, "Chronologia Tractatuum S. Augustini In Evangelium Primamque Epistulam Ioannis Apostoli," *Angelicum* 10 (1933) 52.
3. Marie Comeau, *Saint Augustin exégète du Quatrième Evangile* (Paris: Gabriel Beauchesne, 1930) 2-5.
4. S. Zarb, "Chronologia Enarrationum sancti Augustini in Psalmos," *Angelicum* 10 (1933) 50-110, esp. 54-57.
5. Ibid. 105-108.
6. M. Le Landais, "Deux années de prédication de Saint Augustin: introduction à la lecture de l'*In Iohannem*," *Études Augustiniennes* 28 (1953) 9-95.
7. A.-M. La Bonnardière, *Recherches de chronologie augustinienne* (Paris: Études Augustiniennes, 1965) 46-51. Her conclusions depend on a study of imperial legislation and on the absence of any reference to the Council of Carthage in 411.

2. Homilies 13-16 were perhaps preached in 407-408.[8]

3. Homilies 17-23, in which an anti-Arian emphasis was affirmed, were linked to the invasion of North Africa by Arian Goths in 417 and were preached about 418.

4. Homilies 24-54 were preached between August and Lent either in 419-420 or in 420-421.[9]

La Bonnardière described Homilies 55-124 as the sermon outlines to which Augustine alluded in *Teaching Christianity* IV,29,62.[10] They were produced after 419-420.[11]

David F. Wright effectively demonstrated that Homilies 20-22 were originally separated from the rest, but he did not offer a date.[12] Suzanne Poque combined aspects of the opinions of Le Landais with those of La Bonnardière, dating Homilies 1-6 to January 407 and Homilies 7-12 to the time between February 17 and March 5 or 9, 407.[13]

M.-F. Berrouard accepted La Bonnardière's dating for the first sixteen homilies.[14] He considered Homilies 17-19 and 23-54 a single sequential block, and, due to a similarity of argumentation found in Augustine's anti-Arian and anti-Pelagian works of the period 413-416, he assigns those homilies to 414.[15] On the basis of the similarity with Answer to a Sermon of the Arians, he dates Homilies 20-22 to 418 or 419.[16] Homilies 55-124 would have been prepared beginning in November 419, a conclusion that is based on Augustine's allusion to his work on John's gospel in Letter 23*A.[17] The composition of these homilies, therefore, stretches from 406 to 421 or beyond (see the table below). These dates, however, remain indicative rather than securely fixed in every detail since some debate about them will continue.

---

8. Ibid. 61-62.
9. Ibid. 87-117.
10. Ibid. 124-125.
11. Ibid. 65-87.
12. David F. Wright, "Tractatus 20-22 of St. Augustine's *In Iohannem*," *Journal of Theological Studies* 15 (1964) 317-330.
13. Suzanne Poque, "Trois semaines de prédication a Hippone en février-mars 407," *Recherches Augustiniennes* 7 (1971) 183-187.
14. M.-F. Berrouard, "La date des *Tractatus I-LIV in Iohannis Evangelium* de Saint Augustin," *Recherches Augustiniennes* 7 (1971) 105-168.
15. Ibid. 140-146, 159-163.
16. Ibid. 146-159.
17. M.-F. Berrouard, "Les Tractatus LV-CXXIV dictés à partir de Novembre 419," BA 74A, 9-52 (or Berrouard, BA 71, 177-200).

Dates[1]

406-407 (December-June)

From early December to January 14, the feast of Saint Felix, Augustine preached fifteen times, in this order:
Exposition of Psalms 119, 120
Homily on the Gospel of John 1
Exposition of Psalm 121
Homily on the Gospel of John 2
Exposition of Psalms 122, 123
Homily on the Gospel of John 3
Exposition of Psalms 124, 125
Homily on the Gospel of John 4
Exposition of Psalm 126
Homilies on the Gospel of John 5, 6
Exposition of Psalm 127

After a break of some weeks (from Sunday, March 24 to Tuesday, April 9, 407), he would have preached:
Homily on the Gospel of John 7
Exposition of Psalm 128, 129
Homilies on the Gospel of John 8, 9, 10 (on successive days)
Exposition of Psalm 130
Exposition of Psalms 131, 95 (on successive days)
Homily on the Gospel of John 11
Exposition of Psalms 132, 133
Homily on the Gospel of John 12
Exposition of Psalm 21 (sermon 2) was preached on Wednesday of Holy Week
Homilies on the First Epistle of John (Easter Week, from April 14 to 21, 407)
Homily on the Gospel of John 13
Homilies on the Gospel of John 14, 15, 16 cannot be dated with any assurance, but they were probably preached before Augustine left for Carthage in June, 407.

---

1. See BA 71, 22-27; 90-102; 199-200.

414 (July-November)

Homilies on the Gospel of John 17-19, 23-54 (preached between July and November 414)

419-420

Homilies on the Gospel of John 20-22 (preached on succeeding days after Sermon 125).

419 (November)-??

Homilies on the Gospel of John 54-124

Completing the Commentary
Homilies 55-124

In the surviving manuscripts of the *Homilies on the Gospel of John* from the ninth and tenth centuries, a division of the homilies into two groups was already found, namely 1-54 and 55-124, but both groups have long been regarded as belonging to a single work.[2] A discussion about the differences in length and in style between the two sets of homilies continues. When Augustine returned to his project of completing the commentary on the Gospel of John, did he also alter his style, choosing to dictate short homilies rather than preach them to a gathered community? The question is more complex than it may appear. Three issues need to be addressed: a. Were Homilies 55-124 composed in sequence, beginning with Homily 55? b. Were the homilies preached or dictated? c. What precisely did "dictate" mean for Augustine?

a. In order?

In Letter 23*A, Augustine wrote to Possidius,[3] listing his writing projects between mid-September and early December 419, which he said amounted to six thousand lines. Among those writings he refers to six homilies on the Gospel of John which were *dictated* and which were to be

---

2. Cf. David F. Wright, "The Manuscripts of St. Augustine's *Tractatus in Evangelium Iohannis*: A Preliminary Survey and Check-List," *Recherches Augustiniennes* 8 (1972) 57-104.
3. M.-F. Berrouard, "L'activité littéraire de saint Augustin du 11 septembre au 1er décembre 419 d'après la Lettre 23A* à Possidius de Calama," in *Les Lettres de saint Augustin découvertes par Johannes Divjak* (Paris: Études Augustiniennes, 1983) 301-327.

sent to Aurelius, the bishop of Carthage.⁴ Berrouard suggests that Augustine was referring to Homilies 55-60. His rationale for that conclusion depends upon the use of the word *tractatus* at the beginning of Homily 55, which, as the only instance of that noun in the whole commentary, would thus indicate a certain coordination between his words in Letter 23*A and the series of homilies that begin with Homily 55.⁵ To assume that Augustine commented on the remaining nine chapters of the Gospel of John, beginning with chapter 13, is reasonable—even if it cannot be demonstrated that the homilies he sent to Aurelius were the first six. More about this matter will be discussed shortly.

b. Preached or dictated?

D. J. Milewski's recent overview of the issues relating to the length and style of the second group of homilies appears to be the most acceptable in the light of current research.⁶ Noting that Augustine wanted to provide "a detailed, intricate exegetical and theological discourse to a frequently unpredictable general audience," Milewski affirms Augustine's determined desire "to conclude the series, independent of a particular setting or audience."⁷ His determination to finish the commentary—apparently presuming that there was no time to do otherwise—has been used to say that he dictated the remaining homilies.⁸ Such an inference is not the only way to understand Letter 23A*.

There is no way to know when Augustine began to comment on the last seventy homilies or to affirm clearly that he did them in ordered sequence. Whatever had not yet been treated by the time he wrote to Possidius in 419 refers, undoubtedly, to "what remains of the gospel."⁹ But the evidence for dating the last seventy homilies is scant indeed, and the interpretation of

---

4. *Letter* 23*A, 3: "And, to finish as well what remains of the Gospel of John, I have already begun to dictate some popular and not very long homilies to be sent to Carthage on the condition that, if the same primate of ours wishes that the rest be sent to him, he should say so and not delay in publishing them when he says so. I have already dictated six." (*Ut faciam de Iohannis quoque evangelio ea quae restant, dictare iam coepi populares tractatus non prolixos mittendos Cathaginem ea conditione ut, si vult idem senex noster sibi ceteros mitti, [dicat] neque cum dixerit edere differat. Iam sex dictavi.*)
5. See BA 71, 182-184. Although the noun occurs once here and once in the {commentary} *Exposition of Psalms* (61, 22), its verb form is common; *sermo* occurs frequently.
6. See Milewski, art. cit. 61-77.
7. Ibid. 70.
8. See BA 71, 183-186.
9. See p. 14, note 30.

Letter 23*A, 3 as specifying Homilies 55-60 is not certain—not least because the argument is circular.

Likewise, the use of the length of the second set of homilies as an indicator of a change in the way that Augustine did his work also needs to be questioned. The first fifty-four homilies treat twelve chapters of the Gospel of John and the last seventy only deal with nine chapters; a strict comparison based on the physical length of the homilies is not appropriate. In fact, there is little difference in physical length between the two sets of sermons,[10] and Augustine's decision to preach for shorter periods of time could have been related to the patience of his listeners, to his own strength, or to his busy calendar. By 419, Augustine was preaching two sermons a week rather than several sermons on succeeding days.[11] It is not necessary or even possible to conclude that these homilies were dictated *ex novo*, even if dictation were part of a process of copying some already-preached sermons so that they could be sent to Aurelius in Carthage.

A comparison of Homilies 55-124 with the thirty-two sermons on Psalm 118 (which were dictated) shows that they are of similar length, that is, a little more than three pages each. But the last thirteen *Expositions of the Psalms*, which were believed to have been dictated, average fourteen pages each. As Milewski concludes: "Brevity is no sure warranty of Augustine's dictation ... verbosity is no infallible hallmark of his preaching."[12] More important is the absence of a first-person usage from the psalm commentaries; a detached tone is pervasive. In the psalm commentaries, the first person is rare.[13] In general, when Augustine preaches, he tends to use "us" more often than "you."[14] At least thirty of the last seventy homilies include examples of audience contact

---

10. In his discussion of Homilies 104-111, Milewski, art. cit. 71-72, rightly concludes that a real proportionality with the initial homilies has been preserved, i.e., that the brevity of these homilies does not tell us very much.
11. Augustine did gradually begin to extend the delivery of his homilies over longer periods of time. See Zarb, "Chronologia," 102-104.
12. Art. cit. 73.
13. See ibid. 71-72.
14. G. Lawless, "Listening to Augustine: Tractate 44 on John 9," in *Augustinian Studies* 28 (1997) 54. A. Verwilghen, "Rhétorique et Prédication chez Augustin," in *Nouvelle Revue Théologique* 120 (1998) 240: "Quand il prêchait, il se plaçait, tout comme son peuple, sous la lumière de la Parole, préférant utiliser le 'nous' plutôt que le 'vous.' Comme son peuple, Augustin éprouvait le désir d'être lui-même enseigné."

and direct address.[15] Therefore, even if one can see some difference in the overall tonality, some of these homilies resonate an oral quality which would more readily suggest a real audience than a stenographer.[16]

c. The meaning of "dictation"?

What, in fact, does Augustine mean by "dictate" (*dictare*)? He is known to have delivered sermons, aware that a written version was being recorded: "We have to think of readers as well as hearers."[17] A phrase from Homily 99 on the Gospel of John, which is cited in *The Trinity*, provides an example of a sermon which, after it was preached, was written. Thus he writes about a part of "the utterance of a particular sermon which I delivered to the ears of the Christian people and (which) I later had written down."[18] This final phrase, "and (which) I later had written down," would have to mean that Homily 99 was first preached and then dictated—a practice that Possidius also describes.[19]

Hence, the distinction between preaching and dictation does not say much about the style of the last seventy homilies, at least because such "dictation" may derive from or bear an immediate connection to a preached original. In other words, the criteria for determining which ones may have been preached or dictated or even preached first and dictated later are not now, and may never be, adequate for a firm conclusion.

d. Does it matter?[20]

On the level of the content of Augustine's preaching, it may not matter whether Homilies 55-124 were dictated or preached. But such a discussion,

---

15. For example, Augustine evokes Christ in a way that is reminiscent of his popular preaching in Homily 57,6: *Quando te audimus, exsultant tecum in caelestibus ossa humiliata. Sed quando te praedicamus, terram calcamus ut tibi aperiamus; et ideo si reprehendimur, perturbamur; si laudamur, inflamur. Lava pedes nostros ante mundatos, sed cum ad aperiendum tibi per terram pergimus, inquinatos.* See Milewski, art. cit. 64-65.
16. See ibid. 70-71. Direct address occurs in Homilies 56-64, 67-74, 77-80, 83-87, 96-98 and 101.
17. *Exposition of Psalm* 51, 1: *Neque enim passim praetereunda sunt haec; quandoquidem placuit fratribus, non tantum aure et corde, sed et stilo excipienda quae dicimus; ut non auditorem tantum, sed et lectorem etiam cogitare debeamus.*
18. Homily 99, 8-9: *In sermone quodam proferendo ad aures populi christiani diximus dictumque conscripsimus.* See *The Trinity* XV, 27, 48.
19. Possidius, *Sancti Augustini Vita* 18: *Tanta autem ab eodem dictata et edita sunt, tantaque in ecclesia disputata, excepta atque emendate.*
20. See Milewski, art. cit. 75-77.

by dissolving the connection between the two sets of homilies for technical reasons, can have an insidious effect, i.e., it can appear to suggest that Augustine was not as personally interested in the later homilies as he was in the first ones. But the manner of composition should not obscure the larger interest that this commentary has. Reading and studying these homilies with an interest that is primarily centered on their content is all the more desirable insofar as little more can be said about how they were composed or when they were preached. As Milewski writes about a significant lesson that may be drawn from comments made by the bishop:

It is here that the famous insertion of Holmily 99, 8-9 into *Trinity* 15,27,48 offers perhaps a final significant lesson. It must not be overlooked how telling it is that Augustine could find no better explication of the concluding points in his theological masterpiece than from what he identifies as an excerpt of his preaching. What more eloquent testimony could be given to the priority of Augustine the pastor over Augustine the systematic theologian? And what more obvious sign of the wealth of doctrine contained in his preaching, especially in these homilies, could be offered than that citation?[21]

Excursus: why another commentary on John 5:19-30?

Several homilies are dedicated to the explanation of Jn 5:19-30. The studies of D.F. Wright demonstrated that three of them, namely Homilies 20-22, were inserted some years after Homilies 18, 19 and 23 were written. Even though the two explanations complement one another, the earlier homilies highlight the Son of Man who, one with the Father, seeks not his own will, but, in his humanity, accepts the will of the Father. The later homilies identify the humility of the Word of God; he has come from the Father so as to bring humanity back to God.[22] The addition of Homilies 20-22 to the commentary—presumably in response to the *sermo Arianorum* which Augustine would have read in 418—does demonstrate that Augustine was still preaching his homilies on John's gospel at that time.

---

21. Ibid. 77.
22. L.R. Bastos, " '*Non potest Filius a se facere quidquam, nisi quod viderit Patrem facient*'—L'inserimento tardivo dei Trattiti 20, 21 e 22 in Ioannis Evangelium e il senso di una seconda esegesi agostiniana del brano Gv 5, 19-30" (Dissertatio ad Licentium, Institutum Patristicum Augustianum, 2002) 27-33,103-115.

According to Berrouard, the two series of homilies are not polemical, but fully catechetical. He suggests that Augustine's knowledge of Arianism was changed by his reading of the *Sermo Arianorum*.[23] Rather than claim that Augustine's knowledge of the Arian challenge had grown in the intervening years such that the second set of homilies depended on an understanding of Arianism discovered through the reading of the *Sermo Arianorum*, Bastos prefers to emphasize the pastoral dimensions of this difference, saying that Augustine would have already understood what contemporary Arians were saying, but he recognized a pastoral value in explaining that understanding to his people.[24]

Thus, the new treatment of John 5:19-30 could also have been suggested by the work he was also doing on the *De Trinitate*. For, in the second book of that work (II, 1, 3), he was developing the exegetical rules for interpreting the subordinationist texts of the gospel. In book four (IV, 20, 27-28), in fact, he will insist that the incarnation of the Son was nothing other than the visible manifestation of his eternal mission.[25] Thus, in the first series of homilies on this passage of John (Homilies 19, 20 and 23), the words of Christ (John 5:20.23.30) were attributed to his humanity, but in Homilies 21 and 22 those words are attributed to the person of the Son. For, in the second series, the eternal mission of the Son reveals his origin in the Father, not his subordination to the Father.[26] But Augustine's understanding of John 5:19 had already reached the same conclusion in Homily 23 that was affirmed throughout Homilies 20-22.[27] These homilies, therefore, were primarily pastoral insofar as Augustine was, once again, sharing with his listeners what had already nourished him.[28]

Allan D. Fitzgerald, O.S.A.

---

23. M.-F. Berrouard, *Introduction aux Homélies de Saint Augustin sur L'Évangile de Saint Jean*. Paris: Institut d'Études Augustiniennes, 2004, p. 144.
24. Bastos 106-107. S. Lancel also holds that Augustine did not need the *sermo Arianorum* to change his understanding of Arianism: *Saint Augustin* (Paris: Fayard, 1999) 532. M. Barnes suggests that his understanding of Arianism had evolved: "Exegesis and Polemic in Augustine's *De Trinitate* 1," Augustinian Studies 30/1 (1999) 43, note 2.
25. See Berrouard, *Introduction*, p. 164; Bastos 108.
26. Berrouard, *Introduction*, p. 156.
27. See M.-F. Berrouard, "La date des Tractatus 1-LIV in *Iohannis Evangelium de Saint Augustin*", in *Recherches Augustiniennes* 7 (1971) 151-152; Bastos, 106-107.
28. Homily 2, 1.

Bibliography

Edition

Sancti Aurelii Augustini In Ioannis evangelium tractatus CXXIV, ed. by R. Willems. Turnholti: Brepols, 1954 = Corpus Christianorum. Series Latina 36.

Translations

Homilies on the Gospel of John. Homilies on the First Epistle of John. Soliloquies. Translation by J. Gibb. Edinburgh: T. et T. Clark, 1873-1874; reprinted Grand Rapids, Mich.: Wm. B. Eerdmans, 1986 = A Select Library of the Nicene and Post-Nicene Fathers of the Christian Church 7.
Des heiligen Kirchenvaters Aurelius Augustinus Vortraege ueber das Evangelium des hl. Johannes 1-3. Translation and introduction by T. Specht. Kempten/Muenchen: K el 1913-1914.
Homélies sur l'Evangile de Saint Jean. Translation, introduction and notes by M.-F. Berrouard. Paris: Desclee de Brouwer, 1969-2003.
Tractates on the Gospel of John. Tractates on the First Epistle of John. Translation by John W. Rettig. Washington, D.C.: Catholic University Press, 1988-1995 = The Fathers of the Church 78, 79, 88, 90, 92.

Studies

J.E. Abad, "Christ and the Church in Augustine's Preaching on John 10 (Tractates 45-48 and Sermons 137-139)." Dissertatio ad Licentium, Institutum Patristicum Augustinianum, 2002.
A.A.R. Bastiaensen, *Vite dei Santi*, ed. C. Mohrmann, vol. 3: *Vita di Cipriano, Vita di Ambrogio, Vita di Agostino.* Milan: Arnoldo Mondadori, 1975.
L.R. Bastos, " '*Non potest Filius a se facere quidquam, nisi quod viderit Patrem facientem*'—L'inserimento tardivo dei Trattati 20, 21 e 22 in Ioannis Evangelium e il senso di una seconda esegesi agostiniana del brano Gv 5, 19-30." Dissertatio ad Licentium, Institutum Patristicum Augustinianum, 2002.
M.-F. Berrouard, ed., *Homélies sur L'Évangile de Saint Jean* = Bibliothèque Augustinienne (henceforth BA) 71-75. Paris: Études Augustiniennes, 1969-2003. The introductions to the individual volumes of the BA have been collected in M.-F. Berrouard, *Introduction aux Homélies de Saint Augustin sur L'Évangle de Saint Jean.* Paris: Institut d'Études Augustiniennes, 2004.
M.-F. Berrouard, "L'activité littéraire de saint Augustin du 11 septembre au 1er décembre 419 d'après la lettre 23A* à Possidius de Calama." BA 46B, 301-327.
M.-F. Berrouard, "La date des *Tractatus I-LIV in Iohannis Evangelium* de Saint Augustin." *Recherches Augustiniennes* 7 (1971) 105-168.
M.-F. Berrouard, "L'enseignement de la charité dans les Tractatus." BA 75, 7-38.
M.-F. Berrouard, "L'être sacramentel de l'eucharistie selon saint Augustin. Commentaire de Jean vi, 60-63 dans le «Tractatus XXVII, 1-6 et 11-12 in Iohannis Evangelium.» *Nouvelle Revue Théologique* 99 (1977) 702-721.
M.-F. Berrouard, "L'exégèse de saint Augustin prédicateur du quatrième Évangile. Le sens de l'unité des Écritures." *Freiburger Zeitschrift für Philosophie und Theologie* 34 (1987) 311-38.
M.-F. Berrouard, "Le Tractatus 80,3 in Iohannis Evangelium de saint Augustin: La parole, le sacrement et la foi." *Revue des Études Augustiniennes* 33 (1987) 235-254.
M.-F. Berrouard, "Les Tractatus LV-CXXIV dictée à partir de Novembre 419." BA 74A, 9-52.
A. de Bovis, "Le Christ et la Prière, selon Saint Augustin, dans les Commentaires sur S. Jean." *Revue d'Ascetique et de Mystique* 25 (1949) 180-193.
E. Cassidy, "Per Christum hominem ad Christum Deum: Augustine's Homilies on John's Gospel," in T. Finan and V. Twoney, eds., *Studies in Patristic Christology.* Dublin: Four Courts Press, 1998, 122-143.
J.-L. Chrétien, *Saint Augustin et les actes de parole.* Paris: Presses Universitaires de France, 2002.

J.-L. Chrétien, "Saint Augustin et le Grand Large du Désir," in *La Joie Spacieuse*. Paris: Editions de Minuit, 2007, 33-63.
Marie Comeau, *Saint Augustin exégète du Quatrième Evangile*. Paris: Beauchesne, 1930.
R. Deferrari, "On the Date and Order of Delivery of St. Augustine's Tractates on the Gospel and Epistles of St. John." *Classical Philology* 12 (1917) 191-194.
G. W. Doyle, "Augustine's Sermonic Method." *Westminster Theological Journal* 39 (1976-77) 213-238.
A. Fitzgerald, "Tracing the passage from a doctrinal to an historical approach to the study of Augustine." *Revue des Études Augustiniennes* 50/2 (2004) 295-310.
A. Fitzgerald, "Johannis evangelium tactatus, In," in *Augustine through the Ages - an Encyclopedia*, A.D. Fitzgerald et al., eds. Grand Rapids, Mich.: Wm. Eerdmans, 1999, 474.
R.P. Hardy, "The Incarnation and Revelation in Augustine's *Tractatus in Iohannis Evangelium*." *Eglise et théologie* 3 (1972) 193-220.
R.P. Hardy, *Actualité de la révélation divine. Une étude des Tractatus in Iohannis Euangelium de saint Augustin*. Paris: Beauchesne, 1974.
A.-M. La Bonnardière, "Les commentaires simultanes de Mat. 6, 12 et I Jo. 1, 8 dans l'oeuvre de saint Augustin." *Revue des Études Augustiniennes* 1 (1955) 129-147.
A.-M. La Bonnardière, *Recherches de chronologie augustinienne*. Paris: Études Augustiniennes, 1965^2.
G.P. Lawless, "*Desiderium sinus cordis est*: Biblical Resonances in Augustine's *Tractatus in Evangelium Iohannis* 40, 10." *Augustiniana* 49/3-4 (1998) 305-329.
G.P. Lawless, "infirmior sexus... fortior affectus". Augustine's Jo.ev.tr. 121,1-3: Mary Magdalene." *Augustinian Studies* 34/1 (2003) 107-118.
G.P. Lawless, "Listening to Augustine: Tractate 44 on John 9." *Augustinian Studies* 28/1 (1997) 51-66.
G.P. Lawless, "Profil du ministère chrétien dans le Commentaire de Jean 21,12-19 par Saint Augustin." *Omnis terra* 30 (1991) 234-242.
G.P. Lawless, "The Man Born Blind: Augustine's Tractate 44 on John 9." *Augustinian Studies* 27 (1996) 61-79.
G.P. Lawless, "The Wedding at Cana: Augustine on the Gospel According to John Tractates 8 and 9." *Augustinian Studies* 28/2 (1997) 35-80.
M. Le Landais, "Deux années de prédication de Saint Augustin: introduction à la lecture de l'*In Iohannem*." *Revue des Études Augustiniennes* 28 (1953) 9-95.
G. Madec, *La Patrie et La Voie*. Paris: Desclée, 1989.
D.J. Milewski, *Nec locus Dei sumus*. Augustine's Exegesis and the Theology of John 17 in the light of In Evangelium Iohannis Tractatus CIV-CXI. Doctoral Dissertation, Augustinian Patristic Institute, 2000.
D.J. Milewski, "Augustine's 124 Tractates on the Gospel of John: The *Status Quaestionis* and the State of Neglect." *Augustinian Studies* 33/1 (2002) 61-77.
C. Mohrmann, "Praedicare—Tractare—Sermo," in *Études sur le Latin des Chrétiens* II. Rome: Edizioni di Storia e Letteratura, 1961.
J.M. Norris, "The Theological Structure of Augustine's Exegesis in the *Tractatus in Euangelium Ioannis*," in J. T. Lienhard, E. C. Muller, and R. J. Teske, eds., *Augustine: Presbyter Factus Sum*. New York: Peter Lang, 1993, 385-394.
J.M. Norris, "Augustine and Sign in *Tractatus in Iohannis Euangelium*," in F. Van Fleteren and J.C. Schnaubelt, eds., *Augustine, Biblical Exegete*. New York: 2001, 215-231.
J.J. O'Donnell, "Introduction," in *Confessions* I, xvii-xx. Oxford, Clarendon Press, 1992.
M. Pontet, *L'exégèse de saint Augustin prédicateur*. Marseille: Aubier, 1944.
H. Pope, "Saint Augustine's *Tractatus in Joannem*: a Neglected Classic. *The Ecclesiatical Review* 49 (1913) 161-172.
S. Poque, "Trois semaines de prédication a Hippone en février-mars 407. Le Tractatus in Ioannis Evangelium XI et l'appel aux catéchumènes." *Recherches Augustiniennes* 7 (1971) 183-187.
B. Studer, "I *Tractatus in Iohannem* di sant'Agostino," in L. Padovese, ed., *Atti del I simposio di Efeso sur S. Giovanni apostolo*. Rome: Pontificio Ateneo Antoniano, 1991, 135-146.
B. Studer, "Spiritualità giovannea in Agostino (Osservazioni sul commento agostiniano sulla Prima Ioannis)," in *Atti del II Simposio di Efeso su S. Giovanni Apostolo*. L. Padovese, ed. Roma: 1992, 73-86.
B. Studer, "L'esegesi patristica della 'Prima Ioannis,' " in L. Padovese, ed., *Atti del VIII Simposio di Efeso su S. Giovanni Apostolo*. Roma/Parma, 2001, 143-151.

F. Van Der Meer, *Augustine the Bishop*. New York: Sheed and Ward, 1961.
Luc Verheijen, "Eléments d'un commentaire de la Règle de saint Augustin. La charité ne cherche pas ses propres intérêts." *Augustiniana* 34 (1984) 75-144.
A. Verwilghen, *Christologie et spiritualité selon saint Augustin. L'hymne aux Philippiens*. Paris: Beauchesne, 1985.
A. Verwilghen, "Rhétorique et Prédication chez Augustin." *Nouvelle Revue Théologique* 120 (1998) 233-248.
A. Vita, "Introduzione." *Commento al Vangelo e alla Prima Epistola di San Giovanni*. Rome, Città Nuova, 1968, xi-lix.
F.J. Weismann, "Características eclesiales-comunitarias de la Cristología de los 'Tractatus in Iohannis Euangelium' ", in A. Zumkeller, ed., *Signum Pietatis. Festgabe für Cornelius Petrus Mayer OSA zum 60. Geburtstag*. Würzburg, 1989, 363-367.
F.J. Weismann, "Cristo, Verbo creador y redentor, en la controversia antidonatista de los 'Tractatus in Iohannis Evangelium' I-XVI de S. Agustín." *Stromata* 42 (1986) 301-328.
F.J. Weismann, "Hacia una fundamención antropológica de la cristología en los «Tractatus in Iohannis Evangelium» XVII-LIV de san Agustín." *Omoousios* (1987) 33-45.
F.J. Weismann, "Introducción a la lectura e interpretación de los Tractatus in Johannis Evangelium de San Agustín." *Stromata* 43 (1987) 51-69.
D. F. Wright, "The Manuscripts of St. Augustine's *Tractatus in Evangelium Iohannis*: A Preliminary Survey and Check-List." *Recherches Augustiniennes* 8 (1972) 57-104.
David F. Wright, "Tractatus 20-22 of St. Augustine's *In Iohannem*." *Journal of Theological Studies* 15 (1964) 317-330.
D. Wyrwa, "Augustins geistliche Auslegung des Johannesevangeliums," in J. van Oort and U. Wickert, eds., *Christliche Exegese zwischen Nicaea und Chalcedon*. Kampen: Kok Pharos, 1992, 185-216
S.M. Zarb, "Chronologia Enarrationum sancti Augustini in Psalmos." *Angelicum* 10 (1933) 50-110.
S.M. Zarb, "Chronologia Enarrationum S. Augustini in Psalmos." *Angelicum* 13 (1936) 252-282; 14 (1937) 516-527.

Editor's Note

Since Augustine followed the numbering found in the Septuagint and in the Vulgate, that numbering is followed here, not that of the Hebrew scriptures, where Psalms 10-147 are one digit higher than in Augustine's usage.

As part of the extensive review of the original translation, done by Father Edmund Hill, contractions have been removed so as to avoid the impression that Augustine spoke in an off-handed or informal manner. The original translation also benefited from a fuller, more careful review than would normally be expected of an editor.

This is the first of two volumes.
Complete indexes will appear in the second volume.

Homily 1

On Jn 1:1-5[1]

The challenge of explaining this text to the members of the congregation

1. Thinking about what we have just heard in the reading from the apostle—that *a merely natural human being does not grasp what pertains to the spirit of God* (1 Cor 2:14)[2]—and reflecting further in the midst of this crowd of Your Graces,[3] it is inevitable that many will be merely natural, still of a materialist cast of mind and still not able to raise themselves to a spiritual understanding. Hence, I am very hesitant about how I might say what the Lord may give me to say, or how I might explain, within my limitations, what has just been read from the gospel: *In the beginning was the Word, and the Word was with God, and the Word was God* (Jn 1:1). In fact, a merely natural human being does not grasp it. What then, brothers and sisters? Shall we remain silent for this reason? Then why was the text read aloud if one is to remain silent? Or why listen if it is not to be explained? But then what is the point of explaining it if it will not be understood? And so, since I am once again convinced that some among you are capable not only of grasping the explanation, but even of understanding the text before it is explained, I will not deprive those who can grasp it, even though I fear it may be lost on those who cannot.

Ultimately, the mercy of God will be present, so that all may be satisfied, and each one will grasp what he can; in fact, the speaker only says what he can. For who can state that which *is*? I dare say, my brothers and sisters, that perhaps not even John said what *is*, but only what he could. He, after all, as

---

1. Preached on Sunday, December 9, 406, shortly after Augustine had given his discourses on Pss 119 and 120.
2. *Merely natural human being* (or "the unspiritual person" in the RSV) is *animalis homo* in the Latin; *animalis*, from *anima* or soul, renders the Greek word *psychikos*, which is likewise from the Greek word for soul. In such passages Saint Paul identifies *animalis* with "flesh" and "fleshly" or "carnal," words which he contrasts and opposes to "spirit" and "spiritual." See *The Literal Meaning of Genesis* VI, 19, 30, note 23.
3. *Caritatis vestrae*, literally, "of Your Charity," was an honorific frequently employed in his sermons. Since this and the similar *sanctitas vestra*, "Your Holiness," underline the courtesy with which Augustine habitually treated his congregations, they have to be reproduced in translation. "Your Graces" seems to be the best English equivalent.

a man, spoke about God, and even though inspired by God, he was still a man. Because he was inspired, he said something; if he had not been inspired he would have said nothing. Since he was a human being, even though inspired, he did not say everything, but he said only what he could say as a human being.

The high mountains and the little hills

2. This John, you see, my dearest brothers and sisters, was one of those mountains of which it is written: *May the mountains receive peace for your people and the hills justice* (Ps 71:3). Mountains are lofty souls; hills are ordinary souls. But then the mountains receive peace so that the hills might receive justice. What is the justice which the hills receive? Faith, for *the just person lives by faith* (Rom 1:17; Hab 2:4). Lesser souls, however, would not receive faith unless greater souls—called mountains—were enlightened by Wisdom herself, so that they might pass on to ordinary souls what these ordinary souls can grasp, and thus live from faith as hills because the mountains receive peace.

These same mountains say to the Church, "Peace be with you."[4] And, by proclaiming peace to the Church, these mountains did not separate themselves by acting against the one from whom they received peace; thus could they proclaim peace honestly, rather than deceitfully.

Those who divide the Church are dangerous, wrecking mountains

3. There are, you see, other mountains, shipwrecking ones, and the one who runs a ship into them is undone. It is easy enough, after all, when land is sighted by those in peril on the sea, to make for the land; but sometimes the land sighted is a mountain, and there are rocks lurking at the foot of the mountain, and when someone sets his course for the mountain, he runs into the rocks and finds there, not a safe haven, but a shuddering crash.[5] Some mountains were like that, and they appeared to be great among men; they

---

4. See Jn 20:19 and *Exposition of Psalm* 124, 4. The bishop also greeted the people in this way; hence, the next sentence alludes to the Donatist bishops as those who divided the Church against Christ by proclaiming peace hypocritically.
5. This is an attempt to reproduce the wordplay of the Latin: *non ibi invenit portum sed planctum* might read "finds there not a safe haven and relief but a shuddering crash and grief." The

brought about heresies and schisms and divided the Church of God. But those that divided the Church of God were not the mountains of which it was said, *May the mountains receive peace for your people* (Ps 71:3). How, in fact, could those who divided unity have received peace?

John, a high mountain, received Wisdom

4. But those who did receive peace to proclaim it to the people contemplated Wisdom herself, insofar as human hearts can reach that *which no eye has seen nor ear heard, nor has it entered in the heart of man* (1 Cor 2:9). Well, if Wisdom has not come up into the heart of any human being, how did she enter John's heart? Was John not human? Or perhaps she did not enter John's heart, but rather his heart went up to her? For, what comes up into a man's heart, comes from below to him; but what lifts a man's heart is above man.[6]

Even so, brothers and sisters, it can be said that, if peace did enter John's heart (if this can be said in any way at all), it only came up into John's heart to the extent that John himself was not a man. What does it mean to say he was not a man? To the extent that he had begun to be an angel; for all the saints—because they are announcers of God—are angels. Hence, what did the apostle say to the sensual and merely natural people who do not grasp the things of God? *For when you say, I belong to Paul, I to Apollos, are you not merely human?* (1 Cor 3:4) What did he want to make them, if he was finding fault with them for being merely human? Do you want to know what he wanted to make them? Listen to the answer from the psalms: *I said, You are gods and sons of the Most High, all of you* (Ps 81:6). That is what God called us to—that we not be merely human. But we will become more than merely human if we acknowledge in the first place that we are in fact human, that is, so that we might rise up to that lofty height by humility; otherwise, if we think that we are something, while in fact we are nothing, not only shall we not receive what we are not, but we shall even forfeit what we are.

---

primary meaning of *planctus* is banging or beating, as when one beats a gong; its secondary, more common meaning, from the custom of beating the breast, is grief and lamentation.

6. In the ancient world, for Israelites as well as for Greeks and Romans, the organ which represented thought and practical intelligence was the heart; the tender emotions of pity and compassion were located in the bowels.

John the evangelist was high above the mountains

5. So then, brothers and sisters, John was one of these mountains, and he said, *In the beginning was the Word, and the Word was with God, and the Word was God.* This mountain had received peace, and he was contemplating the divinity of the Word. What was this mountain like? How high was it? It had soared above all the peaks of the earth, soared beyond all the plains of the air, soared beyond the dizzy heights of the stars, soared beyond all the choirs and legions of angels. For, unless he soared above and beyond all these created things, he would never reach the one *through whom all things were made* (Jn 1:3). You can only have a sense of all that he surpassed if you notice where he ended up.

Are you asking about heaven and earth? They were made. Are you asking about the things in heaven and on earth? Obviously, even more clearly were they made. Are you asking about spiritual creatures, about angels, archangels, thrones, dominions, powers, princedoms? They too were made. In fact, once the psalm listed all these things, it finished in this way: *He spoke and they were made; he gave the command, and they were created* (Ps 148:5). If *he spoke and they were made*, then they were made through the Word; but if they were made through the Word, then the only way John's heart could have arrived at what he said, *In the beginning was the Word, and the Word was with God, and the Word was God*, was by soaring above all the things that were made through the Word. What a mountain this man was, how holy, how high among those mountains which received peace for the people of God so that the hills might receive justice!

The psalm just sung says something important about mountains

6. Therefore, brothers and sisters, let us see if John is perhaps one of those mountains about which we sang a few moments ago, *I have lifted up my eyes to the mountains, from where help will come to me* (Ps 120:1). So, if you want to understand, my brothers and sisters, lift up your eyes to this mountain; that is, lift yourself up to the evangelist, raise yourselves up to his meaning. But because these mountains receive peace, while those who place their hopes in man cannot be at peace, take care not to raise your eyes up to this mountain in such a way as to think that your hopes are in man; say, *I have lifted up my eyes to the mountains, from where help will come to*

me, in such a way as to add immediately, *My help is from the Lord, who made heaven and earth* (Ps 120:2).

So let us lift up our eyes to the mountains from where help will come to us; and yet not in those mountains is our hope to be placed; the mountains, in fact, receive what they pass on to us. So then, our hope is to be placed in the one from whom the mountains receive.[7] When we lift up our eyes to the scriptures, because the scriptures have been provided by human beings, we are lifting up our eyes to the mountains from where help will come to us. Even so, because those who wrote the scriptures were human beings, they were not shining on their own, but he *was the true light who enlightens everyone coming into this world* (Jn 1:9). That other John, the Baptist, was also a mountain. He said, *I am not the Christ* (Jn 1:20), so that no one would fall away from the one who lights up the mountains by placing his hope in a mountain. The Baptist also confessed, *And from his fullness we have all received* (Jn 1:16). That is how you ought to say, *I have lifted up my eyes to the mountains, from where help will come to me*, not crediting the mountains with the help that comes to you, but he continued, saying, *My help is from the Lord, who made heaven and earth*.

7. So then, brothers and sisters, this is why I have been reminding you that, when you raise up your hearts to the scriptures at the sound of the gospel, *In the beginning was the Word, and the Word was with God, and the Word was God*, and of the rest of what was read, you should realize that you have lifted up your eyes to the mountains. For, unless the mountains were saying these things, you would not find anything at all for your minds to come to grips with. So then, help has come to you from the mountains, so that you might at least hear these things; but you still cannot understand what you have heard. Call for help from the Lord, who made heaven and earth; because while the mountains have been able to speak, they are not themselves able to enlighten since they too have been enlightened by what they heard. Brothers and sisters, that was where this John, who said these

---

7. See *Exposition of Psalm* 124, 5-6 for a fuller emphasis on the source on which the mountains depend.

things, received them from: he laid his head on the Lord's breast and from the Lord's breast drank in what he would give us to drink.[8]

But he gave us words to drink; then, you have to grasp their meaning from the same source that he who gave them to you drank from. Lift up your eyes then to the mountains from where help is coming to you, so that you may receive a chalice from there, that is, so that you may accept the word given for you to drink; and yet, because your help is from the Lord who made heaven and earth, you may fill your heart from where he filled his—you did say, after all, *My help is from the Lord, who made heaven and earth*. Therefore, let the one who is able be filled.

Brothers and sisters, this is what I have been saying: let each one lift up his heart as best as he can and grasp what is being said. But perhaps you are going to say that I am more immediately present to you than God is. Not at all! He is much more present; while I stand here before your eyes, he watches over your consciences.[9] Lend your ears to me, your hearts to him, that you might fill both. Look, you are lifting up your eyes and these bodily senses to me—no, not really to me, because I am not one of those mountains, but to the gospel itself, to the writer of the gospel; but your hearts are lifted to the Lord to be filled. And lift up your hearts, each one of you, in such a way that you notice what you are lifting up, and where you are lifting it up to. What did I just say, what you are lifting up and where you are lifting it up to? Notice what sort of heart you are lifting up, because you are lifting it up to the Lord; otherwise, weighed down with a load of fleshly pleasure, it will fall before it can be lifted up. But do any of you see yourselves bearing the burden of the flesh? You must work hard by self-denial to purge the heart you are to lift up to God. *Blessed*, after all, *are the clean of heart, for they shall see God* (Mt 5:8).

The difference between the Word and human words

8. Then what is the use of saying these words out loud: *In the beginning was the Word, and the Word was with God, and the Word was God*? While I was talking, I just said some words. Was what I just uttered the Word that

---

8. See Jn 13:23. John's gesture of laying his head on the Lord's breast is repeated in several places in this commentary (see BA 71, 57-60 for the full list).
9. See BA 71, 839-840, where Berrouard recognizes here a reference to Christ who teaches within.

was with God? The words I spoke sounded and ceased, did they not? Did God's Word also make a sound and then come to an end? In that case, how were *all things made through him, and without him was made nothing* (Jn 1:3)? If the Word made noise and then stopped, how can what was created by it be regulated by it? What kind of Word can it be then, that is both spoken and does not come to an end?

Would Your Graces please pay close attention; it is a point of great importance! By being uttered all the time, every day, words have become cheap to us—words just sounding and then ceasing have grown stale; they seem to be nothing more than words. But there is also a word within a human person that abides there, for only the sound comes out of the mouth. There is the word which is really spoken in the spirit, that which you understand from the sound but which is not itself the sound.[10] Look; I utter a word when I say, "God"; what a short word I have uttered, three letters, one syllable![11] Is that really all that God is, just three letters and one syllable? Or rather, is what is understood by these letters cherished all the more insofar as the word is so insignificant? What happened in your heart when you heard "God"? What happened in my heart when I was saying "God"? Something great and supreme occurred to our mind; it soars utterly above and beyond every changeable, carnal and merely natural creature.

And if I say to you, "Is God changeable or unchangeable?" you will answer at once, "Perish the thought that I should either think or feel that God is changeable! God is unchangeable." Your soul, even though small, even though perhaps still flesh-bound, could only answer me that God is unchangeable, even though every creature is changeable. So how could you have that spark in you, leading you toward that which is above every creature, making you sure of your reply to me that God is unchangeable? So what is that thing in your heart, when you are fixing your mind on some substance that is living, everlasting, almighty, infinite, present everywhere, everywhere

---

10. For this relationship between word and meaning, or as Augustine usually says, between the sound or voice and the real word, the meaningful word, see Sermons 28, 4; 120, 2-3; 225, 3, where the theme is applied to the Word incarnate, and the flesh he took is compared to the sound that carries the meaningful word; and Sermons 288, 2, 5; 289, 3, where John the Baptist is the sound or *voice crying in the wilderness* that conveys the Word to the world. The idea is developed more profoundly with regard to the eternal divine Word in *The Trinity*, IX, 10, 15; XV, 10, 20.25.
11. What Augustine actually said was the Latin word for "God," *Deus*; so "four letters, two syllables" was what he went on to say in the original Latin text.

whole and entire, nowhere confined? When you fix your mind on all this, there is a word about God in your heart. But this is surely not mere sound, is it, a sound which consists of three letters and one syllable? So then, whatever things are said and then cease are sounds, letters, syllables. The word that sounds out loud dies away and ceases; but what the sound signified remains both in the thought of the speaker and in the understanding of the hearer; that is what remains when the sounds die away.

The Word is compared to a building plan

9. Turn your attention to this word. If *you* can have a word in your heart—a word that is like a plan born in your mind, such that your mind may give birth to a plan—that plan is like the offspring of your mind, like the child of your heart. For first the heart begets a plan for some building, for putting all you have into some stately monument to be built on your land.[12] The plan is already born and yet the work is not finished. You can see what you are going to make, but no one else can observe and admire it until you have acted and put up that great monument and brought it to its finely sculpted perfection. People notice the admirable building and admire the builder's plan; they are surprised by what they can see and in love with what they do not see. For which of them could see the plan in your heart?

So then, if a human plan wins praise because of some striking monument, do you want to see how the Lord Jesus Christ, that is, the Word of God, is the plan of God? Take a look at the structure of the world, observe what has been made through the Word, and then you will have some idea of what the Word is like. Take a look at the two parts of the world, heaven and earth; who can find words to talk about the splendor of the heavens? Who can find words to talk about the fruitfulness of the earth? Who can fittingly praise the changing seasons, fittingly praise the energy stored in seeds? You will notice how much I am leaving out, because if I went on listing things for a long time I would still in all probability be saying less than you can think up for yourselves.

---

12. See *The Trinity* IX, 17, 12: "When we speak to others we put our voice or some bodily gesture at the disposal of the word that abides within, so that the same sort of thing might happen in the mind of the listener as exists in and does not depart from the mind of the speaker."

From this structure, then, think about what the Word must be like through which it was made—and this structure is not the only thing that was made. All these things, after all, can be seen, because they strike the senses of the body. But, through that Word, angels too were made; through that Word archangels were also made; powers, thrones, dominions, princedoms—through that Word *all things* were made; let that give you some idea of what the Word is like.

10. Now perhaps someone or other will respond to me: "And who thinks about this Word? Well, when you hear "the Word," do not form some trivial idea, nor lump it together with the words you hear every day: "Someone said these words, such words were spoken, you are recounting such words." By endlessly repeating words,[13] it is as if words have become cheap. And when you hear, *In the beginning was the Word*, do not think of something cheap such as you have the habit of thinking of whenever you hear human words; listen to what you should think of: *And the Word was God*.

Arguing against the Arians

11. Now let some misbelieving Arian or other step forward and say that the Word of God was made. How can it be that the Word of God was made, when God made all things through the Word? If the Word of God was also made, through what other Word was it made? If you are saying that there is a Word of the Word through which this Word was made, then I say that this Word is the only Son of God. But if you are not speaking about a Word of the Word, then grant that the Word through which all things were made was not made; for the Word through which all things were made could not be made by himself.

So then, believe the evangelist. For he could have said, "In the beginning God made the Word," just as Moses said, *In the beginning God made heaven and earth*, and then run through all the rest like this: "God said, Let it be made, and it was made." If he asked, "Who said so?"—well, God said so. And what was made? A creature. Between God's "saying" and the creature's being "made," that through which the creature was made is nothing other than the Word; for God said, *Let it be made,* and it was made. Such is the

---

13. Or literally, "the names of words" (*nomina verborum*).

unchangeable Word: although changeable things are made through the Word, that Word is unchangeable.

Through the Word we are also to be created anew

12. Do not therefore believe that the Word, through which all things were made, was made, or else you will fail to be made new by the Word, through which all things are made new. But if you were once made through the Word, you still need to be remade through the Word. If your faith in the Word has grown stale, however, you cannot be remade by the Word. And if it happened that you came to exist through the Word, such that you were made by him, you have turned stale on your own. If you have grown stale on your own, let him who first made you now remake you. If you have deteriorated on your own, let the one who created you recreate you. But how is he going to create you anew through the Word, if you think wrongly about the Word? The evangelist says, *In the beginning was the Word*, and you say, "In the beginning the Word was made." *All things were made through him*, is what he says, and you say that even the Word itself was made. The evangelist could have said, "In the beginning the Word was made;" but what did he say? *In the beginning was the Word*. If he already "was," then he was not "made," so that all things might be made through him, and without him nothing was made. So then, if *the Word was in the beginning, and the Word was with God, and the Word was God*, and if you cannot form any idea of what he is, wait so that you may grow up. He is solid food; accept to be nourished on milk, so that you may become strong enough to take this solid food.[14]

Some wrong ideas about nothing

13. Certainly, brothers and sisters, with the words that follow, *All things were made through him, and without him was made nothing*, see to it that you avoid thinking of *nothing* as being something. Many people, you see, have got into the habit of wrongly understanding *without him was made nothing*, by assuming that there is something called "nothing." Sin indeed was not made through him, and, obviously, sin is nothing, and, when they sin, people

---

14. See 1 Cor 3:2; Heb 5:12.

become nothing. And no idol was made through the Word; it has something like a human shape, but the human being itself was made through the Word, not the shape of the human being you see in the idol; that was not made through the Word, as it is written: *We know that an idol is nothing* (1 Cor 8:4).

So these things were not made through the Word. But whatever was made according to nature, whatever there is among creatures, absolutely everything that is fixed in the heavens, that shines from above, that flies beneath the heavens, and that moves about in the whole of creation, absolutely every single creature—let me put it more plainly, let me say, brothers and sisters, so that you really do understand, everything from angel to maggot—was through the Word. What is there among creatures more noble than an angel, what is there among creatures more lowly than a maggot? The one through whom the angel was made is the one through whom the maggot too was made; but the angel's proper place is heaven, the maggot's proper place is earth. The one who created things also arranged them. If he had put a maggot in the sky, you would find fault, if he had wanted angels to be born of rotting meat, you would find fault—and yet that is just about what God does, and he is not to be faulted. For, all human beings born of flesh, what are they but maggots? And from maggots he makes angels.

After all, if the Lord himself says, *I am a maggot and not a man* (Ps 21:6), can anybody have any hesitation about saying what is also written in Job: *How much more is man than rottenness, and the son of man than a maggot* (Job 25:6)? First he said, *Man is rottenness*, and next, *The son of man a maggot*; because maggots are born of rottenness, he said, *Man is rottenness and the son of man a maggot*. There you are, just look at what he, who *in the beginning was the Word, and the Word was with God, and the Word was God*, was willing to become for your sake! Why did he do this for you? So that you, still unable to eat, could have milk to drink.

That, therefore, brothers and sisters, is certainly the way you are to take the words, *All things were made through him, and without him was made nothing*. Every single creature was made through him, big and small; through him were made the heights, through him the depths; through him what is spiritual, through him what is bodily. There can be no shape, I mean, no organic structure, no harmony of parts, no substance of any sort that is able to have weight, number, measure, except through that Word and from the Word, that is, the creator, to whom it is said, *You have arranged all things in measure and number and weight* (Wis 11:20).

Why did God create flies and fleas?

14. So then, let no one deceive you when, for example, you are bothered by flies. Yes indeed, the devil has had the laugh on many people and caught them with flies. Bird-catchers, you see, regularly put flies in traps, to deceive hungry birds; and that is how these people too are deceived by the devil. I mean, here you have someone or other who was bothered by flies; a Manichee found him feeling irritated, and when he said he could not bear flies and found them utterly loathsome, the other said straightaway, "Who made them?" And because he was fed up with them and loathed them he did not have the nerve to say, "God made them"—Catholic though he was. The other fellow added immediately, "If God did not make them, who did?" "Really," he said, "I think the devil must have made them." Back came the other, "If the devil made flies—as I see you admit, because you are a sensible man—who then made bees, which are a little bigger than flies?" And now he could not bring himself to say that God made bees and flies, because they were much the same sort of thing. And from bees he led him on to locusts, from locusts to lizards, from lizards to birds, from birds to sheep and goats, from there to oxen, from there to elephants, and finally to human beings; and thus he persuaded that man that human beings are not made by God. In this way, the poor guy—from being fed up with flies—was made into a fly himself, taken possession of by the devil. Beelzebub, as a matter of fact, is said to mean "Lord of the flies," about which it is written, *Dying flies ruin sweet-smelling oil* (Qo 10:1).

15. What then, brothers and sisters? Why have I said all this? Shut the ears of your hearts against the wiles of the enemy; understand this clearly, that God made all things whatsoever and set them in their proper places. Why though do we endure so much unpleasantness from a creature that God has made? Because we have offended God. Angels do not endure such things, do they? Perhaps we too would not have such things to fear in this life.[15] Blame your sin, not the judge, for your punishment. Because of pride, in fact, God made this smallest, most useless of creatures to torment

---

15. That is, we would not have such things to fear if there had been no sin.

us. In that way, when man was proud and challenged God, and, even though he was mortal, he terrified other mortals, and even though he was human, he did not acknowledge his neighbors as human, then, just when he flaunts himself, he is afflicted with fleas.

Why do you puff yourself up so, human pride? Someone was rude to you, and you swelled up in wrath; fight off the fleas so that you can get to sleep—recognize who you really are. For, that you might realize, brothers and sisters, that these things were created to molest us so as to curb our pride, notice that God could have curbed the pride of Pharaoh's people with bears, with lions, with serpents; what he did do was send flies and frogs among them, so that pride would be curbed by the most worthless of creatures.[16]

What was made, in him is life

16. So then *all things*, brothers and sisters, *all things* without exception, *were made through him, and without him was made nothing*. But how were all things made through him? *What was made, in him is life* (Jn 1:3-4). It can, in fact, also be phrased: *What was made in him is life*. If we phrase it in that way, then everything is life. What, after all, was not made in him? For he is the Wisdom of God; and the psalm says, *You have made all things in wisdom* (Ps 103:24). So if Christ is the Wisdom of God, and the psalm says, *You have made all things in wisdom*, then just as all things were made through him, so all things were made in him. If then all things were made in him, my dearest brothers and sisters, and what was made in him is life, it would follow that even the earth is life; and therefore wood is life—we do indeed say that wood is life, but we understand by that the wood of the cross, from which we have received life—and therefore even a stone is life.

To understand the phrase in that way is perverse, giving that vile sect of the Manichees another chance to creep in and say that a stone has life, and a wall has a soul, and a rope has a soul, as does wool and clothing too. For that is what they are used to saying in their ravings; when they are challenged and refuted for saying that, they quote the scriptures and say, "Then why does it say, *What was made in him is life*? For if all things were made in him,

---

16. See *Homilies on the First Epistle of John* 8, 6-7 for a fuller explanation of this thinking.

all things are life." Do not let them lead you astray; phrase it like this: *What was made* (pause there, and then carry on), *in him is life*. What does that mean? The earth was made, but the earth itself—that was made—is not life; but in Wisdom herself, in a spiritual way, is found the plan according to which earth was made; that is what is life.[17]

Comparison with a joiner making a chest

17. Let me explain it to Your Graces as best I can. A carpenter makes a chest. First he has a design of the chest in his mind;[18] for, if he did not have the chest in his mind, how could he work to craft it? Yet the chest in his mind is such that it is not the same as the chest which is visible to human eyes. Invisibly in the carpenter's mind, it will be visible once it is produced. Once made, will it no longer be in the artisan's mind? It is both fashioned in fact and still in the mind. For the one can rot and decay, but the other one, which remains in the mind, can fashion another chest. So then, pay attention to the chest in the mind and to the chest that is made. The chest he made is not living; but the chest in his mind is alive, because the soul of the craftsman, where all these things are before they are in fact produced, is living.

So it is, my dearest brothers and sisters, that the Wisdom of God, through whom all things were made, contains all things in the mind before she fashions them; consequently, all the things that are made through such a design are not thereby life, but whatever has been made is alive in him. You see the earth, the earth is there in the design [of the

---

17. With the punctuation of Jn 1:3-4 found in the Revised Standard Version, Augustine's problem does not arise: *All things were made through him, and without him was not anything made that was made. In him was life*. The punctuation Augustine followed is preferred by the Nestle-Aland Greek New Testament (1979) and followed by the Jerusalem Bible. I give my own translation: *All things came to be through him, and without him there came to be not a single thing; what has come to be in him was/is life*. Augustine's problem, in the text so punctuated, arises from the fact that the Latin for "to become, to come to be" is the passive of the verb *facere*, "to make"; and he usually takes it in its strong sense of "to be made," as no doubt did the Manichees. But leaving aside that somewhat outdated argument of theirs, the sentence should be phrased in the way he rejects, *what has come to be in him (more precisely "in it," the Word), was/is life*; for what, after all, has come to be in the Word, what has happened in the Word? *The Word was made flesh and took up residence among us* (Jn 1:14). That indeed was/is life.
18. Throughout this paragraph Augustine contrasts *in arte* with in *opere*: see Homily 2, note 12. The first phrase refers to the ability to conceive of a chest (a blueprint, as it were, in the mind [*concilium*]); the second phrase emphasizes the product or its visible existence (the fact, the construction [*fabrica*]). See Homily 2, 10.

artisan]; you can see the sky, the sky is in the mind; you can see the sun and moon, these too are in the mind. Yet, to the eye, they are physical bodies; in the mind they are living.

Understand it, if you possibly can, for an important matter has been spoken: if it is not great because of me nor great because it comes to you through me; even so, it comes from someone great. All this has not been said by little me, nor is the one to whom I refer in order to speak of little importance. Let each one grasp what he can, to the extent he is able; and if someone cannot grasp it, then let him nourish his heart so as to become able. Where can one find such nourishment? Feed on milk, so as to be able to take solid food.[19] Do not withdraw from Christ born in the flesh, until you reach Christ born of the one Father, the Word God with God, through which all things were made; because that is the life which, in him, is the light of all.

The true light enlightens everyone

18. Notice then what follows: *And the life was the light of all* (Jn 1:4), and it is from that life that human beings are enlightened. Cattle are not enlightened, because animals do not have rational minds, capable of seeing wisdom. But the human being, *made to the image of God* (Gn 1:27), does have a rational mind, with which wisdom may be perceived. So then, that life through which all things were made, that very life is the light, not of all and sundry animate beings, but the light of human beings. That is why a little later he says, *That was the true light who enlightens everyone coming into this world* (Jn 1:9). It was by that light that John the Baptist was enlightened, and John the evangelist as well. Filled with that light was the one who said, *I am not the Christ; but the one who is coming after me, the strap of whose sandals I am not worthy to untie* (Jn 1:20.27). Enlightened by that light was the one who said, *In the beginning was the Word, and the Word was with God, and the Word was God.* That life, then, is the light of all.

Clean the eyes of your heart so as to be able to see the true light

19. But perhaps some foolish hearts here still cannot grasp this light, because they are so weighed down by their sins that they cannot see it. But

---

19. Christ, in his incarnation, is milk for the children that we are; see *Exposition of Psalm* 119, 2.

just because they are unable to see it does not mean that this light is absent; no, because of their sins, they themselves are darkness. *And the light shines in the darkness, and the darkness did not comprehend it* (Jn 1:5). So then, brothers and sisters, just as a blind person, placed in the sun, has the sun present to him, even though he is absent from it, in the same way every fool,[20] every crook, every godless person is blind in heart. Wisdom is present, but while present to a blind person, his eyes are absent from it—not because wisdom[21] is absent from his eyes, but because they are absent from him.

So what is this person to do? Clean up what allows him to see God. Suppose someone could not see because he had sore and dirty eyes, with dust or rheum or smoke getting into them; the doctor would say to him, "Purge your eye of whatever is hurting it, so as to be able to see the light of your eyes." Dust, rheum, smoke, these are sins and wickedness; get rid of all of them, and you will see the wisdom that is present with you, because God is this very wisdom; and it has been said, *Blessed are the clean of heart, for they shall see God.*

---

20. Folly and wickedness are simply equated in the scriptures, as on the other hand are wisdom and virtue.
21. That is Christ, the Wisdom of God.

Homily 2

On Jn 1:6-14[1]

Not fair to those who heard the first homily to repeat it now

1. It is right, brothers and sisters, that I should, as best I can, explain the text of the divine scriptures, and especially of the holy gospel, without leaving anything out, and that I should be nourished by it as much as I can manage, and that I should serve up to you what has nourished me. The first part was dealt with last Sunday, as I remember; that is: *In the beginning was the Word, and the Word was with God, and the Word was God; he was in the beginning with God. All things were made through him, and without him was made nothing. What was made, in him is life; and the life was the light of all; and the light shines in the darkness, and the darkness did not comprehend it.* (Jn 1:1-5) That is, I believe, as much as I dealt with; those of you who were here will remember; those of you who were not here must believe me and believe those who were willing to be here. So now, since we cannot always go back over everything again, we have to think of those who want to hear what comes next; it would be unfair to cheat them out of what follows by repeating the previous parts. So would those who were not here not insist on our going back over the earlier part, but rather listen now—along with those who were here—to what comes next.

On the cross as our way to cross the sea of this world to our home country, seen from afar

2. The gospel continues: *There was a man sent from God, whose name was John* (Jn 1:6). In fact, beloved brothers and sisters, what was said earlier concerned Christ's inexpressible divinity—and it was spoken almost inexpressibly. Who, in fact, will ever comprehend *In the beginning was the Word, and the Word was with God*? And to make sure that the name Word not be of less worth for you because of a familiarity with everyday words, he adds, *and the Word was God.* This Word is Being itself, about

---
1. Preached on Sunday, December 16, 406.

which I spoke at length yesterday;[2] may God grant that, having spoken so much, I succeeded in imparting something to your hearts. *In the beginning was the Word*; it is the same, ever in the same way; as it is, so it always is; it cannot change; that is what *is* means. That is the name he declared to his servant Moses: *I am who am*; and *He who is sent me* (Ex 3:14).

So who then will ever grasp this, when you notice how all things mortal are subject to change, how not only are the features of bodies being continually altered in being born, growing, fading away, dying, but how even their souls are stretched and torn by various desires; when you notice both how people can lay hold of wisdom if they turn toward its light and warmth and how they can forfeit wisdom when, badly disposed, they turn their backs on it? So then, when you see all these changing things, what just *is*, other than something that soars beyond all those things which *are*, as if they are not really to be at all?[3] So who then can grasp this? Or who—no matter how he may have stretched his mental powers so as in some way to touch that which is—who could actually reach what he brushed with the edge of his mind?[4]

It is as if someone could see his home country from a long way away, but is cut off from it by the sea; he sees where to go, but does not have the means to get there. In the same way all of us long to reach that secure place of ours where that which is *is*, because it alone always *is* as it is. But in between lies the sea of this world through which we are going, even though we already see where we are going (many, however, do not see where they are going). Thus, so that we might also have the means to go, the one we were longing to go to came here from there. And what did he make? A wooden raft for us to cross the sea on. For no one can cross the sea of this world unless carried over it on the cross of Christ.[5] Sometimes even someone of ailing eyes embraces

---

2. "Being itself" is a translation of the Latin *idipsum*. The discourse on *idipsum* is an echo of the mysterious, ineffable name of God (see *The Trinity* III, 2, 8; *Confessions* VII, 17, 23) about which Augustine "spoke at length yesterday," refers to the *Exposition of Psalm* 121,5 ("Jerusalem is built as a city, whose sharing is in Being itself"). Augustine preached on Pss 119 to 133 at the same time that he preached on the first twelve homilies on John; see *Homélies sur l'Evangile de Saint Jean*, I-XVI, in BA 71, 29 ff, and 845-848 for the note.
3. See Homily 38, 10.
4. Augustine may be drawing a parallel with his own attempts to ascend there not long before his conversion (*Confessions* VII, 9, 13-14; 10, 16; 17, 23) or to his experience at Ostia with his mother (ibid. IX, 10, 23-25).
5. See Sermon 63, 1, for the image of the cross as a a kind of raft for getting us across the ocean of this life: quoting Wis 10:4 (*Wisdom again healed the world, steering the just man by means of a*

this cross: may the one who does not see from afar where he is going not let go of the cross, and it will take him to that destination.

The high mountains could see the home
country from afar; the lower hills could not

3. And so, my brothers and sisters, this is what I hope I have managed to instill into your hearts: if you wish to live in a devout and Christian way, cling to Christ according to that which he was made for us, so as to come to him according to that which he is and according to that which he was. He came here so that he could become, for us, what he was not, because, for our sakes, he was made into the one who would carry the weak across the sea of this world and so arrive at their home country, where no boat will be needed, because there is no sea there to be crossed. Therefore, it is better to fail to see what *is* with the mind and even so not draw back from the cross of Christ, than to see what *is* with the mind and scorn the cross of Christ. Better than this, even best of all, if it can be done, is that the traveler both see where to go and hold on to what will carry him there.

The great minds of the mountains—those whom the light of justice lit up in a special way were called mountains—were able to do that; they could do that and saw that which is. For, while seeing it, John said, *In the beginning was the Word, and the Word was with God, and the Word was God.* They saw this, and in order to reach what they were seeing from a long way off, they did not let go of the cross of Christ and did not disdain the humility of Christ. Those little ones, however, who cannot understand this, by not backing away from Christ's cross and passion and resurrection, are ferried in this boat to what they do not see; those who do see arrive in the very same boat.

Worldly philosophers could see it, but by disdaining the cross
could not pass over to it

4. Certain philosophers in this world have sought the creator through the creature—because he can indeed be found through the creature, as the apostle clearly tells us, *For his invisible attributes, having been perceived from the foundation of the world through the things that have been made,*

---

contemptible piece of wood), Augustine sees this same function of the cross as prefigured by Noah's ark.

can now be gazed upon; also his everlasting power and divinity, so that they may have no excuse. And he continues, *But because they had come to know God*—he did not say, "Because they have not come to know God," but *because they had come to know God—they did not glorify him as God, or give thanks; but they faded away in their thoughts, and their senseless heart was darkened.* Darkened by what? He continues and says more plainly, *For, calling themselves wise, they became fools.* (Rom 1:20-22)

They saw where they were to go, but, being ungrateful to the one who set what they saw before them, they wanted to take all the credit for the sight themselves; and, grown thus proud, they lost what they saw and turned away from there to idols and images and to the cult of demons, worshiping a creature and disdaining the creator. They did these things once they had been brought down: but pride brought them down, for, when they grew proud, they called themselves wise. So then, those about whom he said, *who though they had come to know God*, saw what John says, because all things were made through the Word of God. In fact, they found such statements in the books of philosophers, as is the fact that God has an only begotten Son *through whom all things are* (Rom 11:36). They were able to see that which is, but from a long way off; they refused to hold onto the humility of Christ, the boat in which they would safely reach what they were able to see from a long way off; and they were disgusted by the cross of Christ.

The sea has to be crossed, and you disdain the cross? O proud wisdom! You mock the crucified Christ; he is the one you have seen from a long way off—*In the beginning was the Word, and the Word was with God.* But why was he crucified? Because you were in need of the wood of his humility. You had swollen up with pride, you see, and had been cast away, far from that home country, and the way back has been cut off by the surging billows of this world, and you have no means of crossing over to the home country, unless you are carried there on the wood. Ungrateful wretch, you mock the one who came to you to help you return! He became the way, the path through the sea; that is why he walked on the sea, to show you there is a path in the sea.[6] But you who cannot walk on the sea like him, let yourself

---

6. See Mk 6:48.

be ferried in a boat, ferried on the wood; believe in the Crucified, and you will be able to reach the further shore.

He was crucified on your account: to teach the lesson of humility and because, if he had simply come as God, he would not have been recognized. After all, if he had come as God, he would not have come to those who were unable to see God. In fact, he did not come or leave according to that which God is, since God is present everywhere and is not contained in any place or space. But how did he come? By appearing as a man.

John the Baptist sent ahead of the Word, a lamp to show us the sun

5. So then, because he was a man in such a way that God was hidden in him, a great man was sent ahead of him; by his witness, he would be found to be more than a man. And who is this? *There was a man.* And how would he be able to speak the truth about God? *Sent from God.* What was he called? *Whose name was John.* Why did he come? *This man came as a witness, to bear witness to the light, so that all might believe through him.* (Jn 1:6-7) What sort of man was the one who would bear witness to the light? This John was someone great, of enormous worth, of great grace, a most lofty peak. Marvel, yes, wonder at him—but as a mountain. A mountain is in darkness unless it be mantled in light; therefore, marvel at John insofar as you listen to what follows, *That man was not the light* (Jn 1:8), lest, by seeing the mountain as light, you end up shipwrecked, not sheltered, by the mountain. But what should you marvel at? Marvel at the mountain as a mountain, but raise yourself up to the one who lights up the mountain, which was itself raised up in order first to receive his rays, and then relay them to your eyes. So then: *That man was not the light.*

6. Why therefore did he come? *To bear witness to the light.* What was that for? So t*hat all might believe through him.* And to what light was he to bear witness? *To the true light* (Jn 1:9). Why did he add *true* ? Because a person who has been enlightened is also called light, but the true light is the one who enlightens. For even our eyes are called lights;[7] and yet unless a

---

7. Augustine makes the same observation in Sermon 4, 6, where he says, "Even the eyes in our heads, after all, are called lights, and everyone swears, 'By my lights.' " See also Homilies 14, 1; 19, 11; 35, 3. I am indebted to Dr. Robert Markus for these references.

lamp is lit during the night, or the sun comes out in the day, these lights open to no avail.

In this way, then, John too was a light, but not the true light because, while yet unenlightened, he was darkness; yet by being enlightened, he became light. If, however, he had not been enlightened, he would have been darkness, like all the godless, to whom, once they were believers, the apostle said, *You were once darkness.* Now, though, because they had come to believe, what were they? *But now*, he says, *you are light in the Lord* (Eph 5:8). If he did not add, *in the Lord*, we would not understand. *Light*, he says, *in the Lord*; as darkness you were not in the Lord. *For you were once darkness*—he did not add *in the Lord* there. Then you are darkness in yourselves, light in the Lord. So not even John *was the light, but he came to bear witness to the light.*

John not the true light

7. But where is the light? *That light was true, who enlightens everyone coming into this world* (Jn 1:9). If he enlightened everyone coming into this world, then he enlightened John as well. Thus, Christ enlightened the one by whom he wished to be made known. Would Your Graces please understand; he came, in fact, to weakened minds, to wounded hearts, to the gaze of the nearsighted human soul. That is what he came for. And how would the soul be able to see that which perfectly *is*? In the way it often happens that the sun's rising, which we are unable to look at with our eyes, is made known to us through some object lit by its rays. After all, even people with bad eyesight are capable of looking at a wall or a mountain or a tree or anything of that sort that the sun is shining on and illuminating. And thus the sunrise, which their eyesight is still too weak to look at directly, is brought to their attention by shining on something else.

That is how all those who came to Christ were; they were not able to see him. He turned his rays on John, who by confessing that he had been lit up by those rays and enlightened—he was not the source of those rays nor of that enlightenment—made the one who enlightens known, made the one who radiates known, and made the one who fulfills known. And who is this one? *The one*, he says, *who enlightens everyone coming into the world*. Because if man had not withdrawn from that light,[8] he would not have needed to be enlightened. But he did need to be enlightened here because he withdrew from that light where man could have been enlightened for ever.

How the Word was both in the world and not in the world

8. So what then? If he came here, where was he? *He was in this world* (Jn 1:10). He was here and he also came here; he was here in his divinity, he came here in the flesh, because though he was here in his divinity, he could not be seen by fools and by the blind and by the wicked. They were the darkness of which it has already been said that *the light shines in the darkness, and the darkness did not comprehend it*. Look, he is here now, and he was here then, and he is always here; and he never departs, never moves anywhere else. But it is necessary for you to have a way to see what never departs from you; necessary for you not to depart from the one who does not move anywhere else; necessary for you not to desert, and you will not be deserted. Do not fall, and he will not "set" on you; if you "set," he will "set" on you;[9] but if you stand, he is present to you.

However, you did not stand up; remember where you fell from, where the one who fell before you cast you down from. He cast you down, you see, not by force, not by pushing you over, but by means of your own will. If you had not consented, after all, to evil, you would still be on your feet, you would have remained enlightened. But now, because you have already fallen, and because your heart, with which the light can be seen, has been wounded, he has come to you in the kind of form you would be able to see; and he has presented himself as a human being so that he might seek the testimony of a human being. God looks for a witness from a human being, and God has a human being give him one. God has a human being bear witness to him—but for the sake of human beings, because we are so weak. We look for daylight with a lamp, because John himself was called a lamp by the Lord: *He was a*

---

8. From the innocence of the garden before the fall.
9. A play on the words *casus*, "fall," and *occasus*, "setting of the sun": *Noli cadere, et non tibi occidet. Si tu feceris casum, ille tibi facit occasum.* God is the sun that may or may not set in relation to one's stance.

burning and shining lamp, and you were willing for a time to rejoice in his light; but my testimony is greater than John's (Jn 5:35-36).

Why the Word wanted John to bear witness

9. So then, he has shown that, for the sake of human beings, he wished to be pointed out to the faith of believers by a lamp, so that his enemies might be put to confusion by means of this lamp. These enemies, you see, were testing him and saying, *Tell us by what authority you are doing these things? I too have a question to ask you*, he said. *Tell me, where is John's baptism from? From heaven or from men? And they were troubled, and said to one another, If we say, From heaven, he is going to say to us, Then why did you not believe him?* Because John bore witness to Christ by saying, *I am not the Christ*, but that man is.[10] *If however we say, From men—we are afraid that the people may stone us; because they regarded John as a prophet.* (Mt 21:23-27)[11] Afraid of being stoned, but more afraid of confessing the truth, they answered the Truth with a lie—*and iniquity has lied to itself* (Ps 26:12); for, they said, *We do not know* (Mt 21:27).

And the Lord, because they had slammed their door in his face by saying they did not know what in fact they did know—the Lord did not open up to them either, because they were not really knocking. It is indeed said, *Knock, and the door will be opened to you* (Mt 7:7). Not only, though, did they fail to knock so that it might be opened, but by their denial they blocked their own entrance. And so the Lord said to them, *Neither am I telling you by what authority I am doing these things* (Mt 21:27). And thus they were put to confusion through John, and the words were fulfilled in their case: *I have prepared a lamp for my Christ; I will clothe his enemies with confusion* (Ps 131:17-18).

The Word in the world compared to a master craftsman

10. *He was in the world, and the world was made through him* (Jn 1:10). Do not think of him being in the world in the same way as the earth is in the

---
10. See Jn 1:20.27.36.
11. This long quotation is really a mix from all three synoptic gospels; see the parallels to Matthew here. Could Augustine have been using a Latin version of Tatian's Diatessaron, a harmony of the gospels that was used in Syrian Churches and may have been available in some African Churches?

world, as the sky is in the world, the sun, moon and stars are in the world, trees, cattle, people are in the world. That is not how he was in the world. But how was he? Like a master craftsman,[12] in command of what he has made. He did not make it, you see, in the way an artisan makes things. The chest an artisan makes is outside him and is in a different place from him while it is being fashioned; it is beside him, of course, but the one who is fashioning it is sitting in a different place, and is outside the thing he is fashioning. But God is present in the world he is fashioning, he does not stand aside from it and handle the matter he is working on, so to say, from the outside. He makes what he makes by the presence of his majesty; by his presence he governs what he has made. That then is how he was in the world, as the one through whom the world was made. For *the world was made through him*, and the world did not know him (Jn 1:10).

Two meanings of world

11. What does it mean: *The world was made through him*? Heaven, earth, the sea and all the things that are in them, that is what is called *the world*? But it has another meaning as well: lovers of the world are called *the world*. *The world was made through him, and the world did not know him*. Did the heavens not know their creator, or the angels not know their creator, or the stars not know their creator, whom even the demons acknowledge? All things from every side bore witness to him. But who then did not know him? Those who, by loving the world, are called *the world*.

By loving, you see, we live from within; yet by loving where they lived, they have deserved to be called by that name. It is like when we say, "That is a bad house," or "That is a good house"; we are not in the first case blaming the walls, or in the second case praising the walls; but by "bad house" we mean bad inhabitants, by "good house," good inhabitants. So it is that those who inhabit the world by loving it are the world. Who are they? Those who put the world first in their affections; for their heart dwells in the world. Yet those who do not put the world first in their affections may

---

12. Here the craftsman is in command of what he constructs from within it; he can be contrasted with the joiner, the *faber*, whose relationship with what he makes is not "interior." Cf. Homily 1, 17 for a similar contrast between that which is made *in arte* (according to a blueprint in the mind) and *in opere* (for the eyes to see).

reside in the world in the flesh; but in their heart they live in heaven, as the apostle says, *But our residence is in heaven* (Phil 3:20). So then, *The world was made through him, and the world did not know him.*

Those who did not receive him

12. *He came to his own*—because everything was made through him. *And his own people did not receive him* (Jn 1:11). Who are *his own*? The people he made: the Jews whom, in the beginning, he made to be over all the nations, because the other nations used to worship idols and serve demons. Yet that people was born of the seed of Abraham, and they are supremely his own, because they are related to him through the flesh which he was good enough to take to himself. *He came to his own, and his own people did not receive him.* Did they fail to receive him without exception? Were none of them saved? After all, nobody will be saved except those who have received Christ at his coming.

And those who did

13. But he added, *As many, though, as did receive him.* What did he bestow on them? Great kindness; great mercy. Singly born, he did not wish to remain the one and only. Many couples who have had no children adopt some when advanced in years and realize by choice what nature was unable to provide; that is what human beings do. But someone who has an only son rejoices in him all the more, because he alone will take possession of the whole inheritance and not have anyone else to divide it with and thus turn out the poorer. Not so God; he sent the very same one and only Son he had begotten, through whom he had created everything, into this world so that he should not be alone but should have adopted brothers and sisters. You see, we were not born of God in the same way as that only-begotten Son of his, but we were adopted through the Son's grace. For the only-begotten Son came to forgive sins, those sins which had us so tied up that they were an impediment to his adopting us; he forgave those he wished to make his brothers and sisters and made them co-heirs.

That, after all, is what the apostle says: *If, however, a son, he is also an heir* (Gal 4:7); and again: *Heirs indeed of God, but co-heirs of Christ* (Rom 8:17). No, he was not afraid of having co-heirs, because his inheritance is not whittled down if many possess it. They themselves, in fact, become the inheritance which he possesses, and he in turn becomes their inheritance. Listen to how they become his inheritance: *The Lord said to me, You are my Son; today I have begotten you. Ask of me, and I will give you nations as your inheritance.* (Ps 2:7-8) How does he, in his turn, become their inheritance? It says in the psalm, *The Lord is my part of the inheritance and my cup* (Ps 15:5). May we possess him and may he possess us—he possesses us as our Lord; we possess him as salvation, we possess him as light. So then, what did he give those who did receive him? *He gave them authority to become children of God, those who believe in his name* (Jn 1:12), that they might thus keep hold of the wood and cross the sea.

How these are born of God

14. And how are they born to him? Because they become children of God and brothers and sisters of Christ, they must of course be born. How, I mean, could they be children, if they were not born? But the children of human beings are born of flesh and blood, and of the will of a man, and the embrace of spouses. But, these, how are they born to him? In what way *not of bloods*, as of a man and a woman. *Bloods* is not Latin; but because the Greek has it in the plural, the translator preferred to keep it and speak what the grammarians would say is not Latin and still spell out the truth so that it could be heard by the weak and feeble. You see, if he said "blood" in the singular, he would not be spelling out what he wished to; human beings after all are born of the bloods of male and female. So let us say it then and not be afraid of a caning from the grammarians, provided we can get at the sure and solid truth. To find fault with what he understands is to be ungrateful for having understood.

Not of bloods, nor of the will of the flesh, nor of the will of the man (Jn 1:13). He used flesh for woman, because Adam said when she had been made from his rib, *This is now bone from my bones and flesh from my flesh* (Gn 2:23); and the apostle says, *He that loves his wife loves himself; for nobody ever hates his own flesh* (Eph 5:28-29). So then, flesh is used for the wife, just as elsewhere spirit is used for the husband. Why? Because he guides, she is guided; he is to command, she to serve; because where the flesh commands and the spirit serves, the household is upside down. What could be worse than a household where the woman rules the man? No, the household is "right" where the man guides and the woman complies. Thus a person is "right" where the spirit guides and the flesh serves.

15. So then, *not of the will of the flesh, nor of the will of man, but of God they were born* (Jn 1:13). But, so that human beings might be born of God, God was first of all born of them. Christ, after all, is God, and Christ was born of human beings. He was only looking for a mother on earth, because he already had a Father in heaven; he was born of God that we might be fashioned and he was born of a woman that we might be refashioned. Do not be astonished, then, O man, at being made a child by grace because you were born of God according to his Word. First, that Word wanted to be born of a human being so that you might be assured of being born of God and might say to yourself, "Not without reason did God choose to be born of a human being; for thus did he regard me of some value, such that he would make me immortal and he would be born mortal for my sake." That is why, after saying, *Of God they were born*, as though to save us from being overwhelmed and flabbergasted at such grace, that it would seem incredible to us that human beings were actually born of God, he says, to set your mind at ease, *And the Word was made flesh and took up residence among us* (Jn 1:14). So why be astonished that human beings are born of God? Observe God himself being born of human beings: *And the Word was made flesh and took up residence among us.*

Why the Word was made flesh

16. Now, because *the Word was made flesh and took up residence among us*, by his very birth he made an ointment with which the eyes of our hearts could be cleaned, that we might see his majesty through his humility. That is why *the Word was made flesh and took up residence among us*; he healed our eyes, and what follows? *And we saw his glory* (Jn 1:14). No one could see his glory without being healed by the lowliness of the flesh. Why would we not have been able to see it? Would Your Graces please pay close attention and see what I am saying. It is as if dust had got into the eye of a person, earth got into it, injured the eye, the eye could not see the light. The injured eye was anointed; it had been injured by earth, and yet earth is put into it for healing. After all, all ointments and medicines have earth as

their source. You were blinded by dust, you are healed by dust; so flesh blinded you; flesh heals you. The soul, you see, had become fleshly-minded by giving its consent to fleshly-minded inclinations, and that is how the eye of the heart had been blinded.

The Word was made flesh; this doctor made you an ointment for the eyes. And since he thus came in the flesh to extinguish the vices of the flesh and with death to slay death, that is why it came to be that you, because *the Word was made flesh*, would be able to say, *And we saw his glory*. What sort of glory? That of becoming the son of man? That is his humility, not his glory. But, once healed by flesh, where is the heart's gaze drawn to? It says, *We saw his glory, glory as of the only-begotten of the Father, full of grace and truth* (Jn 1:14). I shall deal more fully with grace and truth at another place in this gospel, should the Lord be pleased to allow it. Let this now be enough for you to build yourselves up in Christ, to be strong in faith, and to be vigilant in good works. And do not let go of the wood on which you can cross the sea.

Homily 3

On Jn 1:15-18[1]

He will speak on grace and truth, as he promised

1. Filled with the grace and truth of God, the only-begotten Son, our Lord and Savior, showed himself to the saints. That grace and truth, which we have accepted in the name of the Lord and which we promised to present to Your Graces, belongs to the New Testament and thus must be distinguished from the Old.[2] So please give me all your attention so that I may grasp as much as God gives and that you may grasp as much as you hear. If the seed sown in your hearts is not seized by birds nor choked by thistles nor scorched by summer heat,[3] then it will only remain for you to yield a harvest, aided by the falling rain of daily exhortations and by your own good reflections at work in the heart, even as a harrow breaks up the clods in the field, and the seed is covered and it can germinate; thus will the farmer rejoice and be delighted. If, on the other hand, for all the good seed and the good rain, we produce thistles instead of a harvest, it will not be the fault of the seed or a charge to bring against the rain—but the bonfire they deserve is being readied for the thistles.

The law given through Moses; grace and truth through Christ

2. We are Christian people, a fact which I do not think I need to belabor with Your Graces; and if we are Christians, then by that very name we belong to Christ, whose sign we carry on our foreheads; if we also carry it in our hearts, then we are not ashamed of it. His sign is his humility. By a star the magi recognized him; and this was a sign given by the Lord, a heavenly and noble sign. He did not want a star on the foreheads of the faithful to be his

---

1. Preached on Sunday, December 23, 406.
2. For Augustine and his listeners, the Old and New Testaments are not merely two parts of the Bible, but the old and the new covenants. I have decided to use the word "testament" but ask the reader to bear in mind that it does frequently signify covenant. The promise that Augustine made to his listeners may refer not only to the end of Homily 2, but also to the *Exposition of Psalm* 123, 14, given on the previous day. There he elaborates at greater length on the subjects that will be treated in this homily.
3. See Mk 4:3-9.

sign, but his cross. Where he was humbled, that is where he was glorified, from there he lifted up the humble to whom, humiliated, he had come down.

In fact we belong to the gospel, we belong to the New Testament. *The law was given through Moses, while grace and truth came through Jesus Christ* (Jn 1:17). We turn to the apostle and he tells us that we are *not under the law but under grace* (Rom 6:14). *He sent his Son*, therefore, *made of a woman, made under the law, to redeem those who were under the law, that we might receive sonship by adoption* (Gal 4:4-5). See, that is what Christ came for, to redeem those who were under the law, so that we might no longer be under the law but under grace. Who then gave the law? The one who also gave grace, *he* gave the law; but he sent the law through a servant, while he came down himself with grace. And how was it that human beings came to be under the law? By not fulfilling the law. The one who fulfills the law, you see, is not under the law but with the law; while the one who is under the law is not lifted up but pressed down by the law. Thus, the law finds all human beings set under the law guilty; and, therefore, it is held over their head so as to manifest their sins, not to take them away.

So then, the law issues orders; the lawgiver shows mercy in what the law commands. Human beings who have tried to fulfill, by their own strength of character, what was commanded by the law, have been tumbled head over heels by their self-assurance and have fallen; and they are not with the law, but have been found guilty under the law; and since they could not fulfill the law on their own and were guilty under the law, they implored the help of a liberator; and the guilt of the law made the proud sick and the sickness of the proud became the confession of the humble; now the sick confess that they are ill; let the doctor come and heal the sick.[4]

Christ our one and only doctor, the one and only medicine for our ills

3. Who is the doctor? Our Lord Jesus Christ. Who is our Lord Jesus Christ? The one who was also seen by those who crucified him.[5] The one who was arrested, slapped in the face, scourged, smeared with spittle, crowned with thorns, hanged on the cross, died, was wounded with a lance,

---
4. See BA 71, 856 on the ministry of the Law.
5. An allusion to Rev 1:7, quoting Zech 12:10, with a kind of side glance at Jn 14:19. 22, where Jude questioned Jesus about how he was going to show himself to his disciples and not to the world.

taken down from the cross, laid in a tomb. That is who our Lord Jesus Christ is. That is the same one exactly, and he is the one and only doctor[6] for our wounds—that crucified man who was jeered at, whose persecutors wagged their heads at him as he hung on the cross, and said, *If he is the Son of God, let him come down from the cross* (Mt 27:39-40); clearly, he is our one and only doctor.

So why then did he not show those who were jeering at him that he was indeed the Son of God? Having allowed himself to be lifted up on the cross, why did he not come down from it, at least when they said of him, *If he is the Son of God, let him come down from the cross*, and in this way show them that he was in very truth *the* Son of God, whom they had had the audacity to jeer at?

He did not wish to.

Why not? Surely not because he could not do so?

Of course he had the power to do so. But which is greater, coming down from a cross or rising up from a tomb? He put up with their jeers, however, because it was not as a lesson in power that he accepted the cross, but as an example of patience. It was there that he cured your wounds, where he so long endured his own; it was there that he healed your eternal death, where he had the goodness to die in time. He even died—or was it rather death that died in him? What a death it was that slew death!

Christ is no mere man; in him is life and true light

4. Yet, is that the whole Jesus Christ our Lord, the one who was seen and arrested and crucified? Is that the whole of him?

That is indeed the same one, but what the Jews saw is not the whole of him, that is, not the whole Christ.

And what is?

In the beginning was the Word.

In what beginning?

And the Word was with God.

---

6. He is the *totus medicus* in the Latin; but one can hardly translate that phrase as "the whole doctor." An allusion to *totus Christus*, "the whole Christ," it seems best to translate it as "the one and only doctor." Christ's death on the cross is, after all, the cure which he, the one and only doctor, has provided for us.

And what sort of Word?

And the Word was God.

Was this Word, perhaps, made by God?

No. You see, this Word *was in the beginning with God.*

So what then? Are not the other things God has made like the Word?

No. Because *all things were made through him, and without him was made nothing.*

How were all things made through him?

Because *what was made, in him was life* (Jn 1:1-4), and it was life before it was made. What was made is not life, but in the mind, that is, in the Wisdom of God, before it was made, it was life. What has been made passes away; what is in Wisdom cannot pass away. So then, what was made was life in him.[7]

And what sort of life?

In fact, the soul too is the life of the body; our body has its own life, which, when lost, is the death of the body.

So was this life something like that?

No. But *life was the light of men* (Jn 1:4).

Not the life of animals?

In fact, this light is for both human beings and animals; but there is a light just for human beings; so let us see how human beings differ from animals, and then we may understand what their light may be.

The only difference between you and an animal is understanding. Pride yourself on nothing else. Do you presume upon your strength? Wild animals will beat you. Do you presume upon your speed? You will be beaten at it by flies. Do you presume upon your beauty? Think of the beauty in a peacock's feathers! So where does your superiority come from? From the image of God. Where is the image of God? In the mind, in the intelligence.

If then you are greater than an animal because you have a mind with which you understand what an animal cannot understand, and what makes you a human being is your being greater than an animal, then the light of human beings is the light of minds. The light of minds is above minds and surpasses all minds. That is the life through which all things were made.

---

7. See Homily 1, 16-17.

He was in the world, and the world did not know him

5. Where was that life? It was here. Or was it with the Father and not here? Or—more accurately—was it both with the Father and here? Then, if it was here, why was it not seen? Because *the light shines in the darkness, and the darkness did not comprehend it* (Jn 1:5). O, men and women, be not darkness, be not unbelievers, people who are without justice, wicked, rapacious, avaricious, lovers of the world! These, you see, are ways of being darkness. The light is not absent; rather you are absent from the light. The blind man sitting in the sun has the sun present to him, but he himself is absent from the sun. Then be not darkness. For this is perhaps the grace about which I am going to speak, that we might no longer be darkness, as the apostle says to us, *For you were once darkness, but you are now light in the Lord* (Eph 5:8).

So then, because the light of human beings, that is, the light of minds, was not recognized, a man was needed to bear witness to the light, not, of course, a man in darkness, but one already enlightened. Yet it was not because he was enlightened that he could be the light, but he was *to bear witness to the light*. For *that man was not the light*.

And what was the light?

That was the true light, who enlightens everyone coming into the world.

And where was it?

It was in the world.

And how was it in the world? Not like the light of the sun, surely, of the moon, of lamps—that is not how this light too was in the world, is it?

No; because *the world was made through it, and the world did not know it* (Jn 1:8-10); that is the same as saying, *The light shines in the darkness, and the darkness did not comprehend it.* The world, you see, is darkness, because *world* means the lovers of the world.

After all, did the creature fail to acknowledge its creator? The sky bore witness with a star; the sea bore witness, it supported the Lord who walked on it; the winds bore witness, at his command they hushed; the earth bore witness, when he was crucified it quaked.[8] If all these bore witness, how is it that the world did not know him, unless *world* means the lovers of the world, those who are at heart the inhabitants of the world? And the world is

---

8. See Mt 2:2; Mk 6:48; 4:39; Mt 27:51.

bad, because those who live in it are bad, just as a house is bad—not because of its walls, but because of its inhabitants.

The Word came into our midst

6. *He came to his own,* that is, into that which belonged to him, *and his own people did not receive him* (Jn 1:11).[9] So what hope is left then, if not that *as many as did receive him, he gave power to become children of God?* If they become children, they are born; if they are born, how are they born? Not of the flesh—*not of bloods, nor of the will of the flesh, nor of the will of the man, but of God they were born.* So let them rejoice because they have been born of God; let them assume that they belong to God; let them accept the proof that they belong to God: *And the Word was made flesh and took up residence among us.* If the Word was not ashamed of being born of a woman, are men and women to be ashamed of being born of God? By doing this he provided a cure; because he provided a cure, we see. In fact, because *the Word was made flesh and took up residence among us*, he became a medicine for us, so that as we had been blinded by earth we might be healed by earth. And once healed, what were we to see? *And we saw,* he says, *his glory, glory as of the only-begotten of the Father, full of grace and truth* (Jn 1:11-14).

The testimony of John the Baptist

7. John bears witness to him, and shouts out, saying, *This was the one about whom I said, He who is coming after me has come to be in front of me.* He came after me, he stepped ahead of me.[10]

What does it mean, *he has come to be in front of me*? That he was placed ahead of me, and not "he was made before I was made" but "he was placed before me," which is what *he has come to be in front of me* means.

Why has he come to be in front of you, even though he came after you? *Because he was before me* (Jn 1:15).

---

9. To explain the word *propria*, he explains that he came into that which belonged to him: *id est, in sua venit.*
10. *Has come to be in front of me* involves the passive of the verb *facere*, to make, and so would have sounded in their ears as "was made before me." So Augustine's words mean that John was before Jesus as precursor: not "was made before me," but "was placed ahead of me."

Before you, John? What is so great about his being before you? Very well, since you bear witness to him, let us listen to him speaking: *Even before Abraham I am* (Jn 8:58).

But Abraham too had his day in the middle of human history; many came before him, many after him. Listen to what the Father has to say to the Son: *Before Lucifer*[11] *I begot you* (Ps 109:3). The one who was begotten before Lucifer is the one who shed his light on everyone. For it is said that there was a certain Lucifer, who fell; in fact, he was an angel, and he became a devil; and scripture says of him: *Lucifer, the one who was rising at daybreak, fell* (Is 14:12). Why was he called Lucifer? Because as one who was enlightened, he was shining. But how did he become darkness? *Because he did not stand in the truth* (Jn 8:44). So then, he was before Lucifer, before anything was enlightened; because, it is necessary that the one by whom all who can be are enlightened should be there before anything has been enlightened.

The first grace is the faith and the forgiveness received from his fullness

8. That is why it follows immediately: *And from his fullness we have all received.*

What have you received?

And grace for grace (Jn 1:16).

That, you see, is how the gospel text runs, when collated with Greek copies. It does not say, "And from his fullness we have all received grace for grace," but it says it like this, *And from his fullness we have all received, and grace for grace*; that is, we have received something from his fullness, although I do not know what he wanted us to understand by that, and even more, we have received grace for grace. For first we received grace from his fullness, and then we received grace: *grace for grace*. What was the grace we first received? Faith: walking in faith, we are walking in grace. How, after all, did we deserve to have faith? What previous merits did we have to show? Let no one pat himself on the back; let each one return to his conscience, poke into the hiding places of his thoughts, go back to the

---

11. Literally, *Before the light-bearer* or *Before the angel Lucifer fell*. It can also be translated *Before the dawn* or *Before the daystar*.

sequence of his actions; let each one not look at what he now is, if already something, but look at what he was, in order to be something; each one will find that he only deserved punishment.

So then, if what you deserved was punishment, and the one who came would not punish sins, but would pardon them, you have been given a grace—not paid back as per invoice. Why is it called grace? Because it is given *gratis*. You have not, after all, bought what you have received with previous merits. This, therefore, is the first grace that a sinner receives: to have his sins forgiven. What did he deserve? Let him examine justice; he finds penalty. Let him examine mercy; he finds grace. But God had promised this through the prophets; and when he came to give what he had promised, he gave not only grace, but truth as well. How was truth demonstrated? Because he did what was promised.

Grace for grace is eternal life

9. So what then is *grace for grace*? By faith we gain God; and seeing that we did not deserve to be forgiven our sins, by the very fact of receiving such an undeserved gift, that is called grace. What does grace mean? Given *gratis*. What does given *gratis* mean? Bestowed, not paid back. If you were owed it, then it was a payment as per invoice, not a grace bestowed on you. If it really was owed you, that means you were good; if however, and this is the truth, you were bad, but believed in the one *who justifies the godless* (Rom 4:5)—what does *justifies the godless* mean if not "makes godly people out of godless ones"?—then think about what you had coming to you through the law and about what you actually obtained through grace. But, having obtained this grace of faith, as a result of your faith you will be just, since *the just person lives from faith* (Rom 1:17), and you will gain God by living from faith. When you have gained God by living from faith, you will receive immortality and eternal life as your reward. That too is grace. For what merit do you receive eternal life? *For grace*. If faith were a grace, in fact, and eternal life a kind of payment as per invoice for faith, it does indeed look like God is paying you back eternal life as something owed—but owed to whom? To a believer because you have earned it by faith—but because faith itself is a grace, eternal life too is grace for grace.

Paul's example shows the truth of this interpretation

10. Listen to the apostle Paul acknowledging grace and, later on, aspiring to what was his due. What does Paul acknowledge about grace? *I was the one who formerly blasphemed and persecuted and insulted him; but*, he says, *I obtained mercy* (1Tm 1:13). He said he was unworthy to obtain it; but still he did obtain it, not by his own merits but by God's mercy. Now listen to him aspiring to his due, after first receiving that undeserved grace: *For I*, he says, *am now being immolated,*[12] *and the time of my departure is at hand. I have fought the good fight, I have completed the course, I have kept the faith; for the rest a crown of justice has been laid up for me.* Now he asks for his due, now he demands it. Just notice the words that follow: *which the Lord, the just judge, will award me on that day* (2 Tm 4:6-8). To receive grace beforehand, he needed a merciful father; to receive the reward of grace, he needed a just judge.[13] Will the one who did not condemn the godless now condemn the believer? And yet if you think clearly for a moment, it was he who first gave you the faith by which you gained him; for you had nothing of your own by which you were owed anything. So then, later on, he awarded you the reward of immortality; he thus crowned his own gifts, not your merits.

So then, brothers and sisters, *from his fullness we have all received*; we have received from the fullness of his mercy, from the abundance of his goodness. Received what? Forgiveness of sins, that we might be justified by faith. And over and above that, what? *And grace for grace*; that is, for that grace according to which we live by faith, we are going to receive another grace. What else, though, could it be but grace? I mean, if I say that this too is owed me, I am attributing something to myself, as though it were my due. But in fact God crowns the gifts of his mercy in us—provided that we walk with perseverance in that grace which we first received.

---

12. *Immolor*; the Latin verb referred originally to a preliminary rite in Roman sacrifices, in which meal was sprinkled on the victim's head. See Sermon 299A,4, where Augustine also gives the alternative, and in fact the authentic reading: "or *libor*, being poured out as a libation." See also note 13 on that sermon.
13. See *Exposition of Psalm* 39, 3: "At first God is a kindly father, drawing us out of the pit of misery so that he can forgive our sins and disengage us from the slimy mud; then he is a just judge who awards what he has promised to the one who walks well after having received the gift of walking well."

How the law convicts humankind of pride

11. *For the law was given through Moses* (Jn 1:17), and it held us guilty. What is it, after all, that the apostle says? *The law came in, that wrongdoing might abound* (Rom 5:20). It was a benefit to the proud that wrongdoing might abound. For they gave much credit to themselves, as if they attributed it to their own powers; and they were unable to achieve justice without the help of the one who required it. Wanting to curb their pride, God gave the law, as though saying, "There you are, keep that; do not assume that there is no one to command. The one who commands is not lacking; rather the one who keeps the command is lacking."

12. So then, if the one who is to carry out the order fails to do so, what prevents him from doing so? Because he was born with a legacy of sin and death. Born of Adam, he brought what he received back there with him. The first man fell, and all who have been born of him have contracted the lust of the flesh from him. There was a need for another man to be born who had contracted no such lust. One man and another: a man for death and a man for life. That is what the apostle says: *Death through a man, through a man also resurrection of the dead.*

Through which man death? Through which man resurrection of the dead?

Be not impatient, he continues, and says, *For just as in Adam all die, so too in Christ shall all be made alive* (1 Cor 15:21-22).

Which ones belong to Adam?

All who have been born of Adam.

Which ones belong to Christ?

All who have been born through Christ.

Why are all in sin?

Because nobody has been born outside Adam's line. That they were born of Adam was a matter made necessary by a sentence of condemnation; being born through Christ is a matter of choice and grace. People are not compelled to be born through Christ; it is not because they wished to that they have been born of Adam. Still, all born of Adam are sinners and have sin; all born through Christ are justified and just, not in themselves but in him. On the other hand, if you ask what they are in themselves, they are Adam; ask what they are in the other, they are Christ.[14]

Why?

Because the head of the body, our Lord Jesus Christ, did not come with the legacy of sin, but did nonetheless come with mortal flesh.

What do we derive from Adam? from Christ?

13. Death was a punishment for sins; but in the Lord it was a work of mercy, not the punishment of sin. For the Lord had nothing that was a just reason for him to die. He said himself, *Behold, the prince of this world is coming, and in me he has found nothing.*

So why are you dying?

But that all may know that I am doing the will of my Father, arise, let us go hence (Jn 14:30-31). There was no reason for him to die—and he died; there is reason for you to die and do you refuse to die? Have the goodness to suffer with equanimity according to your merits what *he* had the goodness to suffer in order to deliver you from everlasting death.

One man and another; but that one, only a man; this one, the God-man. That one a man of sin, this one a man of justice. You died in Adam, you rise again in Christ; in fact, each is owed to you. You have already believed in Christ; even so, pay back the debt derived from Adam. Yet the chains of sin will not hold you bound for all eternity, because the temporal death of your Lord has slain your eternal death. That is grace, my brothers and sisters; that is also truth, because it was promised and the promise was kept.

The law prepared the ground for the grace of the New Testament

14. This grace was not in the Old Testament, because the law threatened but brought no relief. It gave orders; it did not heal; it manifested frailty; it did not get rid of it. But it was preparing the ground for that doctor who was going to come with grace and truth; as a doctor who wants to cure someone

---

14. Following the manuscript from Carcassonne: *Christus sunt*; other editors follow the reading *Christi sunt*, "they belong to Christ." But the contrast with what they are in themselves, *Adam sunt*, surely requires *Christus*.

first sends along his slave, that the doctor might find the patient bandaged up. The patient was not in good health, did not want to be healed, and, to avoid treatment, was boasting about his health. The law was sent, it bound him; he found himself guilty, and he then cried out from the bandages. The Lord comes, he treats him with bitter and stinging medicines. In fact, he says to the patient, "Bear it"; he says, "Endure it"; he says, "Do not love the world, have patience, let the fire of self-control cure you, let your wounds endure the surgeon's knife of persecution." You were in a panic, although tightly bandaged up; this man, free and not tied up, drinks what he was giving you. He suffered first, to give you some comfort, as though saying, "What you are afraid of suffering for your own sake, I am suffering first for your sake." That is grace for you, amazing grace indeed! Who can worthily sing its praises?

The humility of Christ

15. I am speaking about the humility of Christ, my brothers and sisters. Who will speak about Christ's majesty and divinity? To set out or say anything adequate about the humility of Christ, I am not qualified, indeed, I fail completely. I recommend all of it to your meditations, and I will not satisfy you as my listeners. Meditate on the humility of Christ. But who, you ask, will display it to us, if not you? Let him speak within you. The one dwelling within you says it much better than the one shouting from outside. Let him who has begun to dwell in your hearts show you the grace of his humility. But if I fail to explain fully his humility, who could speak of his majesty? If *the Word was made flesh* stuns us, who will ever unfold *In the beginning was the Word*? So then, brothers and sisters, hold on to this solid certainty.

16. *The law was given through Moses, grace and truth have come about through Jesus Christ* (Jn 1:17). The law was given through a slave; it made people guilty; an indulgence was given by the emperor, it delivered the guilty. *The law was given through Moses*. The slave must not claim credit for any more than what was done by him. Chosen for a great ministry as *one faithful in the household, but still a slave* (Heb 3:2.5), he can act according to the law; he cannot absolve from the guilt of the law. So then, *the law was given through Moses, grace and truth have come about through Jesus Christ*.

Moses did not see God; Christ is in the inner counsel of the Father

17. And in case anyone should say, "Did not both grace and truth come about through Moses, who saw God?" he immediately added, *No one has ever seen God.*

And how was God made known to Moses?

By the Lord revealing him to his servant.

Which Lord?

Christ himself, who sent the law ahead through a slave, in order to come himself with grace and truth. For *no one has ever seen God.*

And how did he appear to that servant, to the extent he was able to grasp what he saw?

He says, *The Only-begotten Son who is in the Father's lap*[15] *has made him known* (Jn 1:18).

What is *in the Father's lap*?

In the Father's inner counsels.[16] God, of course, does not have a lap as we have in our clothes, nor is he to be thought of as sitting as we do, or perhaps as having wrapped himself in something in order to have a lap. But because our lap is intimately close to us, the Father's inner counsels are called the Father's lap. The one in the Father's inner counsels who knows the Father, he it is that has interpreted him; for *no one has ever seen God.*

So then, he came and told what he had seen. But what had Moses seen? Moses saw a cloud, saw an angel, saw a fire, all part of creation. These things bore the image of the Lord, but did not manifest his very presence. You have it plainly in the law: *And Moses used to talk with the Lord, one opposite the other,*[17] *like a friend with his friend.* Continue on, and you find Moses saying, *If I have found favor in your sight, show me yourself openly,*

---

15. *In sinu patris* (Jn 1:18) is variously translated as "in the Father's bosom," "at the Father's side," "close to the Father's heart." Augustine's use appears to fit none of these. He explains it in terms of the Father's *secretum* (see following note); but it is also a place in a tunic or a robe, i.e., as a lap into which is poured the good measure, pressed down, shaken together, running over (see Lk 6:38).
16. *Secretum* means God's private quarters, his study. In Sermon 6,8, I rendered it his "inner sanctum"; but now I think "inner counsels," though less concrete, conveys the meaning better. See Homilies 10, 1; 61, 4.
17. The Latin has *contra in contra*, which the various biblical translations render as "face to face"—even though that expression may seem to imply that Moses was already seeing God in the way in which he would then ask to see him.

that I may see you. And not only did he say it; he got his answer: *You cannot see my face.* (Ex 33:11.13.20) So then, my brothers and sisters, an angel was talking to Moses, representing the Lord; and all the things that were done there through the angel promised this grace and this truth yet to come. Those who have thoroughly searched into the law know this; and when I find an opportunity to say something on the subject myself as well, to the extent the Lord may unveil it to me, I will not withhold it from Your Graces.[18]

The idea that Christ is the visible member of the Trinity is false

18. But what you should know is that all these things which were seen as bodies were not the very substance of God. We see them, after all, with our bodily eyes; what is the substance of God seen with? Put your question to the gospel: *Blessed are the clean of heart, for they shall see God* (Mt 5:8). There have been people so deluded in the futility of their hearts that they could say, "The Father is invisible, while the Son is visible."[19] In what way "visible"? If this is because of the flesh, because he took flesh, then it is obvious. Of those who saw Christ in the flesh, after all, some believed in him, some crucified him, and those who believed tottered in their faith when he was crucified; and unless they had felt and touched his flesh after the resurrection, their faith would not have been restored to them. So if the Son is said to be visible because of the flesh, we too agree, and that is Catholic faith as well. But if they say that it was before the flesh, that is, before his incarnation, then they are simply raving, straying far from the truth. Those visible manifestations, you see, were produced in bodily form through a creature, to provide an image;[20] it certainly was not his very substance that was shown and brought out into the open. May Your Graces pay attention to this brief illustration. God's Wisdom cannot be seen with the eyes. Brothers and sisters, if *Christ is the wisdom of God and the power of God* (1 Cor 1:24), if Christ is the Word

---

18. Augustine may have done so in Sermon 6, which was about the appearance of God to Moses at the burning bush. If that is so, the date I suggested for the sermon, about 400, would have to be revised to several years later.
19. These people, in Augustine's time, were the Arians, even though this idea may be found in earlier works, such as the second-century work by Irenaeus, *Against Heresies*, or in Tertullian and Novatian. The idea took on new meaning after Arius, and Augustine finds it necessary to address it in *The Trinity* II, 9, 15-16, where he deals with Old Testament theophanies.
20. *Typus* is more than "symbolic" insofar as it prefigures a future reality.

of God—a word of a human being cannot be seen with the eyes; how could the Word of God be seen in that way?

The same commandments given to us as to the Jews, but not the same promises

19. So then, sweep such flesh-bound thoughts out of your hearts, so that you may really be under grace, so that you may belong to the New Testament. Read the Old Testament and see how the same commands were given to that still-flesh-bound people as are given to us. For we too are commanded to worship one God. The second commandment, *You shall not take the name of the Lord your God in vain*, is also required of us. *Observe the sabbath day* is a command given more to us, because we are commanded to observe it spiritually. The Jews, you see, observe the sabbath day in a servile fashion, as an occasion for self-indulgence and getting drunk. How much better occupied would their women be spinning wool, instead of dancing on the balconies on that day![21] Heaven preserve us, brothers and sisters, from allowing that they really observe the sabbath! The Christian observes the sabbath in a spiritual way, by abstaining from servile work. What does that mean, after all, "from servile work"? From sin. And how do we prove that? Ask the Lord: *Everybody who commits sin is the slave of sin* (Jn 8:34). So then, the spiritual keeping of the sabbath is enjoined upon us as well. Indeed all those commandments are laid upon us even more than on them, and are to be kept: *You shall not kill; you shall not commit adultery; you shall not steal; you shall not utter false testimony; honor father and mother; you shall not covet your neighbor's goods; you shall not covet your neighbor's wife.* (Ex 20:3-17) Are not all these commands given to us as well?

But now look for the reward, and you will find it said there, "That your enemies may be driven away before you, and that you may receive the land which God promised to your fathers."[22] Because they could not conceive of invisible realities, they were held by visible ones. Why were they held? Lest they should perish utterly and slide away to idols; because that is in fact what they did, my dear brothers and sisters, forgetting, as we are told,

---

21. See Sermon 9, 3 for the same criticism of Jewish behavior on the sabbath.
22. See Ex 23:22-33.

all those great wonders which God performed before their very eyes. The sea was cleft asunder, a road was made in the midst of the waves, their enemies pursuing them were overwhelmed by the very waters through which they themselves had passed. And when Moses the man of God had withdrawn from their eyes, they asked for an idol, and said, *Make us gods to go ahead of us, because that man has left us in the lurch.* They had placed all their hopes, not in God, but in a man. There you are, that man is dead; could God have been dead, the one who had snatched them from the land of Egypt? And when they had made themselves the image of a calf, they worshiped it and said, *These are your gods, Israel, who delivered you from the land of Egypt* (Ex 32:1.4). How quickly they forgot such a manifest grace! So in what other way could such a people be held but by material, flesh-linked promises?

The eternal life promised us consists in knowing God and Jesus Christ

20. The same commands as are also given to us are given there in the Decalogue of the law; but not the same promises as are given to us. What are we promised? Eternal life. *This is eternal life, that they may know you, the one true God, and the one you have sent, Jesus Christ* (Jn 17:3). We are promised knowledge of God; that, yes, that is grace upon grace. Brothers and sisters, we now believe, but do not yet see; the reward for this faith will be to see what we believe. The prophets knew this, but it was hidden before he came.

In the psalms, there is a certain lover, you see, who, sighing, says, *One thing have I asked of the Lord, this will I seek.* And are you wondering what he might be asking for? I mean, maybe he is asking, in a carnal way, for a *land flowing with milk and honey* (Ex 3:8)—though of course in a spiritual way that is indeed to be sought and asked for. Or perhaps he is asking for the subjection of his foes, or the death of his enemies, or worldly power and resources. After all, he is on fire with love, he never stops sighing and sweating and panting. Let us see what he is asking for: *One thing have I asked of the Lord, this will I seek.* What is this thing that he is seeking? *That I may dwell*, he says, *in the house of the Lord throughout all the days of my life.* And supposing you do dwell in the house of the Lord, where will your joy come from? *That I may gaze*, he says, *upon the delight of the Lord.* (Ps 26:4)

We should set our hearts on true and eternal goods,
on God himself as our real reward

21. My brothers and sisters, why this cheering, why this excitement, why this show of love, if not because that is a spark of this charity? What are you longing for, I want to know? Can it be seen with the eyes? Can it be touched? Is it a sort of beauty that delights the eyes? Do we not all have an ardent love for the martyrs and burn with love when we commemorate them? What is it we love in them, brothers and sisters? Their limbs being torn off by wild beasts? What could be more hideous, if you question your eyes of flesh? What more beautiful, if you question the eyes of the heart?

What do you think of a most beautiful young man who is a thief? How horrid he is to the eyes of your heart! But not, surely, in your eyes of flesh? If you question them, nothing could be more graceful, more well-proportioned than that youthful body; beautifully shaped limbs, delectable complexion, both allure the eyes; and yet when you hear he is a thief, you shrink from the man in spirit. Across the road you see a bent old man, leaning on a stick, scarcely able to move, his features ploughed all over with wrinkles; do you see anything there that can please the eyes? You hear he is a just man; you love him, you embrace him.

Such are the rewards that have been promised us, my brothers and sisters. Love things like that, sigh for a kingdom like that, long for that kind of home country, if you want to get to what our Lord came with, that is, to grace and truth. If, on the other hand, you are eager for material, bodily rewards from God, you are still under the law, and for that very reason you are not fulfilling the law; because, you see, when you notice that people who offend God have more than enough of these temporal goods, your steps begin to flag, and you start saying to yourself, "Look, here am I worshiping God, hurrying off every day to church, wearing out my knees in prayer—and I am constantly ill; people commit murder, commit robberies, they have a thoroughly good time and everything they could possibly want; they do very well indeed."

So then, was it such things you were looking for from God? You certainly used to belong to grace. If what God gave you is grace because he gave it *gratis*, for nothing, then give your love to him *gratis*, for nothing. Do not love God for a reward; let him be your reward himself.

Let your soul say, *One thing have I asked of the Lord, this will I seek; that I may dwell in the house of the Lord throughout all the days of my life, that I may gaze on the delight of the Lord.* Do not be afraid of losing interest through boredom. Such will be the beauty of this delight that it will always be present to you, and you will never be satisfied—or rather, you will always be satisfied and never be satisfied. You see, if I say you will not be satisfied, it will imply hunger; if I say you will be satisfied, I fear boredom; where there will be neither boredom nor hunger, I do not know what to say; but God has something to give to those who find no words to say it, and something to give to believers that they will welcome.

Homily 4

On Jn 1:19-34[1]

John heralds Christ the judge, who, silent at his first coming, will not be silent at his second

1. Your Holinesses will have heard often enough, and you know very well that John the Baptist—insofar as he was the most outstanding *among those born of women* (Mt 11:11) and the most humble in acknowledging the Lord—was all the more deserving of being the *friend of the bridegroom* (Jn 3:29), zealous on the bridegroom's behalf rather than on his own, not seeking his own honor, but that of the judge whom he preceded as a herald. And so the prophets before him were allowed to foretell future events in relation to Christ, but John had the honor of pointing him out with his finger.[2] Just as those who did not believe the prophets disregarded Christ before he came, so too did they ignore him when he was actually present. For he came the first time in a humble and hidden way—all the more hidden because he was more humble. Yet those who scorned God's humility through pride crucified their Savior and turned him into the one who would condemn them.

2. But will not the one whose first coming was hidden, because he came in humility, come again openly, because he will come in majesty? You heard the psalm just now: *Our God will come openly and will not be silent* (Ps 49:3). He kept silent so that he could be judged, he will not be silent when he starts judging. It would not say *will come openly* unless he had first come in a hidden way; nor would it say *will not be silent* unless he had kept silent the first time.

How did he keep silent?

Ask Isaiah:

Like a sheep he was led to the slaughter, and as a lamb before the one who was to shear it is without a voice, so he opened not his mouth (Is 53:7).

---

1. Preached on Sunday, December 30, 406.
2. For parallel statements, see paragraph 8 of this homily as well as Homily 5, 6; *Against the Letters of Petilian* II, 37, 87.

He will come openly, though, *and will not be silent.*
In what way openly?
Fire will go before him, and all around him a mighty gale (Ps 49:3). It will be up to the gale to blow away all the chaff from the floor that is now being threshed,[3] and to the fire to burn up what the gale has blown away.

But now, Christ is quiet; quiet in his judgment, but not quiet in his commands. For, if Christ is keeping quiet, what is the point of these gospels? What is the point of the words of the apostles, of the singing of the psalms, of the utterances of the prophets? In all these, you see, Christ does not keep quiet. But he does keep quiet for now insofar as he does not punish; he does not keep quiet by failing to admonish or warn.

He will, however, come in splendor to punish; he will appear openly to everyone, even to those who do not believe in him. But, being present in a hidden way, it was right that he was condemned. After all, if he were not condemned, he would not be crucified; if he were not crucified, he would not shed his blood, the price he paid to redeem us. That he might pay that price for us, he was crucified; that he might be crucified he was despised; that he might be despised, he first appeared humbly.

John the lamp made the humble light known

3. However, because he appeared in a mortal body, as it were at night, he lit a lamp for himself by which he could be seen. That lamp was John, about whom you have already heard a great deal; and today's gospel reading contains John's own words—first and foremost his admission that he was not himself the Christ. John, in fact, was such an outstanding figure, that people could believe that he was the Christ; and it was proof of his humility that he said he was not, when he could well have been thought to be so. Accordingly: *This is the witness of John when the Jews sent priests and Levites to him from Jerusalem to question him: Who are you?* They would not have sent them, surely, unless they had been worried about the greatness of his authority because he dared to baptize. *And he admitted and did not deny.* What did he admit? *And he admitted, I am not the Christ.* (Jn 1:19-20)

---

3. See *Exposition of Psalm* 49, 6.

John's own humility; Christ the stone hewn from the mountain

4. *And they questioned him: What then? Are you Elijah?* (Jn 1:21) They knew, of course, that Elijah was due to come before the Christ. For no one among the Jews was unaware of the title, "the Christ." They did not think this man[4] was the Christ; nor did they ever think that the Christ was not going to come. While hoping for his coming, they stumbled over him already present, they stumbled, as it were, over a humble stone.[5] This stone, you see, was still small, but already hewn from the mountain without being touched by any hands, just as the prophet Daniel says he saw *a stone hewn from the mountain without being touched by any hands.*[6] But what then follows? *And that stone grew*, he says, *and became a great mountain, and it filled the whole face of the earth.* (Dan 2:34-35)

So would Your Graces please note what I am saying: present among the Jews, Christ had already been hewn from the mountain. By the mountain he wants us to understand the kingdom of the Jews. But the kingdom of the Jews had not filled the whole face of the earth. From it was hewn this stone, because from it was born the Lord in this present age. And why without hands? Because the virgin gave birth to the Christ without any male activity. So then this stone, hewn without hands, was already there in the sight of the Jews, but it was humble. Rightly so, because this stone had not yet grown and filled the whole world. That became evident in his kingdom, which is the Church, with which he filled the whole face of the earth.

So then, because he had not yet grown, they stumbled over him as over a stone; what is written has been fulfilled in them: *Whoever trips over this stone will be shattered; and that stone will crush those upon whom it falls* (Lk 20:18). First they tripped over him when he was humble; he is going to come upon them from on high; but in order to crush them when he comes from on high, he first shattered them while he was humble. They stumbled over him and were shattered; not crushed, but shattered;[7] he will come when he is lifted up and crush them. But the Jews can be pardoned for stumbling over the stone which had not yet grown. What about those who have stumbled over the very

---

4. Jesus, of course, not John the Baptist.
5. See Is 8:14; Rom 9:32; 1 Pt 2:8.
6. Actually King Nebuchadnezzar was the one who had this vision.
7. Augustine explains the difference in *Exposition of Psalm* 73, 11, as well as in Sermons 91, 1; 92, 2.

mountain? Yes, you already recognize whom I am talking about;[8] those who reject the Church spread throughout the world are not stumbling over a humble stone, but over the very mountain which this stone became when it had grown. The Jews were blind not to see the humble stone on the ground; what blindness it must be not to see the mountain!

John denies he is Elijah; Christ says he is Elijah

5. So then, they saw him in his humble condition and did not recognize him. He was shown them by means of the lamp. First of all, John—*no one greater than him has arisen among those born of woman* (Mt 11:11) —said, *I am not the Christ*; and he was asked, *Are you Elijah? He replied, I am not.* (Jn 1:20-21) For the Christ sends Elijah ahead of him.[9] And he said, *I am not*, and thereby gives us a problem. For it is to be feared that, failing to understand, some will assume that John was contradicting what Christ said. You see, there is a place in the gospel where the Lord Jesus Christ was saying things about himself, and his disciples answered, *How is it then that the scribes* (that is, those learned in the law) *say that Elijah must first come? And the Lord said, Elijah has already come, and they have done to him what they wished* (Mt 17:10-12); *and if you want to know, it is John the Baptist* (Mt 11:14). The Lord Jesus Christ said, "Elijah has already come, and he is John the Baptist"; while when John was questioned, he admitted that he was not Elijah, any more than he was the Christ. And of course, just as he was telling the truth when he admitted he was not the Christ, so too was it true when he admitted he was not Elijah. So how then are we to reconcile the words of the herald with the words of the judge? Impossible that the herald should be lying; for he was only saying what he was hearing from the judge.[10] So why then does he say, "I am not Elijah," while the Lord says, "He is Elijah"? Because the Lord Jesus Christ wished to prefigure in

---

8. The Donatist schismatics in the African provinces.
9. See Mal 4:5.
10. The judge, as befitted his dignity, always spoke in a low voice; his herald stood beside him to proclaim in a loud voice what the judge had said in a solemn whisper. See Sermon 12,7: "It's the same in public affairs; the judge mostly speaks through the herald, yet it's the judge's name and not the herald's as well which is entered in the official records." The same practice obtained in traditional societies in Southern Africa; at official gatherings, the chief would always speak in a low voice and have someone beside him to act as his personal megaphone or loud-speaker.

John his own second coming in the future, and he wanted to say that John was in the spirit of Elijah, and thus, what John was at his first coming, Elijah would be at the second coming. Just as there are two comings, two advents, so there are two heralds; the judge is the same both times, of course, but while there are not two judges, there are two heralds. For the judge had to come first, that he might be judged. He sent the first herald ahead of him and called him Elijah, because at his second coming Elijah will be what John was at the first.

6. Would Your Graces please notice that what I am saying is true. When John was conceived, or rather once he was born,[11] the Holy Spirit prophesied what would be fulfilled with regard to this man. *And he will be*, he said, *the forerunner of the Most High, in the spirit and power of Elijah* (Lk 1:17). So not Elijah himself, but *in the spirit and power of Elijah*. What does that mean, *in the spirit and power of Elijah*? With the same Holy Spirit, he will have the role of Elijah. Why the role of Elijah? Because what Elijah must be for the second coming, John was for the first coming. Rightly then did John respond with the literal truth; because the Lord was speaking in a figurative way when he said, "He is Elijah," while this man, as I said, meant it literally when he said, "I am not Elijah." If you concentrate on the role of forerunner, John himself is Elijah, for what he was at the first coming, the other will be at the second. If you are asking who was literally who, then John was John and Elijah was Elijah. So the Lord rightly pointed out how John prefigured Elijah by saying, "He is Elijah," while John rightly stated the literal truth, "I am not Elijah." Neither John nor the Lord speaks falsely; nothing false from the herald nor from the judge—as long as you really understand.

Who, though, will understand? Anyone who has imitated the humility of the herald, and recognized the high dignity of the judge. Nothing, you see, is more humble than this herald. My brothers and sisters, John had no greater merit than this humility, such that when he was in a position to deceive people, and to be taken for the Christ, and to be regarded as the Christ (so great was his grace and so excellent his renown), he still admitted openly and said, *I am not the Christ.*

---

11. Although the angel Gabriel spoke to John's father prior to his conception, Augustine emphasizes the fulfillment of those words, not their prophetic quality. Hence, he needed to say, "or rather once he was born."

Can it be that you are not Elijah? If he now said, "I am Elijah," it would mean that Christ was already coming at his second coming to judge, not still at his first coming to be judged. As if to say, "Elijah is still to come," he said, "I am not Elijah." But notice the humble Christ before whom John came, so as not to experience the high and mighty Christ before whom Elijah is going to come. That, after all, is how the Lord finished his statement: "He himself is John the Baptist, who is going to come."[12] John came as a figure of how Elijah will be in his coming. Then Elijah will actually be Elijah; now he was John by comparison. Now John was actually John; by comparison, he is Elijah. Each herald was compared with the other, each retained his own identity; but it is the one Lord and judge, whether this herald or that one precedes him.

John, the voice crying in the wilderness

7. *And they questioned him, What then? Are you Elijah? And he said, No. And they said to him, Are you a prophet? And he answered, No. So then, they said to him, Who are you, that we may give an answer to those who sent us? What do you say about yourself? He said, I am the voice of one crying out in the desert.* (Jn 1:21-23) Isaiah said that. In John the prophecy is fulfilled. *I am the voice of one crying out in the desert. Crying what? Level the road for the Lord, straighten the paths for our God.* (Is 40:3) Does it not seem to you that a herald's job is to say, "Go out, make a path"? But where the herald normally says, "Go out," John says, "Come." A herald usually pushes people away from the judge, John invites them to the judge. Rather, John invites them to the humble one, lest they experience a judge that is mighty.

I am the voice of one crying out in the desert, Level the road for the Lord, as the prophet Isaiah says. He did not say, "I am John," "I am Elijah," "I am the prophet." But what did he say? "This is what I am called, *The voice of one crying out in the desert, Level the road for the Lord.* I am that prophecy."

---

12. Actually, the Lord did not say that Elijah was John but that John was Elijah who was going to come; see Mt 11:14.

John greater than a prophet

8. And those who had been sent were of the Pharisees, that is from the leaders of the Jews. And they questioned and said to him, *If you are not the Christ nor Elijah nor a prophet, why then are you baptizing?* (Jn 1:24-25) As if to baptize were presumptuous; as if to ask, "In what role? We ask whether you are the Christ; you say you are not. We ask if perhaps you are his forerunner, because we know that Elijah is going to come before the coming of the Christ; you deny that you are. We ask whether you may be some herald coming far ahead of him, that is a prophet, and have received that authority; and you say you are not a prophet either." And John was not the prophet either; he was greater than any prophet. The Lord gave this testimony about him: *What did you go out into the desert to see? A reed being shaken by the wind?* Yes, you hear between the lines: Not shaken by the wind because John was not the kind of person who was shifted by the wind, the kind of person blown around by every spirit of seduction. *But what did you go out to see? A man wearing soft garments?* John, after all, wore rough garments, that is, a tunic made of camel's hair.[13] *Those who wear soft garments, you see, are in the houses of kings.* So then, you did not go out to see a man dressed in soft garments. *But what did you go out to see? A prophet? Just so, I tell you; greater than a prophet was this man* (Mt 11:7-9), because the prophets had foretold Christ a long time before; John was pointing to him present in person.

If only the Donatists would imitate John's humility!

9. *Why then are you baptizing, if you are not the Christ, nor Elijah, nor the prophet? John answered and said, I am baptizing in water; but there has stood in your midst one whom you do not know.* Indeed, as a humble person, he was not seen, and that is why a lamp was lit. Notice how the lamp, who could have been thought to be something else, steps aside. *He is the one who came after me, who was made before me,* that is, as we have already explained, was placed ahead of me,[14] *and whose sandal strap I am not worthy to untie.* (Jn 1:25-27) How much lower could he debase

---
13. See Mk 1:6.
14. See Homily 3, 7, note 10.

himself? And that is why he was so highly exalted, because *whoever humbles himself shall be exalted* (Lk 14:11).

From this Your Holinesses should be able to see that, if John humbled himself so far as to say, *I am not worthy to untie his sandal strap*, those who say,[15] "*We* are the ones who baptize, what *we* give is ours, and what is ours is holy," need to become humble. John says, "Not I, but he"; they say, "*We.*" John is not worthy to untie his sandal strap; even if he had said he was worthy to do that, how humble that would have been! Even if he had said he was worthy and had spoken like this: He is the one who is coming behind me, who has been put ahead of me, and I am only worthy to untie his sandal strap, he would have humbled himself greatly. But when he says that he is not even worthy to do that, he truly was full of the Holy Spirit; a servant who acknowledged his Lord like that, and so from being a servant deservedly became a friend.[16]

This is the Lamb of God who takes away the sin of the world

10. This took place in Bethany beyond Jordan, where John was baptizing. The next day John saw Jesus coming to him and said, *Look, there is the Lamb of God; look, there is the one who takes away the sin of the world* (Jn 1:28-29). Let nobody arrogate this power to himself and say that he is the one who takes away the sin of the world. Now exert your minds to see against what proud people John stretched out his finger. Heretics were not even born and they were already being pointed out; then, he was crying out against them from the river bank; now, he cries out against them from the gospel.

Jesus comes, and what does John say? *Look, there is the Lamb of God.* If a lamb is innocent, then John too is a lamb. Was he not innocent as well? But then who is innocent? How innocent? All of us come from that transplant and that cutting, about which David sighs as he chants, *In iniquity was I conceived, and in sins did my mother nourish me in the womb* (Ps 50:7). Only that Lamb, therefore, did not come in such a way. For, he was not conceived in iniquity, because he was not conceived from mortality, nor did his mother nourish him in sins in the womb; he whom a

---

15. The Donatist bishops.
16. See Jn 15:15; 3:29.

virgin conceived was born by a virgin, because she conceived by faith and accepted him by faith.[17] So then, *Look, there is the Lamb of God*. This one does not have Adam's heritage: he took Adam's flesh, but he did not carry Adam's sin. The one who did not take on sin from the lump that we are[18] is the one who takes away our sin. *Look, there is the Lamb of God; look, there is the one who takes away the sin of the world.*

This demolishes the pretensions of the Donatists

11. You know of course that there are people[19] who sometimes say, "We who are holy are the ones who take away sins from people; for if the one who is baptizing is not holy, how can he, a man full of sin, take away another person's sin?" Against such arguments, let me not give you my words; let us read this Word: *Look, there is the Lamb of God; look, there is the one who takes away the sin of the world.* Let not human beings place their trust in human beings; let not the sparrow migrate to the mountains, but trust in the Lord; and if it does raise its eyes to the mountains from where help will come to it, it should understand that its help comes from the Lord, who made heaven and earth.[20]

How immeasurably greater is John! He is asked, "Are you the Christ?" he says, "No." "Are you Elijah?" he says, "No." "Are you the prophet?" "No." "So why are you baptizing, then?" *Look, there is the Lamb of God; look, there is the one who takes away the sin of the world. This is the one of whom I said, A man is coming behind me who has been put ahead of me, because he was before me.* (Jn 1:25. 29-30) *He is coming behind me*, because he was born later; *he has been put ahead of me*, because he has been set over me; *he was before me*, because *in the beginning was the Word, and the Word was with God, and the Word was God* (Jn 1:1).

---

17. See the notes on Christ's innocence and on Mary's conception in BA 71, 864-865.
18. See Rom 9:21.
19. The Donatists. After what he has just been saying about original sin, one would expect him to speak about the Pelagians. Hence, this sermon was probably preached prior to 411. See BA 71, 35-36.
20. See Pss 10:1; 120:1-2; Homily 1, 6-7. For a longer discussion of these texts, see *Exposition of Psalm* 124, 5.

The purpose of John's baptism and its relationship to Christ's

12. *And I did not know him*, he said; *but so that he might be manifested to Israel, that is why I came baptizing in water. And John testified, saying, I saw the Spirit coming down from heaven like a dove, and it rested on him. And I did not know him, but the one who sent me to baptize in water, he it is who said to me, Whomever you see the Spirit coming down upon and resting on him, this is the one who baptizes in the Holy Spirit. And I have seen, and I have testified that this is the Son of God.* (Jn 1:31-34)

Would Your Graces pay attention for a moment. When did John get to know Christ? He was sent, you see, to baptize in water. You ask why? So that he might be manifested to Israel, he said. What was the value of John's baptism? My brothers and sisters, if it had any value, it would have continued to this day, and people would still be baptized with the baptism of John, and, in that way, would come to the baptism of Christ. But what did he say? *So that he might be manifested to Israel*, that is, so that Christ might be manifested to Israel, to the people of Israel, John came to baptize in water. John received the ministry of baptism in the water of repentance to prepare a way for the Lord, although the Lord was not yet present; but once the Lord had become known it was superfluous to prepare a way for him, because he himself had become the way for those who knew him;[21] and that is why John's baptism did not last. But in what manner was the Lord pointed out? As humble, so that John might accept the baptism in which the Lord himself would be baptized.

Why the Lord was baptized

13. And was there any need for the Lord to be baptized? And I immediately answer my own question with a few more: Was there any need for the Lord to be born? Any need for the Lord to be crucified? Any need for the Lord to be buried? So then, if he was going to accept all that humiliation for us, would he not also accept baptism?[22]

And what was the value of receiving the baptism of his servant?

That you would not disdain to accept the baptism of the Lord.

---

21. See Jn 14:6.
22. See Homily 5, 3.

Would Your Graces pay attention. There may be some specially gifted catechumens in the Church. I mean, it sometimes happens that you notice a catechumen who abstains from all sexual intercourse, says goodbye to this world, renounces all his possessions and distributes them to the poor; and he is a catechumen, perhaps better instructed in the doctrine of salvation than many of the faithful. It is to be feared in his case that he might, within himself, speak about the holy baptism in which all sins are forgiven, "What more am I going to receive? Look, here I am better than this or that baptized believer," thinking perhaps of baptized believers who are married or uneducated or hanging onto their own possessions, while he has already distributed his own to the poor; and he reckons that he is better than some fellow who has already been baptized, and he refuses to come to baptism, saying, "I am just going to receive what this fellow and that one already have"; and comparing himself in this way with people he scorns, he may think he will sully himself by receiving what such riff-raff have received, because he already thinks he is better than they are. And yet, all his sins are still on his shoulders; unless he comes to the baptism of salvation where sins are absolved, he cannot, for all his superior excellence of character, enter the kingdom of heaven.

But the Lord came to the baptism of his servant, in order to invite this character of superior excellence to his own baptism, so that his sins might be forgiven; and while he himself had nothing to be forgiven him, nothing in him to be washed away, he still received baptism from his servant; and it was as though he were addressing a proud son, stuck up, proud and perhaps loath to receive with uneducated riff-raff the means by which salvation might be his, as if saying, "How big do you think you are? How high and mighty? What does your excellence amount to? How much grace do you have? Can it be more than mine? If I, then, came to a servant, will you disdain to come to the Lord? If I received the baptism of a servant, do you disdain to be baptized by the Lord?"

Jesus' being baptized is a lesson in humility

14. For, as you know very well, my brothers and sisters, it was not out of the need to be released from any bond of sin that the Lord came to John;

when the Lord, as the other evangelists say,[23] came to him to be baptized, John himself said, *Are you coming to me? It is I who ought to be baptized by you.* And how did the Lord answer? *Let it be for the moment; let all justice be fulfilled.* (Mt 3:14-15) What is the meaning of *Let all justice be fulfilled*? Let all humility be fulfilled. So what then? Was the one who underwent his passion at the hands of bad servants not going to receive baptism at the hands of a good servant? Pay attention, therefore. If the reason John baptized was so that the Lord might demonstrate his humility in receiving his baptism, does that not mean that once the Lord was baptized nobody else would be baptized with John's baptism? But many people were baptized with John's baptism; the Lord was baptized with John's baptism, and John's baptism came to an end. Very soon afterwards John was thrown into prison; from then on you will not find anybody baptized with that baptism.

If, therefore, the reason John came baptizing was that the Lord's humility might be demonstrated to us, so that we might not disdain to receive it from the Lord since he received it from a servant, would the Lord be the only one John baptized? But then if the Lord were the only one John baptized, there would be no lack of people thinking that John's baptism was holier than Christ's; as if to say that Christ alone deserved to be baptized with John's baptism, while with Christ's own baptism it is the whole human race. Pay attention, Your Graces. We have been baptized with Christ's baptism, not only we ourselves, but the whole world as well; until the end, the world will go on being baptized. Which of us can in any respect be compared with Christ, whose very sandal strap John said he was unfit to untie? So then, if this Christ, the God-man so uniquely above us, were alone to be baptized with John's baptism, what would people start saying? "What a baptism John had! A great baptism he had, a sacrament beyond words; why, just think, only Christ deserved to be baptized with the baptism of John!" And thus would the servant's baptism seem to be greater than the baptism of the Lord. Others were indeed baptized with John's baptism, lest John's baptism should seem to be better than Christ's; but the Lord too was baptized, so that with the Lord receiving the baptism of the

---

23. Actually only Matthew; is this an indication that Augustine may have used a harmony of the gospels, like Tatian's Diatessaron?

servant, other servants might not disdain to receive the baptism of the Lord. So that is the purpose for which John was sent.

Once again, the problem of when John first knew who Jesus was

15. But did he know Christ, or did he not? If not, how could he say, when Christ came to the river, *It is I who ought to be baptized by you* (Mt 3:14), which amounts to saying, "I know who you are?" So then, if he already knew him, he certainly recognized him when he saw the dove coming down. It is obvious that the dove only came down on the Lord after he had come up from the water of baptism. The Lord, once baptized, came up from the water, the heavens opened, and John saw the dove coming down on him. So then, if the dove came down after the baptism, and John said to the Lord before he was baptized, *Are you coming to me? It is I who ought to be baptized by you*; it means he knew beforehand the one to whom he said, *Are you coming to me? It is I who ought to be baptized by you.* How then could he say, *And I did not know him; but the one who sent me to baptize in water, he it is who said to me, Whomever you see the Spirit coming down upon like a dove and resting on him, he is the one who baptizes in the Holy Spirit*?

This is no trifling question, my brothers and sisters. If you have seen the problem, you have seen that it is not a small matter. It remains for the Lord to give us the solution. Still, I say again, if you have seen what the problem is, that is no small matter. Look now, there is John set before your eyes; John the Baptist is standing at the river; look again, there is the Lord coming, still to be baptized, not yet baptized. Listen to John's voice: *Are you coming to me? It is I who ought to be baptized by you.* There you are, he already recognizes the Lord, by whom he wishes to be baptized. The Lord, once baptized, comes up from the water, the heavens open, the Spirit comes down, and John recognizes him. If he recognizes him now, why did he say before, *It is I who ought to be baptized by you*? If however it is not just now that he recognizes him, because he already knew him, what is this that he said: *I did not know him; but the one who sent me to baptize in water, he it is who said to me, Whoever you see the Spirit coming down upon, and resting on him like a dove, he is the one who baptizes in the Holy Spirit*?

*The solution has to be put off till next time; it will leave
the Donatists without a leg to stand on*

16. Brothers and sisters, were this problem to be solved today, I am sure it would be too much of a burden for you, because there are so many things that have already been said. You should know, however, that it is the kind of question that can bring down the party of Donatus completely. I say this to Your Graces to heighten your attention, as I usually do, and that you might pray both for me and for yourselves, and that the Lord might enable me to say something worth saying and might make you understand what is worthwhile. But, today, let me put off that discussion.

In the meantime, however, let me say these few words. Until the matter is solved, ask questions about it peaceably, without wrangling, without raising voices, without in-fighting, without mutual hostility; look for answers together and question other people, and say, "This is the problem our bishop put to us today; if the Lord will allow it, he will soon resolve it." But whether it is solved or not, believe me that I have set you a problem that bothers me. Yes, it bothers me a lot.

John says, *It is I who ought to be baptized by you*, as if he knew Christ already. After all, if he did not know the one he wanted to be baptized by, it would be rash of him to say, *It is I who ought to be baptized by you*. So then, he knew him. If he knew him, then what is the point of saying, *I did not know him; but the one who sent me to baptize in water, he it is who said to me, Whomever you see the Spirit coming down upon and resting on him like a dove, he is the one who baptizes in the Holy Spirit*? What are we going to respond? That we do not know when the dove came? But lest they[24] hide behind such a response, let us read the other evangelists, who said it all much more simply, and we find it said as clearly as can be that the moment when the dove came down was when the Lord came up from the water. In fact, it was above the one who was baptized that the heavens were opened, and he saw the Spirit coming down. So if it was when he

---

24. The Donatists, so the Maurists suggest. This cryptic remark would have been clear to Augustine's hearers; earlier editors changed *forte ibi lateant*, "lest they be hiding there," into *forte ibi lateat*, "lest it [the solution to the problem] be hiding there." But the plural form is there in all the manuscripts.

had been baptized that he recognized him, how is it that he says to him as he is coming to baptism, *It is I who ought to be baptized by you*?

For the time being mull over this question, discuss it with each other, debate it among yourselves. May the Lord our God grant that, before you hear any more from me about it, the answer be first revealed to one of you. All the same, brothers and sisters, you should know that, with the solution of this problem, the party of Donatus—even if they have no shame—will have nothing further to say about the grace of baptism, a matter about which they cloud the minds of simple people and spread out their nets to catch flying birds; their mouths will be stopped once and for all.

Homily 5

On Jn 1:33[1]

John, a truthful man, and Christ the Truth cannot contradict each other

1. As the Lord wished, we have come to the day of our promise;[2] he will also grant that I am able to keep this promise. For then, all that I say, if it is useful both to you and to me, will come from him; but what comes from a human being is lies; as our Lord Jesus Christ himself said, *The one who tells a lie is speaking from what is his own* (Jn 8:44).[3] Nobody has anything from what is his own but deception and sin. But if a person does have anything of truth and of justice, it comes from that fountain for which we ought all to be thirsting in this desert, so that, revived by some drops of its spray, we will not fall by the wayside on our pilgrimage and will come to its rest and its fullness.

So then, if the *one who tells a lie is speaking from what is his own*, the one who tells the truth is speaking from what is God's. John is truthful, Christ is truth; John is truthful, but every truthful person gets truthfulness from truth; therefore if John is truthful, and a person can only get truthfulness from truth, from whom did he get his being truthful but from the one who said, *I am the truth* (Jn 14:6)? So then, it would be simply impossible either for Truth to say anything in contradiction of the truthful man or for the truthful man to say anything against the Truth. Truth sent the truthful man, and he was truthful, therefore, because he had been sent by Truth.

If the Truth had sent John, Christ had sent him. But what Christ does together with the Father, the Father does; and what the Father does together with Christ, Christ does. The Father does not do anything separately without the Son, any more than the Son does anything separately without the Father; inseparable charity, inseparable unity, inseparable majesty, inseparable authority, in line with these words which he laid down himself: *I and the Father are one* (Jn 10:30). Then who sent John?

---

1. Preached on Sunday, January 6, 407.
2. See Homily 4, 16.
3. In this passage, Jesus was talking about the devil, not about human beings.

If we say, "The Father," we are telling the truth; if we say, "The Son," we are telling the truth; but it would be more accurate to say, "The Father and the Son." But the one sent by the Father and the Son was sent by the one God, because the Son said, *I and the Father are one.*[4]

So how is it then that he did not know the one by whom he was sent? He said, you see, *I did not know him; but the one who sent me to baptize in water, he said to me.*

I ask John, "The one who sent you to baptize in water, what did he say to you?"

On whomever you see the Spirit coming down like a dove and resting on him, he is the one who baptizes in the Holy Spirit (Jn 1:33).

"This is what the one who sent you said to you, is it, John?"

"Clearly, that is what he said."

"So who was it precisely that sent you?"

"Perhaps the Father."

"God the Father is True (*uerus*) and God the Son is Truth (*ueritas*); so if the Father sent you without the Son, God sent you without Truth. But if the reason you are truthful is that you speak the truth, and speak from Truth, then the Father did not send you without the Son, but Father and Son sent you together. So then, if the Son also sent you together with the Father, how is it you did not know the one you were sent by? The one you had seen in the truth, he it is that sent you so that he would be acknowledged in the flesh, and he said, *On whomever you see the Spirit coming down like a dove and resting on him, he is the one who baptizes in the Holy Spirit.*"

When John saw the Spirit like a dove resting on Christ,
he learned something new about him

2. Did John hear these words so that he might come to know someone he had not known, or so that he might know more fully one whom he knew already? In fact, if he had not known him in any way at all, he would not have said to him when he came to the river to be baptized, *It is I*

---

4. For a detailed treatment of the inseparability of the divine persons in their activity in the created order, see Sermon 52.

who ought to be baptized by you, and are you coming to me? (Mt 3:14) So he did know him. When though did the dove come down? When the Lord had already been baptized and was coming up from the water.

But now, if the one who sent him said, *On whomever you see the Spirit coming down like a dove and resting on him, he is the one who baptizes in the Holy Spirit*; and if he did not know him, but recognized him when the dove came down, then the time the dove came down was when the Lord came up from the water; while again the time when John knew the Lord was when the Lord was coming to the water: then it is being made crystal clear to us that in some respect John already knew the Lord, and in another respect he did not yet know him. Unless we understand the matter in this way, he was a liar.

In what way was he being truthful in saying, *Are you coming to me to be baptized, and I am the one who should be baptized by you*? Is he being truthful when he says this? Once again, how is he being truthful when he says, *I did not know him; but the one who sent me to baptize in water, he it is that said to me, On whomever you see the Spirit coming down like a dove, he is the one who baptizes in the Holy Spirit*? The dove made the Lord known not to someone who did not know him at all but to someone who knew something about him on the one hand and, on the other hand, did not know something. So then, our job is to investigate what John did not know about him yet, and what he learned through the dove.

He learned that baptism would always be accomplished by the Lord, not by the minister

3. Why was John sent baptizing? I remember now that I told Your Graces why, as best I could.[5] For, if John's baptism was necessary for our salvation, it ought to be administered even now. It is not as if people are not being saved nowadays, nor that fewer people are being saved nowadays, nor that salvation was one thing then and another thing now. If Christ has changed, salvation too has changed; if salvation is only to be found in Christ, and Christ is the same now as then, salvation is the same for us now as it was then.

---

5. See Homily 4, 12-14.

But why was John sent baptizing?

Because it was necessary for Christ to be baptized.

Why, though, was it necessary for Christ to be baptized?

Well, why was it necessary for Christ to be born? Why was it necessary for Christ to be crucified? If he came, after all, to demonstrate the way of humility and was going to make himself the way of humility, humility had to be lived fully by him in every situation. Thus did he design to give weight to his own baptism, when he did not disdain to receive the baptism of a servant, so that his servants might realize with what eagerness they should be running to receive their baptism of the Lord. For John had been granted the privilege of calling it his baptism.

Christ's baptism by John is compared with his birth by Mary

4. Would Your Graces please be attentive and make this distinction and understand it? The baptism which John administered is called the baptism of John. He is the only one who ever received such a privilege; none of those who were just before him, no one after him, ever administered a baptism which would be called his baptism. John did indeed receive that ministry; after all, he could not do anything of himself; for, if anyone speaks on his own, he is telling lies from what is his own. And where else did he receive it from, but from the Lord Jesus Christ? From the one whom he would baptize, he received the authority to baptize.

Do not marvel; for Christ did in relation to John just as he did in relation to his mother. After all, it is said about Christ, *All things were made through him* (Jn 1:3); if everything was made through him, then Mary, from whom later on Christ was born, was also made through him. Let Your Graces pay attention: just as he created Mary and was created through Mary, so too did he give John a baptism and was baptized by John.

It was a demonstration of humility

5. So this then is why he received baptism from John: by receiving what was of lesser worth from someone lesser than himself, he wished to encourage all who were of lesser worth to receive what was superior. But then, if the reason John was sent was *to prepare a way for the Lord* (Is 40:3), that is, for Christ, why was it that he was not the only one baptized

by John? We have already spoken about this matter,[6] but I recall it, because it is a necessary part of the present question. If our Lord Jesus Christ had been the only person baptized with the baptism of John—grasp what I am saying; do not let the world prevail such that it erases from your hearts what the Spirit of God has written there; let not the thorns of worldly cares prevail such that they smother the seed that is being sown in you; why, after all, must I repeat these things, if not because I am not sure I can trust the memory of your hearts?—so then, if the Lord had been the only person baptized with the baptism of John, there would have been no lack of people to think that the baptism of John was of more value than the baptism of Christ. For they would say, "That baptism is of so much more value since only Christ deserved to be baptized with it."

So then, for us to be given an example of humility by the Lord and, in this way, to be led to attain salvation through baptism, Christ accepted what he did not need for himself, but what was needed for our sakes. And again, lest this baptism which Christ received from John should be held in greater esteem than the baptism Christ gives, others were allowed to be baptized by John. But John's baptism was not enough for those who received it; they were also baptized, you see, with Christ's baptism, because the baptism of John was not the baptism of Christ.[7] Those who receive Christ's baptism do not seek John's; those who received John's baptism did seek the baptism of Christ.

So John's baptism was enough for Christ. How could it fail to be enough, since it was not even needed? For him, after all, no baptism was needed; but to encourage us to receive his baptism, he accepted the baptism of a servant. And lest the servant's baptism be held in greater esteem than the baptism of the Lord, other people were baptized with the baptism of their fellow servant. But those who had been baptized with the baptism of their fellow servant needed to be baptized with the baptism of the Lord, while those baptized with the Lord's baptism have no need of the baptism of their fellow servant.

---

6. See Homily 4, 14.
7. See Acts 19:1-5.

John's unique privilege was being entrusted with a baptism called his own

6. John therefore received a baptism which would properly be called the baptism of John, but the Lord Jesus Christ did not wish to give his own baptism to anyone else—not that no one would be baptized with the Lord's baptism, but so that it would always be the Lord himself who baptized. Thus would the Lord baptize through the ministry of others, that is, those whom the ministers were to baptize would be baptized by the Lord, not by the ministers. For it is one thing to baptize through a ministry received, another to baptize on one's own authority.[8]

Baptism, you see, is characterized by the one in whose authority it is conferred, not by the one through whose ministry it is conferred. John's baptism was like John: a just baptism has the character of a just man; yes, still a man, but a man who had received this grace—and what a grace it was!—from the Lord, such that he was worthy of going before the judge, pointing him out with his finger and of fulfilling the words of that prophecy: *The voice of one crying out in the desert, Prepare a way for the Lord* (Is 40:3). On the other hand, the Lord's baptism is such as the Lord is; therefore, the Lord's baptism is divine, because the Lord is God.

All subsequent servants of Christ are entrusted with Christ's baptism, not with Peter's or Paul's

7. It is true that the Lord Jesus Christ, if he wanted to, could have given one of his servants authority to confer his baptism in his stead, and could have transferred the baptismal authority from himself and set it up in one of his servants, and could have given just as much force to the baptism he thus transferred to the servant as the baptism he performed would have had. He refused to do this, so that the hope of those baptized would be in that one by whom they accept that they were baptized. So he did not want a servant to place his hope in a servant. That indeed is why the apostle cried out, when he saw people who wanted to place their hope in him, *It was not Paul who was crucified for you, was it? Or were you baptized in the name of Paul?* (1 Cor 1:13) So then Paul baptized as a minister, not on his own authority; while the Lord baptized on his own authority.

---

8. The concise Latin contrast is *per ministerium / per potestatem*; see also Homily 5, 11.

Notice! He could have given this authority to servants, and he was unwilling to do so. For, if he gave this authority to servants, that is, such that what was the Lord's would be theirs, then there would be as many baptisms as there were servants; and just as there was a baptism called John's, so there would also be a baptism called Peter's, and a baptism called Paul's, and a baptism of James, a baptism of Thomas, of Matthew, of Bartholomew; for the baptism of John was called John's baptism. But perhaps someone will refuse that statement and say, "Prove to us that that baptism was called John's." I will prove it in the response of Truth himself to the question of the Jews: *John's baptism, where is it from? From heaven, or from men?* (Mk 11:30) Therefore, to ensure that there would not be as many baptisms as there were servants who had received this authority from the Lord, the Lord kept baptismal authority in his own hands, and gave the ministry of it to servants. A servant says that he baptizes; and he is right to say so, just as the apostle says, *I also baptized the household of Stephanas* (1 Cor 1:16), but as a minister. So it is that if even a bad man happens to have this ministry, and people do not know what he is really like—although God knows—God, who has kept the authority for himself, allows people to be baptized by him.

8. But this was something John did not know about the Lord. That he was the Lord, he knew, that he himself ought to be baptized by him, he knew and he declared it publicly; that the Lord was Truth and that he, a man of truth, had been sent by the Truth, this too he knew. So what was it that he did not know about him? That he was going to retain baptismal authority in his own hands and was not going to hand it over and transfer it to another servant, such that whether the ministry of baptism was exercised by a good servant or a bad servant, the one being baptized would know that he was not being baptized by just anybody but by the one who retained the baptismal authority in his own hands.

And that you may know, brothers and sisters, that this is what John did not know about him, and what he learned through the dove—for he already knew the Lord, but that he was going to retain the baptismal authority in his own hands and not give it to any servant, he did not yet know—that is why he said, A*nd I did not know him*. And that you may know that this is what he then learned, notice what follows: *But the one who sent me to baptize in* *water, he it is who said to me, On whomever you see the Spirit coming down like a dove and resting on him, he is the one.*

He is what?

The Lord.

But he already knew the Lord. So imagine that John had only said this, "I did not know him; *but the one who sent me to baptize in water, he it is who said to me.*"

We ask, "What did he say"?

He goes on: *On whomever you see the Spirit coming down like a dove and resting on him.* (I am not repeating what comes next; wait just a moment).

On whomever you see the Spirit coming down like a dove and resting on him, he is the one.

But what is he? What did the one who sent me wish to teach me through the dove? That he was the Lord? I already knew whom I was sent by; I already knew the one to whom I said, *Are you coming to me to be baptized? It is I who ought to be baptized by you.* So I knew the Lord so well that I wanted to be baptized by him rather than that he should be baptized by me. And then he said to me, *Let it be for now; let all justice be fulfilled* (Mt 3:14-15). I came to suffer; why not also come to be baptized? *Let all justice be fulfilled*, said my God to me; *let all justice be fulfilled*, let me teach humility in its fullness. I know that among my people in the future will be found the proud; I know that some future members will be especially gifted, such that when they see some uneducated persons being baptized, they will see themselves as better, whether in the matter of self-control or of almsgiving or of doctrine, and will perhaps disdain to receive themselves what these inferior people have received. I have to heal them, so that they will not disdain to come to the Lord's baptism, since I myself came to the baptism of a servant.

Though apostles may say my gospel, *they never talk of* my baptism

9. So that is what John already knew, and he knew the Lord. So what did the dove teach him? What did the one who had sent him want to teach through the dove, that is, through the Holy Spirit coming in that form,

when he said to him, *On whomever you see the Spirit coming down like a dove and resting on him, he is the one.*

Who is he?

The Lord.

I know that.

But did you ever know that this Lord who has the authority to baptize would not be giving this authority to any servant, but would be holding on to it, so that those baptized through the ministry of a servant would not attribute his baptism to the servant but to the Lord? You never knew this, did you?

No, I did not know; indeed, what did he say to me? *On whomever you see the Spirit coming down like a dove and resting on him, he is the one who baptizes in the Holy Spirit.*

He did not say, "He is the Lord"; he did not say, "He is the Christ"; he did not say, "He is God"; he did not say, "He is Jesus"; he did not say, "He is the one who was born of the virgin Mary, coming after you, being before you." He did not say any of this, because John already knew all this. But what did he not know? That the Lord himself would have and would hold on to so much authority over baptism; that, whether present on earth or absent in the body and present in majesty in heaven, the Lord would hold on to this baptismal authority, lest Paul should say, "My baptism," lest Peter should say, "My baptism." Look closely, therefore; attend to the voices of the apostles. None of the apostles ever said, "My baptism." But, even though there was only one gospel for them all, you will still find that they said, "My gospel";[9] you will never find them saying "My baptism."

What John learned from the dove, the Church, which is the Dove, must also learn

10. So that, then, is what John learned, my brothers and sisters. May we also learn what John learned through the dove. After all, the dove did not teach John and then fail to teach the Church—the same Church of which it was said, *One is my dove* (Sg 6:9). Let the dove teach the Dove.[10] Let the Dove know what John learned through the dove. The Holy Spirit

---

9. See Rom 2:16; 16:25; 1 Thess 1:5.
10. Augustine uses "dove" (*columba*) in two senses. In English, when the Church is described as a Dove, it will be written with a capital D; the dove that John saw descending on Christ will be written with a small d.

came down in the form of a dove. John was being taught something by the dove, but why by a dove particularly? It was indeed essential for him to learn it; and perhaps it was also essential that he should not learn it except through a dove.

What am I to say about the Dove, my brothers and sisters? Or when will either my heart or my tongue ever have sufficient ability to say it as I would wish? And perhaps the way I would wish to say it does not measure up to how it should be said; and if I cannot even say it as I would wish, how much less can I say it as it should be said! I indeed would much rather hear it from someone better qualified than have to say it myself to you.

Bad ministers of Christ's baptism should not worry the Dove

11. John learns to know the one he already knew, but he learns something about him that he did not know, not something that he already knew about him. And what did he know? That he was the Lord. What was it that he did not know? That the Lord was not going to pass the authority over his baptism to any other person, even though the ministry of baptism was certainly going to be passed on; the authority of the Lord was going to no one, the ministry was going both to good people and to bad people. Let the Dove not shudder at the ministry of bad people, let it look rather to the Lord's authority. What harm can a bad minister do to you, when the Lord is good? How can a malicious minister get in your way, if the judge is benevolent? That is what John learned through the dove. What did he learn? Let him say it again himself, he says, "That one told me," *On whomever you see the Spirit coming down like a dove and resting on him, that is the one who baptizes in the Holy Spirit.* So do not let them deceive you, dear Dove,[11] the seducers who say, "We are the ones who baptize." Recognize, Dove, what the dove taught: *This is the one who baptizes in the Holy Spirit.* Through a dove we learn that he is the one who baptizes; and do you think that you are being baptized according to the authority of the minister who baptizes you? If that is what you think, you are not yet in the body of the Dove; and if you are not in the body of the Dove, it is no surprise that you lack simplicity. Simplicity, after all, is exactly what the dove stands for.

---

11. Thus does he address the members of his congregation as the Church.

Those who wish to baptize again are hawks and kites, not doves

12. Why was it through the simplicity of a dove, my brothers and sisters, that John learned that *this is the one who baptizes in the Holy Spirit*, if not because those who scatter the Church are not doves? They are hawks, they are kites. Doves do not tear things to pieces. And you can see the ill will they have toward us, as if we were responsible for the persecutions which they have suffered.[12] They did indeed suffer bodily—as if they were persecuted—but these were clearly the scourges to which the Lord subjected them to discipline for a time, so as not to have to condemn them for eternity, for failing to acknowledge the Dove and to amend themselves.

They are the ones who persecute the Church; they do so by deceit; they inflict a serious wound on the heart who strike it with the sword of the tongue; they shed blood more ruthlessly who slay Christ—insofar as it is possible for them to do so—in their fellow human beings. They put on a show of being terrified by the judgment of the authorities. But what does an authority do to you, if you are good? Fear authority, however, if you are bad, for they *do not bear the sword in vain*, says the apostle (Rom 13:4). Do not draw your sword, with it you strike at Christ. Christian, what are you persecuting in your fellow Christian? What did the emperor persecute in you? He persecuted the flesh; you for your part are persecuting the spirit in your fellow Christian. You do not slay the flesh. And yet they do not even spare the flesh; they have killed as many as they could by beating them to death; they have not spared either their own people or others. This is something everybody knows about.[13] Because it is legitimate, [state] authority arouses hatred; the one who acts according to the law acts with hatred; the one who acts outside the law acts without hatred!

Would you all pay attention, my brothers and sisters, to what a Christian is. What a human being is, is held in common with everyone else;

---

12. Augustine alludes to the Macarian persecution of the Donatists in the middle of the fourth century, when the Proconsul Macarius enforced the imperial laws against them. They blamed the Catholic bishops for that and for the legislation against them in the first decade of the fifth century. In the latter case, they blamed Augustine. In fact, no Donatists were ever executed for being Donatists; penalties included the confiscation of church properties and the exile of some of their leaders. Hence, Augustine refers to "so-called bodily persecutions."
13. Augustine refers to the Circumcellions, Donatists who used force against their adversaries. The phrases about legitimate authority refer to some Donatist attitudes toward state authorities. See BA 71, 317, note 4.

what a Christian is, sets him apart from everybody else, and being Christian is more important to him than being human. For as a Christian he is renewed according to the image of God, by the one who made human beings according to the image of God.[14] But, as a human being, he could be bad, he could be a pagan, he could be an idolater.

You are persecuting in the Christian the best of what he has; for you want to deprive him of what he lives for. Yes, he lives in time by the spirit of life, which animates the body; but he is living for eternity by the baptism which he has received from the Lord. You want to take away from him what he has received from the Lord; you want to take from him what he really lives for. What bandits want, when they strip people of their goods, is to have more themselves and to leave the others with nothing. You are stealing from the Christian without gaining anything for yourself; for nothing more comes your way because you have stolen it. But, in fact, they do just the same as those who take someone else's life; they take the life of another but fail to end up with two lives.

Argument with Donatists about bad ministers and who gives baptism

13. So what do you want to take away? What do you find displeasing in the one you wish to rebaptize? You cannot give him what he already has, but you make him deny what he does have. Did a pagan, a persecutor of the Church, act any more harshly than that? Swords were unsheathed against the martyrs, wild beasts were let loose on them, red-hot gridirons were applied to them; and why all this? To make him say, "I am not a Christian." What do you teach the one you wish to rebaptize, what else but to say first of all, "I am not a Christian"? In another time, the persecutor used fire for this purpose; you use your tongue; by seductive talk you make him do what the persecutor could not do by killing him.

And what are you going to give him, and to whom are you going to give it? If they tell you the truth and are not seduced by you into telling a lie, each one of them will say, "I have it."[15]

---
14. See Col 3:10.
15. By "having baptism" Augustine means more than "having been baptized." He is referring to what we now call the baptismal character, to having the brand-mark of Christ. That character

"You have baptism?" you ask.[16]

"I do," he says.

As often as he says, "I have it," you say, "I will not be giving it."

"And do not give it; because what you want to give cannot take hold in me, because what I received cannot be taken away from me. But wait a minute; let me see what you want to teach me."

"First say," he says, "I do not have it."

"But I do have it. If I say, 'I do not have it,' I am lying. What I have, after all, I have."

"You do not have it," he says.

"Tell me why I do not have it."

"A bad man gave it to you."

"If Christ is a bad man, then, yes, a bad man gave it to me."

"It is not that Christ is a bad man," he says, "but Christ did not give it to you."

"So who did give it to me?" you must answer. "I know I received it from Christ."

"Someone gave it to you," he says; "not Christ, but some betrayer or other."

"I will look into who the minister was, I will look into who the herald was; but I am not going to argue about the minister, I am paying attention to the judge; and perhaps you are lying when you object to the minister. But I refuse to discuss it; let the Lord of both of us take cognizance of his minister's case. Perhaps, if I insist that you prove your charge, you will not do so; on the contrary, you are lying; it has been shown that you were unable to prove it."[17]

---

signifies that the baptized person belongs to him forever because it cannot be taken away. Nor can it be "over-stamped" by another baptism. The metaphor of "character" (Greek for a stamp or mark) was taken from the imperial stamp branded on the hands of Roman legionaries, thus marking them for life as "belonging" to the emperor.

16. From here to the end of section 13, the argumentative conversation is, for the most part, between the representative member of Augustine's congregation and a Donatist.

17. Augustine is alluding to the charge of betrayal brought against Cecilian, bishop of Carthage at the beginning of the 4th century. During the Diocletian persecution, he was said to have given the sacred books, the scriptures, to the authorities to be burned. The Donatists also objected that he had been ordained bishop by a "betrayer," a *traditor*, and, therefore, they claimed that his

"But that is not what I base my case on, lest, when I begin to defend innocent men and do not give up, you may think that I have placed my hope in innocent men. Whatever those men may have been like, what I received I received from Christ; I was baptized by Christ."

"No," he says, "but that bishop baptized you, and that bishop is in communion with them."

"I was baptized by Christ, that is what I know."

"How do you know that?"

"The dove which John saw taught me. You evil kite, you are not tearing me out of the bowels of the Dove. I am counted among the members of the Dove, because I know what the dove taught. You tell me, 'This man baptized you' or 'That man baptized you.' What I, and you, are told through the dove, is, *This is the one who baptizes*. Which one am I to believe, the kite or the dove?"

The Donatists, like the Pharisees, are confounded by John, the lamp

14. "Tell me clearly so that you may be confounded through that lamp which also confounded earlier enemies, the Pharisees, your equals,[18] who questioned the Lord about his authority for doing those things."

I too will ask you this question, he said. *Tell me where John's baptism comes from. From heaven or from men?* There they were, all set to hurl their deceptions like a javelin, when they were ensnared with a question;[19] they started thinking about the matter among themselves, saying, *If we say that it is from heaven, he is going to say to us, Why did you fail to believe him?* John, you see, had said about the Lord, *Look, there is the Lamb of God; look, there is the one who takes away the sin of the world*. So why are you asking by what authority I am acting? You wolves, I am acting as I do with the authority of the Lamb. But in order to know the Lamb, why did you not believe John, who said, *Look, there is the Lamb of God; look, there*

---

ordination was invalid. The two "litigants" just referred to ("the Lord of them both...") were presumably Cecilian and Donatus. The case went eventually to the court of Constantine, who referred it first to the bishop of Rome, and then to the Council of Arles (314).

18. See the *Letter against Parmenian* II, 8, 17 and the *Letter against Petilian* II, 72, 162 for a similar usage.
19. The metaphor comes from the combats between a gladiator with a javelin and a foe whose weapon was a net.

is the one who takes away the sin of the world? So then, since they knew perfectly well what John had said about the Lord, they said to one another, *If we say that John's baptism is from heaven, he will say to us, Why then did you not believe him? If we say that it is from men, we shall be stoned by the people, because they hold John to be a prophet.* That is how they were afraid of men, that is how they were embarrassed to profess the truth. Darkness responded with darkness, but was overcome by the Light. How then did they answer? *We do not know.* Speaking about something they knew, they replied, *We do not know.* And the Lord said, *Nor will I tell you by what authority I am doing these things.* (Lk 20:1-8)

Thus were the first enemies left in confusion. How? By the lamp. Who was the lamp? John. Can we prove he was a lamp? We can; the Lord, you see, says, *He was a burning and a shining lamp* (Jn 5:35). Can we prove that enemies were put to confusion through him? Listen to the psalm: *I have prepared,* he says, *a lamp for my Christ; I will clothe his enemies with confusion* (Ps 131:17-18).[20]

More about good and bad ministers of baptism

15. Still living in the darkness of this life, we are walking by the lamp of faith; let us too hold on to the lamp which John was, let us use it also to put Christ's enemies to confusion; or rather, let him confound his enemies himself with his own lamp. Let us also ask the question which the Lord put to the Jews, let us ask it and say, *John's baptism, where is it from? From heaven or from men?* What are they going to say? Just see if they too are not put to confusion as enemies by the lamp. What are they going to say? If they say, "From men," even their own people will stone them; while if they say, "From heaven," we will say to them, *Why then did you not believe him?*

Perhaps they say, "We do believe him."

"Then how can you say that you are the ones who baptize, and John says, *This is the one who baptizes?*"

"But," they say, "the ministers of such a great judge, the ministers through whom baptism is given, should be just."

---

20. For a similar treatment of John the Baptist as the lamp, see Sermon 293,4; *Exposition of Psalm* 131, 27.

I too say (and we all say) that the ministers of such a great judge should be just. Let the ministers be just if they are willing; but if they are not willing to be just—those who occupy the chair of Moses—my master, about whom his Spirit said, *This is the one who baptizes*, has assured me. How has he assured me? *The scribes and Pharisees*, he said, *occupy the chair of Moses; do what they say, but do not do what they do; for they say and do not do* (Mt 23:2-3).

If the minister is just, I regard him as I regard Paul, as I regard Peter; with them do I count ministers who are just because ministers who are really just do not seek their own glory; they are, after all, ministers; they do not want to be taken for judges; they shudder at the thought of hope being placed in themselves. So I reckon the just minister as one with Paul. After all, what does Paul say? *I planted, Apollos watered; but God caused the growth. Neither the one who plants nor the one who waters is anything, but God is the one who causes the growth.* (1 Cor 3:6-7)

Yes, a proud minister is to be aligned with Zabulus,[21] but Christ's gift is not contaminated; what flows through the minister remains pure, the liquid that passes through him reaches fertile soil. Think of the proud minister as made of stone, because he cannot produce fruit when watered; and the water passes along a stone channel, the water passes along to the little garden beds. It produces no fruit in the stone channel, but nonetheless it makes the gardens very fruitful indeed.

The spiritual power of the sacrament, you see, is like light; and it is received pure by those to be enlightened,[22] and if it passes through tainted beings, it is not defiled. Certainly let the ministers be just and not seek their

---

21. *Cum Zabulo computatur.* My impression is that Augustine treated Zabulus as a proper name for the devil, and not as just an alternative spelling of *diabolus*. The Maurists spell it with a capital Z, noting that, in most manuscripts, it is written *diabolo*. It occurs, with a capital Z, in three of Augustine's sermons: in Sermon 90, 9, where I just translated it as "the devil." In footnote 26, I mistakenly wrote: "Here spelt *zabulo* instead of *diabolo*, which possibly tells us something about the African pronunciation of Latin at the time." Also found in Sermons 214, 3 and 303, 2, I rendered it there by "the devil." It also occurs in *The City of God* XV, 23; XX, 5. That spelling is found in the Doric dialect of Greek, according to Ducange; so it occurs in Origen and even earlier Greek fathers. It is likely Augustine was not alone in regarding it as one of the devil's proper names. My thanks to Duncan Cloud, Professor emeritus of Classics at Leicester University, for ascertaining the details of its earlier use.
22. A common way at that time of designating the baptizands; the *illuminandi*, the "ones to be enlightened."

own glory but the glory of the one whose ministers they are. Let them not say, "It is my baptism," because it is not theirs. Let them pay attention to John himself. John was full of the Holy Spirit, and he had a baptism from heaven, not from men. But up to when did he have it? He said himself, *Prepare a way for the Lord*. But, when he was made known, the Lord himself became the way; there was no longer any need for the baptism of John which prepared a way for the Lord.

The difference between baptizing after John and rebaptizing after a bad minister

16. However, what are they always saying to us? "But look, baptism was given after John."[23] In fact, before this question was properly dealt with in the Catholic Church, many people, both great and good, were mistaken about it;[24] but because they were members of the Dove, they did not cut themselves off, and what the apostle said was realized in them: *If you think otherwise, God will teach you about that matter* (Phil 3:15). Hence, those who did split off proved unteachable. So then, what are they always saying? "Look, baptism was given after John; why should it not be given after heretics as well?" "Because some of those who had John's baptism were told by Paul to be baptized; for they did not have the baptism of Christ. Therefore, why do you exaggerate John's merits, and then slight the wretched condition of heretics? I grant you that heretics are profane scoundrels; but even heretics gave Christ's baptism, a baptism that John did not give."

17. I return to John, and say, *This is the one who baptizes*. John, after all, is better than a heretic, just as John is better than a drunkard, just as John is better than a murderer. If we have to baptize after those who are not so good because the apostles baptized after one who was better, then everyone among them who may have been baptized by a drunkard—I do not say by a murderer, I do not say by the henchman of a scoundrel,[25] I do not say by a plunderer of other people's goods, I do not say by an oppressor of orphans,

---

23. That is, those who had received John's baptism were again baptized, like the people at Ephesus; they were baptized again on the orders of Paul, to whom Augustine is about to refer.
24. Augustine is most probably referring to those like Cyprian and his fellow bishops who were at odds with the bishop of Rome, Stephen, on this matter. Augustine deals with this in *On Baptism* VI-VII.
25. A reference in all probability to a notorious Donatist bishop, Optatus of Thamugadi (Timgad), who was generally assumed to be the henchman of the rebel Gildo, active in Numidia from 388

I do not say by a breaker-up of marriages; I do not say any of these things; I say what is a common, everyday occurrence, I use a word applied to all of them, and in this city, when people say to them, "Let's go out and get drunk,[26] let's have a good time; you should not fast on a January holiday like this," I just mention little things, everyday things—when baptism is by a drunk man, who is the better, John or the drunkard? Answer, if you can, that your drunkard is a better man than John; you will never have the nerve to say that, will you? So you, then, being a sober man, baptize again after your drunkard. If the apostles, after all, baptized after John, how much more should a sober man baptize after a drunkard! Or do you say, "The drunkard is in communion with me?" So John, then, the friend of the bridegroom, was he not in communion with the bridegroom?[27]

Whether Judas or Peter was baptizing, the baptism of Christ which they gave did not change

18. But to you personally I say, whoever you are, "Are you the better man or is John?" You will not have the nerve to answer, "I am better than John." So then, let your people baptize after you, if they happen to be better than you are. I mean, if baptism was administered after John, then you should be ashamed that it is not being administered after you. You will say, "But I have the baptism of Christ and I teach it."

Well then, bring yourself at some time or other to acknowledge the judge and stop being a proud herald. You give the baptism of Christ, and that is why baptism is not administered after you. Baptism was indeed administered after John, because he was not giving Christ's baptism, but his own; that, after all, is how he had received it, that it should be his own. So you, then, are not a better man than John; but the baptism which is given through your hands is better than John's; for it is Christ's, while that one is John's.

---

until his death in 398. The other kinds of villainy Augustine leaves aside were things Donatist clergy were often accused of, whether fairly or not. See Letter 87 to the Donatist bishop, Emeritus.

26. *Alogiemus*; a verb, *alogio*, which was perhaps Hipponese slang formed from the noun *alogia*, meaning in general irrational conduct or the dinner at which people indulge themselves beyond the bounds of reason. See also Letter 36, 9.11.

27. Augustine's emphasis on personal holiness is in contrast to the Donatist emphasis on being "in good standing." His emphasis is interior; theirs exterior. In this way, he seeks to show why their idea of baptism is not acceptable.

The baptism given both by Paul and by Peter is Christ's; and if any was given by Judas, it was Christ's. Judas gave it, and there was no baptizing again after Judas; John gave it, and there was baptizing again after John, because if baptism was given by Judas, it was Christ's, while what was given by John was John's. We do not rate Judas over John, but the baptism of Christ—even by the hand of Judas—is rightly rated higher than that of John, even higher than the baptism by the hand of John. As a matter of fact, it was said about the Lord before his passion that he was baptizing more people than John; but then it adds, *Although he was not baptizing, his disciples were* (Jn 4:1-2). It was he, and it was not he; he baptized by his authority, they by their ministry; they applied their ministry in baptizing, but the power of baptizing remained with Christ.

So then, his disciples were baptizing, and Judas was there, still among his disciples. Those whom Judas baptized were not baptized again; and were those baptized by John really baptized again? Yes, again, but not by repeating the same baptism. You see, those whom John baptized, John baptized, while those whom Judas baptized, Christ baptized. In the same way, therefore, those whom a drunkard has baptized, whom a murderer has baptized, whom an adulterer has baptized, if it was Christ's baptism, Christ has baptized. I am not worried about the adulterer, about the drunkard, about the murderer, because I am paying attention to the dove, through which I am told, *This is the one who baptizes* (Jn 1:33).

The evil of envy—but even an envious minister does not defile baptism

19. For the rest, my brothers and sisters, it is lunacy to suppose that any human being, not just Judas, was of greater merit than the man of whom it was said, *Among those born of women none has arisen greater than John the Baptist* (Mt 11:11). Thus, no servant is held in higher esteem than this man, but the Lord's baptism—even given through the hands of a bad servant—is held in higher esteem than the baptism of the servant who was also a friend. Listen to the kind of false brethren Paul mentions, preaching the word of God out of envy; and what does he say about them? *And in this I rejoice, yes and I will go on rejoicing* (Phil 1:15. 18), because they were preaching Christ; yes, out of envy, but still they were preaching Christ. Look not at the minister but at the one preached. Is Christ being preached to

you out of envy? Look at Christ, shun the envy.[28] Do not imitate the bad man who is preaching, but the good man who is being preached to you.

And what does being envious amount to? A horrendous evil. Zabulus was cast down by this evil, this malignant cancer with which he cast down many others; and some preachers of Christ had it, yet the apostle still allows them to preach. Why? Because they were preaching Christ. But to envy is to hate; and what is said about the one who hates? Listen to the apostle John: *Whoever hates his brother is a murderer* (1 Jn 3:15). Hence, there was baptizing after John and after a murderer there is no baptizing, because John gave his own baptism, but the murderer gave the baptism of Christ. That sacrament is so holy that a murderer cannot defile it.

More about the dove in the next homily

20. I am not tossing John aside, but rather I am believing John. What do I believe about John? About what he learned through the dove. What did he learn through the dove? *This is the one who baptizes in the Holy Spirit.* So now then, brothers and sisters, hold on to this and impress it firmly on your hearts. You see, although I wished to speak today more fully about the dove, there is not enough time left. I think I have explained to Your Holinesses how John learned from the dove something that he did not yet know about Christ and which he had to learn, even though he already knew Christ; but why this matter had to be demonstrated by means of a dove—well, if it could be stated briefly, I would state it. But it requires a long time to explain, and I do not want to be burdensome to you. However, just as I have been helped by your prayers to carry out what I had promised; so also with the help of your loving determination and good desires, this too will become clear to you—that what John learned about the Lord, that he is the one who baptizes in the Holy Spirit and that he did not bequeath this baptismal authority to any of his servants, he only learned through the dove.

---

28. A little play on words in the Latin, easy to remember: *Vide Christum, vita invidiam.*

Homily 6

On Jn 1:32-33[1]

Continuing the previous homily

1. I must confess to Your Holinesses that I was afraid this cold weather might cool your willingness to come together today. But this big crowd of you gathered here is an ample demonstration of how fervent in spirit you are, and so I have no doubt at all that you have prayed for me that I might be able to pay the debt I owe you. In fact, when the lack of time kept me from explaining why God should have wished to reveal the Holy Spirit in the form of a dove, I promised in the name of Christ to treat that matter today. This day has now dawned just so that it may be explained, and I can feel the desire to hear about it, yes, the avid devotion with which you have gathered together in such numbers to listen. May God satisfy your expectations from my lips! Love, after all, has made you come; but love of what? If love of me, that is fine; for I do want to be loved by you—but I do not want to be loved just for myself. Because I love you in Christ, please, therefore, love me back in Christ, and may our mutual love groan to God: for that love is the groaning of the Dove.

The Spirit's groaning makes us groan; let us moan like a dove out of love, not clamor like crows

2. If, as we all know, moaning is what a dove does, even so, a dove moans in love; then listen to what the apostle says and do not be surprised that the Holy Spirit wanted to be revealed in the likeness of a dove: *For we do not know how to pray as we ought*, he says, *but the Spirit himself intercedes for us with unutterable groans* (Rom 8:26). What then, my brothers and sisters? Are we going to say that the Spirit is groaning in that place where he is in perfect and eternal bliss with the Father and the Son? The Holy Spirit is, after all, God, just as the Son of God is God and the Father is God. Three times I have said "God," but I have not said three gods, because Father and Son and Holy Spirit are one God; you know that

---

1. Preached on Sunday, January 13, 407.

perfectly well. So then the Holy Spirit does not groan within on his own account in that Trinity, in that blessed bliss, in that eternity of being; but he groans in us, because he makes us groan.

Nor is it a small matter that the Holy Spirit teaches us to groan; for he is reminding us that we are on pilgrimage and teaching us to sigh for our home country, and, with that longing, we groan. The one who is doing fine in this world, or rather he thinks that all is going well for the one whose joy is in material, time-bound things and who rejoices in futile bliss, such a person has the voice of a crow; for the sound of a crow is noisy, not sighing. Yet the one who knows that he is crushed by the weight of mortal existence and is wandering far from the Lord, not yet holding the eternal bliss which we have been promised, but has it in hope, and will have it in reality[2] when the Lord (who first came concealed in humility) comes in glory, that person groans. And as long as that is the reason for moaning, he does well to groan; the Spirit has taught him to moan; he has learned to moan from the dove.

Many people, you see, moan about earthly misfortune; whether they have been shaken by financial loss, or weighed down with illness, or shut up in prison, or bound with chains, or tossed about in stormy seas, or fenced in by the snares of enemies, they groan. But they are not moaning with the moan of the dove, because they are not moaning out of love of God, not groaning in the Spirit. Hence, when such people are freed from their distress they jump around with loud noises, making it obvious that they are crows, not doves. How fitting it was that when the crow was sent out from the ark it did not return, while when the dove was sent out it did come back—those are the two birds that Noah sent out![3] He had a crow with him there, he also had a dove; the ark contained each kind of bird; and if the ark was representing the Church, you can of course see how it must be that, in these unsettled times, the Church has both sorts, both the

---

2. This is a favorite contrasting jingle, pointing the difference between *in spe* and *in re*.
3. See Gn 8:6-9. Augustine's more usual treatment of the crow and dove theme is to contrast the dove's moaning, in sorrow for sins, in genuine repentance and readiness to seek absolution, with the crow's cawing cry (in Latin) of *cras, cras*, "tomorrow, tomorrow"; the sinner putting off turning back to God till the last possible moment. "God has given you today," he says, "and promised you forgiveness, even if you do only turn back to him on your deathbed. What he has not promised you is tomorrow." See *Exposition of Psalm* 102,16; Sermons 82,14; 224,3.

crow and the dove. Who are the crows? Those who look after their own interests. Who the doves? Those who look after Christ's interests.[4]

The Holy Spirit is revealed in the dove and in the flame, signs of the simplicity and fervor required of Christians

3. Then that is the reason why, when he sent the Holy Spirit, he revealed him visibly in two ways: by a dove and by fire; by a dove, coming down on the Lord when he was baptized; by fire, coming down on the disciples when they were gathered together. For, when the Lord had ascended into heaven after his resurrection, having spent forty days with his disciples, he sent them the Holy Spirit, as he had promised, when the day of Pentecost arrived. So then, in coming, the Spirit filled that place, and first came a sound from heaven as of a gale force wind blowing, as we read in the Acts of the Apostles: *And there appeared to them*, it says, *divided tongues as of fire, which also settled upon each one of them; and they began to speak in tongues, as the Spirit gave them to proclaim* (Acts 2:3-4). There we saw a dove over the Lord, here divided tongues on the gathering of disciples; there, simplicity was designated; here, fervor.

Some people, in fact, are said to be simple, and they are lazy; they are called simple, but they are lethargic. Stephen, filled with the Holy Spirit, was not like that; he was simple, because he did no harm to anyone; he was fervent because he upbraided the godless. For he was not silent before the Jews; his are these fiery words: *Stiff-necked and uncircumcised of heart and ears, you have always resisted the Holy Spirit* (Acts 7:51). A fierce attack indeed, the ferocious onslaught of a dove without gall. That you might know that he was being ferocious without gall, those who were crows, when they heard these words, immediately rushed to pick up stones against the dove; Stephen began to be stoned; and the man who had just growled at them, fervent in spirit, as if launching an attack on his enemies, inveighing against them with those fiery words that you heard, *Stiff-necked and uncircumcised of heart and ears*, so that anyone hearing them would assume that Stephen, given the chance, would have wished them immediately reduced to ashes; this man, struck by the stones from their hands, knelt

---

4. See Phil 2:21.

down and said, *Lord, do not hold this crime against them* (Acts 7:60). He had clung to the unity of the Dove. His master, you see, had done the same before him, the one on whom the dove had come down, and who said as he hung on the cross, *Father, forgive them, because they do not know what they are doing* (Lk 23:34).

So then, lest those who have been sanctified by the Holy Spirit should be given to trickery, he became visible in the dove; lest their simplicity should remain cold, he became visible in fire. And do not be troubled that the tongues are divided. Languages do differ, after all, so that is why he appeared in divided tongues; *divided tongues as of fire*, it says, *which also settled upon each one of them*. Tongues differ from each other, but differences of languages are not schisms. Do not be afraid of things breaking up through divided tongues; recognize the unity in the dove.

Many Donatists are returning to the Church; Augustine urges the rest to return

4. That then is how, yes, that is the way that the Holy Spirit was to come down upon the Lord, so that everyone could understand that, if he has the Holy Spirit, he should be *as simple as a dove* (Mt 10:16), be truly at peace with his brothers, which is what the billing of doves signifies. Crows too, after all, go in for billing, but among crows peace is false, while among doves peace is true. So not everyone, then, who says, "Peace be with you,"[5] is to be listened to as a dove.

So how then does anyone tell the difference between the billing of crows and the billing of doves? When crows kiss, they tear to pieces; by nature doves are innocent of tearing to pieces. So then, where there is rending and tearing, there is no true peace in kisses. Those who are truly at peace are the ones who have not torn the Church apart. Crows, you see, feed on death, a habit the dove does not have; the dove lives on the fruits of the earth, its food is innocent—which, brothers and sisters, is indeed something marvelous about the dove. Sparrows are the tiniest birds; yet they at least kill flies. None of that with the dove; it does not feed on death. Those who have torn the Church apart are feeding on the dead.

---

5. The usual greeting of a bishop to his flock when they gather for worship.

God is powerful; let us pray for people who are being devoured by them and do not realize it, that they may be restored to life. Many do realize it and are being restored to life; every day, I mean, we can rejoice in the name of Christ at their coming in. As for you, please be as simple as doves in such a way that you are also fervent in spirit; and let your fervor find an outlet in your tongues. Do not just keep quiet; speak with fiery tongues, set fire to the indifferent.

The Donatists are like the crow which refused to come back to the ark

5. What are the facts after all, my brothers and sisters? Who can fail to see what those people do not see? No wonder they do not see, because those who refuse to come back are like the crow which was sent out from the ark. For who could fail to see what they do not see? And what is more, they are ungrateful to the Holy Spirit. Look, there was the dove, coming down upon the Lord, upon the Lord after he was baptized; and that holy and true Trinity, which is for us one God, appeared there. The Lord, you see, came up from the water, as we read in the gospel: *And behold the heavens were opened to him, and he saw the Spirit coming down like a dove, and it rested on him; and right away a voice followed: You are my beloved Son, in whom I am well pleased* (Mt 3:16-17). The Trinity appeared in the clearest possible way: the Father in the voice, the Son in the man, the Spirit in the dove. Let us see what we see about where the apostles were sent in the name of this Trinity and what—surprisingly—those people do not see. Not really that they do not see, after all, but that they shut their eyes to what is staring them in the face. Where were the disciples sent, *in the name of the Father and of the Son and of the Holy Spirit* (Mt 28:19), by the one of whom it was said, *This is the one who baptizes* (Jn 1:33)? For that was said to his ministers by the one who retained this authority in his own hands.[6]

---

6. Not till section 9 will Augustine answer this question, though of course he has already given the obvious clue to the closing words of Matthew's gospel. Both the Maurists and the CCSL editors obscure what the preacher is up to, by punctuating the question as a loose standing relative clause.

The dove is a sign of the unity which is assured by the fact that Christ, not his ministers, baptizes

6. For that is what John saw in him, and he came to know what he had not known—not because he did not know him as the Son of God, or did not know him as the Lord, or did not know him as the Christ, or did not even know that he was going to baptize in water and the Holy Spirit; in fact, he even knew that.[7] But that he would baptize in such a way as to keep the authority to baptize in his own hands, and not transfer it to any of his ministers, this is what John learned in the dove.

By this authority, which Christ kept for himself alone and did not transfer to any of his ministers—even though he chose to baptize through his ministers—the Church's unity stands, the unity signified in the dove, of which it is said, *One is my dove; for her mother she is one* (Sg 6:9). For if, as I have already said, my brothers and sisters, if the authority over baptism were transferred to the minister, there would be as many baptisms as there are ministers, and the unity of baptism would not last.

The Baptist knew, before he baptized him, that Jesus baptizes in the Holy Spirit

7. Pay close attention, brothers and sisters. Before our Lord Jesus Christ came to be baptized—because after his baptism the dove came down and John learned something special, since he had been told, *On whomever you see the Spirit coming down like a dove and resting on him, he is the one who baptizes in the Holy Spirit* (Jn 1:33)—John knew that Christ baptizes in the Holy Spirit. But that he would do so with such a proprietary right that the authority over baptism would not pass from him to anyone else, even by a grant from him, that is what John learned at that moment.

And how can we prove that John already knew that the Lord was going to baptize in the Holy Spirit, so that what he is to be understood as having learned in the dove is that the Lord was going to do this in such a way that this right and authority to baptize would not pass over to any

---

7. These statements are all made in the negative, but the double negative is not a very clear form in English. More literally, it would read: "not that he had not known him as the Son of God, or not known him as the Lord, or not known him as the Christ, or even that he had not known this about him, that he was the one who was going to baptize in water and the Holy Spirit, because this too he had been aware of."

other human being? How can we prove it? The dove came down upon the Lord when he had already been baptized; but before the Lord came to be baptized by John in the Jordan, we have said that he showed he already knew him, by saying, *Are you coming to me to be baptized? It is I who ought to be baptized by you.* (Mt 3:14)

Yes, but that shows he knew him as the Lord, knew him as the Son of God; how are we to prove he already knew that he was the one who would baptize in the Holy Spirit?

Before Jesus ever came to the river, while multitudes were flocking to John to be baptized, he said to them, *I indeed am baptizing you in water; but the one who is coming after me is greater than I, whose sandal straps I am not fit to untie; he it is who will baptize you in the Holy Spirit and fire* (Lk 3:16); he already knew this too. So then, what did he learn through the dove, so as not to be shown up later as a liar (which God forbid we should ever suppose)? What could it be, but that there was going to be a kind of proprietary right in Christ, such that although many ministers—whether just or unjust—were going to baptize, the holiness of baptism would not be attributed to anyone but to him upon whom the dove came down, about whom it was said, *This is the one who baptizes in the Holy Spirit*? Let Peter baptize, this is the one who baptizes; let Paul baptize, this is the one who baptizes; let Judas baptize, this is the one who baptizes.

The holiness of baptism does not depend on the holiness of the minister

8. In fact, if the holiness of baptism varies according to the diversity of merits, there will be as many variations in baptism as there are variations in merit; and the better the person one is baptized by seems to be, the better the baptism one will be thought to have received. The saints themselves, brothers and sisters—and please understand this well—the good people who belong to the Dove, who have a share in the fortunes of that holy city Jerusalem,[8] the good people in the Church of whom the apostle says, *The Lord knows who are his own* (2 Tm 2:19); they all have different graces, they are not all of equal merit; some are holier than

---

8. See Gal 4:26; Rev 21.

others, some are better than others. So why is it, then, that if one person is baptized by that holy and just man, for example, another by that one of inferior merit in God's eyes, of inferior standing, of inferior self-discipline, of inferior quality of life, why is it that what they both receive is nonetheless one and the same and equal, if not because *this is the one who baptizes*?

So then, when a good man baptizes and a better man baptizes, it does not mean that this person receives something good, that person something better; but although one of the ministers was, one good and the other better, what was received was one and the same, not something better in this person, inferior in that one. So too, when a bad person baptizes, with the Church either not knowing what he is like or tolerating it—people's badness, after all, is either not known about or is tolerated, the chaff tolerated until the final winnowing of the threshing-floor—what is being given is one and the same, not something dissimilar because of the dissimilarity of the ministers; no, but the same and equal, because *this is the one who baptizes*.

The Donatists refuse to see that baptism is a gift to all nations

9. So then, dearly beloved, let us look at what they refuse to see: not that they really do not see, but because it hurts them to look at it, as if it were closed to them. Where were the disciples sent, in the name of the Father and of the Son and of the Holy Spirit, to baptize as ministers? Where were they sent? *Go*, he said, *baptize the nations*. You have heard, brothers and sisters, how that inheritance came to him: *Ask of me, and I will give you the nations as your inheritance, and as your possession the ends of the earth* (Ps 2:8); you have heard how the law has gone forth from Zion, and the word of the Lord from Jerusalem;[9] it was there, after all, that the disciples heard, *Go, baptize the nations in the name of the Father and of the Son and of the Holy Spirit* (Mt 28:19).

Our attention was caught when we heard, *Go, baptize the nations*. In whose name? *In the name of the Father and of the Son and of the Holy Spirit*. This is the one God, because it is not in the names of the Father and

---

9. See Is 2:3. They would have heard this and the psalm verse in the readings of the day.

the Son and the Holy Spirit, but *in the name of the Father and of the Son and of the Holy Spirit*. Where you hear that it is one name, it means one God. It is like what was said of the descendants of Abraham, as explained by the apostle Paul: *In your descendants shall all the nations be blessed. He did not say, in descendants, as though in many; but as in one, and your posterity, which is Christ* (Gal 3:8.16). So then, just as the apostle wanted to teach you there that there is one Christ, because it does not say *in descendants*, in the same way here too, when it says *in the name*, not "in the names," as *in the posterity* there, not "in descendants," we have the proof that Father and Son and Holy Spirit are one God.

The Church's unity; the Holy Spirit in the form of a dove

10. But look, the disciples say to the Lord, "We have heard in whose name we are to baptize; you made us ministers and you told us, *Go, baptize in the name of the Father and of the Son and of the Holy Spirit*. But where are we to go?"

"Where? Did you not hear? Go to my inheritance. You ask, 'Where are we to go?' To what I bought with my blood."

"So where to?" He said, "To the nations."

"Oh, I thought he said, 'Go, baptize the Africans[10] *in the name of the Father and of the Son and of the Holy Spirit*.' "

Thanks be to God;[11] the Lord answered the question, the dove has taught us. Thanks be to God; the apostles were sent to the nations; if to the nations, then to all languages. That is what the Holy Spirit—divided in tongues, united in the dove—signified. On the one hand the tongues are divided, on the other the dove unites. The languages of the nations have come together; has the one tongue of Africa separated? What could be clearer, my brothers and sisters? Unity in the dove; community in the tongues of the nations.

---

10. The inhabitants, not of the whole continent as in our usage, but of the north-west littoral, from the gulf of Tripoli to Morocco, constituted the "African" provinces of the Roman Empire. Only one of these, strictly speaking, was the province of Africa, coinciding with modern Tunisia. Further west were the provinces of Numidia, Augustine's native province, and the two Mauritanias.
11. The phrase "Thanks be to God" was a sign of being Catholic, since the Donatists used instead "Praise be to God"; see *Exposition of Psalm* 132, 6.

Some time ago, in fact, through pride, tongues became discordant, and then, out of one tongue, many were made. You see, after the flood a number of proud men, as if trying to protect themselves from God, built a tower—as if anything could be too high for God, anything safe for pride!—as though to avoid being wiped out by a flood, should one come again later. For they had heard and had realized that all iniquity had been wiped out by the flood. Unwilling to moderate their iniquity, they thought a high tower was the answer to a flood; they built a very high tower.[12] God saw their pride, and he introduced this misunderstanding among them, that they would not recognize each other's speech; thus were languages diversified through pride.

If pride brought about the diversity of tongues, the humility of Christ brought the diverse tongues together. Already what that tower had disunited the Church is bringing together. Many tongues were made out of one; do not be surprised, pride did this. One tongue is being made out of many; do not be surprised, charity did this, because even if tongues still make very different sounds, hearts are calling upon one God, are keeping one peace. How better then, dearly beloved, could the Holy Spirit be seen as signifying unity but through a dove, so that the Church of peace might be told, *One is my dove*? How better could humility be signified than through a bird of simple character that moans, rather than through a bird that is proud and self-important like the crow?

A Donatist argument

11. And perhaps they will say, "Because it is a dove and one dove, there cannot be any baptism aside from this one Dove; so if the dove is with you, or if you are the Dove, then, when I come to you, you give me what I do not have." You recognize that this is their approach; in a moment it will be obvious that this is not the voice of a dove, but the rasping of a crow.

In fact, would Your Graces pay attention for a moment and watch out for traps; rather, take care to receive the words of these adversaries as something to be spit out, not swallowed and assimilated. Do with them what the Lord did, when they offered him a bitter drink; he tasted it and spat

---

12. See Gn 11:1-9.

it out.[13] You do the same: listen and reject. What are they saying, after all? Let us see.

Look, he says, "You, O Catholic Church, are the Dove, it is to you that it was said, *One is my Dove; for her mother she is one*; yes, it was certainly said to you."

"Wait; do not question me. Prove first that it was said to me; if it was said to me, I want to hear the proof at once."

He says, "Yes, it was said to you."

I answer, with the voice of the Catholic Church, "Yes, to me."

Brothers and sisters, what has just come from my lips alone has also come, I am convinced, from your hearts, and we have all said together that it is the Catholic Church which was told, *One is my Dove; for her mother she is one*.

"Outside the Dove," he says, "there is no baptism; I myself was baptized outside the Dove; therefore I do not have baptism; if I do not have baptism, why do you not give it to me when I come to you?"

Bad people are found in the Church; hawks and kites as well as doves

12. "I too have some questions. Let us set aside for the moment who was told, *One is my Dove; for her mother she is one*; we will look into it. Either it was said to me or it was said to you; but let us set aside which of us it was said to. So this is my question: if the dove is simple, harmless, without gall, peaceable with its kisses, not savage with its claws, what I want to know is whether members of this Dove include misers, land-grabbers, tricksters, drunkards, knaves; are they members of this Dove?"[14]

"No!" he says.

And indeed, brothers and sisters, who would say this? So as to say nothing more, if I just mention land-grabbers, they could be members of a hawk, not of a dove. Kites grab their prey, so do hawks, so do crows. Doves do not grab, they do not tear apart. So then, land-grabbers are not members of the Dove.

---

13. See Mt 27:34.
14. This argument is a staple of Augustine's thinking: heretics and schismatics are not the only ones who do not belong to the Dove; even sinners are excluded. But neither Catholics nor Donatists baptize sinners again. See *On Baptism* IV, 3, 4; V, 9, 26; VI, 8, 12.

"Has there ever been among you even a single land-grabber? Why does the baptism which a hawk, not a dove, has given, why does it remain? Or why is it that you do not baptize again among your own people after land-grabbers and adulterers and drunkards and after misers? Or are all these members of the Dove? You dishonor your Dove and provide it with vulture-like members."

So what then, brothers and sisters, what are we to say? Are there good and bad people in the Catholic Church, while only bad people are to be found over there? Later, it can be asked whether I may be saying this in an unfriendly spirit. They certainly say that there are good and bad over there, because if they said they only have good people—well, let their own members believe that, and I will vouch for the truth of it. "Among us," let them say, "there are only saints, only holy people, just, chaste, sober; no adulterers, no usurers, no cheats, no perjurers, no tipplers." Let them say it. I pay no attention to their lips, in any case, but I take the pulse of their hearts. Since, however, they are known to us and to you and to their own people, just as you too are known both to yourselves in the Catholic Church and to them, we should not find fault with them, and neither should they flatter themselves.

We admit that in the Catholic Church there are both good and bad, but they are like grains and chaff on the threshing-floor. Sometimes a person baptized by a grain is only chaff, and one baptized by chaff is grain. Besides, if being baptized by a grain is valid and being baptized by chaff is not valid, it means that the words, *This is the one who baptizes*, are false. If, however, *this is the one who baptizes* is true, then not only is what is given by him valid, but, what is more, he baptizes as a dove. That bad man, after all, is not a dove, nor is he one of the members of the Dove; nor can he be said to be either here in the Catholic Church or among them if they say their Church is the Dove. So what then, brothers and sisters, are we to understand the position to be? Since it is obvious and well known to everyone, and they stand convicted, even if against their will, because both there, when bad people give it, baptism is not repeated, and here, when bad people give it, baptism is not repeated. The Dove does not baptize after the Crow; why does the Crow insist on baptizing after the Dove?

If Catholics agree that Donatists also have baptism,
what else can they offer them if they join the Catholic Church?

13. Would Your Graces please take note: just why was the dove chosen as the sign of I-don't-know-what, such that a dove, that is the Holy Spirit in the form of a dove, descended on the Lord when he had been baptized and rested upon him, so that in the coming of the dove, John came to know that, in the Lord, there is a proprietary authority to baptize? Because through this personal authority, the peace of the Church, as I have said, has been firmly established. And it can happen that someone has baptism apart from the Dove, but it is not possible that a baptism apart from the Dove would benefit him.

Would Your Graces please take note and understand what I am saying, for by this trickery[15] they often seduce those of our brothers and sisters who are slack and cold. Let us all be more simple and more fervent.

"Look," they say, "have I received it or not?"

I answer, "Yes, you have."

"So then, if I have received it, you have nothing to give me. Even according to your witness, I am safe. For I too say that I have received it, and you admit that I have received it. Each of our tongues reassures me. So what, then, are you promising me? Why do you want to make me a Catholic, when you will not be giving me anything further, and you admit that I have already received what you say you have? When I say, 'Come over to me,' I am saying that you do not have the baptism that you admit that I have. So why do you say, 'Come over to me?'"

Charity in the peace of the Dove, without which the sacraments are of no avail

14. The dove teaches us the answer. For she replies from above the head of the Lord, saying, "Yes, you have baptism, but you do not have the charity with which I groan."

---

15. *Ista circumventione*; Augustine does not specify what "circumvention" or "trickery" he has in mind; but I think he must mean their ignoring the distinction he has just made.

"What is this?" he says. "I have baptism, but I do not have charity? I have the sacraments,[16] and not charity?"

"Stop shouting; show me how someone who breaks up unity can have charity."

"I," he says, "have baptism."

"You do have it; but the baptism you have is not beneficial to you without charity because, without charity, you are nothing. Indeed, baptism is something—even in someone who is nothing. In fact, it is something great, on account of the one of whom it was said, *This is the one who baptizes*. But lest you think that this great something is of any use to you if you are not in the Unity, the dove came down on the one who had been baptized, as if to say, 'If you have baptism, be in the Dove, or what you have will not do you any good.' So, 'Come to the Dove' is what we are saying; not that you might begin to have what you did not have, but that what you have might begin to be useful to you. Outside, you see, you had baptism to your ruin; if you have it inside, it begins to be useful for your salvation."

Baptism marks us, as with a kind of stamp, *as belonging to Christ*

15. "In fact, baptism will not just fail to be beneficial; it may hurt you."[17]

Even holy things can be harmful; for they are in good people for salvation; in bad people they are for judgment.[18] Yes, of course, brothers and sisters, we know what we receive, and, certainly, what we receive is holy, and nobody says that it is not holy; and what does the apostle say? *But whoever eats and drinks unworthily, eats and drinks judgment upon himself* (1 Cor 11:29). He is not saying that what is received is bad; but because the person is bad, by receiving badly he receives for judgment the good thing he receives. For instance, was the morsel which the Lord handed to Judas bad? Not at all! The doctor would not administer poison;

---

16. The Donatist is referring to the eucharist and to baptism with this statement. The rites would have been much the same in Catholic and Donatist churches.
17. See *On Baptism* VI, 5, 7.
18. What is "in" those who have been baptized, good or bad, is what we now call the baptismal character. See Homily 5,13, note 15.

the doctor gave health. But by receiving unworthily, the one who did not receive in peace received to his undoing.

So then, it is the same too with the person who is baptized.

"I have baptism," he says; "it is mine."

"I agree, you do have it. Notice what you have; by the very fact of having it you will be condemned."

"Why?"

"Because you have what belongs to the Dove apart from the Dove. If you have what belongs to the Dove and are in the Dove yourself, then you have it with nothing to worry about. Imagine you are a soldier; if you have your emperor's mark as one in the army, you have it safely; if you have it as someone outside the army, not only is that mark of no benefit to you as a soldier, it will also get you punished as a deserter. Come on, then, come on and do not say, 'I already have it; that is already enough for me.' Come on; the Dove is calling you, calling you by its gentle moaning."

My brothers and sisters, I am speaking to you: call them with dove-like moaning, not by wrangling; call by praying, call by encouraging them, let them understand from your love that you grieve for them. I have no doubt, my brothers and sisters, that if they see your sorrow for them they will be confounded and will thus be restored to life.

Come then, come, do not be afraid. Be afraid if you do not come—or rather do not be afraid, but lament. Come, you will rejoice if you come; you will moan indeed amid the trials and troubles of this exile, but you will rejoice in hope. Come where the Dove is, who was told, *One is my Dove; for her mother she is one.* You can see one dove above the head of Christ; is it that you cannot see many tongues in the whole wide world? The Spirit being shown in the dove is the same as the Spirit being shown in the tongues. If the Spirit in the dove is the same Spirit as in the tongues, it means the Holy Spirit has been given to the whole world, from which you have cut yourself off, with the result that you clamor with the crow instead of moaning with the dove. Come therefore.

16. But perhaps you are worried, and you say, "I was baptized outside, so I am afraid that makes me guilty, because I received the sacrament outside." Now you have begun to realize what you have to moan about. You are quite right, you are guilty, not because you have received it, but

because you have received it outside. So then, hold on to what you have received, put right your having received it outside. You have received what belongs to the Dove apart from the Dove. There are two things you have just heard: "You have received" and "You have received apart from the Dove." That you have received, I approve of; that you have received outside I disapprove of. So hold on then to what you have received; it will not be changed, but it will be recognized. It is the stamp of my king, I will not be committing sacrilege; I will set right the deserter, I will not alter the stamp.

The problem of bad people in the Church

17. Do not boast about your baptism, just because I say it is true. Yes, I say it is true, the whole Catholic Church says it is true. The Dove observes it and recognizes it and groans because you have it outside of her; she sees there something to recognize, she also sees there something to correct. It is true—come; you boast about it is being true, and you do not want to come?

So what about the bad people who do not belong to the Dove? The Dove says to you, "These bad people too, among whom I moan, who do not belong to my body, and among whom I have to moan—is it that they do not have what you boast of having? Are there not many drunkards who have baptism? Many misers? Many idolaters and—what is worse—stealthy idolaters?" Pagans resort to idols publicly, do they not—or at least they used to?[19] Christians now seek out fortune-tellers and consult astrologers secretly. These people too have baptism, but they are the crows among whom the Dove is groaning; so what are you rejoicing about, just because you have it too? Start having humility, charity, peace; start having the good you do not yet have, so that the good you do have may start doing you some good.

Like Simon Magus

18. What you have, after all, Simon Magus also had. The evidence is there in the Acts of the Apostles, that canonical book which has to be read out in church every year. As you know, it is a solemn yearly custom

---

19. At least they used to, because the laws against pagan sacrifices were being more strictly enforced; hence, they could no longer be open about their idolatry. Augustine thus turns his attention away from the Donatists to his own flock, still influenced by their old superstitious habits, which he saw as part of the sin of idolatry.

for that book to be read after the passion of the Lord,[20] the book in which the story is told of how the apostle was converted and from being a persecutor was made into a preacher; in which also the Holy Spirit was sent on the day of Pentecost, in divided tongues as of fire. We read there that many people in Samaria came to believe after the preaching of Philip; he is understood to have been either one of the apostles or one of the deacons, because we also read there of seven deacons being ordained, one of them with the name of Philip. So then the Samaritans came to believe through the preaching of Philip. Samaria started having plenty of believers. This Simon Magus was there; with his magical tricks he had so bewitched the people that they thought he was the Power of God.[21] All the same, stirred by the signs wrought by Philip, he too believed; what followed showed just how he believed. But Simon too was baptized.

The apostles who were in Jerusalem heard of all this; Peter and John were sent to Samaria, where they found many people baptized; and because none of them had yet received the Holy Spirit, in the way he used then to come down, so that those into whom he came down spoke with tongues (to signify in a demonstrable way the nations that were going to believe), they laid hands on them while praying for them, and they received the Holy Spirit. That man Simon, who was a crow in the Church, not a dove, because he was looking after his own interests, not those of Jesus Christ,[22] and therefore desired power among Christians rather than justice;[23] that man saw the Holy Spirit being given through the laying on of hands by the apostles (not that they themselves gave him, but that he was given while they were praying), and he said to them, "How much money do you want to get from me so that the Holy Spirit may be given through the laying on of my hands as well?" And Peter said to him, *May your money perish with you, since you have thought that the gift of God is to be bought with money* (Acts 8:20).

---

20. Augustine means during the weeks after Easter. The phrase "the passion of the Lord" refers to the whole paschal mystery, to the Passion and Resurrection.
21. See Acts 8:10.
22. See Phil 2:21.
23. For an extended discussion of the relationship between power and justice see *The Trinity* XIII, 10, 13 - 15, 19. Briefly: justice first, power second, power at the service of justice, never the other way round, is how it ought to be.

To whom is he saying, *May your money perish with you?* Clearly, to a man who had been baptized. He already had baptism, but he did not belong to the heart of the Dove.[24] Listen to how he did not belong; notice the very words of the apostle Peter: *You have no part or share in this faith; for I see that you are in the gall of bitterness* (Acts 8:21.23). A dove has no gall, but Simon did; that is why he was separated from the heart of the Dove. What good was his baptism doing him? So do not boast about baptism as though it alone were enough to assure you of salvation; stop being angry, get rid of the gall, come to the Dove. Here you will benefit from what was not merely doing you no good outside but was even doing you harm.

The Church like Noah's ark and its timbers

19. And you must not say, "I am not coming, because I was baptized outside." Look, begin to have charity, begin to bear fruit. When fruit is found in you, the Dove will put you inside. We find this in scripture; the ark was constructed of timbers that would not rot.[25] The seasoned timbers that will not rot are the saints, the believers who belong to Christ. For just as, in the temple, the faithful are said to be the living stones of which the temple is being built,[26] in the same way those who persevere in the faith are seasoned timbers that will not rot. So then in the ark itself there were such seasoned timbers. The ark, you see, is the Church; that is where the dove baptizes.

---

24. Literally: "but he was not sticking to the bowels of the Dove."
25. *Imputribilibus lignis.* The Hebrew has it that the ark was constructed of gopher wood (Gn 6:14). The word only occurs here; modern versions leave it untranslated. The Greek LXX renders it as *tetragonon* timbers, which the Latin text Augustine used rendered as *quadratis lignis* ("squared timbers") (see Sermons 306B, 3 and 306C, 2, both preached in Utica, in honor of a martyred bishop of the town, St. Quadratus). It fit the occasion. These are early sermons, preached in 399 and 397. But in Sermon 361, 21, preached in 411, Augustine follows a text that has the same reading as here. I suggested in note 34 to that sermon that he has mixed up Noah's ark with the ark of the covenant, which Moses is told in Ex 25:10 to make of shittim wood, now generally agreed to be acacia, but rendered by the LXX as "of *asepton* planks," *imputribilibus* in the Latin text Augustine used. But it is clear from what he says here—"we find this in scripture"—that another Latin translator had in fact mixed up the two arks.
26. See 1 Pt 2:4-5. See also Sermon 337, preached at the dedication of a church, for a graphic statement of what it means to be built into the Church as living stones, and indeed as living timbers. The text for the sermon is the title of Ps 30, "A song at the dedication of the temple." Sermon 336, preached on a similar occasion and on the same text, employs the same theme to begin with, but goes on to interpret other verses of the psalm as prophecies of Christ's passion and our association with it.

That ark, after all, was floating in water; the seasoned timbers were baptized inside it. We find that some timbers were baptized outside, all the trees that were in the world. It was all the same water, though, there was no other. It had all come from the sky and from the fountains of the abyss. It was the same water in which the seasoned timbers that were in the ark were baptized, and in which the timbers outside were baptized.

The dove was sent out, and the first time it found nowhere to rest its feet; it came back to the ark. Everything was covered with the waters, you see, and it preferred to come back rather than to be rebaptized. The crow on the other hand was sent out before the waters dried up, and being rebaptized in them it refused to come back; it died in those waters. May God ward off from us the death of that crow! Why, I mean to say, did it not come back? It can only have been because it was cut off by the waters. The dove, by contrast, on finding nowhere to rest its feet, with the water clamoring at it from every side, "Come, come, dip your feet here," in the same way as these heretics clamor, "Come, come, you have it here"—the dove, finding nowhere to rest its feet, returned to the ark.

And Noah sent it out again, as the ark sends you people out to speak to them; and what did the dove do next? Because there were trees that had been baptized outside, it brought back to the ark a branch from an olive tree. The branch had leaves and fruit on it; let there not be just words on you nor just leaves on you; let there be fruit on you and you will be coming back to the ark, not on your own because the dove is calling you back. Let your groan be heard outside, so that you may call them back inside.

The olive branch brought by the dove to the ark signifies charity, without which faith and baptism are useless

20. As for this fruit of the olive tree, try crushing it and you will find out what it was. The fruit of the olive tree signifies charity. How can we prove this? Well you see, oil cannot be pressed down to the bottom by any other liquid, but it bursts through them all, shoots up and overtops them; in the same kind of way, charity cannot be pressed down to the bottom; it simply has to rise to the top. That is why the apostle has this to say about it: *I have a still more excellent way to show you* (1 Cor 12:31). As we have been saying about oil that it rises above other liquids, just in

case the apostle was not saying this about charity, *I have a more excellent way to show you*, let us listen to what follows: *If I speak with the tongues of men and of angels, but do not have charity, I have become like booming bronze, or clashing cymbals* (1 Cor 13:1).[27]

Go out now, Donatus, and shout, "I am a fluent speaker"; go out now and shout, "I am a learned man." How fluent? How learned? You have never spoken, have you, with the tongues of angels? And yet even if you did speak with the tongues of angels without having charity, all I would hear would be booming bronze and clanging cymbals. I am looking for something solid, I would like to find some fruit among the leaves. Let there not be just words; let them have an olive or two, let them come back to the ark.

21. But, you will say, "I have the sacrament." You are right, and a sacrament is something divine. You do have baptism, I too agree with you there. But what does this same apostle say? *If I know all mysteries, and have prophecy and all faith, such that I can move mountains* (1 Cor 13:2)—just in case you should also say, "I have believed, that is sufficient for me." But what does James say? *The demons too believe, and tremble* (Jas 2:19). It is a great thing, faith—but of no use if it does not have charity. Even the demons acknowledged Christ. So then it was by believing, but not by loving, that they said, *What is there between us and you?* (Mk 1:24) They had faith, they did not have charity; that is why they were demons. Do not boast about faith; you are still in the same league as demons. Do not say to Christ, "What is there between me and you?" It is the unity of Christ, after all, that is talking to you. Come, start knowing peace,[28] come back to the bowels of the Dove. You were baptized outside; start bearing fruit, and come back to the ark.

22. And you now retort,

"Why are you looking for us, if we are bad?"

"So that you may be good. It is precisely because you are bad that we are looking for you; I mean, if you were not bad, we would have found you, we

---

27. For a similar explanation of why oil (olive oil, of course) represents charity, again with reference to this text of scripture, see Sermon 93, 5, a sermon on the parable of the wise and foolish virgins, and the oil which the former took for their lamps and the latter did not.
28. "Unity" and "peace" were two of Augustine's names for the Catholic Church.

would not be looking for you. Anyone who is good has already been found; anyone who is bad is still being looked for. That is why we are looking for you. Come back to the ark."

"But I already have baptism."

If I know all mysteries, and have prophecy and all faith, such that I can move mountains, but do not have charity, I am nothing (1 Cor 13:2).

The Donatists both complain and boast about persecutions

23. But what are you saying?

"Look, we are the ones who suffer many evils."

"If only you had suffered these things for Christ's sake, not for the sake of being honored yourselves."

Listen to what comes next. They sometimes pat themselves on the back, you see,[29] because they give much to good causes, they give to the poor; because they are harassed; but it is for the sake of Donatus, not for the sake of Christ.

"Look at how you suffer, because if you suffer for Donatus, you are suffering for a proud man; you are not in the Dove if you are suffering for Donatus. That man was no friend of the bridegroom,[30] because if he had been, he would have sought the bridegroom's honor, not his own. Notice the friend of the bridegroom saying, *This is the one who baptizes*. That man was no friend of the bridegroom, the one for whose sake you are suffering. You do not have a wedding garment on; even if you have come to the banquet, you have to be thrown outside.[31] Or rather, it is because you have been thrown outside that you are in a wretched state. Come back finally—and stop boasting. Listen to what the apostle says: *If I distribute all my goods to the poor, and hand over my body to be burned, but do not have charity.* There you are, that is what you do not have. *If I hand over my body*, he says, *to be burned*—and of course for the name of Christ; but because there are many people who do that ostentatiously, not out of charity, that is why *if I hand over my body to be burned, but do not have*

---

29. Augustine is interrupting his "conversation" with the Donatist to explain the context to the congregation.
30. See Jn 3:29.
31. See Mt 22:11-13.

charity, it does me no good (1 Cor 13:3). Those martyrs who suffered in the time of persecution did this sort of thing with charity, but these people[32] do it all puffed up with pride, because when there is no longer any persecutor around, they throw themselves over cliffs. So then come, in order to have charity."

"But we are the ones who have martyrs."

"What martyrs? They are not doves; that is why they have attempted to fly and have fallen from the rock."

Let Catholics join the simplicity of the dove to fiery pentecostal zeal

24. So then you can see, my brothers and sisters, that everything is crying out against them, all the divine writings, all the prophets, the whole gospel, all the letters of the apostles, all the groaning of the Dove, and still they do not wake up, still they do not rouse themselves. But if we are the Dove, let us groan, let us bear with them, let us hope; God's mercy will be at hand so that the fire of the Holy Spirit may flare up in your simplicity; and they will come. We must not despair; pray, proclaim the truth, love; the Lord is powerful, is he not? They have already begun to be aware of their effrontery, many of them have seen it for what it is. Many have blushed for shame; Christ will be at hand, so that the rest too may come to this awareness. And certainly, my brothers and sisters, at least let it be only the chaff that stays there, let all the grains be gathered in. Anything there that has born fruit, may it return to the ark in the beak of the dove.

The inconsistency of Donatist complaints

25. Now that they are everywhere in full retreat, what is it they hold against us, finding nothing they can really say?

They have taken our villas, they have taken our estates. They produce some peoples' wills. Look here, where his Gaius[33] donated an estate to the Church over which Faustinus presided.

Which church was Faustinus the bishop of? What is a church?

---

32. The Circumcellion fanatics.
33. Both Maurists and CCSL read *Gaiusejus*, which looks a most peculiar name. Berrouard in his text emends to *Gaius Seius*, thus treating it as a double name. This may be the answer; I have translated

The church, he said, over which Faustinus presided.

But Faustinus did not preside over a church; what he presided over was a faction, a party. The Dove, on the other hand, is a Church. We have not devoured estates. Let the Dove have them. Let the question be, which is the Dove? and let her have them. Because of course you know very well, my brothers and sisters, that these villas are not Augustine's. And if you do not know it, and assume that I enjoy possessing villas, God knows it, he is well aware of what I feel about these villas, or what I suffer over them. He is aware of my groans, if he has been pleased to give me some share in the Dove.

"Look, there are the villas; by what right are you laying claim to the villas? By right of divine or of human law?"

Let them reply, "We have divine law in the scriptures, human in the laws of kings."

"By right of which law does anyone possess whatever they do possess? Is it not by right of human law? Because by divine law *the earth is the Lord's and its fulness* (Ps 23:1); God made the poor and the rich from one and the same slime, and one and the same earth supports both rich and poor alike. All the same, it is by right of human law that one says, 'This villa is mine, this house is mine, this slave is mine.' Why? Because God allotted the human race these very laws enacted by the emperors and kings of the world. Would you like us to quote the laws of the emperors and settle about the villas in accordance with them? If you want to gain possession of them by right of human law, let us read out the laws of the emperors; let us see if they really wished anything to be possessed by heretics."

"But what is the emperor to me?"

"It is according to his law that you possess land. Take away the laws of the emperors, and who will presume to say, 'This villa is mine' or 'This slave is mine' or 'This house is mine?' If, however, in order to hold on to these things, people have accepted the laws of kings, do you people want us to quote the laws, so that you may be glad to know that at least you

---

it as if it is indeed two words, *Gaius ejus*, "his Gaius"; whose? Well, Faustinus' friend, supporter, henchman.

have a garden of your own and may put it down to the mildness of none but the Dove that at least you are permitted to stay there? The laws, after all, are publicly available to be read, in which the emperors have commanded that those who make use of the name of Christian outside the communion of the Catholic Church, and refuse to worship the author of peace in the Peace,[34] may not presume to possess any property in the name of the Church."

26. "But what have we got to do with the emperor?"

"But I have already said that the case falls under human law; and in any case the apostle wished kings to be served, he wished kings to be honored, and said, *Respect the king* (1 Pt 2:17).[35] Do not say, 'What have I got to do with the king?' What have you got to do with landed property? It is in accordance with the laws of kings that properties are possessed. You have said, 'What have I got to do with the king?' Do not talk then about your properties, because you have repudiated the very laws, of human origin, by which properties are possessed."

"But I am appealing to divine law," says he.

"So then, let us quote the gospel; let us see to what extent the Catholic Church belongs to Christ, upon whom the dove came which taught, *This is the one who baptizes*. How, then, can it be by divine law that someone possesses things, who says, "I am the one who baptizes," when the dove says, *This is the one who baptizes*, when scripture says, *One is my dove; for her mother she is one*. Why have you been tearing the Dove apart? It is your own entrails, rather, that you have been tearing apart, because in fact you are tearing things apart among yourselves,[36] while the Dove remains whole and entire."

So then, my brothers and sisters, if there is nothing they can say whichever way they turn, I will say here what they can do; let them come to the Catholic Church, and together with us they will have not only land and portions of the earth, but also the one who made heaven and earth.

---

34. That is, in the Catholic Church.
35. Augustine was assuming that these are words from one of St Paul's letters. Had he been thinking of Peter's letter, he would have said "the apostle Peter."
36. An allusion to the schisms which had in fact split the Donatists into rival Churches.

Homily 7

On John 1:34-51[1]

The futility of worldly pleasures

1. I rejoice with you,[2] because you are many and you have come together eagerly, quite beyond my expectations. This is what delights and consoles me in the midst of the toils and dangers of this life: your love for God, loyal efforts, constant hope and fervor of spirit. When the psalm was being read, you heard that the needy and poor person cries to the Lord in this age.[3] It is the voice, after all, as you have so often heard and certainly ought to remember, not of one person, and yet, yes, of one man; not of only one, because the faithful are numerous, many grains groaning under heaps of chaff, scattered throughout the whole world; but just of one, because all are members of Christ, and in this way one body. So then this people, needy and poor, does not know how to rejoice in this age; its sorrow is within and its joy as well where the only one to see is the one who listens to groanings and crowns hopes.

Worldly delight is futile. With great expectation is it hoped for before it arrives; and when it does come, it cannot be held. This day, for example, which is a day of delight for wastrels in this city,[4] will, of course, not be here tomorrow; nor indeed will those same people be tomorrow what they are today. All things pass away, and all things fly away, and vanish like smoke; and woe to those who love such things! Every soul, after all, pursues what it loves. *All flesh is grass, and all the honor of the flesh like flowers in the grass; the grass withers, the flowers droop; but the Word of the Lord abides for ever* (Is 40:6-8). That is what you should love, if you wish to abide for ever. But

---

1. Preached on Sunday, March 24, 407, the third Sunday of Lent.
2. I rejoice with *frequentiae vestrae*, literally, "with your frequency" or "large attendance."
3. The Maurists refer to Ps 74:21; but that verse states that the needy and poor will praise God's name. The psalm verse is more likely to have been Ps 86:1, *Incline your ear, O Lord, and listen to me, for I am poor and needy*, a definite cry, or clamor.
4. Such a day would have been one on which some wealthy citizen put on a show in the city amphitheatre or stadium. Yet, in section 2, Augustine says it is a spectacle of more interest to women than to men, and in section 6 he calls it "the festivity of the blood of some woman or other," a woman from whose ear a gold earring had been torn; when it was placed on the scales, the blood from the wound gave it added weight.

you wanted to say, "How can I possibly grasp the Word of God?" *The Word was made flesh and took up residence among us* (Jn 1:14).

Augustine grieves over those whose frenzied joy lets them avoid knowing themselves

2. Accordingly, dearest friends, it falls to us in our neediness and poverty to grieve over those who think they are prosperous. Their delight, you see, is like that of people who are frenetic. Well, just as a mad person frequently gives vent to joy in his frenzy, while the sane person cries for him, so we too, dearest friends, if we have received the remedy that comes from heaven (for we too used to be delirious), as those who have been saved because we no longer love the things we used to love, so we too groan to God for those who are still frenetic. He is powerful enough, after all, to save them as well. And what they need is to take a good look at themselves and to dislike what they see. What they want, though, is to be seen, and they do not know how to see what is going on in themselves. For if they were to turn their eyes on themselves—just a little bit—they would see how mixed up they are. Until that happens may our interests be different from theirs, may that which holds the attention of our souls be different. Our sorrow is more worthwhile than their delight.

As regards the number of our brothers present, it is hard to see how that celebration could have attracted any of the men. But as for the number of our sisters, it saddens me (and this really is deplorable) that they would not prefer to hasten to church; yet if fear does not keep them away from the crowds, then at least shame should do so. This will be seen by him who sees, and his mercy will be at hand to cure them all. As for us, though, who have come together here, let us feast at God's banquet and find our joy in his word. For he has invited us to hear his gospel, and he is our food; nothing could be more delicious, as long as you have a healthy palate in your heart.

Remember what has been said in the previous
two homilies about John and the dove

3. But now I suspect that Your Graces will remember well that this gospel has been read aloud in continuous, selected sections. And I think

you will not have forgotten what has already been dealt with, especially what was most recently said about John and the dove; with regard to John, in fact, you will remember what the one who already knew to be the Lord learned that was new about the Lord from the dove. And, under the inspiration of the Spirit of God, it was found that John did indeed already know him as the Lord; but the fact that the Lord would baptize in such a way that he would not transmit the baptismal authority to anyone else, this is what John learned through the dove, because he was told: *On whomever you see the Spirit coming down like a dove, and resting on him, this is the one who baptizes in the Holy Spirit* (Jn 1:33). What is the meaning of *this is the one*? No other baptizes, even though it is done by another.

Why, though, did he learn through a dove? Much has been said, and I cannot and do not need to spell it all out again; still, I will say that it was because of peace, because the dove brought some wood[5]—those who were baptized outside—back to the ark, because she found fruit on them. As you remember, a dove sent out by Noah from the ark; the ark was floating over the flood and washed with a kind of baptism; it did not sink.[6] So when the dove was sent out, it brought back the branch of an olive tree; one, what is more, which also had fruit on it and not just leaves. And so this is what we must wish for our brothers and sisters who are being baptized outside, that they may bear fruit; then the dove will not leave them alone outside, but will lead them back to the ark. Now their fruit is all about charity, without which—whatever else he may have—man is nothing.

And we recalled and cited what the apostle most thoroughly asserted, *If I speak with the tongues of men and of angels, but do not have charity, I have become like booming bronze or clashing cymbal; and if I have all knowledge, and know all mysteries, and have all prophecy, and have all faith*—what can he mean precisely by all faith?—*faith such that I can move mountains, but do not have charity, I am nothing. And if I distribute all my goods to the poor, and if I hand over my body to be burned, but do not have charity, it does me no good.* (1 Cor 13:1-3) Now in no way at all

---
5. Literally, *ligna*: some pieces of wood or branches.
6. See Gn 8:1-12.

can those who divided Unity say that they have charity. That has been said; let us look at what follows.

John bore witness to Christ that, no matter who administers baptism, Christ is the one who baptizes

4. John bore witness because he saw. What kind of testimony did he give? *That this one is the Son of God* (Jn 1:34). So then it was fitting that he who is the only Son of God, not a son by adoption, should be the one to baptize. Adopted sons are the ministers of the only Son; the only Son has the authority, adopted sons have the ministry. Even if a minister who is not counted among the sons because of his bad life and bad behavior were to baptize, what reassures us? This is the one who baptizes.

Christ is the Lamb in a unique sense

5. *The next day John was there again with two of his disciples and as he watched Jesus walking by he said, Look, the Lamb of God* (Jn 1:35-36). He is the Lamb in a unique sense, of course, because the disciples were also called lambs: *Look, I am sending you like lambs in the midst of wolves* (Mt 10:16). They were also called light: *You are the light of the world* (Mt 5:14); but in a different way was it said of him: *That was the true light, who enlightens everyone coming into this world* (Jn 1:9). Likewise, he is the Lamb in a unique sense, because he alone is without stain, without sin; not one whose stains had been wiped away, but one who had had no stain to begin with. What, after all, was the significance of John saying about the Lord, *Look, the Lamb of God*? Was not John himself a lamb? Was not John a holy man? Was he not the friend of the bridegroom? So then, he is lamb in a unique sense: This is the Lamb of God because, in a unique sense, only by the blood of this Lamb could human beings be redeemed.

The blood of the Lamb compared with the blood of the woman at the secular festival

6. My brothers and sisters, if we acknowledge that the price paid for us is the blood of the Lamb, who are the people celebrating a festival of blood today, the blood of who-knows-what woman? And how ungrateful they

are! A gold earring, they say, was torn from the woman's ear, and the blood flowed, and the gold was put in the scales or balance, and weighed that much more as a result of the blood.[7] If a woman's blood had sufficient weight to help the gold tip the scales, what weight must the blood of the Lamb have to make the world tip the scales?

And indeed that spirit, whatever it was, was appeased by the blood which made the gold heavier. Unclean spirits knew that Jesus Christ was going to come; they had overheard it from angels, overheard it from the prophets, and they were expecting him to come. I mean, if they had not been expecting him, what would have made them cry out, *What is there between us and you? Have you come to do away with us before the time? We know who you are, the Holy One of God?* (Mk 1:24) They knew he was going to come, but they were ignorant of the time.

But what did you hear in the psalm about Jerusalem? *Since her stones are dear to your servants and her dust moves them to pity, you,* he says, *rising up, will have mercy on Zion, since the time has come for you to have pity on her* (Ps 101:14.13). When the time came for God to have pity, the Lamb came. What a Lamb, whom wolves are afraid of! What a Lamb is this, who being slain slays the lion! The devil, you see, is called *a lion going about and roaring, seeking whom he may devour* (1 Pt 5:8); it was by the blood of the Lamb that the lion was conquered.[8] Such are the public shows of Christians! And what is more, those with the eyes of the flesh are looking at futility; we, with the eyes of the heart, are looking at truth.

For you must not think, brothers and sisters, that the Lord our God has left us without public shows; if there are no public shows, why did you gather here today? Look, there you are, you realized what I said, and you shouted out; you would not have shouted if you had not seen it. And it is a great thing to see it everywhere in the world: the lion conquered by the blood of the Lamb, the members of Christ being snatched from the teeth of lions and joined to the body of Christ. So then, I do not know what spirit has staged an

---

7. The gold *praeponderavit multum de sanguine*; the gold weighed that much more, as a result of the blood on it, than it did when placed in the goldsmith's balance. Berrouard, BA 71, note 48, p. 883, discusses various theories identifying this "festival of blood" with some festival for a pagan deity. He, along with Le Landais, concludes that it was a celebration peculiar to Hippo Regius. Nothing more is known about it.
8. See Rev 12:11.

imitation, as though wishing to have its idol bought with blood, because it knew that some day the whole human race would be redeemed with precious blood. Evil spirits, you see, fashion themselves shadowy resemblances of honor, so that they might, in that way, lead the followers of Christ astray.

Indeed, my brothers and sisters, those who seduce people with their amulets, with their spells, with the machinations of the enemy, even mix the name of Christ into their spells. Because they can no longer lead Christians astray as they used to, they add a little honey in administering the poison, so that, by covering up the bitter taste with something sweet, they can get you to drink it to your ruin. To that extent indeed, I learned some time ago that the priest of a certain Pilleatus[9] used to say, "Even Pilleatus is a Christian." Why did he say that, brothers and sisters, if not because Christians could not be led astray in any other way?

The Father disciplines us with suffering, to fit us for our eternal inheritance

7. So then, do not look for Christ anywhere else, except where Christ wanted to be preached to you; and hold onto him in the way he wished to be preached to you—in that way, write him on your hearts. He is a wall of defense against all the attacks and all the subterfuges of the enemy. Do not fear that one—he cannot tempt you unless he has been given permission. He cannot do anything unless he is given permission or sent. He is sent, like a bad angel, by the authority controlling him;[10] he is given permission when he begs for something;[11] and this, brothers and sisters, only happens for the testing of the just, for the punishment of the unjust. So what are you afraid of? Walk with the Lord your God, be reassured; what he does not wish you to suffer, you will not suffer; what he permits you to suffer is the lash of correction, not the punishment of condemnation.

---

9. This word means literally "wearing a felt cap," and could be applied to any class of persons, such as slaves on being manumitted or soldiers. It was also a name, in the plural, for the divine twins Castor and Pollux, and Attis and Mithras were frequently represented wearing this cap. Which of these deities in particular Augustine was here referring to it is not clear. Since his priest claimed that he was a Christian, it is probably one of the two demigods, Attis or Mithras. See BA 71, 884, note 49.

10. See 2 Cor 12:7, where St. Paul talks of an angel of Satan sent to stop him thinking too highly of himself.

11. Like the legion of unclean spirits begging permission to enter the herd of swine, Mk 5:10-13.

We are being trained for an everlasting inheritance, and we look down on correction! My brothers and sisters, if any boy refused to have his ears boxed or to get a lashing from his father, would he not be called proud, hopeless, ungrateful for paternal discipline! And why does a human father train his human son? To ensure that he does not squander the time-bound things which he has acquired for him, which he has piled up for him, which he does not want him to squander, and which the one who is leaving them could not hold onto for ever.

My brothers and sisters, if a father gives this sort of lesson to the son who will succeed him, and the one he teaches will in turn bypass all those possessions in the same way as the one who warned him is going to bypass them, how would you like to be taught by *our* Father, whom we are not going to succeed, but to whose kingdom we are going to accede and with whom we are going to abide for ever, possessing an inheritance which does not fade away, nor die, nor experience any hailstorms?[12] And he is both the inheritance and Father. That is what we will possess; should we not be taught?

Let us put up with the instruction our Father gives us. Let us not run off to the enchanters, to the fortune-tellers, and their futile remedial amulets as soon as we have a headache. My brothers and sisters, how could I fail to shed tears for you? Every day I find these things going on, and what am I to do? Am I still unable to persuade Christians to put their trust in Christ? Look here; if someone who had some remedy[13] made for him dies—and how many people with such remedies have died, and how many without such remedies have lived!—how will his soul appear before God?[14] He has lost the sign of Christ, he has accepted the sign of the devil.

Or he may perhaps say, "I have not lost the sign of Christ."

---

12. The inheritance which does not fade is an echo of 1 Pt 1:4. The reference to the hailstorm must have been part of a recent experience in Hippo where local vineyards and orchards were damaged. His congregation may have been familiar with meaning that Augustine gave to the hail that was one of the plagues of Egypt, Ex 9:22-26. In his *Exposition of Psalm* 77, 27, discussing vv.47-48, he says, "So it is for the commentator to say, as best he can, what these things signify.... Hail is the iniquity that carries off other people's property, from which are born thefts, robberies and depradations." See Sermon 8,10 as well.
13. Just a few lines beforehand, Augustine spoke of *remedia vanitatis*. Hence, the need to counter superstition was quite real.
14. In the context, Augustine is referring to the sign of the cross traced on the forehead, claiming the person for Christ. To depend on superstitious remedies rather than to trust in Christ is the challenge he places before his people.

Oh, so then you have had the sign of Christ together with the sign of the devil. Christ does not want to share you, he wants to be the sole owner of what he has bought. He paid enough for you to be sole owner; you are making him a partner with the devil, to whom you had sold yourself by sin. *Woe to the double-hearted* (Eccl 2:14), to those who give part of their hearts to God and part to the devil! Angry because the devil was given a share in them, God moves away, and the devil ends up by possessing everything. Not without purpose, then, does the apostle say, *Leave no room for the devil* (Eph 4:27). So then, brothers and sisters, let us get to know the Lamb, let us get to know our price.

John hands over some of his disciples to Jesus

8. *John was there along with two of his disciples* (Jn 1:35). Notice, two of John's disciples: John was the kind of friend of the bridegroom who did not seek his own glory, but bore witness to the Truth. Did he ever want his disciples to stay with him and not to follow the Lord? On the contrary, he pointed him out to his disciples as the one they should follow. In fact, they regarded John as the Lamb; but he says, "Why fix your minds on me? No, I am not the Lamb; *Look, there is the Lamb of God,*" of whom he had already said earlier on, *Look, there is the Lamb of God* (1:29). "And what is the good of the Lamb of God to us?" *Look*, he says, *the one who takes away the sin of the world* (Jn 1:36).[15] On hearing this, the two who were with John followed him.

9. Let us see what comes next. *Look, there is the Lamb of God*, said John. *And the two disciples heard him speaking, and followed Jesus. Jesus though, turning round and seeing them following him, says to them, What are you looking for? They said, Rabbi (which means Teacher), where are you living?* (Jn 1:36-38) They were not following him in such a way as to be ready to stand by him. I mean, it is obvious when they stood by him for good, because he called them from the boat. For, one of these two was Andrew, as you just heard; but Andrew was the brother of Peter, and we know from the gospel that the Lord called Peter and Andrew from the boat, when he said, *Come after me, and I will make you fishers of men* (Mk 1:17). And it was from that moment that they stood by him, so as not to leave him.

---

15. This phrase is omitted in many manuscripts, and in the RSV.

So then, the fact that these two are following him now does not mean they are following him as though never to leave him. But they wanted to see where he was living, and to do what is written: *Let your foot wear out his threshold; rise and come to him constantly, and be instructed by his precepts* (Sir 6:36-37). He showed them where he was staying; they went along and were there with him. What a blessed day they must have spent, what a blessed night! Who could ever tell us what they heard from the Lord? Let us too build a home in our hearts, where he can come and teach us and converse with us!

The symbolic significance of its being the tenth hour

10. *What are you looking for? They said to him, Rabbi (which means Teacher), where are you living? He says to them, Come and see. And they went and saw where he was staying, and they stayed with him that day; now it was about the tenth hour.* (Jn 1:38-39) Do we reckon that the evangelist had no reason to tell us what the time was?[16] Can it be that he did not want us to notice anything, to ask ourselves what it might mean? It was the tenth hour. This number stands for the law, because the law was given in ten commandments. But the time had come for the law to be fulfilled through love, seeing that the Jews were unable to fulfill it through fear. That is why the Lord says, *I have not come to undo the law, but to fulfill it* (Mt 5:17). So it was entirely suitable that it was the tenth hour when these two followed him, on hearing the testimony of the bridegroom's friend, and that it was the tenth hour when he heard "rabbi," which is translated "teacher." If the Lord heard "rabbi" at the tenth hour, and the number ten belongs to the law, the master of the law is nobody else but the lawgiver. Let nobody say that one gave the law, and someone else teaches the law; the one who gave it teaches it; he is the master of his own law and teaches it.[17] Mercy is on his

---

16. The tenth hour was about 4:00 p.m. In addition to the symbolic reason we are to be given, the stating of the time implies very definitely that the two disciples spent the whole night with Jesus, as well as the rest of the day.
17. Contemporary versions here translate what rabbi means as "teacher," which is indeed the only possible rendering of the Greek. But the Latin has *magister*, and Augustine insists on the distinction between the *magister* and the *doctor*, the master and the teacher. The master is the authority, the teacher passes on what the master has taught. And so Augustine as a bishop could not deny that he was, in virtue of his office, a *doctor*, a teacher of the faith to his flock; but he

tongue, and that is why he teaches the law mercifully, as it says about Wisdom, *She carries the law and mercy on her tongue* (Pr 31:26). Do not be afraid that you are unable to keep the law, take refuge in mercy. If keeping the law is too much for you, make use of that agreement, make use of that signed document, make use of the prayers which the heavenly jurist[18] has set out and composed for you.

Christ, the heavenly jurist, shows us how to frame our prayers to his Father

11. You see, people who have cases about which they wish to petition the emperor first look for some scholar learned in the law to compose their petitions for them, in case by presenting them otherwise than in the proper form they should, perhaps, not merely fail to obtain what they were asking for, but should receive a penalty in place of a favor. So then, when the apostles sought to present their petitions, and could not figure out how to approach the sovereign God, they said to Christ, *Lord, teach us how to pray* (Lk 11:1); that is, "As our counsel, court assessor, or better, the one who shares the bench with God, compose our petitions for us." And the Lord taught them from the heavenly law book, taught them how they should pray; and in what he taught he put a certain condition: *Forgive us our debts, as we too forgive our debtors* (Mt 6:12).

If you do not ask in accordance with the law, you will be guilty. Are you trembling with dread of the emperor, on being found guilty? Offer the sacrifice of humility, offer the sacrifice of mercy, say in the petition, "Forgive me, since I too forgive."[19] But if you say it, do it. What, I mean to say, are you going to do, where are you going to go, if you have lied in the prayers? It is not simply, as they say in the law courts, that you will be deprived of the

---

resolutely refused to be thought of as a *magister*. Christ is the only one to have such magisterial authority over the truth he proclaimed and embodied. Mt 23:8 is the crucial text: *Do not you let yourselves be called rabbi; one is your master* [*magister* in the Latin], *and you are all brothers*. This distinction almost exactly parallels that other one between Christ's baptizing, as the one whose baptism it is that is being conferred, and his ministers baptizing, administering a baptism that is not theirs, and not given in their name.

18. See BA 71, 428, note 2: Augustine only uses this title for Christ in relation to the fifth petition of the Lord's Prayer which is an agreement with God that forgiveness is two-way. Forgive us as we forgive.
19. This echoes Luke's version of the Lord's prayer (11:4).

benefit of your rescript; it is that you will not even obtain a rescript.[20] For common law is that anyone who makes a false statement in his petition should not profit from the rescript he has obtained. But that is the case among human beings, because human beings can be deceived. The emperor could have been deceived when you sent your petition; I mean you said what you wanted to, and the one you said it to does not know whether it is true. So he has sent you back to your opponent to establish the truth, so that if you are convicted before a judge of lying—because the emperor, not knowing whether you had lied, could not but grant your petition—you will be deprived of the benefit of the rescript in the place where you sought enforcement. God, however, knows whether you are lying or telling the truth, so he does not arrange for you not to profit from the rescript in the court; he simply does not permit you to obtain anything, because you dared to lie to Truth.

Christ's grace—not superstitious remedies—is the true remedy for all ills

12. So what are you going to do then? Tell me. To keep the law in every particular, so that you do not commit the slightest offence is difficult; so guilt is certain. Are you unwilling to make use of the remedy? Just look, my brothers and sisters, at what a remedy God has set in place against the sicknesses of the soul.

What remedy then?

When you have a headache, we praise you if you have put the book of the gospels to your head instead of having recourse to an amulet![21] For to this has human feebleness been reduced, and to this extent should we lament those who do have recourse to amulets, such that we would even rejoice to see someone bed-ridden, seized by fever and pain, and yet not setting his hopes on anything but having the gospel book placed on his head; not because that is what the gospel book was made for, but because it has been preferred to amulets!

---

20. The rescript was the official response to the petition from the emperor's court, addressed to the local magistrate where the petition came from, instructing him to carry it out. This rescript asks God to forgive our sins.
21. See Letter 245, 2; Sermon 4, 36; *Exposition of Psalm* 70, 1, 17 for other mentions of these *ligaturae*.

So then, if the gospel book is applied to the head to relieve the pain in the head, is it not to be applied to the heart, for that to be cured of sins? Let this be done, then.

Let what be done?

Let the gospel be applied to the heart, let the heart be cured. It is good, yes good, that you should not be concerned with the body's health except by begging for it from God. If he knows it will be to your advantage, he will give it to you; if he has not given it to you, it would not have been to your advantage to have it. How many people there are, sick in bed and doing no harm; and if they had been in good health, they would be committing crimes! How many there are, for whom good health is a disadvantage! The bandit who goes for the throat to kill someone, how much better for him it would be if he were sick! The one who gets up at night to dig through somebody else's wall, how much better for him if he were tossing about with a high temperature! He would have been more innocent sick; healthy, he is a criminal.

So then, God knows what is good for us; let our one concern be that our hearts are cured of sins; and when by any chance we are being scourged with bodily ills, let us pray to him. The apostle Paul begged him to take away the sting of the flesh, and he refused to take it away. Was Paul upset? Did he say in his disappointment that he had been forsaken? What he said, rather, was that he had not been forsaken because what he wanted taken away, for this weakness to be cured, was not in fact taken away. That, after all, is what he discovered from the doctor's words: *My grace is sufficient for you, because strength is made perfect in weakness* (2 Cor 12:8-9).

So then, how do you know that God does not want to cure you? It is still to your advantage to be punished. Do you really know how septic the sore is which the doctor is lancing, pushing the steel through the putrescence? Does he not know the limit of what he should do, know how far he should go with it? Do the wails of the one being cut restrain the hand of the doctor cutting so skillfully? One yells, the other cuts. Is he being cruel by not listening to the yells, or not rather being kind by continuing to attack the wound in order to heal the patient? The reason I have said all this, my brothers and sisters, is so that none of us should go looking for anything apart from God's help, whenever we happen to be corrected by the Lord. Watch out lest you perish, watch out lest you drift away from the Lamb and get devoured by the lion.

While as Christians we share in Christ's anointing,
Christ is uniquely the Anointed One

13. So then, we have said why it was the tenth hour; let us see what follows. *Andrew, Simon Peter's brother, was one of the two who had heard from John and had followed him. Andrew found Simon his brother, and said to him, We have found the Messiah, which means the Christ.* (Jn 1:40-41) Messiah in Hebrew is "Christ" in Greek, "Anointed" in Latin. The word "Christ," you see, comes from anointing. *Chrisma* is the Greek for anointing. So then, Christ is the anointed one. He was uniquely anointed, the main one to be anointed; as a consequence all Christians are anointed, but he is the main one to be anointed. Listen to how he says it in the psalm: *Therefore God, your God, has anointed you with the oil of exultation above all those who take part with you* (Ps 44:8). All the saints share in his anointing; but he is uniquely the saint of saints, uniquely anointed, uniquely the Christ.

The significance of the change of Simon's name to Cephas

14. *And he brought him to Jesus. But gazing at him, Jesus said, You are Simon son of John; you shall be called Cephas (which means Peter).* (Jn 1:42) It is not a great matter that the Lord said whose son this man was. What was great for the Lord? He knew the names of all his saints, whom he predestined before the foundation of the world;[22] and are you astonished at his saying to one man, "You are the son of so-and-so, and you shall be called such-and-such"? It is great that he changed his name and transformed Simon into Peter; the name Peter comes from rock (*petra*); the rock, however, is the Church; therefore, in the name Peter, the Church is signified. And who is safe but the one who builds upon the rock?

And what does the Lord say? *The one who hears these words of mine and acts on them, I will liken him to a sensible man building upon rock* (he does not yield to temptations); *the rain fell, rivers rose, winds blew and beat upon that house, and it did not fall down; for its foundations were upon rock. The one who hears my words and does not act on them* (now let every one of us, please, be afraid and be put upon our guard), *I*

---
22. See Eph 1:5.4.

will liken him to a foolish man who built his house upon sand; the rain fell, rivers rose, winds blew and beat upon that house, and it fell down; and its ruin was total. (Mt 7:24-27) What good does it do him to enter the church if he wants to build upon sand? For by listening and not acting he is indeed building, but upon sand. If he never listens, after all, he does not build anything either; but if he hears, he builds. But we want to know what he builds on. For, if he hears and acts, he builds upon rock; if he hears and does not act, he builds upon sand. There are two kinds of builders; either upon rock or upon sand.

So then, what about those who do not hear? Are they safe? Does he say they have nothing to worry about, because they build nothing? They are exposed to the rain, to the wind, to the waters; when these things happen, they carry these people away before they knock houses down. So then, only one thing is sure—to build and to build upon rock. If you want to hear and not act, you are building; but you are building a ruin; when trials and temptations come, they knock down the house, and with that ruin of yours they carry you away too. If, however, you do not hear, you are without shelter, and you will be dragged away by those temptations.

So then, hear and act; that is the only remedy. How many people today, I wonder, by hearing and not acting, have been swept away by the river of this celebration? By hearing and not acting, you see, along comes the river of this annual celebration, the stream turns into a torrent, which will pass and will dry up; but alas for those whom it has carried away! So then, this is what Your Graces should know; that unless you are both hearing and acting, you are not building upon rock, and you do not belong to that great name, which the Lord recommended to us. He was catching your attention, you see; because if the man had been called Peter before, you would not have seen the mystery of the rock in this way. You would have thought his being called that was just a matter of chance, not part of God's providence. That is why he wanted him called something else first, so that by the change of name the vital power of the mystery[23] might be impressed upon us.

---

23. Of the *sacramentum.*

Nathanael's words when Philip finds him

15. *And on the next day he wished to go to Galilee, and he finds Philip. He says to him, Follow me. But he was from the town of Andrew and Peter. And Philip found Nathanael* (Philip has already been called by the Lord). *And he said to him, The one Moses wrote about in the law, and announced by the prophets, we have found him, Jesus son of Joseph.* He was called the son of the man his mother married. For that he was conceived and born to her while she remained a virgin is well known to all Christians from the gospel. That is what Philip said to Nathanael; and he added the place: *from Nazareth. And Nathanael said to him, From Nazareth, there can be something good.* What is the meaning, brothers and sisters? Not in the way some people speak it; because it is usually said like this: *Can anything good be from Nazareth?* Philip's voice follows, and he says, *Come and see.* (Jn 1:43.45-46) These words, though, can follow both ways of speaking the sentence, whether you speak it like an affirmative statement, *From Nazareth there can be something good*, to which he replies, *Come and see*; or whether in doubt and questioning the whole thing, *Can anything good be from Nazareth? Come and see.* So then, since the words of response, whether spoken in one way or in the other, do not respond to what Nathanael says, my concern is to ask what we should understand by these words.[24]

The Lord's witness to Nathanael; why he was not chosen to be one of the twelve

16. We can show what sort of man this Nathanael was from what follows. Listen to what sort of man he was; the Lord himself bears witness to him. The Lord's greatness is known from John's testimony; Nathanael's blessedness is known from the testimony of the Truth. As for the Lord, even if he were not commended to us by John's testimony, he was, in fact, his own testimony; because truth is its own sufficient testimony. But because human beings could not grasp the truth, they went looking for it with a lamp; and so John, who pointed out the Lord, was sent.

Listen to the testimony that the Lord gives Nathanael: *And Nathanael said to him, From Nazareth can be something good. Philip says to him, Come and see. And Jesus saw Nathanael coming to him, and he says of him,*

---

24. Augustine prefers to take Nathanael's words as a statement. The words in both the Greek and the Latin can be taken either way.

This is truly an Israelite in whom there is no guile. (Jn 1:46-47) Great testimony! What was said of Nathanael was not said of Andrew or said of Peter or of Philip: *This is truly an Israelite in whom there is no guile.*

17. So what do we make of it, brothers and sisters? That this man should be first among the apostles? But not only do we find that he is not first among the apostles; neither the middle one, nor even the last among the twelve is Nathanael, to whom the Son of God bore witness, saying, *This is truly an Israelite in whom there is no guile.* Should the reason be sought? To the extent the Lord suggests a reason, I may have found it. We should realize, you see, that Nathanael was an educated man and learned in the law; that is why the Lord declined to place him among the disciples—because he chose uneducated people, thereby to put the world to shame.

Listen to the apostle saying this: *For observe your own call, brothers and sisters, that not many of you are wise according to the flesh, not many are powerful, not many noble; but God chose the weak of the world in order to put the strong to shame; and the common things of the world and the contemptible ones did God choose, and things that are not as those that are, so that things that are might be rendered void* (1 Cor 1:26-28). If a learned man were chosen, maybe he would say that is why he was picked out, because his learning deserved to be chosen. Our Lord Jesus Christ wished to crush the necks of the proud, and so he did not seek a fisherman through an orator; but by means of a fisherman he gained an emperor. Cyprian was a great orator, but he is outranked by Peter the fisherman, through whom, later on, not only an orator but even an emperor came to believe. No one of noble birth, no learned person was chosen first; because God chose the weak things of the world in order to put the strong to shame.

So this one was a great man and without guile; for this reason alone he was not chosen, to avoid having people conclude that the Lord chose learned men. And from his very teaching of the law it came about that when he heard *from Nazareth*—he had searched the scriptures, you see, and he knew that it was from there the Savior was to be looked for, which the other scribes and Pharisees had not so readily come to know[25]—so this most learned man of law, on hearing Philip say. *We have found Jesus, whom*

---

25. Augustine has in mind that on returning from Egypt Joseph took Mary and Jesus to live in Nazareth, *to fulfill what had been spoken through the prophets, that he shall be called a Nazarene* (Mt 2:23). The prophecy Matthew probably, and Augustine certainly, had in mind

Moses wrote about in the law, from Nazareth, this man who knew the scriptures so supremely well, on hearing the name *Nazareth* felt a surge of hope and said, *From Nazareth there can be something good.*

Nathanael was without guile because he confessed his sins

18. Now let us see the other things said about him. *This is truly an Israelite in whom there is no guile.* What does *in whom there is no guile* mean? Perhaps that he had no sin? Perhaps that he was not sick? Perhaps that a doctor was not needed for him? Not at all! Nobody has ever been born here who did not need that doctor. So then, what does it mean, *in whom there is no guile*? Let us look a bit more attentively; in the name of the Lord, it will shortly become clear.

Guile is what the Lord says, and everyone who understands Latin words knows that it is *dolus* when one thing is being done and another being pretended. Would Your Graces pay close attention? *Dolor*, pain, is not *dolus*; the reason I say this is because many brothers and sisters who are not so good at Latin speak like this, and will say, for instance, "*Dolus* is tormenting him," when they mean *dolor*. *Dolus*, guile, is fraud, is pretence. When someone hides something in his heart and says something else, that is guile, and it is as if they had two hearts; they have one fold[26] in the heart where they see the truth, and another fold where they conceive a lie. And to show you that this is what guile is, it says in the psalms, *Guileful lips*. What are *guileful lips*? It continues: *In heart and heart they have spoken evil things.* (Ps 11:3) What can in heart and heart be but with a two-faced heart?

So then, if there was no guile in this man, it means that the doctor considered that he was curable, not that he was in good health. It is one thing, after all, to be in good health, another to be curable, another to be incurable.[27] When someone is ill but has hope of recovery, he is said to be curable; when ill and without hope, he is said to be incurable; but when he is already well,

---

was the story of Samson in Jg 13:2-5, where the angel of the Lord appears to the barren woman and tells her she will bear a son, and that no razor is to touch his head, *because he shall be called a Nazirite to God.* Now in the Latin Bible "Nazirite" here is spelt Nazaraeus (again in 16:17), which is how "Nazarene" is spelled in Mt 2:23.

26. The Latin, *sinus*, means "fold" or "crease," i.e., an innermost recess in the heart.
27. The Latin wordplay is not reproducible in English: *sanus* is one thing, *sanabilis* is another, and *insanabilis* yet another.

he does not need a doctor. So then, the doctor who had come to cure saw that this man was curable, because there was no guile in him. In what way was there no guile in him? If he is a sinner, he admits he is a sinner; because if he is a sinner and says he is a just man, there is guile in his mouth. So then, he praised the admission of sin in Nathanael; he did not declare that Nathanael was free from sin.

That point is also illustrated in the case of Simon the Pharisee and the woman who was a sinner

19. Hence, when the Pharisees, who thought of themselves as just, found fault with the Lord because as a doctor he mingled with the sick, and said, *Look whom he is eating with, with tax-collectors and sinners*, the doctor replied to these delirious people, *The doctor is not needed for the healthy, but for those who are ill; I have not come to call the just, but sinners* (Mk 2:15-17). That means: "Because you call yourselves just while in fact you are sinners, you present yourselves as being well while in fact you are not well, you are rejecting the cure; you are not keeping your health."

So, that Pharisee who had invited the Lord to dinner thought of himself as healthy; but that sick woman burst into a house where she had no invitation, and being quite shameless in her eagerness for health, she came not to the head of the Lord, nor to his hands, but to his feet. She washed them with her tears, dried them with her tresses, kissed them, anointed them with perfume, made peace as a sinner with the very soles of the Lord's feet. That Pharisee who was reclining there, as if he were in good health, found fault with the doctor, and said to himself, *If this man were a prophet, he would know what kind of woman was touching his feet* (Lk 7:36-39). Now the reason he assumed the Lord did not know was that he had not pushed her away as if to avoid being touched by impure hands; but he knew perfectly well who she was, he allowed himself to be touched so that the very touch might cure her.

The Lord, seeing the Pharisee's heart, put forward a parable: *A certain money-lender had two debtors; one owed him fifty denarii, the other five hundred; since they had nothing to pay him back with, he forgave them both. Which loved him the more? And the Pharisee said, I suppose, Sir, the one he forgave more. Then, turning to the woman, he said to Simon, Do you see this woman? I came into your house, you gave me no water for my feet;*

she, though, has washed my feet with her tears and dried them with her tresses. You gave me no kiss; she has not stopped kissing my feet; you gave me no oil; she has anointed my feet with perfume. For that reason, I tell you, many sins are forgiven her, since she has loved much; but one who is forgiven little, loves little. (Lk 7:40-47) This amounts to saying: "You are sicker than she is, but you think you are in good health; you think there is only a little to be forgiven you, while in fact you are more deeply in debt."

Because there was no guile in her, this woman deserved that cure. What do I mean, there was no guile in her? She confessed her sins. That is what he praises in Nathanael as well, that there was no guile in him; because many Pharisees who were overflowing with sins were saying they were just, and were parading deceit, making it impossible for them to be cured.

Nathanael seen under the fig-tree

20. So then, he now saw this man in whom there was no guile, and said, *Look, this is truly an Israelite in whom there is no guile. Nathanael says to him, How did you know me? Jesus answered and said, Before Philip called you, when you were under the fig-tree, I saw you.*[28] *Nathanael answered him and said, Rabbi, you are the Son of God, you are the king of Israel.* (Jn 1:47-49) This Nathanael could have understood something great indeed in his being told, *When you were under the fig-tree, before Philip called you, I saw you.* I mean, he gave voice to the same sort of expression, *You are the Son of God, you are the king of Israel*, as did Peter somewhat later, when the Lord said to him, *You are blessed, Simon bar Jona, because flesh and blood has not revealed it to you, but my Father who is in heaven* (Mt 16:17). And at that time he spoke of the rock and extolled the solidity and strength of the Church in that faith. This man is already saying, *You are the Son of God, you are the king of Israel.* On what basis? Because he had just been told, *Before Philip called you, when you were under the fig-tree, I saw you.*

---

28. *Sub ficu, vidi te;* he adds, *id est, sub arbore fici*—"that is, under the tree of a fig." It seems that *ficus* was not familiar to most African Latin speakers as meaning a fig-tree, but only as meaning a fig, and that our Lord's words sounded to many of the preacher's audience as if they meant "when you were under the fig I saw you."

Christ looks for us before we ever look for him

21. It should be asked whether this fig-tree has any significance. Listen to him, my brothers and sisters: We found the fig-tree cursed, because it only had leaves and had no fruit.[29] At the origins of the human race, when Adam and Eve had sinned they made themselves aprons out of fig-leaves; thus, fig-leaves are understood to mean sins. Now Nathanael was under the fig-tree as if under the shadow of death. The Lord saw him, and of him it was said, *For those who were sitting under the shadow of death, a light has risen* (Is 9:2). So then, what was said to Nathanael? "You ask me, Nathanael, *How did you know me*? You are talking to me now because Philip called you." The Lord had already seen that anyone called by an apostle belonged to his Church.

O Church, O Israel, in whom there is no guile: if you are the people of Israel in whom there is no guile, you have now already come to know Christ through the apostles, as Nathanael knew Christ through Philip. But his mercy saw you before you came to know him, while you were lying flat on your back under sin. Did we, in fact, first go looking for Christ or was he the one who came looking for us? Did we, the sick, first go to the doctor or was it the doctor who came to the sick? Was that sheep not lost, and did the shepherd not leave the ninety-nine and go looking for it and find it, bringing it back joyfully on his shoulders? Was that drachma not lost when that woman lit a lamp and searched for it everywhere in the house until she found it? And when she found it, she said to her neighbors, *Rejoice with me, because I have found the drachma I had lost* (Lk 15:4-10).

In the same way we too were lost like the sheep and were lost like the drachma; and our shepherd found the sheep—but he first went looking for the sheep; the woman found the drachma—but first she was looking for the drachma. Who is the woman? The flesh of Christ. What is the lamp? *I have prepared a lamp for my Christ* (Ps 131:17). So then, because we were looked for, we have been found; having been found, we speak. Let us not

---

29. See Mk 11:12-14. 20-21, and the parallel passages in the other gospels. The words in this text were not taken from any of these accounts. They may have been taken from the Latin translation of Tatian's Diatessaron.

grow proud, since, before we were found, we were lost for good, if we had not been sought. So then, those whom we love and wish to win over to the peace of the Catholic Church[30] should not be saying to us,

"Why do you want us? Why are you seeking us out, if we are sinners?"

"That is why we are looking for you, lest you should be lost for good; we are looking for you, because we were sought; we want to find you, because we were found."

What greater things than these we shall see?
That, after being called, we were justified by faith

22. And so when Nathanael said, *How did you know me?* the Lord said to him, "*Before Philip called you, when you were under the fig-tree, I saw you.* O Israel without guile, whoever you are, O people living out of faith,[31] before I called you through my apostles, while you were under the shadow of death, and you did not see me, I saw you." The Lord then says to him, *Because I said to you, I saw you under the fig-tree, you believe; you shall see greater things than these.* What is this, *You shall see greater things than these? And he says to him, Amen, amen, I tell you all, you shall see heaven opened, and angels ascending and descending upon the Son of Man.* (Jn 1:50-51)

Brothers and sisters, I have just said something much greater than *I saw you under the fig tree*. That the Lord, you see, justified us after calling us[32] is more important than the fact that he saw us lying under the shadow of death. What good would it have done us, after all, if we had remained there where he saw us? We would still be lying there, would we not? What is greater than this? When we have seen angels ascending and descending upon the Son of Man.[33]

---

30. The Donatists.
31. See Rom 1:17.
32. See Rom 8:30.
33. The Maurists and subsequent editors punctuate this sentence as a question; but Augustine is only repeating Jesus' question.

*The meaning of Jacob's anointing of the stone and dreaming
of the angels climbing up and down the ladder*

23. I have just recently spoken about these ascending and descending angels.[34] But in case you have forgotten, I will speak of it briefly as a reminder; I would say more if it were more than a reminder, but for now I am recalling it.

Jacob saw a ladder in a dream, and on the ladder he saw angels climbing up and down; and he anointed the stone which he had placed under his head as a pillow.[35] You have heard that Messiah means Christ, you have heard that Christ means Anointed. You see, he did not set up the anointed stone in order to come and worship it; that would have been idolatry, not a sign pointing to Christ. So then, a significant pointer was made, to the extent that one was required, and it pointed to Christ. A stone was anointed, but not as an idol. A stone was anointed; why a stone? *Behold, I am placing in Zion a stone, choice and precious, and whoever believes in it shall not be put to shame* (Is 28:16; 1 Pt 2:6). Why anointed? Because Christ took his name from an anointing. But, what did he see on the ladder? Ascending and descending angels. Thus it is also the Church, brothers and sisters; angels of God, good preachers, are preaching Christ; that is, they climb up and climb down to the Son of Man. How do they ascend, and how do they descend? In one man we have an example; listen to the apostle Paul; what we find in him, let us also believe about other preachers of Truth.

Look at Paul ascending: *I know that a man in Christ fourteen years ago was snatched up as far as the third heaven, whether in the body or out of the body I do not know, God knows, and that he heard unutterable words which it is not lawful for a man to speak* (2 Cor 12:2-4). You have heard him ascending, listen to him descending: *I was unable to speak to you as if to spiritual, but only as if to flesh-bound people; as if to little ones in Christ I gave you milk to drink, not solid food* (1 Cor 3:1-2). There you have him descending, the one who had ascended. Ask where he had ascended to; as far as the third heaven. Ask where he descended to; as far as giving milk to

---

34. The reference is to the *Exposition of Psalm* 119,2. See the Introduction on the close connection, in time, between the *Homilies on the Gospel of John* and the *Exposition of Psalms* 119-133.
35. See Gn 28:11-18.

little ones. Hear him descending: *I became a little one*, he says, *in your midst, like a wet-nurse cherishing her children* (1 Thes 2:7).

Well, we see both wet-nurses and mothers coming down to the level of the little ones; and if they know how to say Latin words, they cut them up and somehow or other shake their tongues in order to make baby talk from correct speech; because if they speak correctly the infant does not listen and certainly derives no benefit. And take some learned father or other, an orator of such power that his tongue rattles the windows of the courts, and sets the benches of the judges shaking; if he has a baby son, he lays aside his forensic eloquence when he gets home, and comes down to the little one's level with baby talk.

Listen to the apostle himself in one place, both ascending and descending in a single sentence: *For whether we have been transported*, he says, *in mind, it is toward God; or whether we are moderate, it is toward you* (2 Cor 5:13). What is *We have been transported toward God? That we may see those things which it is not lawful for a man to speak.* What is *We are moderate toward you? Have I ever judged myself to know anything among you, except Jesus Christ, and him crucified?* (1 Cor 2:2). If the Lord himself ascended and descended, it is evident that his preachers too ascend by imitating him and descend by preaching him.

Final exhortation

24. And if I have detained you somewhat longer than usual, the plan has been to let this unseasonable occasion run its course; I reckon those people must now have concluded their nonsense. As for us, though, brothers and sisters, when we have been fed at the banquet of salvation,[36] let us carry out what remains to be done, so that we may complete the Lord's Day with joyful spiritual celebrations and compare the joys of truth with the joys of futility. And if we are horrified by them, let us grieve; if we grieve, let us pray; if we pray, may we be heard; if we are heard, we will win those people too.

---

36. When the eucharist was finished.

Homily 8

John 2:1-4[1]

God's works in nature are more marvelous than his miracles

1. The miracle by which our Lord Jesus Christ made wine out of water is not all that astonishing[2] to those who recognize that God was the one who worked it. For the one who made wine on that day at the wedding in those six jars, which he had ordered to be filled with water, does the same thing every year in the vines. I mean, just as what the waiters put in the jars was turned into wine by the work of the Lord, so too what the clouds pour out is turned into wine by the work of the same Lord. But this does not astonish us, because it happens every year; its familiarity has let the wonder of it slip away. In fact it deserves even more intensive reflection than that which took place in the jars of water. Is there anybody, after all, who can reflect on the works of God by which the whole of this universe is governed and administered and not be stunned and overwhelmed by the miracles? Just reflect on the force in a single grain of any seed you like; it is something tremendous, enough to set you trembling as you think about it.[3]

But because people have been so intent on other things that they have given up reflecting on the works of God and thereby praising the creator every day, it is as if God has kept in reserve some unusual things to do, and thus by miracles to rouse a slumbering humanity to render him due worship. Having died, he rose again; people were amazed; yet how many are born every day, and no one is amazed. If we thought about it a little more rationally, it is a more wonderful miracle for someone who did not exist just to be, than for someone who did exist to come back to life.[4] And yet the same God, the Father of our Lord Jesus Christ, makes all these things through his Word and governs what he created.

---
1. Preached probably on Sunday, March, 31, 407, the fourth Sunday of Lent.
2. His *miraculum is* not *mirum*; this wonder is not to be wondered at. The same point is made about this and other "nature" miracles, like the feeding of the multitudes, in *The Trinity* III, 11; Sermon 126, 4-5.
3. See Sermon 247, 2 for the same reflection.
4. See Sermon 242, 1 for the same idea.

The first miracles were performed through his Word, God with him; the later miracles were worked through the same Word, now incarnate and made man for our sakes. Just as we marvel at the things done through the man Jesus, let us marvel at the things done through the God Jesus. Through the God Jesus were made the heavens and the earth, the sea, and all the embellishments of the heavens, the opulence of the earth, the fecundity of the sea. All these things which are there before our eyes were made through Jesus as God. We see these things and, if his Spirit is within us, they so delight us that the craftsman is praised, not turning our attention to the works and away from the craftsman, nor turning our faces to the things he made and our backs to the one who made them.

Invisible creatures, like the soul, are more wonderful than heavenly bodies

2. And of course these are things that we can see, that are right in front of our eyes; what about those things we cannot see, such as angels, powers, dominions, and every inhabitant of that creation above the heavens which are certainly not right before our eyes? Yet, angels too—when required to—have often shown themselves to human beings. Did not God also make all these through his Word, that is through his only Son, our Lord Jesus Christ?

What about the human soul itself, which cannot be seen, but which—through the works it displays in the flesh—wins the admiration of those who really reflect on it well? By whom was it made if not by God? And through whom was it made if not through the Son of God? I am not yet even talking about the soul of a human being; just think how the soul of any animal you like governs its own mass of matter! It switches on all the senses, the eyes for seeing, the ears for hearing, the nostrils for picking up smells, the judgment of the mouth for distinguishing flavors, finally all the limbs and organs for performing their functions. Is it really the body that does all this, and not the soul, that is to say the host of the body? And the eyes do not see it and it still wins our admiration by these things it does.

So now let your reflections concentrate on the human soul, to which God has granted intelligence for getting to know its creator, for discerning and distinguishing between good and evil, that is between just and unjust; how much it does through the body! Consider the whole wide world set in order by human society, with its regulations, its grades of authority, its political constitutions, its laws, customs, and arts. All this is managed through the soul, and this power of the soul cannot be seen. When the soul is withdrawn from the body, a corpse lies there; but when it is present in the body, the first thing it does is somehow or other to cover up what is rotten. All flesh, you see, is corruptible, disintegrating into rottenness unless it is held together by some sort of seasoning in the soul.

But that, one with the animal soul, is held in common; that which I have already called more amazing belongs to the mind and to the intelligence. That is also where the soul is being renewed according to the image of its creator[5], in whose image man was made.[6] What will this power in the soul be when *this body has put on incorruptibility, and this mortal thing has put on immortality* (1 Cor 15:53)! If it can do such stupendous things through perishable flesh, how much more will it be capable of doing through the spiritual body after the resurrection of the dead![7] And yet this soul, as I have said, wonderful in its nature and its being, is an invisible and intelligible thing; and yet this too was made through Jesus God, because he is the very Word of God. *All things were made through him, and without him was made nothing* (Jn 1:3).

There is a deeper meaning to this miracle at Cana

3. When we see such stupendous things done through the God Jesus, why should we be amazed at water turned into wine through the man Jesus? He was not, after all, made man in such a way as to lose his being God; being man was added to him, being God was not lost. So the same person who did all those other things did this. So let us not be amazed at him, because he did it as God; but let us love him because he did it among us and did it for the sake of our restoration. You see, he was suggesting something to us in the things that were done.[8] It was not without signifi-

---

5. See Col 3:10.
6. See Gn 1:26.
7. The contrast between *animalis* and *spiritalis* can be found in 1 Cor 15:44-46 with reference to the resurrection of the body. Here, a vital principle quickens the body: the soul "animates" the body and the spirit "enspirits" the body.
8. See Sermons 98, 1 and 130, 1.

cance, I think, that he came to the wedding. Quite apart from the miracle, some mystery, some sacrament[9] is hidden in the deed. Let us knock so that he may open, and make us drunk on invisible wine; because we too ourselves were also water, and he has made us into wine, he has made us wise, given us the flavor and taste of wisdom; for we who were previously insipid and flavorless with folly are now wise with the flavor of faith in him.[10] And no doubt it belongs to this same wisdom, one with the honor of God, and the praise of his greatness, and the love of his most powerful mercy, that we should understand what was accomplished in this miracle.

4. The Lord, an invited guest, came to the wedding. What is surprising if the one who came into this world for a wedding went to that house for a wedding? If, in fact, he had not come for a wedding, he would not have a spouse here. And what is the meaning of what the apostle says: *I joined you to one man, to present you as a chaste virgin to Christ*? Why does he fear that the virginity of Christ's bride may be corrupted through the devil's cunning? *I fear*, he says, *that just as the serpent seduced Eve by his cunning, so too your minds may be corrupted from the simplicity and chastity which is in Christ.* (2 Cor 11:2-3) So the Lord has a bride here whom he redeemed with his blood, and to whom he gave the pledge of the Holy Spirit.[11]

He snatched her from bondage to the devil, he died for her transgressions, he rose again for her justification.[12] Who would ever offer his bride such gifts? Let men offer any kind of earthly ornaments—gold, silver, precious stones, horses, slaves, farms, estates; will anyone ever offer his own blood? I mean, if he gives his blood for his bride, there will be no one there to take her home as his wife. The Lord, however, died with no worry on that score, and he gave his blood for the bride he would have as a wife

---

9. Of the *mysterii et sacramenti*; the two words were almost synonyms; *sacramentum* is the Latin translation of the Greek *mysterion*. *Sacramentum*, however, often highlights the expressive dimension of the *mysterium*.
10. In this passage he is playing on the derivation of *sapientia*, wisdom, from *sapere*, which, before meaning "to be wise," means "to taste," "to have a flavor"; hence, the negative, *insipiens*, also has a double meaning.
11. Compare *Exposition of Psalms* 90, sermon 2,13; 122, 5.
12. See Rom 4:25.

when he rose again[13]—to whom he had, in fact, already united himself in the Virgin's womb. The Word, you see, is the bridegroom, and the bride is human flesh; and each is the only Son of God, who is at the same time the Son of Man. When he became the head of the Church, that womb of the Virgin Mary was his bridal chamber, from which he came forth like a bridegroom from his chamber, as scripture had foretold: *And he, like a bridegroom coming forth from his chamber, exulted like a giant to run along the way* (Ps 18:6). He came forth from the chamber like a bridegroom, and, an invited guest, he came to the wedding.

Jesus appears to disregard his mother; what the Manichees try to make of this

5. Certainly, for the sake of a mystery,[14] he seems not to acknowledge the mother from whom he came forth as the bridegroom, saying to her, *What is it to me and to you, woman? My time has not yet come.* (Jn 2:4) What is this all about? Is that why he came to the wedding, to teach us that mothers are to be treated with disrespect? At any rate, the man whose wedding he had come to was marrying a wife to have children, and, of course, he wanted her to be held in honor by those he hoped to have. So then, did Jesus come to the wedding to dishonor his mother, when it is precisely for the sake of having children, who are commanded by God to give due honor to their parents,[15] that weddings are celebrated and wives are married? Clearly, brothers and sisters, something lies hidden here.

It is, you see, a matter of some immediate urgency because, as I mentioned earlier, there are people against whom the apostle warned us when he said, *I fear that just as the serpent seduced Eve by his cunning, so too your minds may be corrupted from the simplicity and chastity which is in Christ*; people who detract from the gospel even say that Jesus was not born of Mary the Virgin; and they attempt to use this passage to support their error by saying, "How could she be his mother, the person to whom he said, *What is it to me and to you, woman*"?

---

13. See *Exposition of Psalm* 122, 5, where Augustine makes the same point, in almost the same words.
14. *Certi sacramenti gratia.*
15. See Mk 7:10; Ex 20:12; Dt 5:16; Ex 21:17; Lv 20:9.

So we have to answer them and to discuss why the Lord said this, so that none of these lunatics will appear to have found, contrary to sound faith, something that will corrupt the chastity of the virgin bride, that is, to violate the faith of the Church. In fact, brothers and sisters, the ones whose faith is being corrupted are those who prefer a lie to the truth. I mean these people, who fancy they are honoring Christ by denying that he had flesh, are quite simply proclaiming him to have been nothing more than a liar.[16] So then, what are those who are building up a lie among human beings expelling from themselves but the Truth? They let the devil in, they shut out Christ; they let an adulterer in, they shut out the bridegroom, making themselves the bridesmen, or rather the brothel keepers of the serpent. They speak, in fact, so that the serpent may gain possession, so that Christ may be excluded. How does the serpent gain possession? When a lie gains possession. When falsehood is in possession, the serpent is in possession; when truth is in possession, Christ is in possession. He said himself, after all, *I am the truth* (Jn 14:6); while about that other one he said, *And he did not stand in the truth, because the truth is not in him* (Jn 8:44). The truth is in Christ, however, in such a way that you must accept it all as true in Christ; true Word, God equal to the Father, true soul, true flesh, true man, true God, true birth, true passion, true death, true resurrection. If you say that any of these is false, rottenness enters; from the serpent's poison are born the worms of lies, and nothing will remain whole.

The way John tells the story explodes their argument

6. "So then," says the adversary, "what is the meaning of the Lord saying, *What is it to me and to you, woman*?" Perhaps, in what comes next, the Lord shows us why he said this: *My time,* he says, *has not yet come* (Jn 2:4). That, you see, is how he put it: *What is it to me and to you, woman? My time has not yet come.* And why this was said has to be investigated. Let us, first of all, stand up against heretics.

What is the age-old serpent saying, the ancient whisperer, hissing forth poisons? What is he saying?

---

16. The heretics he has in mind here are the Manichees; see Sermon 237, 1-3.

"Jesus did not have a woman for mother."

"How do you prove that?"

He answers, "Because he said, *What is it to me and to you, woman?*"

"Who reported this, that we might believe he said it? Who reported this? Was it not John the evangelist? But this same John the evangelist said, *And the mother of Jesus was there.* For thus did he tell the story: *The next day a wedding took place in Cana of Galilee, and the mother of Jesus was there. But he had come, invited to the wedding with his disciples.*" (Jn 2:1-2)

We have two statements from the evangelist. The evangelist said, *The mother of Jesus was there*; the same evangelist also stated what Jesus said to his mother. And notice, brothers and sisters, how he said that Jesus was answering his mother, having first said, *His mother said to him* (Jn 2:3), so that the virginity of your hearts would thus be protected from the serpent's tongue.

There, in the same gospel, reported by the same evangelist, it says, *The mother of Jesus was there*, and *His mother said to him*. Who reported this? John the evangelist. And what was Jesus' answer to his mother? *What is it to me and to you, woman?* Who is reporting this? The very same John the evangelist. O most trustworthy and truthful evangelist, you are telling me that Jesus said to his mother, *What is it to me and to you, woman?* Why did you place him near a mother whom he does not acknowledge? You are the one, after all, who said, *The mother of Jesus was there*, and *His mother said to him.* Instead, why did you not say "Mary was there," and "Mary said to him"? You are reporting each fact on your own: *His mother said to him*, and *Jesus answered her, What is it to me and to you, woman?* Why is this, if not because each is true?

Those people, however, are willing to believe the evangelist when he reports that Jesus said to his mother, *What is it to me and to you, woman?* and they refuse to believe the evangelist when he says, *The mother of Jesus was there*, and *His mother said to him.* Who, on the other hand, is the one who stands up to the serpent and holds on to the truth, whose virginity of heart is not corrupted by the devil's cunning? The one who believes each statement is true, both that the mother of Jesus was there and that Jesus gave his mother that answer. But if they do not yet understand how Jesus could say, *What is it to me and to you, woman?* let them believe for the time being that he did say it, and that he said it to his mother. First let there be piety in believing, and then will fruit be borne in understanding.[17]

7. I ask you, O faithful Christians, "Was the mother of Jesus there?"

You answer, "She was."

"How do you know she was?"

You answer, "The gospel says so."

"What answer did Jesus give his mother?"

You answer, *What is it to me and to you, woman? My time has not yet come.*

"And how do you know this too?"

You answer, "The gospel says so."

Do not let anybody corrupt this faith, if you wish to preserve your chaste virginity for the bridegroom. But if you are asked why he gave his mother this answer, let the one who understands express it; let the one who does not yet understand believe most steadfastly that Jesus did give this answer, and that he gave it to his mother. Such piety will deserve to understand why he answered her like that—as long as, in prayer, not in quarreling, you knock on the door of Truth. But while you think you know, or else are ashamed you do not know, why he replied like that, take care that you are not driven to believe either that the evangelist was lying when he said, *The mother of Jesus was there*, or that Christ himself suffered a false death for our transgressions, and showed false wounds for our justification, and uttered a falsehood when he said, *If you abide in my word, you will truly be my disciples; and you will know the truth, and the truth will set you free* (Jn 8:31-32). For, if she is not truly his mother, then his flesh is not true, his death is not true, the wounds of his passion are not true, the scars of his resurrection are not true; then not Truth but rather falsehood will free those who believe in him.

But no; let falsehood give way to truth, and let those be confounded who wish to be thought truthful themselves, because they try to demonstrate that Christ was a deceiver; and they do not want to be told, "We do

---

17. Augustine is alluding to the sixth and the second of the gifts of the Holy Spirit (Is 11:2-3). See too *Teaching Christianity* II,7,10.

not believe you, because you are lying," while they themselves accuse the Truth of lying. Yet if we say to them, "How do you know that Christ said, *What is it to me and to you, woman?*" they answer that they have believed the gospel. So why do they not believe the gospel when it says, *The mother of Jesus was there*, and *His mother said to him*? Or if the gospel is lying here, how is it to be believed on Jesus having said, *What is it to me and to you, woman*? Why do the poor wretches not rather believe faithfully that the Lord answered, not a stranger, but his mother in that way? Then let them seek respectfully why he answered her like that?

There is, after all, a great difference between the one who says, "I want to know why Christ gave his mother this answer," and the one who says, "I know that Christ did not give his mother this answer." It is one thing to want to understand what is hidden; another to refuse to believe what is obvious. The one who says, "I want to know why Christ answered his mother like that," wants the gospel he believes in to be opened up for him; while the one who says, "I know that Christ did not give this answer to his mother," is accusing the gospel of lying—the gospel which he believed when it said that Christ gave such an answer.

The reason for Christ's apparent disrespect was that his time had not yet come

8. So now then, brothers and sisters, with those people driven off, and left wandering around all the time in their blindness, unless they are humbly healed,[18] it is for us to inquire why our Lord answered his mother like that—he that was uniquely born of the Father without a mother, of a mother without a father; without a mother, as God, without a father, as man; without a mother, before all times, without a father, at the end of the times. What he answered, he answered his mother, because *the mother of Jesus was there*, and *his mother said to him*. That is what the gospel says. From this gospel we have come to know that *the mother of Jesus was there*, just as, from the gospel, we have come to know that he said to her, *What is it to me and to you, woman? My time has not yet come*. Let us believe all this, and let us ask about what we do not yet understand.

---

18. Healed both by the humility of Christ in taking flesh and coming down to our human level at the incarnation; and by their own humility in acknowledging their blindness and their need for healing.

First of all, watch out, lest, just as the Manichees found a pretext for their lack of faith in what our Lord said, *What is it to me and to you, woman?* so the astrologers may find a pretext for their lack of faith when the Lord says, *My time has not yet come.* And if he said that in the way astrologers take it, then we have committed sacrilege by burning their books;[19] but if we did the right thing, as in the time of the apostles, then the Lord did not say in that sense, *My time has not yet come.* This, you see, is what these seducers, themselves seduced, say in their empty chatter, "You can see that Christ was controlled by fate, from his saying, *My time has not yet come.*"

So whom must we answer first, the heretics or the astrologers? Both of them, after all, come from that serpent, eager to corrupt the virginity of the heart which the Church preserves in the integrity of her faith. First, if you agree, let us deal with the ones we mentioned first, whom we have indeed already answered for the most part. But in case they should assume that we have nothing to say about the words with which the Lord answered his mother, I will teach you how to reply to them; for I think that what has already been said should be enough to refute them.

His time for acting as her son would come on Calvary;
by doing what she asked now, he would be acting as her creator

9. So why then did the son say to his mother, *What is it to me and to you, woman? My time has not yet come?* Our Lord Jesus Christ was both God and man; insofar as he was God, he did not have a mother; insofar as he was man, he did. So then, she was the mother of his flesh, the mother of his humanity, the mother of the weakness which he took on for our sakes. But the miracle he was about to do would be done in virtue of his divinity, not in virtue of his weakness; in virtue of his being God, not in virtue of his being born weak. But *the weakness of God is stronger than men* (1 Cor 1:25).

So his mother was demanding a miracle; he, however, as if he were not recognizing the human womb when he was about to perform divine deeds,

---

19. A regular practice of the imperial authorities—supported by the Church. See *Exposition of Psalm* 61, 23, where Augustine presents a repentant Christian astrologer to the congregation at the end of his sermon. The astrologer brought his books with him to be burned. Augustine refers to the burning of magical books which Paul presided over in Ephesus (Acts 19:19).

seemed to say, "You did not give birth to that in me which performs the miracle, you did not give birth to my divinity; but because you did give birth to my weakness, I will acknowledge you when this weakness hangs on the cross." That, you see, is the sense of *My time has not yet come*. For that is when he acknowledged her, he that had, of course, always known her. Even before he was born of her, he had known his mother in predestination; and also before he, as God, had created her of whom he, as man, would be created, he had known his mother. But at a certain time—mysteriously—he did not acknowledge her, and at a certain time which had not yet come—mysteriously—he did again acknowledge her. The time he acknowledged her, you see, was when the one to whom she had given birth was dying. For the one who was dying was not the one through whom Mary had been made; the one who was dying was the one made from Mary. Divine eternity was not dying; fleshly infirmity was dying.

Hence, he gave that answer to mark the difference in the faith of believers between the one who had come and the one by whom he had come. For the God and Lord of heaven and earth came through a woman who was his mother. As Lord of the universe, as Lord of heaven and earth, he was of course Lord of Mary too; as creator of heaven and earth, he was creator of Mary as well. But as the one of whom it was said, *made of a woman, made under the law* (Gal 4:4), he was the son of Mary. He was Mary's Lord, he was Mary's son; he was the creator of Mary, he was created from Mary. Do not let it faze you that he is both son and Lord; for, just as he was Mary's son, so too is he also called David's son, and he is David's son precisely because he is Mary's son. Listen to the apostle openly saying so: *Who was made for him of the seed of David according to the flesh* (Rom 1:3). Listen to him as also David's Lord; let David himself say, *The Lord said to my Lord, Sit on my right* (Ps 109:1). And Jesus himself put this point to the Jews, using it to reduce them to silence.[20]

So then, just as he is both David's son and his Lord; son of David according to the flesh, Lord of David according to his divinity; in the same way he is Mary's son according to the flesh and Mary's Lord according to his majesty. So because she was not mother of his divinity, and because the

---

20. See Mk 12:35-37 and parallels.

miracle she asked for was going to happen through his divinity, he gave her the answer: *"What is it to me and to you, woman?* But do not imagine I am denying you are my mother; *my time has not yet come*; for that is when I will acknowledge you, when the infirmity whose mother you are will be hanging on the cross."

Let us see whether this is true. When the Lord suffered, as the same evangelist says who knew the Lord's mother, and who also introduced the Lord's mother to us at this wedding, he himself tells the story: *There near the cross*, he says, *was the mother of Jesus, and Jesus said to his mother, Woman, see, this is your son; and to the disciple, See, this is your mother* (Jn 19:25-27). He entrusts his mother to the disciple. About to die in front of his mother and to rise before his mother's death, he gives his mother in trust: a human being commits a human being to a human being. To this one did Mary give birth. That time had then come, of which he had previously said, *My time has not yet come.*

So much for the heretics; now for the astrologers and Christ's time

10. In my opinion, brothers and sisters, the heretics have been answered; now let us answer the astrologers. And how do they attempt to convince us that Jesus was under the control of fate? They say, "Because he himself said, *My time has not yet come.*" So then, we believe him; and if he had said, "I do not have a time," he would have precluded the astrologers. "But look," they say, "he said it himself: *My time has not yet come.*" So then, if he had said, "I do not have a time," he would have precluded the astrologers, they would have had no grounds for their false accusation. But now, because he did in fact say, *My time has not yet come*, what can we possibly say against his own words?

Astonishingly, astrologers try to convince Christians that Christ lived under a time determined by fate by trusting in Christ's own words. So let them believe Christ, then, when he says, *I have the authority to lay down my life, and to take it back again; nobody takes it from me, but I myself lay it down of my own accord, and again I take it back* (Jn 10:18). So is this authority then under the control of fate? Let them produce a human being who has authority over deciding how long he will live, when he will die; they most certainly will not be able to. So let them believe God then, when he says,

I have the authority to lay down my life, and to take it back again; and let them inquire why he said, *My time has not yet come*, and no longer find there a reason to place the maker of the skies, the creator of the stars and the one who arranged them in order, under the control of fate. Because if fate were from the stars, then the creator of the stars could not be held to that necessity. Let it be added that not only did Christ not have what you call "a fate," but neither do you, nor I, nor he nor she, nor any human being whatsoever.

11. Having seduced themselves, however, they seek to seduce, and they propose their fallacies to the public. They set up their nets to catch human beings, and that in public places.[21] I mean, those who set up nets to catch wild animals do it in the woods or on the moors; how miserably idiotic must people be, when nets are set up to catch them in the center of town! People who sell themselves to other people accept money; others hand over cash, to sell themselves to idiotic nonsense. For they go to the astrologer to buy themselves such masters as the astrologer wants to give them—whether Saturn, or Jupiter, or Mercury, or anything else with a sacrilegious name. He enters freely so as to pay cash and come out a slave. Or rather, he would not have entered in the first place if he had really been free; but he entered where his master, Error, and his mistress, Greed, dragged him. And that is why Truth says, *Everyone who commits sin is the slave of sin* (Jn 8:34).

12. So why then did he say, *My time has not yet come*? Because he had the time when he would die in his own power, and it was not yet the right time for him to exercise that power. For example, brothers and sisters, this is like when we sometimes say, "Now is the time for us to go out and celebrate the sacraments." If we go out earlier than necessary, are we not just upsetting the order and acting wrongly? So then, because we do not do it until the time is right, does that mean that on such occasions we are calculating our fate when we talk in this way?

So then, what is the meaning of *My time has not yet come*? "When I know that it is the right time for me to suffer, when my suffering will be of value (that time has not yet come), then I shall suffer because it is my will,

---

21. Augustine may have had in mind the women who set about *catching the souls of men* in some mysterious way by attaching veils (RSV, *magic bands*) to their elbows (Ez 13:17-21).

so that you may hold on to each statement; both *My time has not yet come*, and *I have the authority to lay down my life, and to take it back again.*"

So then, he had come with the power over when he would die; but if he were to die before he had chosen any disciples, it would certainly be getting things back to front. If he had been a man who did not have such power over his time, then he could have died before he had chosen any disciples; and if by any chance he did only die after choosing and training disciples, this would be something accorded to him, not something he did himself. But in fact, he did come in control over when he would go and when he would come back, how far he would reach; for, with the underworld open to him not only as he died but also as he rose again—that he might manifest to us the hope of immortality of his Church, showing as the head what the members ought to be looking forward to: the one who rose again as the head will rise again as well in all the members[22]—the time had not yet come, it was not yet the right time.

Disciples had to be called, the kingdom of heaven had to be proclaimed, mighty deeds to be performed, the Lord's divinity to be presented in miracles, the Lord's humanity to be presented in that very sharing with us in the pangs of mortality. The one who was hungry, after all, because he was a man, fed so many thousands on five loaves because he was God; the one who was asleep because he was a man, commanded the winds and the waves because he was God.[23] All these things had first to be gone through, so that there might be something for the evangelists to write down, something to be proclaimed to the Church. But when he had done as much as he judged would be sufficient for the purpose, the time indeed came, set not by necessity but by his will, not by his circumstances but by his power.[24]

The explanation of the story's mystical significance
deferred until the following day

13. So then, what now, brothers and sisters? Because we have answered both these astrologers and those heretics, are we not going to say anything

---

22. See *Exposition of Psalm* 129, 6-12, where the theme of the whole Christ is treated at greater length.
23. See Mk 11:12; 6:41-44; 4:37-41.
24. See Homily 37, 9 for a fuller explanation of that which led Jesus to choose the time.

about what the water jugs mean, and the water turned into wine, about the significance of the steward, of the bridegroom, of the mother of Jesus in the spiritual sense, about the whole wedding itself? It all has to be said, but you must not be overburdened. I did indeed hope in Christ's name to run through it with you all yesterday, when a sermon is usually due to Your Graces, but some pressing business did not allow me to do so. Hence, if Your Holinesses agree, let us put off until tomorrow everything that has to do with the mystery of this event, and thus not overburden your weakness or mine. Perhaps many of you are here today because of the feast and not in order to listen to a sermon. Let those who come tomorrow come precisely in order to listen; in this way we will neither defraud those eager to learn nor bore those who are not interested.

Homily 9

On John 2:1-11[1]

God's works in nature are as wonderful as this miracle

1. May the Lord our God be at hand to enable me to keep the promise I made. Yesterday, you see, if Your Holinesses remember, shortage of time prevented me from completing the sermon I had begun, and so I put off until today the task of opening up, with his help, what is mysteriously contained in the sacraments[2] that are in the event described in the gospel reading. So there is no need to linger now on drawing your attention to this miracle of God. This is the God, after all, who performs daily miracles through the whole of creation. These, though, have grown cheap in people's eyes, not because they are easy, but because they happen all the time; while the rare things done by the same Lord, that is, by the Word who was made flesh on our account, have struck people with greater amazement, not because they were indeed greater than what he does every day in creation, but because the things that are done every day occur, so it seems, in the natural course of events; while the others seem in people's eyes to be manifesting the activity of a power actually present here and now.

I said, you remember, that one dead man rose again, and people were struck dumb with amazement, while nobody marvels at those—who did not exist—being born every day. In the same way, who is not astonished at water being turned into wine, while God is doing the same thing every year in the vines? But all the things done by the Lord Jesus avail not only to stir up our hearts by their miraculous quality, but also to build them up in the teachings of the faith; so it is incumbent on us to investigate what all these things are about, that is, what they mean. We left for today, you will recall, the meanings of all these things.

---

1. Preached probably on the Monday before Palm Sunday, April 1, 407.
2. *In sacramentis*, i.e., in the sacred signs that are part of this gospel narrative.

Christ came to the wedding to confirm the sanctity of marriage

2. By coming to the wedding when he was invited, the Lord intended, quite apart from the mystical significance in his doing so, to confirm that he had instituted marriage. You see, there were going to be people, about whom the apostle spoke,[3] who would forbid marriage and say that it was an evil and that it had been instituted by the devil, while the Lord himself in the gospel, when asked whether it was lawful for a man to put away his wife for any reason at all, said that it was not, apart from the case of fornication. In his reply, if you remember, he said this: *What God has joined together, let no one put asunder* (Mt 19:6). And those who have been well instructed in the Catholic faith know that God established marriage, and that just as the joining of couples together comes from God, so divorce comes from the devil. But the reason why it is lawful in the case of fornication to put away one's wife is that she was first unwilling to be a wife, in that she did not keep marital faith with her husband.

Nor do those women who dedicate their virginity to God by a vow—though they hold a higher rank of honor and holiness in the Church—nor do they go without a wedding, seeing that they too take part with the whole Church in the wedding at which the bridegroom is Christ.[4]

And thus it is, then, that the Lord on being invited came to the wedding to confirm marital chastity, and to show the mystery of marriage; because at that wedding the person of the Lord was also represented by the bridegroom, who was told, *You have kept the good wine until now* (Jn 2:10). Christ, you see has kept the good wine until now, that is to say, his gospel.

The sacraments are hidden in the ancient prophecies

3. Now, let us begin to uncover what is hidden in these sacraments, insofar as the one in whose name I made that promise to you makes it possible. Prophecy was a feature of ancient times, and at no time has prophecy ever ceased; but that prophecy, as long as Christ was not recognized in it, was water. In water, you see, wine is in some way lurking. The apostle tells us what we are to understand about this water: *Up to this very*

---

3. See 1 Tm 4:3.
4. At this stage in the Church's tradition, it seems, consecrated virgins were seen as being the brides of Christ, just as the Church, in her members, was the bride of Christ.

day, he says, *while Moses is being read, the same veil is placed over their hearts, because it is not revealed to them that it is taken away in Christ. And*, he says, *when you cross over to the Lord, the veil will be taken away.* (2 Cor 3:14-16) What he is calling the veil is a wrapping up of prophecy such that it not be understood.

The veil is taken away when you cross over to the Lord; thus is tastelessness taken away when you cross over to the Lord, and what was water is turned into wine for you. Read all the prophetic books without recognizing Christ in them; what could ever be found as so tasteless and foolish? Understand Christ there, and not only does what you read become tasty,[5] it also makes you drunk, moving the mind away from the body, so that *forgetting the past you may reach out to what lies ahead* (Phil 3:13).

Christ to be understood in the law, the prophets, the writings

4. From ancient times, then, from when the series of births in the human race began, prophecy has not been silent about Christ; but then it was hidden, for it was still water. Where do we find proof that, from all earlier times until the age in which the Lord came, prophecy about him was not lacking? The Lord himself said so. When he had risen from the dead, you see, he found disciples doubting about the one they had followed. For they had seen him dead and had no hope of his rising again, and all their hope had collapsed. Why was that robber praised, why did he deserve that same day to be in Paradise? Because nailed to a cross he confessed Christ,[6] at the same time that the disciples had doubts about him.

So then, he found them shaky, and after a fashion criticizing themselves for having hoped for redemption from him. Still, they were grieving that he had been put to death without fault, because they knew he was innocent. And that is what they said after the resurrection, when he found some of them, sad, on the road. *Are you the only pilgrim to Jerusalem not to know about the things done in the place these days? And he said to them, What things? And they said, About Jesus the Nazarene, a man who was a prophet mighty in deeds and words in the sight of God and the whole people; how*

---

5. Again word play on the words *sapientia, insipientia, insipidus,* and *sapere*; see Homily 8, 3, note 9.
6. See Lk 23:40-43.

our high priests and leaders handed him over to be condemned to death and crucified him. We, though, were hoping that he was the one who was going to redeem Israel; and now today is the third day since these things happened. When this and much else had been said by one of the two whom he found on the road going to a nearby village, he himself answered and said, *You witless men, too dull-hearted to have faith in all the things which the prophets spoke! Was it not necessary for the Christ to suffer all these things and to enter into his glory? And he started with Moses and all the prophets, explaining to them what referred to him in all the scriptures.* (Lk 24:18-27)

Again in another place, when he also wanted himself to be touched by the hands of the disciples, so that they might believe that he had risen again in the body: *These are the words*, he said, *which I spoke to you when I was still with you, that it was necessary for all the things to be fulfilled that were written about me in the law of Moses, and the prophets, and the psalms. Then he opened their wits to understand the scriptures, and he said to them that thus it was written that the Christ would suffer, and rise again from the dead on the third day, and that repentance and forgiveness of sins would be preached in his name to all peoples, beginning from Jerusalem.* (Lk 24:44-47)

Changing water to wine means revealing Christ in the scriptures

5. Once all this has been understood from the gospel, where it is certainly plain enough, all those mysteries which are hidden in this miracle of the Lord will be discovered. Notice what he said, that it was necessary that the things written about him be fulfilled in the Christ. Where were they written? *In the law, and the prophets, and the psalms*, he said. He did not pass over any of the Old Testament scriptures. They were the water; and the reason those two were called witless by the Lord was because it still tasted like water to them, not like wine. How though did he make wine out of the water? When he opened their wits and expounded the scriptures to them, beginning from Moses and through all the prophets. Already drunk on all this, they said, *Were not our hearts burning within us, when he opened up the scriptures to us?* (Lk 24:32) For they now understood Christ in the books in which they had not known him.

So then, our Lord Jesus Christ changed water into wine, and what was without taste was tasty; what was not intoxicating was now intoxicating.[7] You see, if he had just ordered the water to be poured out of the jars, and had then put wine into them from the hidden depths of creation, from which he also made bread when he fed so many thousands—five loaves, after all, did not have the quantity in them to satisfy five thousand people, or even to fill twelve baskets,[8] but the Lord's omnipotence was like a source of bread; in that way, after emptying out the water, he could have poured in wine. If he had done that, it would seem that he had expressed disapproval of the old scriptures. But when he turned the water itself into wine, he showed us that the old scriptures too came from him; I mean, on his orders were the water jars filled. Indeed, those scriptures are also from the Lord; but they have no flavor, unless Christ is recognized in them.

The six ages of the world contained in the six water jars

6. But just notice that he says, *The things that were written about me in the law, and the prophets, and the psalms.* Now we know from what times the law tells its story, that is, from the beginning of the world: *In the beginning God made heaven and earth* (Gn 1:1). From there up to this time in which we now live there are six ages,[9] as you have often heard and know very well. The first age is reckoned from Adam up to Noah, the second from Noah up to Abraham; and as the evangelist Matthew follows the series of generations and divides them,[10] the third runs from Abraham up to David, the fourth from David up to the deportation to Babylonia, the fifth from the deportation to Babylonia until John the Baptist; the sixth from there till the end of time.

The reason why it was also on the sixth day that *God made man to his own image* (Gn 1:27) is because, in this sixth age, the refashioning of our minds according to the image of the one who created us[11] is being revealed through the gospel; and water is changed into wine, so that we may get a

---
7. *Non sapiebat—sapit; non inebriebat—inebriat.*
8. See Mk 6:35-44.
9. The text reads, "It is the sixth age," *sexta aetas est.* But Augustine clearly meant to speak about the six ages: *sex aetates sunt.*
10. See Mt 1:17.
11. See Col 3:10; Eph 4:23-24.

taste of Christ, already revealed in the law and the prophets. Hence, *there were six water jars there* (Jn 2:6) which he ordered to have filled with water. So then, those six jars signify the six ages in which prophecy has never been wanting. The six periods of time, therefore, arranged and distinguished, as it were, by six hinges, would be like empty vessels, unless they were filled by Christ. What have I said? Periods of time that would run their course empty of meaning, unless the Lord Jesus were proclaimed in them? The prophecies have been fulfilled, the jars are full; but for the water to be turned into wine, Christ must be recognized in the whole of that prophetic tradition.

The Trinity signified by two or three metretas each

7. So what does it mean then: *They held two or three metretas each* (Jn 2:6)? That expression certainly points to a mystery. *Metretas* are what he calls a kind of measure, as if he were to say urns or pitchers, or something like that. *Metreta* is the name of a measure, and from "measure" this measure takes its name. For the Greeks call a "measure" a *metron*, the word from which the *metretas* get their name. And so, *they held two or three metretas each*.

What are we saying, brothers and sisters? If he had just said *three each*, our thoughts would simply have turned to the mystery of the Trinity. But perhaps we should not be too quick, even so, to turn our minds away from that idea, just because he said *two or three each*, because once Father and Son have been named, the Holy Spirit has in consequence to be understood as well. The Holy Spirit, you see, is not only of the Father, nor merely the Spirit of the Son, but the Spirit of the Father and of the Son. It is written, after all: *If anyone loves the world, the Spirit of the Father is not in him* (1 Jn 2:15); again it is written: *But whoever does not have the Spirit of Christ, this person does not belong to him* (Rom 8:9). The same one is the Spirit of the Father and of the Son. Now when Father and Son are named it is like two *metretas* being named; while when the Holy Spirit is understood there, it is three *metretas*. That is why it does not say "some holding two *metretas*, others three," but all six jars *held two or three metretas each*. It is as though he said, "And when I say two each, I also want the Spirit of the Father and the Son to be understood together with them; and when I say three each, I state the Trinity itself more clearly."

More precision on the trinitarian mystery

8. And so anyone naming Father and Son must also understand there, as it were, the mutual charity of Father and Son, which is the Holy Spirit. Perhaps, you see, when you sift through the scriptures (and I am not suggesting that I could explain this today, that another explanation could not be found), but perhaps, when the scriptures are searched, they will indicate that the Holy Spirit is charity. And please do not think charity comes cheap. But how is *caritas* cheap, when everything that is not said to be cheap is said to be dear (*carus*)? So then if things that are not cheap are dear, what could be dearer than *caritas*!

Thus is charity recommended to us by the apostle who says, *There is a way surpassing all others I can show you. If I speak with the tongues of men and of angels, but do not have charity, I have become like booming bronze or clashing cymbal; and if I know all mysteries and all knowledge and have prophecy and all faith such that I can move mountains, but do not have charity, I am nothing. And if I distribute all my goods to the poor and hand over my body to be burned, but do not have charity, it does me no good.* (1 Cor 12:31-13:3) How great then is charity, if, when it is lacking, all the rest is possessed in vain; when charity is present, everything is possessed to good purpose!

And yet in singing the praises of charity so fully and so richly, the apostle Paul said less about it than what was put briefly by the apostle John, whose gospel this is. For he did not hesitate to say, *God is charity*[12] (1 Jn 4:16). It is also written: *The charity of God has been poured out in our hearts through the Holy Spirit who has been given to us* (Rom 5:5). So who then could name Father and Son, and fail to understand there the charity of Father and Son? When you begin to have the Father and the Son, you will have the Holy Spirit; if you do not have the Father and the Son, you will be without the Holy Spirit. And just as your body, if it is without spirit, which is your soul, is dead, so too your soul, if it is without the Holy Spirit, that is without charity, will be counted as being dead.

---

12. This is usually translated as *God is love*. *Deus caritas est* could mean "charity is God" or "God is charity."

So then, the water jars held two *metretas* each, because in the prophecy of all periods of time the Father and the Son are being proclaimed; but the Holy Spirit is there too, and that is why it adds *or three each*. *I and the Father*, he says, *are one* (Jn 10:30); but in no way is the Holy Spirit lacking when we hear *I and the Father are one*! Still, because he named Father and Son, let the water jars hold two *metretas* each. But listen: *or three*: *Go, baptize the nations in the name of the Father and of the Son and of the Holy Spirit* (Mt 28:19). And so in saying *two each*, the Trinity is not stated, but it is understood; while, in adding *or three*, the Trinity is also stated.

Salvation for all peoples is also signified by the jars

9. But there is also another way of understanding the text which must not be passed over, and I shall present it too; let each one choose the one he prefers—I am not removing what has been suggested to me. This is the Lord's table, after all, and the one who serves must not cheat the guests, especially when they are as hungry as your eagerness shows you are. The prophecy which is served up from the most ancient times concerns the salvation of all peoples. Moses indeed was only sent to the people of Israel, and to that people alone was the law given through him, and the prophets themselves came from that people, and the actual distinction between the various ages of time has been made with reference to the same people—which is why the water jars are said to be there *according to the purification custom of the Jews* (Jn 2:6).

But even so it is quite obvious that prophecy was also announced to other peoples, since Christ—in whom all peoples are blessed—was hidden in this prophecy, as Abraham was promised when the Lord said, *In your seed shall all the peoples be blessed* (Gn 22:18). But this was not yet recognized, because the water had not yet been turned into wine. So then prophecy was being addressed to all peoples. That this may emerge more delightfully, let us remind ourselves, as far as time allows, of certain things about each of the ages of time, as though about each of the water jars in turn.

The first age concerns the mystery of two in one flesh

10. At the beginning Adam and Eve were the parents of all peoples, not just of the Jews; and whatever in Adam stood for Christ naturally concerned all peoples, whose salvation is to be found in Christ. So then, what could I say more powerfully about the water of the first jar than what the apostle said about Adam and Eve? After all, no one will say that I have understood a matter badly when I am presenting the apostle's understanding of it, not my own. So then, what a stupendous mystery about Christ is contained in the one thing of which the apostle reminds us when he says, *And they shall be two in one flesh; this is a great mystery*! And in case anyone should take the greatness of this mystery to lie in each and every man who has a wife, he continues, *I am, however, talking about Christ and about the Church.* (Eph 5:31-32) What is this great mystery, *they shall be two in one flesh*? It is where the Book of Genesis was talking about Adam and Eve, and where it came to these words: *Therefore shall a man leave father and mother and cling to his wife; and they shall be two in one flesh* (Gn 2:24).

If, then, Christ has attached himself to the Church so that they might be two in one flesh, how did he leave the father, how the mother? He left the Father because *while he was in the form of God, he did not reckon being equal to God something to cling to, but he emptied himself, taking the form of a slave* (Phil 2:6-7). That, you see, is "he left the father," not that he forsook or withdrew from the Father, but that he did not appear to men in the form in which he is equal to the Father. How did he leave the mother? By leaving the Synagogue of the Jews, in which he was born according to the flesh, and by clinging to the Church which he has gathered together from all peoples.

So then, the first water jar also held a prophecy about Christ; but as long as these things I am saying were not being preached among the peoples, it was still water, it had not yet been changed into wine. And because the Lord has enlightened us through the apostle, and shown us what we should look for in that one sentence, *They shall be two in one flesh*, namely *a great mystery in Christ and in the Church*, we can look for Christ everywhere and drink wine from all the water jars. Adam sleeps so that Eve may be made; Christ dies so that the Church may be made. While Adam is asleep Eve is made from his side; when Christ is dead his side is pierced with a lance, so that the sacraments, from which the Church is to be formed, might pour out.

Who would not see that in those deeds back then, the future was represented, since the apostle says that Adam himself was a figure of the one to come? *He is*, he says, *a form of the one to come* (Rom 5:14). Everything was mystically prefigured. God, after all, could have formed the woman from a rib taken out while he was awake. Or was it perhaps necessary for him to be asleep so that his side would not hurt him when the rib was pulled out of it? Will anyone, I ask you, sleep so soundly that bones can be extracted from him without his waking up? Or because God was doing the extraction, is that why the man did not feel it? So of course the one who extracted it from him without pain while he was asleep could just as well have done so while he was awake. But without a shadow of doubt the first water jar was being filled to the brim; the prophecy of that time about this time to come was being arranged.

The second age concerns Noah's ark, the wood of the cross

11. Christ was also prefigured in Noah, and the whole world was prefigured in that ark. Why, after all, were all animals included in the ark, if not to represent all peoples?[13] (God, in fact, did not lack the means of creating every kind of animal again. When none of them existed after all, did he not say, *Let the earth produce* [Gn 1:24], and the earth produced them? So, in the same way that he made them then, he could have made them again; he made them with a word, he could have remade them with a word.) Why, if not to present us with a mystery and to fill the second water jar of his prophetic dispensation, so that what stood for the whole world might be delivered through wood, because the life of the whole world was to be nailed onto wood?[14]

The third age recalls the blessing of all peoples in the seed of Abraham

12. Now in the third water jar Abraham himself was told, as I have already mentioned, *In your seed shall all the peoples be blessed*. And can

---

13. See Gn 7:7-9.
14. The wood of the cross prefigured by the wooden timbers of the ark. See *Exposition of Psalm* 103, 3, 2; *The City of God* XV, 27.

anybody fail to see who was represented by his only son, as he carried the wood for the sacrifice to which he was being led to be himself the victim offered?[15] The Lord, you see, carried his own cross, as the gospel says. That must be enough as a reminder of the contents of the third jar of water.

The fourth age is about the messianic prophecies in the psalms of David

13. About David, however, why should I have to say that his prophecy concerned all peoples, when we have just now heard the psalm (and indeed it is difficult to say any psalm where this note is not sounded)? But certainly, as I have said, we have just been singing, *Arise God, judge the earth, since it is you that will inherit in all the peoples* (Ps 81:8). And that is why the Donatists have been, as it were, thrown out of the wedding, like that man who did not have on a wedding garment;[16] he was invited and came, but was thrown out from the number of the guests because he did not have on a garment to honor the bridegroom. The one who seeks his own glory, you see, not that of Christ, is not wearing a wedding garment; for they refuse to sing in harmony with the voice of the one who was the friend of the bridegroom and said, *This is the one who baptizes* (Jn 1:33).

Nor was it undeserved that the one who was not wearing a wedding garment should be reproached for what he was not: *Friend, why have you come in here?* (Mt 22:12) And just as he was silent, so are these people. What is the use, after all, of chatter from the mouth, when the heart is mute? They know perfectly well deep down in themselves that they really have nothing to say. Inside they have become silent, outwardly their chatter never stops. Like it or not, they hear it being sung over at their place too: *Arise, God, judge the earth, since it is you that will inherit in all the peoples*; and by not communicating with all peoples, what else are they doing but acknowledging that they have been disinherited?

---

15. See Gn 22:6-10.
16. See Mt 22:11-13.

All peoples sprung from Adam;
East, West, North, South are contained in his name

14. So then, I was saying, brothers and sisters, that prophecy concerns all peoples—for I wish to point out another meaning in the expression, *Holding two or three metretas each*. That prophecy refers, I say, to all peoples. We have just now reminded ourselves how this is demonstrated in Adam, *who is a form of the one to come*. Is there anybody, though, who does not know that from him have sprung all peoples, and that in the four letters of his name the four quarters of the wide world are indicated, by Greek names? If East, West, North and South, you see, are said in Greek, in the order holy scripture mentions them in many places, you will find Adam contained in the first letters of those words. The four quarters of the world, you see, are called in Greek *anatole, dusis, arktos, mesemthria*. If you write these four names one underneath the other, like a verse, you will read "Adam" in their initial letters.

In the case of Noah this was represented by the ark, which had all the animals in it, which signified all peoples; also in the case of Abraham, who was told more explicitly: *In your seed shall all the peoples be blessed*; also in the case of David, from whose psalms, to say nothing of the others, we have just been singing: *Arise, God, judge the earth; since it is you that will inherit in all peoples*. To which god, after all, can it say, *Arise*, but to one who has gone to sleep? *Arise God, judge the earth*; as though to say, "You fell asleep, judged by the earth; arise, in order to judge the earth." And to what else can this prophecy refer: *Since it is you that will inherit in all peoples*?

The fifth age is seen in Daniel's vision of the stone hewn
without hands from a mountain

15. Next in the fifth age, as if in the fifth water jar, Daniel saw a stone hewn out of a mountain, and not by hands; and it shattered all the kingdoms of the earth; and that stone grew and became a great mountain, such that it filled the whole face of the earth.[17] What could be plainer, my brothers and sisters? A stone is hewn out of a mountain; this is *the stone which the builders rejected, and it has become the corner stone* (Ps 117:22). Which mountain is it hewn from, if not the kingdom of the Jews, of which our

---
17. See Dan 2:31-45.

Lord Jesus Christ was born according to the flesh? And it is hewn without hands, without any human activity, because he was born of the virgin without any marital embrace. That mountain from which it was hewn had not filled the whole face of the earth; the kingdom of the Jews, after all, had not contained all peoples. But as for the kingdom of Christ, we can already observe it occupying the whole world.

The sixth age stretches from John the Baptist to the end

16. To the sixth age now belongs John the Baptist; *none greater than him has arisen among those born of women* (Mt 11:11); it was said of him: *Greater than a prophet* (Mt 11:9). How did he also show that Christ was sent to all peoples? When Jews came to him to be baptized, and to stop them priding themselves on the name of Abraham, he said, *Generation of vipers, who showed you to flee from the wrath to come? So then, produce fruit worthy of repentance*; that is, "Be humble." He was talking to proud people, you see. But what were they proud of? Of their ancestry in the flesh, not of the fruit of imitating father Abraham. What did he tell them? *Do not say, For father we have Abraham; God, after all, has the power to raise up children to Abraham from these stones.* (Mt 3:7-9)

He is calling all peoples stones, not to suggest strength, as the one whom the builders rejected was called a stone,[18] but on account of their rock-hard stupidity and folly, because they had become like the things they worshiped; they worshiped witless images, you see, being equally witless themselves. What made them witless? What it says in the psalm: *May those who make them become like them and all who trust in them* (Ps 113:8). That is why, when people begin to worship God, what is it they hear? *That you may be sons and daughters of your Father in heaven, who makes his sun rise upon the good and the bad, and pours rain upon the just and the unjust* (Mt 5:45).

Accordingly, if people become like what they worship, what is the meaning of *God has the power to raise up children to Abraham from these stones*? We only have to question ourselves, and we see that it has happened. After all, we come from the nations; but we would not come from the nations unless God had raised up children to Abraham from stones. We became children of Abraham by imitating his faith, not by birth in the flesh.

---

18. See Ps 117:22.

Just as they have been disinherited for being untrue to their ancestry, so we by imitating their ancestor have been adopted. So then, brothers and sisters, this prophecy of the sixth water jar also referred to all peoples; and that is why it says of them all, *holding two or three metretas each.*

Two or three each; *the two peoples of Jews and Gentiles;*
the three measures of flour and Noah's three sons

17. But how do we show that all peoples belong to the two or three *metretas* each? It was by a deliberate calculation, you see, that the author said *two each* after saying *three each*; it was in order to focus our attention on the mystery.[19] In what way are there two *metretas* each? *Circumcision and uncircumcision* (Col 3:11). These are the two peoples that scripture mentions, and it does not overlook any human race when it says *circumcision and uncircumcision*; in these two names you have all peoples; they are the two *metretas* each. It was for these two walls coming from different directions to make peace with each other, that *Christ became the corner stone* (Eph 2:20).[20]

Let us also show three *metretas* each, again in all these same peoples. Noah had three sons, through whom the human race was restocked. About this the Lord says, *The kingdom of heaven is like yeast, which a woman took and hid in three measures of flour, until the whole was leavened* (Lk 13:20-21). Who can this woman be, but the flesh of the Lord? What can the leaven be, but the gospel? What can the three measures be, but all peoples, on account of Noah's three sons?[21] Therefore the six water jars holding two or three *metretas* each are the six ages of all the periods of time, holding prophecy that refers to all peoples, whether signified in two kinds of humanity, that is in Jews and Greeks, as the apostle often calls them,[22] or in three, on account of the three sons of Noah. Prophecy, you see, is figuratively represented as stretching out to all peoples; because it is with respect to its stretching out that it is called a *metreta*, as the apostle says, *We have received a measure stretching even to you* (2 Cor 10:13). You see, to evangelize all peoples, it was called *a measure stretching even to you.*

---

19. On *the sacramentum.*
20. On Christ the corner stone joining the two peoples into one see *Exposition of Psalm* 126, 2.
21. See ibid. 101, 2, 11, for a similar connection between the three measures of yeast and the three sons of Noah.
22. See Rom 2:9-10; 1 Cor 1:24; etc.

Homily 10

On John 2:12-21[1]

Introduction; the sighs and groans of the poor

1. In the psalm you heard the groaning of the poor man, whose members suffer tribulations throughout the whole earth until the end of time. Do all you can, my brothers and sisters, to be among these members and to be part of them; because tribulation is going to pass away. Woe to those who rejoice! The Truth says, *Blessed are those who mourn, for they shall be consoled* (Mt 5:4). God has become man; what is man going to become, on whose account God became man? Let this hope console us in every tribulation and temptation of this life. The enemy, you see, never stops persecuting, and if he is not raging openly, he is acting craftily. What then is said? *And over and above wrath, they were acting with trickery* (Ps 34:20). That is why he is called both lion and dragon. But what is Christ told? *And you shall trample on the lion and the dragon* (Ps 90:13); on the lion because of his open wrath, on the dragon because of his craftily hidden snares. As dragon he threw Adam out of Paradise; as lion, the very same one has persecuted the Church, in Peter's words: *Because your adversary the devil goes round roaring like a lion, seeking whom he may devour* (1 Pt 5:8). Do not imagine the devil has lost his fury; when he is flattering you, that is when you need to be most on your guard.

But among all these snares and temptations of his, what else are we to do but what we heard there in the psalm: *Yet I, when they troubled me, used to put on sackcloth and humble my soul with fasting* (Ps 34:13). Someone is listening, do not hesitate to pray; but the one who is listening abides within. Do not turn your eyes to some mountain, do not lift your face to the stars or the sun or the moon; do not think that you will be heard when you pray on the sea; no, loathe such prayers. Just clean up the inner chamber of your heart; wherever you are, wherever you pray, the one who listens is within, in that secret place which the psalmist calls his bosom when he says, *And my prayer will be transformed in my own bosom* (Ps 34:13). The one who is

---

1. Preached probably on the Tuesday before Palm Sunday, April 2, 407.

listening to you is not outside you. Do not set off on a long march, or try lifting yourself up, as though you could reach up and touch him with your hands. It is more likely that if you lift yourself up you will fall; if you humble yourself, he will draw near.[2] He is, after all, the Lord our God, the Word of God, the Word made flesh, Son of the Father, Son of God, Son of Man, mighty that he might make us, humble to remake us, walking about among human beings, suffering human pains, concealing divine power.

Different languages, different idioms

2. *He went down*, as the evangelist says, *to Capernaum, he and his mother and his brothers and his disciples, and they stayed there not many days* (Jn 2:12). There you are, he does have a mother, does have brothers, also has disciples; he has brothers because he has a mother. Our scriptures, you see, are in the habit of calling brothers not only those who are born of the same man and woman, or from the same womb, or of the same father though different mothers, or at any rate cousins of the same degree on father's or mother's side—these are not the only ones whom our scriptures know as brothers. It is in accordance with their way of talking that they are to be understood. They have their own language; anyone who does not know this language gets worried, and says, "How did the Lord get brothers? After all, Mary did not give birth again, did she?" Not at all! It is from her that the dignity of virgins is derived. This female could be a mother, she could not be a woman.[3] But she was called a woman with reference to her feminine sex, not with reference to the breach of virginal integrity —and this too in accord with typical scriptural language; thus Eve, right after being made from her husband's rib, before she was even touched by her husband, was also called a woman, as you know: *And he fashioned it into a woman* (Gn 2:22).

So where did he get brothers from? Mary's relations, of whatever degree of kinship, were the Lord's brothers. How do we prove this? From

---

2. See Jas 4:6-8.
3. *Mulier* ("woman" here) usually means "wife." One cannot say that Mary could not be a wife, because, legally, she was Joseph's wife. The problem is one of Latin, not a problem of "the language of our scriptures." Augustine makes the same point, with reference to Gal 4:4 (*born of woman*), in *The Trinity* II, 5, 8; Sermon 186, 3.

the scriptures themselves. Lot was called Abraham's brother; he was in fact his brother's son. Read, and you will find that Abraham was Lot's uncle, and they were called brothers. How so, if not just because they were related? Again, Jacob had an uncle, Laban the Syrian; Laban, you see was the brother of Jacob's mother, that is of Rebecca, Isaac's wife. Read the scriptures and you will find that an uncle and a sister's son are called brothers. Once you know this rule, you will find that all Mary's relations are the brothers of Christ.

Christ's true relations are those who hear the word of God and keep it

3. But for him the disciples were really his brothers, because even those relatives would not be brothers if they were not also disciples, and they would be brothers to no purpose if they did not recognize their brother as the teacher. You see, in one place, when he was told his mother and his brothers were standing outside, while he was speaking with his disciples, he said, *Who is my mother, or who are my brothers? And stretching out his hand over his disciples, he said, These are my brothers*; and, *Whoever does the will of my Father, he is my mother, and brother, and sister.* (Mt 12:46-50)

So too was Mary, because she did the will of the Father. This is what the Lord glorified in her, not that flesh gave birth to flesh, but that she did the will of the Father. Would Your Graces please listen! Thus, when the Lord seemed wonderful in the eyes of the crowd, performing signs and prodigies and showing what was lying hidden in the flesh, some souls, lost in admiration, said, *Blessed is the womb that bore you*, and he replied, *Blessed, rather, those who hear the word of God and keep it* (Lk 11:27-28); which amounts to saying, "Even my mother, whom you have called blessed, is blessed because she keeps the word of God; not because in her *the Word was made flesh and took up residence among us* (Jn 1:14), but because she keeps the very Word of God through which she was made and which was made flesh in her." Let people exult if they are joined to God in spirit, rather than rejoice over their offspring in time. I have said this because of what the evangelist says when Jesus stayed in Capernaum for a few days with his mother and his brothers and disciples.

Driving the merchants out of the temple

4. What follows after that? *And the Passover of the Jews was near, and he went up to Jerusalem.* The narrator recounts another event, as it occurred in his memory. *And he found in the temple those selling oxen and sheep and doves, and the money-changers sitting there; and when he had made a sort of scourge from strands of rope, he threw them all out of the temple, the oxen as well and the sheep, and he spilled the coins of the money-changers, and overturned their tables; and to those who were selling doves he said, Take these things away, and do not make my Father's house a house of business.* (Jn 2:13-16)

What have we just heard, brothers and sisters? There is that temple—still a figure of the real one[4]—and the Lord drove from there all those who came to market seeking their own interests.[5] And what were those people selling there? Things people needed for the sacrifices of that time. Your Graces know, surely, that for that people, because of their fleshly-mindedness and still stony hearts,[6] such sacrifices were given them as would at least keep them from trickling off to idols; and they used to offer up their sacrifices there, oxen, sheep and doves. You know all this, because you have read it. So it was not all that great a sin, then, if they were selling in the temple what people used to buy to sacrifice in the temple; and yet he threw them out of the place.

What if he had found drunkards there, what would the Lord have done, if he drove out people who were selling what was lawful and was not against justice—things that are bought honestly cannot, after all, be illegal to sell—if, all the same, he drove them out and did not allow the house of prayer to become a house of business? If God's house ought not to become a house of business, ought it really to become a house for carousing?[7] When I say these things, however, they gnash their teeth against me, and

---

4. That is, of the body of Christ and of the Church.
5. See Phil 2:21.
6. That is, in more usual English parlance, "still closed minds."
7. See Letter 29, 3, written to Augustine's friend Alypius in 395, about how he preached against this way of celebrating the feast of St Leontius, the patron saint of Hippo Regius, in the church dedicated to him, and how he managed to suppress the practice. In this case, he is referring to more recent sermons—possibly directed at Donatists who still kept this local custom in their churches and could be heard in the nearby Catholic church.

the psalm which you have heard gives me comfort: *They gnashed their teeth over me* (Ps 34:16). I too know where to look and listen for ways of taking care of myself, even if they double up scourges for Christ, because it is his word that is being scourged: *Scourges,* he says, *were gathered together against me, and they did not know it* (Ps 34:15). He was scourged with the scourges of the Jews, he is scourged with the blasphemies of false Christians; they multiply scourges for their Lord and do not know it. Let us here do what follows, to the extent that he assists us: *Yet I, when they troubled me, used to put on sackcloth and humble my soul with fasting.*

The symbolism of the scourge made of cords

5. Nevertheless, brothers and sisters, insofar as he made a scourge out of strands of rope and scourged that undisciplined bunch who were making a profitable business from God's temple, we have to say that he showed us a sort of sign—for he did not spare them either; the one who was to be scourged by them scourged them first. Indeed all of us braid a rope for ourselves with our sins. The prophet says, *Woe to those who drag sins along like a long rope* (Is 5:18, LXX). Who makes a long rope? The one who adds sin to sin. How are sins added to sins? When the sins that have been committed are covered with other sins.

You commit a theft; in order not to be found out, you look up an astrologer. It should have been enough for you just to have committed a theft; why do you want to join sin to sin? There you are, two sins for you. When you are forbidden to approach an astrologer, you revile the bishop; that makes three sins. When you hear, "Put him out of the church," you say, "I am going over to the party of Donatus"; that adds a fourth. The rope is getting longer; be afraid of the rope. What is good for you is that you should correct yourself by scourging yourself with the rope lest it be said at the end, *Bind him hand and foot, and cast him forth into the outer darkness* (Mt 22:13). *Everyone,* you see, *is entangled in the threads of his own sins* (Prov 5:22). The first is something said by the Lord, the second by another book of scripture; but in fact each is said by the Lord. Human beings are bound by their own sins and cast into outer darkness.

Who are signified by the merchants in the temple?

6. Who though—to look for the mysterious meaning of the event hidden in figurative language—who are the ones selling oxen? Who are the ones selling sheep and doves? They are the ones who *are looking to their own interests in the Church, not those of Jesus Christ* (Phil 2:21). They treat everything as being up for sale, because they do not want to be redeemed. They do not want to be bought, and they want to sell. For it is good for them to be redeemed by the blood of Christ, that they might get to the peace of Christ. What is the good, after all, of acquiring in this age anything that is time-bound and transient, be it money, be it pleasures of the stomach and the gullet, be it honor through human praise? Is all of that no more than smoke and wind? Is it all not passing away, running away? And woe to those who cling to things that pass away, because they will pass away with them! Are not all these things a river rushing down to the sea? And woe to those who fall in, because they too will be swept into the sea!

So then, all of us ought to restrain our longings from all such covetous desires. My brothers and sisters, those who set their hearts on such things are engaged in selling. That fellow Simon,[8] for instance, wished to buy the Holy Spirit because he wanted to sell the Holy Spirit; and he thought the apostles were traders of the same kind as those the Lord threw out of the temple with his scourge. He was the same sort of man you see, and he wanted to buy something he could sell; he was one of those who were selling doves. For the Holy Spirit appeared in the form of a dove.[9] So who then, brothers and sisters, are the ones selling doves, who are they, if not those who say, "We give the Holy Spirit"? I mean, why do they say this, and what price are they selling for? The price of their own honor. The price they get is their *cathedra*,[10] so that they too may appear to be selling doves; they should beware of the scourge of rope strands. The Dove is not for sale; he is given *gratis*, because he is called grace.

---

8. See Acts 8:18-19.
9. See Mk 1:10.
10. Augustine appears to be comparing the *cathedrae*, the presidential chairs of the Donatist bishops, to the chairs of the merchants selling doves; or mixing these up with the money-changers, who were seated at tables.

That is why, my brothers and sisters, it is like what you see with the retailers[11] in the market, each one praising his wares; how many offers they have made! Primian has one thing on offer in Carthage, Maximian has another, Rogatus in Mauretania has another, this, that and the other one here in Numidia, whom I am not up to naming right now, have yet another. So then, someone goes out to buy the Dove, each of them praises his own wares, what he has on offer.[12] May his heart turn away from every salesman, may he come to where the Dove is to be received *gratis*, free of charge. Not even so do they blush for shame, brothers and sisters, because through their bitter and malicious quarrels they have made so many parties of themselves, while they credit themselves with being what they are not, while they put on airs, thinking they are really something, when in fact they are nothing. What, though, is being fulfilled among them, which they refuse to put right, but what you heard in the psalm: *They were rent asunder, and yet not pricked to the heart* (Ps 34:16)?[13]

The genuine oxen are the apostles and prophets

7. So who are the ones selling oxen? Those who have dispensed the holy scriptures to us are understood as being oxen. The apostles were oxen, the prophets were oxen. That is why the apostle says, *You shall not muzzle the ox that is threshing* (Dt 25:4). *Is God concerned about oxen? Or does he say this on our account? You see, it is on our account that he says it, because the one who ploughs should plough in hope, and the one who threshes in the hope of receiving his share.* (1 Cor 9:9-10) So then, the oxen left us the memorial of the scriptures. They were not, you see, dispensing them from their own stock, because it was the Lord's glory they were seeking. For what did you hear in the psalm itself? *And let them always say, Let the Lord be glorified, those who desire the peace of his servant*

---

11. Augustine's word for retailers is *propolarios*, most likely a colloquial African Latin for *propola*, the Greek for a retailer. He here sees the retailers praising their *proposita* (what they are selling) in a way similar to what Donatist leaders had "on offer."
12. The CCSL text omits this sentence altogether, thus making it impossible to make sense of the next one.
13. See *Exposition of Psalm* 57, 20: "You see them torn asunder, and you do not see them pricked to the heart. There you are, they are outside the Church, and they do not repent and come back to where they were torn from."

(Ps 34:27). The servant of God, the people of God, the Church of God. Those who desire the peace of his Church, let them glorify the Lord, not glorify the servant, and *let them always say, Let the Lord be glorified.* Who are the ones that are to say this? *Those who desire the peace of his servant.*

The voice which you heard in the lamentations in the psalm is clearly the voice of his people, the voice of the servant, and you were moved when you heard it, because you belong to that people. What was being sung by one voice echoed in everyone's heart. Happy are those who recognized themselves in those words as in a mirror. So who then are the ones who desire the peace of his servant, the peace of his people, the peace of the one which he calls his only one, and whom he wishes to be snatched from the lion: *Snatch my only one from the hand of the dog* (Ps 21:21.20)? *Those who always say, Let the Lord be glorified* (Ps 34:27).

Thus, those oxen glorified the Lord, not themselves. Look at an ox glorifying his Lord, because *the ox has recognized his owner* (Is 1:3); notice an ox being afraid of people abandoning the ox's owner and relying on the ox instead; how he dreads people wishing to place their hopes on himself! *Was Paul crucified for you, or was it in Paul's name you were baptized?* (1 Cor 1:13) What I gave, it was not I that gave it. You received it *gratis,* the Dove came down from heaven. *I,* he says, *planted, Apollos watered, but it was God who gave the growth; neither the one who plants nor the one who waters is anything, but the one who gives the growth, God* (1 Cor 3:6-7). *And let them always say, Let the Lord be glorified, those who desire the peace of his servant.*

The Donatists are selling these oxen to the devil

8. These others, though, use the scriptures to deceive people, so that they may receive honors and praise from them, and not so that the scriptures might turn people to the truth. But because they deceive the people with the scriptures, the people from whom they are looking for honors, they are in fact selling oxen, selling sheep too, that is to say they are selling the people themselves. And whom are they selling them to, if not the devil? For indeed, my brothers and sisters, if the one and only Church belongs to Christ and is one, then whatever is cut off or removed from it is only for *that roaring and prowling lion, who is seeking whom he may devour*

(1 Pt 5:8). Woe to those who are cut off! Because that Church will remain whole. *The Lord*, you see, *knows who are his own* (2 Tm 2:19).

Still, as far as it is up to them, they are selling oxen and sheep, they are even selling doves; may they pay attention to the scourge of their sins. Indeed, whenever they suffer anything like this on account of their wrongdoings, may they realize that it is the Lord who has made the scourge from strands of rope, thus warning them to be converted and to stop being peddlers; for if they do not change, they will hear at the end: *Bind their hands and feet and cast them into the outer darkness* (Mt 22:13).

May zeal for God's house consume the congregation

9. Then, it was written, *The disciples remembered the words, Zeal for your house has consumed me* (Ps 68:10; Jn 2:17), because it was out of zeal for the house of God that the Lord drove these people out of the temple. Brothers and sisters, may every Christian among the members of Christ be consumed with zeal for the house of God! Who is the one consumed with zeal for the house of God? The one who seeks to correct all the things he may see as evil there, who longs to have them changed, who does not keep quiet about them; if he cannot correct them, he bears with them, he groans over them. Good grain is not swept off the threshing floor; it puts up with the chaff in order to gain entrance to the granary once the chaff has been separated.[14] You, then, if you are a grain, do not get swept off the threshing floor before the granary opens or before you can be gathered into it, you may be picked up by birds. Birds, in fact, powers in the sky, are waiting to snatch something from the threshing floor, and they can only snatch what has been swept off it.

So then, may zeal for the house of God consume you; may zeal for the house of God consume each Christian—in the house of God where he is a member. For no house is more yours than the house in which you have eternal salvation. You go into your own house for earthly rest; you enter God's house for eternal rest. So then, if you make sure that nothing evil is done in your own household, should you just put up with it if you see evil taking place in the house of God where salvation is anticipated and rest

---

14. See Lk 3:17.

without end? For example, have you seen a brother running off to the theatre? If zeal for the house of God consumes you, restrain him, warn him, show your disappointment. Have you seen others running off, wanting to get drunk and wanting to do it in holy places, where it is never right? Hinder those you can, restrain those you can, frighten those you can, plead with those you can; but do not just sit back and keep quiet.

Is it a friend? Let him be admonished gently. Is it your wife? Let her be restrained most strictly. Is it a maidservant? Let her be checked, even with a beating. Do whatever you can, according to your rank and status, and you will fulfill the scripture, *Zeal for your house has consumed me.* But if you are cold and casual about it, thinking only of yourself and almost sufficient to yourself and saying in your heart, "Why should I care about other people's sins? I have more than enough with my own soul, keeping it whole for God." Hey, do you not remember the servant who hid the talent and refused to invest it?[15] Was he ever charged with losing it, and not rather with keeping it without profit?

So then, my brothers and sisters, listen so that you do not just keep quiet. I was about to give you some advice, but let the one who is within you give it, because even if he were to give it through me, he is the one that gives it. You know how you act, each one of you, in your own house with a friend, with a tenant, with a client, with an older or younger person; you know how God provides you with an opening, how he opens a door for his word. Do not rest in gaining someone for Christ, because you yourselves were gained by Christ.

The temple of Christ's body

10. *The Jews said to him, What sign do you show us that lets you do these things?* And the Lord in reply, *Pull down this temple, and in three days I will raise it up.*[16] *So the Jews said, For forty-six years has this temple been in the building and you say, I will raise it up in three days.* (Jn 2:18-20) They were flesh; they had flesh-bound ideas; but he was speaking in a spiritual sense. Who, though, could understand what temple he was talking

---

15. See Mt 25:24-30.
16. For Augustine *excito, suscito, resuscito* and (*re*)*aedificatio* are similar in meaning: "awaken," "raise up," "(re)build."

about? We, however, do not have to look very hard; he has opened the door to us through the evangelist; he said about which temple he was saying, *Pull down this temple, and in three days I will raise it up. Forty and six years has this temple been in the building, and you will raise it up in three days? But*, says the evangelist, *he was talking about the temple of his body.* (Jn 2:21) And it is well known that three days after he was slain, the Lord rose again.

Now this is known to all of us; although it is a closed door to the Jews, because they are standing outside, to us at least the door is wide open, because we know in whom we have believed.[17] We are about to celebrate the solemn annual festival of the pulling down and rebuilding of his temple; and I urge you, if any of you are catechumens, to prepare yourselves to receive God's grace. Now, yes, now is the time; now, yes, now are the labor pains being felt of what is then to be born. So then, that is something we all know.

Both Father and Son raised Christ from the dead

11. But perhaps what is being asked of us is to know whether the temple, built in forty-six years, has some sacramental meaning.[18] There are indeed many things that can be said on the point; but for the time being I will just say what can be said briefly and easily understood. Brothers and sisters, yesterday, I already said, if I am not mistaken, that Adam was one man, and that man is the whole human race.[19] This, I mean, is what I said, if you remember. It is as if he were broken and scattered and then gathered up and kneaded into one fellowship and one spiritual harmony.[20] And now this one poor man groans like Adam, but in Christ he is being made new, because Adam-without-sin has come that in his flesh that he might undo the sin of Adam, and, in himself, might restore Adam to the image of God.

---

17. See 2 Tm 1:12.
18. *Aliquod sacramentum.*
19. See Homily 9, 14 which Augustine recalls in more detail in the next section of this homily. He does not explicitly say that Adam is "the whole human race," but this is the inference to be drawn from the meaning of the letters of his name in Greek.
20. See the *Exposition of Psalm* 95, 15 for a fuller sense of this idea: "Adam was at first in a single place; he fell; and he was somehow fragmented until he filled the earth. But God's mercy collected the shattered pieces, forged them together in the fire of charity and made what was broken into a single whole once more."

So the flesh of Christ comes from Adam; so from Adam comes the temple which the Jews destroyed and which the Lord rebuilt on the third day. For he raised up his own flesh: notice that he was God, equal to the Father. My brothers and sisters, the apostle says, *The one who raised him from the dead.* About whom does he say it? About the Father: *Made obedient,* he says, *unto death, even death on a cross; which is why God also raised him up from the dead, and gave him the name which is above every name.* (Phil 2:8-9) The Lord was raised up and exalted. He raised him up. Who did? The Father, to whom he said in the psalms, *Raise me up, and I will repay them* (Ps 40:11). So then, the Father raised him up. Did he not raise himself up? What does the Father do without the Word? What does the Father do without his one and only Son? I mean, listen to how he too was God: *Pull down this temple, and in three days I will raise it up.* Did he ever say, "Pull down the temple for the Father to raise it up on the third day"? But just as when the Father raises up, the Son also raises up, so too when the Son raises up, the Father also raises up, because the Son said, *I and the Father are one* (Jn 10:30).

The meaning of the forty-six years expounded by looking at the name of Adam

12. What then is the meaning of the number forty-six? You already heard yesterday that, in four Greek letters in four Greek words, Adam is himself found throughout the whole world. You see, if you write these four words under each other, that is, write the names of the four corners of the world, East, West, North and South, which is the whole world (that is why the Lord says he is going to gather his elect from the four winds when he comes to judge[21]), if, therefore, you write these four names in Greek—*anatole,* which is East; *dusis,* which is West; *arktos,* which is North; *mesemthria,* which is South—the first letter of each word gives you "Adam."

So then, how do we also find there the number forty-six? It is because Christ's flesh derived from Adam. The Greeks use letters for numbers. Our letter a they call in their language *alpha,* and *alpha* is written for the number one; while where in counting they write *beta,* which is their b, it means the number two; when they write *gamma* it means for them the

---

21. See Mk 13:27.

number three; where they write *delta* it means for them the number four; and in this way they use all their letters for numbers. What we call m and they call *mu* represents forty. Now see what these letters add up to, and you will find the temple built in forty-six years. "Adam," you see consists of *alpha*, which is one; and of *delta*, which is four—so now you have five; *alpha* again, which is one, gives you six; and finally *mu*, which is forty—there you have forty-six.

All this, my brothers and sisters, has been said in previous times by our ancestors, and the number forty-six has been found by them in these letters.[22] And because our Lord Jesus Christ derived his body from Adam without contracting sin from Adam, he took from that source the temple of his body, not the iniquity which is to be driven from this temple. Now the Jews crucified the actual flesh which he contracted from Adam (Mary, after all, was from Adam, and the Lord's flesh from Mary); and he was going to raise up this very flesh, which they were about to slay on the cross, in three days time; they pulled down the temple built in forty-six years, and he raised it up in three days.

Conclusion: let us rejoice in hope of future happiness, not in present prosperity

13. We bless the Lord our God, who has gathered us together for rejoicing in spirit. Let us always be humble of heart, and let our joy always be in his presence.[23] Let us not be puffed up with any prosperity of this world, this age, but let us realize that our true happiness only comes when these things have passed away. Right now, my brothers and sisters, our joy must be in hope. No one should rejoice as if in present reality, or he may get stuck to the road. Let all our joy be in hope to come, all our desire on eternal life. With all our sighs let us be panting for Christ. May he, the one most beautiful, be the one we desire, he the one who loved the foul and ugly in order to make them beautiful; to him alone let us pant as we run, and *let us always say, May the Lord be glorified, we who desire the peace of his servant* (Ps 34:27).

---

22. The Maurists refer to a work, *On the Mountains of Sinai and Zion against the Jews*, attributed to Cyprian.
23. Augustine is echoing the opening words of the Magnificat, Lk 1:46-48.

Homily 11

On Jn 2:23-25; 3:1-5[1]

This gospel reading is appropriate for the Sunday on which catechumens should be enrolling for baptism at Easter

1. It is quite fitting that the Lord has arranged for us to have this reading on this day. As I am sure Your Graces will have noticed, we are examining and explaining the gospel according to John in sequence. So it was fitting that today you would hear from the gospel that *unless you are born again of water and the Spirit, you will not see the kingdom of God* (Jn 3:5). For it is the time for me to plead with those of you who are still catechumens, who have put your faith in Christ, but in such a way that you are still carrying your sins.[2] But no one will see the kingdom of heaven while burdened with sins, because unless they have been forgiven you, you will not reign with Christ, and they cannot be forgiven you unless you have been reborn of water and the Holy Spirit.

But let us pay attention to how all the words are connected, so that those who are reluctant may discover there how much concern they should have to lay aside the burden. Because if you were carrying some heavy load of stone or wood, or even of some profits, if they were carrying corn, or wine, or money, they would hurry as fast as possible to put their burdens down; they carry a load of sins, and they are too lazy to hurry. They should rush to put aside this load; it weighs heavy and makes one sink.

Why did Jesus not trust himself to his hearers?

2. Look, you have just heard that when the Lord Jesus Christ *was in Jerusalem at the Passover on the feast day, many believed in his name, seeing the signs that he was doing. Many believed*[3] *in his name;* and what follows? *But Jesus for his part did not trust himself to them.* (Jn 2:23-24) So what then does that mean—*they believed in his name,* and *Jesus did not*

---
1. Preached on Palm Sunday, April 7, 407.
2. Augustine is thinking of those who have been catechumens for several years, but who put off enrolling to be baptized.
3. *Crediderunt* means believing and trusting, as it does in Greek, depending upon the context.

trust himself to them? Perhaps they had not really put their trust in him and were just pretending they had, and that is why Jesus would not trust himself to them, is that it? But the evangelist would not say, *Many believed in his name,* unless the testimony he was giving them were true. So it is a serious and surprising matter: human beings put their faith in Christ, and Christ does not put his faith in human beings.

Above all, because he is the Son of God, he suffered willingly, and if he had not been willing, he would never have suffered. If he had not been willing, he would not even have been born; but if the only thing he had wanted was just to be born and that he would not die, whatever he wished he would do because he is the almighty Son of the almighty Father. Let us prove this from the facts themselves. When they had wanted to get hold of him, he withdrew from them—the gospel says, *And when they wanted to hurl him from the crest of the mountain, he withdrew from them unharmed* (Lk 4:29-30). And when they came to arrest him, already sold by Judas the traitor, who thought he had it in his power to betray his master and Lord, there too the Lord demonstrated that he would suffer of his own will, not bound by necessity. When the Jews wished to arrest him, you see, *he said to them, Whom do you seek? They then said, Jesus the Nazarene. And he said, I am he. On hearing this expression they turned away and fell down.* (Jn 18:4-6) In throwing them down by his answer, he showed his power, so that in letting himself be arrested by them he might demonstrate his will. So then, that he suffered was a matter of mercy; *for he was betrayed for our offences, and he rose again for our justification* (Rom 4:25). Listen to his own words: *I have the power to lay down my soul, and I have the power to take it up again. Nobody takes it from me, but it is I who lay it down of myself, so that I may take it up again.* (Jn 10:18)

Since then he had such power, since he proclaimed it in words and demonstrated it in deeds, what does it mean that Jesus did not trust himself to them, as if they were going to injure him against his will, or do something to him against his will, especially because they had already believed in his name? The evangelist says about these same people, *They believed in his name,* and goes on to say that *Jesus for his part did not trust himself to them.* Why not? *Because he himself knew them all, and because he did not need anyone to tell him anything about man; for he was well aware of what was in man* (Jn 2:24-25). The craftsman knew better what was in his work than that work knew what was in itself. Man's creator knew what was in man, which the man created by him did not know. We can use Peter to prove this, can we not, because he had no idea what was in him when he said, *With you even to death.* Listen to the Lord knowing what was in man: "You with me even to death? *Amen, amen I tell you, before the cock crows, you will deny me three times* (Lk 22:33-34)." So then, man was unaware of what was in himself, but man's creator knew very well what was in him.[4]

Nonetheless many believed in his name, and Jesus for his part would not trust himself to them. What are we to say, brothers and sisters? Perhaps what comes next will give us a hint of the meaning of these mysterious words. That people believed in him is plain, it is the truth; nobody doubts it, the gospel is speaking, the truthful evangelist attests it. Again, that Jesus for his part would not trust himself to them, this too is plain, and no Christian doubts it because this too is the gospel speaking and the same truthful evangelist attesting it. So why then did those people believe in his name, and why would Jesus not trust himself to those same people? Let us see what follows.

The solution of the problem provided by Nicodemus

3. *Now there was a man of the Pharisees, Nicodemus by name, a chief of the Jews; this one came to him at night, and said to him, Rabbi*—this is something you know already, that "rabbi" means "master"—*we are aware that you have come from God as a master; for nobody can do these signs which you are doing unless God is with him* (Jn 3:1-2). So Nicodemus then was one of those who had believed in his name, when they saw the signs and prodigies that he was performing. I mean, that is what it said earlier on: *Now when he was in Jerusalem at the Passover on the feast day, many believed in his name.* Why did they believe? It goes on to say, *seeing the signs that he was doing.* And about Nicodemus what does it say? *There was a chief of the Jews, by name Nicodemus; this one came to him at night, and said to him, Rabbi, we are aware that you have come from God as a master.* So this one too had believed in his name. And on what grounds had

---

4. A common theme in Augustine's preaching. See for example *Exposition of Psalms* 36, sermon 1; 41, 13; 43, 20; 55, 2; *Sermons* 137, 3; 181, 1; 284, 6; 285, 3.

he believed? It goes on: *for nobody after all can do these signs which you are doing unless God is with him.*

So if Nicodemus was one of those many who had believed in his name, let us now observe in this Nicodemus why Jesus was not trusting himself to them. *Jesus answered and said to him, Amen, amen, I tell you, unless one is born again, one cannot see the kingdom of God* (Jn 3:3). So then, the ones Jesus trusts himself to are the ones who have been born anew. Look; those people had believed in him, and Jesus was not trusting himself to them. That is what all catechumens are like; they already believe in the name of Christ, but Jesus does not trust himself to them. Would Your Graces please concentrate and try to understand. If we say to a catechumen, "Do you believe in Christ?" he replies, "I do believe," and signs himself. He is now carrying the cross of Christ on his forehead, and he is not ashamed of his Lord's cross. There you are, he has come to believe in his name. Let us question him further: "Do you eat the flesh of the Son of man, and drink the blood of the Son of man?" he does not know what we are talking about,[5] because Jesus has not trusted himself to him.

Comparison of the eucharist with manna;
the catechumens know about manna, not about the eucharist

4. So then, since Nicodemus was one of that number, he came to the Lord; but he came at night; this too may well be a relevant point. He comes to the Lord, and he comes at night; he comes to the light, and he comes in the dark. Those, however, who have been born again of water and the Spirit, what is it they hear from the apostle? *You were once darkness, but now light in the Lord; walk as children of the light* (Eph 5:8); and again: *We, however, who are of the day, let us be sober* (1 Thes 5:8). So then, those who have been reborn were once of the night and are now of the day; were once darkness and are now light. Jesus now trusts himself to them, and they

---

5. According to some, the *disciplina arcana* ("discipline of the secret") meant that catechumens were not told about the sacrament of the eucharist until they had been baptized. However, it more likely meant that, even if they knew some of the facts, they could not understand the mystery before having received it. In this context, therefore, Jesus has not yet entrusted himself to the catechumen; the catechumens do not understand. Instruction will be based on their experience of the eucharist once they have been baptized. See *Exposition of Psalms* 103, sermon 1, 14; 109, 17; Sermons 5, 7; 132, 1; 232, 7; 234, 2.

do not come to Jesus at night like Nicodemus, they do not go looking for the day in the dark. Such people, you see, are now also openly professing the faith; Jesus has stepped right up to them, has wrought salvation in them, because he said himself, *Unless you eat my flesh and drink my blood, you will not have life in you* (Jn 6:53).

Yes, the fact that catechumens have the sign of the cross on their foreheads means that they now belong to a great household; but let them, from being slaves, become sons.[6] They are not, after all, mere nothings, those who already belong to a great household. But when precisely did the people of Israel start eating manna? When they had crossed the Red Sea. As for what the Red Sea stands for, listen to the apostle: *But I would not have you ignorant, brothers and sisters, that all our ancestors were under the cloud, and all passed through the sea.* What did they pass through the sea for? As if you had asked him that, he goes on to say, *And all were baptized through Moses in the cloud and in the sea.* (1 Cor 10:1-2)

So then, if the sea as a prefiguration was so effective, how effective will the reality of baptism be! If what was carried out in a figurative way led the people, once they had been brought across the sea, to the manna as their food, what is Christ going to grant through the truth of baptism, once his people have made the crossing by him? Through baptism[7] he brings believers across after slaying all their sins which were pursuing them like enemies—just as all the Egyptians perished in that sea. What is he bringing them across to, my brothers and sisters? What is he bringing them across to through baptism, this Jesus whose part Moses was then playing, when he was bringing them across the sea? What is he bringing them across to? To manna. What is manna? *I am*, he says, *the living bread, who has come down from heaven* (Jn 6:51).

Manna is what the faithful receive, those who have already been brought across through the Red Sea. Why the Red Sea? Yes it is the sea all right, but why red? That Red Sea was representing Christ's baptism. What makes Christ's baptism red but its consecration by Christ's blood? So to what is he leading those who believe and have been baptized? To the manna. There you are, I say "manna"; it is common knowledge what the

---

6. See Gal 4:7. There are also echoes here of Mt 5:45 and Jn 15:15.
7. That is, Christ's baptism is distinct from John's baptism.

Jews received, that people of Israel, everyone knows what God rained on them from heaven—and the catechumens do not know what Christians receive! So let them blush red then, because they do not know; let them cross through the Red Sea, let them eat manna, in order that just as they have trusted in the name of Jesus, Jesus may entrust himself to them.[8]

We need God; God is in no need of our good things

5. That is why, my brothers and sisters, you must pay attention to the answer this man gave when he came to Jesus at night. Although he had indeed come to Jesus, all the same because he has come at night, he is still talking from the darkness of the flesh. He does not understand what he is hearing from the Lord, he does not understand what he is hearing from *the light who enlightens everyone coming into this world* (Jn 1:9). The Lord has already said to him, *Unless one is born again, one will not see the kingdom of God. Nicodemus says to him, How can a man be born when he is old?* (Jn 3:3-4) The Spirit talks to him, and he only has a taste for the flesh. He savors his own flesh, because he does not yet savor the flesh of Christ.

For, when the Lord Jesus said, *Unless you eat my flesh and drink my blood, you will not have life in you*, some of those who were following him were shocked and said to one another, *This is a hard saying; who can listen to him?* (Jn 6:60) They thought, you see, that what Jesus was saying was that they could carve him up, cook him like lamb and eat him. They were horrified by his words and went away and did not follow him any more. This is what the evangelist says, *And the Lord himself remained with the twelve, and these said to him, Look, Lord, they have left you. And he said to them, Do you also wish to go away?* (Jn 6:67) He wanted to demonstrate that they needed him, not that he needed them; lest someone might deter Christ by saying he would become a Christian—as if Christ would be more blessed if you become a Christian! It does you good to become a Christian, but if you do not, it does no harm to Christ. Listen to the way it is put in the psalm: *I said to the Lord, You are my God, since you have no need of my goods* (Ps 15:2). That is why *you are my God, since you have no need of my goods.*

---

8. See *Exposition of Psalm* 80, 8.

If you are without God, you will be less; if you are with God, God will not be greater. He is not made greater by you, but without him you are less. So grow up in him; do not step back as though that would make him less. You will be restored if you approach him, become weaker if you move away from him. He remains unscathed when you approach him, unscathed when you fall away.[9] So when he said to his disciples, *Do you also wish to go away?* Peter, that rock, speaking for them all, answered, *Lord, to whom shall we go? You have the words of eternal life.* (Jn 6:68) He had savored the Lord's flesh in his mouth. But then the Lord had explained the matter to them and said, *It is the Spirit that gives life,* after he had said, *Unless you eat my flesh and drink my blood, you will not have life in you*, lest they take it all in a fleshly sense. *It is the Spirit*, he says, *that gives life, while the flesh is of no avail; the words which I have spoken to you are spirit and life* (Jn 6:63).

Nicodemus knows only of birth from Adam

6. This Nicodemus, who had come to Jesus at night, did not have a taste for this spirit and this life. Jesus said to him, *Unless one is born again, one will not see the kingdom of God.* And he, still savoring his own flesh, with as yet no taste for the flesh of Christ in his mouth, said, *How can a man, when he is old, be born a second time? Can a man go back into his mother's womb and be born?* (Jn 3:4) This man knew of no birth but the one from Adam and Eve; he did not yet know about the one from God and the Church. He only knew of those parents who produce children for death, he did not know of those who produce them for life. He only knew parents who produce heirs; he did not know of those who, living for ever themselves, produce children who will remain with them for ever.

So then, while there are in fact two kinds of birth,[10] he only understood one of them. One is from the earth, the other from heaven; one is from the flesh, the other from the Spirit; one is from mortality, the other from eternity; one is from male and female, the other from God and Church. But both of these two are unique events, neither the one nor the other can be repeated. Nicodemus had a correct understanding of birth in the flesh; so you should understand birth in the Spirit just as Nicodemus understood

---

9. See *Exposition of Psalm* 65, 19.
10. On the two kinds of birth see Sermons 22, 10; 121, 4; 370, 2.

birth in the flesh. What did Nicodemus understand? *Can a man go back into his mother's womb and be born?* So, to whoever might invite you to be born spiritually a second time, respond as Nicodemus did, *Can a man go back into his mother's womb and be born*? I have already been born of Adam, Adam cannot father me again; I have already been born of Christ, Christ cannot once again give birth to me. Just as the womb cannot be repeated, so neither can baptism.[11]

A comparison initiated with the progeny of the patriarchs

7. Those who are born of the Catholic Church are born as it were of Sarah, are born of the free woman; while those who are born of heresy are born as it were of the slave-girl, but of the seed of Abraham.[12] Would Your Graces please note how great this mystery is.[13] God testifies and says, *I am the God of Abraham, and the God of Isaac, and the God of Jacob* (Ex 3:6). Were there no other patriarchs? Was not Noah before these, that holy man who alone of the whole human race was worthy to be delivered from the flood with his whole family, the man in whom, together with his sons, the Church was prefigured? Carried by the wood, they escape the flood.[14]

Then later on there are the great men we know of, commended to us by holy scripture; there is *Moses, the most faithful in all God's house* (Nm 12:7; Heb 3:5). And yet these three are named, as if they were the only ones who deserved well of God: *I am the God of Abraham, and the God of Isaac, and the God of Jacob; this is my name for ever* (Ex 3:15). A most significant mystery indeed! God is powerful, able to open both my mouth and your hearts, so that I may be able to state it as he has been pleased to reveal it, and you may be able to grasp it as you should.

---

11. Or: "just as one cannot re-enter the mother's womb, neither is it possible to re-enter the waters of baptism."
12. See Gn 16 for the story of Sarah and her maid Hagar, whom she gave to Abraham and who bore him Ishmael; and then look ahead to Gn 21:1-21 for the continuation, where Sarah gives birth to Isaac, and the relationship with Ishmael is described.
13. "Please note *quam magnum sacramentum*" is all that Augustine needed to say in Latin.
14. See Homily 2, 16: "Do not let go of the wood on which you can cross the sea."

The same continued; and the four kinds of human beings

8. So then, these patriarchs are three, Abraham, Isaac and Jacob. You already know that the sons of Jacob were twelve in number, and from them sprang the people of Israel, because Jacob himself was called Israel,[15] and the people of Israel consisted of twelve tribes, belonging to the twelve sons of Israel. Abraham, Isaac and Jacob and the people. Three fathers at the origin of the people; three fathers in whom the people was prefigured, both the first people and the present people. The Christian people, you see, were prefigured in the Jewish people. There in figure, here in truth; there in shadow, here in body;[16] as the apostle says, *Now these things happened to them in figure*—it is the voice of the apostle; *they were written*, says he, *for us, in whom the end of the ages has come* (1 Cor 10:11).

Let your mind now return to Abraham, Isaac and Jacob. With these three we find that free women bear children, slave-girls too bear children; we find there the offspring of free women, and also the offspring of slave-girls. The servant does not represent anything good: *Cast out the slave-girl*, it says, *and her son; for the son of the slave-girl shall not be the heir together with the son of the free woman* (Gal 4:30; Gn 21:10). The apostle recalls this word; and in these two sons of Abraham, the apostle says, the two covenants were prefigured, the old and the new.[17] To the old covenant belong the lovers of time-bound things, the lovers of the world; to the new covenant the lovers of eternal life. That is why that Jerusalem on earth was the shadow of the heavenly Jerusalem, the mother of us all, who is in heaven; these are also the words of the apostle.[18] And about this city, from which we are wandering exiles, you know a lot, you have already heard much.[19]

But there is something rather surprising which we find in these child-births, that is, in their offspring, in the progeny, namely, four kinds of

---

15. See Gn 32:28, on how Jacob's name was changed to Israel.
16. See Col 2:17.
17. See *Exposition of Psalm* 119, 7.
18. See Gal 4:25-26. See also *Exposition of Psalm* 86, 5 and Sermon 4,9, which dwell at length on the theme treated here.
19. Probably in {his sermons on the Gradual Psalms (119-133), *Exposition of Psalms* 119-133, the "Songs of Ascent," of pilgrims "going up to Jerusalem," which were given concurrently with the homilies on John.

human beings; in these four kinds of human beings the image of the future Christian people is made up, so that what was said about those three is not surprising: *I am the God of Abraham, and the God of Isaac, and the God of Jacob.* You see, among all Christians—your attention, please, brothers and sisters—either good ones are born of bad ones, or bad ones born of good ones, or good ones of good ones, or bad ones of bad ones. More than these four sorts you will not be able to find. I will repeat it again, take note of it, hold on to it; examine your hearts, do not be lazy; grasp it, so as not to be taken in: among all Christians there are four sorts. Either good ones are born of good ones, or bad ones are born of bad ones, or bad ones of good ones, or good ones of bad ones. I think that is plain enough.

Good ones are born of good ones, when both those who baptize are good, and those who are baptized believe rightly and are rightly counted among the members of Christ. Bad ones are born of bad ones, when both those who baptize are bad, and those who are baptized approach God with a divided heart and do not keep to the norms which they hear about in church, so that they may not be chaff there on its threshing-floor, but wheat.[20] How many of this sort there are, I mean, Your Graces know very well. Good ones are born of bad ones: sometimes an adulterer baptizes, and the one being baptized is justified.[21] Bad ones are born of good ones: sometimes those who are baptizing are holy; those being baptized refuse to keep to God's way.

New Testament examples of these four kinds

9. I think, brothers and sisters, that what I am saying is well known in the Church, and is proven in everyday examples; but let us look at these four classes in our forefathers, because they too had them. Good ones are born of good ones: Ananias baptized Paul.[22] What about bad ones being born of bad ones? The apostle mentions some preachers of the gospel who he says were not in the habit of proclaiming the gospel sincerely, but whom he tolerates in the Christian community, saying, *What then? Provided that in every way, whether in pretense or in truth, Christ is being proclaimed, and in this I rejoice* (Phil 1:18). Was he being spiteful, rejoicing in someone else's

---

20. See Lk 3:17.
21. See, e.g., Rom 5:1.
22. See Acts 9:18.

evil? On the contrary, it was because the truth was being preached by bad men, and Christ was being preached by the tongues of bad men; if they were baptizing any people like themselves, bad people were baptizing bad ones; if the ones they were baptizing were like what the Lord urges us to be when he says, *Do what they say, but do not do what they do* (Mt 23:3), bad ones were baptizing good ones. Good ones were baptizing bad ones, as in the case of Simon Magus being baptized by the holy Philip.[23]

So then, these four kinds are well known, my brothers and sisters. Look, I will repeat them yet again; hold onto them, count them, take note of them, shun the bad ones, hold onto the good ones. The good are born of the good when holy people are baptized by holy people; the bad are baptized by the bad when both the ones baptizing and the ones being baptized live wicked and godless lives; the good are baptized by the bad when the ones baptizing are bad and the ones being baptized are good; the bad are baptized by the good when the ones baptizing are good and the ones being baptized are bad.

The four kinds typified in the sons of the patriarchs

10. How do we find these four categories in those three names, *I am the God of Abraham, the God of Isaac, and the God of Jacob*? We take the slave-girls as standing for the bad and the free women for the good. Free women give birth to good sons—Sarah bore Isaac; slave-girls give birth to bad sons—Hagar bore Ishmael. In the case of Abraham alone, we have both the case of good ones coming from good ones and the case of bad ones coming from bad ones. Where were the bad ones through good ones represented? The free woman Rebekah was the wife of Isaac; read the story.[24] She gave birth to twins, one was good, the other bad. You have scripture saying openly, with the voice of God, *I have loved Jacob, while I have hated Esau* (Mal 1:2-3; Rom 9:13). These were the two that Rebekah bore, Jacob and Esau; one of them is chosen, the other rejected; one succeeds to the inheritance, the other is disinherited. God does not make his people from Esau, but he makes it from Jacob.

---

23. See Acts 8:13.
24. See Gn 25:21-24; 27:1-40.

There is one father but diversity in those conceived; one womb but diversity in those born. Was it not a free woman who bore Jacob, the same free woman that gave birth to Esau? They were wrestling in their mother's womb, and Rebekah was told, when they were wrestling there, *There are two peoples in your womb* (Gn 25:23). Two men, two peoples, a good people, a bad people; but still it was in one womb that they were wrestling. How many bad ones there are in the Church, and one womb is carrying them, until they are separated at the end! And the good shout against the bad, and the bad shout back against the good, and they are wrestling inside in the belly of the one mother. They will not always be together, will they? They end up coming to the light, the birth which is here being prefigured in this significant mystery is announced,[25] and then it will be seen how *I have loved Jacob, while I have hated Esau.*

How those born of slave-girls shared in the inheritance

11. So then, brothers and sisters, we have now found both the good born of the good, Isaac of the free woman; and the bad born of the bad, Ishmael of the slave-girl; and the bad of the good, Esau of Rebekah. Where shall we find the good born of the bad? There remains Jacob, so that with the three ancestors these four kinds which cover all cases may be duly illustrated. Jacob had free-born wives, he also had slave-girls; the free women give birth, the slave-girls too give birth, and what results is the twelve sons of Israel. If you run through them all to see whom they were born of, they were not all born of the free women, nor all of the slave-girls, but still they were all from the one seed. So what next then, my brothers and sisters? Did not those who were born of the slave-girls take possession of the promised land together with their brothers? We find there good sons of Jacob born of slave-girls and good sons of Jacob born of free women. Birth from the wombs of the slave-girls proved no disadvantage to them when they acknowledged the seed they sprang from in their father, and consequently held the kingdom with their brothers.

So then, just as among the sons of Jacob those who were born of slave-girls found this no obstacle to their holding the kingdom, and receiving the promised land on equal terms with their brothers—their

---

25. Again in *sacramento*. The end which this "sacramental" birth prefigures is the last judgment.

slave-girl origins were no disadvantage to them, being over-ridden by the seed of their father—in the same way, whoever happens to have been baptized by bad people, as though they were apparently born of slave-girls, still spring from the seed of the Word of God which is prefigured in Jacob. So they have no need whatever to be downcast; they will take possession of the inheritance together with their brothers.

So you then, being born of good seed, have nothing at all to worry about; just make sure that you do not imitate the slave-girl if you are born of a slave-girl. No, do not copy the slave-girl in her proudly preening herself. How was it, after all, that the sons of Jacob who were born of slave-girls took possession of the promised land with their brothers, while Ishmael, born of a slave-girl, was barred from the inheritance? Why was this so, if not because he was proud, they were humble? He pushed himself forward, and wanted to lead his brother astray by playing with him.

The significance, the sacrament, of Ishmael playing with Isaac and therefore being hated

12. There is a great mystery here.[26] Ishmael and Isaac were playing together; Sarah saw them playing, and said to Abraham, *Cast out the slave-girl and her son; for the son of the slave-girl shall not be the heir together with my son Isaac* (Gn 21:9-12). And when Abraham showed his distress at the idea, the Lord backed up his wife's demand. Already the mystery is beginning to show itself here, because this episode was laden with I-do-not-know-what future event. She saw them playing and says, *Cast out the slave-girl and her son*. What is this all about, brothers and sisters? What harm, I mean, was Ishmael doing to the child Isaac just by playing with him? But that playing was really mocking;[27] that playing signified deception. Would Your Graces please note the great mystery. The apostle calls it persecution; that playing, that game, he calls persecution. For what he says is this, *But just as at that time the one who was born according to the flesh used to persecute the one born according to the spirit, so also now* (Gal 4:29); that is, those who have been born according to the flesh persecute those who have been born according to the Spirit.

---

26. *Magnum ibi sacramentum.*
27. *Illa lusio illusio erat.* The English expression, "making fun of someone," can have a similar significance; and this is no doubt what Sarah "saw," Ishmael teasing the child.

Who are the ones born according to the flesh? Admirers of this world, lovers of this age. Who are the ones born according to the Spirit? Lovers of the kingdom of heaven, admirers of Christ who long for eternal life, worshiping God freely. They are playing together, and the apostle calls it persecution. After saying these words, you see, *And just as at that time the one who was born according to the flesh used to persecute the one born according to the Spirit, so also now*, he went on to show what kind of persecution he was talking about: *But what does scripture say? Cast out the slave-girl and her son; for the son of the slave-girl shall not be the heir together with my son Isaac* (Gal 4:30). We inquire where scripture says this, to see if there had been any previous persecution of Isaac by Ishmael, and we find it was said by Sarah, when she saw the boys playing together. The bit of play that scripture tells us was seen by Sarah is what the apostle calls persecution.

So then, those persecutors are more dangerous who seduce you by taunting you: "Come along, come and be baptized here; here you get true baptism."[28] Do not play along; there is one true baptism; that one is a game. You will be led astray, and this persecution will weigh heavily on you. It would be better for you if you could gain Ishmael for the kingdom; but Ishmael is not willing, because he wants to play. Hold onto the inheritance of your father and listen: *Cast out the slave-girl and her son; for the son of the slave-girl shall not be the heir together with my son Isaac.*

The Donatist claim that they were being persecuted

13. These people even have the nerve to say that they are quite used to suffering persecution from Catholic kings or Catholic rulers. What persecution do they endure? Physical suffering—but if they suffered at some point or suffered in some way, it is up to them to know and to examine their own consciences; still, they did suffer physically. Yet, the persecution they inflict is more serious. Be on your guard when Ishmael wants to play with Isaac, when he flatters you, when he offers you another baptism. Tell him, "I have already been baptized." I mean, if this baptism which *you* have received is genuine, anyone wishing to give you another seeks to deceive you. Watch out for the persecutor of the soul. In fact, if the Donatist party

---

28. The Donatists.

ever suffered anything from Catholic rulers, they have suffered in body, not by deceiving the spirit.

Listen and observe in the facts of ancient history[29] all the signs and indications of things to come. We find that Sarah made the slave-girl, Hagar, miserable. Sarah is a free woman; after the slave-girl began to grow proud, Sarah complained to Abraham, and said, "Cast out the slave-girl; she has grown haughty toward me"; and as if Abraham were responsible for it all, his wife complained to Abraham. Abraham, however, was not attached to the slave-girl by abusive lust, but merely to beget offspring, since Sarah had given her slave-girl to him for that purpose; he said to her, *Look, she is your maid; treat her as you wish* (Gn 16:6). And Sarah afflicted her sorely, and she ran away from her presence.

Look, the free woman makes the slave-girl miserable, and the apostle does not call that persecution; the slave plays with the master, and he calls it persecution. What is your opinion about that, brothers and sisters? Do you not understand what was signified? In the same way then, when God wishes to stir up the authorities against heretics, against schismatics, against the wreckers of the Church, against those who would blow Christ out of you,[30] against those who make a mockery of baptism, they have no business to be shocked, because this is God stirring up Sarah to give Hagar a beating. Let Hagar come to know herself, set aside her disdain, because when, humiliated, she ran away from her mistress, an angel met her and said, *What is the matter, Hagar, maid of Sarah*? and when she complained about her mistress, what did she hear from this angel? *Go back to your mistress.* (Gn 16:9) So that was what she was afflicted for, to get her to go back. And if only she would return, because then her offspring, like the sons of Jacob, will possess the inheritance with their brothers!

---

29. That is, literally, *in ipsis veteribus factis* ("in the old facts").
30. Augustine is alluding to the exorcism that is one of the preparatory rites of baptism; in that rite the minister breathes into the face of the catechumen to "puff the unclean spirit out of him." The Donatists, by baptizing those who had already been baptized in the Catholic Church, were blowing Christ out of the person, thus "making a mockery of (i.e., blaspheming) baptism" by their denial of the validity of Catholic baptism.

*Nebuchadnezzar's decree that anyone blaspheming
the God of Israel should be put to death*

14. Yet they are astonished at Christian authorities troubling themselves to act against the loathsome wreckers of the Church. So then, should they not be bothered? How in that case would they account to God for their use of authority? Would Your Graces please notice what I am saying, because it is the duty of Christian rulers of this age to ensure peace during their reign for their mother, the Church, of whom they have been born in spirit.

We have been reading the story of Daniel's visions and prophetic actions.[31] The three lads praised the Lord in the fire; King Nebuchadnezzar was amazed at the lads praising God, and the fire around them doing them no harm. And in his amazement what did King Nebuchadnezzar say, this man who was neither a Jew nor circumcised, the man who had set up the statue of himself and forced everyone to worship it? Shaken now by the praises sung by the three lads, on seeing the majesty of God present in the fire with them, what did he say? *And I myself will publish a decree to all tribes and tongues in the whole earth.* And what decree precisely? *Whoever shall utter blasphemy against the God of Shadrach, Meshach and Abednego shall be wiped out, and their houses consigned to perdition.* (Dan 3:29)

There you are, notice what severe measures a foreign king took against anyone blaspheming the God of Israel, because he was able to deliver the three lads from the fire; and these people object to Christian rulers reacting with severity against those who would blow Christ out of you, Christ by whom not just three lads but the whole world with its rulers is being delivered from the fires of Gehenna! For these three lads, my brothers and sisters, were delivered from a fire of this age. Can it be that the God of these three lads is not also the God of the Maccabees? He delivered the former from the fire, while the latter perished physically under fiery tortures, but remained steadfastly loyal in spirit to the commandments of the law.[32] The former were openly delivered, while the latter were awarded victors' crowns in secret. It is more important to be delivered from the flames of Gehenna than from the furnace of a human potentate.

---

31. See Dan 3.
32. See 2 M 7.

So then, if King Nebuchadnezzar praised and proclaimed God and gave him honor and glory, because he delivered the three lads from the fire, and, what is more, gave him such honor as to send out a decree throughout his kingdom, *Whoever shall utter blasphemy against the God of Shadrach, Meshach and Abednego shall be wiped out, and their houses consigned to perdition,* how can these rulers today fail to be stirred, rulers who observe not three lads delivered from flames but themselves delivered from Gehenna, when they see the Christ who so delivered them being blown out of Christians, when they hear of a Christian being told, "Say that you are not a Christian"? These people are prepared to do such things as that, but are not prepared to suffer punishments such as these.

*No comparison between the harm the Donatists do and
the penalties they suffer at the hands of the law*

15. Look, in fact, at what they do and at what they suffer. They kill souls, they are afflicted in the body; they bring about everlasting deaths, and they complain of suffering temporal ones. And yet what forms of death do they suffer? They talk to us about I-do-not-know-which of their martyrs through persecution. "Look, Marculus was hurled down from a crag! Look, Donatus of Bagai was thrown into a pit!"[33] When did the Roman authorities ever decree such punishments as having men thrown off cliffs? What answer, though, do our folk make? What actually happened I do not know; but what have our people told us? That these two jumped to their deaths of their own accord, and they blamed the authorities for it.

Let us call to mind how Roman authorities normally act and see who is to be believed. Our people say they jumped off the cliff; if, nowadays, those who jump off cliffs without anyone persecuting them are not their disciples, let us not believe them. What is surprising at seeing them doing what they usually do? For Roman authorities never practiced such punishments. After all, why not put them to death openly? But men who wanted

---

33. Two of the most popular of the Donatist "martyrs" who suffered under the anti-Donatist laws of the Emperor Constantius in 347. Donatus of Bagai made that Numidian town a center of armed resistance against the imperial commissioner Macarius; he was either killed in battle or executed after it on the commissioner's orders. Marculus was the leading member of a Donatist delegation to Macarius to protest against the measures he was taking, and did so with such violence and insolence that he too was put to death a few months later.

to be worshiped when they were dead could not find a form of death that would more surely win them fame. Finally, whatever the case may be, I myself do not know. And even if you have suffered bodily affliction, O party of Donatists, at the hands of the Catholic Church, you are Hagar suffering at the hands of Sarah; *return to your mistress.*

This important text[34] has kept us a little too long for me to be able to deal with the whole gospel passage. Brothers and sisters, let that suffice Your Graces for the time being, lest what has already been said be pushed out of your hearts by saying more. Hold on to this, talk about it, go out on fire with zeal, inflame those who are indifferent.

---

34. I.e., the text about Sarah and Hagar.

Homily 12

On Jn 3:6-21[1]

About spiritual rebirth

1. I gather that, because I held your attention yesterday, you have now assembled with more eagerness and in greater numbers than usual. But first of all, if you do not mind, let me give you the sermon I owe you on the gospel passage that, in proper order, has been read; then Your Graces will hear about what we have done or what we are still hoping to do about the peace of the Church.[2]

So now, please give the whole attention of your heart to the gospel; let no one's thoughts wander off. I mean, if the one who gives his whole mind to it barely understands, will not the one who lets his mind wander through various thoughts let the little he has grasped get away from him? Now Your Graces will remember that last Sunday, to the extent that the Lord was pleased to assist me, I dealt with spiritual rebirth; and I have had that reading read to you again, so that in Christ's name and with the help of your prayers I may finish what there was not time to deal with then.[3]

Only one spiritual birth, as there is only one birth in the flesh

2. There is only one spiritual rebirth, just as there is only one birth in the flesh. And what Nicodemus said to the Lord was true, that a man, when he is old, cannot go back into his mother's womb and be born. He did indeed say that a man cannot do this when he is old—as though he could do it if he were a baby! In fact, it is impossible for anyone, whether he has just emerged from the womb or has reached a ripe old age, to go back inside his mother's womb and be born. But just as a woman's womb is only intended to give birth once by physical birth, so too the Church's womb is intended to baptize once by spiritual birth.

---

1. Preached on the Tuesday of Holy Week, April 9, 407.
2. In his *Exposition of Psalms* 132 and 133 of the previous day, Augustine spoke of the attacks of Donatist Circumcellions on Catholic monasteries, indicating that he would tell the people what was being done by the bishops for the peace of the Church.
3. See Homily 11, 6.

That is why, so that no one might say, "But this person was born in heresy and that one was born in schism," all such difficulties were excluded, if you remember, by what was discussed with you about our three ancestors of whom God said that he wanted to be called their God,[4] not because he was God of them alone, but because in them alone was the future people as a whole to be fully represented. For we found that a son born of a slave-girl was disinherited, while one born of a free woman was the heir; again we found one born of a free woman disinherited, one born of a slave-girl being the heir. Ishmael born of a slave-girl was disinherited, Isaac born of a free woman was the heir; Esau, born of a free woman was disinherited, those sons of Jacob who were born of slave-girls were heirs. And so in those three ancestors the whole image of the people to come was observed; with good reason did God say, *I am the God of Abraham, and the God of Isaac, and the God of Jacob; this,* he adds, *is my name for ever* (Ex 3:6.15).

More than just that, let us remember what Abraham was promised; the promise, in fact, was also made to Isaac, also made to Jacob. What did we find? *In your seed shall all the nations be blessed* (Gn 22:18; 27:28-29; 35:9-12). At that time, one man believed what he could not yet see; nowadays people see, and their eyes are blinded. What was promised to one man has been fulfilled in the nations, and those who refuse to see even what has been fulfilled separate themselves from the fellowship of the nations. But how does their refusal to see help them? Like it or not, they do see; manifest truth even strikes closed eyes.

The catechumens urged to enroll for baptism

3. An answer was given to Nicodemus, who was one of those who had believed in Jesus, and Jesus for his part was not trusting himself to them. For there were some to whom he would not trust himself, even though they had already believed in him; as it is written: *Many believed in his name, seeing the signs that he was doing. But Jesus for his part did not trust himself to them. For he did not need anyone to tell him anything about man; for he was well aware of what was in man.* (Jn 2:23-25) See, they already

---

4. See Ex 3:15-16 for the story about those born of free women or of slave-girls (Homily 11, 7-8).

believed in Jesus, and Jesus did not trust himself to them. Why not? Because they had not yet been reborn of water and the Spirit.

Hence, I urged and still urge our brothers and sisters the catechumens. For, if you question them, they have already believed in Jesus; but because they do not yet receive his body and blood, Jesus has not yet trusted himself to them. What must they do for Jesus to trust himself to them? Let them be reborn of water and the Spirit; let the Church make known those to whom she has given birth. They have been conceived, let them be brought forth into the light;[5] there are breasts to suckle them, they need have no fear of being suffocated when they are born; let them not withdraw from the maternal breasts.

Comparison with the descendants of Abraham, some born of free women, some of slave-girls

4. No man can go back inside his mother and be born a second time. But someone has been born of a slave-girl. In that time, did those who were born of slave-girls go back into the wombs of the free women to be born again? Abraham's seed was also in Ishmael, and his wife arranged for Abraham to have a son by the slave-girl. Ishmael was born of the seed of the husband and only because of his wife's consent, not from her womb. Was his being born of the slave-girl the reason for his being disinherited? If his birth from the slave-girl was the reason for his being disinherited, then none of the sons of slave-girls would be admitted to the inheritance. The sons of Jacob were admitted to the inheritance; but Ishmael was disinherited, not because he was born of the slave-girl, but because he acted proudly toward his mother and toward his mother's son. His mother, you see, was Sarah rather than Hagar. Hagar lent her womb, Sarah added her consent. Abraham would not do anything Sarah did not want. So then, Ishmael was Sarah's son more than Hagar's.

But because he behaved with pride toward his brother, and he was proud by playing with him because he made fun of him, what did Sarah say? *Cast out the slave-girl and her son; for the son of the slave-girl shall not be the heir together with my son Isaac* (Gn 21:10). So then, it was not the

---

5. See Sermon 260C, 1 to the newly baptized, where those who have remained in the catechumenate for a time are urged to change their condition, i.e., to stop being fetuses and become live babies.

slave-girl's womb that had him thrown out, but his servile pride. Although someone who is proud may be free, he is a slave, and, what is worse, he is the slave of a bad master, of pride itself.

And so, my brothers and sisters, respond to people[6] that no one can be born again; answer without a qualm that it is not possible for someone to be born again. Anything that happens a second time is an illusion; anything happening a second time is a game. Ishmael is playing, let him be thrown out. Sarah, you see, noticed them playing, so scripture tells us, and said to Abraham, *Cast out the slave-girl and her son.* Sarah was not pleased with the game the boys were playing; she saw the boys playing something new. To see their sons playing, is this not what women who have sons really want to see? She saw it and took exception to it. I do not know what she saw in the game; she saw the teasing in that game, she noticed the slave boy's pride; she did not like it, she threw him out.

Those born of slave-girls, who are shameless, are thrown out; the one born of a free woman, Esau, is thrown out as well. So nobody should be presumptuous when born of good parents, nobody should be presumptuous when baptized by holy men. Those baptized by holy men should take care lest they turn out, not like Jacob, but rather like Esau. So then, brothers and sisters, I would say: it would be better to be baptized by people who seek their own advantage[7] and love the world (which is what the name of slave-girl stands for), and to seek the inheritance of Christ in a spiritual frame of mind (which is like being a son of Jacob by a slave-girl), than to be baptized by holy people and remain proud, which is being like Esau, who, even though born of a free woman, was fit only to be thrown out.

Hold on to this teaching, brothers and sisters. I am not just pleasing you; your hope is not in me at all. I am not fooling either myself or you; each of us carries his own burden. Mine is to speak, in order not to come under judgment; yours is to listen, and to listen from the heart, in order not to have what I am giving you demanded of you—or rather, when it is demanded of you, to find that it is to your benefit, not to your loss.

---

6. See section 2 above where Augustine was asked: "What about those who were baptized in heresy or in schism?"
7. See Phil 2:21.

Conversation with Nicodemus

5. The Lord says to Nicodemus and explains to him, *Amen, amen, I tell you, unless one is born again of water and the Spirit, one cannot enter into the kingdom of God.* You are thinking, he says, of child-birth in the flesh when you say, *Can a man go back into his mother's womb?* (Jn 3:5.4) For the sake of the kingdom of God, he has to be born of water and the Spirit. If someone is born for the sake of an earthly inheritance from a human father, he has to be born of the physical womb of a mother; but if he is born for the sake of an everlasting inheritance from a father who is God, he must be born of the womb of the Church. A father who will die bears a son to succeed him by his wife; God bears sons by the Church, not to succeed him, but to remain with him.

And he continues, *What is born of the flesh is flesh, and what is born of the Spirit is spirit.* So then, we are born spiritually, and we are born in the Spirit by word and sacrament. The Spirit is present, so that we may be born; the Spirit, of whom you are born, is invisibly present because you are also born invisibly. For he goes on to say, *Do not be surprised at my saying to you, It is necessary for you to be born again; the Spirit breathes where he will, and you hear his voice, but you are unaware of where he is coming from or where he is going.* Nobody can see the Spirit; how are we to hear his voice? A psalm is sung, it is the voice of the Spirit; the gospel is read, it is the voice of the Spirit; the divine word is read, it is the voice of the Spirit. *You hear his voice, and you are unaware of where he is coming from and where he is going.* But if you also are born of the Spirit, the same will apply to you; as a result, anyone not yet born of the Spirit will not know where you come from and where you are going. That, you see, is what he went on to say, *Such is everyone who has been born of the Spirit.* (Jn 3:6-8)

New birth requires humility

6. *Nicodemus answered, saying to him, How can these things happen?* And indeed, still thinking in terms of flesh, he was in no position to understand. What the Lord had just said was happening with him; he heard the voice of the Spirit and was unaware of where it came from and where it was going. Jesus answered and said to him, *You, a master in Israel, and you do not know these things?* (Jn 3:9) Well what about that, brothers and sisters?

Are we to suppose that the Lord deliberately meant to insult this master of the Jews? The Lord knew what he was doing; he wanted him to be born of the Spirit. Nobody can be born of the Spirit without being humble, because humility is what brings us to birth by the Spirit; because *the Lord is close to those whose hearts are bruised* (Ps 33:19). This master was puffed up, and he saw himself as a person of some consequence because he was a teacher of the Jews; the Lord strips him of his pride, so that he can be born of the Spirit; he treats him as ignorant, but not because he wants to seem to be above him. What is so great about God winning over a man, about Truth beating a lie? Should Christ, can Christ, be said to be greater than Nicodemus? Is that what should be thought about? It would be laughable to say he is greater than the angels; after all, there is simply no comparison in greatness between any created thing and the one through whom everything in creation was made. But he is assailing the man's pride: *You, a master in Israel, and you do not know these things?* As if to say: "Look, you do not know anything, proud leader; be born of the Spirit." For, if you are born of the Spirit, you will keep to God's paths, so as to follow Christ's humility.

What puts him high above all the angels, you see, is that *though he was in the form of God, he did not regard equality with God something to be grasped at; but he emptied himself, taking the form of a slave, being made in the likeness of men; and being found in condition as a man, he humbled himself, becoming obedient to death* (and lest you imagine a pleasing kind of death), *to death on the cross* (Phil 2:6-8). He was hanging there, and they insulted him. He could have come down from the cross, but he waited so that he might rise up from the tomb. The Lord put up with proud slaves, the doctor with arrogant patients. If he, true master in heaven, not of human beings only but of angels too—if he was like that, what should those who need to be born of the Spirit be like? If angels have been taught, after all, they have been taught by the Word of God. If they have been taught by the Word of God, inquire more closely where their teaching comes from, and you will find that *in the beginning was the Word, and the Word was with God, and the Word was God* (Jn 1:1). Man is relieved of his stiff, hard neck, to have it replaced with a neck gentle enough to bear the yoke of Christ, of which he says himself, *My yoke is easy, and my burden is light* (Mt 11:30).

The things of earth Jesus has spoken of; the reference is to the temple of his body

7. And he continues,[8] *If I have spoken to you about things of the earth and you do not believe, how will you believe if I speak to you about the things of heaven?* (Jn 3:12) What things of the earth has he spoken about, brothers and sisters? *Unless one is born again,* is that a thing of the earth? *The Spirit breathes where he will, and you hear his voice, and you are unaware of where he is coming from and where he is going,* is that an earthly thing? I mean, if he said it about ordinary wind, as some people have understood it,[9] when they were questioned about what thing of the earth the Lord meant when he said, *If I have spoken to you about things of the earth, and you do not believe, how will you believe if I speak about things of heaven?*

So when some people were asked what *things of earth* the Lord meant, they found themselves in a jam, and responded that he was talking about the ordinary wind when he said, *The Spirit breathes where he will, and you hear his voice, and you are unaware of where he is coming from and where he is going.* What then did he call *a thing of earth* here? He was talking about spiritual birth; for he went on to say, *Such is everyone who is born of the Spirit.* Brothers and sisters, which of us does not see, for example, Auster coming from the south toward Aquilo,[10] or another wind coming from the east toward the west? So how is it that we do not know where it is coming from and where it is going?

What, therefore, did he mean by *a thing of earth,* which people were not believing? Could it be what he said about raising up the temple? For he had received his body from the earth; and he was getting ready to raise up that very earth which he received from an earthen body. They did not believe the one who was in fact going to raise up that earth. *If I have spoken to you,* he said, *about things of earth and you do not believe, how will you believe if I speak about things of heaven?* that is, "If you do not believe I can raise up the temple that you destroyed, how will you believe that human beings can be reborn through the Spirit?"

---

8. Augustine does not comment on Jn 3:11.
9. Augustine is following earlier writers like Ignatius of Antioch and Origen, and, more immediately, Ambrose, whom he may have heard preaching on the text when he was a catechumen in Milan.
10. Two proper names in Latin for the south wind and the north wind.

*Only those born again of water and the Spirit can ascend
into heaven with the Son of man*

8. And he goes on, *And no one has ascended into heaven but the one who came down from heaven, the Son of Man who is in heaven* (Jn 3:13). There you are, he was here and he was in heaven, he was here in the flesh, he was in heaven in his divinity[11]—or rather, everywhere in his divinity. Born of a mother without departing from his Father. Two births of Christ are thus recognized, one divine, the other human; one through which we would be fashioned, the other by which we would be refashioned; both wonderful; that one without a mother, this one without a father. But because he had received his body from Adam (since Mary came from Adam) and was going to raise that very body, he spoke of that earthly reality, saying, *Destroy this temple and in three days I will raise it up* (Jn 2:19). But he spoke of a heavenly reality, saying, *unless one is born again of water and the Spirit, one will not see the kingdom of God.*

Yes, brothers and sisters; God wanted to be a son of man, and he wanted men to be sons of God! He descended because of us; let us for our part ascend because of him. For, only the one who said, *Nobody has ascended into heaven but the one who came down from heaven,* came down and ascended. So then, are not those he makes sons of God going to ascend into heaven? They certainly will ascend; this is what we have been promised: *They shall be the equals of the angels of God* (Lk 20:36). So how is it that nobody ascends except the one who came down, because just one came down and just one ascended? What about the rest? What else could that mean, except that, since they will be his members, he ascends as one man? That is why he concludes, *No one has ascended into heaven but the one who came down from heaven, the Son of Man who is in heaven.* Does it astonish you that he was both here and in heaven? He put his disciples in the same position. Listen to the apostle Paul saying, *The company we keep is in heaven* (Phil 3:20). If the man Paul the apostle was walking about in the flesh on earth and was keeping company in heaven, was the God of heaven and earth unable to be both in heaven and earth at the same time?

---

11. See Sermon 294, 9, where Augustine quotes this text in support of the unity of the divine and human natures in the one person of Christ.

Our being one in and with Christ the seed of Abraham

9. So if he is the only one who came down and ascended, what hope is there for the rest of us? The hope of the rest is that he came down so that those who were to ascend through him might be one person in him and with him. Scripture, affirms the apostle, does not say, *and to your descendents, as though meaning many; but as referring to one; and to your descendance, which is Christ* (Gal 3:16). And to the faithful he says, *But you are Christ's; and if Christ's, you are therefore the descendance of Abraham* (Gal 3:29). He thus says that we are all the descendance which he called *one*. That is why, at times, many are singing in the psalms: to show that one is being made out of many. At times only one sings to show just what is being made out of many.[12] That is also why one man was healed in that pool, and no one else who went down into it was healed.[13] So this one man commends the unity of the Church.

Woe to those who hate the Unity,[14] and make factions among men! If only they would listen to the one who wanted to make them one in one man for one man! Let them listen to him saying, *Do not make yourselves into many factions; I planted, Apollos watered, but God made it all grow; neither the one who plants nor the one who waters is anything, but only God who makes it all grow.* They were saying, *I belong to Paul, I to Apollos, I to Cephas.* And he said, *Has Christ been divided up?* (1 Cor 3:6-7; 1:12-13) Be in the one, be one thing, be one person. *Nobody has ascended into heaven but the one who came down from heaven* (Jn 3:13). "Look, we want to belong to you," they were saying to Paul. And he answered, "Do not belong to Paul but belong to the one to whom Paul belongs together with you."

Cut down by death, Christ cut death down

10. He came down and died, and by that death he set us free from death; cut down by death, he cut death down. And as you know, brothers and sisters, this death entered the world through the jealousy of the devil. *God*

---

12. See *Exposition of Psalm* 123, 1. Since Augustine says "in the psalms," he is saying that the singer is sometimes one, sometimes many. In the psalms, David, the type of Christ par exellence, sometimes sings in the first person singular, sometimes in the first person plural.
13. See Jn 5:2-9.
14. One of Augustine's names for the Catholic Church.

did not make death—scripture is talking; *nor does he delight*, it says, *in the destruction of the living, for he created all things that they might be*. But what does it say in that book? *But by the jealousy of the devil death entered the whole wide world.* (Wis 1:13-14; 2:24) Man was not dragged to it by force when he came to the death poured out for him by the devil; for the devil had no power of compulsion, only the cunning of persuasion. If you had not consented, the devil would have brought nothing on you; your own consent, O man, swept you down to death. Born from one who is mortal, we are mortal; from being immortal we have become mortal. From Adam all human beings are mortal; but Jesus—Son of God, Word of God through which all things were made, the only Son, equal to the Father—became a mortal, for *the Word became flesh and took up residence among us* (Jn 1:14).

Comparison of Christ with the brazen serpent

11. So then, he accepted death, and hung death on the cross, and from that death mortals are set free. What was enacted in figure among the people of old, the Lord recalls: *And just as Moses*, he says, *lifted up the serpent in the desert, so must the Son of man be lifted up, so that everyone who believes in him may not perish, but may have eternal life* (Jn 3:14). A great mystery![15] Those who have read about this event know what he is talking about. Even those who have not read about it, or who have forgotten what perhaps they once read or heard, should listen.

The people of Israel were brought down in the desert by the bites of serpents,[16] heaps of dead bodies; for the strike was from God, chastising and scourging, so as to teach them. A great mystery about what was to come was enacted there; the Lord himself says as much in this reading, so nobody can give any interpretation other than what Truth points out about himself. Moses, you see, was told by the Lord to make a brazen serpent and lift it up on a pole in the desert, and to advise the people that anyone bitten by a serpent should gaze at that serpent lifted up on the pole. It was done; people were bitten, they gazed, they were healed.

---

15. *Magnum sacramentum.*
16. See Num 21:5-9.

What are the biting serpents? Sins coming from the mortality of the flesh. What is the serpent lifted up on the pole? The Lord's death on the cross. For, since death came from a serpent,[17] it was represented by the figure of a serpent. The serpent's bite is lethal, the Lord's death is life-giving. The serpent is gazed upon, so that the serpent may lose its power. What does that mean? Death is gazed upon so that death may lose its power. But whose death? The death of life, if one can talk about the death of life—or rather, because one can talk about it, such an expression[18] is remarkable. But should not one say what was to be done? Should I hesitate to talk about what the Lord was good enough to do for me? Is not Christ life? And yet Christ was on the cross. Is not Christ life? And yet Christ died. But, in the death of Christ, death died, because life slew death, the fullness of life swallowed death, death was devoured in the body of Christ.

That is what we too shall talk about in the resurrection, when, triumphant, we shall sing, *Where, Death, is your struggle? Where, Death, is your sting?* (Hos 13:14; 1 Cor 15:55) Meanwhile, brothers and sisters, to be healed of sin let us gaze upon Christ crucified, because *just as Moses*, he said, *lifted up the serpent in the desert, so must the Son of man be lifted up, so that everyone who believes in him may not perish, but may have eternal life*. Just as those who gazed on that serpent did not die because of the serpent's bite, so those who gaze in faith on the death of Christ are healed of the bite of sins. They were preserved from death for a life in time, but Christ says *that they might have eternal life*. This, you see, is the difference between that representative image and the real thing; that image bestowed time-bound life; the reality it represented bestows eternal life.

God sent his Son into the world to save it, not to judge it

12. *For God did not send his Son into the world to judge the world, but so that the world might be saved through him* (Jn 3:17). So then, as far as the doctor is concerned, he came to cure the patient. The one who refuses to follow the doctor's prescriptions kills himself. He came as Savior to the world; why was he called Savior of the world, if not because he came to

---

17. Here the reference is to the serpent in paradise, not just to these serpents in the desert.
18. See Jn 14:6, Jesus' answer to Thomas' question, *Lord, we do not know where you are going; how can we know the way? I am the way, the truth and the life.* Augustine now introduces the third title.

save the world, not to judge the world? You do not want to be saved by him? Then, you will be judged by yourself. And why am I saying, "You will be judged"? Notice what he says: *The one who believes in him is not judged; but the one who does not believe*—what are you expecting him to say but "will be judged"?—*has already*, says he, *been judged.* Judgment has not happened yet, but judgment has already been made. *The Lord*, you see, *knows who are his*, he knows who will endure to the crown, who will remain for the flames. He knows the wheat on his threshing floor and knows the chaff; he knows the crop and knows the weeds.[19] Why say "has been judged"? *Because he has not believed in the name of the only-begotten Son of God.* (Jn 3:18)

On doing the truth, and coming to the Light

13. *This, however, is what judgment is, because the Light came into the world, and people loved darkness more than the Light; for their works were evil* (Jn 3:19). My brothers and sisters, whose works did the Lord ever find to be good? No one's; he found everyone's works bad. So how then did some people do the truth and come to the Light? That, you see, is what comes next:[20] *But the one who does the truth comes to the Light, so that his works may be clearly shown to have been done in God* (Jn 3:21). How did some people do good work so as to come to the Light, that is to Christ, and how did others love darkness? I mean, if he found all to be sinners and cures all of sin, and if that serpent by which the Lord's death was represented cures those who had been bitten; and if the serpent was lifted up on account of the bite of the serpent, that is, if the Lord's death was lifted up on behalf of mortal human beings, whom he found to be unjust, then how is this text to be understood: *This is what judgment is, because the Light came into the world, and men loved darkness more than the Light; for their works were evil?*

What does this mean? Whose works, after all, were good? Did you not come precisely to justify the godless?[21] But *they loved darkness*, he says, *more than the Light.* That is the point, for many people loved their sins, many confessed their sins; because the one who confesses his sins and

---
19. See Mt 3:12; 13:24-30.
20. John 3:20 is passed over without comment.
21. See Rom 4:5.

accuses himself of his sins does it together with God. God accuses your sins; if you also accuse yourself, you join yourself to God. There are, so to say, two things: a human being and a sinner; you hear "human being," God made that being; you hear "sinner," the human being made the sinner. Eliminate what you have made, so that God may save what he has made.

You have to hate the word you have done in yourself and love the work God has done in you. When you have started to be displeased by what you have done, that is when your good works begin, because you have found fault with your bad works. The beginning of good works is the confession of bad works. You then are doing the truth and coming to the Light. What does "you are doing the truth" mean? You do not flatter yourself, you do not fool yourself, you do not praise yourself. You do not say, "I am just," when in fact your behavior is iniquitous—then you begin to do the truth. But you come to the light so that your works can be seen as having been done in God. Because, even in being displeased with your sin, that would not displease you unless God had shed his light upon you, unless his Truth had showed it to you.

But the one who prefers his sins even after he has been warned hates the light that warns him and runs from it so that the evil works which he loves will not be criticized. The one who does the truth, on the other hand, finds fault with his own evil deeds; he does not go easy on himself, does not pardon himself so that God may pardon him; because he acknowledges what he wants God to forgive, and he comes to the Light, whom he thanks for showing him what he should hate in himself. He says to God, *Turn your face away from my sins* (Ps 50:11); and with what nerve he would be saying it, unless he added, *since I myself well know my offense, and my sin is always in my presence* (Ps 50:5)! You should notice the sin that you do not want God to notice.[22] But if you place your sin behind your back, God will throw it back in front of your eyes, and he will do that when there is no more time for repentance to bear fruit.

---

22. Since the psalm verse describes sin as *coram me*, "in front of me," Augustine contrasts sin that is in front of or behind the person or God. "In front of" is here translated as "noticing." Literally, however, it is: "Let that be in front of you which you do not want to be in front of God."

The importance of continuing to confess little sins,
after having been forgiven the big ones

14. Run, my brothers and sisters, so that the darkness does not overtake you. Wake up to your salvation, awake while there is time. No one must stay away from the temple of God, no one delay from the work of God, no one be turned away from continuous prayer or be cheated out of his customary devotion. Stay awake then while it is still day; the day is bright, Christ is the day. He is ready to forgive, at least those who acknowledge their sins, punishing those who defend themselves and boast of being just and think they are something, when in fact they are nothing. As for those who are walking in his love and his mercy, even freed from lethal, great sins, from crimes like murder, theft, adultery, they do the truth by confessing those seemingly trifling matters, like sins of the tongue or of thought, like immoderate use of things that are permitted, and they come to the Light in good works. In fact, if many small sins are neglected, they kill.

Indeed, the raindrops that fill rivers are small, the grains of sand are small; but if a big basket of sand is placed on your shoulders, it weighs you down and crushes you. This is what bilge water does, what breaking waves do when neglected; they seep bit by bit into the bilges; seeping in over time and not pumped out, they sink the ship. But how does one pump out your bilges, except by ensuring through good works that sins do not overwhelm you: by sighing and groaning, by fasting, by being generous, and by forgiving?

The journey through this world is complicated, full of trials; when things go well, be not proud, nor let your spirit be broken when things go badly. The one who has given you some of the happiness in this age has given it to console you; likewise, the one who lashes you in this age does it for your correction, not for your damnation. Bear with your father teaching you so as not to experience a punishing judge. I say this kind of thing to you every day, and it has to be said frequently, because it is a genuine help to your salvation.

Homily 13

On John 3:22-29[1]

A glance back at the preceding homilies

1. Our course in the consecutive reading of the gospel according to John, as those of you can recall who are serious about your progress in understanding,[2] requires us to discuss the passage that has just been read. You will remember that the things said from the beginning as far as today's reading have already been dealt with. Even if you may have forgotten much of it, at least the task I have undertaken has not slipped your memories. What you just heard about the baptism of John,[3] even if you have not retained all of it, I am sure that you heard what you should hold on to—even what has been said about why the Holy Spirit appeared in the form of a dove,[4] and how that knottiest of problems was solved: what was it that John did not know about the Lord, which he learned through the dove?[5] For while John already knew the Lord, saying to him when he came to be baptized, *It is I who ought to be baptized by you, and are you coming to me?* the Lord answered him, *Let it be so now, so that all justice may be fulfilled.* (Mt 3:14-15)

Christ's divinity not explicitly stated, only implied by earlier testimonies

2. So then, our consecutive reading of the gospel now obliges us to go back to this same John. He is the one who was predicted by Isaiah: *A voice of one crying out in the desert, Prepare a road for the Lord, straighten out his paths* (Is 40:3). Such was the witness he bore to his Lord and—because Jesus wanted it—his friend; and this same Lord and friend bore witness to

---

1. Preached soon after Ascension Day, 407, which fell on May 23 that year. The next three homilies were preached before Augustine set out for the eleventh Council of Carthage, which opened on June 13, 407.
2. But they needed to remind themselves of it, because it was just over seven weeks since he had preached Homily 12, on the Tuesday of Holy Week, and the weeks of Eastertime had been taken up with homilies on the First Epistle of John.
3. That is, the passage from the gospel that Augustine is about to comment on.
4. In Homily 6.
5. See Homily 5.

John in his turn. For he said about John, *Among those born of women none has arisen greater than John the Baptist.* But because he put himself ahead of John, insofar as he was more than John, he was God. *But the one who is least,* he said, *in the kingdom of heaven is greater than he* (Mt 11:11). Lesser in date of birth, greater in authority, greater in divinity, grandeur, glory, seeing that *in the beginning was the Word, and the Word was with God, and the Word was God* (Jn 1:1).

In previous readings, however, John bore witness to the Lord, calling him indeed *the Son of God* (Jn 1:34); he did not call him God nor did he deny it. He kept quiet about his being God; he did not deny his divinity, and he was not completely silent about his being God. We may, in fact, discover that in today's reading. He called him Son of God, but even human beings have been called sons of God. He said that he so far surpassed all others that he himself was *not worthy to undo his sandal strap* (Jn 1:27). This indeed gives us some idea of the greatness of the one whose sandal strap he—unsurpassed among those born of women—was not worthy to undo. In fact, he was greater than all men and angels. For example, we find an angel forbidding a man to fall at his feet. For, in the Book of Revelation, when an angel was showing the John who wrote this gospel some things, John was so awe-struck by the greatness of the vision that he fell at the angel's feet. And the angel said, *Get up, see that you do not do this; worship God, for I am a fellow servant with you and your brothers and sisters* (Rv 22:8-9). So then, an angel forbade a man to fall at his feet. Is it not obvious that he is above all the angels, the one whose sandal strap such a man said he was unworthy to untie, a man unsurpassed among those born of women?

The psalm praises the divinity of Christ, king of all the earth

3. All the same, let John say something that more obviously shows our Lord Jesus Christ to be God. Let us find it, in fact, in this present reading, because perhaps it is also about him that we have been singing: *God has reigned over all the earth* (Ps 46:2)—which those who think he only reigns in Africa are too deaf to hear. It is not the case, you see, that it was not said about Christ, when it said, *God has reigned over all the earth.* Who else, after all, is our king but our Lord Jesus Christ? *He* is our king. And what did

you hear in the same psalm, in the last verse that was sung? *Sing a psalm to our God, sing a psalm; sing a psalm to our king, sing with understanding*; do not try to limit to one region only the one for whom you sing, *since God is king of all the earth* (Ps 46:6-7).

And how is he king of all the earth, the one who was seen in one part of the earth, in Jerusalem, in Judea, walking about among people, born, suckled, growing up, eating, drinking, keeping awake, sleeping, sitting down tired at the well, arrested, scourged, smeared with spittle, crowned with thorns, hung on the wood, pierced with a lance, dead and buried? So how then is he king of all the earth? What was to be seen in that place was flesh; flesh was evident to eyes of flesh; immortal majesty was concealed in mortal flesh. And what eyes could penetrate the structure of the flesh to gaze upon the immortal majesty? There is another eye, an interior eye.

After all, even Tobit can be said to have had no eyes when, blind in the eyes of his body, he was giving his son rules of life.[6] Tobit was holding his father's hand, that he might walk with his feet; the father was giving his son advice, that he might stay on the way of justice. In one case I see [physical] eyes; in the other I perceive eyes [with my mind]; and the eyes of the one giving advice about life are better eyes than those of the one holding the blind man's hand. Those were also the eyes that Jesus was looking for, when he said to Philip, *Am I with you all for such a long time, and you do not know me?* These were the eyes that he was looking for when he said, *Philip, the one who sees me also sees the Father.* (Jn 14:9) These eyes are in the understanding, these eyes are in the mind. That is why, when the psalm said, *Since God is king of all the earth*, it added straight away, *sing with understanding*.

You see, when I say, *Sing psalms to our God, sing psalms*, I am calling God our king; but you have seen our king among men as a man, you have seen him suffering, crucified, dead; something was hidden in that flesh which you were able to see with eyes of flesh. What was hidden there? *Sing with understanding*; do not go looking with your eyes for what can only be observed with the mind. Sing psalms with the tongue, because he is among you as flesh; but because *the Word was made flesh and took up residence*

---

6. See Tob 4. For a similar comment on the story of Tobit and his son see Sermons 88, 16; 125A, 5.

among us (Jn 1:14), give the flesh its due with sounds, give God his due with the gaze of the mind. *Sing with understanding*, and you see *that the Word was made flesh and took up residence among us.*

By Christ the man, one comes to Christ who is God

4. Let John too bear witness: *After this, Jesus and his disciples came into the land of Judea, and he stayed there with them and baptized* (Jn 3:22). Just baptized, he was baptizing. But he was not baptizing with the baptism with which he had been baptized. The Lord, baptized by a servant, baptizes, thus demonstrating the way of humility and leading people to the baptism of the Lord, that is to say to his own baptism; he gave an example of humility, because he did not spurn the baptism of a servant. And by the servant's baptism *the way was being prepared for the Lord* (Mk 1:3), and after being baptized the Lord made himself into the way for those coming to him. Let us listen to him: *I am the way, the truth and the life* (Jn 14:6). If you are looking for the truth, hold to the way, because that is the way which is Truth. That is the way you are going by, that is the way you are going to. You are not going by one way to another, not coming by something else to Christ; you come to Christ by and through Christ.

How does one come to Christ through Christ? By Christ the man to Christ God; by the Word made flesh to the Word which in the beginning was God with God; from that which man has eaten to that which the angels eat every day.[7] For, that is what is written: *He gave them the bread of heaven, man has eaten the bread of angels* (Ps 77:24-25). What is the bread of angels? *In the beginning was the Word, and the Word was with God, and the Word was God.* How has man eaten the bread of angels? *And the Word was made flesh and took up residence among us.*

This bread is also light; it is not diminished by being eaten, any more than light is by being seen

5. But because I have just said that angels eat, you must not think, brothers and sisters, that it is done by chewing. For if that is what you understand by it,

---

7. An allusion, through the psalm Augustine goes on to quote, first to the manna, and then through the manna to the eucharist.

it is as if God, whom the angels eat, is being torn into shreds. Who can tear justice into shreds? But then someone in return says to me,

"And who ever eats justice?"

What about *Blessed are those who are hungry and thirsty for justice, for they shall have their fill* (Mt 5:6)? The food you eat in the flesh, so that you can be renewed, disappears;[8] it is consumed so as to restore you. Eat justice, and you are restored, and justice continues intact.

Thus, in seeing this bodily light, these eyes of ours are restored,[9] and a material thing is seen by bodily eyes. Many who remained too long in the darkness find their vision weakened, as if by fasting from light. When the eyes are cheated of their food (of course, they feed on the light), they are tired out by such fasting and weakened, such that they cannot look at the light they are restored by; and if the light is lacking too long, the eyes go out and the sharpness of light, as it were, dies in them. So what follows, then? Because so many eyes feed on this light every day, does it grow any less? The truth is both that they are restored and renewed and that the light remains whole and entire. If God has been able to bestow this benefit on bodily eyes with bodily light, will he not bestow on the clean of heart[10] that light which is tireless, remains whole, does not fail at all?

"Which light?"

In the beginning was the Word, and the Word was with God. Let us see if it is light: *Since with you is the fountain of life, and in your light shall we see light* (Ps 35:10).

On earth a fountain is one thing, light another. When you are thirsty you look for a fountain, and in order to get to the fountain you look for light; and if it is not daytime, you light a lamp in order to get to the fountain. Now that fountain itself is the light; for the thirsty it is a fountain, for the blind it is light. Let the eyes be opened to see the light, may the mouth of the heart be opened so as to drink from the fountain; what you drink, that is, what you see, what you hear. God becomes everything for you, because he is for you the fullness of the things that you love.

---

8. The contrast in Latin between *reficere* ("to remake") and *deficere* ("to unmake").
9. Augustine seems to take for granted a pre-Socratic theory of light, as proposed by Anaximander or one of the Ionian philosophers.
10. See Mt 5:8.

If you are thinking of visible things, bread is not God, water is not God, this light is not God, a garment is not God, a house is not God. In fact, these things are visible and distinct from one another; bread is not water, and a garment is not a house; and these things are not God, for they are visible. For you God is everything; if you are hungry, he is bread for you; if you are thirsty he is water for you; if you are in the dark he is light for you, because he abides imperishable; if you are naked he is the garment of immortality for you *when this perishable thing shall put on imperishability and this mortal thing shall put on immortality* (1 Cor 15:54). Everything can be said about God, and nothing that is said is worthy of God. Nothing is more extensive that this poverty of speech. You look for a suitable name, you cannot find one;[11] you look for something to say in any way at all, and you find everything. What have lamb and lion got in common? Each name is applied to Christ: *Look, there is the Lamb of God* (Jn 1:29). How about "lion"? *Look, the Lion from the tribe of Judah has conquered* (Rv 5:5).

Why Jesus had himself baptized by John

6. Let us listen to John:[12] *Jesus was baptizing* (Jn 3:22). We have already said that Jesus was baptizing; but in what way was it Jesus? In what way the Lord? In what way the Son of God? In what way the Word? But *the Word was made flesh. Now John was there too, baptizing in Aenon next to Salim.* Aenon was a lake. How do we know it was a lake? *Because there was a lot of water there, and they were coming and being baptized. John, you see, had not yet been put in prison.* (Jn 3:23-24) If you remember—let me say it yet again—I said why John was baptizing; because it was necessary for the Lord to be baptized. And why was it necessary for the Lord to be baptized? Because there were many people who were going to scorn baptism on the grounds that they were endowed with greater grace than they saw in some of the faithful. For example, a catechumen already living as a celibate would scorn a married man and

---

11. See *Teaching Christianity* I, 6, 6: "While nothing really worthy of God can be said about him, he has accepted the homage of human voices and has wished us to rejoice in praising him with our words."
12. To John the evangelist, giving his testimony that Jesus is God. Augustine thus returns to the question of section 4 above.

say that he was better than that one of the faithful. Such a catechumen could say in his heart, "Why do I need to receive baptism? To have what that man has while I am already better than he is?"

To prevent such presumption from hurling those who were inordinately conscious of the merits of their justice down to their doom, the Lord chose to be baptized by his servant. It is as if he were saying to these proud sons,[13] "What do you praise yourselves? Why are you so full of yourselves, just because you have the virtues, this one of prudence, that one of learning, that other one of chastity, that fellow there of fortitude and patience? Can any of you possibly have as much as I do, I who gave all of it to you? And yet I have been baptized by a servant; you disdain being baptized by the Lord!" That is the meaning of *So that all justice may be fulfilled* (Mt 3:15).

Why other people were also baptized by John

7. But then someone will say, "So it would have been enough for John to baptize the Lord; what need was there for others to be baptized by John?" Here too I pointed out that if the Lord alone had been baptized by John, this thought would not have failed to occur to people, that John disposed of a better baptism than the Lord; I mean, they would say, "The baptism John gave was so great that only the Christ was worthy to be baptized with it." So in order to demonstrate that the baptism the Lord was going to give was the better one, and that the other was to be understood as being that of a servant, this one as being that of the Lord, the Lord was baptized to provide an example of humility; but he was not the only one to be baptized by John, lest John's baptism should appear to be better than the one given by the Lord.

Now what our Lord Jesus Christ was marking out for us all, as you have just heard, brothers and sisters, was a way to stop anyone, who arrogantly claimed to have an abundance of some grace or other, from disdaining to be baptized with the baptism given by the Lord. However outstanding the progress in virtue catechumens may have made, they are still carrying the load of their own iniquity; it is not removed from them until the moment

---

13. *Filios capitales*; they were proud fellows in their own eyes. It is an unusual word for Augustine to use, suggesting that it was part of everyday Latin in Africa. But such pride (*cervix*) may have held overtones relating to "capital punishment" and "capital crimes."

they come to baptism. Just as the people of Israel did not get rid of the people of the Egyptians until the very moment they came to the Red Sea, so too no one is rid of the oppressive weight of his sins until he comes to the baptismal font.

The argument of John's disciples with the Jews

8. *So then, a discussion about purification started among John's disciples with the Jews* (Jn 3:25). John was baptizing, Christ was baptizing. John's disciples were disturbed—people were thronging to Christ, just coming to John. John, you see, would send those who came to him on to Jesus to be baptized; those who were being baptized by Christ were not being sent to John. John's disciples were upset, and they began to argue the point with the Jews, as they were accustomed to do. You must understand that the Jews were saying Christ was the greater, and it was to his baptism that people should throng, while the others did not yet see things like that, and were defending the baptism of John. The argument was brought to John himself to be settled. Would Your Graces please try to understand this; here too the value of humility is being recognized, and we are being shown whether, when people were getting things wrong on this point, John was prepared to boast about himself.

Imagine that he said, "You are right, you have a good argument; my baptism is the better one. So, to convince you that my baptism is the better one, I baptized Christ himself." John could have said this after baptizing Christ. What a way he had there to extend his authority—if that is what he had wished to do! But he knew better before whom he would humble himself; he wanted to give way by acknowledging the one whom he preceded by birth. He understood that his salvation was in Christ. He had already said beforehand, *From his fullness have we all received* (Jn 1:16). That is a profession that he is God. After all, how could all human beings receive from his fullness, unless he were God? Because if he were a human being in such a way as not to be God, then he too would receive from the fullness of God, and thus would not be God. If, however, all human beings receive from his fullness, he is the fountain, they are the ones who drink from it. Those who drink at the fountain are able both to thirst and to drink. The fountain itself is never thirsty, the fountain is not in need. Human beings need the fountain; their vitals dried up, their throats parched, they come running to the fountain in order to be refreshed; the fountain flows in order to refresh them. Such is the Lord Jesus.

John says he himself is the herald, sent on before the judge

9. So let us see then what answer John gave. They came to John and said to him, *Rabbi, the one who was with you over the Jordan, to whom you yourself bore witness—look, this man is baptizing, and all are coming to him*; that is: "What do you say about it? Should they not be stopped, so that they come to you rather than to him?" *He answered and said, A man cannot receive anything, unless it has been given to him from heaven.* About whom do you think John said this? About himself. "As a man," he is saying, "I have received from heaven." Pay close attention, please, Your Graces. *A man cannot receive anything, unless it has been given to him from heaven. You yourselves can bear me witness that I said, I myself am not the Christ.* (Jn 3:26-28)

It is as if he were saying, "Why are you deceiving yourselves? How is it that you are the ones who put this question to me? Why did you say to me, *Rabbi, the one who was with you over Jordan, to whom you yourself bore witness*? So you know then what kind of witness I bore him; am I now going to say that he is not the one I said he was? So then, because I received something from heaven so that I might be something, do you want me now to be an empty nothing, so that I may speak against the truth? *A man cannot receive anything, unless it has been given to him from heaven. You yourselves can bear me witness that I said, I myself am not the Christ.*"

You are not yourself the Christ? But what then, if you are greater than him because you baptized him?

I was sent (Jn 3:28); I am the herald, he is the judge.

Christ the bridegroom, John the bridegroom's friend

10. And now listen to him bearing stronger, more explicit witness. Observe the point being raised with us; observe what we ought to love; observe that to love any human being in place of Christ is adultery. Why

am I saying this? Let us pay attention to John's own voice; it was possible for people to be mistaken about him, there was a real possibility of his being thought to be who he was not. He thrust away from himself a false honor, in order to hold to the solid truth. Observe what he calls Christ, what he calls himself: *The one who has the bride is the bridegroom*. Be chaste, all of you, love the bridegroom. But what are you, though, who are telling us, *The one who has the bride is the bridegroom? But bridegroom's friend, who stands and listens to him, rejoices with joy at the bridegroom's voice.* (Jn 3:29)[14]

May the Lord our God be present to the trouble in my heart, so full of groaning, so that I may say what grieves me. But I beseech you, by Christ himself, that you reflect on what I will not be able to say; for I know that I am not able to give sufficient expression to my sorrow. In fact, I see many adulterers who want to possess the bride that he bought for such a price, loved in her ugliness so that she would become beautiful; she was bought by him, set free by him, bejewelled by him, but they act with their words so as to be loved in place of the bridegroom. About him was it said, *This is the one who baptizes* (Jn 1:33). Who steps up here and says, "I am the one who baptizes"? Who steps up here and says, "What *I* give is holy"? Who goes on to say here, "It is good for you to be born of me"? Let us listen to the friend of the bridegroom, not to the adulterers; let us listen to the one who is jealous, but not for himself.

Christ has entrusted his bride to his friends

11. Brothers and sisters, return in your heart to your own homes; I am now speaking in the language of flesh, in earthly language; *I am speaking in human terms because of the weakness of your flesh* (Rom 6:19). Many of you have wives, many of you would like to have wives, many of you, although unwillingly, had wives, and many of you, who do not wish to have wives at all, were born of the relations of your fathers. No heart at all is untouched by this feeling; no one is so far from human matters, from the human race, that he does not sense what I am saying.

---

14. With the long digression that Augustine begins here, John's answer to his disciples will only be given in Homily 14, 3-4.

Imagine a man who has gone abroad and has entrusted his bride to the care of his friend: "Please see to it, my dear friend, that in my absence no one else is loved in my stead." So what sort of man would he be who, having the custody of his friend's bride or wife, does indeed see to it that she loves no one else, but then seeks himself to be her lover and wants to exploit for himself the woman entrusted to his care? How universally detestable he would appear to be to all human beings! Let him see her looking out of her window a little too gaily or joking with someone there, he stops her as a jealous guardian all over. Yes, I see that he is jealous, but I would like to see whom he is jealous for: his absent friend or himself there present?

Now think about how our Lord Jesus Christ did what this husband did:[15] he entrusted his bride to his friend when he set off abroad to receive a kingdom, as he says in the gospel,[16] but he still remained present in majesty. The friend who has gone overseas may be deceived; and if he is deceived, woe to the one who deceives him! But why do they try to deceive God, God who gazes into the hearts of all and penetrates the secrets of all? Some heretic stands up and says, "I am the one who gives, I am the one who sanctifies, I am the one who justifies; I do not want you to go to that sect." He is rightly jealous, but on whose behalf? "Do not go off to idols": a proper jealousy. "Do not go off to the fortune-tellers": a proper jealousy. But let us see on whose behalf he is being jealous. "What *I* give is holy, because I am the one who gives it; the one whom *I* baptize really is baptized, the one I do not baptize has not been baptized."

Now listen to the friend of the bridegroom, learn how to be jealous on behalf of your friend; listen to that voice: *This is the one who baptizes.* Why do you want to claim for yourself what is not yours? How absent is the one who left his bride behind? Do you not know that he has risen again from the dead and is seated at the right hand of the Father? If the Jews despised him while he was hanging on the tree, you despise him seated in heaven.

---

15. See Sermon 268, 4.
16. See Lk 19:12.

Your Graces should know what great pain I suffer in this matter; but as I said, I leave the rest to your reflections. I mean, I could not say it all if I were to speak all day; if I were to cry all day, it is not enough. I am not saying, like the prophet, if I had *a fountain of tears* (Jer 9:10); but if I were turned into tears and became nothing but tongues, it would still be too little.

The humility of the bridegroom's friend; the bride's virginity of mind and heart

12. Let us go back; let us see what John says: *The one who has the bride is the bridegroom*; the bride does not belong to me.

And do you not rejoice at the wedding?

Of course I rejoice, he says. *But the bridegroom's friend, who stands and listens to him, rejoices with joy at the bridegroom's voice.* "I am not," he says, "rejoicing at my own voice, but I am rejoicing at the bridegroom's voice. My being consists in listening, his in speaking. For I need enlightening, he is the light; I am an ear, he is the Word."

So then, the friend of the bridegroom stands and listens to him.

Why does he stand?

Because he does not fall.

Why does he not fall?

Because he is humble. Observe him standing on a solid foundation: *I am not worthy to untie his sandal straps* (Jn 1:27). You are right to humble yourself; rightly you do not fall, rightly you stand, rightly you listen to him and rejoice with joy at his voice.

In the same way the apostle too is a friend of the bridegroom, he too is ardent, not on his own behalf but on behalf of the bridegroom. Listen to the voice of his zeal: *I am jealous for you with God's jealousy* (2 Co 11:2-3), he said. "It is not mine, it is not on my behalf, but it is with God's jealousy."

Why? How so? Whom are you jealous for, or rather on whose behalf are you jealous?

For I betrothed you to one man, to present you to Christ as a chaste virgin.

So what are you afraid of? Why are you jealous?

But I fear, he says, *that just as the serpent led Eve astray with his cunning, so your senses may be corrupted from the chastity which is in Christ.* (2 Cor 11:3)

The whole Church is being called a virgin. The members of the Church are diverse; you can see and rejoice that they have a variety of gifts: some are married men, some are married women, some are widowers who are no longer looking for wives, some are widows not looking for husbands, some are men who have remained chaste from their youth, some are women who have vowed their virginity to God; many are the gifts, but together they are all one virgin. Where is this virginity found? It is not, after all, in the body. Bodily virginity is something that few women enjoy, and, if one can talk about virginity in men, that holy purity of body is something that few men in the Church have. And these are the Church's more honorable members. Other members have not kept virginity in the body, but all keep virginity of the mind.

What is virginity of the mind? Integral faith, solid hope, sincere love. The man who was jealous on behalf of the bridegroom feared that this virginity might be corrupted by the serpent. Just as a particular part of the body gets violated, so too does the seductive tongue violate the virginity of the heart. Let the one who does not wish to preserve the virginity of the body in vain take care not to be corrupted in the mind.[17]

The Donatist virgins not really betrothed to Christ

13. So what am I to say then, brothers and sisters? The heretics too have virgins, there are many virgins among the heretics. Let us see if they love the bridegroom, in such a way as to safeguard this virginity.

Whom is it being kept safe for?

"For Christ," she says.

Let us see if it is for Christ, not for Donatus. Let us see whom this virginity is being kept safe for; you will be able to test it quickly enough. Look, I am showing you the bridegroom, because he is showing you himself. John bears witness to him: *This is the one who baptizes*. O virgin, if you are keeping your virginity safe for this bridegroom, why do you go running off to the one who says, "I am the one who baptizes," when your bridegroom's friend says, *This is the one who baptizes*?

---

17. See *Exposition of Psalm* 90; Sermon 2, 9.

Then, your bridegroom holds the whole world; why do you, in one part of the earth, ruin it? Who is the bridegroom? *God is king of all the earth* (Ps 46:8). This bridegroom holds the whole world because he bought it all. See how much he bought it for, to get the right idea of what he bought; what was the price he gave? He gave his own blood. When did he pay it, when did he shed his blood? In his passion. Do not you sing to your bridegroom, or pretend to sing, when the whole world has been bought, *They have dug my hands and feet, they have counted all my bones; they however have inspected and observed me; they have divided my clothes among themselves, and over my garment they have tossed dice* (Ps 21:16-18)? You are the bride, identify your bridegroom's garment. Over which garment were they tossing dice? Interrogate the gospel, see there to whom you have been engaged, from whom you receive the engagement ring.

See what it is saying to you in the Lord's passion. *There was a tunic there*; let us see what kind of tunic; *woven from the top*. What can the tunic woven from the top stand for but charity? What can the tunic woven from the top stand for but unity? Pay attention to this tunic, which not even Christ's persecutors divided. After all, the psalm says, *They said to one another, Let us not divide it, but toss dice for it.* (Jn 19:23-24) There you are, that is what you heard the psalm say. The persecutors did not tear the garment; Christians do divide the Church.

Psalm 21 tells us the extent of the domain Christ bought with his blood

14. But what am I to say, brothers and sisters? Let us see clearly what he bought. For he bought it in the place where he paid the price. How much did he pay? If he paid just for Africa, let us be Donatists, not calling ourselves Donatists but Christians, because Christ only bought Africa (although there are not just Donatists here). But, in this transaction, he did not keep quiet about what he bought. He kept a record. Thank God, he has not misled us. The bride needs to hear and then to understand to whom she has vowed her virginity; the record is there, in the psalm, where it said, *They have dug my hands and feet, they have counted all my bones*. The Lord's passion is described most clearly; the psalm is read every year in the last week before Easter as the passion of Christ approaches with all the people attentive—this psalm is read both among us and among them.

Notice carefully, brothers and sisters, what he bought there; read the commercial records. Listen to what he bought there: *All the ends of the earth shall remember and shall turn to the Lord; and all the countries of the nations together shall worship in his sight; since his is the kingdom, and he shall lord it over the nations* (Ps 21:28-29). Look, that is what he bought. Look at how your bridegroom is God, *the king of all the earth.* So why do you want a bridegroom of such wealth reduced to rags? Admit it, he bought it all, and you say, "Your part is here." Oh, if only you were out to please the bridegroom! Oh, if only you were not talking as someone who has been corrupted and, what is much worse, corrupted in the heart, not in body! You are in love with a mere man in Christ's place, in love with one who says, "I am the one who baptizes." You do not listen to the bridegroom's friend who says, *This is the one who baptizes*; you do not listen to him saying, *The one who has the bride is the bridegroom.* "I do not have the bride," he said, "but who am I?" *But the bridegroom's friend, who stands and listens to him, rejoices with joy at the bridegroom's voice.*

No amount of virginity or good works is of any value without the charity signified by the seamless robe

15. Evidently, therefore, my brothers and sisters, it does these people no good to preserve virginity, to be continent, to give alms. All these things that are thought of so highly in the Church are no good to them at all, because they are tearing the Unity to shreds, that is, the tunic of charity. What are they doing? Many among them are eloquent, great speakers with torrents of words. Are they speaking angelically? Let them listen to a friend of the bridegroom, being jealous on the bridegroom's behalf, not his own: *If I speak with the tongues of men and of angels but do not have charity, I have become like booming bronze or clashing cymbals* (1 Cor 13:1).

Baptism of no effect outside the Unity, the Church

16. But what are they saying?

"We have baptism."

You do, but it is not yours. It is one thing to have it, another to own it. You have baptism because you have received the grace of being baptized, you have received it as being enlightened by it—provided, that is, you have not been darkened by yourself and, in giving it, you do so as minister, not as proprietor; you speak as a clerk, not as a judge. The judge speaks through the clerk of the court, and yet what is written in the record is not "The clerk said" but "The judge said." So then, see if what you give is really yours, as something in your power. But if you have received it, then confess with the bridegroom's friend: *A man cannot receive anything unless it has been given him from heaven.* Confess with the bridegroom's friend: *The one who has the bride is the bridegroom; but the bridegroom's friend stands and listens to him.*

But oh, if only you would stand and listen to him, and would not fall to the point of listening to yourself! By listening to him, you see, you would be standing and listening; in fact, you are always talking and filling your head with hot air. "If I am the bride," says the Church, "if I have received the engagement ring, if I have been redeemed at the price of that blood, then I am listening to the bridegroom's voice; and I am then also listening to the voice of the bridegroom's friend, if he sings the praises of my bridegroom, not his own." Let the friend say, *The one who has the bride is the bridegroom; but the bridegroom's friend stands and listens to him, and rejoices with joy at the bridegroom's voice.*

Look, you have the sacraments, and I grant you that. You have the form,[18] but you are a twig cut off from the vine; you show the shape, but I am looking for the root. Fruit does not come from the shape except where it is attached to the root; and where is the root to be found if not in charity? And listen to something about the form of the twigs; let Paul speak: *If I know*, he says, *all the mysteries,*[19] *and have all prophecy and all faith* (and how much faith?), *such that I can move mountains, but do not have charity, I am nothing* (1 Cor 13:1. 2).

---

18. The form or shape, as opposed to the substance; Augustine is not using the word in the sense it has in our catechisms when applied to the sacraments, which consist of "form," the operative words, and "matter," the material over which the words are spoken.
19. All *sacramenta*.

Donatist stories about their miracle workers

17. So do not let anyone sell you stories: "Pontius too performed a miracle; Donatus too prayed, and God answered him from heaven."[20] In the first place, they are either being deceived or deceiving; and then, make Pontius "move a mountain." *But do not have charity*, he says, *I am nothing*. Let us see if he had charity. I would believe it if they had not broken up the Unity. For my God has also put me on my guard against these wonder-mongers,[21] if I may so call them, by saying, *In the last times false prophets will arise, performing signs and prodigies, so as to lead into error, if that can happen, even the elect; behold, I have told you beforehand* (Mk 13:22-23). So then, the bridegroom put us on our guard, because we ought not to be taken in even by miracles. Sometimes, you see, a deserter will scare country folk; but the man who is not prepared to be scared or to be led astray will notice whether he belongs to the garrison and whether that mark he has been branded with stands him in good stead.[22]

So let us stick, my brothers and sisters, to the Unity; outside the Unity, even the one who performs miracles is nothing. The people of Israel, you see, were in the Unity and were not performing miracles; Pharaoh's magicians were outside the Unity and were doing things as Moses did.[23] The people of Israel, as I said, were not performing them. Who were the ones saved by God, those who were performing them or those who were not? The apostle Peter raised up a dead person; Simon Magus did many wonderful things.[24] There were a number of Christians at that time who could not do such things, neither what Peter did, nor what Simon did; but what was there for them to rejoice about? That their names were written in heaven. In fact, our Lord Jesus Christ said this for the sake of the faith of the nations to the returning disciples. The disciples themselves, you see, said

---

20. Pontius had been a Donatist bishop who had moved to Rome when the Emperor Constantius issued an edict against the Donatists in 347. In 362 he obtained a rescript from the Emperor Julian restoring the legal status of Donatism and returned in triumph to Africa, so that the Donatists came to regard him almost as the second founder of their movement.
21. *Mirabiliarios*, a word that Augustine clearly coined for the occasion.
22. When young men joined the Roman army, they were branded on the back of their hands with the mark, the *character*, of the reigning monarch. See Homily 5, 13, and note 15 there.
23. See Ex 7:12.22; 8:7.
24. See Acts 9:40; 8:10. On Peter's miracle the text says he raised a *mortuum*, a dead man, though it was in fact the widow Tabitha; perhaps the masculine form was generally used to mean a corpse.

boastfully, *Look, Lord, in your name even the demons were subject to us.* They were indeed stating it very well, giving all the credit to the name of Christ; and yet what did he say to them in reply? *Do not boast that the demons were subject to you; but rejoice that your names are written in heaven.* (Lk 10:17-20)

Peter cast out demons; heaven knows what poor old widow, heaven knows what ordinary layman, having charity, holding on to the integrity of the faith, does not do this. Peter is the eye in the body, these two are fingers in the body; but they are in the same body as Peter is, and even if fingers are of less worth than eyes, they still have not been cut off from the body. It is better to be a finger and be in the body than to be an eye and to have been plucked out of the body.[25]

Conclusion; let us love Christ faithfully and one another in Christ

18. So then, my brothers and sisters, do not let anyone deceive you, do not let anyone lead you astray. Love the Peace[26] of Christ, who was crucified for you, even though he was God. Paul says, *Neither the one who plants is anything, nor the one who waters, but the one who makes things grow, God* (1 Cor 3:7); and is there anybody among us who says he is something? If we say we are something and do not give Christ the credit, we are adulterers; we want ourselves to be loved, not the bridegroom. You then, all of you, love Christ and love me in him, in whom you also are being loved by me. Let his members love each other, but let them all live under the head. Brothers and sisters, I have indeed been forced by my pain to say too much—and I have said too little! I have not been able to finish the passage read; the Lord will be on hand to see that it is finished in due course. I do not want to burden your hearts any further; I would like to give you time to groan and to pray for those who are still deaf and do not understand.

---

25. In his *Exposition of Psalm* 130, 6—a sermon preached shortly before Easter 407, a few days before Homily 11—Augustine develops this comparison between eye and finger at greater length.
26. Like "the Unity," one of Augustine's favorite names for the Catholic Church.

Homily 14

On John 3:29-46[1]

The difference between the God-man and John, a mere man

1. This reading from the holy gospel teaches us about the divine pre-eminence of our Lord Jesus Christ and about the humility of the man who was worthy to be called *the bridegroom's friend* (Jn 3:29), so that we might note the difference between a man who is just a man and a man who is God. In fact, our Lord Jesus Christ is a man who is God: God before all ages and a man in our time; God from the Father, man from the Virgin, but still one and the same Lord and Savior, Jesus Christ, Son of God, God and man. John, however, a man of pre-eminent grace, was sent ahead of him, enlightened by the one who is light.

About John, you see, it was said, *He was not the light, but came to bear witness to the light* (Jn 1:8). He can indeed be called a light, and he is properly called a light;[2] but he is a light that is enlightened, not one that enlightens. For a light that is lit is one thing, and a light that gives light is another. I mean, our eyes are called lights; and yet when opened in the dark they do not see anything.[3] The light, though, which enlightens, is light of itself and is light for itself, and needs no other light for it to shine; but other lights do need light if they are to shine.

John, the bridegroom's friend, rejoicing in the bridegroom's voice, not in his own

2. So then, you have heard the profession of John. Because when Jesus was making many disciples, and the news was brought to John as if to stir him up—they told him, you see, assuming he would be jealous, "Look, he is making more disciples than you are"—he confessed what he was, and

---

1. Probably preached a few days after Homily 13, shortly after the feast of the Ascension, May 23, 407; the next two homilies were preached before Augustine left for the eleventh Council of Carthage, which met on June 13, 407. However, La Bonnardière allows that Homilies 14, 15 and 16 could have been preached a year later at this time.
2. See Jn 5:35.
3. For Augustine's theory of vision, that our eyes see by emitting rays, but which are only "empowered" to do this by exterior light, see *The Trinity* IX, 3 and note 10 there. It is Plato's theory (in the *Timaeus*), rejected by Aristotle.

thereby earned the right to belong to Jesus, because he did not have the gall to say that he was Jesus. So this then is what John said, *A man cannot receive anything unless it has been given him from heaven*. So then, Christ gives, and man receives. *You yourselves can bear me witness that I said, I am not the Christ* (Jn 1:20), *but that I have been sent ahead of him. The one who has the bride is the bridegroom; but the bridegroom's friend, who stands and listens to him, rejoices with joy at the bridegroom's voice.* (Jn 3:27-29)

He did not rejoice about himself. The one who wants to rejoice in himself will be sad; but if you want to rejoice in God, you will rejoice for ever, because God lasts for ever. Do you want to have everlasting joy? Stick to the one who is everlasting. That is the sort of man John said he was. Because of the bridegroom's voice, he said, the bridegroom's friend rejoices, not because of his own voice; he is standing and listening to him. So if he falls, then, it means he is not listening to him, for it was said about the one who fell, *And he did not stand in the truth* (Jn 8:44); yes, it was said about the devil. So then, the bridegroom's friend ought to stand and listen. What does standing mean? Remaining in the grace of the bridegroom, which he has received. And he listens to the voice at which he can rejoice.

That is what John was like; he knew what he was rejoicing at, he did not claim what he was not. He was well aware that he was the one who was enlightened, not the one who enlightens. *He, however, was the true light*, says the evangelist, *which enlightens everyone coming into the world* (Jn 1:9). So, if every man was enlightened, then John too was enlightened, because he came from among men. And indeed, although *among those born of women none has arisen greater than John the Baptist* (Mt 11:11), he was, all the same, one of those born of women. Is he to be compared with the one who, because he wished to be, was born—and by a new birth, therefore, because a new kind of infant was born? For both of the Lord's births, the divine and the human birth, are out of the ordinary; in the divine birth he has no mother, in the human birth he has no father.

Thus, John was one of the rest of us, yet still of greater grace, such that no one born of women has arisen greater than him; and he gave our Lord Jesus Christ this splendid testimony of calling him the bridegroom and of calling himself the bridegroom's friend, even if *not worthy to undo his sandal straps* (Jn 1:27). Your Graces have already heard a great deal about this; let us look at what comes next, for it is somewhat difficult to understand. But since John himself says, *A man cannot receive anything unless it has been given him from heaven*, let us ask the one who gives from heaven[4] about anything we will not understand, because we are human beings, and we cannot receive anything unless the one who is not a human being gives it.

We must give God the credit for the gifts he has given us, not claim it for ourselves

3. This then is what follows;[5] John says, *So this joy of mine has been made complete* (Jn 3:29). What is his joy? To be able to rejoice at the bridegroom's voice. "It has been made complete in me. I have my grace, I am not grabbing at anything more for myself, lest I should lose what I have received." What is this joy? *He rejoices with joy at the bridegroom's voice.*

Let everyone, therefore, understand that they ought not to rejoice over their own wisdom, but over the wisdom they have received from God. Let them look for nothing more, and they will not lose what they have found. The reason, you see, that many have become foolish is that they have said they are wise. The apostle challenges them and says about them, *Because what can be known of God*, says he, *is evident to them; God, after all, has manifested it*; listen to what he is saying about some ingrates, about some who are godless: *God, after all, has manifested it to them. For his invisible attributes are there to be gazed upon from the creation of the world, being understood from what has been made; also his everlasting strength and divinity, so that they are inexcusable.* Why are they inexcusable? *Because knowing God*—he did not say, "because they did not know him" —*knowing God, they did not give him glory as God nor give thanks; but they became vain in their reasoning, and their unwise heart was darkened; calling themselves wise, you see, they became fools.* (Rom 1:19-22)

If they had known God, after all, they would have known at the same time that it was none other than God who had made them wise. So they would not have given themselves credit for what they did not have, but

---
4. That is, let us ask God the Father, the giver from heaven.
5. Augustine seems to refer back to what John had said about the bridegroom and his friend as following the words, *A man cannot receive anything unless it has been given him from heaven* —an inference based on the fact that what follows does not reflect on what has just been said, but on the passage from Rom.

they would have given credit to the one from whom they had received it. So then, what God had given *gratis* he took away from the ungrateful. That is not what John wanted to be; he wanted to be grateful to God.[6] He confessed that he had received and affirmed that his joy came from hearing the bridegroom's voice, and he said, *So this joy of mine has been made complete.*

Problems raised by Jesus' having to grow, John's having to decrease

4. *He must increase, but I must decrease* (Jn 3:30). What does this mean? He is to be exalted, but I am to be humbled.[7] How can Jesus increase, how can God increase? The one who is perfect does not increase; no, God neither increases nor decreases. I mean if he increases he is not perfect; if he decreases, he is not God. How does Jesus, who is God, increase? If he comes to be of age, it is because he became a man, and he was a boy; and although he is the Word of God, he lay as an infant[8] in the manger; and although he himself had fashioned his mother, he sucked the milk of infancy from his mother. So because Jesus grew in years in the flesh, therefore, that is perhaps why it was said, *He must increase, but I must decrease.*

But, why this? As regards the flesh, John and Jesus were the same age —with only six months' difference between them, they grew up together; and if our Lord Jesus Christ had wished to stay here longer before his death, and to have John himself here with him, they could have grown old together just as they had grown up together. So then, why *He must increase, but I must decrease*? First of all, because the Lord was already thirty[9]—will you ever find a youth still growing if he is already thirty? That is the age from which people begin to slide down toward maturity, and then into old age. But even if they had both been boys, he would not have said, *He must increase, but I must decrease*, but "We both must grow together." Now though, in fact this one is thirty, that one is thirty; the six months' difference between them does not make them different ages; only the writings tell you about that, not their looks.

---

6. *Gratus* in the Latin; Augustine is playing on the words *gratis, ingratus,* and *gratus* (and *gratia*).
7. For both similar and different treatments of this point see Sermons 287, 3-4; 293D, 5.
8. *Infans* means literally "not speaking."
9. See Lk 1:36; 3:23.

Various figurative solutions to the problems

5. So what does it mean that *he must increase, but I must decrease*? This is a great mystery.[10] Would Your Graces please try to understand! Before the Lord Jesus came, people used to credit the glory to themselves; he came as a man to decrease the glory of man and to increase the glory given to God. Indeed, he came without sin and found everyone else in sin. If he came so as to forgive sin, God may be generous, man may confess. The confession of man is the humility of man; the mercy of God is the greatness of God. So then, if he came to forgive the sins of human beings, let each one acknowledge his lowliness and let God exercise his mercy.

He *must increase, but I must decrease*; that is, he must give, but I must receive; he must be given the credit and glory, but I must confess. Let each one recognize his status and confess to God and listen to the apostle saying to the proud and puffed-up man who wants to praise himself: *What do you have, after all, that you did not receive? But if you received it, why are you boasting as if you did not?* (1 Cor 4:7) So let man know that he received what he wanted to call his own, and let him be decreased; it is good for him, in fact, that God be glorified in him. Let him become less in himself, so that he may increase in God.

In the passion that each of them suffered, Christ and John confirmed this witness and this truth: John was decreased by the loss of his head, Christ was lifted up on the cross, so that the meaning of the words, *He must increase, but I must decrease*, might be evident. Then again, Christ was born when the days were already beginning to grow longer, John was born when the days had started to decrease.[11] So creation itself, as well as the deaths they suffered, confirm John's words, *He must increase, but I must decrease*.

So then, let God's glory increase in us, and our own glory be decreased so that even our glory may increase in God. This, after all, is what the apostle says, what scripture says: *Let the one who glories glory in the Lord* (1 Cor 1:31; Jer 9:23-24). Do you want to glory in yourself? You want to grow, but you grow badly to your own harm; for the one who grows badly is justly decreased. So let God, who is always perfect, increase; let him

---

10. *Magnum hoc sacramentum.*
11. Jesus on Christmas Day just after the winter solstice, John just after the summer solstice; see Sermon 192, 3.

increase in you. The more you know God, after all, and the more you understand, the more God seems to grow in you—in himself, of course, he does not grow, but he is always perfect. Yesterday, you were understanding a little, today, you are understanding more, you will understand much more tomorrow; the very light of God is growing in you; in that way it is as if God is growing, who always remains perfect.

It is as if a person's eyes were being cured of their former blindness, and he began to see a little bit of light, and the next day saw more of it, and on the third day much more and further still. It would seem to him that the light was growing; the light nonetheless is perfect, whether he can see it or whether he cannot see it. It is like that too with your inner self; you make progress in God, and God seems to grow in you; yet in fact you are diminishing, so that you may fall away from your own glory and rise up to the glory of God.

How John, being of the earth, speaks of the earth

6. And now what we have just heard becomes clear and distinct. The one who comes from up above is over all. Notice what he is saying about Christ. About himself, what? *The one who is from the earth is of the earth, and it is of the earth he speaks. The one who comes from up above is over all* (Jn 3:31)—that is Christ. *But the one who is of the earth is earthly, and his language is earthly* (Jn 3:31)—that is John. And is that everything? that John is of the earth and speaks an earthly language? Is all of the testimony he gives to Christ in an earthly language? Does not John utter the words of God when he bears witness to Christ? How is it that he is speaking an earthly language? But John was saying this about a man. In regard to man, he is from the earth and his language is earthly; if however he speaks anything divine, it is because he has been enlightened by God. I mean, if he was not enlightened, earth would only be speaking an earthly language.

So then, the grace of God is one thing, the nature of man is another. Ask now about the nature of man; he is born, he grows, he learns about ordinary human things. What does he know but earth and what is from the earth? He has a human language, a human knowledge, a human taste; a being of flesh, he judges according to the flesh, presumes according to the flesh. There you have everything about man.

Let the grace of God come; let it light up man's darkness, as he says, *You, Lord, will light my lamp; my God, light up my darkness* (Ps 17:29). Let it lift up the human mind, turn it toward its own light, and he now begins to say what the apostle says, *Not I, though, but God's grace with me* (1 Cor 15:10); and *I live, though no longer myself, but Christ is living in me* (Gal 2:20). That is what *He must increase, but I must decrease* amounts to. So then John, simply as John, *is of the earth and speaks an earthly language*; if you have heard anything divine from John, it comes from the one enlightening him, not from him who receives it.

How the Word of God speaks himself;
the remote analogy of the concepts in our minds

7. *The one who comes from heaven is above all; and he bears witness to what he has seen and heard, and no one accepts his testimony* (Jn 3:31-32). He comes from heaven, he is above all—our Lord Jesus Christ, about whom he said earlier, *Nobody has ascended into heaven but the one who came down from heaven, the Son of Man who is in heaven* (Jn 3:13); but he is above all, *and he speaks about what he has seen and heard.* The Son of God himself, you see, also has a Father; yes, he has a Father too, and he listens to the Father; and what he hears from the Father, what is it? Who can explain it? When will my tongue, when will my heart be enough: my heart to understand or my tongue to express what the Son has heard from the Father? Did the Son perhaps hear the Father's Word? But no, the Son is the Father's Word. You can see how every conjecture of our heart will fail, every thought of a darkened mind.

I hear scripture saying that the Son speaks what he hears from the Father; and again I hear scripture saying that the Son is himself the Father's Word: *In the beginning was the Word, and the Word was with God, and the Word was God* (Jn 1:1). We speak words that fly off and are gone; as soon as the word has sounded on your lips, it is gone; it makes its own noise, and passes on into silence. Can you chase the sound your word makes, and hold it so that it stands still? Your thought, however, lasts; and from that thought which remains you say many fleeting words. What are we saying, brothers and sisters? When God was speaking, did he make use of a voice, make use of sounds, make use of syllables? If he did make use of these things, what language did he speak? Was it Hebrew or Greek or Latin? Languages are necessary where you have distinct peoples. But nobody can say that God spoke in this language or in that.

Pay attention to your heart. When you conceive the word you will say—let me say, if I can, what we might notice in ourselves, without explaining how we might understand it—when you conceive the word which you will utter, then, you want to say a particular thing, and the concept of that thing is already a word in your heart; it has not come out yet, but it has already been born in the heart and remains ready to come out. But you are paying attention to the one it is meant for, to the one you are talking to; if he is a Latin-speaker, you look for a Latin expression; if he is Greek, you think up some Greek words; if he is a Punic-speaker, you ask yourself whether you know the Punic language. According to the diversity of your hearers, you make use of different languages in order to utter the word you have conceived; but the word you have conceived in your heart was being held there in no particular language.

Since God was not looking for a language to speak with and, indeed, since he did not adopt a kind of oratory, how was he heard by the Son, seeing that it is the Son himself that God spoke? For, when you have the word you are going to speak in your heart, and it is there in you, and this concept is a spiritual reality—because just as your soul is spirit, so too the word you have conceived is spirit, for it has not yet received a sound so as to be divided into syllables, but it remains as a concept in your heart, as perceived in your mind's eye—so God, in similar fashion, gave birth to the Word, that is, he begot the Son. You indeed also beget a word in your heart at a moment in time; God begot the Son, through whom he created all times, outside of time. Since, therefore, the Son is God's Word, and the Son spoke to us, not his own word, but the Word of the Father, the one who uttered the Word of the Father wanted to speak himself to us.[12]

So then, John has said all this in a way that was fitting and proper, while I have been expounding it as best I could. If a person has not come to an understanding in his heart that is worthy of so great a thought, he has someone to turn to, someone at whose door to knock, someone from whom to seek, someone from whom to ask, someone from whom to receive.[13]

---

12. See *The Trinity* I, 12, 26 where this matter is also raised. This complicated thought builds on the active and passive dimensions of the Word: the Word speaks, but that which speaks is also the spoken Word.
13. See Mt 7:7-8.

Those who do not accept Christ's testimony about himself, and those who do

8. *The one who comes from heaven is above all; and he bears witness to what he has seen and heard, and no one accepts his testimony.* If no one accepts it at all, why did he come? So then, *no one* means no one in a particular group. There is a people, prepared for the wrath of God, who will be damned with the devil; among these no one accepts the testimony of Christ. For, if absolutely no one, not a single human being accepts it, how could what follows make sense: *But whoever has accepted his testimony certifies that God is trustworthy* (Jn 3:33)?[14] So perhaps if John were questioned on the point, he would answer and say, "I know what I meant by *no one*. You see, there is a certain people born for the wrath of God and foreknown for this. For God knows who will believe and who will not; God knows those who are going to persevere in what they have believed, and those who are going to slide away; and all those who will have eternal life have been counted by God, who already knows that other people which has been set aside."[15] And if he knows it himself and if he has also given knowledge of it to his prophets through his Spirit, he has also given it to John.

So then, John was taking a look—but not with his eyes, for as far as he is concerned himself, *he is of the earth and speaks an earthly language*—but, in that grace which he received from God, he saw a particular people, ungodly, unbelieving. Looking at its infidelity, he says, "No one accepts the testimony of the one who comes from heaven." No one in which particular group? Of those who are going to end up on the left-hand side, of those who will be told, *Go into the eternal fire which has been prepared for the devil and his angels.* So who then do accept it? Those who are going to end up on the right-hand side, those who will be told, *Come, you blessed of my Father, receive the kingdom which has been prepared for you from the origin of the world.* (Mt 25:41.34)

So then, in the Spirit he paid attention to this division, even though in the human race as it is they are all mixed up together; and what has not yet been sorted out in distinct places he sorted out with his intelligence, sorted out with a penetrating glance of the heart; and he saw two peoples, of believers

---

14. The Latin, *verax*, can be rendered "truthful" or "true," but in context it can also mean "trustworthy," "faithful."
15. For a somewhat more ample statement of God's foreknowledge in this matter, see Homily 12, 12.

and unbelievers, of the faithful and the faithless, and said, *The one who comes from heaven is above all; and he bears witness to what he has seen and heard, and no one accepts his testimony.* Then he switched from the left hand and glanced at the right hand, and said, *But whoever has accepted his testimony certifies that God is trustworthy.*

What can *certifies that God is trustworthy* mean but that man is deceitful and God is trustworthy?[16] Because no human being can say what belongs to the truth, unless enlightened by the one who is unable to lie.[17] So then, God is truthful; but Christ is God. Do you want to prove it for yourself? Accept his testimony, and you will discover that *whoever has accepted his testimony certifies that God is truthful.* Who? The one who came down from heaven and is above us all, he is the true God. But if you do not yet understand him to be God, you have not accepted his testimony; accept this testimony, and you assent, you understand by anticipation, you acknowledge distinctly, that God is trustworthy.

How God's unsurpassable charity ensures that Father and Son are one God

9. *For the one whom God has sent speaks the words of God* (Jn 3:34). He is the true God, and God sent him. God has sent God. Join them both, one God, the true God sent by God. Ask them singly, each is God; ask them both, they are God. Not that each is God and both are gods, but each one of them is God and both together are God. For so great is the charity of the Holy Spirit, so great the unitive force of peace, that when you ask about each, the answer you get is "God"; when you ask about the Trinity, the answer you get is "God."

After all, if the spirit of a human being when it clings to God is one spirit, as the apostle says in the clearest terms, *The one who clings to God is one spirit* (1 Cor 6:17), how much more must the co-equal Son clinging to the Father be together with him one God! Listen to another piece of evidence. You know what a great many there were who believed, *when they sold everything they had, and laid the proceeds at the feet of the apostles, so that it might be shared out to each according to his needs* (Acts 2:44-45;

---

16. It goes better in the Latin: *homo mendax est, et Deus verax est.* Augustine is echoing Paul in Rom 3:4, where the apostle cites Ps 116:1, as rendered by the Greek LXX.
17. See Homily 5,1 on truth and truthfulness.

4:34-35); and what does scripture say about that community of saints? *They had one soul and one heart in the Lord* (Acts 4:32). If charity made one soul out of so many souls, out of so many hearts made one heart, how much charity must there be between the Father and the Son! Yes, greater than among all those who were of one heart!

So then, if because of charity many are of one heart, and because of charity many are of one soul, are you going to say that God the Father and God the Son are two?[18] If they are two gods, then you do not find there the summit of charity. For, if charity is so great that it makes your soul and your friend's soul into one soul here below, how could Father and Son not be one God up there? May sincere faith never entertain such an idea! And here is something else from which you can form a clear notion of how much that charity up there surpasses absolutely everything. Many souls are many human beings, and, if they love one another, there is one soul; but, among men, they can still also be called many souls, because there is no question here of their being totally joined together. Up there, however, while it is right for you to say one God, it is certainly not right to say two gods, or three. This should drive home to you the pre-eminence and the absolute totality of charity, such that none greater can there be.

God does not give Christ the Spirit by measure,
while he does measure out the Spirit to us

10. *For the one whom God has sent speaks the words of God.* He was saying this, of course, about Christ, to distinguish him from himself. But wait a minute—God sent John, did he not? Did he not say, *I was sent ahead of him*, and, *The one who sent me to baptize in water* (Jn 3:28; 1:33)? And was it not said about him, *Behold, I am sending my angel ahead of you, and he will prepare the way for you* (Mt 11:10)? Did he not also speak the words of God, seeing that it was also said of him that he was *more than a prophet* (Mt 11:9)? So then, if God also sent him and he speaks the words of God, how can we take it as distinguishing Christ from others that he said, *The one whom God has sent speaks the words of God*?

---

18. See *The Trinity* VI,4,8-9 for a fuller discussion. Augustine may have written these texts at the same time.

Notice what he adds: *For not by measure does God give the Spirit* (Jn 3:34).[19] What is this, though: *Not by measure does God give the Spirit?* We find, in fact, that God does give the Spirit by measure. Listen to the apostle saying, *According to the measure of the giving of Christ* (Eph 4:7). He gives by measure to human beings, to his only Son he does not give by measure. How by measure to human beings? *To one indeed there is given through the Spirit a word of wisdom, to another a word of knowledge according to the same Spirit, to another faith in the same Spirit, to another prophecy, to another the discernment of spirits, to another kinds of tongues, to another the gift of healing. Are they all apostles? Are they all prophets? Are they all teachers? Do all have powers? Do all have gifts of healing? Do all speak with tongues, do all interpret them?* (1 Cor 12:8-10.29-30) This person has one thing, that another; what that one has, this one does not have; there is a measuring out, a division of gifts.

So then, human beings are given things by measure, and harmony here makes one body out of them. Just as the hands receive one thing so that they may work, the eyes another for them to see, the ears another for them to hear, the feet another in order to walk; but still there is just one soul which does all these things, working with the hands, walking with the feet, hearing with the ears, seeing with the eyes; in the same way there is a variety of gifts among the faithful, shared out by a measure appropriate to each, as to parts of the body. But Christ, who gives these things, does not himself receive by measure.

In sending us his Son, the Father sends his other self

11. You must continue to observe what comes next, after his saying about the Son, *For not by measure does God give the Spirit: The Father loves the Son and has placed all things in his hand* (Jn 3:35). He added *He has placed all things in his hand* to let you know here too in what distinct way he said the Father loves the Son. What is the reason, then? Does not the Father love John? And yet he has not placed all things in his hand. Does not the Father love Paul? And yet he has not placed all things in his hand. The Father loves the Son, but as a father loves a son, not as a master loves a

---

19. Jn 3:34 can also be translated: *He does not ration his gift of the Spirit.*

slave; loves him as his only Son, not as an adopted son. And so he placed all things in his hand. What does *all things* mean? That the Son should be as great as the Father. You see, he begot as his equal the one for whom it would not be robbery for him to be, in the form of God, equal to God.[20] *The Father loves the Son and has placed all things in his hand.* So then, when he was good enough to send his Son to us, we must not suppose that we were sent anything less than the Father. In sending the Son, the Father sends his other self.

Whoever has seen me has seen the Father

12. The disciples, in fact, were still assuming that the Father was something greater than the Son, when, seeing his flesh and not understanding his divinity, they said to the Son, *Lord, show us the Father, and that will satisfy us* (Jn 14:8). It is as if they were saying, "We already know you, and we bless you because we know you; yes, we are most grateful to you for having shown yourself to us. But we do not know the Father yet; that is why our heart is on fire, is bursting with a holy eagerness to see your Father who sent you. Show *him* to us, and we will desire nothing more from you; for we shall be completely satisfied when we are shown the one than whom there can be none greater."

A good eagerness, a good desire, but little understanding. The Lord Jesus himself, you see, on observing these little ones wanting and seeking great things, and aware of himself as being great among little ones—and little among little ones[21]—answered Philip, one of the disciples who had spoken, *Have I been with you for such a long time, and you have not come to know me, Philip?* Philip could have answered at this point, "We certainly do know you; but we did not say, did we, 'Show us yourself?' We know you already, but we are still wanting the Father." So Jesus added straightaway, *Anyone that has seen me has seen the Father* (Jn 14:9).

So then, if he was sent as the Father's equal, let us not form our assessment of him from the frailty of the flesh, but let us fix our thoughts on the

---

20. See Phil 2:6.
21. Great among them as God, little among them as a fellow human being; see Homily 21, 1.

grandeur that was clothed in the flesh and not weighed down by the flesh. Abiding as God with the Father, he became a man among us, so that through him you, for whose sake he became man, might become such a one as can grasp God. A human being, indeed, was unable to grasp God; he was able to see a human being, unable to grasp God. Why could a human being not grasp God? Because he did not have that eye of the heart needed to grasp him. So something inside was sick, something outside was healthy; the eyes of the body were healthy, the eyes of the heart were ill. Christ was made man for the eyes of the body to see, so that by believing in him who could be seen in a bodily way, you might be cured for seeing the same "him" that you had not been able to see in a spiritual way.

Have I been with you for such a long time, and you have not come to know me, Philip? Anyone that has seen me has seen the Father. Why were they not seeing him? Look, they were seeing him, and were not seeing the Father; they were seeing the flesh, but the divine grandeur was hidden. What the disciples who loved him were seeing was also being seen by the Jews who crucified him. So within that flesh was the whole of him, and in such a way within the flesh that he remained with the Father; he did not, after all, forsake the Father when he came to the flesh.

By sharing with us God's wrath, Christ changes it into God's grace for us

13. Those with flesh-bound thoughts will not grasp what I am saying. Let them put off trying to understand and start from faith. Let them listen to what follows: *He that believes in the Son has eternal life; while he that puts no trust in the Son will not see life, but the wrath of God remains upon him* (Jn 3:36). He did not say, "the wrath of God comes upon him," but *the wrath of God remains upon him*. All who are born as mortals carry God's wrath with them. What wrath of God? The wrath that overtook the first Adam. You see, if the first man sinned, and heard, *You shall die the death* (Gn 2:17), he became mortal, and we began to be born mortal; so we are born with the wrath of God. The Son of God came from up there having no sin, and he clothed himself with sin, clothed himself with mortality. If he shared the wrath of God with us, are we going to be lazy in sharing the grace of God with him?

So then, whoever refuses to believe in the Son, *the wrath of God remains upon him.* What wrath of God? The wrath about which the apostle says, *We too were by nature children of wrath, like the rest* (Eph 2:3). So then, we are all children of wrath, because we stem from the death curse. Believe in Christ who became mortal for your sake, so that you may grasp him as immortal; you will not be mortal either, you see, when you have grasped his immortality. He was alive, you were dying; he died so that you might live. He brought along God's grace, took away God's wrath. God conquered death and mortality, to prevent death from conquering humankind.[22]

---

22. For themes dealt with in this section see Sermons 80, 5; 144, 2; 232, 5; 265B, 4.

Homily 15

On John 1:1-42[1]

Great mysteries are contained in the story of the woman at the well

1. It will not come as a shock to Your Graces' ears to learn that the evangelist John, like an eagle, flies higher than the others, soaring above the foggy atmosphere of the earth, and gazing with steadfast eyes upon the light of Truth. After all, through my ministry and with God's help, many things in his gospel have already been dealt with; and this passage that has been read today follows upon them in due order. The things I am going to say, as the Lord allows, will be heard by many as something you recognize, rather than as something you need to learn. But your attention should not therefore be lazy because you will be recalling what you know rather than learning something you did not know.

This passage has been read, and in my hands I am holding this reading to be discussed, namely, that the Lord Jesus Christ was at Jacob's well, talking with a woman from Samaria. Indeed, great mysteries and figures of great realities, which can nourish the hungry soul and revive the faint and weary, were uttered there.

Why Jesus left Judea after being baptized by John

2. The Lord, you see, said these things *when he had heard that the Pharisees had come to know that he was making more disciples than John and baptizing more (though it was not Jesus who was baptizing, but his disciples), and so he left the land of Judea and went again into Galilee* (Jn 4:1-3). We must not spend too long discussing this; if we linger over what is perfectly clear, we will not leave ourselves enough time to investigate and explain what is obscure. Of course, if the Lord had known that the Pharisees, as a result of learning that he was making more disciples and baptizing more than John, would realize that following him would benefit them for salvation such that they would be his disciples and would wish to be baptized by him, then he would not have left the land of Judea but would

---

[1]. Preached early in June 407, soon after Homilies 12-14.

have stayed on there for their sakes. But in fact because he knew that they were aware of all this and, at the same time, knew that they were jealous, and that they would use what they had learned not to follow him but to attack him, he left that place.

Of course, even if he had stayed there, he did not have to be seized by them if he did not want to; he did not have to be killed if he did not want to—after all he could have avoided being born if he had not wanted to. But in every action that he performed as a human being he was giving an example to the human beings who were going to believe in him. Now although a servant of God commits no sin by withdrawing to another place when he observes the rage of those who are attacking him or seeking to ruin his soul, he might still think he is sinning in doing so, unless the Lord had done it before him. So the good master did it himself in order to educate and not because he was afraid.

How Jesus was both baptizing and not baptizing

3. Perhaps someone is also concerned about why it was said, *Jesus was baptizing more than John*, and afterward is said, *he was baptizing*, adding, *though it was not Jesus who was baptizing, but his disciples*. So what does this mean? That the first statement was untrue and was corrected by the addition of *though it was not Jesus who was baptizing, but his disciples*? Or is each statement true, because Jesus *was* both the one baptizing and the one not baptizing? He was the one baptizing, because he was the one who was cleansing; he was not the one baptizing, because he was not the one immersing. His disciples were providing a service to the body, he was providing the assistance of his majesty.[2] When, in fact, will he ever give up baptizing, as long as he does not stop cleansing? John the evangelist, speaking in the person of John the Baptist, says of him, *This is the one who baptizes* (Jn 1:33). So Jesus is still baptizing; and as long as we are to be baptized, Jesus baptizes. Untroubled, let each one approach this lesser ministry,[3] for he has a Master above him.

---

2. See Homily 5,18.
3. That is, without concern for their reputation or for their moral standing.

Christ baptizes both in the Spirit and in the body, by water with a word

4. But perhaps someone is saying, "Christ indeed baptizes spiritually, not physically"—as if it could be by the gift of someone else that anybody is infused with this physical, visible sacrament of baptism. Do you wish to be assured that he baptizes not only spiritually but also with water? Listen to the apostle: *Just as Christ*, he says, *loved the Church and gave himself up for her, cleansing her by the bath of water with a word, so that he might present himself with a glorious Church, not having any spot or wrinkle or any such thing* (Eph 5:25-27). *Cleansing her.* How? *By the bath of water with a word.* Take away water, there is no baptism; take away the word, there is no baptism.

Christ's strength and weakness as he comes to sit at the well, worn out from the journey

5. So then, having treated all that led up to his conversation with that woman, let us look at what follows, full of mysteries, pregnant in symbols.[4] *Now it was necessary*, he says, *for him to pass through Samaria. So he came to a town of Samaria which is called Sichar, next to the estate which Jacob gave to his son Joseph. Now Jacob's well was there.* (Jn 4:4-6) There was a well; but every well is a spring, while not every spring is a well. Wherever water flows up from the ground, you see, and provides a source to be used by those who come to draw water, it is called a spring. But if it is readily available on the surface it is just called a spring, while if it is only to be found deep down it is called a well, without losing the name of spring.[5]

6. *So then Jesus, weary from the journey, went to sit down there at the well. It was about the sixth hour.* (Jn 4:6) Now the mysteries are already beginning; for it is not for nothing that Jesus is tired, not for nothing that the strength of God is weary; not for nothing that the one by whom the weary are re-made is tired; not for nothing that the one whose absence wears us out, whose presence makes us steadfast, is weary. Still, Jesus is tired; he is tired from the journey and he sits down, and he sits down by the well, and it is at the sixth hour that, weary, he sits down. All these details are hinting at

---

4. *Gravida sacramentis.*
5. Note that "spring" ("fountain" or "font"), which translates the Latin *fons*, is a source from which to draw strength, grace, etc.

something, they want to suggest something; they are making us alert, they are encouraging us to knock. Therefore, may the one who was good enough to encourage us by saying, *Knock, and it will be opened to you* (Mt 7:7), open the door both to me and to you.

For you was Jesus weary from the journey. We find a strong Jesus and we find a weak Jesus; Jesus is weak and strong; strong, because *in the beginning was the Word, and the Word was with God, and the Word was God; in the beginning he was with God.* Do you want to see how this Son of God is strong? *All things were made through him, and without him was made nothing* (Jn 1:1-3)—and they were made without effort. So what could be stronger than him through whom all things were made without effort? Do you want to see him as weak? *The Word was made flesh and took up residence among us* (Jn 1:14). The strength of Christ created you, the weakness of Christ recreated you. The strength of Christ caused that which was not to be; the weakness of Christ caused that which already was not to perish. He fashioned us in his strength, came looking for us in his weakness.

Christ's weakness—like that of a hen with her chicks—is stronger than that of men

7. So then, as a weak one, he nourished the weak, like a hen who nourishes her chicks—for that is what he compared himself to: *How often*, said he to Jerusalem, *have I wanted to gather your children under my wings, like a hen with her chicks, and you were unwilling!* (Mt 23:37) But you can see, brothers and sisters, how a hen makes herself weak with her chicks. No other bird can be so immediately recognized as a mother. We see sparrows of all sorts building their nests before our very eyes; swallows, storks, doves, we see them every day building their nests; but we cannot recognize them as parents except when they are in their nests. But a hen makes herself weak among her chicks, to such an extent that even if the chicks are not following her and you do not see them, you still recognize her as a mother. Wings drooping, feathers ruffled, her hoarse clucking, as she droops and brings her limbs down to them, you recognize her as a mother, even if, as I said, you do not see her chicks.

So then, that is how Jesus was weak, *weary from the journey*. His journey is the flesh he took on for our sake. How, in fact, can the one who is everywhere, who is absent from no place whatever, make a journey? What does it mean to talk about where he goes from or where he goes to—if not that he would not have come to us if he had not taken on the form of visible flesh? So then, because he was good enough to come to us that he would appear, with the flesh that he took to himself, in *the form of a slave* (Phil 2:7), the very taking of flesh to himself is his journey. Accordingly, what else can *weary from the journey* mean but weary in the flesh? Jesus is weak in the flesh. But do not weaken: *you* must be strong with his weakness, because *the weakness of God is stronger than men* (1 Cor 1:25).

The Church is made from Christ's strength, like Eve from Adam's rib

8. In this matter, Adam, who was *the model of the one to come* (Rom 5:14), provided us with a most telling pointer of the mystery[6]—or rather God did so in him. For not only was he privileged to receive a wife while he was asleep, but besides that his wife was made for him from his rib, because from Christ asleep on the cross the Church was going to issue from his side, from the side of one sleeping, that is; because it was from his side, pierced by the lance as he hung on the cross, that the Church's sacraments flowed out.[7]

But why have I mentioned this here, brothers and sisters? Because Christ's weakness makes us strong. In that story a most telling comparison has been made in advance. God could have taken flesh out of the man, with which to make the woman; and it does seem that that could well have been more appropriate. It was the weaker sex, after all, that was being made, and weakness should have been made out of flesh rather than bone; the bones, after all, are the stronger element in the flesh. Well, he did not take out flesh to make the woman of; he took out a bone, and the woman was formed from the bone that had been taken out, and the bone's place was filled in with flesh. He could have replaced bone with bone; he could have taken out not a rib but flesh to make the woman. So what did it all signify? The woman was

---

6. *Magnum indicium sacramenti.*
7. See Gn 2:21-22; Jn 19:34; the Church's sacraments, baptism and the eucharist, represented by the water and the blood. For a brief statement of the doctrine see Sermon 218, 14. For a longer discussion, see Homily 9, 10.

made, as it were, strong in the rib; Adam was made as it were weak in the flesh. It is Christ and the Church; his weakness is our strength.

Jesus sitting on the well at the sixth hour means his humbling himself in the last age of the world

9. So why the sixth hour then? Because it is the sixth age of the world. In the gospel, count from Adam up to Noah as one hour, one age; a second from Noah up to Abraham; a third from Abraham up to David; a fourth from David to the exile in Babylon; a fifth from the exile in Babylon up to the baptism of John; from then on the sixth is running its course.

Why be surprised? Jesus came, and, humbling himself, he came to the well. He came weary, because he carried the weakness of the flesh. He came at the sixth hour, because it was the sixth age of the world. He came to a well, because he came into the very depths of this dwelling place of ours—which is why it says in the psalms, *Out of the depths have I cried to you, Lord* (Ps 129:1). He sat down, as I said, because he humbled himself.

The woman represents the Church of the gentiles

10. *And a woman comes*, a model of the Church not yet justified, but ready to be justified; for that is what the conversation will deal with. She comes, all unaware, she finds him there, and he converses with her. Let us see what that conversation was, and why it came about. *A woman comes from Samaria to draw water* (Jn 4:7). The Samaritans did not belong to the Jewish people; in fact, they were foreigners, though they lived in neighboring territories. It would take a long time to unravel the origin of the Samaritans, thus holding on to many details and not saying what needs to be said. Let it be enough to count the Samaritans as foreigners. And in case you think I have said this rashly rather than truly, listen to the Lord Jesus himself, and to what he said about that Samaritan among the ten lepers whom he had made clean, the only one who came back to thank him: *Were not ten made clean? And where are the nine? There was not one other who would give God the glory, except this foreigner.* (Lk 17:17-18)

It is part of the symbolism of this episode that this woman, who was a type of the Church, came from a foreign people. In fact, the Church, a foreigner to the Jewish people, was going to come from the nations. So then, let us listen to ourselves in her and recognize ourselves in her, and in her give thanks to God for ourselves. She, after all, was a figure, not the true reality, and because she prefigured the reality, that is what she became. For she came to believe in the one who proposed her to us as a figure. So then, *she comes to draw water*. She had just come to draw water, as both men and women are in the habit of doing.

Jesus is thirsting for the woman's faith

11. *Jesus says to her, Give me a drink. For his disciples had gone off to the town to buy food. So this Samaritan woman says to him, How is it that you, who are Jewish, can ask for a drink from me, a Samaritan woman? The Jews, you see, do not consort with the Samaritans.*(Jn 4:7-9) As you see, they were foreigners; the Jews would not even make use of their vessels. And because the woman brought a vessel with her to draw the water, she was astonished that a Jew should be asking her for a drink, something Jews were not in the habit of doing. But the one who was asking for a drink was thirsting for the woman's own faith.

12. Just listen, in fact, to who was asking for a drink: *Jesus answered and said to her, If you knew the gift of God, and who it is that is saying to you, Give me a drink, you would perhaps have asked him, and he would have given you living water* (Jn 4:10). He asks for a drink, he promises a drink. He needs water as if to slake his thirst, and he pours forth water so as to satisfy fully. *If you knew*, he says, *the gift of God*. God's gift is the Holy Spirit. But he is still speaking in veiled terms to the woman, and little by little finding a way into her heart. Perhaps he is already teaching. What, after all, could be kinder and more friendly than this exhortation? *If you knew the gift of God, and knew who it is that is saying to you, Give me a drink, you would perhaps ask him, and he would give you living water*. So far he is keeping her in suspense.

What is called living water in ordinary speech is water as it comes from a spring. I mean, water that is collected from the rain in ponds or cisterns is not called living water. Even if it has flowed from a spring and has been stored in some place, and the source from which it flowed has been cut off and its movement stopped, such that it has been separated from the spring, it is not called living water. That water is called living which is drawn as it flows. Such was the water in that spring.[8] So why was Jesus promising what he was asking for?

The woman knocking on the door with her ignorance

13. However, the woman held in suspense said, *Sir, you do not even have something to draw water with, and the well is deep* (Jn 4:11). Notice how she understood *living water*, that is, as the water that was in that spring. "You want to give me living water, and I am the one who has something to draw it with and you have nothing. The living water is right here; how are you going to give it to me?" While understanding him in a different sense, and thinking in terms of the flesh, she is in some way knocking on the door so that the master might open what was closed. Ignorance—not desire—was knocking; she was still worthy of compassion and not yet of instruction.

The true living water, the water of life

14. The Lord says something even clearer about that living water. The woman, you see, had said, *Are you greater than our father Jacob, who gave us the well and drank from it himself with his children and his flocks* (Jn 4:12)? "You cannot give me any of this living water, since you do not even have a bucket; perhaps you are promising us another spring? Could you be better than our father, who dug this well, and used it himself together with his own family?"

So let the Lord tell her what he had called living water. Jesus answered and said to her, *Everyone who drinks of this water will get thirsty again; but whoever drinks of the water that I shall give him will never get thirsty again; but the water which I shall give him will become in him a spring of water, bubbling up into everlasting life* (Jn 4:13-14). The Lord has spoken more openly: *It will become in him a spring of water, bubbling up into everlasting life; whoever drinks of this water will never get thirsty again*. How could it be any clearer that he was promising not visible but invisible water? How could it be any clearer that he was speaking not in terms of the flesh but in terms of the spirit?

---

8. In section 5 of this homily, Augustine included wells in the category of springs, thus making wells a source of living water.

The woman still thinking in material terms

15. However, that woman was still understanding according to the flesh. She was delighted at the thought of not getting thirsty and, according to the flesh, supposed that the Lord had just made that promise. Well, that is also going to happen, but only in the resurrection of the dead; she wanted it already. For there was a time when God gave his servant Elijah the power to go forty days without getting hungry or thirsty.[9] If he could give this power for forty days, could he not give it for ever?

Still, she heaved a great sigh, longing to be done with the need, longing to be done with the toil. Time and again was she constrained to come to that well, and to carry the load which met her needs, to come back again when what she had drawn was finished. This was her daily toil, because the water assuaged that need, but it did not extinguish it. So then, delighted at the prospect of such a favor, she asks him to give her this living water.

The water in the well stands for the pleasures of life;
the bucket stands for human greed

16. However, we must not overlook the fact that he was promising something spiritual. What is the meaning of *Whoever drinks of this water will get thirsty again*? It is indeed true both for this water and for what this water was representing. Thus the water in the well is worldly pleasure in the dark depths. People draw it from there with the bucket of their lusts; bent over they submit to lust so that they may attain the pleasure drawn up from the depths and may enjoy the pleasure which was preceded by the lust sent down to it. In fact, the one who does not first put his lust forward cannot reach the pleasure.

So then, take the bucket as being lust, the water from the depths as being pleasure; when anyone attains the pleasure of this world—that is food, drink, the baths, the stadium, intercourse—will he not get thirsty again? So then, Jesus says, *Whoever drinks of this water will get thirsty again*; but if he accepts water from me, *he will never get thirsty again*. *We shall be satisfied*, says the Psalmist, *by the good things of your house* (Ps 65:4). So from what water is he going to give us a drink, if not that of which it says, *With*

---

9. See 1 K 19:8.

you is the spring of life? How, after all, will those ever get thirsty who *shall be made drunk on the abundance of your house* (Ps 35:10.9)?

Jesus was promising the water of life, the Holy Spirit

17. So then, he was promising a lavish meal and her fill of the Holy Spirit, and she did not yet understand, and in her failure to understand, what was her reply? *Sir, give me this water, so that I may not be thirsty nor have to come here to draw* (Jn 4:15). Need forced her to this toil and weakness objected to it. If only she could hear, *Come to me, all you who toil, and I will refresh you* (Mt 11:28)! That, in fact, is what Jesus was saying to her, so that she need no longer toil. But she did not yet understand.

Call your husband *means* Apply your intelligence

18. Finally, wanting her to understand, *Jesus says to her, Go, call your husband and come back here* (Jn 4:16). What does that mean, *Call your husband*? Did he want to have her husband give her that water? Or perhaps, since she did not understand, he wanted her husband to teach her. Perhaps, as the apostle said about women, *But if they wish to learn, let them question their husbands at home* (1 Cor 14:35)? But what is said there, *Let them question their husbands at home,* refers to a case where Jesus is not teaching. In fact, it is being said to women whom the apostle was forbidding to speak in the Church. But when the Lord himself was present and was talking to the woman face to face, what need was there for him to talk to her through her husband? Did he talk through her husband to Mary, as she sat at his feet drinking in his words, while Martha, all too busy with the cares of service, grumbled about her sister's good fortune?[10]

So then, my brothers and sisters, let us listen and understand what the Lord is saying with the words, *Call your husband*. Perhaps, you see, he is also saying to our souls, *Call your husband*. So then, let us also ask about the soul's husband. Why would Jesus himself not already be the soul's true husband?[11] Concentrate your minds, because what I am going to say can only be grasped by those who are paying close attention. Concentrate your

---

10. See Lk 10:39-40.
11. Since he is now the bridegroom of the Church, and hence of every Christian soul.

minds, then, so that you may understand—and perhaps the intelligent mind itself will turn out to be the soul's husband.

19. So then, seeing that the woman was not understanding and wanting her to do so, Jesus said, *Call your husband.* You do not know what I am talking about because your understanding is not present. I am talking with reference to the spirit, you are hearing with reference to the flesh. The things I am talking about have no relation to the pleasure of the ears, or to the eyes or the sense of smell, or to taste or touch. They are only grasped by the mind, only drunk in by the understanding. Your understanding is not here with you; how can you grasp what I am saying? *Call your husband,* bring your intelligence here.

After all, how does having a soul benefit you?[12] Not much, since even cattle have souls. But what makes you better than them? Having intelligence, which cattle do not have. So what do I mean by *Call your husband*? You do not comprehend, you do not understand me. I am talking to you about the gift of God, but you are thinking of the flesh. It is with reference to the flesh that you do not want to get thirsty any more, while I am speaking to your spirit. Your understanding is absent; *call your husband. Do not be like horse and mule, which have no understanding* (Ps 31:9).

So then, my brothers and sisters, having a soul and not having intelligence—that is, not applying it, not living as it dictates—is to live an animal life. There is, to be sure, something of the animal in us, by which we live in the flesh, but it is meant to be directed by the intelligence. The intelligence directs from above the motions of the soul, which follows the promptings of the flesh and longs to spread itself without moderation in flesh-bound delights. Which of these ought to be called the husband, the one directing or the one being directed? Without doubt, when a life is well regulated, the intelligence—which belongs to the soul—is directing the soul. The intelligence, you see, is not something other than the soul but is part of the soul, just as the eye is not different from the flesh, but is part of the flesh. But while the eye is something in the flesh, it alone is capable of enjoying light; the other fleshly parts of the body can be

---

12. Note the relationship, almost identification, in Augustine's use of terms, between "soul" and "flesh"—and the contrast, the opposition almost, between "soul" and "spirit."

bathed in light, but they cannot perceive light; only the eye is bathed in it and also enjoys it.

In the same way there is something in our soul which is called intelligence. This part of the soul, which is called intelligence and mind, is enlightened by a higher light; this higher light, by which the human mind is enlightened, is God. *That, you see, was the true light which enlightens everyone coming into the world* (Jn 1:9). That is the kind of light Christ was; that is the kind of light that was talking to the woman; and she was not there with her intelligence, which could be enlightened by that light, and not only be bathed in it but also enjoy it. It is as if the Lord were saying, "I want to enlighten, and no one is here to enlighten." *Call your husband*, he said; "summon the intelligence by which you can be taught, can be directed."

So then, think of a soul without intelligence as a woman, of a soul which has intelligence as a man. But this man does not direct his wife well, unless he is directed from above. For *the head of the woman is the man, while the head of the man is Christ* (1 Cor 11:3). The head of men was speaking with the woman and the man was not present. It is as if the Lord wanted to say, "Bring along your head[13] so that he might welcome his head." So *call your husband and come back here* means, "Be present, be truly with me; I mean, you are elsewhere as long as you do not understand the voice of Truth here present; be present yourself, but not alone; be present with your head."

The matter of the five husbands

20. But, not yet calling her husband, she did not understand; she still knew according to the flesh, for her husband was not there. *I do not have a husband*, she says. And the Lord follows her line of thinking and speaks in mystery. In fact, you must understand that it was quite true; this woman did not then have a husband, but was living with who-knows-which illicit partner, an adulterer rather than a husband. And the Lord says to her, *You have said well, I do not have a husband* (Jn 4:17). "So then, why did you say, *Call your husband?*" Notice that the Lord knew very well that she did not have a husband. *He said to her.* So then, lest the woman should think the reason the Lord said, *You have said well, I do not have a husband*, was that

---

13. That is, the one who is "above" you according to Paul's usage.

he had learned about it from her, and not that he knew it by divine knowledge, he said to her, Listen to what you did not say, *You have had five husbands, and the one that you have is not your husband; that you have said truly* (Jn 4:18).

Augustine understands the five husbands as the five senses

21. Once again, he compels us to take a closer look at these five husbands. Many commentators,[14] in fact, have understood the five husbands of this woman to be the five books of Moses; that is neither absurd nor improbable. The Samaritans, after all, accepted these books and followed the same law as the Jews; for, on that basis, they also practiced circumcision.

But, faced with a difficulty in what follows, *And the one that you have now is not your husband*, it seems to me that it is easier for us to take the first five husbands of the soul as being the five senses of the body. As soon as anyone is born, you see, before they can use their reason, their actions are directed only by the senses of the flesh. In a small child, what is heard, what is seen, what smells, what has a taste, what is perceived by touch, is what the soul wants or shrinks from. It wants whatever flatters these five senses; it shrinks from whatever offends them. Of course, pleasure flatters these five senses; pain offends them. The soul lives according to these five senses as subject to five husbands because the soul is ruled by them.

Her true husband is intelligence, imbued with wisdom

But why are they called husbands? Because they are lawful partners, made by God and bestowed upon the soul by God. The soul which is directed by these five senses is still weak, and she[15] acts in submission to these five husbands. But when she comes to the years of discretion—as long as she has accepted the best of discipline and the teaching of wisdom—what follows these five husbands in directing her is none other than her true, lawful husband, a better one than those, who will give her better direction, directing her toward eternity, training her for eternity,

---

14. E.g., Ambrose, *Commentary on Luke* IX, 38.
15. "Soul" is feminine in Latin. Hitherto I have referred to the soul as "it," but it is represented by a woman here, and the feminine pronoun is appropriate. Masculine pronouns will be used for intelligence or understanding.

educating her for eternity. These five senses, I mean to say, do not direct us toward eternity, but to seeking or shunning these things of time.

But when intelligence, imbued with wisdom, begins to direct the soul, she now knows not only how to avoid the ditch and walk on level ground which her eyes make clear to her weak soul, nor only to listen with pleasure to harmonious voices and close her ears to discordant ones, nor to take delight in agreeable smells and thrust aside foul stenches, nor to be enthralled by what tastes sweet and offended by what tastes bitter, nor to be soothed by things smooth to the touch and find rough things painful. Knowing about all these things, after all, is necessary for a weak soul. So what kind of direction, then, is provided by that intelligence? The intelligence will not just distinguish between black and white, but between just and unjust, good and evil, useful and useless, chastity and shamelessness, in order to love the one and shun the other; between charity and hatred, in order to live in the first and not in the second.[16]

Her actual adulterous partner is error

22. In this woman's case, this husband was not the one who had succeeded those five husbands. Where *he* does not take their place, you see, error rules. For, when the soul begins to be capable of reason, she is directed either by a wise mind or by error—error, however, does not guide but leads astray. So then, after [the rule of] those five senses, that woman was still all off track, and error was playing with her. This error, though, was not a legitimate husband, but an adulterer. That is why the Lord said, *You have said well, I do not have a husband, for you have had five husbands.* The five senses of the flesh directed you at first; you reached the age for making use of reason, and you did not get as far as wisdom but fell into error. So then, after those five husbands, *the one that you have is not your husband.*

And if he was not a husband, what was he but an adulterer? "So then, call not an adulterer but your husband, in order that you may grasp me with your intelligence, not from some false idea about me through error." The woman, you see, was still in error, thinking about that water when the Lord was already talking about the Holy Spirit. What else was leading her astray

---

16. See *Exposition of Psalm* 42, 6.

but having an adulterous partner instead of a husband? "So get rid of this adulterer who is corrupting you, and go, call your husband. Go and come back, so that you may understand me."

The differences between Samaritans and Jews

23. *The woman says to him, Sir, I see that you are a prophet* (Jn 4:19). The husband is beginning to come, he has not yet come completely. She was taking the Lord for a prophet. He was indeed also a prophet; I mean, he said about himself, *A prophet is not without honor except in his home country* (Mk 6:4). Again, it was about him that Moses was told, *I will raise up a prophet like you from their brothers* (Dt 18:18); *like you*, that is, in the form of the flesh, not in his surpassing majesty. So then, we find the Lord Jesus called a prophet. Hence, the woman is now not far off. *I see*, she says, *that you are a prophet*. She is beginning to call the husband, to keep out the adulterer. *I see that you are a prophet*; and she begins to question him about that which normally rouses her interest.

Of course, there was a dispute between Samaritans and Jews, because the Jews worshiped God in the temple built by Solomon; the Samaritans, settled far from there, did not worship in that temple. Therefore, the Jews boasted about being better, because they worshiped God in the temple; *the Jews, you see, do not consort with the Samaritans*, because they would say to them, "How can you boast, pretending to be better than us, just because you have a temple that we do not have? Did our ancestors, who found favor with God, worship in that temple? Did they not worship on this mountain, where we are? So then, it is better for us," they say, "to pray to God on this mountain where our ancestors prayed." Both were quarreling in ignorance, because neither of them had a husband; they were all puffed up against each other, the ones flaunting their temple, the others their mountain.

Worship in spirit and truth, the starting point, the foundation being faith

24. However, what does the Lord now start teaching the woman, as one whose husband had started to be present? The woman says to him, *Sir, I see that you are a prophet. Our ancestors worshiped on this mountain, and you say that Jerusalem is the place where one ought to worship. Jesus says to*

her, Woman, believe me. (Jn 4:19-21) In fact, the Church is coming, as it says in the Song of Songs, *She will come and pass through from the beginning of faith* (Sg 4:8, LXX). She will come in order to pass through, and she can only pass through if she begins from faith.[17] Most appropriately does she hear, with her husband now present, *Woman, believe me.* Now, in fact, someone in you believes, because your husband is present. You began to be present here with your intelligence, your understanding, when you called me a prophet. *Woman, believe me, because unless you believe you will not understand* (Is 7:9, LXX).

So then, *Woman, believe me that the hour is coming when neither on this mountain nor in Jerusalem shall you worship the Father. You worship what you do not know, we worship what we do know, because salvation is from the Jews. But the hour is coming.* When? *And now is.* So what hour then? *When true worshipers will worship the Father in spirit and truth. Not on this mountain, not in the temple, but in spirit and truth—for the Father is looking for such people to worship him.* (Jn 4:21-23)

Why is the Father looking for such people to worship him, not on the mountain, not in the temple, but in spirit and truth? *God is spirit.* If God were a body, it would be necessary for him to be worshiped on the mountain, because a mountain is something physical; necessary for him to be worshiped in the temple, because the temple is something physical. *God is spirit, and those who worship him must worship him in spirit and truth* (Jn 4:24).

The necessity of humility

25. We have heard and it is obvious; we had been leaving, we were sent back inside. You were saying,

"Oh, if only I could find some high and solitary mountain! For I believe that God is on high, that he listens to me more readily from a high place."

"You think that, because you are on a mountain, God is near you, and that, as one who cries out from nearby, you will be quickly heard, is that it? He dwells in the heights, but looks on the lowly."

"The Lord is near."

---

17. See also *Exposition of Psalms* 33, 1, 10; 67, 41; Sermon 105, 6. Augustine usually quotes this text in conjunction with Is 7:9, LXX, as he will shortly be doing here; both texts support his doctrine of "faith seeking understanding."

"Near whom? Perhaps to those who are high up?"

He is near those who have crushed their hearts (Ps 33:19).

What a wonderful thing; he dwells in the heights and draws near to the humble. *He looks on the lowly, while he knows what is high up from afar* (Ps 137:6). He sees the proud from afar, and the higher they think they are, the less he draws near to them.[18] So, were you looking for a mountain? Come down in order to reach him. But you want to ascend? Ascend, by all means, but do not look for a mountain. *The mountains were in his heart*—says this psalm—*in the valley of weeping* (Ps 83:6-7). A valley is low-lying. So then, do everything within; and if perchance you are looking for some high place, some holy place, present the temple within you to God. *For the temple of God is holy, and that is what you are* (1 Cor 3:17). Do you want to pray in the temple? Pray in yourself. But first *be* a temple of God, because he will listen to anyone praying in his temple.

Christ, the cornerstone between Jews and gentiles

26. *So then, the hour is coming and now is, when true worshipers will worship the Father in spirit and truth. We worship what we know, you worship what you do not know, because salvation is from the Jews.* He credited the Jews with a great deal; but do not take the Samaritans as being rejected. Think of them as that wall to which another was joined, so that, reconciled in the cornerstone which is Christ, they might be bound together.[19] One wall, you see, is from the Jews, one from the gentiles; these walls are a long way away from each other, until they are joined at the corner. But the foreigners were guests, strangers to God's covenants. So it was in that connection that he said, *We worship what we know*. It was said of the Jews as a people, but not of all Jews, not of the Jews who were rejected, but of Jews such as the apostles were, such as the prophets were, such as all those saintly people were who sold all their possessions and laid

---

18. See Sermon, 21, 2 for an almost identical treatment of this theme, also triggered by the quotation of Jn 4:24. Note 1 on that sermon indicates the difficulty with dating the sermons. But when that paragraph is compared to this homily (given in early June 407), there is some reason to date Sermon 21 to that same time.
19. See Eph 2:12-22, to which allusion is made again several times in the next paragraph.

The expectation of the Messiah

27. This woman heard all this and made a further contribution; she had already called him a prophet; she saw that the man she was talking to was saying the kind of things that would be beyond a prophet;[21] and notice what she answers: *The woman says to him, I know that Messiah is coming, who is called Christ; so when he has come, he will show us everything* (Jn 4:25). What is that all about? "Right now the Jews," she is saying, "are arguing in favor of the temple, while we here are arguing in favor of the mountain. When he has come, he will both spurn the mountain and overthrow the temple; he will teach us all we need to know in order to worship in spirit and truth." She knew who would be able to teach her, but did not yet recognize him, already teaching her. So she was already worthy that he reveal himself to her. But *Messiah* means "anointed." "Anointed" in Greek is *Christos*, in Hebrew *Messiah*; even in Punic *messe* means "anoint." Of course, these languages, Hebrew, Punic and Syriac, are closely related.[22]

Christ reveals himself to the woman as her true husband

28. So then, the woman says to him, *I know that Messiah is coming, who is called Christ; so when he has come, he will announce everything to us. Jesus says to her, I am he, talking to you now.* (Jn 4:25-26) She has called her husband; her husband has become the head of the woman, Christ has become the head of the husband.[23] The woman is already being guided in faith and directed toward living a good life. After hearing, *I am he, talking to you now*, what more could she say, since Christ the Lord wanted to reveal himself to the woman, to whom he had said, *Believe me*?

---

20. See Acts 4:34-35.
21. Reading *quae jam plus essent a propheta*, with six manuscripts, instead of *plus essent ad prophetam*, with the Maurists and our given text: "things that would be beyond a prophet." In fact, she goes on to ask about the coming of the Messiah.
22. See Sermon, 113, 2, note 7. The word Augustine is commenting on in that sermon is *mammon*.
23. See 1 Cor 11:3.

The disciples return, and the woman goes back to the town

29. *And at that moment his disciples came, and they were surprised that he was talking to a woman.* What surprised them was that the one who had come to seek what was lost[24] was seeking this lost woman. They were surprised, I mean, at something good, not suspecting anything bad. *Yet no one said, What are you asking for? or Why are you talking to her?* (Jn 4:27)

30. *So then the woman left her bucket* (Jn 4:28). On hearing, *I am he, talking to you now,* and having received Christ the Lord in her heart, what else should she do but abandon the bucket and run off to evangelize? She threw away earthly passion, and hurried off to proclaim truth. Let those who want to evangelize learn; let them abandon the bucket at the well. Remember what I said earlier on[25] about the bucket; it was a vessel for drawing water, called by the Greek name *hydria,* because water in Greek is *hydor,* as if one were to say *aquarium* in Latin. So she abandoned the bucket, which was now not useful, but just a burden; of course she eagerly desired to be filled with that other water. To proclaim Christ, her burden now left aside, *she ran to the town and told those people, Come and see the man who has told me everything I have ever done.* She went about it step by step, lest any of them might get angry, take umbrage and assail her. *Come and see the man who has told me everything I have ever done. Could he be the Christ? They went out of the town and came to him.* (Jn 4:28-30)

The fields ripe for harvesting; the woman already at work

31. *And meanwhile the disciples were urging him, saying, Rabbi, eat.* For they had gone to buy food and had now come back. But he said, *I have food to eat, which you do not know about. So the disciples said to one another, Could someone have brought him something to eat?* (Jn 4:31-33) What is surprising about that woman's failure to understand about the water? Look, the disciples did not yet understand about the food! He, though, heard their thoughts and now taught them as the master,[26] not in a roundabout way, as with the woman whose husband he asked for, but quite plainly. *My food,* he said, *is to do the will of him who sent me* (Jn 4:34).

---

24. See Lk 19:10.
25. In section 16.
26. As the *rabbi,* which they had called him.

So then, in terms of that woman, his drink was also that he should do the will of the one who had sent him. Therefore, he said, *I am thirsty; give me a drink* (Jn 19:28; 4:7),[27] so that he might produce faith in her and drink her faith and make it part of his body; his body, you see, is the Church. So then, he said, *My food is to do the will of him who sent me.*

The seed for the harvest had been sown by the prophets and by Abraham, Isaac and Jacob

32. *Do you not say that there are still four months and then harvest will be here?* He was on fire for the work to start and was getting ready to send out workers: "You count four months before the harvest; but I am showing you another harvest, already white and ready. *Look, I am telling you; lift up your eyes and see that the fields are already white for the harvest.*" So then, he was going to send harvesters. *In this case, indeed, the saying is true, that one sows and another reaps, so that both the one who sows and the one who reaps may rejoice together. I have sent you to reap what you have not worked for; others have labored, and you have entered into their labors.* (Jn 4:35-38)

So what is this, then? He sent out reapers, did he, not sowers? Where did he send the reapers? Where others had already labored. Obviously, where they had already labored, something had been sown, and what had been sown was already ripe, waiting only for the sickle and the threshing sledge.[28] So where were the reapers to be sent to? To where the prophets had already preached; for they were the sowers. For, if they were not the sowers, how had the word come to that woman, *I know that Messiah is coming*? This woman was already ripe fruit, and the harvest was white and asking for the sickle. So then, *I have sent you.* Where to? *To reap what you have not sown; others have sown, and you have entered into their labors.*

Who thus labored? Abraham, Isaac and Jacob. Read about their labors; in all their labors are found prophecies of Christ, and that is why they are the sowers. Moses and the rest of the patriarchs, and all the

---

27. The combining of the cry on the cross with the request to the woman is surely deliberate.
28. For the whole of this section see Sermon, 101, 2, much of it almost word for word the same.

prophets—when they were sowing, how much they had to endure in that cold! So then, in Judea, the harvest was already ready. Rightly can we say that that is where the crop was already ripe, when so many thousands[29] brought the price of their possessions and, laying it all down at the feet of the apostles, relieved their shoulders from the burdens of this age and started following the Lord. Truly a ripe harvest!

What came of it? From that harvest a few grains were scattered, and they sowed the whole wide world, and another harvest sprang up, which is to be reaped at the end of the age. Of this harvest it is said, *Those who sow in tears shall reap in joy* (Ps 125:6). So into this harvest it is not apostles but angels who will be sent; *the reapers* he says, *are the angels* (Mt 13:39). So this harvest is growing among weeds and waiting to be rid of them at the end.

That other harvest, though, was already ripe, into which the apostles were sent, where the prophets had labored. All the same, brothers and sisters, notice what was said: *So that both the one who sows and the one who reaps may rejoice together.* Their labors were unequal, according to the season; but they will share in the joy equally; they are going to receive the reward of life together.

Jesus stays two days, gives the two commandments of charity

33. *Now from that town many Samaritans came to believe in him because of the woman's word, testifying that, He told me everything I have ever done. But when the Samaritans came to him, they asked him to stay with them, and he stayed there two days. Many others came to believe in him because of his word, and they said to the woman, We no longer believe because of your word; for we have heard for ourselves, and we know that this is truly the savior of the world.* (Jn 4:38-42)

And this must be noted briefly, because that is the end of the reading. The woman first brought the news, and on her evidence the Samaritans came to believe, and they urged him to stay with them; and he stayed there two days, and more of them came to believe; and when they had come to believe, they said to the woman, *We no longer believe because of your word; for we have heard for ourselves, and we know that this is truly*

---

29. Three thousand in Acts 2:41.

the savior of the world. First, by a report, afterwards by his presence. That is how it happens today with those who are outside and are not yet Christians; they are told about Christ by Christian friends; Christ was proclaimed through that woman, who was the Church proclaiming him; they come to Christ; they believe by her account; he stays with them two days, that is, he gives them the two commandments of charity, and many more believe in him, and more firmly too, since he truly is the savior of the world.

Homily 16

On John 4:43-53[1]

A prophet is without honor in his own country

1. Today's gospel reading, which follows yesterday's reading, is set before us for discussion. No difficult inquiries are needed into its meaning, but it is worth a sermon, worth admiration and praise. Accordingly, let me go over this passage of the gospel again, more to commend it to your attention than to deal with any difficulty. Jesus, you see, *after the two days* he spent in Samaria, *went on to Galilee* (Jn 4:43), *where he had been brought up* (Lk 4:16). The evangelist, however, goes on to say, *For Jesus himself bore witness that a prophet has no honor in his home country* (Jn 4:44).[2] That is not the reason why Jesus departed from Samaria after two days, because he was not getting any honor in Samaria; Galilee, not Samaria, after all, was his home country. Since therefore he had left that place so soon and had come to Galilee where he had been brought up, how can he be asserting that a prophet has no honor in his home country? It would seem he could more suitably have asserted that a prophet has no honor in his home country if he had rejected the idea of going on to Galilee and had stayed on in Samaria.

The problem set by this saying of Jesus

2. So would Your Graces please pay close attention to the mystery, of no trifling significance,[3] being presented to us; the Lord will suggest and provide what I am to say. You know the question proposed; work out its solution. But let us repeat the challenge, so that the solution will be more desirable. What provokes us is why the evangelist said, *For Jesus himself bore witness that a prophet has no honor in his home country*. Goaded by this, we returned to the previous words to find out why the evangelist wanted to say this; and we found that in his previous words he was saying how after two days Jesus traveled from Samaria into Galilee.

---
1. Preached the day after Homily 15, early in June 407.
2. See Mk 6:4 and its parallels in Mt and Lk.
3. *Non modicum sacramentum.*

Is that then, O evangelist, why you said that Jesus bore witness that a prophet would have no honor in his home country? Is it because he left Samaria after two days and hurried on to reach Galilee? On the contrary, I think I would find it more reasonable to suppose that, if Jesus would not have any honor in his home country, he would not be hurrying off to it and leaving Samaria. But, if I am not mistaken—or rather because it is true, and I am certainly not mistaken—the evangelist saw better than I do what he was saying; he saw the truth better than I can, since he was drinking it from the Lord's breast. John the evangelist, you see, is the one among all the disciples who reclined on the Lord's breast, the one for whom the Lord, while owing all of them his love, loved more than the rest.[4] So could that man be mistaken, while I have the right idea? On the contrary, if I have a sense of piety, I will listen obediently to what he said, so that I may deserve to perceive what he perceived.

*Augustine's suggestion; the royal official in Cana
who asked him to come and heal his son*

3. And so, my dearest friends, let me tell you what I think about the subject, without prejudice to anything better that you may have perceived. We all have one Master, after all, and we are fellow pupils in the same school. So then, this is my opinion, and it is for you to see whether what I think is true, or comes close to the truth.

He spent two days in Samaria, and the Samaritans came to believe in him; he spent as many days in Galilee, and the Galileans did not believe in him.[5] Think back to yesterday's reading and sermon, and go over them in your minds. He came to Samaria, where first of all the woman, with whom he had spoken great mysteries at Jacob's well, had proclaimed him; and when the Samaritans had seen and heard him, they believed in him because of the woman's words, and more firmly because of his words, and they believed in greater numbers; that is what is written. Having spent two days there—by this number of days the two commandments, *on which depend*

---

4. See Jn 13:23-26.
5. As Berrouard remarks in BA 71, 818, n. 2, it is astonishing that Augustine never refers to v. 45, where it says that *the Galileans received him.* Is it possible or likely that the verse was omitted from the copy of the gospel in Hippo Regius?

the whole law and the prophets (Mt 22:40), are mystically suggested, as you will remember my suggesting to you yesterday—he moved on into Galilee, *and came to the town of Cana in Galilee, where he had made the water into wine* (Jn 4:46). There, however, when he changed the water into wine, as John himself writes, his disciples believed in him—and the house, of course, was full of a crowd of banqueters. A great miracle was performed, and no one but his disciples believed in him!

This was the town in Galilee that he now revisited. *And behold a certain royal official, whose son was ill, came to him and began to ask him to come down*, to the town or to his house, *and heal his son; for he was near death* (Jn 4:46-47). Was the one who was asking not also believing? What answer do you expect to hear from me? Question the Lord how he felt about the man. When he was asked, you see, for such a favor he replied, *Unless you have seen signs and wonders, you do not believe* (Jn 4:48). He was reproving the man for being tepid or cold in faith, or for not having any faith at all, but just wanting to use the health of his son as a test, to see what sort of Christ this man was, who he was, how much he could do. While we have heard the words in which he makes his request, we do not see the doubt in his heart. But the one who pronounced judgment both heard his words and looked into his heart.

In any case, the evangelist himself also shows, by the way he tells the story, that the man who desired the Lord to come down to his house and heal his son had not yet come to believe. Thus after he was told that his son was in good health, and found that he had been healed at the very time when the Lord had said, *Go, your son lives* (Jn 4:50), the writer says, *And he and his whole household believed* (Jn 4:53). So then, if the reason he and his whole household believed was that he was told his son was better, and comparing the time they told him with the time Jesus had told him, it means that when he asked him to come, he was not yet believing.[6]

The Samaritans had been expecting no sign, they simply believed his words, while his fellow citizens were good enough to hear, *Unless you have seen signs and wonders, you do not believe*; and yet even there, after such a great miracle, no one believed but the man and his household. Many more

---

6. Augustine ignores some words in v.50 where Jesus tells the man his son lives: *and the man believed the word that Jesus said to him, and went off.*

Samaritans believed on his word alone; on that miracle, only that household believed, where it was performed.

What is it, therefore, my brothers and sisters, what is it that the Lord is drawing our attention to? In those days, Galilee of Judea was the Lord's home country, because that is where he was brought up. In our days, however, because this episode predicted something—not without reason, you see, were they called wonders (*prodigia*) because they predicted something; in Latin, *prodigium* is short for *porrodicium*, which means "say in advance," "signify in advance," and predicts something in the future—thus, because all those things were predicting something, all those things foretelling something, let us, for the moment, make the home country of our Lord Jesus Christ in the flesh (after all, he did not have a home country on earth except in the flesh, which he received from the earth), let us make the Lord's home country the Jewish people. See there. In his home country he has no honor.

Now, turn your attention to the crowds of Jews, turn your eyes to that nation, dispersed over the whole wide world and torn away from its roots. Notice the branches broken off, chopped up, dispersed, withered: into the place from which they were broken off, *the wild olive* had the privilege of being *grafted in* (Rom 11:17). Look at the throng of Jews, what are they saying nowadays? "The one you worship, the one you bow down to, was our brother." And let us reply, *A prophet has no honor in his home country.* The Jews in those days saw the Lord Jesus walking on earth, performing miracles, enlightening the blind, opening the ears of the deaf, loosening the tongues of the dumb, tightening up the limbs of the paralyzed, walking over the sea, commanding the winds and the waves, raising the dead, performing such tremendous signs, and barely a few of them believed.

I address the people of God: so many of us have believed; what signs have we seen? So then, what happened then predicted what is going on now. The Jews were, still are, like the Galileans; we are like the Samaritans. We have heard the gospel, together we have adhered to the gospel, through the gospel we have come to believe in Christ. We have seen no signs, nor have we asked for any.

A comparison of the case with that of doubting Thomas

4. Although he was one of the twelve chosen and holy apostles, the Thomas who wanted to put his fingers in the places left by the wounds was nonetheless an Israelite, a fellow countryman of the Lord. The Lord reproved him in the same way as he reproved the royal official. To this man he said, *Unless you have seen signs and wonders, you do not believe*; to that one he said, *Because you have seen, you have believed* (Jn 20:29). He came to the Galileans, after being with the Samaritans, who had believed his words, among whom he had performed no miracles, and from whom he had parted fully assured of their steadiness in the faith, because he had not parted from them in his omnipresent godhead. So then, when the Lord said to Thomas, *Come, put your hand in, and do not be unbelieving, but believe*; and when, on touching the places of the wounds, he cried out and said, *My Lord and my God*, he is rebuked and told, *Because you have seen, you have believed* (Jn 20:27-29). Because, however, this prophet does have honor among foreigners, what comes next? *Blessed are those who do not see, and who believe* (Jn 20:29).

Thus, we have been foretold here, and what the Lord first praised he has had the goodness to fulfill in us. Those who crucified him saw him, touched him, and even so only a few believed; we have not seen, have not handled him; we have heard, we have believed. May the blessing he promised come to pass in us, be fully accomplished in us, both here, because we have been preferred to his home country, and in the age to come, because we have been grafted in as replacements of the branches that were broken off.

The contrast with the case of the Roman centurion

5. In fact, he also indicated that he was going to break off these branches and graft in this wild olive, when he was moved by the faith of that centurion, who said to him, *I am not worthy that you should come in under my roof; but only say the word, and my servant will be healed. For I too am a man set under authority, having soldiers under me; and I say to this one, Go, and he goes, and to this one, Come, and he comes, and to my servant, Do this, and he does it. Jesus turned to those who were following*

him, and said to them, Amen, I say to you, in no one in Israel have I found such great faith. (Mt 8:8-10; Lk 7:6-7)[7] Why did he fail to find such great faith in Israel? Because *a prophet does has no honor in his home country.*

Could not the Lord also have said to the centurion what he said to this royal official, *Go, your son lives*? Mark the difference; this royal official wanted the Lord to come down to his house, that centurion said he was unworthy of having him come. To him Jesus had said, *I will come and heal him* (Mt 8:7), to the other, *Go, your son lives*. He was promising his actual presence in the first case, healing with a word in the second. And yet this man would wrench his presence from him, the other was saying he was not worthy of his presence. In this case he submitted to self-importance, in that one he gave in to humility. It is as though he were saying to this man, "*Go, your son lives*; do not wear me out. *Unless you have seen signs and wonders, you do not believe*; you want my presence in your house; but I can command with a word. Stop needing signs in order to believe. That foreign centurion believed I could do it with a word, and he believed before I did it; as for you people though, *unless you have seen signs and wonders, you do not believe.*"

So then, if that is how it is, let the proud branches be broken off, the humble wild olive grafted in; let the root nonetheless remain, after those have been cut away, these received in their place. Where does the root remain? In the patriarchs. Yes indeed, Christ's home country is the people of Israel, because he came from them in the flesh. But the root of this tree is found in Abraham, Isaac and Jacob, the holy ancestors. And where are these now? At rest with God, in great honor, such that, after his departure from the body, the poor man,[8] helped by God, was raised up to the bosom of Abraham, and was seen by the proud rich man from a long way off. So then, the root remains, the root is praised; but the proud branches were deservedly cut off and left to wither, while the humble wild olive found a place in the root as a result of their being cut off.

---

7. Both gospels are used in this long quotation; another instance perhaps of the church of Hippo Regius' using a harmony of the gospels? Or just Augustine quoting from a memory in which the two were blended?
8. Lazarus, Lk 16:22; his full Hebrew name is Eleazar, which means "My God helps." Augustine explains this fully in *Exposition of Psalm* 69, 7.

*Where the wild olive comes from and what happens
to it and to the broken-off branches*

6. So then, listen to how the natural branches are cut off, how the wild olive is grafted in, from the centurion himself, whom I thought we should remind ourselves of as a comparison with this royal official. *Truly, I tell you*, says Jesus, *I have not found such great faith in Israel; therefore, I tell you, many from East and West* (Mt 8:10-11). How wide the land over which the wild olive had spread! This world was indeed one of bitter woods, but because of humility, because of *I am not worthy that you should come in under my roof, many from East and West shall come*. And suppose they do come, what will be done with them? If they come, you see, it means they have now been cut out of the woods; where are they to be grafted in, so that they do not wither? *And will sit down*, he says, *with Abraham and Isaac and Jacob*. At what banquet, lest you not invite them to enjoy life everlasting, but to do some heavy drinking? *And will sit down with Abraham and Isaac and Jacob*. Where? *In the kingdom of heaven* (Mt 8:11), he says. And how will it fare with those who have come from the stock of Abraham? What will happen to the branches that filled the tree? What else but that they will be cut off, so that these may be grafted in? Show us that they will be cut off: *But the children of the kingdom will be cast into the outer darkness* (Mt 8:12).[9]

How we should honor him in his new home country; brief meditation on Ps 86:5

7. So then, may the prophet have honor among us, because he did not have any honor in his home country. He did not have honor in the home country in which he was brought up; let him have honor in the home country which he himself has founded.[10] In that one, you see, was brought up the founder of all things, brought up there in *the form of a slave* (Phil 2:7). For he founded the city in which he was brought up, Zion itself, the nation of the Jews, Jerusalem itself; being the Word of God with the Father, he founded all this; *all things*, after all, *were made through him, and without him was made nothing* (Jn 1:3).

---

9. For similar treatment of the story of the centurion, as illustrating what Paul says about the olive and the wild olive in Rm 11:16-21, see Sermon 77, 12.15; *Exposition of Psalm* 134, 7.
10. The play on the meanings of the verb *condo* (contrasting *patria in qua conditus est* with *patria quam condidit*) is lost.

Now, a psalm also spoke beforehand regarding that man whom we have heard about today, *the one mediator of God and men, the man Christ Jesus* (1 Tm 2:5); it says, *The man will say Mother Zion* (Ps 86:5). A man, mediator of God and men, says *Mother Zion*. Why does he say *Mother Zion*? Because it was from there that he took flesh, from there came the Virgin Mary, from whose womb he received the form of a slave, being good enough to be manifested in this way as the most lowly. *Mother Zion*, says the man; and this man who says *Mother Zion* was made in her; *the man was made in her* (Ps 86:5). In fact, before her he was God, and in her he was made man. The one who was made man in her, *the Most High*, not the most lowly, *founded her* (Ps 87:5). But then, as the most lowly, *the man was made in her*, because *the Word became flesh and took up residence among us* (Jn 1:14); the Most High founded her himself because *in the beginning was the Word, and the Word was with God, and the Word was God; all things were made through him* (Jn 1:1.3). But because he founded *this* home country too, let him have honor here. He was rejected by the home country in which he was born; may he be received by the home country which he has caused to be born anew.

Homily 17

On John 5:1-18[1]

The healing of souls from their vices is more important than curing the ills of bodies

1. We should not be astonished at a miracle performed by God; what would be astonishing would be one performed by a human being. Instead, we should rejoice and be in wonder[2] that our Lord Jesus Christ was made man, rather than that he, as God, performed divine deeds among men. Our salvation, after all, depends more on what he was made on our behalf, than on what he did among us; and it is more important that he healed the sins of souls than that he healed the ills of bodies which were going to die. But because the soul itself did not know the one it was to be healed by and because it had eyes in the flesh with which to see things done with bodies and did not yet have eyes in the heart healthy enough to recognize God in disguise, therefore he did what it was able to see, so as to heal its inability to see.

He went into a place where a big crowd of sick people was lying, blind, lame, with withered limbs; and since he was the doctor of both souls and bodies, and had come to heal the souls of all those who were going to believe, out of all those sick people he chose just one to be healed, in order to signify Unity. If we bring a lukewarm heart, a merely human capacity and disposition to bear on what he was doing, knowing what he had the power to do, then he did not do very much; in regard to his kindness, he did too little. So many were lying there, and just one was cured, even though, by one word, he could have set them all on their feet! So then, what are we to understand but that he used his power and his kindness to help souls grasp in his deeds what their eternal health and salvation required, rather than what their bodies needed for health in time?

You see, the true health of bodies, which we are expecting of the Lord, will come at the end in the resurrection of the dead. What comes to life then

---

1. Preached on a day in mid-July 414.
2. Following a suggestion of the Maurists, and reading *et ammirari* instead of what all the manuscripts have, *quam mirari*, which gives the sense: "what we should much more rejoice over than wonder at."

will not die; what is healed then will not get sick; what is filled then will not get hungry or thirsty; what is made new then will not grow old. Now though, notice the deeds of our Lord Jesus Christ: the eyes of the blind that were opened have been closed in death; the limbs of the paralyzed that were steadied have fallen apart in death; and whatever was healed in mortal limbs in this world of time has ended up as nothing; but the soul which believed has won its passage to eternal life.

So then, he gave a great sign in this one man that was healed to the soul that was going to believe, whose sins he had come to forgive, whose ills he had humbled himself to heal. About the profound mystery of this event and of this sign[3] I shall speak as best I can, as far as the Lord is pleased to grant me, with all of you paying careful attention and supporting our weakness by your prayers. Whatever I cannot manage will be supplied for you by the same one who helps me do what I can.

The pool signifies the Jewish people, the five porticoes the five books of Moses

2. I remember that I have often dealt with this pool surrounded by five porticoes,[4] under which a huge number of the sick were found, and, with me, several of you will recognize rather than have to learn what I am going to say. Still, it is by no means pointless to repeat even things that are known, both to instruct those who do not know them and to encourage those who do. All the same, since these things are known, they are to be treated briefly, not taught at leisure.

That pool and that water signified, in my opinion, the people of the Jews. John's Apocalypse, after all, openly points out to us that peoples are signified under the name of *waters*, where *many waters* were shown to him, and he asked what they were, and was given the answer, *they are peoples* (Rv 17:15). So then, this water, that is this people, was enclosed by the five books of Moses, as by five porticoes. But those books only manifested the

---

3. *Profundum sacramentum.*
4. Although Augustine says that he preached often (*assidue*) on this topic, we have few sermons that would have been preached before this one: Sermons 124; 125; 125A; *Exposition of Psalms* 70, 1, 19; 83, 10; 102, 5. This statement, therefore, suggests that some of Augustine's sermons have been lost.

sick, they did not heal them.⁵ The law, you see, found sinners guilty and did not absolve them. That is why the letter of the law without grace made everyone guilty, until grace delivered those who acknowledged their fault. That is, after all, what the apostle says: *For if a law had been given which could bring life, justice would most certainly have come from the law.* So why was the law given, then? He continues, and says, *But scripture enclosed all things under sin, so that what was promised through faith in Jesus Christ might be given to those who believe.* (Gal 3:21-22)

What could be more obvious? These words have explained to us, have they not, both the five porticoes and the crowd of the sick? The five porticoes are the law; why were the five porticoes not healing the sick?

Because if a law had been given that could bring life, justice would most certainly have come from the law.

So why then were they confining those that they were not healing?

Because scripture enclosed all things under sin, so that what was promised from faith in Jesus Christ might be given to those who believe.

The stirring of the water signified Christ's presence among the Jews; the healing of the one signified Unity

3. How was it happening that those who were not healed under the porticoes were healed in that water when it was stirred up? For all of a sudden the water was seen to be stirred up, but the one who agitated it was not seen. You may believe this was commonly done by the power of some angel, but not, all the same, without some mystery being signified.⁶ After the water was stirred, the one who was able to do so threw himself in, and he alone was healed; anyone who threw himself in after that would be doing so in vain.

What can this mean but that the one Christ came to heal the people of the Jews, and by doing great deeds and teaching useful doctrine stirred up sinners, stirred up the water by his presence, and stirred it up to bring about his passion? But he did so while remaining hidden; *for if they had known, they would never have crucified the Lord of glory* (1 Cor 2:8). So then, to step down into the water that is agitated is to believe humbly in the Lord's

---

5. The same point is made briefly in Sermon 272B and, in one way or another, in the sermons and homilies mentioned in the previous note.
6. *Sine significante aliquo sacramento.*

passion. One man was healed then, signifying Unity; anyone who came after him was not healed, because anyone who is outside the Unity will not be able to be healed.

The number 38 signifies sickness; its relation to 40 and to 50

4. Let us see then what he—intent on observing the mystery of Unity, as I said earlier on—wished to signify in that one man, whom alone out of so many sick persons he was good enough to restore to health. He found, in the years the man had been sick, a number symbolizing sickness; *he lived thirty-eight years in his infirmity* (Jn 5:5). How this number pertains more to sickness than to health calls for a rather more detailed explanation. I want you to be attentive; God will be present so that I speak fittingly and you hear sufficiently.

The sacred number forty is commended to us by a certain completeness. I think that Your Graces know this; the divine scriptures bear witness to it very often. Fasting was consecrated by this number, as you well know. Moses fasted forty days and Elijah for just as many, and our Lord and Savior Jesus Christ observed this number in fasting.[7] Moses represents the law, Elijah represents the prophets, the Lord represents the gospel. Also these three appeared on that mountain when he showed himself to the disciples, his features and garments transfigured in brilliant light. He appeared, you see, in the middle between Moses and Elijah, the law and the prophets thus bearing witness to the gospel.[8] So then, whether in the law or the prophets or the gospel, the number forty is commended to us in connection with fasting.

The great fast and fasting in general, however, is to abstain from wickedness and from the unlawful pleasures of the world; this is the perfect fast, *that renouncing ungodliness and worldly desires, we may live temperately, justly and devoutly in this world.* What reward does the apostle attach to this fast? He continues, saying, *awaiting that blessed hope and manifestation of the glory of the blessed God and of our Savior Jesus Christ* (Tit 2:12-13). So then, in this world we celebrate, as it were, forty days of fasting when we live well and abstain from wicked actions and unlawful pleasures. But because

---

7. See Ex 34:28; 1 K 19:8; Mt 4:2.
8. See Mt 17:1-3.

this abstinence will not go unrewarded, we are looking forward to *that blessed hope and the revelation of the great God, and of our Savior Jesus Christ.* In that hope, when hope has become fact, we are going to receive a denarius as our wages. That is the wage, you see, paid to the laborer working in the vineyard according to the gospel,[9] which I think you all remember; we do not have to go over everything again, after all, as with illiterate and uneducated people. So then the denarius, which has its name from the number ten, is paid; and joined to forty it makes fifty. Thus we celebrate the forty days of Lent before Easter with toil; but the fifty days after Easter with joy, as having now received our reward. For to this salutary and saving labor of good work, which goes with the number forty, is added the denarius of rest and of happiness, becoming fifty.

40 plus 10 represented by the laborers in the vineyard

5. The Lord Jesus also signified this meaning much more clearly when he spent forty days after his resurrection with his disciples; then, after ascending into heaven on the fortieth day, he sent them the reward of the Holy Spirit ten days later.[10] These same events were signified, and these realities were preceded by certain signs. We are nourished by signs such that we can, through perseverance, reach the realities themselves. We are laborers, after all, and still at work in the vineyard; at the end of the day, with the work finished, the day's pay will be handed out. But can any laborer last out the day, to receive his wage at the end, without having anything to eat while working? After all, even you will not merely pay your workman his wage; will you not bring him the wherewithal to renew his strength while he is working? Of course, you feed the one you are going to pay.

Accordingly, the Lord also feeds us with scriptural meanings while we work. I mean, if this joy of understanding these mysteries were taken from us,[11] we would falter in the work and no one would be left to reach the reward.

---

9. See Mt 20:1-16. The Jerusalem Bible calls the denarius "a fair wage."
10. See Acts 1:1-10; 2:1-4.
11. *Intelligendorum sacramentorum.* See Sermons 56, 10; 229E, 4. This latter sermon relates the laborer's lunch box to his wages, thus signifying the relationship of the incarnate Word (humanity) to divinity.

Other ways to explain how 40 stands for the law:
it combines 38 (the law minus love) with 2 (love)

6. So then, how is the work accomplished indicated by the number forty? Perhaps it was because the law was given in ten commandments, and the law was to be proclaimed throughout the whole world—this whole world which presents itself to us in its four quarters, East and West, South and North; and thus the denarius multiplied by four reaches forty. Or else because the law is fulfilled by the gospel, of which there are four books, because it is said in the gospel, *I did not come to do away with the law, but to fulfill it* (Mt 5:17). So whether for this reason or that one or for some other more likely one which escapes us—but which does not escape those who are more learned—the number forty certainly stands for a kind of perfection in good works, which are above all practiced by a kind of abstinence from unlawful desires of the world, that is, by fasting in its widest sense.[12] Listen to the apostle also, as he says, *Love is the fullness of the law* (Rom 13:10). Where does love come from? From the grace of God, from the Holy Spirit. We would not, after all, get it from ourselves, as if we could make it ourselves. It is a gift of God, and a great gift too: *Because the love of God*, he says, *has been poured out in our hearts through the Holy Spirit who has been given to us* (Rom 5:5). So then, love fulfills the law, and it is most truly said that *love is the fullness of the law*. Let us investigate how this love is commended to us by the Lord.

Remember what I have proposed; I wish to explain the number of thirty-eight years in that sick man, to see why this thirty-eight is a number more related to sickness than to health. So then, as I was saying, love fulfills the law. What belongs to the law in all good works is the number forty; but as regards love, we are presented with two precepts. Take a good look at them, I beg you, and fix what I am saying in your memories, so that you not be those who despise the word, or your souls will become the path where the scattered grains of wheat do not germinate, *and the birds of heaven*, it says, *will come and pick them all up* (Mk 4:4.15). Learn it yourselves, and store it away in your hearts. The precepts of charity enjoined by the Lord are two: *You shall love the Lord your God with your whole heart,*

---

12. See Sermons 263A,4; 270,3.

and with your whole soul, and with your whole mind; and, *You shall love your neighbor as yourself. On these two commandments hangs the whole law, and the prophets.* (Mt 22:37-40)

How right it was for that widow, with two little coins as a gift to God, to give all she had to live on. How right it was, too, in the case of that sick man wounded by robbers, for the innkeeper to receive two coins to look after him! How right it was for Jesus to spend two days with the Samaritans,[13] to confirm them in their love! So then, when anything good is being signified by this number two, it is above all this twofold love that is being brought to our attention. If then the number forty contains the perfection of the law, and the law is only fulfilled by the twin commandments of charity, why be surprised that the sick man should be sick for two less than forty years?

The significance of the man being given two orders by Christ

7. Accordingly, let us see what significant mystery is involved in this sick man's being cured by the Lord.[14] For the Lord comes, a teacher of charity, filled with charity, *shortening*,[15] as was foretold of him, *the word upon the earth* (Is 10:23), and he shows that the law and the prophets depend upon the two precepts of love. So then, Moses depended on them for his forty-days' fast, Elijah also depended on them for his fast; the Lord also upheld this number in his own witness. This sick man is cured by the Lord's present in person; but what does Jesus say to him first? *Do you want to be healed?* That man replies that he does not have anyone to put him into the pool. Truly, in order to return to health, he needed the help of a man, but of that man who was also God. *For there is one God, the mediator also of God and men, the man Christ Jesus* (1 Tm 2:5). So then, along comes the very man he needed; why should there be any delay in his getting his health back? *Get up*, he says, *pick up your stretcher and walk* (Jn 5:6-8).

He said three things: *Get up—pick up your stretcher—and walk.*

---

13. See Lk 21:2-4; 10:33-35. Augustine symbolically identifies the man who fell among thieves with the sick man whose thirty-eight years he is explaining.
14. *Quo sacramento iste languidus curetur.*
15. Following the Septuagint, Augustine uses Is 10:23 or Rom 9:28 to speak about how the Word is compressed into the double commandment of love; see too Letter 189, 2.

But *get up* was not a command to do something but the act of healing. The man, once healed, was commanded, *Pick up your stretcher and walk.* I ask you, why would not *walk* be enough? Or why would not *get up* be enough? After all, that man would not have stayed in the place once he had got up with his health restored. Would he not have got up in order to go on his way? So what thrills me is that the man whom he found lying there in need of two things to reach forty was given two commands, as though, by prescribing two things, he was fulfilling that man's need.

Pick up your stretcher *means* Love your neighbor; Walk *means* Love God

8. So how then are we to find that, in the two things ordered by the Lord, the two precepts of love are signified?[16] *Pick up your stretcher*, he says, *and walk*. Join me, brothers and sisters, in recalling what these two precepts are. They ought to be so well known to you that they do not just spring to mind when I mention them; no, they ought never to be wiped away from your hearts. Always be thinking, the whole time, that one must love God and neighbor—God with the whole heart, with the whole soul, and with the whole mind; and one's neighbor as oneself. Always think about them, reflect on them, observe them, practice them, fulfill them.

In terms of precept, the love of God comes first; but, in terms of practice, the love of neighbor comes first. The one who prescribed this command of love for you in two precepts would not first commend your neighbor to you and then God after that; but God comes first and the neighbor after that. But, because you do not yet see God, you will deserve to see him by loving your neighbor; for, by loving your neighbor, you clean up your eye for seeing God, as John plainly says, *If you do not love the brother whom you see, how will you be able to love the God whom you do not see?* (1 Jn 4:20) Look, you are told, *Love God*. If you say to me, "Show me the one I am to love," what else will I say in reply but what John himself says, *No one has ever seen God* (Jn 1:9)? And, to stop you from supposing that seeing God is altogether beyond your scope, he says, *God is love, and the one who remains in love remains in God* (1 Jn 4:16). So then, love your neighbor,

---

16. The first command, *Get up*, as a word of healing, is followed by two orders to the man just restored to health.

and contemplate in yourself the source of your loving your neighbor; there, as best as you can, you will see God.

Begin, therefore, by loving your neighbor. *Break your bread to the hungry, bring the one who is needy, without a roof over his head, into your house. If you see him naked, clothe him, and do not look down upon your own.* If you do this, what will you gain by it? *Then your light will burst forth like the dawn.* (Is 58:7-8) Your light, your dawn, is God, because he will come to you after the night of this world; he, of course, neither rises nor sets, because he always remains the same. He will be the dawn to those of you who come back to him, just as he will set for those of you who were perishing. So then, *Pick up your stretcher* means, in my opinion, *Love your neighbor.*

Pick up your stretcher *means* Bear one another's burdens

9. But there is still something, I think, that needs explaining: why should love of neighbor be represented in the picking up of the stretcher—unless perhaps what we really find offensive is our neighbor being represented by a stretcher, a brutish object, without sense or feeling. Please do not be angry, dear neighbor, at being presented to us in the form of a thing that lacks both soul and sense. Our Lord and Savior Jesus Christ was himself called *the cornerstone* (Eph 2:20), so as to join two walls together in himself; he was also called the rock from which water poured out: *the rock was Christ* (1 Cor 10:4). So if Christ is rock, what is surprising about the neighbor being wood? Not just any wood, however, even as Christ was not just any rock, but one from which water had poured out for the thirsty people; nor any stone, but a cornerstone, binding together two walls coming from different sides. In the same way it is not any piece of wood you have received as your neighbor, but a stretcher.

So what is it about a stretcher, I ask you? What else, but because that man, while sick, was being carried on the stretcher, while restored to health, he carries the stretcher? What did the apostle say? *Carry one another's burdens, and in this way you will fulfill the law of Christ* (Gal 6:2). So then, the law of Christ is the law of love, and love is not fulfilled unless we carry one another's burdens, *putting up with each other*, he says, *in love, careful to preserve unity of spirit in the bond of peace* (Eph 4:2-3). When you were sick your neighbor was carrying you; you have been restored to health—carry your neighbor. *Carry one another's burdens, and in this way you will fulfill the law of Christ.* In this way, you will fulfill what you were lacking.[17]

So then, *pick up your stretcher*; but when you have picked it up, do not just stay there: *walk*. By loving your neighbor and taking care of your neighbor you set out on a journey. Where are you heading for but toward the Lord God, the one whom we should be loving with the whole heart, with the whole soul, and with the whole mind? In fact, we have not yet reached the Lord, but we have the neighbor right here beside us. So carry the one whom you are walking along with, in order to reach him with whom you long to remain. Therefore, *pick up your stretcher and walk*.

The Jews are careful not to blame Christ for the cure;
they blame the man for work on the sabbath

10. That is what the man did, and the Jews were scandalized. For they saw a man carrying his stretcher on the sabbath day. They were not going to blame the Lord for restoring him to health on the sabbath, because he could have answered that, if any of them had a draught animal which had fallen into a pit on the sabbath, he would for sure haul it out on the sabbath and save his animal.[18] And so they were not objecting to him that the man's health had been restored on the sabbath day, but that the man was carrying his stretcher. Granted that healing was not to be put off, was such a work required? *It is not lawful*, they say, *for you to do what you are doing, to carry your stretcher*. He in turn, calling on the one who healed him, objected to his critics, *The man who restored me to health*, he said, *he said to me, Pick up your stretcher and walk*. Should I not accept the order of the one from whom I had received back my health? They in turn said, *Who is that man who said to you, Pick up your stretcher and walk?* (Jn 5:9-11)

Christ to be sought in solitude, not in the crowd

11. *But the man who had been restored to health did not know who it was* from whom he had heard these words. For *Jesus*, after doing this and

---

17. The two years less than the perfection of forty.
18. See Lk 14:5.

giving these instructions, *had slipped away from him into the crowd* (Jn 5:13). Notice how this too is fulfilled in us. We carry the neighbor, and we walk toward God; but we do not yet see the one we are walking toward. Hence, even that man did not yet know Jesus. A mystery is suggested[19] because we believe in someone we have not yet seen, and in order not to be seen he slips away into the crowd. It is difficult to see Christ in a crowd; our minds need some solitude; someone who is attentive in solitude may see God.[20] A crowd means bustle; this vision requires separation. *Pick up your stretcher*; after being carried, carry your neighbor; *and walk* to reach the end.

Do not look for Jesus in the crowd; he is not like just one of the crowd, he comes ahead of every crowd. That great fish[21] was the first to come up from the sea, and is now seated in heaven interceding for us; like the high priest, he alone has entered within the veil; the crowd is standing outside. *Walk*, you that are carrying your neighbor—if you have learned how to carry, after being so used to being carried. In any case, at present you do not yet know Jesus, do not yet see Jesus. What comes next? Because the man did not stop carrying his stretcher and walking, *Jesus saw him later on in the temple*. He did not see him in the crowd, he saw him in the temple. The Lord Jesus indeed could see him both in the crowd and in the temple; while the sick man himself does not know Jesus in the crowd, he knows him in the temple. So then, he arrived, he reached the Lord; he saw him in the temple, saw him in the sacred place, in the holy place. And what did he hear from him? *Look, you have now been restored to health; do not sin, lest something worse should happen to you* (Jn 5:14).

---

19. *Sacramentum hoc commendatum est.*
20. The word *intentionis* suggests that there is a stretching of one's attention.
21. Using "fish' to designate Jesus (*ichthys*, in Greek, has the first letters of 'Jesus Christ, God's Son, Savior') would have been well known. The earliest written evidence for the name comes from the epitaph of Abercius, written toward the end of the second century, in which Christ is called "the fish from the spring of the virgin, mighty and pure." By Augustine's time the title was found in the *Sybilline Oracles* 8, which Augustine quotes in *The City of God* XVIII, 23, explaining its significance in this way: " 'Fish' is the name by which Christ is mystically understood, in that he was able to exist alive, that is without sin, in the abyss of this mortal state, as in the deepest waters."

The Jews raging against Christ in their frustration

12. Then that man, after seeing Jesus and learning that Jesus was the one who had restored his health, lost no time in proclaiming the good news about the one he had seen. *He went off and announced to the Jews that it was Jesus who had restored his health* (Jn 5:15). He brought the news and they raged; he proclaimed his salvation; they were not looking for their own salvation.

Christ's reply to the Jews will show how the sacrament of the sabbath is fulfilled in himself

13. *The Jews started persecuting the Lord Jesus because he did this on a sabbath* (Jn 5:16). So let us listen then to the answer the Lord now gave the Jews. I have already mentioned what he would answer with regard to those healed on the sabbath: that the Jews themselves never neglected their animals on the sabbath, whether in rescuing them or feeding them.[22] What answer did he give about carrying the stretcher? Clearly, a material work had been done before their eyes, not for bodily health but for bodily activity which did not seem to be as necessary as health. So then, let the Lord openly explain that the mystery of the sabbath and the sign of observing one day was given to the Jews only for a time, but that the natural fulfillment of the sacrament had been realized in himself. He says, *My Father is working until now, and I too am working* (Jn 5:17). Yes, he provoked a lot of confusion among them; the water is stirred up at the Lord's coming, but the one stirring it up remains hidden. Even so, when the water is stirred up, a single sick person was to be healed; when the Lord suffered, the whole world was healed.[23]

God's working and his resting coincide

14. So then, let us take a look at the answer given by Truth: *My Father is working until now, and I too am working*. So then, was what scripture said false, that *God rested from all his works on the seventh day* (Gn 2:2)? And can the Lord Jesus be speaking against this text of scripture, given to us

---

22. See section 10 above, with its reference to Lk 14:5.
23. On the identification of the Lord's passion with the troubling of the waters, see section 3 above.

through the ministry of Moses, seeing that he says to the Jews, *If you believed Moses you would also believe me; for he wrote about me* (Jn 5:46)? So then, see whether Moses spoke of God's rest on the seventh day to signify something deeper. After all, God was not tired out by working on his creation, and God did not need a rest like a human being. How was the one who made everything with a word tired?[24] And yet, it is true that *God rested from his works on the seventh day*; and what Jesus says here is also true: *My Father is working until now*.

But who can explain with words—a human being to human beings, a weak person to the weak, an unlearned man to those longing to learn—who can explain something that is difficult even for those who are able, maybe, to grasp it, even if what is to be grasped could be explained? Who, I say, brothers and sisters, can find words to explain how God both works while resting and rests while working? I beg you to put off seeking an answer until you make more progress. This vision, you see, requires the temple of God, requires the holy place; carry your neighbor and walk; that is where you will see him, where you will not be requiring any human words.

Christ too both rests and works at the same time

15. Perhaps we should instead say this: that in telling us that *God rested on the seventh day* scripture signified in a great sacrament our Lord Jesus Christ himself, who said as he was talking about these things, *My Father is working until now, and I too am working*; because the Lord Jesus is, of course, also God. He is, after all, the Word of God, and you have heard that *in the beginning was the Word*, and not just any word, but *the Word was God, and all things were made through him* (Jn 1:1.3). So perhaps it meant that he was going to rest on the seventh day from all his works. Read the gospel, I mean, and see at how many great things Jesus worked. He worked our salvation on the cross, so that all the predictions of the prophets might be fulfilled in him; he was crowned with thorns, hung up on a tree; he said, *I am thirsty* (Jn 19:28), received vinegar in a sponge, in fulfillment of what was said: *And in my thirst they gave me vinegar to drink* (Ps 69:21). But

---
24. See Sermon 125, 4 (and note 12), where Augustine elaborates on this point at the expense of "the Jews." That sermon may have been preached a year or two later than this homily.

when all his works had been completed, on the sixth day of the week *he bowed his head and yielded up the spirit* (Jn 19:30), and rested in the tomb on the sabbath from all his works.[25]

So then, it is as if he were saying to the Jews, "Why do you expect me not to work on the sabbath? The sabbath day was enjoined upon you to signify *me*. You observe the works of God; I was there when they were done; all things were made through me; I know that. *My Father is working until now*. The Father made light; but he simply said that light should be made; if he said it, he worked by a Word. His Word is what *I* was, what *I am*. Through me the world was made in those works, through me the world is governed in these works. My Father did not just work then when he made the world, he is also working now as he governs the world; accordingly, when he made the world, he made it through me; and as he governs it, he does so through me." This in effect is what he said—but to whom? To the deaf, the blind, the lame, the sick, who would not even acknowledge the doctor, and, being out of their minds in a kind of frenzy, wanted to kill him.

The Jews understood that Christ claimed equality with God;
the Arians, though Christians, deny it

16. What was it, accordingly, that the evangelist went on to say? *For this reason the Jews tried all the more to kill him, because he was not only doing away with the sabbath, but was also saying God was his Father*. Not just in any kind of way, but how? *Making himself equal to God* (Jn 5:18). In fact, all of us say to God, *Our Father who art in heaven* (Mt 6:9); we read that the Jews also said, *Since you are our Father* (Is 63:16; 64:8). So then, what made them angry was not just that he called God his Father, but that he did so in a much different way from human beings.

Look! The Jews understand what the Arians do not understand! In fact, the Arians say that the Son is not equal to the Father, and, then, this heresy disturbed the Church. Look, these blind people, these Christ-slayers, still understood Christ's words. They did not understand that he was the Christ,

---

25. This "sacramental" application of God's resting on the seventh day to Christ's "resting" in the tomb on the sabbath appears to be Augustine's own invention. He mentions it again in *The Literal Meaning of Genesis* IV, 11, 21, where he is engaged in reconciling these two texts, as he is here. But he also suggests ibid. IV,9,16 that the literal meaning of God's resting on the seventh day is his granting rest in himself to his rational creation.

they did not understand that he was the Son of God; but still they did understand that with these words a Son of God was being set before them of such a kind that he was God's equal. Who he was they did not know; still, they acknowledged it was as such that he was being advertised, because *he called God his Father, making himself equal to God.*

So was he not then equal to God? He did not make himself equal, but God begot him as his equal. Were he to make himself equal, he would fall by committing robbery.[26] The one, you see, who did want to make himself equal to God when he was not, well, he did fall and from being an angel became the devil; and it was this pride that he served up as a drink for man, which is why he too was cast down. This, you see, is what he said to man,[27] whom he envied for still standing on his two feet while he himself had fallen.[28] *Taste, and you will be like gods* (Gn 3:5); that is, "Seize illegally what you are not according to your creation because I too fell by stealing what was not mine." This is not what he actually said in so many words, but it is what he was persuasively suggesting.

Christ however was born equal to the Father, not made so; born of the Father's substance. Thus the apostle presents him in these terms: *Who, since he was in the form of God, did not regard being equal to God as something to be grasped at* (Phil 2:6). He did not usurp divine equality, but had it by being born with it. And what about us, how should we ever reach God's equal? *He emptied himself, taking on the form of a slave* (Phil 2:7). So then, he did not empty himself through losing what he was, but by taking on what he was not. The Jews despised this slave form, and so could not understand the Lord Christ as equal to the Father, although they had not the least doubt that that is what he said about himself; and that is why they were frantic with rage. And still, for all that, he put up with them and sought to cure his persecutors.

---

26. See Phil 2:6.
27. In fact to Eve; but she too, like Adam, represents man, *homo sapiens*, the human race.
28. And was now crawling on his belly on the ground.

Homily 18

On John 5:19[1]

The special gift of the evangelist John

1. John the evangelist was the one among his colleagues and fellow evangelists who received this particular and personal gift from the Lord (on whose breast he reclined at the banquet,[2] indicating by this that he was drinking profound secrets from the inner depth of the Lord's heart), that he would say things about the Son of God which might stir up the attentive minds of little ones, but without satisfying those still lacking the necessary capacity; but by these words he gives more grown-up minds, who have reached an inner maturity, something that both exercises and nourishes.

You heard the passage when it was read, and you will remember the occasion for this sermon. Yesterday, in fact, the reading said that *the Jews wanted to kill Jesus, because he was not only doing away with the sabbath, but he was also calling God his Father, making himself equal to God* (Jn 5:18). While this displeased the Jews, it pleased the Father. Undoubtedly it also pleases those who honor the Son just as they honor the Father, because if it does not please them, they will be the one to displease. God, after all, will not be any greater because he pleases you, but you will be all the less if he displeases you. But the Lord is speaking against this false charge of theirs, whether it stems from ignorance or malice, not saying something they can grasp, but what might trouble and upset them, and thus perturbed, they may seek a doctor. He said things that would be written down so that, later on, they might also be read by us. So then, we have already seen what happened in the hearts of the Jews when they heard these things; but let us think about what happens in us when we hear them.

In fact, heresies and some perverse doctrines, which ensnare souls and toss them into the deep, are only born when the good scriptures are wrongly understood, and what is wrongly understood in them is then asserted with rash, bare-faced audacity. And so, my dearest friends, we

---

1. Preached the day after Homily 17 in mid-July 414. See also Sermon 126, 5.7-11; *The Trinity* II, 3, 5; XV, 14, 23-24.
2. See Jn 13:25.

should listen to these things with great caution, little ones that we are when it comes to grasping them; and, with a devout heart and with trembling, we should hold on to this wholesome rule, as it is written: that we should enjoy as food what we have come to understand according to the rule of the faith in which we were baptized; as for what we have not been able to understand in accord with the sound rule of faith, let us put doubt aside and put off understanding, so that, even if we do not know what something means, we should not have the least doubt that it is good and true.

And as for me, brothers and sisters, who have accepted to talk to you, you should think about the one who has accepted this task, and about what I have accepted. For I, a mere man, have accepted to discuss divine matters; a creature of the flesh, to discuss spiritual matters; a mortal being, to discuss eternal matters. Let vain presumption, my dearest friends, be far from me, if I want to be in good health in the house of God,[3] *which is the Church of the living God, the pillar and buttress of the truth* (1 Tm 3:15). Given my limitations I grasp what I set before you; when the door is opened, I am nourished together with you; when it is shut, I knock together with you.[4] The Catholic rule of faith: Christ equal to the Father as Word, less than the Father as man.

2. So then, the Jews were upset and indignant, and indeed rightly so, because a man dared to make himself God's equal; but wrongly so, precisely because they were failing to perceive God in the man. They saw the flesh but did not know God; they perceived the dwelling, but ignored the one dwelling there. That flesh was a temple, God was dwelling in it. So then, Jesus was not equating the flesh with the Father, nor comparing the *form of a slave* (Phil 2:7) with the Lord, nor talking about what he was made because of us, but about what he was when he made us. Who Christ is, after all—I am speaking to Catholics[5]—you know because you have believed rightly that he is not just the Word only, and not just flesh, but that *the Word was made flesh* so as to take up residence among us. Let me recall what you know about the Word: *In the beginning was the Word, and the Word was with God, and the Word was God*; that is his equality with the Father. But

---

3. An allusion to Jesus' finding the man he had cured in the temple, Jn 5:14.
4. See Mt 7:7.
5. Distinguishing them perhaps from catechumens or even from any pagan or Arian present in the congregation.

the Word was made flesh and took up residence among us (Jn 1:1.14); there the Father is greater than this flesh.

Thus the Father is both equal and greater; equal to the Word, greater than the flesh; equal to the one through whom he made us, greater than the one who was made because of us. In accord with this sound Catholic rule let us align the things we understand, the rule which above all you ought to know, which those of you who do know it keep, from which your faith ought never to slip, which must never get twisted round in your hearts by any human arguments; let what we understand be directed by this rule and let the things we do not understand be put off until we become ready for them to be directed by this rule.

So then, we know the Son of God is equal to the Father, because we know the Word of God from the beginning. So why then were the Jews wanting to kill him? *Because he was not only doing away with the sabbath, but he was also calling God his Father, making himself equal to God*; they saw the flesh, they did not see the Word. So then, let the Word speak against them through the flesh, let the one who dwells within resound through his dwelling, so that the one who is able may know who dwells within.

The Arian argument from Jn 5:19

3. So then, what does he say to them? And so Jesus answered and said to those who were upset that he was making himself equal to God, *Amen, amen, I tell you, the Son can do nothing on his own, but only what he sees the Father doing* (Jn 5:19). How the Jews replied to this is not written, and perhaps they kept quiet. Some people all the same, who want to be considered Christians, do not keep quiet, and somehow devise things from these words that can be said against us, things which, both for their sake and for ours, we must not just shrug aside.

I am referring to the Arian heretics, who say that the Son, who took flesh, is less than the Father, not through the flesh but before the flesh,[6] and that he is not of the same substance as the Father is. They seize on these words as a handle for their fallacy, and they answer us, "You see how the

---

6. "The flesh" in this phrase appears to be shorthand for the Incarnation.

Lord Jesus, on noticing how upset the Jews were because he was making himself equal to God, added the kind of words that would demonstrate that he was not equal. After all," they say, "he was turning the Jews against the Christ by making himself equal to God," and so Christ, wishing to allay their anxiety and to demonstrate that the Son is not equal to the Father, that is, not equal to God, he said, as it were, "Why are you getting angry, why this indignation? I am not equal," he says, *"because the Son can do nothing on his own, but only what he sees the Father doing."* "For the one," they say, "who *can only do what he sees the Father doing*, is obviously less, is not equal."

The Father and Son are one God by union of love

4. May the heretic who follows this crooked and twisted rule of his own heart listen to us, not yet critical of him, but still seeking, as it were. You see, I rather think, whoever you are—let us pretend, in fact, that he is actually present among us[7]—that you hold, together with us, that *in the beginning was the Word.*

"I do," he says.

"And that *the Word was with God*?"

"I hold this too," he says.

"Carry on then, and hold this even more firmly, that *the Word was God*."

"This too I hold," he says; "but that one is greater God, the other one lesser God."[8]

"Now here is a whiff of who-knows-what kind of paganism; I thought I was talking to a Christian. If there is a greater God and there is a lesser God, we are worshiping two gods, not one God."

"Why?" says he. "Do you not also say two gods equal to each other?"

"I do *not* say that; for, I understand this equality in such a way that I also perceive undivided charity there; and if undivided charity, then perfect unity. If the charity, after all, which God has sent among human beings makes one heart out of many human hearts, and makes many human souls one soul, as is written in the Acts of the Apostles about the believers and

---

7. As some Arians almost certainly were.
8. See *Exposition of Psalm* 130, 11, probably delivered about the same time as this homily.

their love for each other, *They all had one soul and one heart in God* (Acts 4:32); then, if my soul and your soul, when we have the same tastes and when we love each other, become one soul, how much more must the Father God and the Son God be, in the source and font of love,[9] one God!

A poor comparison: artisan and apprentice versus Father and Word

5. "But now take a look at these words which were bothering you, and recall with me what questions we were asking about the Word. Let me add one more thing, that after saying, *He was in the beginning with God*, the evangelist added right away, *All things were made through him* (Jn 1:2-3). Now, in my questioning, I am going to unnerve you, now I am going to have you contradict yourself and have you plead against yourself. Just keep in mind these things about the Word: that *the Word was God* and that *all things were made through him*. Listen now to the words which bothered you and pushed you into saying the Son was less, namely that he said himself, *The Son can do nothing on his own, but only what he sees the Father doing*."

"That is right," he says. "Explain it to me a little."

"This, I rather think, is how you understand it—that the Father makes some things, while the Son watches how the Father does it, so that he himself can also make what he has seen the Father making. You have set up, as it were, two artisans, Father and Son, like master and apprentice, in the way artisans who are fathers generally teach their sons their craft. Look at me here, coming down to your carnal-minded level;[10] for the time being I am thinking in the same way as you are; let us see if this way of thinking of ours can find a way out for us, a way that accords with what we have already said together and agreed on together about the Word; that *the Word is God*, and that *all things were made through him*.

"Imagine the Father, therefore, as an artisan engaged in some work, with the Son as an apprentice, *who can do nothing on his own, but only what he sees the Father doing*; in fact, he watches the Father's hands, so that, as he sees him fashioning things, he too may, in his own works, fashion something. But now this Father who is making all these things and

---

9. That is, in the Holy Spirit.
10. *Ad carnalem sensum tuum*; Augustine does the same thing in Sermons 126, 8-9;135, 3-4.

wishes the Son to observe him and make such things himself as well—through whom does he do it? Aha! Now is the moment for you to notice your previous judgment which you agreed on with me and held with me, that *in the beginning was the Word*, and *the Word was God*, and *all things were made through him*. So then, along with me, you held that all things were made through the Word; again, with your carnal-minded and childish approach, you form a picture in your mind of God making something and the Word observing him at it, so that when God has made it the Word can make it too.

"What, after all, does God make apart from the Word? If he makes anything thus, then not all things were made through the Word; you have lost what you were holding on to. But if all things *were* made through the Word, correct what you understood wrongly. The Father made things, and he did not make them except through the Word. How can the Word watch to see the Father making things without the Word, for the Word to make them too in a similar way? What the Father has made, he has made through the Word, or else the statement is false: *All things were made through him*. But it is true; all things *were* made through him. Did that strike you by any chance as being too little? *And without him was made nothing* (Jn 1:3).

The Son's seeing to be investigated before his doing

6. "So move away then from this prudence of the flesh, and let us ask the meaning of what was said, *The Son can do nothing on his own, but only what he sees the Father doing*. Let us ask if we are worthy to understand. I confess, in fact, that it is a great matter, singularly difficult, to see the Father doing things through the Son; not Father and Son each doing their own thing, but the Father doing every kind of work through the Son, so that there are no works whatever done either by the Father without the Son or by the Son without the Father, because *all things were made through him and without him was made nothing*.

"All that rests most firmly on the foundation of faith, but what sort of seeing is involved in the Son's being unable to do anything *on his own, but only what he sees the Father doing*? You seek to know, I suppose, the Son at work; seek to know the Son first in what he sees. Just what does he say, after all? *The Son can do nothing on his own, but only what he sees the Father doing.* Pay attention to what he said: *but only what he sees the Father doing.* Seeing comes first, doing follows; he sees, after all, in order to do. You though, why are you already seeking to know how he does and makes things, while you do not yet know how he sees things? Why are you chasing after what comes second, leaving aside what comes first? He talked of himself seeing and doing, because *the Son can do nothing on his own, but only what he sees the Father doing.*

"Do you want me to explain to you how he acts? Then you explain to me how he sees. If *you* cannot explain this, then neither can *I* explain that; if *you* are not able to perceive this, then neither am *I* able to perceive that. So then, let each of us *seek*, each of us *knock*, so that each of us may deserve to *receive* (Mt 7:7). Why, as a learned person, find fault with someone less learned? Let us both, as unlearned men, seek from the Master: I about his doing, and you about his seeing; let us not engage in childish wrangles in his school.[11]

"Still, we have already learned together that *all things were made through him.* Clearly, therefore, the Father is not doing some works for the Son to see, so that he can do similar ones, but the Father does those same works through the Son, because through the Word was everything made. Now who knows just how God makes things? I am not talking about how he made the universe, but how he made your eye, to whose vision you are materialistically attached, putting visible things on a par with the invisible. In fact, you are thinking about God just as you were used to seeing with these eyes. But if God could be seen with these eyes, he would not say, *Blessed are the clean of heart, for they shall see God* (Mt 5:8). Therefore, you have physical eyes to see the artisan, but you do not yet have the eye of the heart for seeing God; that is why you want to transfer to God what you are used to seeing in the artisan. Let earthly things be of the earth; but lift up your heart."

To understand such mysteries, our desire for them must grow

7. What then, my dearest friends? Will I have to explain what I have asked, about how the Word sees, about how the Father is seen by the Word,

---

11. On this topic see also Sermons 126, 3; 270, 1; 291, 1; 340A, 4.

about what it means that the Word sees? I am not so confident, so rash as to promise both myself and you that I will explain it; while I can only guess about your limitations, I am aware of my own. So then, if you agree, let us not delay any longer; let us go over the reading and see how the Lord's words disturb hearts of flesh; they are so disturbed that they might not continue to hold the opinions they once held.

It is like having to wrest some toy from the hands of children, a toy with which they may get into mischief, so that more useful things can take its place in them as they grow, so that those who crawl on the earth might make progress. Get up, search, sigh, pant with desire, and knock at the closed door. But if we do not yet have any desire, are not yet craving, not yet sighing, we will be casting pearls before whomever, or else we will only find pearls worth next to nothing.[12]

So then, my dearest friends, I hope I have stirred up some longing in your heart; good habits lead to understanding; the kind of life lived here leads to the kind of life lived hereafter. An earthly life is one thing and a heavenly life is another; there is the life of a herd, the life of human beings, the life of angels. The life of a herd burns for earthly pleasures, it only seeks earthly things, toward which it is inclined and driven; the life of angels is just heavenly; the life of human beings is in the middle between that of angels and that of the herd. If human beings live according to the flesh, they are on a par with the herd; if they live according to the spirit, they associate with angels.

When you are living according to the spirit, ask yourself, even in this angelic life, whether you are little or big. If you are still a little one, in fact, the angels say to you, "Grow; we are eating bread; you are being nourished on milk, the milk of faith, so as to come eventually to the solid food of sight." However, if there is still a craving for sordid pleasures, if fraud is still being considered, if telling lies is not being avoided, if perjury is piled on top of lying, would such an unclean heart have the nerve to say, "Explain to me how the Word sees," even if I could explain, even if I could already see?

Well now, if I, by any chance, am not involved in such bad morals, and, for all that, am still a long way off from attaining such vision, how

---

12. See Mt 7:6; 13:45-46.

much further from it must be those who are not yet caught up by this heavenly desire, still weighed down by earthly desires!

There is a big difference between someone who shuns something and someone who desires it, and again a big difference between someone who desires it and someone who enjoys it. You live like an animal, shunning heavenly life, the angels fully enjoy it. But if you do not live like an animal, are not shunning heavenly life, you desire something and do not grasp it; by that very desire you have begun to live the life of the angels. Let it grow in you and be perfected in you, and you will grasp it, not from me, but from the one who made both me and you!

The significance of the Son's acting in like manner

8. All the same, the Lord did not leave us without a clue, wanting it to be understood that, when he said, *The Son can do nothing on his own, but only what he sees the Father doing,* he did not mean that the Father does some works for the Son to see, and the Son does other ones when he has seen the Father's actions, but that the Father and the Son do exactly the same works. In fact, he went on to say, *For whatever the Father has done, the Son does in like manner* (Jn 5:19), not "When he has done them, the Son does others in like manner," but *Whatever the Father has done, the Son does in like manner.*

If the Son does the things the Father has done, the Father does them through the Son; if the Father does what he does through the Son, then it is not the case that the Father does some things, the Son does others, but that the works of Father and Son are the same. And how does the Son also do the same things? Both *the same* and *in like manner.* In case by any chance they should be the same but in a different manner, he says, *the same* and *in like manner.* Take an example which I think will be familiar to you; when we write letters,[13] our heart does so first of all, and then our hand. Yes, of course.... Why did you all shout and applaud, if not because you got the point? What I said is certain and obvious to everyone. Letters are first made in our heart, and next by our body; the hand serves at the heart's command,

---

13. Presumably letters of the alphabet rather than epistolary letters since many, or even most, were barely literate.

both heart and hand make the same letters; the heart does not make one set, does it, and the hand another? The hand makes the same letters, but not in like manner; our heart, I mean, makes them intelligibly, our hand makes them visibly. There, that is how the same works can be done in a different manner.

Thus it would be too little for the Lord to say, *Whatever the Father has done, the Son does*, unless he added *and in like manner*. What after all, if you understood this in the same way as whatever the heart does, that the hand also does, but not in like manner? But here, he added, *the Son does these things in like manner*. If he both does these things and does them in like manner—wake up!—let the Jews be tied up in knots, let the Christian believe, let the heretic be confounded and convinced: the Son is equal to the Father!¹⁴

Seeing and hearing in the Word are identical

9. *For the Father loves the Son and shows him all that he does himself* (Jn 5:20). Look, there is that word, *shows*. *Shows* to whom? Obviously, to one who can see. We return to the point we are unable to explain—how the Word sees. Here is a man created by the Word; but a man has eyes, he has ears, he has hands, he has different organs in the body; with his eyes he can see, with his ears he can hear, with his hands he can work; different organs have different functions. This organ cannot do what that one can; still, because of the body's unity, the eye sees for itself and for the ear, and the ear hears for itself and for the eye. Are we to think of anything like that in the Word, since *all things were made through him*? And scripture said in the psalm, *Understand, you that lack wisdom among the people, and you fools, get wise at last. Shall the one who planted the ear not hear, or does the one that fashioned the eye not look closely?* (Ps 93:8-9) So then, if the Word fashioned the eye (because all things are through the Word), if the Word planted the ear (because all things are through the Word), we cannot say, "The Word does not hear, the Word does not see," or the psalm will rebuke us and say, *You fools, get wise*.

---

14. Augustine is still addressing his Arian fall guy, urging him to wake up to the truth: *expergiscere*. For similar statements of this doctrine, quoting the same text, see Sermons 135, 2-3; 261, 7, both probably preached a few years after this homily.

And so if the Word hears and the Word sees, the Son hears and the Son sees; but are we for all that going to look for eyes and ears in him in different places? Does he hear in one part, see in another, and is his ear unable to do what his eye does, and his eye to do what his ear does? Or is he all sight and all hearing? Is that perhaps so? Not at all. There is no "perhaps" about it; that is really and truly so—provided, however, that his seeing and hearing happen in a far different way from how ours do. Both seeing and hearing are one and the same in the Word; hearing is not one thing there and seeing another; but hearing is sight and sight is hearing.

Come back to the heart and find the image of God

10. And we, who hear in one way, see in another, how do we come to know this about the Word? Perhaps we return to ourselves, provided we are not transgressors, like those who were told, *Go back, transgressors, to the heart* (Is 46:8).[15] Go back to the heart; why go away from yourselves and get lost out of yourselves? Why walk the ways of loneliness? You are going astray, wandering around like that. Return.

Where to?

To the Lord. He is ready:[16] return, first of all, to your heart. You are wandering about outside, exiled from yourself. You do not know yourself, and you are looking for the one by whom you were made! Return, return to the heart, lift yourself up from the body. Your body is your dwelling; your heart also senses through your body, but your body is not what your heart is. Leave aside your body, return to your heart.

In your body you were finding eyes in one place, ears in another; you do not find that in the heart, do you? Or do you not have ears in the heart? About what then was the Lord saying, *Those who have ears for hearing, let them hear* (Lk 8:8)? Or do you not have eyes in the heart? How then can the apostle say, *With the eyes of your heart enlightened* (Eph 1:18)? Return to the heart; see there perhaps what you may sense about God,

---

15. A much quoted text, understood as calling on us not so much to examine our feelings as to practice self-knowledge, to return to our deepest thoughts. See *Exposition of Psalms* 70, 1, 14; 75, 15; 101, 1, 10; *Confessions* IV, 12, 18-19; Sermon 112A, 4.
16. *Cito est.* Here I differ from F.-M. Berrouard, who takes this to mean "But it's too soon for that." Could it also mean "It is a short enough journey" or "He has urged it"? In any case returning to oneself is the first stage of returning to the Lord.

because that is where God's image is. Christ is dwelling in the inner self; in the inner self you are being renewed after the image of God;[17] in his image get to know its author.

Notice how all the senses of the body convey within to the heart what they have sensed outside; notice how many ministers the one who rules within has in his service and what he does by himself, even without these ministers. The eyes inform the heart about white and black, the ears inform the same heart about melodious and discordant sounds; the nostrils inform the same heart about perfumes and rottenness; the sense of taste informs the same heart about things bitter and sweet; the sense of touch about things smooth and rough; and the heart informs itself about things just and unjust. Your heart both sees and hears and distinguishes between the other senses, and—what the senses of the body do not aspire to—it distinguishes between things just and unjust, things evil and good.

Show me the eyes, ears, nostrils of your heart. Various things are conveyed to your heart, yet no variety of organs is found there. In your flesh you hear with one part, see with another; in your heart you hear with what you see with. If that is how it is with the image, how much more radically with the one whose image it is! So then, the Son hears and the Son also sees, and the very seeing and hearing is the Son; and for him to hear is the same as to be, and for him to see is the same as to be. For you, to see is not the same as to be, because even if you lose your sight you can still exist, still be; and even if you lose your hearing, you can still exist, still be.

To see into the Word our hearts need the stinging eye-salve of the commandments

11. Do you think that we have knocked?[18] Has something come up in us so as to make us suspect—however faintly—where the light comes from to us? I think, brothers and sisters, that when we say these things and reflect on them, we exercise ourselves through them. And when we exercise ourselves in these things, and then return again, as it were by our own weight, to that which is habitual, we are just like bleary-eyed people who (if we presume that they previously had no sight at all), when brought into

---

17. See Eph 3:16-17; 4:22-24; Col 3:10; 2 Cor 4:16.
18. See Mt 7:7.

the daylight, also begin to recover some of their sight, thanks to the doctor's treatment. And when the doctor wants to test how much they have recovered healthy vision, he tries to show them what they were longing to see and could not see when they were blind; and so, with some sight now coming back to their eyes, they are brought out to the light; and when they have seen it they are somehow or other beaten back by its brilliance, and they answer the doctor who is showing them the light, "Yes now, now I have seen it—but I cannot see."

So what does the doctor then do? He calls them back to what they were used to and adds an eye-salve to help them cherish the desire for what was seen and could not be seen; and, by that desire, he leads them to a fuller healing. And if ointments that sting are applied for restoring healthy sight, they must bear it bravely, and on fire with love of that light must say to themselves, "When will the time come that I can see with healthy eyes the light I have been unable to see with them damaged and weak?" They press the doctor, and beg him to go on with the cure.[19]

So then, brothers and sisters, if by any chance something like that has happened in your hearts, if you have lifted up your heart to see the Word, and, stunned by his light have fallen back into your old habits, ask the doctor to apply some stinging eye-salve—the precepts of justice. There is something to see, but you do not succeed in seeing it. Earlier, you were not believing me that there was something for you to see, but you were led forward with some reasoning as a guide; you drew near, you took a good look, your heart beat faster—you took to flight.[20] You certainly now know that there is something for you to see, but that you are not fit to see it. So then, carry on with the cure. What are the eye-salves? Do not lie, do not perjure yourself, do not commit adultery, do not steal, do not defraud. But you have gotten into the habit of such things, and you are called away from your usual habits with some pain. That stings—but it cures. For I can speak all the more freely insofar as I am speaking out of my fear and yours. If you give up being cured, and neglect getting fit enough to enjoy this light with health restored to your eyes, you will be loving the dark; and by loving the dark you will be staying in the dark; and by staying in the dark you will be

---

19. See *The Trinity* V, 16, 17; VIII, 2, 3.
20. See Sermon 52, 16; *The Trinity* XII, 24, 23; XV, 6, 10; *Exposition of Psalm* 41, 10.

cast forth *into the outer darkness where there will be weeping and gnashing of teeth* (Mt 22:13). If love of the light was not doing anything in you, let it be done by fear of pain.

Conclusion; appeal from the bishop

12. I think I have been talking long enough, and still I have not finished the gospel reading. If I have my say about the rest of it, I will be burdensome to you, and I am afraid that even what has been drawn from it may be wasted. So let that be sufficient for Your Graces. We[21] are your debtors, not only now but always, as long as we live, because it is for your sakes that we live. Nonetheless, please bring some comfort in this world to this life of ours, so weak, so laborious, so full of danger, by living good lives; do not grieve us and wear us out by your bad behavior. Were we to flee when offended by your bad lives and distance ourselves from you and no longer approach you, would you not complain and say, "Even if we were sick, would you not take care of us; even if we were ill, would you not visit us?" Look, we are taking care of you, we are visiting you; but may what you have heard from the apostle, *I fear I may have labored among you in vain* (Gal 4:11), not happen to us.

---

21. From here on Augustine lapses into the episcopal plural, and for once I think his translator must lapse with him, to point the formality, the seriousness of the pastoral exhortation with which he concludes.

Homily 19

On John 5:19-30[1]

A literal understanding of 5:19 ruled out by the doctrine of 1:3

1. In my last sermon, to the extent that my feelings and the poverty of my understanding allowed, I spoke about the words of the gospel where it is written, *The Son can do nothing on his own, but only what he sees the Father doing* (Jn 5:19), about what it is for the Son to see, that is, what it is for the Word to see, because the Son is the Word. And because all things were made through the Word, we questioned how that text could be understood as meaning that after the Son first sees the Father making things, then he also makes what he has observed being made; the Father, you see, has made nothing except through the Son; *all things*, after all, *were made through him, and without him was made nothing* (Jn 1:3). However, I did not explain it, and yet, although it was not explained, something was understood. Sometimes, you see, a word is lacking even as understanding is making progress; how much more deficient is the word, when understanding has no perfection![2]

And so now, as the Lord may grant, let us run briefly through the reading, and at least today let me finish the appointed task. If by chance any time and strength remains, I shall again consider—insofar as that becomes possible for me and for you—what it means that the Word sees, what it means to be shown to the Word.[3] If everything said here, in fact, is understood in relation to human senses or in a literal-minded way, the soul, stuffed with fancies, only comes up with some images of Father and Son or as two human beings, one showing something, the other seeing it; one talking, the other listening; all of that provides idols for the heart. If idols have now been thrown out of their temples, how much more should they be thrown out of the bosoms and heads of Christians![4]

---

1. Preached a few days after Homily 18.
2. See Homily 18, 11 for a longer statement of this idea, and also *Teaching Christianity* I, 2, 2.
3. Only in Homily 23, preached the day after this homily, will Augustine get a hold on this problem.
4. The removal of idols from temples had been ordered by a decree of the Emperor Honorius in 407.

Both statements of scripture are true; they must be harmonized

2. *The Son*, he says, *can do nothing on his own, but only what he sees the Father doing*. This is true; hold onto this, provided, that is, you do not let go of what you held onto at the beginning of this same gospel, that *in the beginning was the Word, and the Word was with God, and the Word was God*; and in particular that *all things were made through him* (Jn 1:1.3). For you must join what you have just heard to what you heard before, and let them both be harmonized in your hearts. And so *the Son* indeed *can do nothing on his own, but only what he sees the Father doing*, but in such a way, all the same, that the things the Father does he only does through the Son, because the Son is his Word, and *in the beginning was the Word, and the Word was with God, and the Word was God, and all things were made through him. For whatever things he has made, the Son makes these things too, in like manner* (Jn 5:19). Not other things, but *these things*; not differently, but *in like manner*.

The Father shows the Son all that he is going to do

3. *For the Father loves the Son, and shows him all the things that he does* (Jn 5:20). What he said just before, *but only what he sees the Father doing, and also shows him all the things that he does*, seems to go with this. But if the Father shows him the things he has made, and the Son cannot make anything except what the Father has shown him, and the Father cannot show him anything except what he has made, the consequence will be that the Father does not make all things through the Son; accordingly, if we hold as unshakably fixed and certain that the Father does make all things through the Son, this text must mean that he shows them to the Son before he makes them. If, you see, the Father shows them to the Son after he has made them, for the Son to make the things shown him, things already made before being shown, then the Father without a shadow of doubt makes them without the Son. But the Father does not make anything without the Son, because the Son of God is the Word of God, and *all things were made through him*.

Perhaps therefore one issue remains: that the Father shows the things that he is going to make as having to be made, so that they might be made through the Son. In fact, if the Son makes the things the Father shows as already made, then the things the Father shows as already made were certainly not made through the Son. After all, they could not be shown to the Son unless they were already made; the Son could not make them unless they had been shown; therefore they were made without the Son. But the truth stands: *All things were made through him*; therefore, they were shown before they were made. But I said that we would defer this point and come back to it after we had run through the reading if, as I said, I have any time and strength left to go back over the things we have deferred.

Further difficulties with 5:20

4. Listen to something more, something even more difficult: *And greater works than these*, he says, *will he show him, in order to astonish you* (Jn 5:20). *Greater than these*—greater than which? The answer readily suggests itself: greater than the cures of bodily illnesses that you have just heard about. In fact, the occasion for this whole discourse arose from this man who had been sick for thirty-eight years and had had his health restored by a word from Christ; and it was because of this that the Lord was able to say, *Greater works than these will he show him, in order to astonish you.* There are, after all, greater works than these cures, and the Father will show them to the Son. Not "has shown," as if in the past, but *will show*, in the future; that is, he is going to show them.

Again a difficult question arises. I mean, does the Father have anything which he has not yet shown to the Son? Did the Father have anything that was still hidden from the Son when he said all this? For if *he will show them*, that is to say, is going to show them,[5] it means he has not yet shown them, and is going to show them to the Son at the same time as he shows them to these people; it does continue, after all, *in order to astonish you.* And this is what is so difficult to see, how the eternal Father shows things to the co-eternal Son in a time sequence, to the Son who knows everything that the Father has.

---

5. Augustine may have needed to explain a future verb form because of a possible confusion between *demonstrabit* ("will show") and *demonstravit* ("has shown") To the ears of his audience *demonstrabit* and *demonstravit* would have sounded almost identical. See too Homily 21, 5.

The Son's power and will are the same as the Father's;
but how does the Father give all judgment to the Son?

5. What nonetheless are those greater things? Well, this is easily grasped, no doubt. For *as the Father*, he says, *raises the dead and gives them life, so too the Son gives life to whom he will* (Jn 5:21). So then, raising the dead is a greater work than restoring health to the sick; but *as the Father raises the dead and gives them life, so too the Son gives life to whom he will.* So does the Father give it to some, the Son to others? But, remember, *all things are through him*; and so the Son gives it to the same ones as the Father does, because he does not do different things, nor do them differently, but *the Son does these things too, in like manner* (Jn 1:10).[6] That clearly is what is to be understood, and what is to be held; but remember that *the Son gives life to whom he will.* So here then you must hold on not only to the power of the Son but also to his will. And *the Son gives life to whom he will*, and the Father gives life to whom he will, and the Son gives it to the same ones as the Father does; and hence Father and Son have both the same power and the same will.

So then, what comes next? *The Father, in fact, does not judge anyone, but he has given all judgment to the Son, so that all may honor the Son just as they honor the Father* (Jn 5:22-23). These words were added here as a kind of explanation of the previous assertion. It raises a great matter; pay close attention.

The Son gives life to whom he will, the Father gives life to whom he will; the Son raises the dead, just as the Father raises the dead. *For the Father does not judge anyone.* If the dead are to be raised at that judgment, how come the Father raises the dead, if he does not judge anyone? Well, *he has given all judgment to the Son.* But it is at that judgment that the dead are raised; and some rise up to life, others to punishment.[7]

If the Son does all this, while the Father does not do it, for the very reason that *the Father does not judge anyone, but he has given all judgment to the Son*, this will appear to contradict what has just been said: *Just as the Father raises the dead and gives them life, so too the Son gives life to whom he will.* So they raise them together; if they raise them together, they give them life

---
6. See Homily 18, 8.
7. See Mt 25:46; Jn 5:29.

together; therefore they judge together. And so how is this true: *The Father, in fact, does not judge anyone, but he has given all judgment to the Son?*

Let the questions proposed disturb us for the time being; the Lord will delight us with the solutions. That is how it is, brothers and sisters; unless a problem rouses your interest when it is set before you, its explanation will afford you no pleasure. So let the Lord himself carry on talking, and let us see if perhaps, in the things he adds, he may not open up his meaning a little. You see, he has covered up his light under a cloud; and it is difficult to soar on eagle's wings above the whole cloud with which the whole earth is covered, and see the purest light in the Lord's words.[8] So in the hope that the heat of its rays may disperse our foggy darkness, and that he may be good enough to open up a little in what follows, let us leave these problems on one side and take a look at what comes next.

The Father is not truly honored unless the Son is honored as equal to the Father

6. *Whoever does not honor the Son does not honor the Father who sent him* (Jn 5:23). This is true and it is plain enough; I mean, *He has given all judgment to the Son,* as he said just now, *so that all may honor the Son just as they honor the Father* (Jn 5:22-23).

What if some are to be found who honor the Father and do not honor the Son?

It cannot happen, he says. *Whoever does not honor the Son does not honor the Father who sent him.*

So no one can say, then, "I was honoring the Father only, because I did not know the Son"?

If you were not yet honoring the Son, you were not honoring the Father either. What is it after all to honor the Father, but to acknowledge that he has a Son? It is one thing, you see, when God is brought to your attention as being God, and another when God is brought to your attention as being the Father. When he is presented to you as God, it is the creator being presented to you, the almighty being presented to you, some supreme spirit, eternal, invisible, unchanging being presented to you; but when he is being brought to your

---

8. On the eagle's reputed ability to gaze directly at the sun see Homily 36, 5; *On Genesis against the Manichees* I, 3, 6.

attention because he is the Father, it can only be the case that the Son is also being brought to your attention, because he cannot be called the Father unless he has a Son, just as the Son cannot be called Son unless he has a Father.

But perhaps you are honoring the Father indeed as greater, the Son on the other hand as lesser, and so will say to me, "I honor the Father, since I know that he has a Son; and I am not mistaken in the name of Father, because you see I do not envisage the Father without the Son. But still I honor the Son too as lesser." In that case the Son himself puts you right and gives you a warning with the words: *So that all may honor the Son*, not in a lesser degree but *just as they honor the Father. Whoever*, therefore, *does not honor the Son does not honor the Father who sent him.*

I want to give higher honors, you say, to the Father, lower honors to the Son. That is how you are depriving the Father of honor, where you give less to the Son. If that is how you feel, I mean, what else can you be thinking but that the Father either did not wish or was not able to beget the Son as equal to himself? If he did not wish to, he was being jealous; if he was unable to, he lacked the ability. So do you not see then that, by feeling that you may give greater honor to the Father, you are in fact slandering the Father? If you wish to honor both Father and Son, give the same honor, therefore, to the Son as you give to the Father.

Peace reigns in the scriptures

7. *Amen, amen, I tell you that whoever listens to my word and trusts the one who sent me has eternal life; and he does not come under judgment, but has passed,* not is passing now, *but has* already *passed from death into life* (Jn 5:24).[9] Note this as well: *Whoever listens to my word*, and he did not go on to say "trusts me" but *trusts the one who sent me*. So let him listen to the word

---

9. In *The Trinity* I, 13, 30 Augustine quotes the same passage but reads: *and he will not come under judgment, but will pass from death into life*; i.e., *veniet* and *transiet* in each case. In *The City of God* XX, 5, 4; 6, 2 the manuscripts are divided. According to the Maurists, while all have the first verb in the future, *veniet*, some have the second one in the past tense, as in our text here, *transiit*, others in the future, *transiet*. The variation in *The City of God* manuscripts is presumably the result of scribal correction one way or the other, probably from the reading in *The Trinity* to the one we have here, which accords with both the Greek and the Latin Vulgate texts. I think this may be an indication that at least this first book of *The Trinity* was written before the preaching of our homily here on John; here Augustine is careful to stress the correct as against the incorrect reading; there he just comments on the incorrect reading as something to be taken for granted.

of the Son, in order to trust the Father. Why does he listen to your word and trust someone else? When we hear someone's word, do we not believe the very person uttering the word, place our trust in the person speaking to us?

So what did *Whoever hears my word and believes the one who sent me* mean but that his word is in me? And what does *listens to my word* mean but "listens to me"? But he believes the one who sent me, because when he believes him he believes his Word; while when he believes his Word he believes me, because I am the Word of the Father.

So then, peace reigns in the scriptures, everything is in agreement; there are no contradictions at all. So rid your heart of conflict, appreciate the harmony of the scriptures. Would Truth ever contradict himself?

The two resurrections

8. *Whoever listens to my word and believes the one who sent me has eternal life; and he does not come under judgment, but has passed from death into life* (Jn 5:24). You all remember of course what we had established earlier on, that *as the Father raises the dead and gives them life, so too the Son gives life to whom he will.* Now he is beginning to reveal himself and talk about the resurrection of the dead; and lo and behold, the dead are already rising.

You see, *whoever listens to my word and trusts the one who sent me, has eternal life and will not come under judgment.*

Prove that he has risen again.

But has passed, he says, *from death into life*. After all, he would not pass from death to life unless he were first of all in death and not in life; but when he has passed, he will be in life and not in death. So then, *he was dead and has come to life; he was lost and is found* (Lk 15:32).

There is accordingly already a kind of resurrection, and people pass from the death of infidelity and unbelief to the life of faith, from the death of falsehood to the life of truth,[10] from the death of iniquity to the life of justice. So all this then is also a kind of resurrection of the dead.

---

10. One could, in contemporary parlance, also translate this "from the death of unreality to the life of reality," but Augustine was primarily thinking of the simple difference between telling lies and telling the truth.

The hour is coming, and now is, when the dead are already rising to eternal life

9. Let him explain the matter in more detail, and let his light that has started to dawn on us grow still brighter. *Amen, amen, I tell you, that the hour is coming, and now is* (Jn 5:25). What we for our part were expecting was the resurrection of the dead at the end, because we have already believed in that—or rather we were not expecting it, but we certainly should be expecting it; after all, there is nothing false about our belief in the resurrection of the dead at the end. So then, the Lord Jesus was suggesting to us a kind of resurrection of the dead before the resurrection of the dead—not like that of Lazarus, or that widow's daughter, or the daughter of the synagogue official,[11] who were all going to die eventually after rising again (I mean, these were dead people who also underwent a kind of resurrection before the resurrection of the dead). No, but what he says here is, *He has eternal life, and does not come under judgment, but has passed from death to life*. To what kind of life? To the eternal kind. So not then like the body of Lazarus; he too after all passed from the life of the tomb to the life of men, but not to eternal life, as he was going to die again, while the dead who are going to rise again at the end of the age will pass into eternal life.

So then, when our Lord Jesus Christ, our heavenly teacher, the Word of the Father and the Truth, wished to demonstrate to us a kind of resurrection of the dead into eternal life, before the resurrection of the dead into eternal life, he said, *The hour is coming*. You, baptized in faith in the resurrection of the flesh, were expecting without a shadow of doubt that hour at the end of the world, the day of judgment; but to stop you from expecting that resurrection in this passage, he added, *and now is*. So then, in saying *The hour is coming*, he is not saying it about that last hour, when *at the command and the voice of an archangel, and at the signal of God's trumpet the Lord himself will come down from heaven, and the dead in Christ will rise first; then we, the living who are left, shall be snatched up with them in the clouds to meet Christ in the air, and in this way we shall always be with the Lord* (1 Thes 16-17).

That hour will come, but it is not now. But as for this hour, just notice what it is: *The hour is coming, and now is*. What takes place in it? What

---

11. See Jn 11:43-44; Lk 6:14-15; Mk 5:41-42.

but the resurrection of the dead? And what sort of resurrection? That those who rise again may live for ever. This will also happen at the last hour.

In the resurrection now, those who hear, that is those who obey, will live

10. So what now? How are we to understand these two resurrections? Can it by any chance be that those who rise now will not rise then, so that now there is a resurrection for some, then for others? No, that is not how it is. In this resurrection, you see, if we have believed with the right kind of faith, we have ourselves risen again; and we who have already risen again ourselves are certainly expecting the other resurrection at the end. But even now we have risen again into eternal life, if we persevere steadily in this faith; and then too we shall rise again into eternal life, when we are put *on a level with the angels* (Lk 20:36).

So let him then distinguish them, let him explain what we have dared to say: how there can be a resurrection before the resurrection, not of different people, but of the same ones both times, and not like the one of Lazarus, but into eternal life. Let him explain it clearly. Listen to the master's dawning light, and to our sun slipping into our hearts; not the sun the eyes of flesh long for, but the one to which the eyes of the heart are in a fever to be opened. So then, let us listen to him.

Amen, amen, I tell you that the hour is coming, and now is, when the dead—notice that a resurrection is being described—*when the dead will hear the voice of the Son of God, and those who have heard will live* (Jn 5:25). Why did he add, *those who have heard will live*? Could they hear, after all, unless they were living? So then, it would have been enough to say, "The hour is coming and now is, when the dead will hear the voice of the Son of God"; we then would already grasp that he is talking about the living, seeing that they would not be able to hear if they were not alive.

No, he says, it is not because they are alive that they hear, but it is by hearing that they come to life again; *they will hear, and those who have heard will live.*

So what is the meaning of *they will hear* but they will obey? You see, as regards the hearing done by the ear, not everyone who hears shall live;

many, after all, hear and do not believe; by hearing and not believing, they do not obey; by not obeying, they fail to live.

And so in this place *those who will hear* just means those who obey.[12] Then, those who have obeyed shall live; they can be quite certain, be absolutely sure about it, they shall live. Christ is being proclaimed here, the Word of God, the Son of God, *through whom all things were made*, who taking flesh by the grace of a predetermined plan was born of the virgin, a baby in the flesh, a young man in the flesh, suffering in the flesh, dying in the flesh, rising again in the flesh, ascending in the flesh, promising resurrection to the flesh, promising resurrection to the mind, to the mind before the flesh, to the flesh after the mind. Whoever hears and obeys shall live; whoever hears and does not obey, that is, hears and shrugs it aside, hears and does not believe, shall not live.

Why shall he not live?

Because he does not hear.

What is the meaning of "he does not hear?"

He does not obey. Therefore, *those who have heard will live*.

What it means for the Son to have life in himself

11. Pay attention now to what we said had to be put off for a while,[13] so that now, if that can happen, its meaning may be discovered. He added right away about this very resurrection: *For just as the Father has life in himself, so he has given the Son also to have life in himself* (Jn 5:26). What is the meaning of *the Father has life in himself*? He does not have life elsewhere; he has it in himself. His being alive, in fact, is in him; it is not from outside, it is not foreign to him. He does not as it were borrow life, nor come to life as a participant, in a life which is not what he is himself; but *he has life in himself*, so that he is himself that life.

Let me see if I can say a little more about this, by proposing examples to inform your understanding; I will be able to do that with the Lord's help and with your steadfast attention. Well now, God is alive, and the soul is alive; but God's life is unchanging, the soul's life is changeable. God does not

---

12. In Latin "to obey," *obaudire*, has an obvious relationship with "to hear," *audire*, that is lacking in English.
13. In sections 1, 3 and 5 of this homily.

make progress nor falter, but he is always in himself; he is just as he is; no different now than he will be later, than he was before.[14] The soul's life on the other hand is very much one thing one minute, another the next; it lived foolishly, it lives wisely; it lived a wicked life, it lives a just life; now it remembers, then it forgets; now it learns, then it is unable to learn; now it loses what it had learned, now it recovers what it had lost. Yes, the life of the soul is changeable.

And when the soul lives in wickedness, that is its death; but when it becomes just, it becomes a participant in the life of another, in a life which is not what it is itself; by raising itself up to God, in fact, and clinging to God, it is justified by him. For it has been said, *To the one believing in him who justifies the impious, his faith is accounted as justice* (Rom 4:5). By withdrawing from him it becomes wicked, by moving toward him it becomes just. Does it not strike you as being as it were something cold which starts to melt and bubble when set by the fire, to turn solid and stiff again when removed from the fire? Does it not strike you as being something dark which starts to shine when brought into the light, to darken again when removed from the light? That is the sort of thing the soul is, not the sort of thing God is.

People can also say they have light now in their eyes. So let your eyes say in their own words, if they can, "We have light in ourselves." The answer to that is: "You are wrong in saying you have light in yourselves; you do have light, but it is in the sky that you have light; you do have light if it happens to be nighttime, but in the moon, in lamps, not in yourselves; after all, when your eyes are closed you lose the light which you perceive when open. You do not have light in yourselves. Hold on to the light when the sun sets, if you can; it is night now, and you are enjoying lamps lit at night; hold on to the light when the lamp is withdrawn; but, when the lamp is withdrawn, in fact you remain in the dark, you do not have any light in yourselves."

This then is to have light in oneself: not to be in need of light from someone else. That is where, if anyone can understand, he shows that the Son is equal to the Father, where he says, *Just as the Father has life in himself, so he has given the Son also to have life in himself,* so that the only

---

14. See Homily 2, 2; Sermon 182, 3; *The Literal Meaning of Genesis* V, 16, 34.

difference between Father and Son is this: that the Father has life in himself which no one has given him, while the Son has life in himself which the Father has given him.

The soul receives light and life from the Word

12. But even here something of a cloud crops up that has to be blown away. Let us not give up, let us concentrate; these are the pastures of the mind, we must not be fussy if we are to live.

You say, "Look, you admit yourself that the Father has given the Son life, so that he has it in himself just as the Father has life in himself, that he does not stand in need of it just as the other does not stand in need of it, that he is life just as the other is, and that both of them are one life, joined together, not two lives, because they are one God, not two gods; and that is what it is to be life. So how then has the Father given life to the Son? It cannot be as though the Son were without life, and received life from the Father in order to live, because if that were the case, he would not have life in himself."

See, I was also talking about the soul. The soul is; even if it is not wise, even if it is not just, it is a soul; even if it is not pious, it is a soul. So then, it is one thing for it to be a soul, but quite another thing for it to be wise, to be just, to be pious. There is therefore something about it which results in its not yet being wise, not yet just, not yet pious. Even so, it is not a nothing, even so, it does not lack life; for it shows itself to be life by a number of its activities, even though it does not show itself to be wise, pious, just. Unless it were alive, you see, it would not move the body around, it would not command the feet to step out, the hands to work, the eyes to look around, the ears to hear; it would not open the mouth to utter sounds, would not wag the tongue to articulate the sounds. And thus by these activities it shows itself to be alive and to be something that is better than the body; but does it show itself by these activities to be wise, pious, just? Do not those who are unwise and impious and unjust walk around, work, see, hear, speak?

But when the soul lifts itself up to something which it is not, and which is above it, and from which it itself is, it receives wisdom, justice, and piety; without these virtues it was dead and did not have the life by which to live, but only the life by which the body would be enlivened. Of course, it is better than the body; but better than the soul itself is God. So then, it is the life of the body, even if it is unwise, unjust, and impious. But because its own life is God, just as when it is in the body it bestows vigor, comeliness, agility, and the functioning of its parts upon it, so too when God, who is its life, is in it, he bestows wisdom, piety, justice, and charity upon it. Therefore, what is bestowed upon the body from the soul is one thing, quite another what is bestowed upon the soul from God. It brings to life and is brought to life; even as dead it brings to life while not being brought to life.[15]

And so, when the Word comes and inserts itself into its hearers, and they both hear it and obey it, then the soul rises again from its death to its life; that is, from wickedness, from folly, from impiety to its God, who is for it wisdom, justice, splendor. *Approach him*, he says.

And what is there in that for us?

And be illuminated (Ps 33:5). If you are illuminated by approaching, and by withdrawing are plunged into darkness, your light, obviously, was not in yourselves but in your God. Approach, in order to rise again; if you withdraw, you will die. If by approaching you live and die by withdrawing, you did not have your life in yourselves. Your life, you see, is the same as your light. *Since with you is the wellspring of life, and in your light shall we see light* (Ps 35:9).

Giving life to the Son, the Father begets the Son from eternity

13. So then, it is not the case that, just as the soul is something else before being illuminated and, when illuminated by participation in something better, becomes better, so too the Word of God, the Son of God, was something else before receiving life, such that, by participation, he has life; on the contrary, he has life in himself, and thus he is himself that very life.

So why then does he say, *He has given the Son to have life in himself*?

Let me put it as briefly as possible: He has begotten the Son. It is not, you see, that he was without life, and received life; but that by being born he is life. The Father is life, not by being born; the Son is life by being born. The Father is not from any father, the Son is from God the Father. That the Father is, he gets from no other; but that he is Father, he is because of the Son. As for the Son though, both his being Son is because of the Father, and

---

15. See Sermon 65, 6: "So marvelous a thing is the soul, so noble a creature, that it is capable, even though it is dead, of making flesh live." See also Letter 120, 4, 18.

his simply being is from the Father. So that is what he said here, *He has given the Son to have life in himself*, as though to say, "The Father who is life in himself has begotten the Son to be life in himself." For, he wanted *has given* to be understood as "has begotten."

It is as if we were to say to someone, "God has given you being." Whom has he given it to? If he has given being to someone already in existence, then he has not given him being, because there already was someone there, able to receive before things were given. So when you hear, "God has given you being," it means you were not there to receive it, and it was in coming into existence that you received being. The builder gave this house its being. But what, to be more exact, did he give it? Its being a house. But now if it was a house, to what would he give being a house, when it already was a house? So what does it mean, then, that he gave it its being a house? He made it to be a house.

So then, what did he give the Son? He gave him to be the Son, he begot him to be life. That is the meaning of *He has given him to have life in himself*, so that he would be life, not be in need of life, so that he should not be understood to have life as a participant. If, you see, he had life as a participant, it would also be possible for him, by losing his share, to be without life. Do not ever accept such a thing about the Son, do not even think it, do not believe it. So the Father then is life abiding, the Son too is life abiding; the Father's life in himself, not from the Son; the Son's life in himself, but from the Father. He was begotten by the Father to be life in himself, while the Father is unbegotten life in himself. Nor did he beget the Son as younger than himself, to become equal to himself by growing up. He was not helped by time, after all, to reach his full perfection, he through whom in his full perfection the times were created. Before all times he is co-eternal with the Father. The Father, you see, was not ever without the Son; but the Father is eternal; therefore the Son too is co-eternal.

What about you, soul? You were dead, you had lost life; listen to the Father through the Son. Arise, receive life, in order that the life which you do not have in yourself you may receive in the one who does have life in himself. So then, the Father quickens you, and so does the Son; and the first resurrection is enacted, when you rise again to participate in the life which you yourself are not; and, by participating, you are brought to life. Arise from your death into your life, which is your God, and pass from death into eternal life. For the Father does have eternal life in himself; and unless he had begotten such a Son as would have eternal life in himself, it would not have happened that just as the Father raises the dead and gives them life, so too the Son would give life to whom he would.

We believe in the resurrection of the soul now and in the resurrection of the body at the end

14. So what about that resurrection of the body, then? I mean, those who hear and live, how do they come to live except by hearing? In fact, *the bridegroom's friend stands and listens to him, and he rejoices with joy at bridegroom's voice* (Jn 3:29), not at his own voice; that is, it is by participating, not by existing, that they hear and live; and all who hear, live, because all who obey, live. Say something too, dear Lord, about the resurrection of the flesh. There were people, you see, ready to deny it and to say that the only resurrection is this one which happens through faith.[16] It is of this resurrection that the Lord reminded us just now and set our hearts on fire, because some of the *dead will hear the voice of the Son of God and will live.* He was not talking about those who hear, of whom some will die and others will live; but saying that all *who hear will live,* because all who obey will live. There you are: what we see here is the resurrection of the spirit; so let us not let go of faith in the resurrection of the flesh.[17] And unless you, Lord Jesus, had said something about it, whom would we put up to oppose those who speak against it?

None of the sects, after all, that have presumed to sow seeds of some kind of religion or other among humankind have ever denied this resurrection of the spirit, lest someone should say to them, "If the soul does not rise again, why are you talking to me? What is it you want to do for me? If you are not making a better person out of me than the bad one I was, why are you talking? But if you are making a just person out of a wicked one, making someone pious who used to be impious, someone wise who used to be foolish, you are admitting that my soul will rise again if I go along with you, if I believe you."

---

16. Augustine probably had the Valentinians in mind, a Gnostic sect founded by Valentinus in the second century, against whom Tertullian wrote a polemical tract.
17. So nearly all the manuscripts, reading: *non ergo amittamus de fide resurrectionem carnis.* But the Maurists and the received text follow the few others who correct this slightly unusual use of "faith," meaning the creed, to read: *amittamus fidem de resurrectionem carnis,* "lose faith about the resurrection of the flesh."

So all founders of any sect, even of some false religion or other, wanting to be believed, have been unable to deny this resurrection of the spirit; they have all agreed about that, but many of them have denied the resurrection of the flesh, saying that the resurrection has already taken place in faith. The apostle takes his stand against such people, when he says, *Among them are Hymenaeus and Philetus, who have gone astray about the truth,*[18] *saying that the resurrection has already taken place, and they are undermining some people's faith* (2 Tm 2:17-18). They were saying that a resurrection had already taken place, but in such a way that another should not be hoped for; and they were reproving the people who were hoping for the resurrection of the flesh, as though the promise made of resurrection would be fulfilled here and now in the spirit by believing.

The apostle censured them.

Why did he censure them? Were they not saying what the Lord was talking about just now: *The hour is coming, and now is, when the dead will hear the voice of the Son of God, and those who hear will live*?

"But I am still talking about the life of minds," Jesus says to you, "I am not yet talking about the life of bodies; but I am talking about the life of the life of bodies, that is, about the life of souls; it is in them that the life of bodies is to be found. Yes, I know there are bodies lying in graves; I know your bodies too are going to end up in graves; I am not yet talking about that resurrection, I am talking about this one. Make sure of rising again in this one, in order not to rise again to punishment in that one. But to convince you that this is the one I am talking about, what is it I go on to say? *For as the Father has life in himself, so he has given the Son also to have life in himself.* This life which is what the Father is, what the Son is, to what is it related? To the soul, or to the body? Well, it is not the body, after all, that experiences that life of wisdom, but the rational mind. Nor is every soul able to experience wisdom; an animal too, after all, has a soul; but the soul of an animal cannot experience wisdom. So then, the human soul can experience this life which the Father has in himself and has given the Son for him to have life in himself; because *that is*

---

18. Berrouard writes (BA 72, 202, note 107) that in Sermon 362, 22. 24 (preached perhaps at the beginning of Lent, 411), Augustine says that Paul accused these nay-sayers of error *about* truth, not of straying *from* truth; they did not totally deny the resurrection, accepting that of the mind or soul and denying that of the body.

the true light which enlightens, not every soul, but *everyone coming into this world* (Jn 1:9). So then, since I am speaking to the mind itself, let it listen, that is, let it obey, in order to live."

The Lord himself goes on to teach expressly
the resurrection of the flesh at the end of the world

15. And so do not keep quiet, dear Lord, about the resurrection of the flesh, lest people refuse to believe it, leaving us as mere debaters, not preachers. So then, *Just as the Father has life in himself, so has he given the Son also to have life in himself.* Let those who hear understand, let them believe in order to understand, let them obey in order to live. Let them hear this word too, lest they should think resurrection stops here. *And he has given him authority also to pass judgment.*

Who has?

The Father.

To whom has he given it?

To the Son. Having *given him, you see, to have life in himself, he has given him authority also to pass judgment, because he is the Son of Man* (Jn 5:27). This Christ, you see, is both the Son of God and the Son of Man. *In the beginning was the Word, and the Word was with God, and the Word was God; he was in the beginning with God* (Jn 1:1-2). There you are, that is how *he has given to him to have life in himself.* But because *the Word was made flesh and took up residence among us* (Jn 1:14), being made man from the virgin Mary, he is the Son of Man.

What, then, has he received because he is the Son of Man?

The authority also to pass judgment.

Which judgment?

At the end of the world; and that will be a resurrection for you of the dead, but of bodies. So then, God raises souls through Christ the Son of God; through the same Christ, the Son of Man, God raises bodies. He has given him authority. He would not have this authority unless he had received it, he would simply be a man without authority.

But the same one is the Son of Man who is also the Son of God. For, by his cleaving to the unity of person, the Son of Man to the Son of God, one person is constituted, the same person being the Son of God who is also the Son of Man. But what he has and why he has it has to be distinguished. As

Son of Man he has a soul, he has a body. As Son of God, which is the Word of God, he has the man in the way a soul has a body. Just as a soul having a body does not constitute two persons but one human being, so the Word having the man does not constitute two persons, but one Christ. What is a human being? A rational soul having a body. What is Christ? The Word of God having a man. I can thus see what things I am talking about, and who it is that is talking, and to whom I am talking.

It is as the Son of Man, not as God the Son, that Christ
will be seen at the last judgment by those who sat in judgment on him in this life

16. Now listen, not to me, but to the Lord, who is going to talk about the resurrection of bodies, for the sake of those who have risen again by rising from death, cleaving to life.

To what life?

To the kind that does not know death.

Why does it not know death?

Because it does not know change.

Why does it not know change?

Because it is life in itself. *And he has given him authority also to pass judgment, because he is the Son of Man.*

What judgment, what sort of judgment?

Do not be surprised at this, because I said, *He has given him authority also to pass judgment. For the hour is coming* (Jn 5:28).

He did not add *and now is*; so he wants to suggest some hour or other at the end of the world.[19] The hour now is for the dead to rise, the hour at the end of the world will be for the dead to rise; but to rise now in the spirit, then in the flesh; to rise now in the spirit through the Word of God, the Son of God; to rise then in the flesh through the Word of God made flesh, the Son of man. Nor, you see, is the Father himself going to come to the judgment of the living and the dead; and yet, for all that, the Father does not distance himself from the Son.

How is it then that he is not going to come himself?

---

19. See Sermons 127, 14; 362, 26.

Because he himself will not be seen at the judgment. *They shall gaze at the one they have pierced* (Zech 12:10; Jn 19:37; Rv 1:7). He will be the judge in that form[20] in which he was placed in judgment; he will pass judgment in the form in which judgment was passed on him; the judgment passed on him, you see, was an iniquitous one, while the judgment he passes will be just.

So it is the form of a slave that will come, and that is the one that will appear and be seen. I mean to say, how could the form of God be seen by the just and the wicked? If a judgment were only to be made between the just and the just, then the form of God would appear and be seen by them precisely as just; but because it is going to be a judgment of the just and of the wicked, and the wicked are not permitted to see God—for *blessed are the clean of heart, for they shall see God* (Mt 5:8)—the judge will appear in such guise as can be seen both by those whom he is going to crown, and by those whom he is going to condemn. So then, the form of a slave will be seen, the form of God will be concealed. In the form of a slave the Son of God will be concealed, and the Son of man will appear. The Father on the other hand will not appear, because he has not been clothed with the form of a slave; that is why he said earlier on, *The Father does not judge anyone, but has given all judgment to the Son* (Jn 5:22).

So we did well then to defer things, so that the one who proposed the problem might himself solve it. Earlier on, after all, the matter was wrapped in obscurity; now, I rather think, it has finally been made clear that *he has given him authority also to pass judgment*, because *the Father does not judge anyone, but he has given all judgment to the Son*; and this because the judgment is going to be made in that form which the Father does not have. And what kind of judgment? *Do not be surprised at this, because the hour is coming*, not the one which now is for souls to rise again, but which is going to come, when what will rise again will be bodies.

More about the distinction between the two resurrections

17. Let him say this more expressly, to stop the heretic who denies the resurrection of the body from finding any slur he can cast on it, though it should already begin to be light for the mind. When he said earlier on, *The hour is coming*, he added, *and now is*; here, though, *the hour is coming*; he

---

20. See Phil 2:6-7; *Exposition of Psalm* 48, 1, 5.

has not added, *and now is*. Still, with the truth out in the open, he shatters every pretext, disrupts every opening to calumny, and cuts every knot of their snares. *Do not be surprised at this, because the hour is coming when all who are in the graves* (Jn 5:28). What could be more clearly, what more expressly said? Bodies are in graves, not souls—neither those of the just nor of the wicked. The soul of the just man was in Abraham's bosom, the soul of the wicked man was being tormented in hell;[21] in a grave is found neither the one nor the other. Earlier on, when he said, *The hour is coming, and now is*—please, I implore you, pay attention. You know very well, brothers and sisters, that getting food for the stomach is laborious; how much more so is getting food for the mind! You work at standing and listening, I work even harder to stand and speak. If I labor for your sakes, should you not—for your own good—also join me in that labor?

So then, earlier on, when he said, *The hour is coming*, and added, *and now is*, what did he go on to say? *When the dead will hear the voice of the Son of God, and those who hear will live.* He did not say all the dead will hear and those who hear will live, because by the dead he meant us to understand the wicked;[22] and since when are all the wicked obedient to the gospel? The apostle says clearly, *But not all are obedient to the gospel* (Rom 10:16). Yet those who hear shall live, because all who are obedient to the gospel pass over to eternal life through faith; nonetheless not all are obedient, and that is what is happening now. But at the end, however, *all who are in the graves*, that is both just and unjust, *will hear his voice, and come forth* (Jn 5:28). Notice how he was unwilling to say "and shall live." All, you see, will come forth, but not all will live. When he said earlier on, *And those who hear will live*, he wanted us to understand, in this very act of obedience, eternal and blessed life, and this is something that not all will have who come forth from the graves. So now then, both by the mention of graves and by the express statement of coming forth from the graves, we are clearly meant to understand the resurrection of bodies.

---

21. See Lk 16:22-25.
22. See Sermon 127, 8.

At the last judgment there will be open and public separation of the just from the wicked

18. *All will hear his voice, and come forth.*

And where is the judgment, if all hear, and all come forth? It looks like total confusion; I cannot see anything separated out. Certainly, you have received the authority to judge, because you are the Son of Man; look, here you are at the judgment, bodies will rise; say something about the actual judgment, that is, about separating the good and the bad.

Listen to this too: *Those who have done good to the resurrection of life, those who have done evil to the resurrection of judgment* (Jn 5:28-29).

When he was talking earlier on about the resurrection of minds and souls, did he do any sorting out? But then all who hear shall live, because it is by obeying[23] that they shall live. But now on the contrary, by rising again and coming forth from the graves, they will not all go off to eternal life, but only those who have done good; while as for those who have done evil, off with them to judgment. Here, by the way, he put *judgment* for "punishment." And there will be a cleaving asunder, and not like the one there is now. Now too, after all, we are separated from one another, not in different places, but in morals, dispositions, desires, in faith, hope and charity. We live together, you see, with the wicked, but we do not all lead the same kind of life; we are being cleft asunder in secret, separated in secret, like the grain on the threshing floor, not like the grain in the granary. The grain on the threshing floor is both separated from the chaff and mixed up with it; separated when it is stripped of the chaff, mixed up with it because it has not yet been winnowed.

Then there will be open, public separation, a distinction of life just as of conduct, a distinction of bodies just as of wisdom. Those who have done good will live with the angels of God; those who have done evil will be tormented with the devil and his angels. And the servant form will pass away. The reason, after all, that he had shown himself as a servant was to pass judgment; after the judgment he will depart from here, he will take with him the body whose head he is and offer it as his kingdom to God.[24]

---

23. Remember, hearing (*audire*) is the same as obeying (*obaudire*).
24. See 1 Cor 15:24. It is with reference to this text that Augustine has just said: "And the servant form will pass away." Berrouard wonders if Augustine may not mean that Christ's humanity, in which he took on the form of a servant, will be totally absorbed into his divinity after the final judgment (see BA 72, 219, note 153; 827, note 67). He refers to *Revisions* I, 24, 1, where Augustine clarifies

Then will that form of God which could not be seen by the wicked—those whose sight needed the form of the servant—be seen plainly.

He also says something similar elsewhere: *These will go off to eternal fire* (about those on the left hand); *but the just will go to eternal life* (Mt 25:46); he speaks about that in another place: *Now this is eternal life, that they should know you, the one true God, and Jesus Christ whom you have sent* (Jn 17:3). Then will be seen there the one *who, since he was in the form of God, did not think being equal to God was a thing to be grabbed* (Phil 2:6); then he will show himself in the way he promised he would show himself to his lovers; *for whoever loves me*, he said, *keeps my commandments; and whoever loves me will be loved by my Father, and I too will love him, and show myself to him* (Jn 14:21). There he was, in the presence of those he was speaking to; but what they could see was the form of a servant, while they were not able to see the form of God; they were being taken on the mule to the inn to be healed;[25] but once they have been healed they will see it, because *I will show myself*, he says, *to him*. How is he shown?[26] As equal to the Father, when he says to Philip, *Whoever sees me, also sees my Father* (Jn 14:9).

---

what he wrote in his *Commentary on Galatians*, written at least fifteen years before this homily, and to *The Trinity* I, 8, 15, where the reference is to writers who did hold this opinion. But in neither of these works does Augustine even hint that he held it himself, nor does he admit to having done so in *Revisions*. It is a mistake to assume that he regarded the phrase "the form of a servant" as being simply equivalent to the human nature of Jesus, contrasted with his divine nature or substance. What he says in one or two places is that it means the mortality of human nature in its present condition. So when Christ laid aside his mortality by rising from the dead, and ascended in glory into heaven, still the man who was born of the virgin (as was already said earlier on in section 11), his humanity, his human substance, while still remaining human, and thus creaturely, and entirely distinct from his uncreated divinity, no longer wore "the form of a servant." Augustine does talk about its being seen by the wicked when Christ comes again to judge the living and the dead; at that point the phrase represents the visibility of his human body. After he hands over the kingdom to God and his Father, his human visibility is overshadowed by his being seen as God, as he hinted in his discourse at the last supper; see Jn 14:9-10; 16:16-22. But this in no sense means his human nature is absorbed or eliminated by his divine nature. See *Against a Sermon of the Arians* 34, 37; *The Trinity* I, 8, 15.

25. See Lk 10:30-35. Jesus is the good Samaritan, his humanity in "the form of a servant" is the mule, the inn is the Church. See Sermon 264, 5, where in quite a different context he says, "The Lord's beast is his flesh."
26. The Maurists and all subsequent texts punctuate: *Quomodo ostenditur aequalis Patri?*; and that too is how Berrouard translates it: 'How does he show himself equal to the Father?' I think it makes more sense to punctuate: *Quomodo ostenditur? Aequalis Patri*; which is what I translate.

How to make the will of one's superior one's own

19. *I myself cannot do anything on my own; as I hear, so I judge, and my judgment is just* (Jn 5:30). We were on the point of saying, "You then will judge, and the Father will not judge, because *he has given all judgment to the Son*; so you will not then be judging in accord with the Father." To meet this objection he added, *I myself cannot do anything on my own; as I hear, so I judge, and my judgment is just, because I do not seek my own will but the will of the one who sent me* (Jn 5:30). For sure, *the Son gives life to whom he will*. He does not seek his own will but the will of the one who sent him. Not mine, not my own interest; not that of the Son of Man; not mine, which resists God.

People do their own will, you see, not God's, when they do what they want, not what God requires; when, however, they do what they want in such a way that they still follow God's will, they are not doing their own will, even though they are doing what they want. Do willingly what is required of you, and in this way you will both do what you want and you will not be doing your own will but that of the one who commands.

Conclusion; the solving of much earlier problems deferred until the morrow

20. What then? *As I hear, so I judge*. The Son hears, and the Father shows him something, and the Son sees the Father doing it. We set aside this problem so as to deal with it more directly, if any time and strength had been left us after we had gone through the reading. If I say I cannot continue speaking, you may not be able to listen any more. Perhaps you will say, in your eagerness to hear, "We can." So it is better that I then should admit my weakness, because I am too tired to go on talking, rather than pouring into you, who have already had your fill, what you could not properly digest. Accordingly, hold me tomorrow as your debtor to keep with the Lord's help the promise I had put off yesterday until today.[27]

---

27. The homily preached the next day is in fact Homily 23. The reason for this has been given in the Introduction.

Homily 20

On John 5:19[1]

On the Lord's own words in Jn 5:19

1. The words of our Lord Jesus Christ—especially those which John the evangelist, who reclined on the Lord's breast for good reason,[2] that is, to drink of the secrets of his lofty wisdom, and to proclaim by evangelizing what he imbibed by loving—are so mysterious and of such profound significance that they disturb every twisted heart and exercise all the upright of heart. Would Your Graces then turn your attention to this short passage that has been read. If we can by any means do so with the grace and help of the one who wished his words to be read to us, words which were heard at that time and committed to writing in order to be read now, let us see what he meant by what you just heard him saying, *Amen, amen, I tell you, the Son can do nothing on his own, but only what he sees the Father doing; for whatever the Father does, the Son does these same things in like manner* (Jn 5:19).

The true meaning of the sacrament of the sabbath

2. But you need to remember that this discourse was based on the passage before this reading, where the Lord cured one of those who were lying in the five porticoes surrounding that pool of Solomon[3] by telling the man, *Pick up your stretcher, and go home* (Jn 5:8).[4] But he did this on the sabbath, whereby the Jews were so upset that they accused him falsely of overturning and breaking the law. That was when he had said to them, *My Father is working until now, and I am working* (Jn 5:17). For they understood the observance of the sabbath in a materialistic sense, and thought that God, after the work of

---

1. Preached on the feast of St. Cyprian, September 13, 420.
2. See Jn 13:23; Homily 18, 1.
3. This, according to Berrouard, is the only time Augustine refers to the pool as the pool of Solomon; there is no justification for this in any version of the text. But in Jn 10:23 we are told that Jesus was walking about in the temple in the portico of Solomon. Augustine may have transferred Solomon's name from that single portico to these five porticoes and the pool they encircled.
4. In fact, these words were addressed to the paralytic in Mk 2:11.

making this world, went to sleep until this day, and for that reason sanctified the day on which he began as it were to rest from his labors. In the sacrament of the sabbath, however, our fathers of old were enjoined to abstain from all servile work, and we Christians keep that spiritually by abstaining from sin, because the Lord says, *Everyone who commits sin is the slave of sin* (Jn 8:34), and by giving rest to our heart, that is, a spiritual tranquility. And although we strive to do so in this world, we will nevertheless only attain to perfect rest when we depart from this life.

But the reason God is said to have rested is that he did not build anything else once everything was accomplished. Scripture, though, called it rest, to admonish us that we should only rest after good works. That, you see, is how we find it written in Genesis, *And God made all things very good, and God rested on the seventh day* (Gen 1:31; 2:2), so that you, O man, on observing that God rested after having done good works, should only hope for rest after performing good works. And just as God rested on the seventh day after making man in his own image and likeness on the sixth day, and after completing all his works that were very good, so you also should not hope for rest until you have returned to the likeness in which you were created, and which you lost by sinning. God, after all, cannot be said to have toiled or labored, since he just spoke and they were made. Is there anyone who after working with such ease would want to rest as if after hard labor? If he gave an order and somebody withstood him, if he gave an order and it was not carried out, he might rightly be said to have rested after toil and labor. But in fact we read in the Book of Genesis: *God said, Let there be light, and light was made; God said, Let there be a firmament, and a firmament was made* (Gen 1:3.6); and the other things made immediately at his word. The psalm also bears witness to this, where it says, *He spoke and they were made, he commanded and they were created* (Pss 148:5; 32:9). So how, after making the world, could he need rest, as if he had stopped working, when, in fact, he never had to toil in giving commands? So then, these words are mysterious, and put there like that so that we should hope for rest for ourselves after this life—as long as we have done good works.

That is why, to give the impudence and error of the Jews a good hammering, and show up their distorted notions about God for what they were, the Lord said to them, scandalized as they were by his restoring people to health on the sabbath,[5] *"My Father is working until now, and I am working.* So do not imagine that my Father rested on the sabbath in such a way that he would do no more work from then on; but just as he is still working now, so I too am working." But just as the Father does it without any toil and sweat, so too does the Son act without any toil and sweat. *God spoke and they were made*; Christ said to the sick man, *Pick up your stretcher, and go home*, and it was done.

Just as Father and Son are inseparable, so are their works inseparable

3. Now the Catholic faith maintains that the works of Father and Son cannot be separated. This is what I want to talk about to Your Graces, if I can, but in accordance with those words of the Lord, *Whoever is able to understand, let him understand* (Mt 19:12). Whoever though is unable to grasp it should not put it down to me, but to his own slow wits, and should turn to the one who opens the heart, so that he may pour in what he has to give. Finally, if the reason anyone does not understand is that the matter has not been stated by me as it should have been, let him excuse human weakness and throw himself on divine goodness. For we have Christ, the teacher within. When anything comes to your ears from my lips that you are not able to take in, turn within your heart to the one who is both teaching me what to say and distributing understanding among you as he thinks fit. He knows what he has to give and who he is giving it to, and so will present himself to the one who asks, and open to the one who knocks.[6] And if maybe he does not give anything, nobody should say that he has been abandoned; perhaps, you see, he is putting off giving something, but he does not leave anyone starving. I mean, if he does not give for the time being, he is putting seekers through their paces, not showing contemptuous indifference to beggars. So then, pay close attention to what I wish to say, even if I cannot do it very well.

This is what the Catholic faith maintains, upheld by the Spirit of God in his saints, against every warped doctrine of the heretics, that the works of

---

5. In Homily 17, 10 Augustine is careful to point out that the Jews did not in fact find fault with Jesus for curing the man on the sabbath, in order not to bring on themselves once again the rebuke they had received from him in Lk 14:5, after he had cured the man with dropsy on the sabbath. This time they picked on the man who had been cured for carrying his stretcher on the sabbath.
6. See Mt 7:7.

Father and Son are inseparable. What have I actually said? Just as Father and Son are themselves inseparable, so too are the works of Father and Son inseparable. In what way are Father and Son inseparable? In the way he said himself, *I and the Father are one* (Jn 10:30); in the way Father and Son are not two gods, but one God, the Word and the one whose Word he is, the one and only God, Father and Son bound together by love, and theirs is the one Spirit of love, so that Father and Son and Holy Spirit constitute the Trinity. So then, just as all three persons are equal and inseparable, in the same way it is not just the works of the Father and the Son but also those of the Holy Spirit that are inseparable.

Let me say still more plainly what it means that their works are inseparable. The Catholic faith does not say that the Father has done something, and the Son has done something else, but that what the Father has done, that is, what the Son has also done, that is what the Holy Spirit has also done. All things, after all, were made through the Word; when he spoke and they were made, they were made through the Word, they were made through Christ. *In the beginning*, after all, *was the Word, and the Word was with God, and the Word was God; all things were made through him* (Jn 1:1.3). If all things were made through him, *God said, Let there be light, and light was made.* He made it in the Word, he made it through the Word.

The Son gets both his being and his power from the Father; and with them being and power are identical, which is not the case with us

4. So then, we have now heard the gospel, when he answered the Jews, who were indignant *because he was not only doing away with the sabbath, but he was also calling God his Father, making himself equal to God* (Jn 5:18); that, you see, is how it is written in the previous section. In answer to their misplaced indignation, therefore, the Son of God who is the Truth said, *Amen, amen, I tell you, the Son can do nothing on his own, but only what he sees the Father doing* (Jn 5:19). It is as if he were saying, "Why are you scandalized that I call God my Father, and that I make myself equal to God? I am equal, such that he begot me; I am equal, such that he is not from me, but I am from him." That, you see, is what is to be understood in these words, *The Son can do nothing on his own, but only what he sees the Father doing.* That means that, whatever the Son has the power to do, he has that power from the Father.

How is it from the Father that he has that power?

Because he has his being as Son from the Father.

How is it from the Father that he is the Son?

Because he has the power from the Father, because he has being from the Father; for the Son, in fact, power is the same as being.[7] That is not how it is with human beings. Lift up your hearts in some way from a comparison with human frailty, lying prostrate far below; and if, by chance, anyone of us should reach the mystery, and, struck with dread at such a dazzling flash of light, should understand something that keeps him from remaining ignorant, let him not think that he has understood everything, lest he become proud and lose hold of the little he has understood. For a human being "can" is one thing, "is" is another. Sometimes, after all, a person is, and cannot do what he wants, while sometimes he is in such a condition that he can do what he wants; and this shows that in him "is" is one thing, "can" is another. For, if "is" were the same in him as "can," he "could" whenever he "would."

With God on the other hand there is not one thing, substance, by which he is, and another, power, by which he can, but whatever he has, it is all consubstantial with his very self, and he is whatever he is, because God simply is. It is not the case that he is in one way, can in another, but he has "is" and "can" together, because he has "will" and "do" together, all simultaneously, identically. So then, because the Son's power is from the Father, that is why the Son's substance too is from the Father; and because the Son's substance is from the Father, that is why the Son's power too is from the Father. And so, because the Son is from the Father, that is why he said, *The Son can do nothing on his own*. Because the Son does not get "is" from himself, that is why he does not get "can" from himself either.

The difficulty the heretics have with their "solution"

5. Yes, it does seem on the face of it that he made himself less when he said, *The Son can do nothing on his own, but only what he sees the Father doing*. At these words heretical vanity stiffens its neck,[8] those people, namely, who say the Son is less than the Father, of less power, less majesty,

---

7. "Power (*posse*) is the same as being (*esse*)" could also be expressed as " 'Can' is the same as 'is.' "
8. The stiff-necked heretics are the Arians.

less ability, because they fail to understand Christ's words as stating a mystery. Would Your Graces please pay close attention, and see how with their literal-minded, materialistic[9] understanding they are now disturbed and tripped up by the very words of Christ. I referred to this a little while ago,[10] how God's word disturbs all whose hearts are twisted, just as it exercises devout hearts. This is above all the case with God's word as you find it in John's gospel, in which sublime matters are being stated, not just things of any old sort, not just things that can be easily understood.

If the heretic happens to hear these words, look at him; he stiffens his neck and says to us, "See, the Son *is* less than the Father; here, just listen to the words of the Son who says, *The Son can do nothing on his own, but only what he sees the Father doing.*" Wait, just as it is written, *Be quiet to hear the word, in order to understand* (Sir 5:11). Yes, let us suppose I am disturbed by these words, since I say the Father's and the Son's power and majesty are equal, so I am tripped up when I hear, *The Son can do nothing on his own, but only what he sees the Father doing.* Deeply disturbed by these words, I enquire of you, already sure in your own opinion that you have understood them, "We know from the gospel that the Son walked on the sea;[11] when did he ever see the Father walking on the sea?" Now it is his turn to be disturbed! Suppose then that you had understood correctly, and let us examine the matter together. What are we to do? We have heard the Lord's words, *The Son can do nothing on his own, but only what he sees the Father doing*; he walked on the sea, the Father never walked on the sea. Surely, the Son does nothing, but only what he sees the Father doing!

The Catholic solution deals with all difficulties

6. So then, come back with me to what I was saying, and perhaps the problem is to be understood in such a way that we can both get out of this puzzle. For, in accord with the Catholic faith, I see how I can get out of it without stumbling, without scandal, while you are still hemmed in, and looking for a way to get out. Notice which way you came in. Perhaps you have not understood this either, my saying, "Notice which way you came

---

9. Simply "their fleshly understanding," *carnali suo intellectu*.
10. At the beginning of the sermon, section 1.
11. See Mk 6:48, and parallels.

in." Listen to him saying himself, *I am the door* (Jn 10:7.9). The reason you are looking for a way out, and not finding one, is that you did not enter through the door but tumbled in over the wall. So then, pick yourself up as best you can from your collapse, and come in through the door, in order to come in without stumbling and not go astray when you get out. Come through Christ, and do not bring along what you are going to say from your own heart, but only speak what he has shown you.

Here then is how the Catholic faith gets out of this puzzle. The Son walked upon the sea, he placed his feet of flesh upon the waves; his flesh was walking, his godhead controlling. So then, while his flesh was walking, his godhead controlling, was the Father absent? If he was absent, how can the Son himself say, *It is the Father dwelling in me who performs his works* (Jn 14:10)? So then, if it is the Father dwelling in the Son who performs his works, that walking on the sea by the flesh was being done by the Father, was being done through the Son. I see each of them working there; the Father did not abandon the Son, nor did the Son depart from the Father. So it is that whatever the Son does, he does not do it without the Father, because whatever the Father does, he does not do it without the Son.

The Father acts through the Son

7. That is how to get out of that one. Notice that we are right in saying the works of Father and Son and Holy Spirit are inseparable. The way you, I mean, understand it, well, God made light, and the Son saw the Father making light, according to your literal-minded understanding, by which you want to understand him as being less, because he said, *The Son can do nothing on his own, but only what he sees the Father doing*. God the Father made light; what other light did the Son make? God the Father made the firmament, the sky between the waters and the waters;[12] the Son saw him, according to your gross and sluggish understanding; because the Son saw the Father making the firmament, and said, *The Son can do nothing on his own, but only what he sees the Father doing*, give me another firmament. Or have you by any chance lost a firmament?[13] Those, however, *who are built upon the foundation of the apostles and the prophets, Christ himself*

---

12. See Gen 1:3. 6-7.
13. The Latin has *fundamentum*, "foundation"; but I cannot help feeling that what Augustine said, making fun of his opponents, was *firmamentum*, and that this was changed by the earliest copyists into *fundamentum* to accord with the contrasting quotation he goes on to employ.

being the chief cornerstone (Eph 2:20), are at peace in Christ, and do not quarrel and stray off into heresy.

So then, we understand that the light was made by God the Father, but through the Son; that the firmament was made by God the Father, but through the Son. *All things*, after all, *were made through him, and without him was made nothing* (Jn 1:3). Give your intelligence a good shaking—nor indeed should it be called intelligence, but downright silliness. God the Father made the world; what other world did the Son make? Give me the Son's world; this world in which we find ourselves, whose is it? Tell us, by which of them was it made? If you say, "By the Son, not by the Father," you have strayed from the Father. If you say, "By the Father, not by the Son," the gospel answers you, *And the world was made through him, and the world did not know him* (Jn 1:10). So then, acknowledge him through whom the world was made, and do not be found among those who did not know the one through whom the world was made.

The Son not being able to do anything from himself simply means his being from the Father[14]

8. So then, the works of Father and Son are inseparable. But to say, *The Son can do nothing on his own*, is the same thing as if he said, "The Son is not from himself."[15] Obviously, if he is the Son he was born; if he was born he is from the one of whom he was born. But he, all the same, begot his equal. The begetter, after all, was not in need of anything, looking either for a time to beget, seeing that he begot one co-eternal with himself; or looking for a mother to beget by, seeing that he uttered the Word from himself. So in begetting, the Father did not come before the Son in age, or beget a Son younger than himself. And perhaps someone is saying to himself that after many eons the Father had the Son in his old age. But just as the Father does not experience old age, so too

---

14. Berrouard points out (BA 72, 202, note 107) that in Sermon 362, 22. 24 Augustine emphasizes that they went astray *about* the faith, not *from* it, in that they still believed in the resurrection of the mind or soul. That sermon was devoted to the subject of the resurrection of the dead, like the one before it, both of a length almost to outdo this homily on John.
15. "On his own": *a se*; "from himself": *a se*.

the Son does not have to grow up; just as the one did not grow old, so the other did not grow up, but equal begot equal, eternal begot co-eternal.[16]

"How," someone says, "does eternal beget eternal?"

In the same way as time-bound flame begets time-bound light. Now the flame begetting is coeval with the light it begets, and the flame begetting does not precede in time the light begotten; but from the moment the flame begins, from that very moment the light begins too. Give me a flame without light, and I will give you God the Father without the Son.

That then is the meaning of *The Son can do nothing on his own, but only what he sees the Father doing*; because seeing for the Son is the same as being born of the Father. His seeing is not one thing and his substance another; nor is his power one thing and his substance another. Everything that he is, he is from the Father; just as his "can" and his "is" are one thing, and all of it is from the Father.

The Son not only does the same things as the Father,
he also does them in like manner

9. He continues in his own words, and thereby upsets those who misunderstand it all, in order to call them back from where they go wrong to a right understanding of what he is saying—in case some literal-minded understanding should creep in, and turn your mind away from the truth, and you set up for yourself something like two cabinetmakers, a master craftsman, and an apprentice paying attention to the master as he is making, for example, a chest; so just as he has made a chest, the other one makes another chest in accordance with his observation of the way the master set about his work. But to stop any such literal-minded understanding seeing double, so to say, in the single godhead, he went on to say, *Whatever things the Father does, the Son does these same things in like manner* (Jn 5:19). The Father does not do some things, and the Son others like them, but he does the same things in like manner. He did not say, after all, "Whatever things the Father does, the Son too does others like them," but, *Whatever things the Father does, the Son does these same things in like manner.*

---

16. See Sermon 118, 2.

What one has made, the other has made also; the Father has made the world, so has the Son, so has the Holy Spirit. If they are three gods, then there are three worlds; if Father, Son and Holy Spirit are one God, then it is one world that was made by Father, Son and Holy Spirit. So then, the Son makes these things that the Father also makes; and he does not make them differently; as well as making these same things, he makes them in like manner.

An illustration from how the mind and body do the same thing, but not in like manner

10. He had already said, *He does these same things*; why did he add, *in like manner*? So that another twisted understanding or mistake might not be born in the spirit. Thus you observe a man's work; in the man there is both spirit and body, the spirit giving orders to the body. But there is a vast difference between body and spirit; while the body is visible, the spirit is invisible; between the powers and capacities of the spirit and of any kind of body you like, even heavenly ones, there is a vast difference. Still, the spirit gives an order to its own body and the body does what it is told, and what the spirit appears to do the body does also. So then, the body appears to do the same thing as the spirit, but not in like manner.

How does it do the same thing, but not in the same manner?

The spirit forms a word within itself, gives an order to the lips, and these utter the word which the spirit has formed; the spirit has formed it, the lips have formed it too; the body's master has formed it, the servant has formed it too; but for the servant to form it, he received what he should form from his master, and formed it on the master's orders. The same thing has been formed by each of them; but in like manner? Surely not. "How not in like manner?" somebody asks. Look, the word which my spirit has formed remains in me; what my lips have formed vibrates the air, ceases and is no more. When you have spoken the word in your spirit, and it has made a sound through your lips, return to your spirit, and notice that the word you formed is still there. Has it remained on your lips just as it has remained in your spirit? Surely not. Your lips formed it by making a sound, your spirit formed it by thinking; but the sound made by your lips has ceased; the thought formed by your spirit remains. So then, the body has made what the spirit has made, but not in like manner. The spirit, after all, has made what the spirit can hold on to, while the lips have made a sound which strikes the ear, passing through the air. You do not chase after the syllables and make them stay put, do you?

So then, that is not how it is with Father and Son; no, he does the same things and does them in like manner. If God made the heaven which abides, this is the heaven which abides that the Son made. If God the Father made man who dies, the Son too made the same man who dies, because he made him in like manner; and whatever things the Father made to be time-bound and temporary, these same things the Son made to be time-bound and temporary, because he not only made them, but also made them in like manner.[17] The Father, after all, made them through the Son, because the Father made all things through the Word.

One must take a leap beyond oneself to attain to God, Father, Son and Holy Spirit

11. Look for separation between Father and Son, and you will not find it; even if you have risen above yourself, you will not find it then; if you have touched something above your mind, you will not find it then. In fact, if you keep going over the things that a spirit which deludes itself does, you are conversing with your imagination, not with the Word of God, and your imagination deceives you. Rise above the body and savor the things of the spirit; rise above the spirit and savor the things of God. You cannot touch God unless you also rise above the spirit; how much less can you touch him if you remain stuck in the flesh! How far then are those who think in a flesh-minded way from appreciating what God is, because they would not even get that far if they were thinking with the spirit! He withdraws far from God when he thinks according to the flesh, and there is a great difference between flesh and spirit; yet there is an even greater difference between spirit and God. You then, being in the spirit, are in the middle; look down below, there is the body; look up above, there is God. Lift yourself up from the body, go even beyond yourself.

---

17. While here Augustine applies the *in like manner* to the things made by both Father and Son, elsewhere he applies it to the manner of working of the divine persons, as for example in Sermon 135, 3-4, where he uses it to refute the Arian idea that the Father acts by commanding, and the Son by obeying and carrying out the order. There, incidentally, I translated *similiter* by "likewise." See also *Exposition of Psalm* 108, 23; *Against the Sermon of the Arians* 9, 114-15.

Look, in fact, at what the psalmist said, and you will learn how God is to be savored: *My tears*, he says, *have become crumbs of bread for me day and night, when I am being asked every day, Where is your God?* (Ps 41:3) It is as if the pagans were to say, "Look, these are our gods; your God, though, where is he?" They are showing us, you see, something that can be seen; we worship what cannot be seen. And whom are we being asked to show him to in any case? To a person who does not have the wherewithal to see. Because of course, if they can see their gods with their eyes, we too have other eyes with which we may see our God. These eyes need to be cleaned up if we are to see our God; *Blessed*, after all, *are the clean of heart, for they shall see God* (Mt 5:8).

So then, after saying how troubled he was when he was asked every day, *Where is your God? These things I remembered*, he goes on, *because I am being asked every day, Where is your God?* And he says, as if in his eagerness to grasp his God, *"These things I remembered and I poured out my soul over myself* (Ps 41:4). So then, in order to reach up and touch my God, about whom I was being asked, *Where is your God?* I did not pour my soul over my flesh but over and above myself; I passed beyond myself so as to touch him. For the one who is above me made me; no one will reach him without first going beyond himself."

How the spirit of man must climb beyond all created things to attain to God

12. Think about the body; it is mortal, earthy, fragile, corruptible. Leave it aside. But is it just the flesh that is subject to time?[18] Think about other bodies, think about heavenly bodies; they are greater, better, dazzling; take a look at them too. They revolve from east to west, they do not stand still; they can be seen by the eyes of animals as well as of human beings. Pass beyond them too.

"And how," you will ask, "am I to pass beyond the heavenly bodies when I am walking about on earth?"

---

18. The sequence of thought is not easy to follow here. By "flesh" Augustine does not just mean body, but in the Pauline sense, the flesh of sin; that is what has subjected the children of Adam to the ravages of time which he has just listed. By including other material bodies which are not "flesh" Augustine shows that his concern is mutability or things that change, not just flesh.

"You pass beyond them with the mind, not with the flesh. But leave them aside too. Even though they provide light, they are bodies; although they shine from the sky, they are bodies. Come, because you may be thinking that you have nowhere else to go, once you have considered all these things."

"And where am I to go beyond the heavenly bodies," you say, "and what am I supposed to pass beyond with the mind?"

"Well, have you reflected on all these things?"

"I have," you say.

How have you reflected on them? Let the one who examines them all appear. For the one who examines all these things, discriminating, distinguishing, and after a fashion weighing them in the balance of wisdom, is the soul. Without doubt the spirit, by which you thought about all these things, is better than all these things you have thought about.

So the mind then is spirit, not body; pass beyond this too. First of all compare this spirit, just to see what you are to pass beyond, compare it with flesh. Perish the thought! Do not even dream of making such a comparison. Compare it with the brilliance of the sun, the moon, the stars; the brilliance of the spirit is greater. Observe, to begin with, the speed of spirit. See if just a spark of a thinking spirit is not more swift than the splendor of the sun shining. With your spirit you see the sun rising; how slow its movement is, compared with that of your spirit! In a flash you have been able to think what the sun is going to do. It is going to travel from east to west, now it is rising tomorrow at the other end. While your thought finished the course, the sun continues to its route; you have traveled it all.

The spirit therefore is something great. But how am I saying "is"? Go beyond it too. Because, although it is better than every kind of body, the spirit too is subject to change. Now it knows, now it does not; now it forgets, now it remembers; now it wills, now it does not; now it sins, now it is just. So then, pass beyond every kind of change; not only beyond everything that can be seen, but everything that can change. You have passed, you see, beyond flesh, which can be seen, passed beyond sky, sun, moon and stars which can be seen; pass next beyond everything which can change. When you went beyond those, after all, you came to your spirit, but there too you discovered the mutability of your spirit. God is not mutable, is he? Go beyond your spirit too. Pour your soul over yourself, so as to touch the God, about whom they say to you, *Where is your God?*

The example of the evangelist making this leap

13. Do not imagine that you are going to do something that is beyond the powers of human beings. John the evangelist did it. He passed beyond the flesh, passed beyond the earth on which he was treading, passed beyond the seas which he was observing, passed beyond the air in which the birds fly around, passed beyond the sun, beyond the moon, beyond the stars, beyond all spirits that cannot be seen, beyond his own mind by the reasoning powers of his spirit. Passing beyond all these things, pouring out his soul over himself, what did he reach, what did he see? *In the beginning was the Word, and the Word was with God* (Jn 1:1).

So then, if you see no separation in the Light, why look for it in the work? Observe God, observe how his Word cleaves to the one speaking the Word. In speaking, after all, he does not speak in syllables, but flashing with the brilliance of wisdom, that is what speaking is. What does it say about his wisdom? *She is the radiance of eternal light* (Wis 7:26). Notice the radiance of the sun; it is up there in the sky, and it spreads its radiance over all lands, over all seas; and this of course is material, bodily light. If you can separate the sun's radiance from the sun, then separate the Word from the Father. I am talking of the sun; one slight flame of a lamp, which can be blown out by a single puff, sheds light over everything around it. You see the light shed by the flame that begets it, you see its emission, you do not see any separation.

So then, my dearest brothers and sisters, understand that Father and Son and Holy Spirit cleave inseparably to one another; that this Trinity is the one God; and that all the works of the one God are works of the Father, works of the Son, works of the Holy Spirit. As for the rest that follows in the sermon of our Lord Jesus Christ himself in the gospel, be sure to come along to hear it tomorrow, when you are also owed a sermon.

Homily 21

On Jn 5:20-23[1]

Divine mysteries far above human understanding;
that is why the Word became a human being

1. Yesterday, to the extent the Lord was pleased to grant it, we discussed to the best of our ability and understood according to our capacity how the works of Father and Son are inseparable; nor does the Father do some things, the Son others, but the Father does all things through the Son as through his Word, about which it is written: *All things were made through him, and without him was made nothing* (Jn 1:3). Let us take a look today at the words that follow, and let us both beg and hope for mercy from the same Lord, so that first of all, if he thinks it fitting, we may understand what is true; but if we cannot manage that, we may at least not turn to what is false. Ignorance, after all, is better than error; but knowing is better than ignorance. And so we should above all make every effort to know; if we manage to do so, God be thanked; while if we do not manage just now to reach the truth, let us at least not turn aside to falsehood.

We should take account, you see, of what we are and what we are discussing. We are human beings, flesh-bearers as we walk through this life; and if we have already been born again through the seed of the word of God,[2] even so, we have been made new in Christ, without being stripped of the old Adam altogether.[3] In fact, it is obvious that the mortal and perishable in us weighs down the soul and clearly derives from Adam; while what is spiritual in us lifts up the soul and is the gift of God and of his mercy; for he sent his only Son to share our death with us and to lead us toward his undying life. We have him as the teacher of how to avoid sinning; as counsel for the defense if we have sinned and confessed and turned back to him; as intercessor on our behalf if we desire some good gift from the Lord;[4] as giver of such gifts with the Father, because Father and Son are the one God.

But, as a human being, he was saying these words to human beings; concealed as God, visible as human, so as to make visible human beings

---
1. Preached the day after Homily 20, probably in 420.
2. See 1 Pt 1:23.
3. See Sermon 351, 6.
4. See 1 Jn 2:1.

into gods; the Son of God became the Son of Man, so as to make the sons of men into sons of God.[5] We can recognize in his words the art of his wisdom, the wisdom by which he does this. A little one speaks to little ones; but he is little in such a way that he is also great; we, however, are little, but in him we are great; thus does he speak as one who nurtures and nourishes the newborn[6] so that they grow by loving.

It is in himself that the Father shows the Son everything he has done

2. He had just said, *The Son can do nothing on his own, but only what he sees the Father doing* (Jn 5:19). We realized, however, that this does not mean the Father's doing something on his own, and when the Son has seen this he too can do something similar after taking a good look at the Father's work; but his saying *The Son can do nothing on his own, but only what he sees the Father doing* means that the Son is totally from the Father, and his total substance and power is from the one who begot him.[7] Now, however, after saying that what the Father does he himself does in like manner, to keep us from thinking that the Father does some things, the Son others, while in fact the Son does the same things as the Father with the same power, since the Father does them through the Son, he went on to say what we have heard read out today, *For the Father loves the Son, and shows him all the things which he himself does* (Jn 5:20).

Once again our mortal way of thinking is upset. The Father shows the Son what he is doing himself. Therefore, someone will say, the Father does things on his own, so that the Son can see what he is doing. Again, the picture conjured up by the human mind is one of two craftsmen, as of an artisan teaching his craft to his son, and showing him whatever it is he is making, so that he too can make it. *He shows him all the things*, it says, *which he himself does.* So is the Son then not doing anything while the Father is making it, so that the Son can see what the Father is doing? It is certain that *all things were made through him, and without him was made nothing.* From this we can see precisely how the Father shows the Son what he is doing, since the Father makes nothing except what he makes through the Son. So what has the Father made? The world.

---

5. See Sermons 119, 5; 121, 5; 342, 5; *The Trinity* XIII, 9, 12.
6. That is, literally, those feeding at the breast.
7. See *Against a Sermon of the Arians* 9, 14.

Having made the world, did he show it to the Son so that he too could make something of the same kind? Give us the world, then, which the Son also made. But then not merely *were all things made through him, and without him was made nothing*, but in particular *the world was made through him* (Jn 1:3). If the world was made through him, and all things were made through him, and the Father makes nothing except what he makes through the Son, where does the Father show the Son what he is making, if not in the Son himself through whom he does the making?

What place can there be, after all, in which the Father's work is shown to the Son, as though he were seated apart and making things apart, and the Son were watching the Father's hands to see how he was making them? Where is that inseparable Trinity? Where is the Word, of whom it is said that he is himself *the power and the wisdom of God* (1 Cor 1:24)? Where do we fit in what scripture says about this very wisdom, *For she is the brilliance of eternal light* (Wis 7:26)? Where too what is again said about her, *She reaches mightily from end to end, and arranges all things sweetly* (Wis 8:1)? If the Father makes anything, he does it through the Son; if he makes it through his power and his wisdom, it is not outside of himself that he shows him something to see, but it is in his very self that he shows him what he is doing.

God is not the Father of Christ in the same way as he is our Father

3. What does the Father see, or rather, what does the Son see in the Father, in order to do it himself as well? Perhaps I could say what, but then you would have to give me someone who could grasp it; or perhaps I could think it without saying it; or perhaps I could not even think it.[8] That divine reality, after all, is as much beyond us as God is beyond mere human beings, as the immortal one is beyond mere mortals, as the eternal one beyond mere time-bound creatures. May he grant us the inspiration and the grace needed, may he be pleased to sprinkle us from that *fountain of life* (Ps 35:9) with a few drops of water to assuage our thirst, lest we wither away in this desert. We say "Lord" to the one we have been taught to call "Father." Let us have the courage, indeed, to say this to him, because he

---

8. See *The Trinity* V,1, 1; 3, 4; VII, 4, 7.

wanted us to have the courage to say it—provided, that is, that we live in such a way that he does not say to us, *If I am Father, where is the honor due to me? If I am Lord, where is the reverence that is my due?* (Mal 1:6)[9]

Let us say to him, then, *our Father* (Mt 6:9). To whom are we saying *our Father*? To the Father of Christ. So whoever says *our Father* to Christ's Father, what else is he saying to Christ but "our Brother?"[10] All the same, he is not Christ's Father in the same way as he is also our Father; Christ, after all, never joined us to himself so as to make no distinction between himself and us. He, I mean, is the Son equal to the Father, and co-eternal with the Father; we on the other hand have been made sons through the Son, adopted through the only Son. That is why such words were never heard from the lips of our Lord Jesus Christ, when he was talking to the disciples; he was never heard to say about almighty God, his Father, *our Father*, but he said either *my Father* or *your Father*. He avoids saying *our Father* to the extent of putting these two phrases together in one place: *I am going*, he said, *to my Father and to your Father* (Jn 20:17). Why did not he say *our Father*? He said both *my Father* and *your Father*; he did not say *our Father*. He joins them in such a way as to distinguish them; he distinguishes them in such a way as not to unjoin them. One is what he wants us to be in himself, while one is what he himself and the Father are.[11]

In the Son seeing is the same as being; not so with us

4. So however much then we understand and however much we see, even when we have been *put on a level with the angels* (Lk 20:36), we shall not see as the Son sees. We, after all, even when we do not see, still are something. And what else are we when we do not see but non-seeing people? Even as non-seeing people, all the same, we are; and in order to see we turn round toward the person we want to see; and actual vision occurs in us, which was not there before when we, for all that, were. For first there is a non-seeing person, and when the very same one does see, he is called a seeing person. So for him seeing is not the same thing as just being a person, a human being. I mean, if seeing were for him the same as being a human person, he would never be anything but a seeing person. But since

---
9. See Sermons 57, 2; 58, 2.
10. See Sermon 224, 1.
11. See Sermons 229L, 2; 246, 5.

he is first a non-seeing person, and wants to see what he does not see, there is someone there to want this, and someone there to turn round in order to see; and when he has well and truly turned round and seen, he becomes a seeing person, having previously been a non-seeing person. So seeing, then, comes upon him and departs from him; comes upon him when he turns round, departs from him when he turns away again.

That, surely, is not how it is with the Son, is it? What an idea! The Son was never non-seeing, and then seeing; but seeing the Father is for him the same thing as being the Son.[12] We, after all, by turning to sin lose enlightenment, and by turning back to God receive enlightenment. The light, you see, by which we are enlightened is one thing, we who are being enlightened are another. But the light by which we are enlightened does not turn away from itself, nor does it ever cease to shine, because it is itself the light.[13]

So then, the Father shows the Son a thing he is making in such a way that the Son sees all things in the Father, and that the Son *is* all things in the Father. It is by seeing, after all, that he is born, and by being born that he sees. But there was a time when he was not, and then later he was born, just as there has not been a time when he did not see, and then later he saw. No, seeing is for him is the same as being is for him, not changing at all is the same for him as existing without beginning and without end.

So then, let us not take it in a literal-minded way that the Father sits and makes something and shows it to the Son, and that the Son sees what the Father is making and makes it himself in another place or from other material. *All things*, I mean to say, *were made through him, and without him was made nothing*. The Son is the Word of the Father; the Father said nothing which he did not say in the Son. For by saying in the Son what he was going to make through the Son, he begot this Son through whom he would make all things.

Difficulty about the future tense's introducing time into God's activity

5. *And greater works than these will he show him, to fill you with astonishment* (Jn 5:20). Once more this upsets us. Is there anyone indeed who can worthily plumb the depths of such a great mystery as this? But since he

---

12. See *The Trinity* II, 1, 3.
13. See Jn 1:4.9; 8:12.

has seen fit to speak to us, he is opening it already. He would not, after all, wish to say something he did not wish to be understood; because he has seen fit to say it, he has undoubtedly stirred up his audience; would the one who stirred the interest in listening then abandon what he stirred up?

I have said as best I could that the Son does not know things in a time-bound way, nor is the Son's knowledge one thing and the Son another, nor is the Son's vision one thing and the Son another. Rather that vision *is* the Son, and that knowledge or wisdom of the Father *is* the Son, and this eternal wisdom and vision is from the eternal one, and co-eternal with the eternal one; and nothing there changes as if in time, nor is anything born there which was not, nor does anything that was perish. Yes, I have said it as best I could.

So what then is time all about here when he says, *Greater works than these will he show him*? That means "he is going to show him"; that is what *will show him* means. It is one thing to say "has shown" and another to say "will show." We say "has shown" about the past, "will show" about the future. So what are we dealing with here, brothers and sisters? We have said that he is co-eternal with the Father, knowing no variations in time, no movement through spaces or times or places, remaining always with the Father, seeing him; seeing the Father and existing by seeing him; and yet, once again, he speaks to us about times: *Greater than these*, says he, *will he show him*. So is he still going to show the Son something the Son does not know? So what are we to do? How are we to understand this?

Look, our Lord Jesus Christ was up above, he is down below. When was he up above? When he said, *Whatever the Father does, these things too the Son does in like manner* (Jn 5:19). How is he now down here below? *Greater works than these will he show him*.

O Lord Jesus Christ, our Savior, the Word of God through which all things were made, what is the Father going to show you that you do not yet know? What is there about the Father that is hidden from you? What is there in the Father that is still hidden from you, to whom the Father is not hidden? What greater works is he going to show you? Or in relation to what works are the ones he is going to show you greater? After all, since he said *greater than these*, we must first understand what those works are than which these will be greater.

Raising the dead a greater work than curing the sick

6. Let us recall how this talk came to be. When the man who had spent thirty-eight years in his illness was healed and returned to health, Jesus ordered him to pick up his stretcher and go home.[14] That, in fact, is what bothered the Jews with whom he was talking—in this verbal exchange he did not address the meaning. In a certain way, he was hinting at the meaning to those who understood, concealing it from those who were angry. So then, when the Jews were bothered that the Lord acted in this way on the sabbath, they gave him the opportunity for this talk. So do not listen to these words as if we had forgotten what was said earlier, but let us look back to that man who had been sick for thirty-eight years and was suddenly restored to health, filling the Jews with astonishment and anger. They sought the darkness from the sabbath more than light from the miracle.

So, in speaking to these indignant hearers, he said, *Greater works than these will he show him. Greater than these!* Than which? You have seen a man restored to health whose sickness had lasted up to thirty-eight years; greater things than these will the Father show the Son. He continues and says, *For just as the Father raises the dead and gives them life, so too the Son gives life to whom he will* (Jn 5:21). Obviously these things are greater. It is much more significant, after all, that a dead person should rise again than that a sick person should get better. Such things are greater. But when will the Father show them to the Son? I mean, is the Son unaware of them? And did the one speaking really not know how to raise the dead? Did he still have to learn how to raise the dead, the one through whom all things were made? Did the one who gave us life while we were still non-existent still have to learn how to raise us from death? So what does he really mean?

Christ speaks differently as God and as man;
as man he learns things in us, his members

7. He is coming down to our level, you see, and the one who a short while ago was talking as God has begun to talk as a man. He is the man, all the same, who is God, because God has become man; become what he was not,

---

14. See Jn 5:1-16. In fact this command was given to the paralytic in Mk 2:11. See Homily 20, 2, note 4.

though, without losing what he was.¹⁵ So then, a man was attached to God,¹⁶ in order that the one who was God might now be man, not that he might now be man and not be God. So let us listen to him now as also our brother, whom we were listening to as our creator; he was creator in the beginning as Word; he is brother because born of the virgin Mary; creator before Abraham,¹⁷ before Adam, before the earth, before the heavens, before all things bodily and spiritual; but brother from the seed of Abraham, of the tribe of Judah,¹⁸ of an Israelite virgin. If we are aware then that this person talking to us is both God and man, we should be able to take his words as being those of God and of man; sometimes, you see, he says to us the sort of thing that suits his majestic loftiness, sometimes the sort that suits his humble lowliness. He indeed is the Most High who stoops low down to the depths in order to lift our lowliness up on high to the heights.

So what does he say then? *Greater works than these will the Father show me, to fill you with astonishment.* So then, it really is to us that the Father is going to show them, not to him.¹⁹ Since the Father then is going to show them to us, that is why he said, to fill you with astonishment. He thereby explained, you see, what he meant by *the Father will show me*.

Well, why did he not say, "The Father will show you," instead of saying, *The Father will show the Son*?

Because we too are members of the Son, and it is as if he is learning in his members what we are learning as his members.

In what way is he learning in us?

In the same way as he is suffering in us.

How do we prove he is suffering in us?

From that voice from heaven, *Saul, Saul, why are you persecuting me?* (Acts 9:4)

Is he not the one who will take his seat at the end of the age and, after setting the just on his right hand, the wicked on his left, is going to say,

---

15. See Sermons 121, 5; 123, 3; 127, 9; 184, 1; 186, 1; 187, 3.
16. The phrase, *accessit homo Deo*, may appear to say that the man existed before being attached to God. Augustine would repudiate such an idea.
17. See Jn 8:58.
18. See Heb 7:14.
19. Since the Father wants to provoke our admiration, we have to be the ones who benefit from his action. Given the unity between Christ and his members, it is permissible for Christ to say that the Father will show *me* rather than say that he will show *you*.

Come, you blessed of my Father, receive the kingdom; for I was hungry, and you gave me something to eat? And when they answer him, *Lord, when did we ever see you hungry?* he is going to say to them, *When you gave it to one of the least of mine, you gave it to me.* (Mt 25:34.40) Let the one then who said, *When you gave it to one of the least of mine, you gave it to me,* submit to interrogation from us, and let us say to him, "Lord, when will you ever be learning, since it is you that teach everything?" Immediately, of course, he will answer us in our faith, "When one of the least of mine learns anything, I too am learning."

In becoming members of Christ's body we become Christ himself

8. Let us congratulate ourselves then and give thanks for having been made not only Christians but Christ. Do you understand, brothers and sisters, the grace of God upon us; do you grasp that?[20] Be filled with wonder, rejoice and be glad; we have been made Christ. For, if he is the head, and we the members, then he and we are the whole man. That is what the apostle Paul says: *So that we should no longer be little ones, tossed about and surrounded*[21] *by every wind of doctrine.* In the previous sentence he had just said, *Until we all arrive at the unity of faith, and at the recognition of the Son of God, at the perfect man, at the measure of the age of the fullness of Christ.* (Eph 4:14.13) The fullness of Christ, then, is head and members.

What is that, head and members?

Christ and the Church.

It would be pride, in fact, to claim this for ourselves, unless he had seen fit to promise it; he says through the same apostle, *Now you are the body of Christ and the members* (1 Cor 12:27).

---

20. *Intelligitis, fratres, gratiam Dei super nos capitis?* I treat *capitis* as the second person plural of *capio,* and as reinforcing, so to say, the initial *intelligitis.* Berrouard treats it as the genitive singular of *caput,* and translates: "Do you understand, brethren, the grace which God has shown us in giving us Christ as Head?" Apparently, he is thinking about what Augustine will say about the body of Christ, head and members. He is working up to that idea, but here it is still a matter of our personal and corporate identity with Christ. See *Exposition of Psalm* 54, 3 and Sermon 133, 8, both cited by Berrouard on this point.
21. *Circumdati*; it would seem that the original translators from the Greek wrote *circumlati,* meaning "carried around," an exact translation of the original, if not quite in the right tense (Latin lacks the present passive participle of the Greek). This may have been changed into the more common word in Augustine's text.

Given this unity of head and body, the Father shows things to Christ through Christ

9. So then, when the Father shows something to the members of Christ, he shows it to Christ. A kind of great miracle takes place, but one that is true; something has been shown to Christ which Christ already knew, and it has been shown to Christ through Christ.[22] A marvelous thing it is and a great one, but that is the way scripture talks. Are we going to contradict the divine statements, and not rather going to penetrate their meaning, and give thanks for his gift to the one who has given it?

What then is this that I have said: Christ is shown something through Christ? The members are shown it through the head. Here is an example; look at the same thing in yourself. Imagine yourself with your eyes shut, wanting to take hold of something. Your hand does not know where to go, and of course your hand is one of your members; it has not after all been separated from your body. Open your eyes; now your hand sees where to go; with the head showing the way, the member has followed. So if it has been possible to find something of the sort in you, with your body showing something to your body, and with something being shown your body through your body, do not be surprised at what has been said, that Christ is shown something through Christ.

The head, you see, is pointing something out for the members to see, and the head is teaching something for the members to learn; but it is still one human person, head and members. He did not wish to separate himself, but was willing to glue himself onto his body. He was far away from us, very far indeed; what is so far apart as creature and creator? What so far apart as God and man? What so far apart as justice and wickedness? What so far apart as eternity and mortality? There you have how far apart was the Word, in the beginning God with God, through whom all things were made.[23] So how did he draw near, in order to be what we are, and for us to be in him? *The Word was made flesh, and took up residence among us* (Jn 1:14).

Father and Son work together in raising the dead

10. This then is what he is going to show us, this is what he showed his disciples, who saw him in the flesh. Well, what is *this*? *Just as the Father*

---
22. See Sermon 354, 1.
23. See Jn 1:1.3.

raises the dead and gives them life, so too the Son gives life to whom he will. Does the Father give life to some, and the Son to others? What is certain is that all things were made through him. What am I getting at, my brothers and sisters? The Lazarus whom Christ raised—did the Father raise him when he had died so that Christ would see how to raise Lazarus? Or when Christ raised Lazarus did the Father not raise him, and did the Son alone do it without the Father? Read that passage for yourselves, and see how he there calls upon the Father, so that Lazarus might rise up.[24] As a human being he is calling upon the Father; as God he is doing it with the Father. So then, Lazarus who rose again was raised by both Father and Son through the gift and the grace of the Holy Spirit; and thus it was the Trinity that performed that marvelous work.[25] So then, let us not understand *Just as the Father raises the dead and gives them life, so too the Son gives life to whom he will* as meaning that we should reckon some were raised and given life by the Father, others by the Son; but the very same ones that the Father raises and gives life are also raised and given life by the Son, because *all things were made through him, and without him was made nothing.*

It is also to show that the power he has, though given by the Father, is equal to the Father's, that he said, *So too the Son gives life to whom he will.* He shows that his own will is involved, in case anyone should say, "Yes, the Father raises the dead through the Son, but he does it as the powerful one, as the one having the power and authority, while the other does it by the power and authority of another, as an agent does things, like an angel." He signified power and authority by saying, *So too the Son gives life to whom he will.* The Father, after all, does not want anything different from the Son; but just as they have one and the same substance, so too one and the same will.

In saying this, Jesus is really referring to
the resurrection of the dead on the last day

11. And who in fact are these dead to whom the Father and the Son give life? Are they really the ones we have mentioned, like Lazarus, or the son of that widow, or the daughter of the leader of the synagogue?[26] These, after all, are the ones raised by the Lord Jesus that we know about. No, there is

---
24. See Jn 11:41-42.
25. See Sermon 126, 10.
26. See Jn 11:1-44; Lk 7:11-15; Mk 5:35-43.

something else he wishes to suggest to us, the resurrection of the dead, that is, which we are all waiting for; not the one which some experienced so that the rest might believe. Lazarus, you see, after rising again was going to die once more; we on rising again are going to live for ever. Does the Father bring about this kind of resurrection or the Son? Well, it is the Father in the Son. So then it is the Son, and the Father in the Son.

How can we prove that he is talking about this resurrection? After saying, *Just as the Father raises the dead and gives them life, so too the Son gives life to whom he will*, he did not want us to take it as that resurrection of the dead which he performs for the sake of a miracle and not for eternal life, and so he went on, *For neither does the Father judge anyone, but he has given all judgment to the Son* (Jn 5:21-22). What does this mean? Well, he was still talking about the resurrection of the dead, because *just as the Father raises the dead and gives them life, so too the Son gives life to those whom he will*. So why, as though giving a kind of explanation of this, did he immediately add these words about judgment, saying, *For neither does the Father judge anyone, but he has given all judgment to the Son*; why, if not because he had said it about that resurrection of the dead which is going to take place at the judgment?

If all this is confusing us, Christ is doing it deliberately to liven us up

12. *For neither*, he says, *does the Father judge anyone, but he has given all judgment to the Son*. A moment ago we were imagining the Father making something which the Son does not make, when he said, *For the Father loves the Son, and shows him all the things he has made*, as though the Father were making something, with the Son looking on. Thus a literal-minded understanding was creeping into our minds, as if the Father were making what the Son was not making, while the Son watched the Father showing him what was being made by the Father. So it is as if the Father were doing what the Son was not doing; now, though, we are seeing the Son doing something which the Father does not do. How he twists us around and juggles with our minds, leading them hither and thither! He will not let them stay in any single place favored by the flesh, but he twists them about to exercise them, exercises them to clean them up, cleans them up to make them spacious, makes them spacious so as to fill them.

What are all these words doing to us? What was he talking about? What *is* he talking about? A moment ago he was saying that the Father shows the Son whatever he makes, and I pictured the Father making, the Son watching. Now on the other hand I picture the Son doing something, the Father standing by doing nothing, *for neither does the Father judge anyone, but he has given all judgment to the Son*. So when the time comes for the Son to judge, will the Father stand idly by and not judge? What is all this? What sense am I to make of it all?

Lord, what *are* you saying? You are God the Word, I am a human being. You say that the Father does not judge anyone, but has given all judgment to the Son. In another place I read of you saying, *I do not judge anyone; there is another to investigate and to judge* (Jn 8:15.50).[27] That is the one who investigates your wrongs, that is the one who passes judgment about your wrongs. How then does the Father here not judge anyone, having given all judgment to the Son? Let us interrogate Peter as well, let us listen to him talking in his letter: *Christ suffered for us*, he says, *leaving us an example, so that we might follow in his footsteps; he committed no sin, neither was deceit found in his mouth; when he was reviled, he did not revile in return, when he was treated with violence he did not utter threats, but commended himself to the one who judges justly* (1 Pt 2:21-23). In what way is it true that *the Father does not judge anyone, but has given all judgment to the Son*?

We are confused by all this; may our confusion make us work; may it purify us. Let us try hard, by his gift, to penetrate the lofty secrets of these words. Perhaps we are brash in discerning God's words and examining them? Yet, why were they spoken if not to be known? Why have they sounded if not to be heard? Why have they been heard if not to be understood? May he strengthen us and grant the understanding he thinks fit; and if we cannot yet penetrate to the very wellspring, let us drink from the brook. Notice, John poured himself out for us like a running brook, he brought us the Word from on high, humbled him and, in a way, lowered him to ground level, so that we might not dread the exalted one, but might approach the humble one.

---

27. Whether it was Augustine's memory that conflated these two verses of Jn 8, or his Latin text that did so, there is no telling; very possibly the latter. What the other seeks, or in the context of juridical judgment investigates, and judges in v. 50 is Christ's glory.

All judgment has been given to the Son, because at the last judgment he will be seen, by the wicked as well as the just, in the form of a slave

13. The phrase, *The Father does not judge anyone, but he has given all judgment to the Son,* has a true and powerful meaning, if we can in any way appreciate it. This was said, you see, because the Son alone will appear visibly to human eyes at judgment. The Father will be hidden, the Son openly visible. In what way will the Son be openly visible? In the form in which he ascended; because *in the form of God* he will be hidden with the Father, while it is *in the form of a slave* (Phil 2:6.7) that he will be manifest to human eyes. So then, *the Father does not judge anyone, but he has given all judgment to the Son,* manifest judgment that is, and it is at that manifest judgment that the Son will judge, because he will appear visibly to those to be judged.[28] We have the clearest evidence of scripture that he is the one who will appear visibly. On the fortieth day after his resurrection he ascended into heaven, as his disciples watched; and by angelic voices they were told, *Men of Galilee, what are you standing here for, looking up into heaven? This man who has been taken up from you into heaven will come in the same way as you have seen him going into heaven.* (Acts 1:11)[29] How were they seeing him go? In the flesh, which they had touched, which they had felt, whose wounds they had verified by feeling them; in that body in which he had gone in and come out with them for forty days, manifesting himself to them in truth, not by some kind of make-believe, not as a ghost, not as a shade, not as a spirit;[30] but as he said himself without deceit, *Touch, and see that a spirit does not have flesh and bones, as you can see that I have* (Lk 24:29). That body has indeed already the right to dwell in heaven, not being subject to death nor to change by growing older.[31] You see, it was not like the way he had grown up to that age from infancy, that he went on growing older from a young man toward being an old man. He remains the same age as when he ascended, and that is how he is going to come to those by whom he wished his word to be proclaimed before he does come.[32]

---

28. See *The Trinity* I, 13, 29; *Against a Sermon of the Arians* 11, 9.
29. See Sermons 127, 10; 214, 9; 265, 2; 265D, 6; 277, 17.
30. See Sermon 362, 27.
31. *Per aetates*; Berrouard simply translates "with time." But surely it cannot just mean the same as *per tempora,* especially in view of what Augustine goes on to say in the next sentence.
32. See Lk 24:47; Acts 1:8.

So that is how he will come, then, in human form. This is what even the godless will see; both those placed at his right hand will see it, and those set apart on his left will see it; as it is written: *They shall look upon the one they have pierced* (Zech 12:10; Rv 1:7). If they shall look upon the one they have pierced, they shall look upon the very body which they struck with a lance; it is not the Word that was struck by the lance. So this is what the godless will be able to see, the same body as the one they had been able to wound. They will not see God lying hidden in the body; after the judgment he will be seen by those who will be on his right. This then is what he meant by *The Father does not judge anyone, but he has given all judgment to the Son*—that the Son will come to the judgment openly visible, appearing in his human body to human beings, saying to the right hand ones, *Come, you blessed of my Father, receive the kingdom*; saying to the left hand ones, *Go into the eternal fire, which has been prepared for the devil and his angels* (Mt 25:34.41).

The vision of God reserved for the just

14. There you are: the form of a man will be seen both by the godly and the ungodly, both by the just and the unjust, both by believers and unbelievers, with both jubilation and lamentation, with both confidence and confusion; yes, that is how he will be seen. Once that form has been seen at the judgment, and the judgment has been completed of which it was said that *the Father does not judge anyone, but he has given all judgment to the Son*, because the Son will appear at the judgment in the form he took on from us, what is going to happen next? When will the form of God be seen, which all the faithful are thirsting for? When will that be seen which *was the Word in the beginning, God with God, through whom all things were made* (Jn 1:1)? When will that form of God be seen, about which the apostle says, *Although he was in the form of God, he did not regard being equal to God as something to be grasped at* (Phil 2:5)? Great indeed is that form in which the equality of Father and Son is apprehended—something beyond words, beyond comprehension—by little ones in particular. When will it be seen?

Look, there on the right are the just, on the left the unjust; all equally see the man, see the Son of Man, see the one who was pierced,[33] see the one who

---

33. See Rv 1:7.

was crucified, see him as he humbled himself, see him as born of the virgin, see the lamb of the tribe of Judah; when will they see the Word, *God with God*? He will be present then as well, but will only appear in *the form of a slave*. The form of a slave will be shown to slaves; the form of God will be reserved for sons.[34] So let the slaves become sons; let those on the right move into the eternal inheritance promised of old, which the martyrs believed in though they did not see it, shedding their blood without hesitation on the strength of that promise; let them move into it and there see what they shall see. When will they move there? Let the Lord himself answer: *So those shall go into eternal burning, but the just into eternal life* (Mt 25:46).

What constitutes eternal life? Knowing the one true God,
and Jesus Christ whom he has sent

15. But look here, all he has mentioned is eternal life. He has not told us, has he, that there we shall see and comprehend the Father and the Son? Suppose we live for ever, but never even see that Father and Son?

Listen to where he mentioned eternal life in another place, and expressly stated what eternal life is. "Never fear," he says, "I am not cheating you; it is no vain promise I made to my lovers when I said, *The one who has my commandments and keeps them, that is the one who loves me; and the one who loves me shall be loved by my Father, and I will love him and will show myself to him* (Jn 14:21)."

Let us answer the Lord and say, "Well what, dear Lord our God, what is so great about that? What is so great about it? You are going to show us yourself, are you? So what? Did you not also show yourself to the Jews? Did those who crucified you not also see you? But you will show yourself at the judgment, when we shall be standing on your right; will those who are standing on your left not also be seeing you? What is so special about your showing yourself to us then? Do we not see you now, after all, while you are speaking?"[35]

He will answer, "I will show myself in the form of God; what you now see is the form of a slave.[36] I will not cheat you, dear loyal believer; believe that you will see this. You love now, and you do not see; but is this very love not leading

---

34. See Gal 4:7.
35. Presumably Augustine means we see Jesus now in our imaginations, as we picture him to ourselves.
36. For this interpretation of Jn 14:21, see also *Sermon* 127, 12; *The Trinity* IV, 19, 26.

you onward toward that sight? Love, persevere in loving; I will not defraud your love," he says, "having cleansed your heart. Why, after all, did I cleanse your heart, if not so that God could be seen by you? *For blessed are the clean of heart, for they shall see God* (Mt 5:8)."

"But you did not expressly state this," says the slave, having the nerve, it seems, to argue with the Lord, "when you said, *The just shall go into eternal life*. You did not say, 'They shall go into seeing me in the form of God, into seeing the Father whose equal I am.'" Listen to what he said somewhere else: *This is eternal life, that they may know you, the one true God, and Jesus Christ whom you have sent* (Jn 17:3).

Final words, to clinch the argument against the Arians

16. And now, therefore, after the judgment just recalled, which the Father, not judging anyone himself, has given to the Son, what is going to happen next? *That all may honor the Son just as they honor the Father* (Jn 5:23). The Father is honored by the Jews, the Son despised. The Son, you see, was being seen as a slave, the Father being honored as God. The Son too will appear as equal to the Father, *that all may honor the Son just as they honor the Father*. So now we hold onto this in faith. Do not let the Jew say, "I honor the Father, what business of mine is the Son?" Let the Son answer him, *Whoever does not honor the Son does not honor the Father* (Jn 5:23). You are lying in your teeth, you are speaking ill of the Son and doing wrong to the Father. The Father, after all, sent the Son; you there are speaking ill of the Son; how can you be honoring the sender, when you speak ill of the one sent?

The Father is not greater than the Son just because he sent him

17. "Look here," someone will say, "the Son was sent; and that makes the Father greater, because he sent him."[37] Give up this flesh-governed way of thinking. The old man is suggesting some old nonsense; you now should acknowledge in the new man a new line of thought. For you he is new, but ancient from the beginning of time, everlasting, eternal; let him recall you to this right understanding. The Son is less, because the Son is said to have been sent, you say? I hear sending mentioned, not a word about separation.

---

37. This is the line taken in *A Sermon of the Arians*, which Augustine has in mind in Homilies 20-22.

"But this," says he, "is what we see in human affairs, that the one who sends is greater than the one who is sent."

But human affairs are deceptive to human beings; let divine affairs purge them. Do not pay any attention to human affairs, in which the one who sends seems to be greater, and the one who is sent to be of less importance—though as a matter of fact these human affairs too can bear witness against you. For example, if someone wishes to ask for a lady's hand in marriage, and is unable to do it personally, he sends a friend who is of greater dignity than himself to ask on his behalf. And there are many situations in which a person of greater dignity is chosen to be sent on behalf of a less important person. So why do you still want to go on making a fuss, because one did the sending, the other was sent? The sun sends out rays without separating them from itself; the moon sends out its gleams without separating them; a lamp sheds its light without separating it. I see sending in these instances, and I do not see any separation.

I mean, if you are looking for examples in human affairs, O heretical vanity—although, as I said just now, in some cases these very affairs refute and convict you—pay attention all the same to how different it is in human affairs, from which you want to draw examples in illustration of divine affairs. The person who sends stays where he is, and the one being sent goes off; the first one does not go along with the one he is sending, does he? The Father, on the other hand, who sent the Son, never left the Son. Listen to what the Lord himself has to say: *Behold, the hour is coming when each one of you will drift away about his own affairs, and you will all leave me alone; but I am not alone, because the Father is with me* (Jn 16:32). So how did he send the one with whom he came along? Elsewhere he said, *The Father abiding in me performs his works* (Jn 14:10). There you are, he is in him; there you are, he is working. The sender has not withdrawn from the one sent, because the sender and the one sent are one.[38]

---

38. See Jn 10:30. The concluding words are in exact and explicit contradiction of *Against a Sermon of the Arians* 32 (PL 42, 682) where it says, "It is impossible that the one who has been sent and the one who has sent him ... should be one and the same." So Berrouard, BA 72, 313, note 128.

Homily 22

On John 5:24-30[1]

The text presents us with divine matters altogether beyond our feeble intelligence

1. Today's gospel reading follows on the sermons you were given yesterday and the day before; let me discuss it in due order, not as it deserves but insofar as I have strength, because even you will understand it according to the limits of your capacity, not according to the abundance of the overflowing fountain; and I am not saying as much in your hearing as that fountain pours forth, but only as much as I can understand; that is what I pass on to your senses, while he is at work in your hearts more richly than any action of mine in your ears.[2] For something great is being discussed, and it is not treated by great people but rather by truly little people. But the one who was great and who made himself small for our sakes gives us hope and confidence. For, if we were not being urged on by him nor invited to understand him, if he were pushing us aside as beneath his notice because we could not grasp his divinity, if he had not put on our mortality and come down to us to announce the gospel to us, if he had been unwilling to share with us what in us is base and of no importance, we would have thought that the one who took our smallness upon himself was unwilling to give us his greatness.

I have said this so that no one will take me to task for daring to discuss this text nor despair of being able to grasp—with the help of God's grace—what the Son of God has been good enough to say to him. So then, we should firmly believe that he wished us to understand, what he has had the goodness to say to us.[3] But if we are unable to do so, the one who gave the gift of his word without being asked gives understanding when asked.

---

1. Preached the day after Homily 21, in September 420.
2. See Homily 20, 3.
3. See Homily 21, 12.

Seeing that Christ was willing to speak to us,
he must have wanted us to understand as well as to believe

2. Look then and notice what is hidden in these words. *Amen, amen, I say to you, that whoever hears my words and believes the one who sent me has eternal life* (Jn 5:24). Eternal life is certainly what we are all reaching for; and he is saying, *Whoever hears my words and believes the one who sent me has eternal life.* Could it be that he wanted us to hear his words and did not want us to understand them? If eternal life is to be found in hearing and believing, much more will it be found in understanding.

But faith is an attitude of devotion, while the fruit of faith is understanding, so that we might come to eternal life,[4] where no gospel will have to be read to us; rather will the one who has now provided us with the gospel—setting aside the reading of pages and the voice of the reader and of the preacher—will appear in person to those who are his own, who are present with purified hearts and with immortal bodies, never to die again; he will purify them and enlighten the living and they will see that *in the beginning was the Word, and the Word was with God* (Jn 1:1).[5]

So now, then, let us be aware of who we are, and think about the one we are listening to. Christ is God, and he is talking to human beings; he wishes to be understood; let him give us the capacity; he wishes to be seen, may he open our eyes. Not without reason is he speaking to us, because what he promises us is true.

There is a resurrection in this life already,
a crossing from death to life by faith

3. *Whoever hears my words, he says, and believes the one who sent me, has eternal life and will not come under judgment, but has crossed from death to life* (Jn 5:24). Where and when do we cross from death to life without coming under judgment? It is in this life that there is a crossing from death to life; from here in this life, which is not yet life, there is a crossing from death to life. How does this crossing come about? *Whoever hears my words, he said, and believes the one who sent me.* Keeping to this, you believe, and you cross over.

---

4. See Homily 3, 20; *Exposition of Psalm* 109, 8; Sermons 43, 1; 97A, 2; 142, 8; *The Trinity* XIV, 2, 4.
5. See *Exposition of Psalms* 83, 8; 93, 6; 103, serm. 3, 3; 119, 6; 146, 8; Sermons 57, 7; 59, 6.

Is there really anyone who crosses over while staying here?

Clearly there is. In fact, you stay here in the body; you cross over in the mind.

Where was the place from which someone would cross over and where does he cross to?

He crosses over from death to life.

Imagine someone standing here, in whom all that is being said is taking place. He is standing here, he is listening, he was not believing perhaps, but, on listening, he believes; a moment ago he did not believe, now he does believe; he has made the crossing as it were from the region of unbelief to the region of faith, and the movement of his heart, not that of his body, has come to something better; for those who forsake the faith again move to something worse. That is how, in this life which, as I said, is not yet life, someone crosses over from death to life so as not to come under judgment.

But why did I say that it is not yet life? If this were life, the Lord would not say to someone, *If you wish to come into life, keep the commandments* (Mt 19:17). You see, he did not say to him, "If you wish to come into eternal life"; he did not add "eternal," but simply said *life*. So then, this one is not to be called life, because it is not true life.[6] Which is the true life, if not the one which is eternal life? Listen to the apostle saying to Timothy: *Command the rich of this world not to be proud in their thoughts, nor to pin their hopes on the uncertainty of riches, but on the living God, who bestows all things on us in abundance to be enjoyed; let them do good, let them be rich in good works, be ready to give things away, to share.* Why all this? Listen to what follows: *Let them store up for themselves a good foundation for the future, in order to lay hold of true life.* (1 Tm 6:17-19) If they should be storing up for themselves a good foundation for the future, in order to lay hold of the true life, it follows that this one in which they found themselves is false life. I mean, why should you want to lay hold of true life, if you already possess it? Is true life to be laid hold of? Then one must move away from false life. How is one going to move away? Where is one to move? Listen and believe and you cross from death to life and you do not come under judgment.

---

6. See *Exposition of Psalm* 118, 19, 4; Sermon 346, 1.

This seems to contradict what Paul says in 2 Cor 5:10

4. What is this, " 'And you do not come under judgment?' Will anyone say it better than Paul: *It is necessary for all of us to be brought before the judgment seat of Christ, in order for each one to receive there what he has earned through the body, whether good or evil* (2 Cor 5:10)? Paul says, *It is necessary for all of us to be brought before the judgment seat of Christ*; and do you have the nerve to promise yourself that you will not come under judgment?"

"Perish the thought," you say, "that I should have the nerve to promise this to myself; but I believe the one who does promise it. The Savior is speaking, Truth is making the promise, he is the one who told me, *Whoever hears my words, and believes the one who sent me, has eternal life, and is making the crossing from death to life and will not come under judgment* (Jn 5:24). So I, then, have heard the words of my Lord, I have believed. Thus, having been an unbeliever, I have become a believer; just as he taught me, I have crossed from death to life, I am not coming under judgment—and that is not my presumption, it is his promise."

But is Paul speaking against Christ, a slave against his Lord, a disciple against his master, a man against God, such that, while the Lord says that *whoever hears and believes crosses over from death to life and will not come under judgment*, Paul says, *It is necessary for all of us to be brought before the judgment seat of Christ*? Well, if you can be brought before a judgment seat and still not come under judgment, I do not know what sense to make of it.

Two meanings of judgment: first, the equivalent of punishment; second, as distinguishing between cases

5. Well then, it is the Lord our God who discloses the truth of the matter, and advises us through his scriptures how things are to be understood when judgment is mentioned. So then, let me urge you to pay close attention. Sometimes it is called judgment when you are punished, sometimes it is called judgment when a decision is made, one way or the other. In the way that such a decision is called judgment, *it is necessary for all of us to be brought before the judgment seat of Christ, in order for a man to receive there what he has earned through the body, whether good or evil*; that, you see, is the decision either way, that good things should be handed out to the

good, bad things to the bad. I mean, if judgment were always to be taken in a bad sense, the psalm would not say, *Judge me, God* (Ps 42:1). Maybe somebody hears it saying, *Judge me, God*, and is astonished. What people usually say, after all, is, "May God forgive me," or, "Spare me, God"; is anyone going to say, *Judge me, God*? And sometimes that very verse of the psalm is put as the refrain[7] which is first proposed by the reader and then repeated by the people. Is anyone not pierced to the heart by this and afraid to sing to God by saying, *Judge me, God*? And yet the crowd of believers does sing it, and they do not think they are making a bad choice for themselves by singing what they have learned from the reading of the divine scriptures; and if they hardly understand how, they still believe that what they are singing is something good.

And even that psalm did not send them away without understanding. It went on, you see, to show in the next few words what kind of judgment was asserted: not a verdict of condemnation but of discretion.[8] For it says, *Judge me, God*. What does it mean, *Judge me, God, and distinguish my case from that of an unholy nation* (Ps 42:1)? So then, according to this judgment of discretion, *all of us must appear before the judgment seat of Christ*. But according to the judgment of condemnation, *Whoever hears my words*, he says, *and believes the one who sent me, has eternal life, and will not come under judgment, but makes the crossing from death to life*. What is *will not come under judgment*? It means "will not come under condemnation."

Let us prove from the scriptures that the judgment mentioned was the one to be understood as paying the penalty; although even in this very reading you will hear in a moment or two that this word *judgment* is only put here for condemnation and penalty.[9] All the same the apostle says somewhere or other, writing to those who showed no respect for the body which you, the faithful know about,[10] and who were being chastised with a beating by the Lord for their lack of respect—in fact, he says to them, *For*

---

7. Augustine uses the Greek term *diapsalma*, which primarily means a pause in the music, or a pause in the singing of the psalm. Then it came to mean the refrain; sometimes the one that occurs in the actual text of a psalm, as for example in Ps 67,3.5; sometimes for the refrain chosen for use in the liturgy, as here, for the people to repeat at the end of each verse of the psalm being sung by the cantor or read by the reader.
8. *Non est damnationis, sed discretionis* contrasts condemnation with good judgment, a legal conviction with mature decision-making that distinguishes or separates what is or is not good.
9. See Jn 5:29.
10. That is, the faithful have experienced the eucharist and therefore are presumed to understand.

that reason many among you are sick, and those in ill health are falling asleep in considerable numbers; many, that is, were even dying for that reason. And he went on: *For if we were to judge ourselves, we would not be judged by the Lord*; that is, if we were to chastise ourselves, we would not be chastised by the Lord. *But when we are judged, we are being chastised by the Lord, so that we may not be condemned with this world.* (1 Cor 11:30-32)

So then, here, some are being judged in terms of being punished, so that, over there, they may be spared; others are being spared here so that they may be racked more thoroughly over there; but there are those to whom these punishments are dealt without being punished[11] since they were not corrected by the flail of God; so, after having despised the father's beating here, they will feel the hand of the judge condemning them to punishment over there. So then, there is a judgment into which God, that is the Son of God, is going to send the devil and his angels at the end, along with all the unfaithful and ungodly; those who, by believing now, make the crossing from death to life will not come under this judgment.

Rise again by faith in this life, and so make sure
of rising again to life on the last day

6. Of course, though, you must not think that by believing you will escape dying in the flesh; you must not take it in a flesh-bound manner, and say to yourself, "My Lord said to me, *Whoever hears my words, and believes the one who sent me, has crossed over from death to life*. So as for me, then, I have believed, I am not going to die." What you must realize is that by dying you are going to pay the debt which you owe thanks to the penalty incurred by Adam.[12] That man, you see, in whom all of us were then contained, received the sentence, *You shall die by death* (Gen 2:17), and the divine judgment cannot be annulled. But when you have paid the death penalty of the old man, you will be taken up into the life of the new man, and you will make the crossing from death to life.

---

11. Augustine says most succinctly, and hence obscurely, *sine flagello poenae*; literally, "without the whip of punishment." Taken in that sense, it means that they are punished without being punished, i.e., without any result. Lewis and Short says that *flagellum* could also refer (in late Latin) to the flail used for threshing corn; hence, "without the flail of punishment" can mean without the flail achieving the separation of the grain from the husks.

12. See Homily 3, 13.

Meanwhile, for the time being, make the crossing to life.

What is your life?

Faith. *The just man lives by faith* (Rom 1:17; Hab 2:4).

What about unbelievers?

They are dead. Living in the body among the dead of that sort was the man about whom the Lord says, *Let the dead be, they can bury their own dead* (Mt 8:22). So then, even in this life there are the dead and there are the living, and almost all appear to be alive.

Who are the dead ones?

Those who do not believe.

Who are the living?

Those who have believed.

What are the dead told by the apostle?

Get up, sleeper.

"But he spoke of sleep," he says, "not death."

Listen to what follows: *And arise from the dead*—and as though he were saying, "Where will I go?"—*and Christ will shine upon you* (Eph 5:14). Right now, when Christ has shone upon you as you believe, you are making the crossing from death to life; stay in what you have crossed over to, and you will not come to judgment.

Resurrection by faith in this life compared to the raising of Lazarus

7. He now explains it all himself and continues, *Amen, amen, I tell you*—lest we should take what he said about crossing over from death to life as referring to the resurrection to come in the future, he wants to show how the one who believes makes the crossing, and how this crossing from death to life means crossing over from unbelief to faith, from injustice to justice, from pride to humility, from hatred to charity—so now he says, *Amen, amen, I tell you, that the hour is coming and now is*. What could be clearer? Now he has assuredly given us the key to what he was saying, that what Christ is urging us on to is happening at this very moment. *The hour is coming.*

Which hour?

And now is, when the dead shall hear the voice of the Son of God, and those who have heard shall live (Jn 5:25).

We have already spoken about these dead. What are we to think, my brothers and sisters—that in this crowd listening to me here there are none who are dead? I mean, those who believe and act in accordance with the faith are alive and not dead; those however who either do not believe, or like the demons *believe and tremble* (Jas 2:19), living bad lives, acknowledging the Son of God and having no charity, are to be reckoned as dead. And yet this hour is still running its course. The hour, surely, which the Lord spoke about will not be one hour of the twelve that make up one day. From the time he was speaking to this present time, and right on to the end of the world, this hour is still running its course, about which John says in his letter, *Little children, it is the last hour* (1 Jn 2:18). So then, it is right now.

Those who are alive, let them live; those who are dead, let them live. Let the one who was lying there, a corpse, hear the voice of the Son of God, let him rise and come to life. The Lord shouted at the tomb of Lazarus, and the one dead for four days rose again, The one who was stinking came out into the fresh air. He had been buried, the stone had been placed on top of him, the Savior's voice shattered the hardness of the stone[13]—and is your heart so hard that still that divine voice does not shatter you?

Rise in your heart, come forth from your tomb. You see, you were lying dead in your heart as in a tomb, and were being weighed down as if by the rock of your evil habits.[14] Rise and come forth.

What does that mean, Rise and come forth?

Believe and profess your faith. The one who has believed, you see, has risen again, the one who professes his faith has come forth. Why have I said that the one who professes his faith has come forth? Because before he did so, he was hidden; while when he does so he comes forth from darkness into light. And when he has made this profession, what are the ministers told to do? What they were told to do for the body of Lazarus: *Unbind him and let him go* (Jn 11:44).

How do they do this?

The apostles as ministers were told: *What you unbind on earth shall be unbound in heaven* (Mt 18:18).

---

13. See Jn 11:38-43.
14. See Sermons 67, 2; 98, 5; 128, 14; 139A, 2.

Christ is the life the dead who rise again shall live by

8. *The hour is coming, and now is, when the dead shall hear the voice of the Son of God, and those who have heard shall live.*

What will they live by?

By life.

By what sort of life?

By Christ.

How can we prove that they live by the life which is Christ?

I am, he says, *the way, the truth and the life* (Jn 14:6).

Do you want to walk? *I am the way.* Do you want to avoid being deceived? *I am the truth.* Do you want to avoid death? *I am the life.* This is what your Savior is saying to you: "There is no place you can go to, except to me; there is no way you can go by, except by me." So now is this hour running its course; yes, certainly running its course, and it does not stop at all. People who were dead are rising, they are crossing over to life at the voice of the Son of God, they are living by him, persevering in his faith.[15] The Son, you see, has life; he has the life by which those who believe also live.

The meaning of Christ's having life in himself,
just as the Father has life in himself

9. And how does he have it? As the Father has it. Listen to him saying so himself, For, *as the Father has life in himself, so too he gave the Son the possession of life.* (Jn 5:26). Brothers and sisters, let me talk about this as best I can. For these are the very words which trouble tiny minds like ours. Why did he add *in himself?* It would have been enough to say, surely, *For, as the Father has life in himself, so too he gave the Son the possession of life.* But he added *in himself.* In fact, the Father does have life in himself; the Son has life in himself as well. When he said in himself, he wanted us to understand something and the secret is locked away here in this saying. Let us knock, that he might open.[16]

---

15. Augustine does not say "in faith in him," but "in his faith," *in fide ipsius*, which probably means "in the faith he demands or proclaimed"—in this instance that means faith in his Father, *believing the one who sent me.*
16. See Lk 11:9; Mt 7:7.

O Lord, what is this that you have said? *In himself*—why did you add it? The apostle Paul, after all, whom you caused to live, did not he have life?

"Yes, he did," says he.

"All those countless dead whom you have caused to live again and to cross over by believing your word, will not they have life in you when they have crossed over?"

"Yes, they will; after all, I just said a moment ago, *Whoever hears my words, and believes the one who sent me, has eternal life*."

"So those who believe in you, then, have life; and you did not say 'in themselves.' When, though, you were talking about the Father, it was, *As the Father has life in himself*; and again, when you were talking about yourself, you said, *so too he gave the Son the possession of life in himself*. Just as he has it, so he gives you to have it."

"Where does he have it?"

"*In himself*."

"Where did he give the Son to have it?"

"*In himself*."

"Where does Paul have it?"

"Not in himself but in Christ."

You there, one of the faithful, where do you have it? Not in yourself, but in Christ. Let us see if the apostle says the same. *I am living, however, now not I, but Christ is living in me* (Gal 2;20). Our life, precisely as ours, as lived from our very own wills, cannot be anything but bad, sinful, wicked; but a life that is good is in us from God, not from ourselves; it is given us by God, not by ourselves. Christ on the other hand has life in himself just as the Father does, because he is the Word of God. He does not live a bad life at one time, a good life at another; while human beings do—bad at one time, good at another. The one who was living a bad life was living his own; the one who is living a good life has crossed over to the life of Christ. Having been made a shareholder in life, you were not what you have received, and you were there previously, open to receiving it. The Son of God on the other hand was not, so to say, first of all without life, and then received it. If that is how he had received it, you see, he would not have it in himself. What then does this mean, *in himself*? It means he received it so as himself to be life itself.[17]

Christ is life, is light, just as the Father is; his receiving life and light from the Father means his being eternally begotten by him

10. Perhaps I can put it still more clearly. Everyone has lighted a lamp; that lamp there, for example,[18] as regards the little flame that is shining in it, that fire has light in itself; but your eyes, which were lying as if dead and not seeing anything in the absence of the lamp, now also, once it has been lit, have light, but not in themselves. Accordingly, if they turn away from the lamp, they are darkened; if they turn round toward it, they are enlightened. That flame of fire, on the other hand, goes on shining as long as it exists; if you want to take its light away, you douse it also at the same time, because it cannot go on being fire without light.

But the light which Christ is cannot be doused; it is co-eternal with the Father, always glowing, always shining, always at white heat; I mean, if it was not white hot, would it say in the psalm, *Nor is there anyone who can hide from his heat* (Ps 18:6)? You for your part were icy cold in your sin, then you turn round toward him to get warm; if you turn your back on him, you get cold. In your sin you were in the dark, you turned toward him to be lighted on your way; if you turn away again, you will be left in the dark. Accordingly, because in yourself you were darkness, you will not, when lit up, be light yourself, though you are in the light. That is what the apostle says, after all: *You all were once darkness, but now light in the Lord* (Eph 5:8); after saying *but now light*, he added *in the Lord*.[19] Why light at all? Because you are light by sharing in that light. If, however, you turn your back on the light you are being lit up by, you go back to your own darkness.

That is not how it is with Christ, nor how it is with the Word of God.

Well, how is it with him?

---

17. See Homily 19, 11-12.
18. So it seems clear, as the Maurists suggest, that this sermon was being preached by lamplight, the light of the little lamps which almost everyone in the congregation had brought along with them. Perhaps the sermon had started in daylight, but most of them had brought lamps with them, knowing it would be dark before the bishop had finished, and had just been passing the light from one lamp to the next—little clay lamps holding some olive oil, with a wick emerging from their spouts.
19. See Homily 2, 6; Sermon 67, 5.

As the Father has life in himself, so too he gave the Son the possession of life in himself, so that he does not live as one who participates, but lives without change, and is himself entirely life. So he gave the Son the possession of life; just as he has, so has he given.

Then what is the difference between them?

That the former has given, the latter has received.[20]

Was he already there before receiving?

Can we really think of Christ as having been some time without light, seeing that he is himself the wisdom of the Father, of which it is said, *She is the brilliance of eternal light* (Wis 7:26)?[21] So then, to say *gave the Son* is exactly the same as saying "has begotten the Son."[22] Just as he gave him simply to be, so he gave him to be life, so he gave him to be life in himself. What does that mean, to be life in himself? Not to be in need of life from anywhere else, but himself to be the fullness of life, from which others who believe might draw life as long as they live. So then, he gave him the possession of life in himself. He gave it to him precisely as to whom? As to his own Word, as to the one who *in the beginning was the Word, and the Word was with God.*

*Christ given authority to judge as the Son of Man,
in order to be seen by those who judged and pierced him*

11. After that, when he had become man, what did he give him? *And he gave him authority to pass judgment, since he is the Son of Man* (Jn 5:27). Insofar as he is the Son of God, *as the Father has life in himself, so too he gave the Son the possession of life in himself,* while insofar as he is the Son of Man, *he gave him authority to pass judgment.* That is what I explained to Your Graces yesterday,[23] that at the judgment the man will be seen, while God will not be seen; but after the judgment God will be seen by those who have been victorious in judgment, while God will not be seen by the godless. So then, because the man will appear at the time of judgment in the form he had when he ascended[24] and will have when he comes again, that is

---

20. See Homily 19, 11.
21. For a similar use of this text, see *The Trinity* IV, 20, 27-28; Sermons 117, 11; 118, 2.
22. See Homily 19, 13.
23. See Homily 21, 12-14.
24. See Acts 1:11.

why he previously said, *The Father does not judge anyone, but he has given all judgment to the Son* (Jn 5:22). He also repeats that fact here, when he says, *And he gave him authority to pass judgment, since he is the Son of Man.* As though you there were to ask, "He gave him authority to pass judgment, but why? Was there a time when he did not have this authority to pass judgment? When *in the beginning was the Word, and the Word was with God, and the Word was God, when all things were made through him* (Jn 1:1.3), did he not have authority to pass judgment?"

But what I am saying is that the very reason the Father gave him authority to pass judgment was that he is the Son of Man; yes, the reason he received authority to judge is that he is the Son of Man. Because, of course, as the Son of God, he has always had this authority. It is the one who was crucified that received it,[25] the one who was in death is in life. The Word of God was never in death, was always in life.

The resurrection of the dead in the flesh at the end is not precluded by the resurrection of faith here and now

12. So now, I suppose, someone among us here was already saying about the resurrection, "Look, we have risen; the one who listens to Christ, the one who believes crosses from death to life and will not come under judgment; the hour is coming, and now is, that whoever hears the voice of the Son of God shall live; he was dead, he heard, and behold he rises again;[26] what is all this talk about a resurrection to come later on?"

Do not be so hard on yourself, so hasty in passing sentence, or you may have to follow it through. There is indeed this resurrection which takes place now; unbelievers were dead, the wicked were dead; the just live, they cross over from the death of unbelief to the life of faith; but do not conclude from that that there is not going to be any resurrection of the body later on; believe as well that there is going to be a resurrection of the body.

You must listen, after all, to what follows on the statement about this resurrection which takes place through faith, to prevent anybody from thinking it is the only one, and so falling into despair, and into the error of those people who went about subverting the understanding of others,

---

25. See Homilies 19, 16; 21, 13-14.
26. See Jn 5:24-25.

saying that the resurrection has already happened; about them the apostle says, *And they overthrow the faith of some* (2 Tm 2:18). I think, you see, that they went about saying something like this to them, "Look, here is the Lord saying, *And whoever believes in me has crossed over from death to life*; this resurrection has already happened with the faithful who had been unfaithful. How can you talk about another resurrection?"[27]

The Lord our God be thanked, he shores up the shaky ones, shows the way to the hesitant, confirms the doubters. Listen to what comes next, because you have no grounds for shrouding yourself in the fog of death. If you have come to believe, believe the whole of it.

What is the whole of it, you say, that I am to believe?

Listen to what he says: *"Do not be surprised at this*, that he has given the Son authority to pass judgment. I am talking about the end," he says.

In what way about the end?

Do not be surprised at this, that the hour is coming—here he does not say, *and now is*. What did he say about the resurrection of faith? *The hour is coming, and now is*. With this resurrection, which he is representing as being one of dead bodies to come in the future, *the hour is coming*, he said; and he did not say *and now is*, because it is going to happen at the end of the world.[28]

At the resurrection for the final judgment, some will rise to life, others to eternal punishment

13. "And how," you say, "are you going to prove to me that he said this about that resurrection?"

If you listen patiently, you in person will prove it to yourself in a moment. So then, let us continue: *Do not be surprised at this, that the hour is coming, in which all who are in the tombs*. How could it be put more plainly which resurrection he is talking about? A short while ago he did not say, *who are in the tombs*, but, *The dead shall hear the voice of the Son of God, and those who have heard shall live*. He did not say, "Some shall live, others shall be condemned," because all who believe shall live. But what does he say about the tombs? *All who are in the tombs*

---

27. See Homily 19, 14 for a fuller account of these heretics, who denied the resurrection of the dead.
28. See Jn 5:28. See also Homily 19, 16-17.

shall hear his voice, and come forth (Jn 5:28). He did not say, "shall hear and live." If they had lived bad lives, you see, and were lying there in the tombs, they will rise to death, not to life.

So let us see, then, who will come forth. Although a few moments ago the dead were coming to life by hearing and believing, there was no distinction being made then;[29] it did not say, "The dead shall hear the voice of the Son of God, and when they have heard, some will live, others shall be condemned," but *all who have heard shall live*, because those who believe shall live, those who have charity shall live, and none of them shall die. About the tombs though: *They shall hear his voice and come forth, those who have done good to the resurrection of life, those who have done evil to the resurrection of judgment* (Jn 5:28-29). This is the judgment, the penalty, about which he had said a short while beforehand, *Whoever believes in me has crossed over from death to life, and will not come under judgment.*

The Word is both the speaking of the Father and the hearing of the Word;
his being spoken by the Father is his being eternally begotten of the Father

14. *I myself cannot do anything of myself; I judge as I hear, and my judgment is just* (Jn 5:30).

If you judge as you hear, whom do you hear it from?

If from the Father, it is clear that *the Father does not judge anyone, but he has given all judgment to the Son* (Jn 5:22).

Is it insofar as you are in some sense the Father's herald that you just repeat what you hear?[30]

What I hear is what I say, because what the Father is, is what I am. Speaking or saying, after all, is my very being, because I am the Father's Word.

That, you see, is what Christ is saying to you in your heart. What else can *As I hear, so I judge* mean but "As I am?" How does Christ hear, after all? Brothers and sisters, let us really tackle this question, I implore you. Does Christ hear from the Father? How does the Father speak to him? Obviously if he speaks to him, he utters words to him; I mean, everyone who says

---

29. See Homily 19, 18.
30. In Roman courts the judge or presiding officer spoke, as befitted his dignity, in a quiet voice, and then his herald (*praeco*), who was standing beside him, repeated his words in a voice loud enough to be heard by all.

anything to anyone, says it with a word. How does the Father say anything to the Son, when the Son is the Father's Word? Whatever the Father says to us, he says with his Word; the Word of the Father is the Son,[31] so with what other word does he say anything to the Word himself? God is one, he has just one Word, in that one Word he embraces all things.[32] So what is the meaning of *As I hear, so I judge*? As I am from the Father, so I judge. That is why *my judgment is just*.

Well, but if you do nothing of yourself, Lord Jesus, in the way we flesh-bound creatures understand that; if you do nothing of yourself, how is it you said a short while ago, *So too the Son gives life to whom he will* (Jn 5:21)? Now you are saying, *By myself I do nothing*. But what else does the Son ever draw our attention to, but that he is from the Father? If he is from the Father, he is not from himself. If the Son were from himself, he would not be Son; it is from the Father that he *is*. The Father, in order to be, is not from the Son; the Son, in order to be, is from the Father. Equal to the Father; but still, this one from that one, not that one from this one.

Concluding exhortation to do the will of God and a statement against the Arians

15. *Because I do not seek my own will, but the will of the one who sent me* (Jn 5:30). The only begotten Son says, *I do not seek my own will*, and mere human beings want to do their own will! To such an extent does he humble himself, the one equal to the Father; and to such an extent does the other vaunt himself, the one lying at the bottom of the heap, unable to get up unless a hand is reached down to him! So then, let us do the will of the Father, the will of the Son, the will of the Holy Spirit; because this Trinity has just one will, one authority and power, one majestic greatness. Still, the reason the Son says, *I have not come to do my own will, but the will of the one who sent me* (Jn 6:38), is that Christ is not from himself, but from his Father.[33] What, however, he had in order to appear visibly as a human being, he took to himself from the creature which he himself had fashioned.

---

31. See Homily 21, 4.
32. For another wrestling bout with this trinitarian conundrum, see in particular *Against a Sermon of the Arians* 9, 17; also for a more leisurely and profound treatment *The Trinity* VII,1,1; 2,3.
33. See Homily 19, 19. There Augustine interpreted Jn 5:30 as referring to Christ as man, while here, in a later homily, he is referring it to Christ as the eternal Son of the Father—not exactly a more mature interpretation, but a more difficult one that also needed to be made, particularly against the Arians.

Homily 23

On John 5:30-40[1]

Introduction; we must build on the rock of Christ's own testimony

1. Somewhere in the gospel the Lord says that the good and sensible listener to his words ought to be like someone intending to build, who digs down until he reaches a solid foundation of rock on which he erects whatever he is building, safe against a river in spate, such that when it comes, it is warded off by the strength of the building, not causing that house's collapse by its onslaught.[2] Let us imagine God's scriptures as being a site where we want to build. Let us not be lazy, content with building on the surface; let us dig deep until we reach the rock; *now the rock was Christ* (1 Cor 10:4).[3]

On the light of lamps compared with the sun

2. Today's reading spoke to us about the testimony given to the Lord—how he has no need of any testimony from human beings, but has one that is greater than theirs could ever be; and he told us what that testimony is: *The works that I perform,* he says, *bear witness to me.* Then he added, *And the Father who sent me bears witness to me* (Jn 5:36-37). He also says that he has received the works he performs from the Father. So then, the works bear witness, the Father bears witness.

Did not John bear witness? Of course he bore witness; but like a lamp, not to satisfy friends, but to confound enemies;[4] after all, it had already been foretold in the name of the Father: *I have prepared a lamp for my Christ; his enemies I shall clothe with confusion; over him, however, my sanctification shall burst into flower* (Ps 131:17-18). Put yourself in the dark of night; you have waited for a lamp, and you have admired it, and you have reveled in the light of the lamp; but that lamp tells you that there is a sun, in which you really ought to revel; and though it is burning during the night, it bids you look forward to the day.

---
1. Preached the day after Homily 19. See the Introduction for an explanation.
2. See Mt 7:24-25.
3. See Sermons 46, 10; 129, 8; 358, 5.
4. See Homilies 2, 8-9; 4, 3; 5, 14-15; Sermons 127, 1-2; 293, 4; 293D, 4; 308A, 6.

That does not mean, then, that there was no need for that man's testimony; why after all was he sent, if he was not needed? But, lest people stay with the lamp and imagine that the light of the lamp was enough for them, therefore the Lord does not say that this lamp was superfluous, nor that one should remain in its light.

He says that the scriptures of God are another witness; that, of course, is where God bore witness to his Son, and the Jews pinned their hopes on those scriptures, that is, on God's law brought to them by God's servant, Moses.[5] *Scrutinize the scriptures,* he says, *in which you imagine that you have eternal life; they bear witness to me, and you do not wish to come to me so as to have life* (Jn 5:39-40).

Why do you imagine you have eternal life in the scriptures? Question those scriptures about the one to whom they bear witness, and understand what eternal life really is. And because they wanted to repudiate Christ for opposing the institutions and laws prescribed by Moses, he once again confounds them with the aid of another lamp.

The oil that feeds the light of the lamps is God's grace

3. In fact, all human beings are lamps because they can be illuminated and put out, and they really are[6] lamps when they are wise, shine and burn with the Spirit;[7] while if they were burning and have gone out, they stink. The good lamps, you see, have persevered as servants of God, kept alight from the oil of his mercy, not from their own strength. God's freely-given grace, I mean, that is the oil in the lamps. *I toiled, you see, more than all of them,* says a certain lamp; and in case he should seem to be burning from his own powers, he added, *Not I, however, but the grace of God with me* (1 Cor 15:10).

So then, every prophecy before the coming of the Lord is a lamp; about this the apostle Peter says, *We hold as more certain the prophetic word to which you do well to pay attention, as to a lamp shining in a dark place, until the day dawns and the morning star rises in your hearts* (2 Pt 1:19).

---

5. See Jn 5:45.
6. See Sermons 133, 6; 182, 5; 289, 4.
7. See Rom 12:11.

The prophets, therefore, were lamps, and all prophecy one huge lamp.[8] What about the apostles? Were they not lamps as well? Clearly they were lamps. Only the Christ was not a lamp; for he is not illuminated nor extinguished; because *as the Father has life in himself, so he gave the Son the possession of life in himself* (Jn 5:26).

So the apostles too were lamps; and they give thanks for having been lit by the light of truth, and they are aglow with the Spirit of charity, who supplies them with the oil of God's grace. If they were not lamps, the Lord would not have said to them, *You are the light of the world* (Mt 5:14). After saying to them, though, *You are the light of the world*, he showed them that they were not to think of themselves as being the light of which it was said, *That light was true, who enlightens everyone coming into this world* (Jn 1:9). That was said of the Lord to distinguish him from John.[9] For it had just said about John the Baptist, *He was not the light, but to bear witness to the light* (Jn 1:8). And to keep you from asking, "How was he not light, the one of whom Christ says that he was a lamp?" it is by comparison with another light that he was not light, for *that light was true, who enlightens everyone coming into this world*.

So then, when he had also told the disciples, *You are the light of the world*, to stop them from thinking they were being credited with something that was to be understood of Christ alone, and thus would the lamps be blown out by the wind of pride, after saying, *You are the light of the world*, he added right away, *A city set on top of a mountain cannot be hidden, nor do they light a lamp and put it under a basket, but on top of a lampstand, to give light to all who are in the house* (Mt 5:14-15).

But what if he was not calling the apostles the lamp, but the lighters of the lamp, which they were to put on the lampstand? Listen to him calling them the lamp itself: *So let your light*, he says, *shine before men, that on seeing your good works they may glorify*, not you, but *your Father who is in heaven* (Mt 5:16).

4. So then, Moses bore witness to Christ, and John too bore witness to Christ, and the other prophets and apostles also bore witness to Christ. To the testimony of all these witnesses he preferred the testimony of his own works, because, while through those men none but God was bearing witness

---

8. See Sermon 43, 5.
9. See Homilies 2, 6-7; 3, 5; 14, 2.

to his Son, there is yet another way in which God bears witness to his Son. Through the Son himself, God points to the Son, points to himself through the Son. If anyone can get as far as the Son, he will not need lamps, and by truly digging deeper, he will lay his building's foundations on the rock.

Taking up the debt left over from yesterday

5. So today's reading, then, brothers and sisters, is straightforward, but on account of yesterday's debt (for I am well aware of what I put off, did not unilaterally break off, and the Lord has been good enough to let me talk to you today as well), please recall what you should require of me, if we are to reach out, with due piety and healthy humility, not against God but toward God. And let us lift up our soul to him, pouring it out over ourselves like that man in the psalm, to whom people were saying, *Where is your God? These things*, he said, *I reflected, and I poured out my soul over myself.* (Ps 41:2-4) And, with his help, let us lift up our soul, for it is heavy.

What on earth makes it heavy? The fact that *a corruptible body weighs down the soul, and this earthy dwelling presses down on the spirit musing on many things* (Wis 9:15).[10] So lest we not be able to collect our thoughts from many things to one, tear them away from many things and lift them up again[11] to the One—which indeed we will not be able to do, as I said, unless helped by the one who wants our souls to be lifted up to him—and appreciate in some way, how the Word of God, the only-begotten of the Father, co-eternal and equal to the Father, only does what he has seen the Father doing, although in fact the Father himself does not do anything except through the Son who sees him.[12] It seems to me that, in this passage, the Lord Jesus wished to suggest something of great importance to those bent on hearing it, and to fill the minds of those who are capable, to incite those not yet capable to study so that, in their

---

10. On the translation and the interpretation of this verse, see A.-M. Bonnardière, *Biblia augustiniana. A.T. Le livre de la Sagesse* (Paris: Mame, 1970) 206-215.
11. *Relevare*; the verb in classical Latin means, basically, "to relieve." Here however it is clearly almost synonymous with simple *levare*, "to lift up"; but the prefix *re* must be given due weight; it normally means "again," which is how I render it. The question then arises, when were they previously lifted up to the One? That was in the age of innocence, before the fall.
12. See Jn 5:19, and Augustine's long discussion of the problems raised by this verse in Homilies 18, 3-6 and 19, 2-3, on the previous two days.

lack of understanding, those who do not understand might—by living good lives—acquire the capacity to do so.[13]

He taught us that the human soul and the rational mind, which human beings possess and animals do not, is not given life, not rendered blessed, nor filled with light except by the very substance of God; and that this soul acts through the body and by means of the body, and rules the body as its subject, and the senses of the body can be soothed or hurt by material bodies, and for this reason, that is, because of a certain companionship or intertwining of soul and body in this life, the soul can feel pleasure when the body's senses are soothed, or pain when they are hurt; and that the soul's happiness, by which it is rendered blessed, is only achieved by sharing in that life of the ever-living, unchanging and eternal substance, which is God; so it is that, just as the soul which is inferior to God gives life to what is inferior to itself, namely the body, in the same way nothing will give the blessed life to the soul except what is superior to the same soul. The soul, you see, is superior to the body, and God is superior to the soul. It bestows something on its inferior, it has something bestowed on it by its superior. Let it serve its Lord so as not to be trampled on by its servant.

This, my brothers and sisters, is the Christian religion, which is preached throughout the world, to the horror of its enemies, who moan and groan where they are overcome, and who act in anger where they prevail. This is the Christian religion, that the one God, not many gods, be worshiped, because only the one God can make the soul happy. Participation in God makes the soul happy. It is not the participation in a holy soul that gives happiness to a soul that is sick; nor is a holy soul made happy by sharing with an angel; but if the sick soul seeks happiness, let it seek from that source of the holy soul's happiness. For no angel will give you happiness, but the source of the angel's happiness will be the source of yours.

Soul and body in relation to the divine substance and the humanity of Christ; the resurrection of souls and of bodies

6. With this introduction, I think, we have established that the rational soul is rendered blessed by none but God, and that the body is given life by

---

13. See Homily 18, 7.

nothing but the soul, and that the soul is thus a mid-point between God and the body.[14] So now listen closely and go over again with me, not today's reading (which we have sufficiently talked about), but yesterday's reading, to which we return for the third time[15] discussing it and digging down in it until we get to the rock.

Christ is the Word, Christ is the Word of God, Christ is the Word with God and Christ is God the Word, and God and the Word are one God.[16] Go that far, my soul, after scorning or indeed rising above everything else; proceed that far. Nothing is more potent than this creature which is called the rational spirit, nothing is more sublime than this creature; all that is above it now is only the creator. Now I was saying that Christ is the Word, and Christ is the Word of God, and Christ is God the Word; but Christ is not only the Word, because *the Word was made flesh and took up residence among us* (Jn 1:14). So then Christ is both Word and flesh. For when *in the form of God, he did not regard being equal to God as something to be grasped at.* And what about us at the bottom, infirm and crawling on the earth, we were unable to reach up to God, were we to be abandoned? Not at all! *He emptied himself, taking the form of a slave* (Phil 2:6-7), not, therefore, losing the form of God. So then, the one who was God was made man, taking on what he was not, not losing what he was; that is how God became man. There you have something for your infirmity, something for your becoming perfect. Let Christ set you on your feet by that in him which is man, let him lead you forward by that in him which is God-man, let him lead you right through to that which is God.

Everything that has been preached and achieved by Christ, brothers and sisters, is this and nothing else: that souls should rise again, that bodies should also rise again. Each, of course, was dead; the body from sickness, the

---

14. See Homily 20, 11.
15. Augustine is going back to Jn 5:19-30, which had been the previous day's reading, the subject of Homily 19. But the key opening verse had already been the subject of Homily 18, 2-3; so that is why he talks here about "the third day running," *triduo*. In fact it would seem from other internal evidence that Homily 18 was delivered a few days before Homily 19, not on the day immediately preceding it.
16. I here follow Berrouard in adopting the punctuation of the Louvain edition. Others put the last comma in such a place as to require the last phrase to be construed, "Christ and God and the Word are one God," which, as Berrouard rightly remarks, is a strange expression and fails to refer to the prologue of John, unlike the preceding phrases.

soul from wickedness. Because each was dead, each had to rise again. What do you mean, "each"? Soul and body. So how would the soul rise again, but through Christ as God? How would the body rise, but by Christ as man?[17]

In Christ too, you see, there was a human soul, a complete soul; not just the non-rational element in this soul, but the rational one as well, which is named mind. For, there have been some heretics, and they have been expelled from the Church, who maintained that the body of Christ does not have a rational mind, but just a kind of brute soul;[18] cut out the rational mind, after all, and you are left with life that is brutish. But since they have been expelled—expelled in truth—you must now take the whole Christ as Word, rational mind, and flesh. That is the whole Christ; let your soul then rise from wickedness through that which is God, let your body rise again from corruption through that which is man.

Accordingly, dearly beloved, listen to the great depth, so does it seem to me, of this reading, and see how Christ is talking about nothing but the goal of his coming, namely, that souls should rise again from wickedness, bodies from corruption. I have already said how souls may rise again, through the very substance of God; how bodies may rise again, through the human achievement of our Lord Jesus Christ.

The Father showing the Son what he is doing means
God making all things through the Word

7. *Amen, amen, I tell you, the Son can do nothing on his own, but only what he sees the Father doing; for whatever things the Father does, these things the Son also does in like manner* (Jn 5:19); the sky, the earth, the sea, everything in the sky, everything on earth, everything in the sea, things visible, things invisible, animals in the countryside, shrubs in the fields, fishes in the waters, birds in the air, lights in the sky; in addition to all these things, angels, virtues, thrones, lordships, princedoms, powers; *all things were made through him* (Jn 1:3). Did God make all these things, and show

---

17. See Homily 19, 15-19.
18. Augustine is referring to the followers of Apollinaris, bishop of Laodicea in the middle of the 4th century and a friend and staunch supporter of St. Athanasius against the Arians. To defend the full divine nature of Jesus Christ he maintained that the Word took the place of the rational mind, saying in effect that Jesus, the eternal Word of God, did not need a human mind. Augustine affirms the need for a rational mind so that Jesus is true man and true God. The heresy was condemned at the First Council of Constantinople in 381.

them ready made to the Son, so that he too might make another universe, full of all these things? Of course not. But what, then? For whatever that one has done, you see, these things, not others, but these things the Son too does, not in a different way but in like manner.

The Father, you see, loves the Son, and shows him all the things which he himself does (Jn 5:20). The Father shows the Son that souls are to be raised up, because through the Father and the Son souls are raised up, nor can souls be alive unless God is their life. So if souls then cannot be alive unless God is their life, just as they are the life of bodies, what the Father shows the Son, that is, what he is doing, he does through the Son. In fact, he does not show it to the Son while doing it, but while showing it he does it through the Son. The Son, I mean, sees the Father showing it before anything is made, and as a result of the Father's showing and the Son's seeing, everything is made which is made by the Father through the Son. Thus souls are raised up, if they have been able to see this bond of unity; the Father showing and the Son seeing, and creation being brought into being through the Father's showing and the Son's seeing; and all that being made through the Father's showing and the Son's seeing which is neither Father nor Son, but beneath the Father and the Son; everything that is ever made by the Father through the Son. Who sees this?

A comparison with a human father showing his son how to make something

8. I see it is time for me to return to the physical senses; I must once again humble myself and come down to you—if, indeed, I had ever risen even a little above you. You want to show something to your son, so that he may make what you are making; you will make it yourself, and in this way you will show it to him. What therefore you are going to make in order to show your son, you do not of course make through your son, but you alone make something for him to see when it is made, so that he can make another similar thing in like manner. That is not how things are there; why turn to your own likeness, and erase in yourself the likeness of God? That is not at all how it is up there. I have found an example of how you show what you are making to your son before you make it, so that when you have shown him, you can make through your son what you are making yourself.

Here perhaps an example occurs to you. "Look," you say, "I am thinking of putting up a house, and I want to have it constructed by my son; before I build it, I show my son what I want him to do, and he himself does it and I make it through him, by having shown him my wishes." You have certainly moved away from the previous comparison, but you are still caught in a vast difference. Notice, in fact, that before you build the house, you give your son some indication and show what you wish him to put up, so that by showing your wishes before you do anything, he himself can do what you have shown, and thus you are doing it through him. But you are going to speak words to your son, and words were exchanged between you and him; and between the one showing and the one seeing, or the one speaking and the one listening, articulated sounds are flying back and forth—sounds which are not the same as what you are, not the same as what he is. The sounds, that is, which issue from your mouth, and by lashing the air in between strike the ears of your son, and by filling his sense of hearing bring your thought to his heart; those sounds, then, are not you yourself, are not your son himself. A sign has been given by your spirit to your son's spirit, and the sign is neither your spirit nor your son's spirit, but something else.

Are we to suppose that the Father spoke with the Son in that way? Did words pass between God and the Word? How did that happen? If the Father wished to say something to the Son, if he wanted to say it with a word, well, the Son is the Word of the Father; would he ever use a word to speak to the Word? Or because the Son is the Word par excellence, were lesser words going to run back and forth between Father and Son? Was a sound of some sort, a kind of time-bound and fleeting creature, going to issue from the Father's mouth and strike the Son's ear? Does God have a body, so that this can somehow issue from his lips? Does the Word have bodily ears which a sound can reach?

Put aside all bodily things, concentrate on simple things, if you are a simple person. But how are you to become simple? If you are not all tied up in the world, but have disentangled yourself from the world, you will in fact be simple by disentangling yourself. And notice, if you can, what I am saying; or if you cannot see it, believe what you cannot see. You speak to your son, you speak with words; you are not the word which makes a sound, nor is your son.

The simplicity of God; he is not anything that can change

9. "I have another way of showing him," you say; "my son has been so well brought up that he does not even need to hear me speaking, but I just give him the nod to show him what he is to do." Fine, show him your wishes by giving him the nod, it is still undoubtedly your spirit wanting to show what it has in mind. What do you give him the nod with? With a bodily sign, with your lips, that is to say, your expression, with eyebrows, eyes, hands. None of these is your spirit; even these are means; something, which is not your spirit, is understood through these signs; it is not your son's spirit either; but everything that you do with the body is less than your spirit and less than the spirit of your son. Nor can your son get to know what your spirit has in mind, unless you give him bodily signs. What am I to do then? That is not how it is in God where all is simplicity.[19] The Father shows the Son what he is doing, and by showing he begets the Son.

I know what I just said; but because I also know to whom I have said it, let there be understanding at some time or other. If you cannot understand what God is right now, at least understand what God is not. You will have made great progress if you do not think God is something different from what he really is. You cannot yet get as far as what he is, but get as far as what he is not. God is not a body, not earth, not the sky, not the moon, not the sun, not the stars, none of these bodily things. If not things in the heavens, how much less anything earthly![20] Remove every body!

Listen to something else; God is not a changeable spirit. Yes, I admit, it has to be admitted, because it is the gospel speaking: *God is spirit* (Jn 4:24). But pass beyond every changeable spirit, pass beyond any spirit that now knows, now does not know, now remembers, now forgets, wants what it did not want, does not want what it did; whether it undergoes all these changes, or whether it is just able to;[21] pass beyond all of this. You will not find any change in God, anything that is now like this, a moment ago like that. Where you find "now like this, now like that," a kind of death has taken place there; it is a death, after all, for something not to be what it was.

---

19. On the simplicity of the Trinity and of the divine persons, see *The Trinity* VI, 6, 8-7, 9; VII, I, 2; VIII, 2, 3; Homily 20, 9.
20. See *The Trinity* VIII, 2, 3.
21. Spirits that can change, but do not, are the blessed angels and souls of the just in heaven; their desires, wholly satisfied with the vision of God, do not change; as created, however, they could change. See Homily 19, 11.

Yes, the soul is said to be immortal, because the soul is always alive, and there is in it a kind of abiding but changeable, life. As regards the changes of this life, it can also be called mortal, because if it was living wisely and turns foolish, it has died for the worse; if it was living foolishly and turns wise, it has died for the better.[22]

Scripture teaches us that there is a death for the worse and a death for the better. They died for the worse, of whom it says, *Let the dead be, let them bury their own dead* (Lk 9:60); and *Get up, you who are sleeping, and arise from the dead, and Christ will enlighten you* (Eph 5:14); and from this reading: *When the dead shall hear, and those who have listened shall live* (Jn 5:25). They were dead for the worse; therefore they come to life again. By coming to life again they die for the better, because by coming to life again they cease to be what they were; but for something to cease being what it was is a kind of death.

But perhaps if it is for the better, it should not be called death? The apostle called it death: *But if you have died with Christ from the elements of this world, why do you still go on laying down the law as if you were drawing life from this world?* (Col 2:20) And again: *For you have died, and your life is hidden with Christ in God* (Col 3:3). He wants us to die in order to live, because we have been living in such a way that we would die.

So whatever dies—both from better to worse and from worse to better—is not what God is, because it is not possible either for the highest good to become better or for the truly eternal to become worse. The truly eternal, after all, is where nothing is about time. Was it now this, now that? Once time is introduced, the eternal is no longer. That you might know that it is not with God as it is with the soul, the soul is certainly immortal, but what did the apostle mean by saying about God, *Who alone has immortality* (1 Tm 6:16), if not that God alone is beyond all change, because he alone has true eternity? So then, there is no change where God is.

Even if we cannot know what God is, it is no trifling matter to know what he is not

10. Recognize in yourself something which I want to talk about, something within, deep inside you; not in you as inside your body, although that

---

22. See Homily 19, 12.

too can be spoken about as "in you." Indeed, health is in you, your age is in you—whatever age you may be—but those things are about the body; thus you have hands, you have feet. But something is in you, as inside you, another is in you as your clothing. But leave aside what is outside—both your clothing and your flesh; go within yourself, visit your secret chamber, your mind, and see there, if you can, what I want to say. After all, if you are far from yourself, how will you be able to draw near to God?[23] I was talking to you about God, and you thought you would understand; I am talking about the soul, I am talking about you; know that that is where I will put you to the test.

I do not have to go very far for examples, when I want to find something in your mind to show a likeness to your God; because not in the body but in the mind was man made in the likeness of God.[24] Let us seek God in his own likeness, let us recognize the creator in his own image. There, inside of us, let us find, if we can, what we are talking about: how the Father is showing to the Son and how the Son sees what the Father is showing, before anything is made by the Father through the Son. Even so, when I have spoken and you have understood, do not imagine that the reality is anything like that; in that way you may preserve the devotion which I want you to preserve, and about which I remind you above all, that is, while you cannot grasp what God is, do not imagine that it is a small matter to know what he is not.[25]

Our memory shows things to our thought; but the Father shows the Son himself

11. Here then, in your mind I see two things, your memory and your thought, which is, in some way, the sight and gaze of your soul.[26] You see something, and you perceive it with the eyes and commit it to memory; there inside you is what you have committed to memory, tucked away in a corner, as in a granary, as in a treasure, as in some secret place and inner

---

23. See Homily 18, 10.
24. See Gn 1:27. For Augustine's comments on this theme see *The Trinity* IX, 12, 18; XI, 5, 8; XII, ii, 2; XIV, 8,11; 10, 13; 12, 15.
25. See Sermons 21, 2; 52, 16; *The Trinity* I, 3, 4; VIII, 2, 3.
26. *Aciem quandam et obtutum animae tuae*. Elsewhere Augustine will talk of the *acies animi/ae, acies mentis* without any qualifying *quaedam*. It could be paraphrased it as "the concentrated gaze" of the mind—as he says here, its *obtutum*. In *The Trinity* XI, 6, 11; XIV, 6, 8 I translate it as "conscious attention."

sanctuary. You are thinking about something else, your attention is elsewhere; the thing you have seen is in your memory, and you do not really see it, because your thought is directed elsewhere. I will now prove this, speaking as I am to knowledgeable people: I mention Carthage; all of you who know the place instantly "see" Carthage in an interior way. Are there as many Carthages as there are souls among you? You have all seen it through this name; through these two syllables[27] coming forth from my mouth and which are known to you, your ears were touched; the sense of your soul was touched through the body, your mind was turned away from some other preoccupation to what was already in it, and it "saw" Carthage. Was that the moment at which Carthage was formed there? No, it already was there, but it was hidden. Why was it hidden? Because your mind was paying attention to something else. But when your thought was turned back to what was already in your memory, it took on a shape, and a kind of sight was formed in your mind. Previously there was no sight, what there was, was memory; once thought returned to the memory, sight resulted.

So then, your memory demonstrated Carthage to your thought, and what was already there was shown by memory to your thought, which turned back to pay attention to it. So there you are; a demonstration has been made by the memory, sight has been made in thought; and no words have run in between, no sign has been given from the body; you have not given the nod, you have not written, you have not made a sound; and yet thought has seen what memory has shown. They are, however, of the same substance, that which has done the showing and that to which it has shown it.[28] But for your memory to have Carthage in it, this image of it was drunk in through the eyes; you have seen, after all, what you would tuck away in your memory. In the same way you have seen a tree which you remember, a mountain, a river, the face of a friend, of an enemy, of your father, mother, brother, sister, son, neighbor. In the same way you remember the letters written in a book, the book itself, this basilica; all these things you have seen, and having seen them because there they were in front of your eyes, you have committed them to memory. You have as it were deposited them there to

---

27. He actually said "four syllables," *Car-tha-gi-nem*. See *The Trinity* VIII, 6, 9; IX, 6, 10 for the same point.
28. See *The Trinity* X, 11, 18; XI, 3, 6-4, 7.

look at by thinking about them whenever you wanted to, even when they were no longer there in front of your eyes.

You saw Carthage, after all, when you were in Carthage, your soul took in its appearance through your eyes; this appearance has been tucked away in your memory, and as a visitor to Carthage you kept something inside you, which you could refer to even when you were no longer there. All these things you have taken in from outside.[29] The Father does not take in from outside what he shows to the Son; the whole process is carried on inside, because there would not be any creature outside, unless the Father had made it through the Son. Every creature has been made by God; before it was made it just was not. So then, after being made, it was not then seen and retained in the memory so that the Father could show it to the Son, like memory showing something to thought; no, the Father showed it as something to be made, as something to be made the Son saw it, and the Father made it by showing it, since he made it through the Son who was seeing it.

And that is why we should not be alarmed because it says, *but only what he sees the Father doing*; it does not say "showing." This, you see, indicates that it is the same thing for the Father to do as it is to show, so that we may understand from this that the Father makes all things through the Son who sees. Neither this showing nor this seeing is time-bound. Because all times, after all, are made through the Son, they could not, obviously, be shown to him at some particular time as things to be made. Now the Father's showing begets the Son's seeing in the same way as the Father begets the Son. It is the showing, of course, that gives rise to the seeing, not the seeing to the showing. Now if we enjoyed keener, more perfect sight with which to gaze into the mystery, we might perhaps discover that neither is the Father one thing, and his showing another, nor the Son one thing, and his seeing another.[30]

But if we have scarcely been able to explain, scarcely been able to grasp how memory shows to thought what it has taken in from outside, how much less shall we be able to grasp or explain how God the Father shows the Son what he does not have from anywhere else, or how his doing so is not anything other than he is himself! We are so little; I am speaking to you about

---
29. See *The Trinity* XI, 5, 8; 7, 11; XII, 1, 1; XV, 3, 5.
30. See Sermon 126, 15; Homily 18, 10.

what God is not, not showing you what he is; so in order to grasp what he is, what shall we do? Will you ever be able to get it from me, through me? I will say this to little ones, both to you and to myself; there is in fact someone through whom we can learn this. We have just been singing, just been hearing, *Cast your care upon the Lord, and he will nourish you* (Ps 54:22). The reason you cannot do this, O man, is that you are little; if you are a little one, you must be nourished; nourished, you will grow up, and what you could not see as a little one you will see as a grown up. But in order to be nourished, *cast your care upon the Lord, and he will nourish you.*[31]

The bodily raising of the dead will be shown to the Son of Man

12. So now let us run briefly through what remains, and notice here how the Lord suggests what I have explained. *The Father loves the Son and shows him everything he himself does.* He raises souls, but through the Son, so that the souls thus raised up may delight in the substance of God, that is, of the Father and of the Son. *And greater works than these will he show him.* Greater than which? Than healing bodies. We have already explained this beforehand[32] and do not need to attend to it now. Raising up a body for ever, after all, is greater than a bodily healing which was done for a time in the case of that sick man.[33] *And greater works than these will he show him, to fill you with astonishment* (Jn 5:20). *Will show him,* as if in time, so as if to a man in time, because God the Word, through whom all times were made, was not made; but Christ was made man in time. During which consulate and on what day Mary gave birth to Christ—who was conceived by the Holy Spirit—is evident.[34] He was, therefore, made man in time, he through whom, as God, times were made. That is why he will show him, in time, greater works, that is, the raising up of bodies, so that you may be astonished at the resurrection of bodies brought about through the Son.

---

31. See Homily 18, 7.
32. See Homily 19,4-5.
33. At the pool with the five porticoes; see Jn 5:1-9.
34. *Apparet.* Not in the gospels; Luke's dating is much vaguer than this, just *in the days of king Herod* (Lk 1:5), and then *when Quirinius was governor of Syria* (Lk 2:2). He is more precise about the beginning of John the Baptist's ministry (Lk 3:1-2); but nowhere does he or anyone else in the New Testament say in whose consulate any event occurred. (Rome dated events by naming consulates). Some early tradition must have supplied Augustine and his contemporaries with evidence for the date of Christ's birth.

*How one passage refers to the resurrection of souls,
another to the resurrection of bodies*

13. Next he turns back to the resurrection of souls: *For just as the Father raises the dead and gives them life, so too the Son gives life to those whom he will* (Jn 5:21), that is, life according to the spirit. The Father gives life, the Son gives life, the Father to whom he will, the Son to whom he will, but the Father to the same ones as the Son, because *all things were made through him* (Jn 1:3). In fact, *just as the Father raises the dead and gives them life, so too the Son gives life to those whom he will*; this is said about the resurrection of souls;[35] what about the resurrection of bodies? He turns back to that and says, *Neither*, you see, *does the Father judge anyone, but he has given all judgment to the Son* (Jn 5:22). The resurrection of souls is brought about by the eternal and unchanging substance of Father and Son; the resurrection of bodies, on the other hand, is brought about through the efficacy of the Son's humanity, which is not co-eternal with the Father. That is why, when reminding us of the judgment, where the resurrection of bodies will take place, he says, *Neither does the Father judge anyone, but he has given all judgment to the Son*; while about the resurrection of souls he says, *Just as the Father raises the dead and gives them life, so too the Son gives life to those whom he will.*

So the Father and Son together bring about the resurrection of souls; while it is said about the resurrection of bodies, *The Father does not judge anyone, but he has given all judgment to the Son, so that all may honor the Son, just as they honor the Father* (Jn 5:22-23). This returns to the resurrection of souls. *That all may honor the Son.* How? *Just as they honor the Father.* The Son, you see, works the resurrection of souls in the same way as the Father; the Son gives them life in the same way as the Father. So then, for the resurrection of souls, that all may honor the Son just as they honor the Father. What about honor paid for the resurrection of bodies? *Whoever does not honor the Son does not honor not the Father who sent him* (Jn 5:23). He did not say "just as," but simply *honors* and *honors.* The man Christ, you see, is honored, but not "just as" God the Father is. Why not? Because it is in this respect that he said, *The Father is greater than me* (Jn 14:28). But when is the

---

35. The day before, in Homily 19, 6, Augustine referred this verse to the resurrection of bodies; he will also do that some years later in Homily 21, 11. The interpretation of this section of John is more consistent, more lucid, and more rational in those homilies than it is here.

Son honored just as the Father is honored? When *in the beginning was the Word, and the Word was with God, and all things were made through him* (Jn 1:1.3). And that is why in this second honoring—well what precisely did he say? *Whoever does not honor the Son does not honor the Father who sent him;* the Son was only sent insofar as he was made man.

More about the resurrection of souls through the Son of God

14. *Amen, amen, I tell you.* Once more he returns to the resurrection of souls, to help us grasp what he was constantly saying; because we could not follow a word "in flight," as it were, notice this: God's Word stays with us; notice: it is as if he dwells with our infirmities. He returns again to recommend the resurrection of souls. *Amen, amen, I tell you that whoever hears my word and believes the one who sent me has eternal life,* but insofar as it comes from the Father. *That whoever hears my word and believes the one who sent me has eternal life from the Father,* by believing in the one who sent him. *And will not come under judgment, but has crossed over from death to life* (Jn 5:24).

But he is given life by the Father, in whom he believes. What about you, do you not also give life? Notice that the Son too gives life to those whom he will. *Amen, amen, I tell you, that the hour is coming when the dead shall hear the voice of the Son of God, and those who hear shall live* (Jn 5:25). He did not say, "They will believe the one who sent me, and that is why they shall live," but by hearing the voice of the Son of God, those who hear, that is, who obey the Son of God,[36] shall live. So then, they will live both from the Father when they believe the Father and from the Son when they hear the voice of the Son of God. Why will they live from the Father and also live from the Son? *For just as the Father has life in himself, so has he given the Son the possession of life in himself* (Jn 5:26).

The resuscitation of bodies through the Son of Man

15. He has finished what he has to say about the resurrection of souls; it remains for him to say something more definite about the resurrection of

---

36. In Homily 19 Augustine dwelt at some length on how hearing (*audio*) in this context means obeying (*obaudio*).

bodies. *And he gave him authority also to pass judgment*; not only to raise up souls through faith and wisdom, but *also to pass judgment*. But why this? *Because he is the Son of Man* (Jn 5:27). So the Father then does something through the Son of Man, which he does not do from his very substance, in which the Son is equal to him: for example, his being born, his being crucified, his dying, his rising again; none of these things, after all, happened to the Father. So also with the resuscitation of bodies. For the Father brings about the resuscitation of souls from his substance through the substance of the Son, because there he is his equal; souls, indeed, become participants in that unchanging light, but bodies do not; but the Father brings about the resuscitation of bodies through the Son of man.[37] *And he also gave him authority*, you see, *to pass judgment, because he is the Son of Man*; this agrees with what he said earlier: *For neither does the Father judge anyone*.

And to show that he said this about the resurrection of bodies he said, *Do not be surprised at this, because the hour is coming*. Not "it now is,"[38] but *the hour is coming, in which all who are in the tombs* (you already heard more than enough about this yesterday) *shall hear his voice and come forth*. And where to? To judgment? *Those who have done good to the resurrection of life; those who have wrought evil to the resurrection of judgment* (Jn 5:28-29). And are you doing all this by yourself, because the Father has given all judgment to the Son, and does not himself judge anyone? "I," he says, "do it." But how do you do it? *I cannot do anything of myself; I judge as I hear, and my judgment is just* (Jn 5:30).

When it was a matter of the resurrection of souls he did not say "I hear" but *I see*. "I hear," after all, rather implies a command of the Father telling him to do something. So now then as a man, as one than whom *the Father is greater*,[39] speaking from *the form of a slave*, not from *the form of God* (Phil 2:7.6), *I judge as I hear, and my judgment is just*. What makes a man's judgment just? My brothers and sisters, pay close attention: *Because I am not seeking my own will, but the will of the one who sent me* (Jn 5:30).

---

37. See Homily 19, 15-19.
38. As in Jn 5:24.
39. See Jn 14:28.

Homily 24

On John 6:1-14[1]

God performs miracles because we have become so inured to his wonderful works in nature

1. The miracles which our Lord Jesus Christ performed are indeed divine works, and, from visible things and events, they encourage the human mind to come to some understanding of God. God, after all, is not the kind of substance that can be seen with the eyes, and his miracles, by which he governs the whole world and administers every creature, have grown cheap in our estimation through their regularity, so that almost no one bothers to pay attention to the wonderful and stupendous action of God in every grain of seed.[2] So with his usual kindheartedness he kept back some things for himself, to perform them at a suitable time apart from the usual course and order of nature, so that wonders that were not greater than the daily ones, but just more out of the ordinary, would amaze people who had ceased to value those that occur every day.[3]

Governing the whole cosmos, after all, is a greater marvel than satisfying five thousand men on five loaves of bread, and yet nobody marvels at it; people marvel at the latter because it is uncommon. Who, after all, even now feeds the whole world but the one who creates the crops from a few grains? So, on this occasion, the Lord acted as God. Just as he multiplies a few grains into the crops, so too did he multiply the five loaves in his hands. For there was power in the hands of Christ.[4] Those five loaves were seeds of a kind, not indeed committed to the earth but seeds which were multiplied by the one who made the earth.[5]

Something therefore was brought to the attention of the senses whereby the mind would be alerted, something displayed before the eyes whereby the understanding could be exercised, so that we might marvel at the invisible God through his visible works; and so, being thus raised up to faith and puri-

---
1. Preached just a few days after Homily 23.
2. See Homily 9, 1.
3. See Homily 8, 1-2; Sermons 130, 1; 252, 1; *The Trinity* III, 9, 19.
4. See Homily 9, 5.
5. See Sermon 126, 2-4.

fied through faith, we might even long to see in an invisible manner the one we recognized through things visible as invisible.

Christ's miracles are like the script of a master scribe:
beautiful to look at and admire and meant to be read and understood

2. It is not enough all the same just to observe this truth in the miracles of Christ. Let us question the miracles themselves about what they are telling us about Christ. For, if properly understood, they have their own language. In fact, because Christ is himself the Word of God, even the deeds of the Word are a word for us. So then, let us inquire about this miracle, since we have heard that it was great, and ask how deep is its meaning; let us not just delight in its appearance; let us also scan its depths. After all, there is an inner meaning to the outer form that fills us with wonder.

We have seen, we have looked upon something great, something outstanding and altogether divine, which could only be done by God; the deed has led us to admire the doer. But if, for example, we were to look at the beautiful letters on the pages of some book, we would not be satisfied with admiring the scribe's skilful fingers in producing such a regular, neat and even script, without also reading what he was saying to us with it. Well, in the same way anyone who just takes a look at this deed is delighted by its beauty and filled with admiration for the craftsman; anyone though who takes the trouble to understand it is after a fashion reading it. Pictures, after all, are looked at in one way, letters in another. When you see a picture, that is all there is to it, to see it and admire it; when you see letters, that is not all there is to it, because you are being urged also to read them.

Even if you do not know how to read some letters when you see them, you say, do you not, "What are we to suppose is written here?" You inquire what it is, when you have already seen something; the person you ask to help you understand what you have seen will show you something else, something more. He has eyes of one sort, you of another. Do you not both see the marks on the page in the same way? But you do not both know the signs in the same way. So you, then, see them and admire; he sees, admires, reads and understands. Because, then, we have seen this miracle and admired it, let us read it and come to understand it.[6]

---

6. See Sermon 98, 3.

The meaning of the mountain; how the sacrament
of the five loaves will speak to us after Philip has been tested

3. The Lord is on the mountain;[7] let us more fully understand that the Lord on the mountain means the Word on high. Accordingly what was done on the mountain is not like something down to earth or lowly, not something to step over and to pass by casually, but to which we should raise our eyes.

He saw the crowds, he realized they were hungry, he fed them out of the kindness of his heart, not just in virtue of his goodness but of his power as well. What use, after all, would goodness alone have been, where there was no bread on which to feed the hungry multitudes? Unless power had been joined to goodness, that crowd would have remained fasting and hungry. Finally, even the disciples, who were with the Lord and who were hungry, wanted to feed the crowds,[8] so that they would not remain with empty stomachs, but they had nothing to feed them with. The Lord asked them where they might buy enough bread to feed the crowds. And scripture adds, *But he said this by way of testing him,* namely the disciple Philip, to whom he addressed the question; *for he himself knew what he was going to do* (Jn 6:6).

So what was the point of testing the disciple, if not to show up his ignorance? And perhaps by demonstrating the disciple's ignorance, he was signifying something. What this is, in fact, will be obvious when the actual sacrament[9] of the five loaves begins to talk to us and to indicate what it signifies; I mean, we shall see then why the Lord, on this occasion, wished to manifest the disciple's ignorance by asking him about something that he already knew. For sometimes we ask a question about something we do not know, wishing to hear the answer in order to learn; sometimes we ask about what we do know, wishing to find out whether the one we are asking also knows the answer. The Lord of course knew both things; he knew the answer to his question, being quite aware, after all, of what he was going to do; and in the same way he knew that Philip did not know. So why else did

---

7. See Jn 6:3. Augustine is treating this verse as a kind of scene-setting; so its deeper meaning governs all that follows: the Word will be speaking to us in signs.
8. See Mk 6:35-36, and the parallel passages in Mt and Lk.
9. *Sacramentum* in the full Augustinian sense of a sacred, significant action or thing. That usually applies to what is found in the scriptures.

he ask, if not to show up the man's ignorance? And why he did this, as I have just said, we shall shortly understand.[10]

A short account of the miracle

4. Andrew said, *There is a lad here who has five loaves, and two fish; but what are these for so many?* (Jn 6:9) When Philip was questioned, he had said that 200 denarii would not be enough to buy bread to feed such a huge crowd; whereupon a boy with five barley loaves and two fish was there. *Jesus said, Make the people sit down. There was plenty of grass there, and almost five thousand people sat down. The Lord Jesus, then, took the loaves, gave thanks,* directed them, the loaves were broken and set before those sitting down to eat[11]—no longer just five loaves, but what had been added by the one who created the increase. *And the same for the fish as much as was sufficient.* (Jn 6:10-11) It is too little that such a crowd was given its fill; there were even fragments left over, and he ordered these to be collected, so that they should not be wasted; and *they filled twelve baskets with the fragments* (Jn 6:13).

The sacramental elements of the story speak;
the barley loaves, the lad, the two fish

5. Let us run through this briefly. The five loaves are to be understood as the five books of Moses;[12] it is right that they were not wheat loaves but barley, because they belong to the Old Testament. You know, of course, that barley was created in a way that makes it hard to get at the kernel; for the kernel is clothed with a hairy husk, and it is tenacious and clinging, so that it is stripped with great effort. Such is the letter of the Old Testament, clothed in the husks of material, this-worldly symbols;[13] but if one does get to its kernel or heart, it nourishes and satisfies.

So then, some boy brought five loaves and two fish; if we inquire who this boy may have been, perhaps he was the people of Israel; he carried the bread

---

10. See section 5 below.
11. The Latin word here and earlier on is *discumbere*, which means "to recline at table." So in our modern context it means more than just "sit down;" precisely "sit down to eat."
12. Genesis, Exodus, Leviticus, Numbers, Deuteronomy. See Sermon 130, 1.
13. Rather more succinctly, *carnalium sacramentorum* in the Latin.

as a child and did not eat it. The things he carried, after all, were a burden when they were all wrapped up; once opened, they were nourishing.

But the two fish, it seems, represent for us those two eminent Old Testament figures, who were anointed to sanctify and to govern the people, the priest and the king. And the one whom they prefigured eventually came in mystery; the one who finally came was concealed by the barley husk and revealed in the barley kernel. He came, one man bearing in himself each of these roles, of priest and of king; that of priest insofar as he offered himself to God as victim for our sakes; that of king, insofar as we are ruled by him; and then what was carried all wrapped up was opened.

Let thanks be given to him, for he realized in himself everything that was promised through the Old Testament. And he gave orders to break the bread; by being broken the loaves were multiplied. Nothing could be more true: to how many more books have those five books of Moses—by being commented upon, by being broken open, and explained—given rise! But the ignorance of the first people, the people of whom it is said, *As long as Moses is read, there is a veil placed over their hearts* (2 Cor 3:15), was wrapped up in that barley. And the veil, in fact, had not yet been taken away, because Christ had not yet come; the veil of the temple had not yet been torn to ribbons as he was hanging on the cross.[14] So it is because the people's ignorance was embodied in the law that the Lord—by testing him—showed up the ignorance of the disciple.

The meaning of the crowd of five thousand, and of the twelve baskets of fragments

6. No detail, therefore is pointless, everything has a meaning, but someone has to understand what that is. For instance, even the number of the people who ate signified the people which was established under the law. Why, after all, were there five thousand of them, if not because they were under the law, the law which is explained in the five books of Moses? That is why the sick were laid out by those five porticoes and were not cured.[15] But the one who cured the sick man there fed the crowds here on five loaves. That is also why they were reclining on the grass; theirs was a

---

14. See Mt 27:51; Sermon 300, 3-4.
15. See Jn 5:2-9; Homily 17, 2.

wisdom of the flesh, and they were taking their ease in the things of the flesh. *All flesh, you see, is grass* (Is 40:6).

But what are those fragments, but that which this people could not eat? Let them be seen as more mysterious truths which the crowd cannot grasp. What remains, then, but to entrust these more mysterious things—which the multitude cannot grasp—to the intelligence, to those capable of also teaching others, such as the apostles were? That is why twelve baskets were filled.

This deed was both amazing because it was extraordinary and useful because it was spiritual. Those who saw it at that time were amazed; we on the other hand are not amazed when we hear the account of it. It was done, I mean, for them to see, while it has been written down for us to hear. What their eyes could do for them, faith is able to do for us. We discern with our minds what we have not been able to see with our eyes, and we have an advantage over them because about us it was said, *Blessed are those who do not see, and yet believe* (Jn 20:29). I must add, though, that maybe we have also understood what that crowd did not understand; and we have truly been fed, because we have been able to get at the kernel of the barley.

Jesus a prophet, as the Lord of the prophets;
just as he is an angel, and the Lord of the angels

7. Finally, what did the people who saw all this think about it? *When the people*, it says, *had seen what a sign he had done, they started saying, This man is truly a prophet* (Jn 6:14). They may have still been thinking of Christ as a prophet because they were reclining on the grass.[16] But he was the Lord of the prophets, the one who inspired the prophets, the one who sanctified the prophets; even so he was also a prophet, since Moses had been told, *I will raise up for them a prophet like yourself* (Dt 18:18), like him as regards the flesh, not as regards dignity; and that this promise of the Lord's might be understood as referring to Christ, it is openly stated and explained in the Acts of the Apostles.[17] And the Lord said about himself, *A prophet is not without honor, except in his own country* (Mk 6:4). The Lord

---

16. That is, because they were still thinking according to the flesh. So they were thinking he was a prophet in the same way and the same sense as the Old Testament prophets.
17. See Acts 3:22.

is a prophet, and the Lord is the Word of God, and no prophet prophesies without the Word of God; the Word of God is with the prophets, and the Word of God is a prophet. Previous ages were thought worthy of inspired prophets and prophets filled by the Word of God; we have been thought worthy of a prophet who is the very Word of God.

Christ however is a prophet, the Lord of prophets, in the same way as Christ is an angel, the Lord of angels. For he was also called the *angel of great counsel* (Is 9:6 LXX). And yet what does the prophet Isaiah say in another place? *That not an ambassador nor an angel, but he himself will come and save them* (Is 63:9 LXX); that is, to save them he will not send an ambassador, will not send an angel, but will come in person. Who will come? The angel himself. Certainly not acting through an angel, except insofar as this one is an angel in such a way as to be also the Lord of angels. In Latin, in fact, angels are heralds. If Christ had had nothing to announce, he would not be called an angel. He exhorted us to believe, and by faith to lay hold of eternal life; he announced something present, foretold something to come in the future. Insofar as he announced something present, he was an angel; insofar as he foretold something to come, he was a prophet; insofar as *the Word was made flesh* (Jn 1:14), he was, of both angels and prophets, the Lord.

Homily 25

On John 6:15-44[1]

*Why the five thousand of yesterday's reading
must have been fed on lower ground, not on the mountain*

1. This gospel reading follows the one from yesterday and so it will be the focus of the sermon which is due to you today. After the performance of that miracle by which Jesus fed five thousand men on five loaves, when the crowds were so astounded that they said he was the great prophet who was coming into the world, this is what follows: *So when Jesus realized that they were coming[2] to seize him and make him king, he fled once more to the mountain by himself alone* (Jn 6:15). So we are being given to understand that when the Lord had been seated up on the mountain with his disciples and had seen the crowd coming toward him, he had gone down from the mountain and fed the crowd at some lower level. I mean, how could he flee up there again, if he had not previously come down from the mountain? So it is significant in some way or other that the Lord came down from the high ground to feed the crowd.[3] He fed the crowd and went up again.

*All the details of Christ's actions are words;
he is here refusing to let his kingdom be anticipated*

2. Why though did he go up, when he realized that they wanted to seize him and make him king? What was the point, after all? Was he not, in fact, king, this man who was afraid of being made king? He most certainly was; and not of the sort either that could be made king by human beings, but the kind of king who would give human beings the kingdom. Is not Jesus, whose actions are words,[4] pointing something out to us here as well? So then, was the fact that they wanted to seize him and make him king, and the

---

1. Preached the day after Homily 24 and a few days before Homily 26.
2. Reading *quia venirent* with the Maurists, instead of *quia venerant*, "that they had come."
3. Augustine does not tell us what he thinks this "coming down" and "going up" might signify. Perhaps it would not have been fitting to feed them on the heights, because feeding was an "earthly sacrament," a sign of the presence of Christ through his Church. Any teaching given on the heights was to be about the mystery of God, about the Father and the Son and the Holy Spirit in their eternal relationships and substance.
4. See Homily 24, 2.

fact that he fled up the mountain by himself alone for that reason, was that fact silent, does it say nothing, does it signify nothing; is that it?

Or was it perhaps that the desire to seize him would have anticipated the time of his kingdom; could that be it? He had come at this time, then, not to reign already in the way he will reign, about which we say, *Your kingdom come* (Mt 6:10). Indeed, he reigns eternally as king with the Father insofar as he is the Son of God, the Word of God, the Word through whom all things were made.[5] The prophets though had foretold his kingdom insofar as Christ was also made man, and in turn made his faithful believers into Christians. So there will be a kingdom of Christians, which is now being gathered together, now being acquired, which is now being bought by the blood of Christ. The time will come when his kingdom will be manifest, when the glory of his saints will be disclosed after the judgment over which he will preside, the judgment which earlier on he said the Son of Man was going to pass.[6]

This is the kingdom of which the apostle also said, *When he has handed over the kingdom to God and the Father* (1 Cor 15:24); about which he himself also said, *Come, you blessed of my Father, receive the kingdom which has been prepared for you from the beginning of the world* (Mt 25:34). The disciples, though, and the crowd who believed in him, thought that he had come that he might already reign; wanting to seize him and make him king was wanting to anticipate the time which he was keeping to himself, so as to make it known at the right moment and declare it rightly at the end of the world.

Proof from other passages that the kingdom
in its fullness was not to be anticipated

3. Know now that they wanted to make him king, that is, to anticipate and already have the kingdom of Christ out in the open; first, however, he had to be judged and only then would he judge.[7] When he had been crucified, even those who were hoping in him had lost all hope of his resurrection; on rising from the dead he found two of them talking to each other of

---

5. Cf. Jn 1:3.
6. See Homilies 19, 16.18.19; 23, 15.
7. See Homily 19, 16; 28, 6.

their despair and discussing in mournful tones what had happened. He appeared to them as a stranger, and while their eyes were kept from recognizing him, he joined in their conversation, and they, in telling him what they were talking about, said that he had been a great prophet in word and deed and had been put to death by the chief priests; *and we*, they went on, *were hoping that he was the one who would redeem Israel* (Lk 24:21).

You were right to hope; in truth were you hoping: the redemption of Israel is in him. But why are you rushing? You want to seize him—something that is also indicated by another text; when the disciples were questioning him about the end, they said to him, *Is this the time at which you will manifest yourself, and when will the kingdom of Israel come to be?* (Acts 1:6) They were longing for it already, already wanting it; that is what their wanting to seize him and make him king meant. But he told the disciples that for the time being he alone was going to ascend. *It is not for you*, he said, *to know times which the Father has placed under his own authority; but you shall receive power from on high, the Holy Spirit coming down upon you, and you shall be witnesses to me in Jerusalem, and in the whole of Judea and Samaria, and as far as the ends of the earth* (Acts 1:7-8). You want me to display the kingdom here and now; first let me gather together what I am to display; you love the heights and you shall gain the heights; but follow me first in humility.

That was what had also been foretold of him: *And the peoples shall congregate around you, and you, for their sake, return on high* (Ps 7:7). That is: so that the assembly of peoples might gather around you, that you might assemble many together, return to the heights. That is what he did; he fed them and went back up.

The deeper meaning of saying that he fled

4. But why does it say that *he fled*? After all, he would not be caught if he really did not wish to be, would not be seized if he did not wish to be,[8] would not even be recognized if he did not wish to be. I mean, to convince you that this action was symbolic, not done out of necessity, but with the intention of signifying some mystery, you will shortly see in what follows

---

8. See Homily 11, 2.

that he showed himself to these very same crowds who were seeking him, and that he talked to them and told them many things, starting a long discussion with them about the heavenly bread; was he not arguing about the bread with the very same people from whom he had fled to escape being caught by them? So could he not have made sure they did not lay hands on him that earlier time, just as he did later on, when he was talking to them? So then, he meant to signify something by fleeing. What then is the meaning of *he fled*? That it was impossible to understand his lofty greatness.[9] If there is anything, after all, that you do not understand, you say, "It flees from me."[10] So then *he fled again up the mountain by himself alone* (Jn 6:15), the firstborn from the dead, mounting above all the heavens and interceding for us.[11]

The boat in difficulties on the lake represents the Church in the world at the present time

5. Meanwhile, the great priest stood alone on the heights, the one who entered within the veil[12] while the people stood outside—that priest of the old law, in fact, who did this once a year, was the one who prefigured him. So while he stood on the heights, what was happening to the disciples down below in the boat? For that boat prefigured the Church, while he stood on the heights. But if we do not first understand what was happening in that boat as referring to the Church, then those things had no meaning, but were just happenings. If however we see the true meaning of these signs verified in the Church, then it becomes clear that the deeds of Christ really are a kind of language.[13]

But as it had grown late, the gospel says, *his disciples went down to the sea; and when they had got into a boat, they came across the sea to Capernaum* (Jn 6:16-17). Right away, he describes as finished something that happened later on. *They came across the sea to Capernaum*. Then he goes back to explain how they came, because they crossed the lake by boat. And while they were going by boat toward the place which he has already

---

9. See Sermon 75:3; Homily 24, 3.
10. We would say, "It escapes me."
11. See Col 1:18; Eph 4:10; Rom 8:34.
12. See Homily 17, 11.
13. See Homily 24, 2. See also *Teaching Christianity*, III, 22, 32; Sermon 2, 7.

said they had reached, he goes back to explain what was happening: *It had already grown dark, and Jesus had not yet come to them* (Jn 6:17)—for sure it was dark, because the Light had not come. *It had already grown dark, and Jesus had not yet come to them.*

As the end of the world approaches, errors increase, terrors multiply, wickedness spreads, infidelity increases. Then the light, which John the evangelist identifies clearly and often as charity, such that he even says, *The one who hates his brother is in darkness* (1 Jn 2:11)—the light is time and again extinguished; the darkness of hate among brothers spreads further day by day—and Jesus has not yet come. How can we tell that it is spreading? *Because evildoing thrives, the charity of many will grow cold* (Mt 24:12). Darkness is increasing, and Jesus has not come. Growing darkness, charity growing cold, thriving wickedness, these are the waves tossing the boat about; storms and winds are the cries of adversaries. That is what makes charity cold, what increases the waves and rocks the boat.

The significance of the number of furlongs

6. *With a strong wind blowing, the sea was rising* (Jn 6:18). Darkness was spreading, understanding was decreasing, evildoing increasing. *So when they had rowed about twenty-five or thirty furlongs* (Jn 6:19). Meanwhile they were advancing, making progress, and neither those winds and storms nor the waves and darkness kept the boat from making progress or managed to break it up and sink it; rather, in the midst of all these evils, it kept on going. Indeed, because evildoing has flourished and the charity of many is growing cold, the waves are rising, the darkness is spreading, the wind is raging; but all the same the boat is advancing. *For the one who perseveres to the end is the one who will be saved* (Mk 13:13).

We must not ignore the actual number of furlongs. After all, what is said—*When they had rowed twenty-five or thirty furlongs, then Jesus came to them* (Jn 6:19)—could not be without meaning. It would have been enough to say *twenty-five*, enough to say *thirty*, especially as it was only a rough estimate, not a precise statement. Would the truth have been imperiled in this rough guess if he had said "about thirty" or "about twenty-five furlongs"? But in fact out of twenty-five he made thirty. Let us first look into the number twenty-five.

What is it made up of, where does it come from? From five; that number five belongs to the law. There are those five books of Moses, there are those five porticoes surrounding the sick people, there are the five loaves feeding five thousand people.[14] So then, the number twenty-five signifies the law, since five by five, that is five times five, makes twenty-five, the square of five. But before the gospel came this law was lacking in complete perfection. Now perfection is to be understood in the number six.[15] That is why God completed the world in six days, and why those five are multiplied by six—so that the law may be fulfilled by the gospel—to make thirty out of six times five.

So then, Jesus comes to those who fulfill the law. He comes, but how does he come? Trampling on the waves, keeping all the puffed-up pretensions of the world under his feet, putting down all the high-and-mighty of the world. This happens as time passes and the older the world gets. Trials are on the increase in this world, evils on the increase, grinding oppression on the increase, all these things are accumulating; Jesus is crossing over, trampling the waves under foot.

Jesus walking on the water is Jesus overcoming the world

7. And yet so great are the tribulations that even those who have come to believe in Jesus, and who are striving to persevere until the end, are terrified of falling away; though Christ is trampling on the waves, putting down the ambitious and the high-and-mighty of the world, Christians are terrified. Were not all these things foretold them? Understandably were they afraid, even at Jesus walking on the waves, just as Christians, in spite of their hope in the world to come, on seeing the high-and-mighty of this world being put down are frequently disturbed over this turning upside down of human affairs.[16]

They open the gospel, they open the scriptures, and there they find all these things foretold, because the Lord does all this. He puts down the high-and-mighty of the world, so that he may be glorified by the humble

---

14. See Jn 5:2-3; 6:9-11.
15. See Homily 9, 6; also 17, 4 where the perfection of the number six is explained.
16. Berrouard suggests, correctly in my opinion, that Augustine has in mind the dismay, the crisis of faith, felt by so many Christians over the sack of Rome in 410 by Alaric and his Goths. See Sermons 81, 8-9; 113A, 11; 296, 6.9-11.

and lowly. About these great powers it was foretold, *The strongest cities shall you destroy* (Mic 5:11; Sir 28:14 LXX), and, *The sabers of the enemy have come to nothing at the end, and their cities you have destroyed* (Ps 9:6). So what are you afraid of, Christians? Christ is speaking: *It is I, do not be afraid. So then they willingly took him aboard the boat,* rejoicing and reassured on recognizing him. *And immediately the boat was at the land they were going to.* (Jn 6:20-21) The end came on landing; from the waves to dry ground, from a turbulent sea to solid footing, from being on the way to the end.

Various points to emphasize the sacramental significance both of the five thousand and of Jesus going up the mountain

8. *The next day the crowd which had stayed on the other side of the sea,* from which the disciples had come, *saw that there had only been one small boat there, and that he had not gone aboard the boat with his disciples, but his disciples had gone off alone; other boats, however, came over from Tiberias, near the place where they had eaten the bread, when the Lord had given thanks. So then, when the crowds saw that Jesus was not there, nor his disciples, they got into the small boats, and came to Capernaum looking for Jesus.* (Jn 6:22-24)

They had, all the same, been given an inkling of such a great miracle, for they had seen that only his disciples had boarded the boat, and that there was not any other boat there. Later, though, boats did come near the place where they had eaten the bread, and in them the crowds followed him. So then, he had not gone aboard with his disciples, there was no other boat there at the time; how then did Jesus suddenly get to the other side of the sea, if not by walking over the sea, to emphasize the miracle of the loaves?[17]

9. *And when the crowds found him.* Look at him, presenting himself to the crowds which he had feared would seize him, and from which he had escaped up the mountain. This fully confirms and suggests to us that all

---

17. Literally, "to demonstrate the miracle." What follows in paragraph 10 will show that Augustine is referring to the miracle of the loaves and not to the walking on the water. In that way he can show the importance of the previous miracle and suggest that there is more to it than the mere fact that it took place.

this had been said as a great mystery which means something.[18] Look, here is the man who had fled up the mountain to escape the crowds; is this not the one who is now talking to the crowds? Now let them catch him, let them make him king now. *And when they found him on the other side of the sea, they said to him, Rabbi, when did you come here?* (Jn 6:25)

Work for the food which abides to eternal life

10. He then, after the symbolic sacrament of the miracle, also adds a word so that, if possible, those who were fed might be nourished, and those whose stomachs he satisfied with loaves might have their minds satisfied with his words—as long as they take them in. And if they do not receive those words, let what they do not take in be picked up, lest any fragments should be lost.[19] So then, let him talk, and let us listen: *Jesus answered and said, Amen, amen, I tell you, you are looking for me, not because you have seen signs, but because you ate of my loaves* (Jn 6:26). You are looking for me because of the flesh, not because of the spirit. How many there are who do not look for Jesus, except when they want him to do them a temporal favor![20] Someone has a business, he seeks the intervention of the clergy; someone else is pursued by a man stronger that he is, and he takes refuge in the church; another wants a plea made to someone with whom he has little influence; one wants this, another that. The church is filled every day with such people.[21] Rarely does anyone seek Jesus for the sake of Jesus.

You are looking for me, not because you have seen signs, but because you ate of my loaves. Work not for the food which perishes, but for that which abides to eternal life. You are all seeking me for the sake of something else, not for my own sake. You see, he is hinting that he is himself the

---

18. As Berrouard points out, one of the "laws" of mystical, sacramental, spiritual interpretation is in play when we are, as it were, forced to such an interpretation by the incoherence of a narrative, which does not make sense in literal terms.
19. See Sermons 56, 10; 57, 7; 58, 5; 59, 6, all on the Lord's Prayer, in which the petition *Give us this day our daily bread* is treated in a manner similar to the way Augustine is here interpreting the feeding of the five thousand—bread for the body being a symbol, or a sacrament of the bread of the word broken for the mind and heart. But both have to be "taken in," or eaten, if they are to nourish either body or spirit.
20. See Sermon 47, 18, where Augustine has a good word for those Christians who do not seek the Lord for personal gain, i.e., to find influential friends or a good wife!
21. It was the bishop's help they were almost always seeking, help that Augustine never refused, although this sort of thing took up a huge amount of his time and energy.

food, and this will become as clear as daylight in what follows. *Which the Son of man will give you.* (Jn 6:26-27) You there were expecting, I am sure, to eat bread again, again to sit down, again to have your fill. But he had said, *not the food which perishes, but that which abides to eternal life*, just as he had said to that Samaritan woman, *If you knew who is asking you for a drink, you would perhaps make a request of him, and he would give you living water.* This was when she said, "Where will you get it from, seeing that you have not got a bucket, and the well is deep?"[22] He answered the Samaritan woman, *If you knew who is asking you for a drink, you would have asked him for the water from which anyone who drinks will not be thirsty any more; for anyone who drinks of this water here will get thirsty again.* (Jn 4:10-14) And she was delighted and wanted to receive it, as if she were not going to suffer bodily thirst, she who tired herself out with the labor of coming to draw water, and by this kind of conversation she reached the point of spiritual drinking. Well, exactly the same thing is happening here.

The Son of Man is also sealed with the sign of the Son of God

11. So then, *this food which does not perish, but which abides to eternal life, is what the Son of Man will give you; for God the Father has signed him with his seal* (Jn 6:27). Do not regard this Son of Man in the same way as the other sons of men, of whom it is said, *But the sons of men shall hope in the protection of your wings* (Ps 35:7). This Son of Man—set apart by a special grace of the Spirit, son of man as regards the flesh, and set apart from the tally of human beings—is the Son of Man. This Son of Man is the Son of God, this man is also God. In another place, where he is questioning the disciples, he says, *Who do people say that I, the Son of Man, am? And they said, Some say John, others Elijah, others Jeremiah, or one of the prophets. He in turn said, but you, who do you say that I am? Peter answered, You are the Christ, the Son of the living God.* (Mt 16:13-16) He himself said he was the Son of Man, and Peter said he was the Son of the living God.

---

22. See, however, Homily 15, 10-14.

Rightly he called to mind what he had shown us out of kindness, while Peter called to mind that he remained in his glory. The Word of God points out his humility, a man acknowledges the glory of his Lord. And truly, brothers and sisters, that is, I think, right; he humbled himself for our sakes, let us in turn declare his glory; not for his own sake, after all, is he the Son of Man, but for ours. So then, he was the Son of Man in this way when *the Word was made flesh, and took up residence among us* (Jn 1:14).

That, you see, is why *the Father signed him with his seal*. What is the point of signing with a seal, if not to mark something as your own? I mean, to seal is to mark something so that it will not be confused with other things. Whatever you seal with your mark, you therefore place that sign so that it will not be confused with other things and then not be recognizable to you. So then, *the Father signed him with his seal*.

What does that mean, *he signed*?

He gave him something to prevent his being compared with the rest of humankind. That is why it is said of him, *God, your God, has anointed you with the oil of exultation, ahead of your fellows* (Ps 44:7). So what does it mean to sign, then? To treat as special, that is, *ahead of your fellows*.

"And so," he says, "do not scorn me because I am the Son of Man; instead, seek from me *food which does not perish, but which abides to eternal life*. I am the Son of Man, you see, in such a way that I am not just one of you; I am the Son of Man such that the Father, God, has signed me."

What does that mean, *he signed*?

"Has given me something that was mine, so that I would not be confused with the human race, but through me the human race will be freed."

The work of faith; comparison with Moses and the manna

12. *So they said to him then, What shall we do, to work the works of God?* For he had said to them, *Work not for the food which perishes but for that which abides to eternal life. What shall we do?* they say. "What observances must we keep, if we are to comply with this instruction?" Jesus answered and said to them, *This is the work of God, to believe in the one whom he has sent.* (Jn 6:27-29) So this is to eat *the food which does not perish, but which abides to eternal life*. Why are you getting your teeth and stomachs ready? Believe and you have eaten.

Faith indeed is distinguished from works, as the apostle says, *A person is justified by faith without the works of the law* (Rom 3:28); and there are works which appear to be good, without any faith in Christ, but they are not good, because they are not seen in relation to him, the end from which they are good. *For the end of the law is Christ, for the justification of every believer* (Rom 10:4). That is why he did not wish to distinguish faith from work, but said that faith is itself a work. This is the faith, after all, *which works through love* (Gal 5:6). He did not say, "This is your work," but *This is the work of God, that you believe in the one whom he has sent*, so that *whoever boasts may boast in the Lord* (1 Cor 1:31).

So, because he invited them to faith, they were still looking for signs to lead them to believe. Notice whether *the Jews ask for signs* (1 Cor 1:22). *So they said to him, What sign then do you give, for us to see and believe you? What work are you doing?* (Jn 6:30) So, was it too little to have fed them on five loaves? They were of course aware of this feat, but they preferred the manna from heaven to this food. But the Lord Jesus spoke of himself as superior to Moses. Moses, after all, had not dared to claim that, on his own, he could give them *food which does not perish, but which abides to eternal life*. This man was promising something more than Moses. Obviously, Moses had promised a kingdom and a land flowing with milk and honey, temporal peace, abundance of children, bodily health, and all the rest; they were indeed temporal goods, but they were, all the same, symbols of spiritual goods because they were promised to the old man in the Old Testament.[23]

So then, the Jews were listening carefully to the promises made through Moses and to the promises made through Christ as well. The first was promising a full stomach here on earth, but on food that perishes; the second was promising *food which does not perish, but which abides to eternal life*. They listened to him promising more, but it was as if they did not yet see him doing greater works. And so they were aware of the kinds of things Moses did, and wanted this man, who was promising such great things, to perform something more. *What*, they said, *will you do, for us to believe you?* And to prove to you that they were comparing those old miracles to this miracle, and that they judged what Jesus did as less than those, they said, *Our fathers ate manna in the desert.*

---

23. See Homily 3, 19.

But what is manna? Perhaps you have little respect for it.

As it is written: *He gave them manna to eat* (Jn 6:31). Our fathers received bread from heaven through Moses. Moses did not tell them, *Work for the food which does not perish.* You are promising *food which does not perish, but which abides to eternal life*, but you are not performing works like those that Moses did. He did not give them mere barley loaves, but he gave them manna from heaven.

The true bread from heaven, who gives life to the world

13. So Jesus said to them, *Moses did not give you bread from heaven, but my Father has given you bread from heaven. For the true bread is that which comes down from heaven and gives life to the world.* (Jn 6:32-33) So that bread is true which gives life to the world, and he himself is the food about which he spoke a little earlier on: *Work for the food which does not perish, but which abides to eternal life.* So then, that is what the manna signified and all those signs were mine as well. You delighted in my signs; have you no time for the one signified by them?

So Moses did not give bread from heaven; God gives bread. Which bread? Manna, perhaps? No, but the bread which manna stood for, namely the Lord Jesus himself. *My Father gives you the true bread. For the bread of God is the one who came down from heaven and gives life to the world. So they said to him, Lord give us this bread always.* (Jn 6:32-34) Like that Samaritan woman, who was told, *Whoever drinks of this water will never be thirsty*, right away she took it in a material sense, but still eager to be rid of a need, she said, *Give me, Lord, some of this water*[24] (Jn 4:14-15); so too these people: *Lord, give us this bread*, which refreshes us and never runs out.[25]

Coming to Jesus, entering the inner shrine

14. *But Jesus said to them, I am the bread of life; whoever comes to me will not be hungry, and whoever believes in me will never be thirsty* (Jn 6:35). *Whoever comes to me* means the same as *whoever believes in me*; and when he says *will not be hungry* that means the same as *will never be*

---

24. See Homily 15, 15.17.
25. An attempt to echo the much neater word play in the Latin: *qui nos reficiat, nec deficiat.*

thirsty. After all, both signify that fulfillment which is eternal and where there is no need.[26] You long for the bread from heaven; you have it in front of you and you do not eat. *But I have told you that you have seen me and have not believed in me* (Jn 6:36). But I am not the one who has lost the people; is it not your infidelity, rather, that has nullified God's fidelity?[27]

Look, in fact, at what comes next: *All that the Father gives me will come to me, and I will not cast out the one who comes to me* (Jn 6:37). What is that inside like, where there is no casting out? A vast inner shrine,[28] and a lovely quiet place. O that inner quiet, where there is no boredom, no bitterness from evil thoughts, no harassment by temptations and sorrows! Is this not the place of inner quiet which will be entered by the servant who has well deserved it, to whom the Lord is going to say, *Enter into the joy of your Lord* (Mt 25:21.23)?

Not my will, but the will of him who sent me; *the divine humility of the new Adam*

15. *And I will not cast out the one who comes to me, because I have come down from heaven, not to do my own will, but the will of him who sent me* (Jn 6:37-38). So that then is the reason why you will not cast out the one who comes to you, because you have come down from heaven, not to do your own will, but the will of the one who sent you. A great mystery! I beg you, together, let us knock; may something come to us to feed us, in accord with that which delights us. Indeed a great and lovely secret: *Whoever comes to me*; your attention, please, pay close attention and weigh well these words.[29] *I will not cast out the one who comes to me*.

"So then, whoever comes," he says, "I will not cast out."

"Why not?"

Because I have come down from heaven, not to do my own will, but the will of him who sent me.

---

26. See Homily 3, 21.
27. See Rom 3:3.
28. *Magnum penetrale*; as well as being an inner chamber, the *penetrale* was also the place where pagan households kept the household gods, the *lares et penates*. Augustine may also be referring to the holy place in the Jerusalem temple which has the holy of holies just beyond it.
29. *Attende, attende, et appende*. The play on words is clear in the Latin.

"Is that then the reason you do not cast out the one who comes to you? Is it the fact that you have come down from heaven, not to do your own will, but the will of the one who sent you?"

"Yes, that is it."

Why keep asking whether that is it? That is it, he says so himself. It is not lawful for us to suppose anything different from what he says himself. *I will not cast out the one who comes to me.* And as if you were to ask why not; *because I have not come to do my own will, but the will of him who sent me.*

I fear that the reason the soul went outside far from God is that it was proud; or rather, I have no doubt about it at all. It is written, after all: *The beginning of all sin is pride*, and, *The beginning of man's pride is to distance himself from God* (Sir 10:13.12). It is written, it is convincing, it is true. Then, what does scripture say about the proud mortal, wrapped in the rags of the flesh, encumbered with the weight of the perishable body, and yet for all that exalting himself and forgetting what skin he is clothed with? *What does earth and ashes have to be proud of?* What is it proud of? Let scripture tell us what he has got to be proud of: *Because in his life he has thrown away his inwardness.* (Sir 10:9) What is the meaning of *thrown away* but "thrown far away?"[30] That is what going outside amounts to. Entering within, that is seeking the inner realities; casting forth one's inwardness, that is going outside. Proud people throw away their inwardness, the humble seek the things within.[31] If we are thrown away by pride, the way back is by humility.

---

30. Augustine is interpreting the prefix *pro* in *proiecit* as derived from and equivalent to the adverb *porro*; he has done the same in Homily 16, 3.
31. Berrouard has a note at 793-796 on Sir 10:9 which ties pride to being outside oneself. He shows that Augustine's understanding of the "outwardness" of pride had perhaps been formed from the time of his earliest writings. To some extent, it also depends on his neo-Platonic notion of the true self being the soul, the mind, the spirit inside the outer garment of the flesh, the body. The self finds its truest, most real self within itself; God is more deeply within me than my deepest self (*Deus interior intimo meo*). But pride means moving away from God, thus rejecting one's essential dependence on him. Rejecting one's inwardness and seeking one's "independence" from God affirms self-importance and living in the outer, material world. The story of Adam and Eve expresses all of that, as it were, "sacramentalizes" it. Grasping at equality with God, they were cast out of the inner world of Eden, into the outer darkness; to follow Adam's example is to cast oneself out, wandering through the outer world of the flesh and material things, like Cain.

Pride the root of all evil; God's example of humility,
the incarnation; man's imitation of this, self-knowledge

16. The origin of all sicknesses is pride, because the origin of all sins is pride. When a doctor diagnoses some illness, he may care for the symptoms brought on by some cause without caring for that cause; for a while the sickness appears to be healed, but, since the cause remains, it soon reasserts itself. For example, if I may say this more clearly; some fluid in the body produces sores or ulcers; there is then a high fever and no little pain in the body. Some medicines are prescribed to check the sores and reduce the fever brought on by that ulcer, and they are applied and prove effective. You see the man healed, whose skin was thitherto covered with sores and ulcers; but because that fluid has not been drained away, the sores and ulcers come back again. When the doctor realizes this, he purges the fluid, thus eliminating the cause, and there will now be no more ulcers.

Why does wickedness abound? Because of pride. Treat the pride, and there will be no wickedness. So then, in order that the cause of all sicknesses, that is pride, might be treated, the Son of God came down and was made humble. Why are you proud, O man? For your sake, God was made humble. You might perhaps be ashamed to imitate a humble human being; imitate, at least, a humble God. The Son of God came in a human being,[32] and was made humble; he instructed you to be humble; he did not instruct you to turn the human being that you are into an animal; God has become man; you, man, recognize that you are a human being. The sum of humility for you consists in knowing yourself.[33]

So then, because God is teaching humility, he said, *I have come, not to do my own will, but the will him who sent me.* This, after all, is the approval of humility. Pride, of course, does its own will; humility does God's will. Therefore, *I will not cast out the one who comes to me.*

Why not?

Because I have not come to do my own will, but the will of him who sent me. I came humble, I came to teach humility, I came as the master of humility; the one who comes to me is embodied in me; the one who comes

---

32. See Homily 8, 3.
33. The advice inscribed over the shrine of Apollo at Delphi. See Sermons 137, 4; 166, 4; 341A, 2.

to me will be made humble; the one who clings to me will be humble,[34] because he does not do his own will, but God's; and that is why he will not be cast out, because when he was proud he cast himself out.[35]

It is within that the upright of heart will drink of the abundance of God's house

17. Notice how that inwardness is recommended in a psalm: *But the sons of men shall hope in the protection of your wings*. Notice what it is to go within, notice what it is to take refuge under his protection, notice what it is even to run within reach of the Father's lash;[36] for *he punishes every son that he takes in* (Heb 12:6; Prov 3:12). But *the sons of men shall hope under the cover of your wings*.

And what is there within?

They will get drunk on the abundance of your house. When you have brought them inside, on entering into the joy of their Lord,[37] *they will get drunk on the abundance of your house, and you will give them to drink of the torrent of your delight, since with you is the fountain of life* (Ps 35:8-9); not outside, away from you, but inside, with you, that is where the fountain of life is found. *And in your light shall we see light. Stretch out your mercy to those who know you, and your justice to those who are upright of heart.* (Ps 35:9-10)

Those who follow the will of their Lord, not seeking their own interests, but those of the Lord Jesus Christ,[38] these are the upright of heart whose feet do not stumble. For, *the God of Israel is good to the upright of heart. My feet however*, says he, *almost stumbled.*

Why is that?

Because I was envious of sinners, observing the peace of sinners (Ps 72:1-3). So to whom is God good, if not to the upright of heart? For,

---

34. Compare Homily 12, 6.
35. I have here translated the passive, *proiectus est*, as a reflexive; it accords much better with what Augustine was saying earlier about the proud casting forth their inwardness; and my justification is that Latin has no mood to correspond with the Greek middle, and so the passive could occasionally be used as a reflexive.
36. Shortly, Augustine will explain that the upright of heart who follow the will of the Father know how to accept the trials that come their way.
37. Cf. Mt 25:21.23.
38. Cf. Phil 2:21.

when my heart was all twisted, I did not like God. Why did I not like him? Because he gave happiness to bad people; and that is why my feet stumbled, as if I had been serving God to no purpose. So that then is why my feet had almost stumbled, because I was not upright of heart.

So then, what does it mean to be upright of heart?

To follow the will of God. One man is successful, another in distress; that one is bad in the way he lives and he prospers, this one is just in the way he lives and struggles. The one who lives justly and struggles must not feel unfairly treated; he has within himself something which that prosperous man does not have; so he should not be downcast, should not be distressed, should not give up. That fortunate man has gold in his coffers, this man has God in his conscience. Now compare gold and God, coffers and conscience. That man has something which can be lost and has it in a place from which it can be lost; this man has God, who cannot be lost, and has him in a place from which he cannot be taken away—as long as he is upright of heart; then, in fact, he enters within and does not go out.

So then, what was this man saying? *Since with you is the fountain of life*; it is not with us. Therefore we have to enter within so as to live, not as if we were self-sufficient, such that we perish; not as if we could be satisfied with what is our own, such that we wither up; but we should put our mouth to the fountain where the water never fails. Because Adam wanted to live his life on his own terms, he slipped and fell through the deception of the one who previously fell through pride, who gave him the cup of pride to drink.[39] So then, because *with you is the fountain of life, and in your light shall we see light*, let us drink within, let us look within.

Why, in fact, did anyone ever come out from there?

Listen to the reason. *May the foot of pride not come to me* (Ps 35:11). So the one to whom the foot of pride came is the one who came out.

Prove that that is why he came out.

And may the hands of sinners not move me (Ps 35:11), on account of the foot of pride.

Why do you say this?

Thereby they fell, all those who work iniquity (Ps 35:12).

Whereby did they fall?

---

39. He is referring to Satan. See Homily 17, 16.

By pride itself. *They were driven out, nor were they able to stand* (Ps 35:12).

So if pride has driven out those who were unable to stand, humility brings back within all those who will be able to stand for ever. That is why the one who said, *The bones that have been humbled shall exult*, said just before, *To my hearing you will give exultation and rejoicing* (Ps 50:8).

What is the meaning of *to my hearing*?

Hearing you makes me glad, your voice makes me glad; drinking inside makes me glad. That is why I do not fall, that is why *the bones that have been humbled shall rejoice*; that is why *the friend of the bridegroom stands and listens to him* (Jn 3:29). The reason he is standing is because he is listening. He is drinking from the inner fountain, that is why he is standing. Those who have not wished to drink from the inner fountain, *they fell, they were driven out, nor were they able to stand*.

Christ, the teacher of humility, does not cast out those who do God's will, not their own

18. And so the teacher of humility came, not to do his own will but *the will of him who sent him*. Let us come to him, let us enter to him, let us be embodied in him, so that we too may do not our own will, but the will of God; and he will not cast us out, because we are his members, because he was willing to be our head, teaching us humility. Finally, listen to him preaching: *Come to me, all you who are in difficulties and overburdened; take my yoke upon you and learn from me, because I am meek and humble of heart*; and when you have learned this, *you shall find rest for your souls* (Mt 11:28-29). You will not be thrown out from there, *because I have come down from heaven, not to do my own will, but the will of him who sent me*; I teach humility; only the humble can come to me. Pride alone sends you outside; how can anyone who maintains humility go out and not fall away from the truth?

I spoke, brothers and sisters, as much as I could about the hidden meaning of this passage. Its meaning, after all, is deeply concealed, and I do not know whether I have found the right words to draw out and make plain why he does not cast out the one who comes to him because he has not come to do his own will but the will of the one who sent him.

This teaching of humility tied in with the doctrine of two resurrections, of the spirit and of the flesh

19. *But this,* he goes on, *is the will of the Father who sent me, that I should lose nothing of all that he has given me* (Jn 6:39). That person has been given to him, who maintains humility; this one he accepts; whoever does not maintain humility is far away from the master of humility. *That I should lose nothing of all that he has given me. So it is not the will of your Father that any one of these little ones be lost* (Mt 18:14). Someone who is puffed up can be lost, but none of the little ones, because *unless you are like this little child, you shall not enter into the kingdom of heaven* (Mt 18:3).[40]

That I should lose nothing of all that he has given me; but I shall raise it up on the last day (Jn 6:39). Notice how here too he is sketching that double resurrection.[41] *Whoever comes to me* is now rising up, by being made humble among my members; but *I shall* also *raise him up on the last day* (Jn 6:40) in the flesh. For *this is the will of my Father who sent me, that everyone who sees the Son and believes in him should have eternal life; and I shall raise him up on the last day* (Jn 6:40). Earlier he said, *Whoever hears my word, and believes the one who sent me* (Jn 5:24); now, however, it is *who sees the Son and believes in him.* He did not say, "sees the Son and believes in the Father"; believing in the Son, after all, is the same as believing in the Father, because *just as the Father has life in himself, so too has he given the Son the possession of life in himself* (Jn 5:26), so that *everyone who sees the Son and believes in him should have eternal life,* by believing and crossing over to life, as in that first resurrection. And because that is not the only one, he adds, *and I shall raise him up on the last day.*

---

40. See Sermons 67, 8; 68, 7-8; 340A, 1; 353, 1.
41. Augustine is alluding to what he had to say, at considerable length, in Homilies 19, 8-19; 23, 12-15.

Homily 26

On John 6: 41-59[1]

Christ, the bread from heaven, is the justice for which we should hunger

1. When our Lord Jesus Christ, as we heard when the gospel was read, said that he was the bread which came down from heaven, the Jews muttered, and said, *Is this not Jesus, the son of Joseph, whose father and mother we know? So how then can this man say, I have come down from heaven?* (Jn 6:42) These people were a long way away from the bread from heaven, and did not know how to hunger for it. The jaws of their hearts were listless, with their ears open they were deaf, they saw but they remained blind. This bread for the inner man certainly requires a hunger—which is why he says somewhere else, *Blessed are those who hunger and thirst for justice, for they shall be satisfied* (Mt 5:6). Our justice is Christ, as the apostle Paul says.[2] And so whoever is hungry for this bread is hungry for justice—but for the justice which comes down from heaven, the justice which God gives, not the sort which human beings fashion for themselves.[3] If human beings, after all, did not fashion any justice for themselves, the same apostle would not have said about the Jews, *For ignoring the justice of God and wishing to establish their own, they did not submit to the justice of God* (Rom 10:3).

These people were such that they failed to grasp the meaning of the bread coming down from heaven; because they were full of their own justice, they were not hungry for the justice of God.

What does it mean to talk about the justice of God and the justice of man?

The justice of God does not refer to the justice with which God is just, but to that justice which he gives to someone so that he might be just with his help.

---

1. Preached a few days after Homily 25.
2. See 1 Cor 1:30.
3. Augustine is speaking about the virtue of justice by which a person is just, not the justice of the courts. Many distinguish the two by translating it as "righteousness," a word that is so closely associated with "self-righteousness" that I avoid it.

Well, what was their own justice?

That for which they presumed on their own strength, claiming that they, with their own virtue, perfectly fulfilled the law. But no one fulfills the law without the assistance of grace, that is, without the bread which comes down from heaven. *The fullness of the law*, in fact, as the apostle sums it up, *is charity* (Rom 13:10); that charity is the love of God, not of money. it is not the love of earth nor of heaven, but of the one who made both earth and heaven.

Where do human beings get this charity from?

Let us listen to him: *The charity of God*, he says, *has been poured out in our hearts through the Holy Spirit who has been given to us* (Rom 5:5). So then, the Lord, who was going to give the Holy Spirit, said he was himself the bread who came down from heaven, urging us to believe in him. To believe in him, in fact, is to eat the living bread. The one who believes, eats; he is invisibly filled, because he is invisibly reborn; inside, he is an infant; inside he is new; where he is newly planted,[4] that is where he is filled up.

Does being drawn by the Father not mean being subjected to violence, being forced to believe?

2. So what answer then did Jesus give to murmurers like these? *Do not murmur to one another*, as if to say, "I know why you hunger not and have no understanding of this bread nor do you seek it." *Do not murmur to one another; no one can come to me unless the Father who sent me draws him* (Jn 6:43-44). What splendid praise of grace! Nobody comes unless drawn. Which one he draws and which one he does not, why he draws this one and does not draw that one, is not for you to judge, if you do not want to err.[5] Hold on to this once and for all and understand it. Are you not yet being drawn? Pray to be drawn.

---

4. Augustine uses a rare word, *novellatur*, whose use is principally agricultural (referring to setting out new vines or new fields); it cannot just be translated as "being renewed." It would have struck his hearers as being as an unexpected usage—as my translation may strike readers. The reference is to baptism—not so much to the ritual as to the permanent realization or effect within the baptized; thus is there an unceasingly rebirth, a permanent status as *infantes* (as the newly-baptized are called) within the heart. See Homily 12, 5, for similar metaphorical references to baptism.

5. When Augustine deals with the mystery of predestination, he almost invariably refers to Rom 9:14.20; 11:33. See also Sermons 26, 23.25; 27, 4.6.7. He treats predestination just as St. Paul does.

What are we saying here, brothers and sisters? That, if we are being dragged to Christ,[6] then we are believing unwillingly; then force is being applied, not a stirring of the will. Someone can enter a church against his will, approach the altar against his will, receive the sacrament against his will; but he cannot believe unless he wants to. If believing were done with the body, it could happen in those not wanting it; but one does not believe with the body. Listen to the apostle: *With the heart one believes unto justice.* And what comes next? *But with the mouth one makes confession unto salvation.* (Rom 10:10) Confession rises up from the root of the heart. Sometimes you hear someone confessing the faith, and you do not know if he is a believer. But you should not even call it confessing when you decide that he does not believe. To confess, after all, is to say what you have in your heart; but if you have one thing in your heart and say something else, you are just talking, not confessing.[7] So then, one believes in Christ with the heart; that is something that no one does unwillingly. But whoever is drawn to do so would appear to be forced to believe unwillingly. So how are we to solve the problem of *No one comes to me unless the Father who sent me draws him?*

The inwardness of faith; the case of the woman who touched Jesus' garment

3. If he is drawn, someone may say he comes unwillingly. If he comes unwillingly, he does not believe; if he does not believe, he does not come. After all, one does not go to Christ by walking, but by believing; we approach Christ not by moving the body, but by a choice of the heart. That is why the woman who touched the hem of his cloak touched him more genuinely than did the crowd which was pressed against him. Hence, the Lord said, *Who touched me?* And the disciples, astonished, said, *The crowds are crushing against you, and you say, Who touched me?* And he repeated, *Someone touched me.* (Mk 5:27-31; Lk 8:4-46[8])

---

6. *Traho* primarily means "to haul" or "to drag along," not "to draw gently" or "to attract." So in the Latin, *unless the Father draws him* suggests forced attraction.
7. Regarding the invisibility of faith and the visibility of the confession, whether in word or by bodily gesture, see *The Trinity* XIII, 2, 5 and Sermon 49, 2, n. 5.
8. Is Augustine referring to the two gospel accounts by memory, or does he have a Latin translation of Tatian's *Diatessaron* in hand?

She touches him, the crowd is merely pressing against him. What does "touch" mean, if not "believe"? That is why he said after his resurrection to that other woman who wanted to throw herself down at his feet, *Do not touch me; for, I have not yet ascended to the Father* (Jn 20:17). "You think that I am only what you see; *do not touch me*." What does that mean? "You think I am only what is visibly apparent to you; do not believe like that." This is the meaning of *Do not touch me; for, I have not yet ascended to the Father*: "I have not ascended for you; in fact I never withdrew from where he is." She did not really touch the one who was standing there;[9] how was she to touch the one ascending to the Father? That, however, is the way he wished to be touched; that is the way he is touched by those who touch him rightly: as the one ascending to the Father, abiding with the Father, equal to the Father.

One can be drawn by love or pleasure

4. From there, if you pay attention to this, *No one comes to me except whom the Father has drawn*, do not imagine that you are being drawn against your will; the soul is also drawn by love. Nor should we fear being taken to task over this gospel text of the holy scriptures by people who weigh words scrupulously and are far from understanding, especially from understanding divine realities. Fear not their saying to us, "How can I believe by choice if I am being drawn?" I in turn say, "Your will is less important than you think;[10] you are also drawn by pleasure."

What does it mean to be drawn by pleasure?

Delight in the Lord, and he will give you the appeals of your heart (Ps 36:4). There is a pleasure of the heart for the one for whom that heavenly bread is sweet. If the poet could once say, "Each one is by his pleasure drawn,"[11] not by necessity but by pleasure, not by obligation but by delight, how much more strongly should we say that those whose delight is in the

---

9. See Sermons 229L, 2; 244, 2; 246, 4.
10. The Latin, *Quid est trahi voluptate . .?*, is exceedingly concise. An even more colloquial translation: "Forget about your freedom since you do not complain about being drawn by pleasure."
11. Virgil, *Second Eclogue* 65: *Trahit sua quemque voluptas*, where Corydon's pleasure, by which he is being drawn, is the handsome Alexis. See Sermon 131, 11, note 5, where the reference in the *Eclogue* is mistakenly given as 657.

truth, whose delight is in happiness, whose delight is in justice, whose delight is in eternal life, are drawn to Christ, because each of those is Christ.

Or is it true that the senses of the body have their pleasures, while the mind is denied its pleasures? If the mind does not have its pleasures, how is it said, *But the sons of men shall hope under the cover of your wings; they will get drunk on the abundance of your house, and you will give them to drink of the torrent of your delight, since with you is the fountain of life, and in your light shall we see light* (Ps 35:7-9)? Give me a lover, and he will know by experience what I am saying here. Give me a man of desires, give me someone who is hungry, give me someone traveling thirsty through this wilderness, and panting for the fountain of eternal life, and he will know what I am saying. If on the other hand I am talking to some cold-hearted so-and-so, he has not the slightest idea of what I am talking about. Such were these people who were murmuring to one another. *Whom the Father has drawn*, he said, *comes to me*.

That the Father draws to the Son is an indication that the Father begot the Son

5. But what does it mean, *whom the Father has drawn*, when Christ is the one who does the drawing? If we have to be drawn, let us at least be drawn by one to whom a lover says, *We shall run after the fragrance of your perfumes* (Sg 1:3-4). But let us notice what he wished us to understand, brothers and sisters, and grasp it as best we can. The Father draws those who believe in him to the Son, precisely because they think of him as having God as his Father.[12] God the Father, in fact, begot the Son as his equal; so then, the one who imagines, who experiences in his faith, and who meditates on the one he believes in as equal to the Father, he is the one whom the Father draws to the Son. Arius believed he was a creature; the Father did not draw him, because, by not believing that the Son was equal, he did not show any consideration to the Father.

What are you saying, Arius? What are you talking about, heretic? What is Christ?

"Not," he says, "true God, but one who was made by the true God."

---

12. See Homily 19, 6.13.

The Father did not draw you; for, by denying his Son, you did not understand him as Father. You are thinking of something else, not of the Son. You are neither drawn by the Father nor drawn by the Son. The Son after all is one thing, quite another is what you are talking about.

Photinus[13] said, "Christ is only a man, he is not God as well." Anyone who believes that has not been drawn by the Father. The one whom the Father draws says, *You are the Christ, the Son of the living God*; not like a prophet, not like John the Baptist, not like some great and just man, but as the only, as the equal, *you are the Christ, the Son of the living God*. Now see how he was drawn, and drawn, what is more, by the Father: *Blessed are you, Simon Bar-Jona, because it is not flesh and blood that has revealed this to you, but my Father who is in heaven.* (Mt 16:16-17) This revelation is the same as attraction. You show a bunch of green leaves to a sheep, and you draw her. Nuts are shown to a small boy, and he is drawn; and he runs where he is drawn to, he is drawn by love, drawn without any harm to his body, drawn by a cord of the heart. So, if these things, which are revealed to their lovers among earthly delights and pleasures, draw, how true it is that "each one is by his pleasure drawn." Will not Christ draw us, when revealed by the Father? After all, what can the soul desire more eagerly than Truth? What ought to make its mouth water more, what better reason could it have for wanting a healthy inner palate, sensitive enough to judge the truth of things, than the prospect of eating and drinking Wisdom, Justice, Truth, Eternity?

Our hunger for justice will be satisfied when Christ raises us up on the last day

6. But where is that to be? Much better up there,[14] more truly, more fully. Here, after all, even if we have a good hope, we can hunger more easily

---

13. Photinus, bishop of Sirmium, was a critic of Arius and his doctrine in the middle of the fourth century; so he was several times deposed by Arian synods, and as frequently restored to his see by orthodox ones, with the full consent of contemporary Roman bishops. Augustine saw the difference between him and Arius in this way: Arius believed in a real incarnation of the Word of God; but the Word itself was made and adopted, not begotten. Hence the Word was a kind of super creature, higher even than the angels. Photinus taught that Christ was a human being in whom the Word came to abide; but he seems to have seen the Word as God in an odd way; for God expanded himself into a trinity somehow, without, however, a distinction of persons. See Sermons 71, 4, note 12; 92, 3.
14. *Ibi* means "there." It refers to life after death. See section 10 of this homily.

than be satisfied.¹⁵ In fact, he says, *Blessed are those who hunger and thirst for justice*—but here below! *for they shall be satisfied*—but up there! That is why, after saying, *No one comes to me, unless the Father has drawn him,* what did he add? *And I shall raise him up on the last day* (Jn 6:44). I shall give him what he loves, I shall give him what he longs for; he shall see what he believed in while he still did not see it; he shall eat what he hungers for, be satisfied with what he thirsts. Where? At the resurrection of the dead, because I shall raise him up on the last day.

God in Christ teaches us inwardly

7. For *it is written in the prophets, They shall all be taught by God* (Jn 6:45). Why have I said that, my dear Jews? The Father has not been your teacher, how can you recognize me?

All those who belong to his kingdom will be taught by God, they will not hear about it from human beings. And if they do hear about it from human beings, what they understand is, all the same, given within, illuminates within, is revealed within.¹⁶ What do those who preach on the outside accomplish? What am I doing now, when I talk? Striking your ears with the noise my words make. So unless the one who is within reveals the meaning, why am I talking, why am I speaking?¹⁷ The one who cares for the tree is outside, inside is the creator. The one who plants and who waters acts on the outside; that is what we do. But *neither the one who plants nor the one who waters is anything, but the one who makes things grow, God* (1 Cor 3:7). That is the meaning of *They shall all be taught by God.*

Who are these *all*? *Everyone who has heard from the Father and has learned comes to me* (Jn 6:45). Notice how the Father draws; he delights by his teaching, without imposing by force. Notice how he draws: *They shall all be taught by God*—that is how God draws. *Everyone who has heard from the Father and has learned comes to me*—thus is God drawing them.

---

15. See Sermons 53, 4; 170, 7.
16. See Homily 1, 6-7.
17. See Sermon 153, 1.

The Father teaches us in Christ because Christ is the Father's Word

8. What then, brothers and sisters? If each one who has heard from the Father and learned from him comes to Christ, did Christ not teach anything? What about the people that did not see the Father as teacher, but did see the Son? The Son was talking but the Father was teaching.[18] I, a human being, whom do I teach? Whom but the one who has heard my word? If I, a human being, teach the one who hears my word, then the Father also teaches the one who hears his Word. If the Father teaches the one who hears his Word, ask what Christ is, and you will find he is his Word:[19] *In the beginning was the Word* (Jn 1:1). Not "in the beginning God made the Word,"[20] in the way that *in the beginning God made heaven and earth* (Gn 1:1). There you are, it is not something created. Learn how to be drawn to the Son by the Father; let the Father teach you, listen to his Word.

You ask, "What Word of his do I hear?"

In the beginning was the Word (not "was made" but *was*), *and the Word was with God, and the Word was God* (Jn 1:1).

"How can human beings, made of flesh, hear such a Word?"

Because *the Word was made flesh and took up residence among us* (Jn 1:14).[21]

Only the Father's Word knows the Father

9. He also explains this himself and shows us what he had said: *Whoever has heard from the Father and has learned comes to me.* Right away he added something which we can think about: *Not that anyone has seen the Father, except the one who is from God—he has seen the Father.* (Jn 6:46)

What is this he is saying?

"I have seen the Father, you have not seen the Father; and yet you do not come to me unless you are drawn by the Father. What, though, does being drawn by the Father mean but that you learn from the Father? What is learning from the Father but hearing from the Father? What is hearing from the Father but hearing the Father's Word, that is, hearing me?

---

18. Neat word-play: *Filius dicebat, sed Pater docebat.*
19. See Homilies 14, 7; 19, 7.
20. See Sermons 119, 2; 135, 4; 183, 4; 225, 1; 293, 5; Homily 1, 11.
21. See Homily 7, 1.

"So then, when I say to you, *Whoever has heard from the Father has learned*, you may say to each other, 'But we have never seen the Father, how could we have learned from the Father?' Hear it from me: *Not that anyone has seen the Father, but the one who is from God—he has seen the Father*. For I know the Father; I am from him, but from him as a word comes from the one whose word it is—not a word that resounds and fades away, but one that stays with the one speaking and draws the one hearing."

Eternal life died in order to slay death

10. Let that which follows remind us: *Amen. Amen, I tell you, whoever believes in me has eternal life* (Jn 6:47). He wanted to reveal what he was, because he could have said in a word, "Whoever believes in me has me." Christ himself, after all, is true God and eternal life. So then, "Whoever believes in me," he is saying, "comes to me; and what comes to me possesses me. What though does it mean to possess me? To have eternal life."

Eternal life took on death, eternal life was willing to die;[22] but to die in what is yours, not in what is his; he took from you that in which he would die for you. I mean he took flesh from human beings, but not like human beings take on flesh. Having a Father in heaven, you see, he chose a mother on earth; and up there he was born without mother, and here he was born without father.[23] So then, life took on death, so that life might slay death. Because *whoever believes in me*, he said, *has eternal life*, not obviously, but in a hidden way.[24] Eternal life, after all, was the Word in the beginning with God, and *the Word was God, and the life was the light of men* (Jn 1:1.4). He is eternal life, and he gave eternal life to the flesh he took on. He came to die, but on the third day he rose again. Between the Word taking flesh and flesh rising again, death has been swallowed up.

---

22. See Homily 12, 11.
23. See Homily 8, 8.
24. More rhyming word-play: *non quod patet, sed quod latet*.

Those who ate manna in the desert died there,
because they did not understand it spiritually

11. *I*, he says, *am the bread of life*.

And what were they proud of?

"*Your fathers*," he says, "*ate manna in the desert, and they died* (Jn 6:48-49). What are you so proud of? They ate manna, and they died. Why did they eat and die? Because they believed in what they could see; they had no understanding of what they could not see. That is why I mention your fathers, because you are like them."

After all, my dear brothers and sisters, as far as this visible and bodily death goes, do we too not die, we who eat the bread that comes down from heaven? Those people died too, just as we are going to die—speaking, as I said, about the visible and bodily death of this body. But as for that other death, about which the Lord means to terrify us, by which death the fathers of these people died, Moses also ate manna, Aaron also ate manna, Phineas also ate manna, many at that time who found favor with the Lord ate manna, and did not die.[25]

Why not?

Because they had a spiritual understanding of that visible food, they were hungry in a spiritual way, tasted it in a spiritual way, in order to have their fill in a spiritual way. After all, we too receive a visible food today; but a sacrament is one thing, quite another is the benefit[26] of the sacrament.

How many receive from the altar and die, die by receiving! Of such the apostle says, *One eats and drinks judgment upon himself* (1 Cor 11:29). The morsel offered by the Lord, after all, was not poison for Judas; and yet he took it, and when he did so the enemy entered into him, not because he had taken something bad, but because a bad man took something good in a

---

25. See Num 14:26-45. As a matter of fact, both Moses and Aaron did die before entering the promised land; see Num 20:24-29, Dt 34:4-6. So they did die, unlike Joshua and Caleb and Phineas. But to this objection Augustine would perhaps reply that, while they were punished for their sins in the desert, they understood that the manna was a "sacrament" of something infinitely greater and more spiritual.
26. The word Augustine uses is *virtus*. The force or effect of the sacrament is to confirm, to strengthen the recipient's membership in the body of Christ. Christ's presence is thus part of the sacramental sign which—more than just bread and wine—is also the Church, the body of Christ.

bad way.[27] See to it then, brothers and sisters; eat the heavenly bread in a spiritual way; bring innocence along to the altar. Even if there are sins every day, at least do not let them be deadly. Before you approach the altar, pay attention to what you say: *Forgive us our debts, just as we too forgive our debtors* (Mt 6:12). You forgive, you are forgiven; approach without a qualm, it is bread, not poison. But mind you really do forgive; because if you do not forgive, you are lying, and you are lying to one whom you do not deceive. You can lie to God, you cannot deceive God.[28] He knows what to do. He sees right into you, he examines you within, he inspects you within, within he judges, within he either condemns or crowns you[29].

But the fathers of these people, that is to say, bad fathers of bad people, unbelieving fathers of unbelieving people, grumbling fathers of perpetual grumblers,[30] well, that people of old is said to have given the Lord no greater offence than by its grumbling against God.[31] That is why the Lord himself, wishing to show that they are the descendants of such a crew, began what he had to say to them from this point: "Why are you grumbling to each other, you grumblers, sons of grumblers? Your fathers ate manna, and died, not because the manna was bad, but because the spirit in which they ate it was bad."

The manna signified Christ, the bread from heaven

12. *This is the bread which has come down from heaven* (Jn 6:50). This bread was signified by the manna, this bread is signified[32] by the altar of God. Those things were sacraments, differing from each other as signs,

---

27. See Homily 6, 15; Sermon 266, 7.
28. See Homily 7, 11.
29. See Sermon 90, 4, where God alone is said to discern the good from the bad in the heart, depending upon a presence or an absence of faith working through love.
30. See Homily 9, 16.
31. See Ex 16:12; Num 14:1-12; Ps 95:8-11.
32. Most manuscripts have the verb here in the present tense, *significat* (in translation I have changed the sentence into the passive); but the Maurists have gone along with the minority in reading the aorist, *significavit*, doubtless because it goes better with the tense of the verb in the following sentence, "those things were sacraments." If one were to keep the past tense here, then the altar of God referred to would be the altar of holocausts in the Old Testament Jewish temple. But Augustine has not been talking about that altar, whereas he has been talking, very insistently too, about the altar of God in the Christian church in Hippo Regius, on which the eucharist was celebrated, which is indifferently referred to by him as both altar and table, *altare* and *mensa*. So the present tense fits the whole context better than the past. As for the following

equivalent in the thing they signify. Listen to the apostle: *I would not have you ignorant,* he says, *brothers and sisters, that our fathers were all under the cloud, and all went through the sea, and all were baptized into Moses in the cloud and in the sea, and all ate the same spiritual food* (1 Cor 10:1-3). Yes, as spiritual it is the same; as bodily food it is different, since for them it was manna, for us something else; as spiritual food, however, it was the same as for us.

But as such it was eaten by our fathers, not theirs, by the fathers we are like, not the fathers they were like. And he added, *And all drank the same spiritual drink.* They one kind, we another, but in visible appearance; the spiritual force of both, all the same, would be to signify the same thing. How, after all, is it the same drink? *They were drinking,* he says, *of the spiritual rock that was following them; and the rock was Christ* (1 Cor 10:4). That is where the bread comes from, where the drink comes from: the rock was Christ as sign, the real Christ is Word and flesh. And how did they drink? The rock was struck twice with a rod;[33] the double striking signifies the two bars of the cross.[34] *This then is the bread coming down from heaven, so that if anyone eats of it, he may not die* (Jn 6:40). This refers to the grace of the sacrament, not to the sacrament we can see; to those who eat inwardly, not outwardly, who eat in the heart, who do not just chew with the teeth.

In order to live by the Spirit of Christ, we must be in the body of Christ

13. *I am the living bread that came down from heaven*—living, therefore, because I have come down from heaven. Manna also came down from heaven; but manna was the shadow, this is the truth. *If anyone eats of this bread, he will live for ever; and the bread which I shall give is my flesh for the life of the world.* (Jn 6:51) When would flesh be able to grasp that he

---

sentence, by "these things" he no doubt had in mind, as much as anything, the things he is going on to quote from 1 Cor.

33. See Num 20:11. That the rock which Moses struck on that occasion followed the people through the wilderness as a perpetual water supply was a rabbinic legend that was certainly a spiritual one!

34. See Sermon 352, 3, where the fact of Moses' rod being of wood, not iron, signifies the wood of the cross in contact with Christ. That sermon may have been preached in 398, almost 20 years before this homily; so this interpretation may be regarded as the one he favored in his maturer years. The two "woods" (*ligna*) of the cross are the upright and the horizontal bars.

called bread flesh? What flesh does not understand is called flesh, and flesh grasps even less because it is called flesh. This, after all, is what horrified them, this is what they said was too much for them, this is what they thought could not possibly happen.

My flesh, he says, *is for the life of the world*. The faithful know the body of Christ, if they do not neglect to be the body of Christ. Let them become the body of Christ, if they wish to live by the Spirit of Christ. Only the body of Christ lives by the Spirit of Christ.[35]

Understand, my brothers and sisters, what I have been saying. You are a human being, you have both a spirit and a body. I am calling spirit what is usually called soul, by which you exist as a human being; you consist, after all, of soul and body. Thus the spirit you have is invisible, the body you have is visible. Tell me which draws life from which; does your spirit draw life from your body, or your body from your spirit? The answer given by everyone who is alive—anyone who cannot answer this question, well, I do not know if they really are alive—so what answer is given by anyone who is alive? My body of course draws life from my spirit.

So then, do you also wish to draw life from the Spirit of Christ? Be in the body of Christ. Does my body, after all, draw life from your spirit? Mine draws life from my spirit, and yours from yours. That is why, when the apostle Paul is explaining this bread to us, he says, *We being many are one bread, one body* (1 Cor 10:17). O sacrament of piety, O sign of unity, O bond of charity! The one who wants to live has somewhere to live, has something to live on. Let him approach, let him believe, let him belong to the body so as to be given life. Let him not shudder at the make-up of its members, let him not be a festering member which needs to be amputated, nor a crooked member of which it would be ashamed; let him be beautiful, well suited, healthy; let him cling to the body, live for God and by God. Let him work now on earth so as to reign later on in heaven.

---

35. See Sermons 267, 4; 268, 2, both preached on the day of Pentecost. In both instances, and here too, Augustine had the Donatists in mind. That is why he could say, "Let the faithful *become* the body of Christ," instead of something like "Let the faithful make sure they are the body of Christ." He thus invited the Donatists to join the Catholic Church, the true body of Christ.

The Jews wrangled with each other,
having no understanding of the bread of concord

14. *So then, the Jews started wrangling with each other, saying, How can this man give us his flesh to eat?* (Jn 6:52) They were wrangling with each other, of course, because they had no understanding of the bread of concord, nor were they willing to take it; for, those who eat such bread do not wrangle with each other, since *we being many are one bread, one body.* And through this bread *God makes people with the same way of life dwell in the house* (Ps 67:6, LXX).[36]

Eating this food means having fellowship in the body of Christ, the Church

15. What they want to know as they wrangle with each other is how the Lord can give us his flesh to eat; they do not hear the answer right away, but he tells them, *Amen, amen, I say to you, unless you have eaten the flesh of the Son of Man and have drunk his blood, you shall not have life in you* (Jn 6:53). How indeed it may be eaten and in what way this bread is eaten, you do not know; even so, *unless you have eaten the flesh of the Son of man and have drunk his blood, you shall not have life in you.* He was not saying this, obviously, to corpses, but to living people. To stop them from applying it to this life and from wrangling over it in that context, he went on to add, *Whoever eats my flesh and drinks my blood has eternal life* (Jn 6:54). Eternal life then is what is missed by the one who does not eat this bread or drink this blood; after all, people can have life in this world of time without this food; on the other hand, they certainly cannot have eternal life.

So then, if you do not eat his flesh, nor drink his blood, you do not have life in him; and if you do eat his flesh and drink his blood, you do have life. In each case, though, it is, as he said, eternal life. That is not how it is with this food, food that we take for sustaining this temporal life. For the one who does not take it does not stay alive; but, even so, the one who does take it will not necessarily stay alive. It can happen, after all, that most of those who do take it still die of old age, or of illness, or in some accident. But with this other food and drink, that is with the Lord's body and blood, it is not like that. For, if you do not take it, you do not have life, and if you do take it, you do have life, and that life is eternal.

---

36. See *Exposition of Psalm* 67, 7 for a fuller treatment of this verse.

Thus by this food and drink he wishes that the fellowship of his body and of his members be grasped; that fellowship is the holy Church in his saints and his faithful, who have been predestined, and called, and justified, and glorified;[37] of these stages the first has already happened, that is, predestination; the second and third both have happened and are happening, that is, calling and justification; while the fourth, that is, glorification, is now only to be had in hope, to be realized in the future. The sacrament of this reality, that is, of the unity of Christ's body and blood, is placed on the Lord's table and received from the Lord's table—in some places every day, in others at fixed intervals of time,[38] leading some to life and others to ruin. But, the reality itself, of which this is the sacrament, means life for all, ruin for none, no matter who shares it.

One eats and drinks in order to have eternal life, and to be raised up on the last day

16. But lest they should think that eternal life is promised in this food and drink, such that those who take it will no longer die in the body, the Lord countered this kind of thinking.[39] Thus after saying, *Whoever eats my flesh and drinks my blood has eternal life*, he immediately added, *and I will raise him up on the last day* (Jn 6:54), so that, in the meantime, he may have eternal life according to the spirit in the rest which welcomes the spirits of the saints; as far as the body is concerned, though, he will not be cheated of its eternal life either, but will have it in the resurrection of the dead on the last day.

Out of many grains, one bread; out of many grapes, one cup

17. *For my flesh*, he says, *is really food, and my blood is really drink* (Jn 6:55). What people desire when it comes to food and drink is to stop being hungry or thirsty, but that is only truly provided for by the food and drink which makes those who take it immortal and imperishable, by this fellowship of the saints, in which there will be peace and full and perfect unity. That is the reason, as men of God before our time understood perfectly

---

37. See Rom 8:30.
38. Berrouard (819-822) documents the fact that a daily celebration of the Eucharist was the practice in the African Churches of Augustine's time, as also in the Church of Milan.
39. See Homily 3, 13.

well,[40] why our Lord Jesus Christ presented us with his body and blood in those things which are made one out of many. Thus one bread is brought together as one from many grains, the other flows together from many grapes.

Eating Christ's flesh and drinking his blood means our abiding in him and his abiding in us

18. Finally, he explains how what he is talking about happens and what it means to eat his body and to drink his blood. *Whoever eats my flesh and drinks my blood abides in me and I in him* (Jn 6:56).[41] This, therefore, is eating that food and drinking that drink: abiding in Christ and having him abide in oneself. And thus if someone does not abide in Christ and Christ does not abide in him, there can be no doubt that he does not eat his flesh or drink his blood, but rather he is eating and drinking the sacrament of such a great reality to his own condemnation, because he had the presumption to approach the sacraments of Christ in an unclean state; those sacraments can only be worthily received by someone whose conscience is clean, of whom it says, *Blessed are the clean of heart, for they shall see God* (Mt 5:8).[42]

I live by the Father because I humbled myself; you live by me because I exalt you

19. *Just as the living Father*, he says, *sent me, and I live because of the Father, so whoever eats me, he too will live because of me* (Jn 6:57). He did not say, "Just as I eat the Father, and I live because of the Father, so whoever eats me, he too will live because of me." The Son, you see, because he was born the Father's equal, is not made better by having shares in the Father, in the way that we are effectively made better by sharing in the Son through the unity of his body and blood, which is signified by that eating and drinking. We, then, live because of him by eating him, that is, we receive him as eternal life, which we did not have from ourselves. But he lives because of the Father, in that he was sent by him, because *he emptied himself, becoming obedient even to the death of the cross* (Phil 2:7-8).

---

40. Augustine appears to have Cyprian of Carthage in mind, particularly his Letters 63, 13, 4; 69, 5, 2.
41. See Sermons 71, 17; 131, 1.
42. Most editors also think that several words were added to this text so as to emphasize a merely spiritual reception of the sacraments. The edition of the Corpus Christianorum, which retains some of them, is the text followed here.

After all, if we interpret *I live because of the Father* as equivalent to what he says elsewhere, *The Father is greater than me* (Jn 14:28), just as we live because of him, who is greater than us, this came about through his being sent. His being sent is certainly the same as his emptying himself and taking the form of a slave, which is rightly understood to have happened without the Son's forfeiting his equality in nature with the Father. The Father, after all, is greater than the Son as man, but has the Son as God as his equal, since the one Christ is at the same time both God and man, Son of God and Son of Man.

If these words are rightly taken to have this meaning, then the statement, *Just as the living Father sent me, and I live because of the Father, so whoever eats me, he too will live because of me*, can be rephrased as follows: "That I might live because of the Father, that is, that I might attribute my life to him as greater, was the effect of my self-emptying, into which he sent me; but that anyone should live because of me is effected by his sharing in me through eating me. Thus I, on being humbled, live because of the Father, while that person, on being promoted, lives because of me." If however it says, *I live because of the Father*, because the Son is from him, not he from the Son, it says this without detriment to his equality with the Father.[43] All the same, by saying, *And whoever eats me, he too will live because of me*, he did not signify our equality with him, but manifested the grace of the mediator.

Christ is life everlasting

20. *This is the bread which came down from heaven*, so that we might live by eating it, because we cannot have life everlasting from ourselves. *Not*, he says, *as your fathers ate manna, and died; whoever eats this bread will live for ever* (Jn 6:58). So then, by saying that those people died, he wants it to be understood that they do not live for ever. After all, those who eat Christ will, to be sure, also die a temporal death; but they live for ever, because Christ is life everlasting.

---

43. See Homily 19, 13.

Homily 27

On John 6:60-72[1]

Really to eat Christ's flesh and drink his blood means
our abiding in him and his abiding in us

1. We have just heard from the gospel the words of the Lord which follow on what he was saying in the reading a few days ago. So your ears and your minds have a right to a sermon, and today is a good day for that; it is about the Lord's body, you see, which he said he was giving them to eat for the sake of eternal life.[2] He has just explained what it meant for him to hand over this gift, how he would give his flesh to be eaten, saying, *Whoever eats my flesh and drinks my blood abides in me and I in him* (Jn 6:56). The sign that someone has really eaten and drunk is that he abides in Christ and Christ in him, that he dwells in Christ and Christ in him, that he sticks to Christ so as not to be left behind.

So this then is what he taught us and impressed upon us with those mysterious words, that we should be in his body, under him as our head, among his members, eating his flesh, not forsaking his Unity.[3] But a great many of those who were present did not grasp what he was getting at and were scandalized; on hearing these words, you see, they only thought about the flesh, which is what they were.[4] Now the apostle says, and says truly, *Being wise according to the flesh is death* (Rom 8:6). The Lord gives us his flesh to eat, and being wise according to the flesh is indeed death, because what he was saying about his flesh was that it is the means of eternal life. So then, not even about flesh should we be wise according to the flesh—as is clear from these words.

---

1. Preached a few days after Homily 26, on the feast of St. Laurence; see sections 10 and 12.
2. A sermon on the eucharist, which is also a sermon on the Holy Spirit, is appropriate for the celebration of a martyr's feast day, since it is from full participation in the eucharist, and by the gift of the Holy Spirit, that the martyr derives the constancy to witness to Christ to the death. As St. Laurence, the senior deacon of the Roman Church, was responsible for taking the eucharist to the confessors, imprisoned for the faith, before he was arrested himself, such a sermon was particularly suitable on his feast day.
3. This is one of the names Augustine likes to use for the Church. For this general theme see Homilies 2, 5; 6, 21; 26, 18.
4. See Homily 26, 13.

A hard saying—if understood according to the flesh

2. *Many of those who were listening, therefore, not of his enemies but of his disciples, said, This is a hard saying; who can listen to it?* (Jn 6:60) If his disciples considered this a hard saying, what about his enemies? And yet it was right for it to be said in such a way that it would not be understood by everyone. The mysteriousness of God should make us keen, not hostile. These disciples, though, quickly fell away, when the Lord Jesus said such things; they did not believe the one speaking of a great matter whose words contained a hidden gift of grace; they understood what they wanted and, in a merely human way, took them to mean that Jesus was able, or even that he was preparing, to slice up the flesh with which the Word was clothed, and distribute it to those who believed in him.[5] *This is a hard saying*, they said; *who can listen to it?*

Understanding will come, when the Son of man ascends into heaven

3. *But Jesus, knowing in himself that his disciples were murmuring about this.* They said this among themselves, you see, in such a way as not to be overheard by him; but he who knew them within himself, also heard them within himself, and said in reply, *Does this scandalize you?* Because I said I am giving you my flesh to eat and my blood to drink, this evidently scandalizes you. *What then if you see the Son of Man ascending where he was before?* (Jn 6:61-62) What is this all about? Is this how he solved the problem that was troubling them? Is this how he cleared up what had scandalized them? Indeed it is—if only they would understand. For they were thinking he was going to give them helpings of his body; but he said that he was going to ascend into heaven—the whole of him, of course. *When you see the Son of Man ascending where he was before,* then at least you will see that he is not giving you helpings of his body in the way you are thinking; then at least you will understand that his grace is not something finished off in mouthfuls.

How the Son of Man was in heaven before; the unity of person in Christ

4. And he said, *The Spirit gives life, the flesh is no use at all* (Jn 6:63). Before we try to explain this, as far as the Lord may concede, we must not

---

5. See Homily 11, 5; Sermon 131, 1.

carelessly pass over his saying, *What then if you see the Son of Man ascending where he was before?* Christ, after all, is the Son of Man from the virgin Mary. So he began to be the Son of Man here on earth, when he took flesh from earth, which is why it is said in prophecy, *Truth has sprung from the earth* (Ps 84:11). What then does he mean by saying, *When you see the Son of Man ascending where he was before?* I mean, no question would arise if he had said, "If you see the Son of God ascending where he was before." But as he said, *the Son of Man ascending where he was before,* well, was the Son of Man ever in heaven before, seeing that he began his existence on earth?

He did indeed say *where he was before* as if he were not there while speaking these words. But in another place he says, *No one has ascended into heaven except the one who came down from heaven, the Son of Man who is in heaven* (Jn 3:13); he did not say "was," but he says *the Son of Man who is in heaven.* He was speaking on earth and saying he was in heaven. Nor did he say it like this: "No one has ascended into heaven except the one who came down from heaven, the Son of God, who is in heaven." What is this about other than to help us understand, as I also put it to Your Graces in a previous sermon,[6] that Christ, God and man, is one person, not two, lest our faith should not be in a Trinity but in a quaternity? So then, Christ is one being: Word, soul and flesh, one Christ; Son of God and Son of Man, one Christ. Son of God always, Son of Man from a point in time, but still one Christ as regards the unity of person. He was in heaven, when he was speaking on earth. The Son of Man was in heaven in the same way as the Son of God was on earth; the Son of God on earth in the flesh he had taken, the Son of Man in heaven in the unity of person.

The involvement of the Holy Spirit in the eucharist

5. So then, what is this that he added, *The Spirit gives life, the flesh is of no use at all?* Let us say to him—he puts up with us, you see, as longing to know, not as contradicting him, "Dear Lord, good teacher, how is the flesh no use at all, when you yourself have just said, *Unless you eat my flesh and drink my blood, you shall not have life in you* (Jn 6:53)? Is life no use at all,

---

6. See Homily 26, 19 (see a similar idea in Homily 12, 8-10).

then? And to what end are we what we are, but that we may have eternal life, which you promise by means of your flesh? So what is this then, *the flesh is no use at all?*" It is no use at all, but in the way those people understood it; they understood flesh as that which is torn off a cadaver or sold at the butcher's, not as that which is animated by the spirit.

Thus *the flesh is no use at all* is being said in much the same way as *knowledge puffs up.* Should we then hate knowledge? Not at all! And what does it mean, *knowledge puffs up?* Knowledge alone, without charity. That is why he added, *but charity builds up* (1 Cor 8:1). So add charity to knowledge, and knowledge will be useful; not of itself, but through charity. So too here: *The flesh is no use at all,* but that means flesh by itself; let spirit be joined to flesh, in the way charity is attached to knowledge, and flesh is very useful.

In fact, if flesh had been of no use, the Word would not have become flesh to dwell among us. If it was through the flesh that Christ was of the greatest use to us, how is the flesh of no use at all? Yet, through the flesh, the Spirit[7] did something for our salvation. The flesh was a container; concentrate on what it contained, not on what it was. The apostles were sent out; can we say their flesh was no use to us? If the flesh of the apostles was of use to us, could the Lord's flesh have been of no use? How has the sound of the Word reached us, after all, if not through the voice of the flesh? What about a pen, about writing? These are all works of the flesh, but they are moved by the Spirit as an instrument. "So then, *The Spirit gives life, the flesh is of no use at all* refers to the way those people understood flesh, but I do not give my flesh to be eaten in that way."

---

7. Should "Spirit" here be written with a capital or in the lower case? I follow the Latin text of the Maurists and other editors; Berrouard prefers the lower case, on the grounds that the whole context shows Augustine to be referring to the Word, not to the Holy Spirit. It is true that the context shows that Augustine has the Word in mind as what is "contained" by the flesh; but he had previously repudiated the notion that the flesh of Christ was animated by the Word; no, it was animated by the soul of Christ, and to say otherwise is to fall into the heresy of Photinus. Again, the incarnation took place through the Holy Spirit; as the angel said to Mary, *The Holy Spirit will come upon you, and the power of the Most High will overshadow you* (Lk 1:35). So where the Word is, there too is the Holy Spirit, cooperating with the Word in enabling the flesh to be of use and value—even in the celebration of the eucharist.

The Spirit gives you life in the body of Christ;
but not if you are separated from it

6. Then he continues, *The words which I have spoken to you are spirit and life* (Jn 6:63). After all, brothers and sisters, I have just said that what the Lord has impressed upon us in the eating of his flesh and the drinking of his blood is that its whole purpose is for us to abide in him and him in us.[8] Now we abide in him when we are his members, while he abides in us when we are his temple. But for us to be his members, we have to be bonded together by unity. What makes unity bond us together? What else but charity? And where does the charity of God come from? Question the apostle. *The charity of God*, he says, *has been poured out in our hearts through the Holy Spirit who has been given to us* (Rom 5:5). So then, *the Spirit gives life*; it is the Spirit after all who makes sure the members are alive. Nor does the Spirit make sure any members are alive, unless they are in the body which the Spirit itself animates.[9]

Take the spirit, after all, that is in you, a human being, which sets you up precisely as human; does it keep any limb or organ of yours alive which it finds separated from your flesh? By your spirit I mean your soul; your soul only keeps those parts alive which are in your flesh; if you remove one, it is no longer kept alive by your soul, because it is not bound in with the unity of your body. I am saying this in order to make sure that we love unity and fear separation. There is nothing, after all, that Christians should be more afraid of than being separated from the body of Christ. If they are separated from the body of Christ, in fact, they are no longer his members; if they are not his members, they are not being kept alive by his Spirit. *But whoever*, says the apostle, *does not have the Spirit of Christ does not belong to him* (Rom 8:9).

So then, *the Spirit gives life; but the flesh is of no use at all. The words which I have spoken to you are spirit and life.* What is the meaning of *are spirit and life*? These words are to be understood in a spiritual way. Have you understood in a spiritual way? *They are spirit and life.* Have you understood in a carnal way? Even so, they are still spirit and life, but not for you.[10]

---

8. See Homily 26, 18.
9. That is, in the body of Christ, the Church. See Sermons 71, 18; 267, 4.
10. See Homily 26, 11.

Belief comes first, as a gift of grace; understanding second

7. *But there are some among you*, he says, *who do not believe* (Jn 6:64). He did not say, "There are some among you who do not understand," but he gave the reason for their lack of understanding. *There are some among you who do not believe*, and that is just why they do not understand; because they do not believe." The prophet said, after all, *Unless you have believed, you shall not understand* (Is 7:9, LXX). By faith, we are bonded together,[11] by understanding that we are made alive. First of all let us be attached to him by faith, so that there may be something which can be made alive by understanding. The one who is not attached to him, in fact, is resisting him. The one who resists does not believe. If someone resists how can he be given life? He opposes the ray of light which ought to penetrate him; he is not simply averting his gaze; he closes his mind.

So then, there are some who do not believe. Let them believe and open up, let them open up and be enlightened. *Jesus, after all, was aware from the beginning who the ones were that believed, and who was going to betray him* (Jn 6:64). Yes, Judas too was there. Some were scandalized; he, though, stayed to work against Christ, not to understand him. And because he stayed, the Lord did not keep quiet about him. He did not name him explicitly, but neither did he keep silent, so that all might fear, though only one would be lost. But after he had spoken and distinguished those who believed from those who did not, he stated the reason why they did not believe: *That is why I told you that no one can come to me unless it has been given him by my Father* (Jn 6:65). So then, even believing is something given to us. Believing, in fact, is not a mere nothing. But if is something great, rejoice because you have believed, but do not be proud; *for what do you have that you have not received?* (1 Cor 4:7)

---

11. See Sermon 144, 2, where Augustine makes it clear that the faith which bonds us into the body of Christ is faith working through love. What he goes on to say here, about being made alive through understanding, sounds rather strange, as he is in general quite clear that knowledge without love is nothing. But just as the presence of charity to faith is assumed in the first part of the sentence, so is its presence to understanding assumed in the second. The understanding in question is that the sacrament of the eucharist is precisely the sacrament of our incorporation into the body of Christ, of our union with Christ in his Church. Augustine never denied the real presence of Christ in the sacrament, as some theologians feared that he did; but his eucharistic theology did not stop there. It always went on to emphasize the ultimate thing signified by the sacrament (and by the sacrament, incidentally, he understood the eating and drinking of the consecrated elements, not just the consecration of them); and that is the grace we receive through it, the grace of union with Christ in his Church. See Homilies 11, 3-4; 26, 10.

Many turned back; if Jesus could carry on regardless,
so can we when the same happens today

8. *From this moment many of his disciples turned back, and no longer accompanied him* (Jn 6:66). They *turned back*, but to follow Satan, not Christ. In fact, Christ once called Peter Satan, more because he wanted to get out in front of his Lord and advise the one who came that he might die so that we might not die forever to avoid dying; and he said to him, *Get behind me, Satan, for you do not savor the things of God, but the things of men* (Mt 16:23). He did not push him back so that he would follow Satan, but he called him Satan so that he would come after him, so that he would not be a Satan[12] while following behind the Lord.

These others, however, turned back, in the way the apostle says some women did: *For there are some women who have turned back behind Satan* (1 Tm 5:15). They no longer walked with him. Look at them; cut off from the body they have forfeited life, because they were perhaps never in the body. They too are to be counted as ones who did not believe, even though they were called disciples. Those who turned back were not few, but many.

Perhaps this occurred to reassure us, because it sometimes happens that someone says what is true, and what he says is not understood, and those who hear it are scandalized and depart. But he regrets having said what is true and says to himself, "I should not have spoken like that, I should not have said that." Look, it happened to the Lord; he spoke and lost many, he carried on with a few. But he was not disturbed, because he knew from the beginning both who the believers would be and who would not believe. If this sort of thing happens to us, we are upset. Let us find reassurance in the Lord—and, all the same, let us be careful about the words we utter.

Peter's confession: You have the words of eternal life

9. Turning then to the few who did stay, *Jesus said to the twelve*—that is, to those twelve who stayed with him—*Do you also*, he said, *wish to go away*? (Jn 6:67) Not even Judas had drifted away; but it was already clear to the Lord why he stayed, while to us it was manifested later on. Peter

---

12. Augustine clearly knew the meaning of the Hebrew word "satan," *shaitan*, which means adversary, prosecutor, one who specializes like a prosecuting counsel in tripping someone up.

answered for them all, one for many, unity for all of them together.[13] *So then, Simon Peter replied, Lord, to whom shall we go?* Are you turning us away from you?[14] Give us yourself in another guise. *To whom shall we go?* If we part company with you, *to whom shall we go? You have the words of eternal life* (Jn 6:68).

Just see how Peter, by God's gift, made new by the Holy Spirit, how he understood. How could he have done so, unless he had first believed? *You have the words of eternal life*; after all, you have eternal life in serving us with your body and blood. And we have believed, and we have come to know. Not "We have come to know and have believed," but *We have believed and have come to know.* You see, we have believed in order to know, because if we wanted to know first and then believe, we would be incapable of either knowing or believing. What have we believed and what have we come to know? *That you are the Christ, the Son of God* (Jn 6:69),[15] that is, that you are eternal life itself, and do not give anything in your flesh and blood other than what you are.

While the wicked make bad use of good things,
God makes good use even of the wickedness of Judas

10. So then, the Lord Jesus said, *Did I not choose you twelve, and one of you is a devil?* (Jn 6:70) So should he not have said, "I chose eleven?" Or is a devil also chosen, and there is a devil among the elect? "Elect" is usually said in praise. Or is this man also chosen, through whom such a great benefit would be brought about without his either willing or knowing it? This is how God is, quite the opposite to what the wicked do. Just as the wicked, you see, make bad use of the good works of God, so on the contrary God makes good use of the bad works of wicked men.

How good it is that the members of our body are disposed in a way only a divine craftsman could have done! And yet what bad use wantonness makes of the eyes! What bad use deceitfulness makes of the tongue! Does a false

---

13. For this representative role of Peter's see Sermons 149, 7; 232, 3; 270, 2; 295, 2).
14. I treat this phrase as a question against the authority of all manuscripts and all editors; it seems to me to make better sense, so punctuated.
15. Here Augustine's text, indeed probably nearly all Latin texts, including the Vulgate, has allowed the text of Mt 16:16, Peter's confession of faith at Caesarea Philippi, to override the original of Jn 6:69: *that you are the Christ, the Holy One of God.*

witness not first butcher his own soul with his tongue, and having done for himself then make every effort to injure another? He is making bad use of the tongue, but that does not mean the tongue is bad; the tongue is a work of God, but that evil malice is making bad use of God's good work. How regularly the feet are used by those running to commit their crimes! How commonly their hands are used by murderers, and what bad use is made by bad men of those good creations of God external to us! With gold they corrupt judges, oppress the innocent. This light of day is made bad use of by the bad; by living bad lives, after all, they misappropriate the very light they see by to serve their crimes. A bad man, I mean, on his way to do something bad wants the light to see by in case he stumbles, having already stumbled and fallen inwardly; what he is afraid of for his feet has already occurred in his heart.

So then, in a word, since it would take far too long to run through all the good works of God one by one, all of them are made bad use of by the bad; while good people on the other hand make good use of the bad deeds of the bad. And is there anything as good as the one God, seeing that the Lord himself said, *No one is good but the one God* (Mk 10:18)? So then, being all that much better than us, all the better is the use he makes even of our bad deeds. Could anything be worse than Judas? Among all those who accompanied the Master, among the twelve, it was to him that the funds were entrusted, and the distribution of them to help the poor. Ungrateful for such a privilege, for such a great honor, he accepted the money, forfeited justice; being dead himself, he betrayed life; the one in whose tracks he followed as a disciple, he tracked down as an enemy.[16] All this was the evil doing of Judas, but what good use the Lord made of his evil doings! He permitted himself to be betrayed in order to redeem us. There you are, that is how the evil of Judas was turned into good. How many martyrs Satan hunted down to death! If Satan had stopped tracking them down, we would not be celebrating Saint Laurence's glorious crown today. If then God makes such good use of the evil deeds of the devil himself, by making bad use of God's goodness the bad man does not in any way falsify it, he just harms himself. The craftsman makes use of him; so great is the craftsman that if he did not know how to use him, he would not allow him to exist.

So then, *One of you is a devil*, he said, *while it was I who chose you twelve*. His saying *I chose twelve* can also be understood in this way;

---

16. A neat play on words in the Latin: *quem ut discipulus secutus, ut inimicus persecutus est.*

because twelve is a sacred number. This number, you see, was not deprived of its honor, just because one of them was lost, seeing that another was chosen to take his place.[17] The sacred number, the number twelve, remained intact, because throughout the whole world, to all four corners of the earth, they were going to proclaim the Trinity; so three times four. So Judas then killed himself, but he did not dishonor the number twelve. He forsook his teacher,[18] while, to him, God appointed a successor.

In all this the Lord is telling us to make sure we share in his Spirit by sharing in the sacrament

11. All of this that the Lord said about his flesh and blood and about the promise he made us of eternal life in the grace of its sharing, and about his wish that we should thereby understand that those eating and drinking his body and blood do so as to abide in him and have him abiding in them,[19] and about the fact that those who did not believe did not understand, and about those who were scandalized who knew spiritual things in a carnal way, and about those who were scandalized and on the point of being lost so that the Lord stood by to reassure them, and about those whom he tested by asking, *Do you too wish to go away?* (Jn 6:67) so that we could learn of their intention to stay with him (because he himself knew they would stay)—all this, my dearest friends, is of value to us so that we not feed on the body of Christ and the blood of Christ in a merely sacramental way (which many bad people do), but that we eat and drink to the extent of a participation in the Spirit, staying in the Lord's body as members, and being energized by his Spirit, not scandalized even in this time, if many who will end up in eternal torment eat and drink the sacraments with us now.

At the present time, you see, the body of Christ is all mixed up, as on a threshing floor; but *the Lord knows who are his own* (2 Tm 2:19). If you, when you are threshing, know that there is a mass of grain hidden there, and that the threshing does not destroy what the winnowing is going to sort out

---

17. See Acts 1:15-26.
18. His *praeceptorem*. It is scarcely translatable, as it is being contrasted with the concluding *successorem*, and also has a subsidiary meaning of one who goes ahead. Berrouard translates by "the one who preceded him," contrasted with the one who succeeded him. But Jesus was above all his teacher; and at least in English a predecessor would signify one who occupied his place before him, which would not be true, nor what Augustine was saying.
19. See Homilies 25, 15-16; 26, 13.

and clean, then we can be sure, brothers and sisters, that all of us, who are in the body of the Lord and are abiding in him so that he too may abide in us, must live among bad people in this world until the end of time. I am not speaking about those bad people who revile Christ with their tongue—who are not many today—but about those who revile him with their lives. So we will have to live among them until the end.

How the eucharist sustained the martyrs; How St. Sixtus encouraged St. Laurence

12. But what is this that he said: *Whoever abides in me, and I in him* (Jn 6:56)? What else but what the martyrs listened to: *The one that perseveres to the end is the one that shall be saved* (Mt 10:22; 24:13)? How did Saint Laurence, whose feast we are celebrating today, abide in him? He abided through every temptation, staying with him through the tyrant's interrogation, staying with him under the severest threats, staying with him to the death; that is saying little enough; he stayed with him through the most brutal torture. He was not killed quickly, after all, but tortured by fire; he was allowed to live a long time—or rather it is not that he was allowed to live a long time, but that he was compelled to die slowly. So in that long-drawn-out death, amid those torments, because he had eaten well and drunk well, as if that food had sated him and that cup had made him drunk, he did not feel the torments. There beside him, you see, was the one who had said, *The Spirit gives life.* His flesh was burning, but the Spirit gave life to his soul. He never submitted and into the kingdom was promptly admitted.[20]

Now the holy martyr Sixtus, whose feast day we celebrated four days ago, had said to him, "Do not grieve, son." He was the bishop, you see, Laurence his deacon. "Do not grieve," he said, "you will follow me after three days." He said three days, meaning the three days in between the day of Saint Sixtus' martyrdom and the martyrdom of Saint Laurence today. Three days in between. What encouragement![21] He did not say, "Do not grieve, son, the persecution will soon end, and you will be safe," but, "Do not grieve; where I am going ahead, you will follow. Nor is your attaining the end being deferred; three days and you will be with me." He accepted the prophecy, overcame the devil, and attained victory.

---

20. *Non cessit, et in regnum successit.*
21. Above all, I am sure Augustine means, in the trinitarian number three.

Homily 28

On John 7:1-13[1]

Christ presenting himself here above all as human

1. In this section of the gospel, brothers and sisters, our Lord Jesus Christ commended himself to our faith above all as human. Of course, in his words and actions he always does what will ensure that we believe him to be both God and man; the God who made us, the man who sought us; God for ever with the Father, man with us from a point in time.[2] He would not, you see, come looking for the one he had made, unless he himself was made into what he had made. But just remember this, and do not ever put it out of your minds, that Christ was made man in such a way that he did not stop being God; remaining divine, the one who made humanity took on humanity himself.[3]

So then, when he lay hidden as a man, he must not be thought to have lost his power, but he presented our weakness with an example. After all, he was arrested when he wanted, put to death when he wanted. But since there were going to be members of his, that is his faithful, who would not have the power which he, our God, possessed, his disappearing, his going into hiding so as to avoid being killed, he showed what his members were going to do, those, of course, in whom he would himself be present. Christ, after all, is not in the head and then absent from the body, but the whole Christ is found in head and in body. So what his members are, he is—even though it does not necessarily follow that what he is, his members also are.[4] After all, if his members were not he himself, he would not say, *Saul, why are you persecuting me?* (Acts 9:4) Saul, I mean to say, was not persecuting him in person, but persecuting his members on earth, that is his faithful.[5] All the same, he did not wish to refer to "my holy ones," "my servants," or finally,

---

1. Preached a few days after the previous homilies.
2. See Homily 8, 12.
3. See Sermon 127, 9, note 15.
4. See Sermon 91, 8, where Augustine uses the metaphor of bride and bridegroom (see Is 61:10) and shows that they are one person—in relation to Christ's flesh or human nature.
5. See Homily 21, 7.

more honorably, "my brothers and sisters." He said rather *me*, that is my members, for whom I am the head.[6]

*By concealing himself from his enemies Christ reassured
Christians who did the same during persecutions*

2. With this introduction, I do not think we are going to struggle with the passage that has just been read; often, in fact, what was going to happen in the body was often seen in sign in the head. The evangelist says, *After this Jesus went around in Galilee; for he did not wish to go around in Judea, because the Jews were seeking to kill him* (Jn 7:1). As I just said, he was presenting our weakness with an example. He had lost no power, but was consoling our frailty. After all, in the future it was going to happen, as I said, that a faithful Christian would go into hiding so as not to be discovered by the persecutors; and, so that they not be blamed with a serious sin for going into hiding, the action which would be sanctioned in the members was first taken by the head.

Thus, in fact, is it said, *He did not wish to go around in Judea, because the Jews were seeking to kill him*, as if Christ were unable either to walk about among the Jews or to avoid being killed by the Jews. He did demonstrate this power, after all, when he wanted to. I mean, when they wanted to arrest him just before he was due to suffer, he said to them, *Whom are you searching for? They answered, Jesus. He in turn said, I am he*,[7] not concealing, but revealing himself. At this revelation, however, they could not stand their ground, but *turning away, they fell down.* (Jn 18:4-6) And yet, because he had come to suffer, they got up again, arrested him, led him to the judge, and killed him. Yet what did they achieve? What another text of scripture says, *Earth was handed over into the hands of the impious* (Jb 9:24); flesh was given over to the Jews to deal with as they wished. And all for this reason: so that, as it were, the purse from which the price for us would be spilled[8] might be torn open.

---

6. See Sermons 116, 7; 122, 6; 169, 9; 361, 14.
7. See Homily 11, 2.
8. See Jn 19:34, Christ's side pierced with a lance, and blood and water flowing from it; a theme frequently taken up by Augustine in this manner. See Sermons 296, 2; 329, 1; 336, 4; BA 72, 571, note 15.

Who the Lord's brothers were

3. *Now the feast of the Jews, the Skenopegia,*[9] *was at hand* (Jn 7:2). Those who have read the Scriptures know what the Skenopegia is all about. On the feast day they used to make tents or huts, on the model of the tents in which they had lived when they were wandering in the desert after being brought out of Egypt. This was a feast day of great solemnity.[10] Those Jews, who were going to kill the Lord, celebrated it in memory of the goodness shown them by the Lord.

So on this day of the feast—because the feast comprised several days; in fact, the day of the feast among the Jews consists not of a single day but of several—*his brothers* (Jn 7:3) said to the Lord Christ. Take *his brothers* in the sense you are familiar with. Blood relations of the virgin Mary were called the brothers of the Lord.[11] For that was the custom of the scriptures, to call any blood relations and near kin brothers, but that is foreign to our way of talking, not at all what we are used to. Who, in fact, would call his maternal uncle or his sister's son his brother? Yet scripture also calls these relations brothers. Thus Abraham and Lot are called brothers, though Abraham was Lot's paternal uncle; and Laban and Jacob are called brothers, though Laban was Jacob's maternal uncle.[12]

So then, when you hear *the brothers of the Lord*, think of Mary's relatives, not of her having any other children. You see, just as no dead person had been in the tomb where the Lord's body was placed, either before or after, so neither did Mary's womb carry any mortal child either before or after.

The advice his brothers gave Jesus

4. We have said who his brothers were; let us hear what they said: *Move on from here and go to Judea, so that your disciples too may see your*

---

9. Augustine's Latin text, like the Vulgate, keeps the Greek word (literally "tent-pitching"). "Tabernacles" of course is as foreign to English as that Greek word was to Latin, but it has a number of connotations and may not convey the feeling of foreignness, which would be misleading. The Latin *tabernaculum* (the diminutive of *taberna*) was commonly used for the huts or booths Roman soldiers put up when on campaign.
10. As the greatest solemnity in the Jewish calendar at that time, it was known quite simply as "The Feast."
11. See Homily 10, 2.
12. See Gn 13:8; 14:14; 11:27. Latin distinguished between *avunculus*, a mother's brother, and *patruus*, a father's brother. Hence the translation, "maternal uncle" and "paternal uncle."

works, which you perform (Jn 7:3). The works of the Lord did not escape the notice of the disciples, but they quite escaped the notice of these others. In fact, these brothers, that is, these blood relatives, may have had Christ as their relation, but they were squeamish about believing someone so close to them. That is what the gospel says; after all, we would not dare to express such an opinion on our own; you heard it just now. They go on to give him advice: *No one who wants to be known acts in secret; if you are going to do these things, show yourself to the world.* And then: *In fact, even his brothers were unable to believe in him.* (Jn 7:4-5) Why could they not believe in him? Because they were looking for human fame and glory.[13] Even the advice his brothers seem to be giving him only refers to his fame: "Perform miracles, get yourself known; in other words, show yourself to everybody, so that you can be praised by everyone." Flesh was talking to flesh; flesh without God was talking to flesh united to God. *The prudence of the flesh* (Rom 8:6) was talking to the Word which was *made flesh and took up residence among us* (Jn 1:14).

The way of humility the only road to the home above the stars

5. How did the Lord respond? *So then, Jesus says to them, My time has not yet come, but your time is always at hand* (Jn 7:6). What can this mean? Christ's time had not yet come? So why had Christ come, if his time had not yet come? Have we not heard the apostle saying, *When the fullness of time came, God sent his Son* (Gal 4:4)? If then he was sent in the fullness of time, was sent when he should have been, came when the time was right, what is the meaning of *My time has not yet come*? Understand, brothers and sisters, the design of those who spoke to him as if they were advising him as a brother. They counseled him about winning fame, worldly advice, as it were, based on an earthy affection for him, so that he not remain unknown and hidden. So the Lord said, *My time has not yet come*; he was responding to those advising him advice about fame; "The time of my fame has not yet come."

Notice how profound this is; they were advising him about fame, but he wanted such prominence to be preceded by humility; he wanted to pave the

---

13. Literally, "human glory."

way to that lofty eminence with humility. For those disciples, who wanted seats, one at his right hand, the other on his left, were also looking for fame and glory. Their attention was fixed on where they were going, they did not see the way to get there. Just so that they might reach their home, the Lord called them back to the way.[14] For home is on the heights; the way to get there is humble. Home is the life of Christ, the way there is his death; home is the dwelling of Christ, the way there is his suffering. Why seek to go home, if you refuse to take the way? In sum, that is the answer he gave those who sought the first places: *Can you drink the cup which I myself am going to drink?* (Mk 10:38) That is how to get to the heights you are so eager for. Of course, he was recommending the cup of humiliation and suffering.

Now is the time for being just, later the time for judging

6. So here too then: *My time has not yet come, but your time*, that is, for worldly fame, *is always at hand* (Jn 7:6). This is the time about which Christ, that is, the body of Christ, declares in prophecy, *When I welcome the time as my own, I will pronounce just judgments* (Ps 74:2).[15] Now, you see, is not the time for judging, but for tolerating the wicked. Let the body of Christ therefore bear with and tolerate the wickedness of those who live badly. All the same, let it have justice now, before having judgment; for, through justice, it will come to judgment. What does scripture say in a psalm to the members of the body who are tolerating the wickedness of this world? *The Lord will not thrust aside his people.* His people indeed labors among the unworthy, among the wicked, among denigrators, among grumblers, detractors, those with hostile intentions, who will, if allowed, destroy this people.[16] It labors, certainly, but *the Lord will not thrust his people aside, nor will he forsake his inheritance, until justice is turned into judgment* (Ps 93:14-15). *Until justice*, which is now to be found in his saints, *is*

---

14. See Homily 25, 3. For this contrast between the home country (*patria*) and the way to it (*via*), see Sermon 92, 3, where the one is the divinity of Christ, the other his humanity, with no specific reference to his passion—though of course that was where the incarnation was inevitably leading; also *The Trinity* VII, 3, 5, where the way is more explicitly stated to be Christ's humility, i.e. his humiliation, leading to the eternal abode of his divinity.
15. For his full comments on this verse see *Exposition of Psalm* 74, 5. While the theme is frequently dealt with in the Sermons, nowhere does Augustine actually refer to this particular verse.
16. See Homily 27, 11.

turned into judgment, when what they were told will be fulfilled: *You shall take your seats upon a bench of twelve, judging the twelve tribes of Israel* (Mt 19:28). The apostle had justice, but not yet that judgment of which he says, *Are you not aware that we shall be judging angels?* (1 Cor 6:3)

So let the present, therefore, be the time for living justly; later on will come the time for judging those who have lived bad lives. *Until justice*, it says, *is turned into judgment.* That will be the time for judgment, about which the Lord said just now, *My time has not yet come.* That, you see, will be the time for fame and glory, the time for the one who came in lowliness to come in majesty. The one who came to be judged will come to judge; the one who came to be slain by the dead will come to pass judgment on the living and the dead. *God*, says the psalm, *will come openly, and will not keep silent* (Ps 49:3). Why will he come openly? Because he came in a hidden way. Then, he will not keep silent, because when he came in a hidden way, *he was led like a sheep to the slaughter, and like a lamb in the presence of its shearers he did not open his mouth* (Is 53:7). He will come, and will not keep silent. *I kept quiet*, he said; *shall I always keep quiet?* (Is 42:14 LXX)

Being upright of heart means not blaming God for the evils of the world

7. Now, however, what do those who do have justice need? The response can be read in the same psalm: *Until justice is turned into judgment and all the upright of heart have it* (Ps 93:15). Perhaps you are asking who the upright of heart are. We find in scripture that the upright of heart are those who put up with the evils of the world, and do not blame God for them. Look, brothers and sisters, I am talking about a rare bird.[17] For I do not know how it is that when something bad happens to someone, he rushes to blame God, when he should blame himself. When you do anything good, you give yourself the credit, when anything bad happens to you, you put the blame on God. So that is a twisted heart, not an upright one. If you correct this twistedness and viciousness, you will change what you used to do to the opposite. What did you, in fact, previously do? You gave yourself

---

17. *Rara avis*, a phrase from Horace's *Satires*, II, 2, 26, which had become a popular saying. On not blaming God, see Homily 25, 17.

credit for God's good actions and put the blame on God for your own bad ones; once your heart has turned in the right direction, you will give God the credit for his good actions, taking the blame yourself for your bad ones. Such are the upright of heart.

Indeed, someone who was not yet upright of heart, and who was offended by the way bad men did well and good men were in constant difficulty—after he had straightened himself out—said, *How good is the God of Israel to the upright of heart! But my feet,* when I was not upright of heart, *almost stumbled, my steps were on the point of slipping.* Why? *Because I was envious of sinners, noticing the peace of sinners.* (Ps 72:1-3) "I saw," he is saying, "bad men who were happy, and I was annoyed with God; for what I wanted was that God not allow bad men to be happy." Let it be known, man: it is never God who allows this, but the bad man is thought to be happy because real happiness is not known.[18]

So then, let us be upright of heart; the time for our fame and glory has not yet arrived. Let the lovers of this world, who are like the brothers of the Lord, be told, *Your time is always at hand; our time has not yet come* (Jn 7:6). Let us too be bold enough to say these words. Since we are the body of our Lord Jesus Christ, since we are his members, since we gratefully acknowledge him as our head, let us most definitely say it, since he was good enough to say it on our behalf. When the lovers of this world deride us, let us say to them, *Your time is always at hand;* our *time has not yet come.* After all, the apostle said to us, *For you have died, and your life has been hidden with Christ in God.* When will our time come? He says, *When Christ, your life, appears, then you too will appear with him in glory.* (Col 3:3-4)

The problem of Christ's going up anonymously to the feast

8. What did he go on to say? *The world cannot hate you.* What does this mean, if not that the world cannot hate its lovers, its false witnesses? For you say that something good is bad, and that something bad is good. *But the world hates me because I testify to it, that its works are bad. You go up to this feast.* (Jn 7:7-8) What does he mean by *this feast*? The one where you

---

18. The Latin word here is *felicitas*, which combines the notions of happiness and well-being, and can rarely be translated by just one of these English words. For this theme see Homily 25, 17.

seek human fame. What does he mean by *this feast*? The one where you want to prolong the delights of the flesh, without thinking about those that are eternal. *I am not going up to this feast, because my time is not yet fulfilled* (Jn 7:8). On this feast day you are looking for human fame and glory; my time, however, that is, the time of my glory, has not yet come. That will be the day of my feast, not the one that runs by and passes away with these days, but the one that abides for ever; that will be a celebration, joy unending, eternity unfailing, cloudless serenity.

After saying this, he stayed in Galilee. When his brothers, though, had gone up, then he went up to the feast as well, not publicly, but as it were in secret. (Jn 7:9-10) The reason he had said *not to this feast* was that he did not want temporal fame and glory, but to teach something salutary, to correct some people, to warn people about the eternal feast day, to turn them away from love of this world, and to turn them to God. But what does it mean that he went to the feast, *as it were, in secret*? This behavior of the Lord is not pointless. It seems to me, brothers and sisters, that by going up, as it were, in secret, he meant to signify something; what follows, after all, will inform us that he went for the middle day of the feast, that is, halfway through those days, so as to teach openly. But the writer said *as it were in secret*, meaning he did not want to parade himself before men. It is not without point that Christ went to the feast in secret, because he indeed hid himself on that feast day. What I have just said still remains obscure. So let it be made known then, let the veil be removed,[19] and let what was a secret be apparent.

The things to come of which Tabernacles was the shadow

9. Everything said to the ancient people of Israel in the many writings of the holy law about what they should do, whether about sacrifices, or about priests, or about feast days, and in all the things that concerned their worship of God, in all that they were informed and instructed about—all these were shadows of things to come.[20]

---

19. Again an allusion to the veil in the temple which hid the holy of holies from the common gaze; also of course, and perhaps even more, to St. Paul's words about the veil that Moses put over his face after speaking to the Lord, and the veil over the hearts of the Jews (see 2 Cor 3:12-18), preventing them from seeing the glory of the new covenant in Christ.
20. See Col 2:17.

What things to come?

Everything fulfilled in Christ. That is why the apostle says, *For however many are the promises of God, their yes is in him* (2 Cor 1:20), that is, they are fulfilled in him. Then he said in another place, *All things that ever happened to them did so in figure; but they were written down for our sake, upon whom the end of the ages has come* (1 Cor 10:11). And he said elsewhere, *For the end of the law is Christ* (Rom 10:4); again in another place, *Let nobody judge you over food or over drink, or in the matter of a feast day, or of the new moon, or of sabbaths, which is all a shadow of things to come* (Col 2:1-17).

So then, if all those things were shadows of things to come, the Skenopegia too was a shadow of things to come. Here then is the feast day; let us ask of which thing to come it was the shadow. I have explained what Skenopegia was; it was celebrated in booths or tents, because on being liberated from Egypt and traveling through the desert toward the promised land the people lived in booths or tents. Let us understand what this is all about and we will be there, we, I say, who are members of Christ—as long as we are members; but members by his grace, not by our own merits. So let us now pay attention, brothers and sisters; we have been brought out of Egypt, where we served the devil as our Pharaoh, where we spent time with works of mud according to our earthly desires and labored mightily in it. Indeed, Christ cried out to us as we made bricks, *Come to me, all you that toil and are overburdened* (Mt 11:28).

Brought out from there through baptism as through the Red Sea, red precisely because consecrated by the blood of Christ, and our enemies who were pursuing us all dead, that is, all our sins blotted out, we ourselves have been ferried across.[21] So for the time being then, before we come to the promised homeland, that is to the eternal kingdom, we are in the wilderness in tents. Those who recognize these realities are in tents; some were meant to recognize all these things. The one living in a tent realizes that he is a

---

21. See Homily 11, 4.

foreigner[22] in the world. He understands that he is wandering as someone who knows himself as a person longing for his homeland.

But as long as the body of Christ is living in tents, Christ is living in tents. Then, however, the mystery was not evident, but hidden. For, the shade still obscured the light; when the light had come, the shade withdrew. Christ was there in secret, Christ was there in the Skenopegia, but Christ was hidden. Now that all these things have been brought to light, we recognize that we are on a road in the wilderness; for, if we recognize that, then we are in the wilderness.

What is "in the wilderness?"

In the desert.

Why in the desert?

Because in this world, where we endure thirst along a waterless way.[23] But let us thirst, so as to be satisfied. *Blessed,* after all, *are those who hunger and thirst for justice, for they shall be satisfied* (Mt 5:6). And our thirst is slaked from the rock in the wilderness; *the rock was Christ* (1 Cor 10:4), you see, and it was struck with a rod, to make water gush out. For it to gush out, though, it was struck twice[24]—because the cross had two beams.

All these things then which were happening in figure have been made manifest, and it is not without meaning what was said about the Lord, that *he went up to the feast day, not publicly, but as it were in secret.* After all, it was foreshadowed about him in secret, because on that feast day Christ was in hiding, because that feast day signified the members of Christ who would be wandering around.

The Jews looking for Christ on the feast day

10. *So the Jews then were looking for him on the feast day* (Jn 7:11), before he went there. His brothers went there first, but, when they thought he should and wanted him to, he did not go up then, so that he might fulfill what he had said, *Not yet* (Jn 7:8), that is, not on the first or second day,

---

22. *Peregrinus,* the word from which we get "pilgrim." To translate it "pilgrim" misses the connotation of exile in a foreign land.
23. See Homily 5, 1.
24. See Num 20:11; Homily 26, 12.

when you want to go.[25] However, he went up later, as the gospel puts it, *on the middle day of the feast* (Jn 7:14), that is when as many days of the feast had preceded it as still remained. Their celebration of the festival, after all, so we must understand, lasted for several days.

When the grain is sorted out from the chaff

11. *So they started saying, then, Where is he? And there was much murmuring about him in the crowd.* (Jn 7:11-12)

What caused the murmuring?

The disagreement.

What was the disagreement about?

For some were saying, He is a good man, while others said, No, but he is misleading the rabble (Jn 7:12). These words are to be understood about his servants; that is still said nowadays. Anybody, you see, who has gained prominence for some spiritual grace, certainly has others say, *He is a good man*, and others, *No, but he is misleading the rabble*.

Why does this happen?

Because *our life has been hidden with Christ in God*.

Thus you can say to people throughout the winter, "This tree is dead, a fig tree, for example, a pear tree, any fruit tree of that sort; it looks as if it is quite withered." And as long as winter lasts, you cannot tell the difference. The summer shows the difference, the summer makes the judgment. Our summer is the manifestation of Christ. *God will come openly, and will not keep silent* (Ps 49:3); *fire will go before him, fire that will burn up his enemies* (Ps 96:3); the fire will catch hold of the withered trees. That is when they will be shown up as withered, when they will be told, *I was hungry, and you gave me nothing to eat* (Mt 25:42). On the other side, though, that is, on the right, the abundance of fruit and the splendor of the foliage will be on display; the greenery is eternity. The first ones then, as withered and dry, will be told, *Go into everlasting fire* (Mt 25:41). Then, he says, *The axe has been laid to the root of the trees. So every tree that does not bear good fruit will be cut out and thrown into the fire.* (Lk 3:9)

---

25. See Sermon 133; which, however, is only concerned to show that Jesus was not lying.

So let them say about you, if you are making progress in Christ, let people say, *He is misleading the rabble*. This is being said about the whole body of Christ. Think of the body of Christ still in the world, think of the body of Christ still on the threshing floor; notice how the chaff reviles it. Indeed, they are beaten all together, but the chaff and straw is crushed, the grain is cleansed. So what was said then about the Lord is good to reassure any Christian about whom insults are being spoken.

What was being shouted then is nowadays only whispered;
what was whispered then is nowadays being shouted aloud

12. *No one, however, was speaking openly about him for fear of the Jews* (Jn 7:13). But who were the ones not speaking about him for fear of the Jews? Those of course who were saying, *He is a good man*, not those who were saying, *He is misleading the rabble*. As for those who were saying, *He is misleading the rabble*, the noise they made was like that of withered leaves. *He is misleading the rabble*, people were trumpeting it aloud; *He is a good man*, people were whispering. Now, though, brothers and sisters, while that glory of Christ which is going to make us eternal has not yet come, now at least his Church is growing. She is spreading so much everywhere that now they are whispering, *He is misleading the rabble*, and *He is a good man* is being loudly trumpeted.

Homily 29

On John 7:14-18[1]

Different opinions among the Jews about Jesus

1. Let us also look at the next passage from the gospel which was also read today and say whatever the Lord may give. Yesterday it was only read this far, because although they had not seen the Lord Jesus during the festival, they were still talking about him: *And some were saying, He is a good man, while others said, No, but he is misleading the rabble* (Jn 7:12). This was said to reassure those who would preach the word of God later on,[2] and would be *treated as seducers and yet are truthful men* (2 Cor 6:8). If to seduce or to mislead,[3] after all, means to deceive, then neither Christ nor his apostles were deceitful; nor should any Christian be a seducer; but if to seduce means to persuade someone from thinking one thing to thinking another, then we have to ask from what to what; if from bad to good, then the seducer is good; if from good to bad, then the seducer is bad. So in the sense that you can say people are seduced from the bad to the good, then all of us should be called and are seducers!

The amazement of the Jews at Jesus' ability to teach, when he had never learned

2. So then, afterwards the Lord *went up* to the feast, *on the middle day of the feast, and began teaching. And the Jews were astonished, saying, How does this man know his letters, when he has not studied?* (Jn 7:14-15) The man who was hiding was teaching and speaking openly, and he was not arrested. While he was hiding to set an example, his teaching without being arrested showed his power.[4] But when he began teaching, the Jews were astonished. All of them indeed, I think, were astonished, but they were not all converted.

---

1. Preached the day after Homily 28.
2. See Homilies 27, 8; 28, 11.
3. In English "to seduce" or "to mislead" can only be used in a bad sense. In Latin the noun *seductor* can only be used in a bad sense; the verb *seducere* means "to seduce" or "to lead astray" or "to mislead," even in a moral sense. So, in his interpretation of Jn 7:12 and of 2 Cor6:8, Augustine is reinterpreting the word in a positive sense.
4. See Homily 28, 1-2.

And what gave rise to this astonishment?

The fact that many of them knew where he was born, how he had been brought up; they never saw him learning letters, yet now they were hearing him discussing the law, producing evidence from the law, which nobody could produce unless he had read it, nobody could read it unless he had learned letters; and that is why they were astonished.

Their astonishment, however, provided the Master with the occasion for putting forward the truth in a deeper way. Taking his cue from their astonishment and their words, the Lord said something very profound, which calls for much more thorough examination and discussion. That is the reason why I am asking Your Graces to be attentive, not only to hear what is beneficial for yourselves but also to pray for me.

The problem of My teaching is not mine

3. What then did the Lord respond to those who were astonished at how he knew letters which he had not learned? *My teaching*, he said, *is not mine, but from him who sent me* (Jn 7:16). This is a first depth-to-be-explored;[5] He seems, in fact, to have contradicted himself in these few words. He did not say, "This teaching is not mine," but *My teaching is not mine*. If not yours, how is it yours? If yours, how is it not yours? After all, you are saying each thing, both *my teaching* and *not mine*.

So if he had said, "This teaching is not mine," there would be no question. But, for the moment, brothers and sisters, concentrate first of all on the question, and then look for its solution. For, if you do not see the problem which is set before you, how can you understand the way it is dealt with? His saying "Mine not mine" is what poses a problem, because it appears to be a contradiction in terms; how is "mine" also "not mine?"

If, then, we take a close look at what the holy evangelist says at the start, *In the beginning was the Word, and the Word was with God, and the Word was God* (Jn 1:1), the resolution of the question depends on that text. What, therefore, is the teaching of the Father but the Word of the Father? So, if he is the Word of the Father, then Christ is the teaching of the Father.[6] But since a word must belong to someone and cannot be no one's, Christ both

---

5. *Profunditas prima.* It is clear that Augustine is not just referring to an insight he wants to share; rather is he inviting his listeners into the depths of the Lord's words.
6. See Homily 14, 7.

called himself his teaching and said that his teaching was not his, because he is the Word of the Father. If what you are belongs to someone else, what is so fully yours as you? And what is so fully not yours as you?[7]

Words signify things; The Word of God both sign and thing signified

4. So the Word then is both God and the Word of a steadfast teaching, which is not uttered in syllables that vanish once heard, but which abides with the Father; to this abiding teaching we are to turn, once summoned by the transient sounds of spoken words. Such transient words, after all, are not summoning us to the pursuit of transient realities. We are being summoned to love God. Everything that I have said was a bunch of syllables; they lashed the air with their vibrations to reach your sense of hearing, and that was the end of them, once they had made their sounds. But it should not be the end of what I summoned you to, because the one I summoned you to love does not pass away; and once you have turned to him on being summoned by these transient syllables, you will not pass away either, but will abide with him as he abides.

This then is the great, lofty and eternal reality in the teaching that abides, to which all the things that pass away in time call us, when they signify well and are not presented falsely. All the signs, of course, that we present when we utter sounds signify something that is not a sound. God, I mean to say, is not one brief syllable,[8] and we do not worship one brief syllable, and bow down to one brief syllable, and long to attain to one brief syllable, which almost ceases to be heard before it has begun; nor is there room in it for the last two letters before the first has disappeared.[9] So then, there abides something great which is called "God," though the sound made when you say "God" does not abide. Understand the teaching of Christ in this way, and

---

7. See *The Trinity* I, 12, 27; II, 2, 4. In the first of these texts Augustine explains Jn 7:16 in terms of the two natures of Christ; as a human being his teaching is really the Father's who sent him; as the eternal Word, his teaching is indeed his own. But in the second he advances more deeply into the divine mystery; so that Christ, as the Word, can identify himself with his teaching, as Augustine is saying in this homily; and yet the same eternal Word can say that he is not his own, but the Father's Word, the Father's teaching, because he is eternally from the Father, eternally begotten of the Father, and is not from himself.
8. Augustine said "two brief syllables," of course, viz. *Deus*.
9. With his two syllables to play with, Augustine said: "Nor is there room for the second before the first has disappeared." For all this explanation of the difference between the Word and words see Homily 1, 8.

you will arrive at the Word of God; when you have arrived at the Word of God, turn your minds to *the Word was God*, and you will see the truth of his saying *my teaching*; turn your minds also to whose Word it is, and you will see how right he was to say *is not mine*.

This sentence means that Christ is not from himself, but from the Father

5. So then, let me briefly tell Your Graces that, with the words, *My teaching is not mine*, I think the Lord was saying, "I am not from myself." For, while we indeed say and believe that the Son is equal to the Father, and that there is no difference of nature or substance between them, and that there was no interval of time interposed between begetter and begotten; all the same, with that being assured and maintained, we still say that one is the Father, the other is the Son. The one would not be the Father unless he had a Son; the other would not be the Son unless he had a Father. Nonetheless, the Son is God from the Father, while the Father is God, but not from the Son. The Father of the Son is not God from the Son, while the other, the Son of the Father, is also God from the Father. The Lord Christ, remember, is called "Light from Light."[10] So then there is Light which is not from Light, and an equal Light which is from Light, together one Light, not two Lights.

To understand, you must first believe;
the will of the Father is that we believe in the one he sent

6. If we have understood, then God be thanked! If someone, however, has understood little—a human being has thus done what he could—let him see in the rest the basis he has for hope.[11] We preachers, like laborers, can work outside by planting and watering, but God is the one who makes things grow.[12] *My teaching*, he says, *is not mine, but from him who sent me* (Jn 7:16). Let the one who says, "I have not yet understood," listen to a counsel. Once this great and profound matter had been broached, the Lord Christ realized that not all were going to understand such a profound matter, and added some advice. Do you want to understand? Believe. God himself, you see, said through the prophet, *Unless you have believed, you shall not understand* (Is 7:9 LXX). What the Lord went on to add here is

---
10. Augustine is quoting the Nicene creed. For the whole of this topic see Homily 19,6.13.
11. See Homily 23, 11.
12. See 1 Cor 3:6.

also relevant: *If anyone wants to do his will, he will know whether the teaching is from God, or whether I am speaking on my own* (Jn 7:17).

What does it mean, *If anyone wants to do his will*? I had said, *If anyone believes*, and I gave this advice: "If you have not understood," I said, "believe." For understanding is the reward of faith.[13] So then, do not try to understand in order to believe, but believe in order to understand, because *unless you have believed, you shall not understand*. So then, to make understanding possible, I advised you to practice the obedience of faith and said that the Lord Jesus Christ added the same advice in the next sentence, where we find that he said, *If anyone wants to do his will, he will know about the teaching*.

What is *he will know*? The same as "he will understand." But what is *If anyone wants to do his will*? That means "to believe." But everyone understands that *he will know* is the same as "he will understand;" but when he says, *If anyone wants to do his will*, that is a matter of believing; if we are to understand that more thoroughly, we need the Lord himself as our interpreter, to show us whether doing his Father's will really and truly is a matter of believing. Who is not aware of the fact that to do God's will means performing his work, something, that is, which pleases him? Now the Lord himself says openly in another place, *This is the work of God, that you should believe in the one whom he has sent* (Jn 6:29). *That you should believe in him*, not that you should believe him. If you believe in him, you believe him; while it does not immediately follow that if you believe him, you also believe in him. After all, even the demons believed him, and did not believe in him. Again, we can say about his apostles, "We believe Paul" but not "We believe in Paul;" "We believe Peter" but not "We believe in Peter."

For *to the one who believes in him who justifies the ungodly, his faith is credited to justice* (Rom 4:5). What then does it mean, to believe in him? By believing to love (*amare*) him, by believing to cherish (*diligere*) him,[14] to go to him by believing and be incorporated in his members. That then is the faith which the Father requires of us; and he does not find what he requires,

---

13. See Homilies 18, 1; 27, 7.9.
14. The distinction between the two Latin words, *amare* and *diligere*, is delicate. *Amare* refers to love in general terms; *diligere* means having a high regard or valuing someone. But Augustine does not always make a distinction, occasionally using these two words as synonymous, or switching their meanings.

unless he has given us what he may find in us.¹⁵ What can this faith be, but what the apostle gave the fullest definition of in another place, saying, *Neither being circumcised nor being uncircumcised is worth anything, but faith which works through charity*¹⁶ (Gal 5:6). Not any old faith, but faith which works through charity; have this within you, and you will understand the teaching. Yes, what is it you will understand? That *this teaching is not mine, but from him who sent me*; that is, you will understand that Christ the Son of God, who is the teaching of the Father, is not from himself, but is the Son of the Father.

This sentence of Christ rules out Sabellianism

7. This affirmation has destroyed the Sabellian heresy.¹⁷ The Sabellians, you see, had the nerve to say that the Son is the same as the Father; two names but one reality. Well, if they were two names and one reality, he would not say, *My teaching is not mine*. Obviously, dear Lord, if your teaching is not yours, whose can it be, if the one whose it is is not someone else? The Sabellians do not understand what you have said; they have not, after all, seen the Trinity but have followed the error of their own heart.

We who worship the Trinity and Unity of the Father and the Son and the Holy Spirit and the one God, let us be sure to understand about the teaching of Christ, that it is not his own. And this is the reason why he said that he does not speak from what is his own, that Christ is the Son of the Father, and the Father is the Father of Christ, and the Son is God from God the Father; while God the Father is not God from God the Son.

Antichrist will be the one who pre-eminently seeks his own glory

8. *Whoever speaks on his own is seeking his own glory* (Jn 7:18). This one will be called the Antichrist, *exalting himself*, as the apostle says, *above all that is called god and is worshiped* (2 Thes 2:4). The Lord in fact

---

15. See Homilies 26, 2;27, 7.
16. Here the Latin is *dilectio*, a translation of the Greek *agape*. The usual English is "charity," "holding dear."
17. A heresy which arose and flourished in the middle of the third century. Augustine's description of it is accurate; one could say it was a simplification of the Christian doctrine of God. Sabellius, a native of Cyrenaica, who came to Rome about the year 210, picked it up from a man called Praxeas, a Christian in Asia Minor.

announced someone who would seek his own glory, not the Father's, when he said to the Jews, *I now have come in my Father's name, and you have not acknowledged me; another will come in his own name, him you will acknowledge* (Jn 5:43). He meant they were going to acknowledge Antichrist, who was going to seek the glory of his own name, puffed up and hollow and therefore unable to stand and ready to fall into ruin.[18]

Our Lord Jesus Christ, on the other hand, has offered us a wonderful example of humility; yes, equal to the Father; yes, *in the beginning was the Word, and the Word was with God, and the Word was God*; yes, the one who said and said with total truth, *Am I with you all this time, and you do not know me? Philip, whoever has seen me, has also seen the Father* (Jn 14:9); yes, the one who said and said with total truth, *I and the Father are one* (Jn 10:30). If then he, one with the Father, equal to the Father, God from God, God with God, co-eternal, immortal, equally unchanging, equally timeless, equally creator and disposer of times, if he, because he came in time, *took the form of a slave, and was found in appearance as a man* (Phil 2:7), then he seeks his Father's glory, not his own. What should you, O man, do, you who seek your own glory whenever you do anything good, while when you do something bad, you figure out ways to blame God?[19]

Take a look at yourself; you are a creature, acknowledge the creator; you are a slave, do not disdain the master; you have been adopted, but not on your merits. Seek the glory of the one from whom you have received this grace, O adopted child, seek the glory of the one whose glory was sought by his only true born Son. *But the one who seeks the glory of him that sent him, he is truthful, and there is no injustice in him* (Jn 7:18). In the Antichrist, however, there is injustice, and he is not truthful, because he will seek his own glory, not that of the one who sent him—although he was not sent, but permitted to come.[20] So then, all of us who belong to the body of Christ, let us make sure of not being enticed into the snares of Antichrist, let us not seek our own glory. But if Christ sought the glory of him that sent him, how much more should we be seeking the glory of him that made us?

---

18. Literally, *Inflatus, non solidus* would be "full of wind, not solid." The whole sentence is an allusion to the one who builds a house on sand (see Mt 7:26). Antichrist is thought of here as the final false Messiah. On pride the origin of all sins, see Homily 25, 17.
19. See Homily 28, 7.
20. See Homily 7, 7.

Homily 30

On John 7:19-24[1]

As we are hearing Truth speaking in the gospel,
we are listening to the Lord himself, as if present here and now

1. The reading from the holy gospel, which I recently spoke to Your Graces about, is followed by the passage that was read today. Listening to the Lord speaking were both disciples and Jews; listening to Truth speaking were people both truthful and deceitful; listening to Charity speaking were both friends and enemies; listening to Goodness speaking were people both good and bad. They were all listening, but he was discerning among those for whom his words were or would be beneficial; he saw and foresaw them both.

So then, let us listen to the gospel as if the Lord himself were present here; and let us not say, "Oh how fortunate were those who could actually see him!" because many of those who saw him also killed him, but many of us who have not seen him have also come to believe. The precious words, after all, that fell from the lips of the Lord were written down on our behalf, and preserved for us, and have been read aloud for our sake, and will also be read out loud for our descendants, and right on till the end of the world. The Lord is above, but the Lord, the Truth, is also here. The body of the Lord, you see, in which he rose again, can only be in one place; but his truth has been spread everywhere.[2] So then, let us listen to the Lord, and may I also say whatever he may grant me to say about his words.

The crowd says Jesus has a demon

2. "*Did not Moses*, said he, *give you the law, yet none of you keeps the law? Why are you seeking to kill me?* (Jn 7:19) In fact, the reason for trying to kill me is that none of you keeps the law," because if you did keep the law, you would recognize Christ in these writings and would not kill him when he is present. And they answered him. *The crowd answered him.* The

---
1. Preached a few days after Homily 29.
2. See Homily 27, 3.

crowds did not answer in a calm way but—as is the way with crowds—in a disturbed way.³ Anyway, see what answer the agitated crowd gave: *You have a demon; who is seeking to kill you?* (Jn 7:20)—as if it were not worse to say "You have a demon" than to kill him! In fact, the one who was being told he had a demon was casting out demons. What else could a crowd in turmoil say? What other smell could come from churned-up mud? The crowd was disturbed; what by? By truth. The clarity of light disturbed the sore unhealthy eyes of the crowd. Those who do not have healthy eyes, after all, cannot bear bright light.⁴

The Lord is the source of all health

3. The Lord, however, clearly not disturbed but tranquil in his truth, *did not pay back evil for evil, nor cursing for cursing* (1 Pt 3:9). If he had said to them, "You are the ones that have a demon," he would undoubtedly have spoken the truth. After all, they would not have said such a thing to him, Truth in person, unless they had been put up to it by the deceit of the devil. So what answer did he give them? Let us calmly listen and drink in his serenity: *One work have I performed, and you are all amazed* (Jn 7:21), as if he were saying, "What if you could see all my works?" For his were the works they saw in the world, but they were not seeing the one who made them all.

He did one thing; they were troubled, because he restored a man to health on the sabbath.⁵ Indeed, it was as if—when a sick person recovered his health on the sabbath—someone else were restoring him to health, someone other than the one who scandalized them by healing on the sabbath! Who else, in fact, restored others to health than Health itself, the one who also gives to animals the same health he gave to this man? This was, after all, bodily health. The health of the flesh is both restored and dies; when it is restored, death is postponed, not removed. Yet even this health,

---

3. Throughout the rest of this section there is a play on words related to the word for crowd, *turba*, i.e., disturbed, turbulent, perturbed; but it cannot always be replicated in English.
4. See Homilies 17, 3; 18, 11.
5. The man who had been lying beside the pool of Bethesda for thirty-eight years (see Jn 5:2-16). When Augustine speaks about anyone else getting better on the sabbath, he may have the other sick people by the pool in mind, those who may have jumped into it when its waters were disturbed by an angel. That would not have scandalized the Jews, because jumping into the pool would not be performing a work.

brothers and sisters, comes from the Lord, no matter who restores it; whoever prescribes the cure and nurses you back to health, it is given by the one from whom all health comes, to whom it says in the psalm, *Men and beasts, Lord, will you save, just as you have multiplied your mercy, O God* (Ps 35:6-7). Because you are God, after all; your mercy is multiplied and also reaches to the health of human flesh, also reaches to the health of speechless animals; but you who give health of the flesh to man and beast alike, is there no health[6] which you keep for human beings alone?

There certainly is another health which is not only not shared by man and beast but is not even shared by good and bad human beings. So, after talking there about the health which is shared by cattle and human beings, the psalm went on to add something about the health which human beings—those who are good—ought to hope for: *But the sons of men shall hope under the cover of your wings; they will get drunk on the abundance of your house, and from the torrent of your delight you will give them to drink, because with you is the fountain of life, and in your light shall we see light* (Ps 35:7-9). This is the health reserved for good people, for those called *the sons of men*, although previously it had said, *Men and beasts, Lord, will you save.*

What is that about? Were those *men* not *sons of men*, such that, after saying *men*, it went on to say *sons of men*, as if *men* were one thing, *sons of men* another? I hardly think the Holy Spirit said this without giving some significance to the distinction. Perhaps *men* refers to the first man, but *sons of men* refers to the Son of Man.

Circumcision on the sabbath, healing on the sabbath

4. *One work have I performed, and you are all amazed*; and right away he added, *That is why Moses gave you circumcision*. It was good that you received circumcision from Moses. *Not that it came from Moses, but from the ancestors* (Abraham, of course, was the first to receive circumcision from the Lord),[7] *and you perform circumcision on the sabbath* (Jn 7:21-22). Moses has exposed you; you learned in the law that you

---

6. The Latin *salus* means both "health" and "salvation." *Salvos facere* means "to save" in both senses of the English word.
7. See Gn 17:10-13.

should circumcise on the eighth day; you learned in the law that you should rest on the seventh day;[8] if the eighth day after a child's birth should occur on the seventh day of the sabbath, what are you going to do? Are you going to rest, in order to keep the sabbath, or are you going to circumcise, in order to fulfill the sacrament of the eighth day?[9]

"I know," he said, "what you do; you circumcise a man. Why? Because circumcision refers to a particular sign of salvation, and people should not give themselves a rest from salvation on the sabbath. So then, *do not be angry with me, because I have saved the whole man on the sabbath* (Jn 7:23). *If*, he says, *a person receives circumcision on the sabbath, so that the law of Moses may not be broken* (something salutary, you see, was instituted by Moses in that ordinance about circumcision), why are you indignant with me for a work of healing on the sabbath?"

The multiple significance of circumcising on the eighth day with knives of flint

5. Perhaps that circumcision was, in fact, a sign of the Lord, with whom these people were so indignant for curing and restoring to health. The commandment, after all, was to administer circumcision on the eighth day; and what is circumcision but a removal of flesh?[10] So then, this circumcision signifies the stripping from the heart of the desires of the flesh. Not without reason, then, was the command given to perform it on that particular organ, since it is through that organ that mortal creatures are procreated.[11] *Through one man death came*, and *through one man comes the resurrection of the dead* (1 Cor 15: 21), and *through one man sin entered the world, and through sin death* (Rom 5:12).[12]

---

8. See Lv 12:3; Ex 20:10.
9. Remembering that, for Augustine, any sign signifying something sacred was a sacrament, why not speak of the sacrament of circumcision? Because the sacrament of the eighth day, or rather of the number eight, was a key element in his general interpretation of the scriptures; it signified the Lord's resurrection on the first day of the week, which was also the eighth day. See 1 Pt 3:20, where the eight souls in all saved from the flood in Noah's ark have the same sacramental significance.
10. See Col 2:11.
11. See Sermons 231, 2; 260A, 4.
12. See Sermon 331B, 1 and note 5.

Therefore, every male is born with a foreskin because all human beings are born with the sin of their origin;[13] and God only cleanses us, whether from the vice with which we are born or the vices which we add by bad lives, by means of a knife made from rock, by means of the Lord Christ; for *the rock was Christ* (1 Cor 10:4). The Jews, in fact, used to circumcise with flint knives,[14] and through the name of this rock they represented Christ, and when he was present they did not acknowledge him, but, even more, they wanted to kill him.

But why was circumcision on the eighth day, if not because, after the seventh day of the sabbath, the Lord rose on Sunday, the Lord's Day? So then, the resurrection of Christ—which indeed happened on the third day after his passion, and on the eighth day in a seven-day week—that is what circumcises us. Listen to the exhortation of the apostle to those circumcised by the true rock: *If then you have risen with Christ, seek the things that are above, where Christ is, seated on God's right; savor the things that are above, not the things on earth* (Col 3:1-2). He is speaking to the circumcised;[15] Christ has risen; he has rid you of the desires of the flesh, rid you of evil lusts, rid you of the superfluity you were born with and the much worse extras you have added by bad lives; circumcised with rock, why do you still savor the earth?

And to conclude, because Moses gave you the law, and you circumcise a man on the eighth day, you must understand that by this is signified the good work which I did in making the whole man well on the sabbath, because he was both cured, and thus had health restored to his body, and he believed, and thus had health restored to his soul.

The Jews should judge between Jesus and Moses without respect of persons

6. *Do not judge because of the person, but render judgment justly* (Jn 7:24). What does this mean? "You that now circumcise on the sabbath according to the law of Moses are not angry with Moses, but because I have

---

13. Berrouard interprets *vitio propagationis* as the excessive concupiscence involved in the sexual act. I think rather that Augustine is referring to original sin, as is clear from his references to Adam, the old man, and the new man.
14. See Jos 5:2.
15. That is, to Jewish Christians, or perhaps to all those spiritually circumcised by Christ. In either case, "the superfluity you were born with" in the next sentence refers to original sin (signified perhaps by the foreskin).

restored a man to health on the day of the sabbath, you are angry with me. You are judging because of the person; pay attention rather to the truth." The Lord, the very one who was the Lord of Moses, says, "I am not putting myself before Moses. Think about us as if we were just two men. Judge between us as two men, but render a true judgment; do not condemn him by honoring me, but honor me by understanding him." This is what he said to them in another place, *If you believed Moses, you would surely believe me; after all, he wrote about me* (Jn 5:46). But he did not want to say that in this place, where he was, as it were, setting Moses and himself before them on equal terms. "You circumcise according to the law of Moses, even when the sabbath occurs on the eighth day; and as for me, do you not want me to give people the benefit of healing them well on the sabbath?"

Because the Lord of circumcision and *the Lord of the sabbath* (Mk 2:28) is the author of salvation, and because you are forbidden to perform servile works on the sabbath, if you really understand what servile works are, you do not sin.[16] *Whoever commits sin, after all, is the slave of sin* (Jn 8:34). Is it, I ask you, a servile work to restore a person to health on the sabbath? You eat and drink—if I may borrow something from a warning given by our Lord Jesus Christ and in his own words[17]—well, why do you eat and drink on the sabbath, if not because what you are doing is concerned with health? Thereby you show that works which have to be done for health's sake are in no way to be omitted on the day of the sabbath. So then, *do not judge because of the person, but render judgment justly.* "Take notice of me as a man, take notice of Moses as a man; if you judge in accordance with the truth, you will condemn neither Moses nor me; and once you have come to know the truth, you will come to know me, because *I am the Truth* (Jn 14:6)."

Respect of persons a difficult vice for us too to avoid

7. This vice, brothers and sisters, which the Lord spoke about in this place, is really hard to avoid in this world, not judging because of the person, but making right judgment. The Lord was indeed admonishing the

---

16. See Ex 20:8-11. About the true meaning of abstaining from servile works, see Homilies 3, 19; 20, 2.
17. Augustine may be referring to Jesus' admonition in Luke 7:33-34: *John the Baptist came, neither eating bread nor drinking wine, and you say, He has a demon; the Son of Man came, eating and drinking, and you say, Look, a gluttonous man and a wine-bibber.*

Jews, but he was warning us too; they were convicted by him, we were being instructed; he confuted them, he alerted us. Let us not think that this was not said to us, just because we were not there at the time. It was written down, it is read, we heard it when it was recited, but we heard it as something that was said to the Jews. Let us not put ourselves behind our backs, looking keenly, as it were, to find something to blame in our enemies, and then we ourselves do what Truth itself can reproach us with.[18]

The Jews were indeed judging because of the person, but that is why they do not belong to the New Covenant, that is why they do not possess Christ in the kingdom of heaven; that is why they are not admitted to the company of the holy angels. They were looking for earthly things from the Lord: the promised land, victory over enemies, fecundity in parenting, many children, abundance of crops, all the things that the God who is indeed true and good did promise them; but they were promised to fleshly-minded people; all these things constitute for them the Old Covenant.[19] What is the Old Covenant? You could say it is the inheritance belonging to the old man. As for us, we have been renewed, we have been made into the new man, because that man, Christ, came as the New Man.

What could be newer than being born of a virgin? So, because there was nothing in him for the commandment to renew, since he had no sin, he was granted a new kind of birth. In him a new birth, in us a new man. What is a new man? One renewed from what is old. Renewed for what purpose? That he might desire heavenly things, yearn for eternal things, desire the homeland which is above and fears no foe, where a friend is not lost, an enemy is not feared; where we live in inner peace without any want; where no one is born, because no one dies; where no one makes greater progress, and no one falls away; where there is no hunger, no thirst,[20] but fulfillment is immortality, and food is truth. Having these promises, and belonging to the New Covenant, and made heirs of the new inheritance, and co-heirs of the Lord himself,[21] we have another great hope; so let us not judge because of the person, but hold to judgment because it is right.

---

18. See Sermon 129, 2; Homily 12, 13.
19. See Homily 3, 20.
20. See Sermon 127, 3; Homily 3, 21.
21. See Rom 8:17.

Conclusion; honor where honor is due; but always equity in judgment

8. Who are the ones who do not judge because of the person? The one who loves everyone with equal respect. Loving people with equal respect is not acting because of the person. Not that, when we honor people in different ways according to their station in life, we should fear that we are acting because of the person. But when we are judging between two individuals, and sometimes between relatives—often is there a judgment between father and son, the father complaining about his bad son, or the son complaining about his father's harshness[22]—we observe the courtesy which the son owes to the father, and we do not make the son equal to the father in the respect due him; but, if his cause is just, we put him ahead of his father. Let us make the son equal to the father in the truth of the matter, and render the honor that is due without letting their equal rights be lost. Thus shall we profit from the Lord's words, and to do so shall we be assisted by his grace.

---

22. Such quarrels were continually being brought to the bishop's tribunal for his judgment on them. He certainly knew what he was talking about in this matter!

Homily 31

On John 7:25-36[1]

*The mystery signified by Jesus going up secretly,
and then speaking openly at Tabernacles*

1. Your Graces will remember that in the sermons of the last few days I have, to the best of my ability, discussed what was also read in the gospel, namely, that the reason why the Lord Jesus went, as it were, secretly to the feast day, was not because he was afraid of being arrested, since it was in his power not to be arrested, but to signify that he was concealed even on the feast day being celebrated by the Jews, and that the mystery of the feast was his own.[2] So, in today's reading, what was thought to be cowardice was revealed as power; he was talking openly, you see, on the feast day, such that the crowds were amazed and they began to say what we heard when the reading was read, *Is he not the one they are trying to kill? And look, he is talking openly, and they say nothing to him. Have the authorities in fact realized that he is the Christ?* (Jn 7:25-26)

Those who knew with what grim determination he was wanted were amazed at his power in holding off arrest. Then, not fully understanding his power, they thought that the authorities had come to know that he was the Christ, and, for that reason, they spared the man they had sought unremittingly to arrest so as to put him to death.

They knew where he came from; but nobody will know where the Christ is from

2. Next, these people who had been saying in themselves, *Have the authorities realized that he is the Christ?* proposed a question among themselves which seemed to show that, for them, he was not the Christ; for they added, *But we know where this man comes from; while when the Christ comes, nobody knows where he is from* (Jn 7:27). Let us ask ourselves how this opinion arose among the Jews, that *when the Christ comes, nobody*

---

[1]. Preached not long after the previous three homilies.
[2]. See Homily 28, 9 where what is signified by the feast of Tabernacles is related to New Testament events. In this homily Augustine is suggesting that the feast signifies Jesus Christ, the Word made flesh, both in his hiddenness and in his visibility.

knows where he is from; that opinion did not, after all, come to be without purpose, if we look at the scriptures; because we find, brothers and sisters, that the holy scriptures said about Christ that *he shall be called a Nazarene* (Jg 13:5; Mt 2:23). So they had foretold where he was from.

Again, if we inquire about the place of his birth, assuming that he is from the place where he was born, even this did not escape the Jews because the scriptures foretold this as well. I mean, when the Magi, having seen his star, were looking for him so as to worship him, they came to Herod and told him what they were seeking and what they wanted to do; Herod, after summoning those who knew the law, asked them where the Christ would be born; they said, *In Bethlehem of Juda* (Mt 2:5-6); and they also produced the evidence from the prophets.[3]

So then, if the prophets had foretold both the place where he came from in the flesh, and the place where his mother gave him birth, how did this opinion arise among the Jews, which we heard just now: *When the Christ comes, nobody knows where he is from*? How else but by the scriptures having predicted and foretold each thing? The scriptures had foretold where he would be from insofar as he was human; insofar as he was God, he was hidden from the ungodly and was seeking the godly. That is what they had in mind when they said, *When the Christ comes, nobody knows where he is from*, because what had given rise to this opinion was what had been said through the prophet Isaiah, *But his begetting who shall declare?* (Is 53:8 LXX) Finally, the Lord himself also answered them on both points, both that they knew where he was from and that they did not know, in order to corroborate the holy prophecies that had been made about him, with reference both to his infirmity as a man and to his majesty as God.

Jesus goes on to confirm each point

3. Listen then, brothers and sisters, to the Word of God; see how he corroborated for them both the things they had said—both *We know where this man is from* and *When the Christ comes, nobody knows where he is from*. So then, *Jesus cried out in the temple area as he was teaching, You know me, and you also know where I am from; yet I have not come on my own, but the*

---

3. See Mic 5:1.

one who sent me, whom you do not know, is true (Jn 7:28). This amounts to saying, "You both know me and do not know me." It amounts to saying, "You both know where I am from and do not know where I am from."

Where I am from you know: Jesus of Nazareth; his parents, you also know. In fact, the only point hidden from them here was his birth from the Virgin, to which nonetheless her husband could give witness; in fact, he could give loyal testimony, just as he could have shown a husband's jealousy. So then, apart from this virginal birth, they knew everything about Jesus as a man; his face was known to them, his native town was known to them, his family was known to them, where he was born was public knowledge. So he was justified in saying about the flesh and the human form which he was wearing,[4] *You recognize me, and you also know where I am from.* And about the divine nature, *Yet I have not come on my own, but the one who sent me, whom you do not know, is true.* Even so, to know him, believe in the one whom he has sent and you shall know him. After all, *no one has ever seen God, except the only begotten Son who is in the bosom of the Father, who has made him known* (Jn 1:18); and, *No one knows the Father but the Son, and those to whom the Son may wish to reveal him* (Lk 10:22).

Christ's being sent by the Father is a sign of his being eternally begotten by the Father

4. Finally, after saying, *But the one who sent me, whom you do not know, is true*, he went on to show them from where they could learn what they did not know by adding, *I know him myself.* Ask me, therefore, if you want to know him. But how is it that I know him? *Because I am from him, and he sent me* (Jn 7:29). A magnificent demonstration of each point. *I am from him*, he says, because the Son is from the Father, and whatever the Son is, it is from the one whose Son he is. That is why we call the Lord Jesus God from God; we do not call the Father God from God, but just God; and we call the Lord Jesus Light from Light;[5] we do not call the Father Light from Light, but just Light. So his saying *I am from him* goes along with all that.

---

4. Augustine's characteristic description of Christ's humanity as "worn" (*gerebat*) suggests that it was assumed or taken up, and not that it can be easily separated from him.
5. When we recite the Nicene Creed.

But as for your seeing me in the flesh, *he sent me*. When you hear the words *he sent me*, do not take it as suggesting any unlikeness of nature, but only that the authority is in the Father.[6]

Christ's hour, willed by God, not decreed by fate, was the fullness of time

5. So then, *they were looking for ways of arresting him, and nobody laid hands on him, because his hour had not yet come* (Jn 7:30); that is, because he was not willing. What, after all, is the meaning of *his hour had not yet come*? The Lord, I mean, was not born subject to fate. That is not to be believed even of you, and even less of the one through whom we were made. If your hour is his will, what can his hour be, but his own will? So he did not mean the hour in which he was bound by fate to die, but the one in which he would deign to be put to death.

After all, he was waiting for the time to die, because he had waited for the time to be born. Speaking of this time, the apostle says, *But when the fullness of time had come, God sent his Son* (Gal 4:4). That is why many people say, "Why did Christ not come before?" and the answer to give them is that the fullness of time had not yet come, as planned by the one through whom all times were made; for he knew when he ought to come. First of all he had to be foretold through a whole series of times and years. For it was not something trivial that was going to come; he had to be foretold for a long time, since he has to be held onto for ever. The greater the judge who was coming, the longer the ranks of heralds preceding him.

Finally, when the fullness of time did come, the one who would set us free from time also came. Set free from time, in fact, we will come to that eternity in which there is no time; nor does anyone say, "When will the hour come?" It is an everlasting day, you see, neither preceded by a yesterday, nor concluded by a tomorrow. In this age, however, the days stretch out, some passing by, others coming along. None of them lasts, and the moments when I am speaking push one another aside, nor does the first syllable stand still, but it has to make way for the second to be heard. From the moment I started speaking I have grown a little older, and without a

---

6. The words, *noli intellegere naturae dissimilitudinem, sed generantis auctoritatem*, maintain the balance: the same nature and the Father as generating the Son. See Sermon 71, 18: "In the Father is authority, in the Son is birth, in the Holy Spirit is communion of Father and Son."

shadow of doubt I am now older than I was this morning. Thus it is that in time nothing stands still, nothing remains fixed.[7]

Accordingly, we ought to love the one through whom times were made, in order to be set free from time and to be fixed in eternity, where there is no longer any changing around of times. Great indeed therefore must be the mercy of our Lord Jesus Christ, that he through whom the times were made should for our sake have been made in time; that he through whom all things were made should himself have been placed in the middle of all things; that he should have been made what he made. Yes, he was made what he had made; he was made man, you see, he that had made man, so that what he had made might not be lost.[8] In accordance with this dispensation, the hour of his birth had already come, and he was born; but the hour for him to suffer had not yet come; that is why he had not yet suffered.

Proof from the passion story that Christ's hour was in his power

6. In summary, so that you may know that he died not by necessity but by his own power—I am speaking now for the sake of some who, on hearing *his hour has not yet come*, are thereby confirmed in believing in fate, and thereby make their hearts foolish—so then, that you may know the power of the one who died, just recall his passion, gaze on the crucified one. Hanging on the tree, he said, *I am thirsty* (Jn 19:28). When they heard this, they offered him on the cross vinegar in a sponge on a cane; he accepted it, and said, *It is finished; and bowing his head, he gave up the spirit* (Jn 19:30). You can see this dying man's power, because he was waiting for the fulfillment of all the things that had been foretold about him as going to happen before his death. The prophet, in fact, had said, *For my food they gave me gall, and in my thirst they gave me vinegar to drink* (Ps 68:21). He was waiting for all this to be fulfilled; when it was, he said, *It is finished*, and departed this life under his own power, because he did not enter it under any constraint.

That is why some people were more amazed by this power of the man dying than they had been by the power of the man working miracles. They came to the cross to take the bodies down from the tree, because the

---

7. See Sermons 77, 14; 117, 10; 124, 4; 157, 4.
8. See *The Trinity* IV, 1, 2; 18, 24.

sabbath was about to dawn; the bandits were found to be still alive. The punishment of the cross, in fact, was harder because its agony lasted longer, and those crucified were subjected to a slow death. But so that those two might not remain on the tree, their legs were broken to make them die, so that they could be taken down from there.[9] The Lord, however, was found to be already dead, and people were astonished; and those who had despised him when alive so marveled at him when dead that some of them said, *Truly this man is the Son of God* (Mt 27:54).

The same goes, brothers and sisters, for his saying to those who were seeking him, *I am he* (Jn 18:5-6); and they drew back and all fell down. So then, in him there was sovereign power. Nor was he forced to die; but he waited for the hour in which his will might most suitably be done, not the hour in which necessity might be fulfilled unwillingly.

Some of the Jews believed in him, because of the signs he did; others tried to arrest him

7. *Now many from the crowd came to believe in him* (Jn 7:31). The humble and the poor were being saved by the Lord; the authorities were raging against him; and that is why they not only failed to recognize the doctor but were even longing to have him put to death. There was one kind of crowd which was quick to see their own sickness, and not at all slow to be aware of his remedy for it. Just notice what the people in this crowd, moved by his miracles, said to one another: *When the Christ comes, will he perform more signs than this man has done?* (Jn 7:31) Clearly, if there are not going to be two of them, this man is the one. So then, in saying such a thing, they showed they believed in him.

8. But when the authorities heard the multitude expressing their faith like this, and glorifying Christ by this murmuring, *they sent their guards to arrest him* (Jn 7:32). Whom were they to arrest? One still not willing to be arrested.[10] So because they were unable to arrest him while he was not willing, they were actually sent to hear him teaching. Teaching what? *So then*

---

9. See Jn 19:31-33.
10. The Maurists, and subsequent editions, treat this short sentence as a question. However, the text Berrouard is using punctuates it as a statement; he so translates it, and so do I, because on the whole I think it makes better rhetorical sense this way.

Jesus says, "I will be with you for a little while; and then I go to the one who sent me (Jn 7:33). What you want to do now, you will do in due course, but not now, because I do not wish it now. Why do I not wish it now? Because *I am still with you for a little while, and then I go to the one who sent me.* I have to complete my mission, and in this way come to my passion."

How they will seek and not find him after his resurrection

9. *You will look for me and not find me; and where I am, you cannot come* (Jn 7:34). Here he was already foretelling his resurrection; they refused, you see, to acknowledge his presence among them, and later on they looked for him, when they saw the multitudes already believing in him. Great signs were also performed, even after the Lord had risen and ascended into heaven. At that time these great things were done through the disciples; but he was acting through them, just as he had acted on his own; indeed, he had said to them, *Without me you can do nothing* (Jn 15:5).

When that lame man who used to sit at the gate stood up at Peter's voice, and walked about on his own feet, so that people were amazed, Peter addressed them to the effect that he did not do such things by his own power, but by the power of the one whom they had put to death.[11] Many were pricked to the heart, and said, *What shall we do?* (Acts 2:37) For they saw they had been guilty of a momentous crime of contempt, when they slew the one whom they ought to have venerated and worshiped; and they thought that it could not be forgiven. It was, after all, an action of such proportions, that the thought of it led them to despair; but they were not to despair, since the Lord had seen fit to pray for them as he hung on the cross. He had said, *Father, forgive them, because they know not what they do* (Lk 23:34). Among many who did not know him, he had eyes for some who were his own; he was already asking pardon for those by whom he was still being wronged. What concerned him was not the fact that he was dying at their hands, but that he was dying for their sake.

This unique favor was granted them, that it was both at their hands and for their sake that he died, so that none should despair about having their sins forgiven, when those who put Christ to death were found fit to be

---

11. See Acts 3:2-16. Augustine inverts the order of events here. He goes on to mention Peter's address at Pentecost, described in Acts 2:14-36.

pardoned. Christ died for us; but not at our hands, surely. These people, however, watched Christ dying as a result of their wicked misdeed, and believed in the Christ who pardoned their wicked misdeeds. Until they drank the blood they had shed, they were in despair about their salvation.[12] So then, what he meant by saying, *You will look for me and not find me; and where I am, you cannot come*, was that being pricked to the heart they were going to look for him after his resurrection.

He did not say, either, "where I shall be" but *where I am*.

Christ, you see, was always in the place he was going to return to; he came in such a way, after all, as not to leave where he was. That is why he says elsewhere, *Nobody has gone up to heaven except the one who came down from heaven, the Son of Man, who is in heaven* (Jn 3:13). He did not say "who was in heaven." He was speaking on earth and saying he was in heaven. He came in such a way as not to depart from there; he returned in such a way as not to abandon us. Why be surprised? God is doing this. A human being, after all, is in a place as regards the body, and moves from that place, and after coming to another place will not be in the place he came from. God however fills all things and is wholly everywhere; he is not contained in places as occupying so much space. The Lord Christ, all the same, as regards his visible flesh was on earth, as regards his invisible majesty both in heaven and on earth; that is why he says, *Where I am, you cannot come*.

And he did not say "you will not be able to" but *you cannot*; at the time, you see, they were the kind of people who could not. You can tell, though, that this was not said to reduce them to despair, because he also said something similar to his disciples, *Where I am going, you cannot come* (Jn 13:33); while in his prayer for them we will find him saying, *Father, it is my wish that where I am, they may also be with me* (Jn 17:24). Anyway, he explained this all to Peter, and said to him, *Where I am going you cannot follow me now, but you shall follow later on* (Jn 13:36).

---

12. Augustine's attention is fixed on Acts 2:37, where the crowd listening to the apostles are pricked to the heart at the proclamation of the resurrection of the one they crucified. Their compunction shows they now believed in Christ risen from the dead; but they have not yet heard anything about his having died for their sins. Peter tells them what they are to do. Augustine frequently follows the same sequence, speaking about Christ's prayer on the cross, the miracles of the Apostles after Pentecost, repentance among the Jews in the face of the greatness of their fault and the offer of pardon, and finally, communion in the blood of Jesus (not mentioned here). See Sermons 60A, 2; 77, 4; 80, 5; 87, 14, 89, 1; 229E, 2; 229I, 3; 313B, 4; 313E, 4; 352, 1.

How the Jews unwittingly prophesied the mission to the gentiles

10. *So the Jews then said* not to him but *to one another, Where is he going that we will not find him? Is he going to those dispersed among the nations,*[13] *and going to teach the nations?* (Jn 7:35) They did not know, you see, what they were saying; but because that was his will, they were prophesying. The Lord was indeed going to go to the nations, not present in the flesh, to be sure, but still on his own feet.[14]

Who were his feet?

The feet Saul was wanting to stamp on by persecuting them, when the head cried out to him, *Saul, Saul why are you persecuting me?* (Acts 9:4)

What is the meaning of his saying, *You will look for me and not find me; and where I am, you cannot come* (Jn 7:36)? They did not know why the Lord said this, and yet without knowing it, they foretold something that would happen in the future. The Lord said this, after all, because they had no notion of the place (if indeed it is to be called a place), that is, of the bosom of the Father, from which the only-begotten Son never departed; nor were they capable of forming any idea about where Christ was, from where Christ had not withdrawn, where Christ was going to return to, where Christ still remained. How indeed could the human heart conceive it? Even more, how could the human tongue explain it?

So then, they did not understand him at all, and yet, on this occasion, they foretold our salvation, that the Lord was going to go to those dispersed among the nations, and he would fulfill what the Jews read and failed to understand: *A people I did not know served me and obeyed me when their ear heard me* (Ps 17:43-44). Those who had him before their eyes did not hear; those others listened who had only the sound of him in their ears.[15]

Christ, visibly present to the Jews and invisibly present among the gentiles

11. The woman suffering from an issue of blood was a type of the Church of the nations that was to come; she touched him without being

---

13. *To those dispersed among the nations* refers to the Jewish communities scattered among the nations. Augustine chose to take the phrase at its most literal, meaning among the gentiles scattered all over the world. Christ was going to these Jewish believers and teaching them.
14. See Sermons 99, 13; 345, 4.
15. The Jews saw him and did not hear; the pagans did not see him and yet heard.

seen; still unknown, she was cured. In fact, the Lord asked, as a sign, *Who touched me?*[16] (Lk 8:45) He healed this unknown woman as if she were unknown to him; he did likewise to the gentiles. For we did not know him in the flesh, and yet we were found worthy to eat his flesh and to be his members in his flesh.

Why?

Because he sent to us.

Whom?

His heralds, his disciples, his slaves, the creatures he redeemed, who were also his brothers—but what I have just spoken about is little; he sent his members, he sent himself. You see, he sent his members to us and made us his members.

All the same, Christ was not among us in the bodily form which the Jews saw and despised, because it was also said of him, as the apostle also says, *For I say that Christ became a minister of the circumcised to show God's truthfulness, to confirm the promises to the fathers* (Rom 15:8). He was obliged to come to the people to whose ancestors and by whose ancestors he had been promised; that is why he too spoke in this way, *I was only sent to the lost sheep of the house of Israel* (Mt 15:24). But what does the apostle go on to say? *But the gentiles glorify God for his mercy* (Rom 15:9). And what about the Lord himself? *I have other sheep, who are not of this fold* (Jn 10:16). He had said, *I was only sent to the lost sheep of the house of Israel*; so how can he have other sheep to whom he was not sent, unless it was that he was indicating that he was only going to show his bodily presence to the Jews who, in fact, saw him and slew him? And yet many of them, both before and afterwards, still came to believe.[17] The first harvest was thus winnowed from the cross, to provide seed from which another harvest might rise up.

But now that he has faithful—stirred by the renown of the gospel and its good odor[18]—he will be *the one expected by the nations* (Gen 49:10) until the one who has already come comes again; until the one who, the first time, was not seen by some and was seen by others; until the one who came to be judged comes to judge; until the one who did not come to be set apart

---

16. See *Teaching Christianity*, II, 3, 4; Sermon 77, 5-7.
17. See Sermons 51, 14; 60A, 2.
18. See 2 Cor 2:15.

comes to discern among them. For Christ was not distinguished from the godless, but was judged together with them; in fact, it was said of him, *He shall be reckoned among the wicked* (Is 53:12). A brigand was freed, Christ was condemned. A criminal received pardon, the one who pardoned the crimes of all who confess them was condemned.[19]

Nonetheless the cross itself, if you pay careful attention, was a court of justice; for the judge was placed in the middle; the thief who believed was freed, while the one who jeered was condemned. He was already indicating what he was going to do with regard to "the living and the dead,"[20] placing some at his right hand and others at his left. So one brigand was like those who were going to be on the left, the other like those who were going to be on the right. Christ was judged, and he threatened judgment.

---

19. See Jn 18:38-40.
20. Quoting the words in the creed recited by those about to be baptized, on the final judgment, when Christ comes again in glory.

Homily 32

On John 7:37-39[1]

Christ's summons to go to him and drink

1. Among the disagreements and doubts of the Jews about the Lord Jesus Christ, among all the other things he said which would throw some of them into confusion, while instructing others, *on the last day of that feast* (Jn 7:37), which is called Skenopegia, that is, "the pitching of tents" (for that is when all this was happening). Your Graces will remember that we have already discussed this festival on previous occasions; on that day the Lord Jesus Christ cries out, and he does not merely speak, he cries out, that anyone who is thirsty should come to him.

If we are thirsty, let us go not on our feet but on our heartfelt sentiments; let us go by loving, not by traveling. It is one thing for the body to travel, another for the heart; the body travels by moving from place to place; the heart by changing its feelings and sentiments. If you now love one thing where you used to love another, your heart is not in the same place as it used to be.

The refreshment offered to the interior person is the Holy Spirit

2. So then, the Lord is crying out to us. He was standing and crying out, *If anyone is thirsty, let him come to me and drink. Whoever believes in me, as scripture says, streams of living water shall stream from his belly.* (Jn 7:37-38) We have no need to linger on what this might mean, since the evangelist explained it himself by saying, *But he said this about the Spirit, which those who believed in him were going to receive. For the Spirit had not yet been given, because Jesus had not yet been glorified.* (Jn 7:39)

So then, there is an inner thirst, and an inner belly, because there is an inner man. And this inner man is invisible, while the outer one is visible; but the inner one is of greater value than the outer. And what is not seen is loved all the more; it is universally agreed, after all, that the inner person is loved more than the outer. How is this agreement seen? Let each one verify it in himself.

---

1. Preached soon after the previous homily.

While those who live bad lives do indeed hand over their souls[2] to their bodies, they do, for all that, want to stay alive, which is a matter of the soul alone, and they identify themselves with the ruling element rather than with the one which is being ruled; rational souls, after all, do the ruling, bodies are what they rule over.[3] Everyone enjoys pleasure, and gets pleasure from the body; but remove the rational soul, nothing is left in the body to do the enjoying; even if enjoyment is in the body, the rational soul does the enjoying.[4] If the soul gets enjoyment from its home, should it not get enjoyment from itself? And if the rational soul finds diversion in things outside itself, is it to remain without any delights within? Yes, it is as certain as can be that people love their souls more than their bodies.

But what they love more in another person too is the soul rather than the body. What do you love in your friend, where love is more loyal, more chaste? What do you love in your friend, the soul or the body? If he loves fidelity, the soul is loved; if he loves kindness, the soul is the seat of kindness; if what you love in someone else is that he also loves you, you are loving his soul, because it is his soul, not his flesh, that is loving you. You love, in fact, that he loves you; ask yourself how he loves you, and you will see what you love. So then, it is loved more, and it cannot be seen.

Proof of this universal preference for souls over bodies

3. I also wish to say something which may make it clearer to Your Graces how much the soul is loved, and how it is preferred to the body. Those licentious lovers, who delight in the beauty of bodies and are inflamed by the sight of shapely limbs, love all the more when they are loved in return. Indeed, if one of them loves and then finds that he is an object of hatred, he is angry rather than loving.

Why is he angry rather than loving?

Because he is not given in return what he is spending.[5]

---

2. The Latin here, and throughout this section is *animus*, not *anima*. It refers to the rational or human soul; Augustine does not, I think, ever speak about animals having an *animus*—although they are animated by an *anima*.
3. See Sermon 20, 4; *The Trinity* XIV, 14, 18-19.
4. See *The Literal Meaning of Genesis* III, 5, 7; XII, 24, 51.
5. See Sermon 34, 4.

So then, if those who love bodies want to be loved in return, and if what gives them most enjoyment is being loved, what must it be like with the lovers of souls? And if it is great to be lovers of souls, what must it be like with the lovers of God, who gives souls their beauty? Just as the soul, after all, makes the body beautiful, so does God do in the case of the soul. In fact, the soul is that which makes the body lovable; when it departs, the corpse is an object of disgust; and however beautiful those limbs that you loved, you hasten to bury them. So then, the beauty of the body is the soul; the beauty of the soul is God.

What streams from the interior belly is kindness

4. If we thirst within, therefore, the Lord calls out to us, that we might come and drink; and he says that, when we have drunk, streams of living water will flow from our belly. The belly of the inner person is the conscience of the heart. So once this liquid has been quaffed, the purified conscience comes alive, and, drinking more deeply, it will have its own spring, or better, it will be a well.

What is this spring, and what is the river that flows from the belly of the inner person? The kindness with which you look after your neighbor. I mean, if someone assumes that what he drinks should be enough for himself alone, living water is not flowing from his belly; but, if he hastens to think about his neighbor, then, because it flows, it does not dry up. We shall now see what those who believe in the Lord drink; because we are Christians, and, if we believe, we drink. And each one ought to recognize in himself whether he drinks, and whether he has life from what he drinks; the spring, after all, will not forsake us, if we do not forsake that spring.

The spring of living water is the Holy Spirit

5. As I said, the evangelist went on to explain why the Lord called out, and to what drink he invited us, what he poured out for the drinkers, saying, *But he said this about the Spirit, which those who believed in him were going to receive. For the Spirit had not yet been given, because Jesus had not yet been glorified.* What Spirit is he talking about but the Holy Spirit? For every human being has his own spirit in him, which is what I was talking about when I was discussing the soul. Everyone's soul is his own

spirit, about which the apostle Paul says, *Who among men, in fact, knows what is in a human being, but the spirit in him?* Then he adds, *So too, no one knows what is in God but the Spirit of God.* (1 Cor 2:11) No one knows what is going on in us but our own spirit. After all, I do not know what you are thinking, nor you what I am thinking; all this, you see, is our own business, what we are thinking within ourselves; and the spirit of each one of us bears witness to each one's thoughts.[6]

So too, no one knows what is in God but the Spirit of God. We with our spirit, God with his—with this difference though, that God with his Spirit also knows what is going on in us, while we without his Spirit cannot know what is going on in God. God, though, knows in us even what we do not know in ourselves. Indeed, Peter did not know his own weakness, when he heard from the Lord that he was going to deny him three times,[7] and he did not know that he was sick; the doctor recognized the one who was sick.[8] So there are some things then that God is aware of in us which we do not know about. Still, as far as human beings are concerned, no one knows himself like the person himself; another person does not know what is going on in him, but his own spirit knows.

But once we have received the Spirit of God, we learn even what is going on in God—not the whole of it, because we have not received the whole of it. We know many things about the pledge; it is the pledge, after all, that we have received, and of this pledge the fulfillment will be given later on. Meanwhile, during these wanderings of ours, let the pledge be our comfort and consolation, because the one who has been kind enough to pledge us is preparing to give us so much. If this is what the token is like, what can that be of which it is just the token?[9]

Why Jesus did not wish to give the Spirit before he was glorified

6. But what is this that it says, *For the Spirit had not been given, because Jesus had not yet been glorified?* The meaning is clear enough. It does not mean that there was no Spirit of God; the Spirit was with God but not yet in those who had come to believe in Jesus. The Lord Jesus had planned that he

---

6. See Sermon 217, 2.
7. See Mt 26:33-35.
8. See Sermons 4, 2; 137, 3; 231, 1; 285, 3; 295, 3; 297, 1; 299, 7.
9. See Sermons 23, 8-9; 156, 16.

would not give them this Spirit we are talking about until after his resurrection—and for good reason. And perhaps, if we look into it, he will agree to our finding it; if we knock, he will open to let us in. Piety knocks, not the hand—although the hand too knocks if it does not stop performing works of mercy. What therefore is the reason why the Lord Jesus Christ had decided only to give the Holy Spirit when he had been glorified?

Before I say what I can, we must first inquire, so that no one is bothered about it, how it is that the Spirit was not yet there in holy people, since we read in the gospel about the Lord himself just after he was born, that Simeon recognized him in the Holy Spirit, that the widow Anna, a prophetess, also recognized him; John too, who baptized him, also recognized him; Zachary had much to say, when filled with the Holy Spirit; Mary herself received the Holy Spirit in order to conceive the Lord.[10] So we have many earlier inklings of the Holy Spirit before the Lord was glorified in the resurrection of his flesh. After all, it was not some other spirit that the prophets also had, who foretold that Christ was going to come.

But there was going to be a way of giving him of which there had been no prior instance whatsoever; that is what is referred to here. In no previous instance, after all, do we read about those gathered together receiving the Holy Spirit and then speaking in the languages of all nations.[11] After his resurrection, however, when he first appeared to his disciples, he said to them, *Receive the Holy Spirit* (Jn 20:22). About this, then, it is said, *The Spirit had not been given, because Jesus had not yet been glorified. And he breathed in their faces* (Jn 20:22), he that had given life to the first man by his breath, raising him from the mud; by this same breath he gave a soul to his members, indicating that he was the same one breathing in their faces, so that they might rise up from the mud, and renounce their muddy works.

After his resurrection, which the evangelist calls his glorification, that was the first time when the Lord gave his disciples the Holy Spirit. Next, after staying on with them for forty days, as the book of the Acts of the Apostles makes clear, while they were watching and following him with their eyes, he ascended into heaven. Then after ten days had passed, on the

---

10. See Lk 2:25-38; Lk 1:41; Jn 1:26-34; Lk 1:67-79; Lk 1:35.
11. See *The Trinity* IV, 20, 29.

day of Pentecost, he sent the Holy Spirit from above.[12] Filled with what they received, as I said just now, those who were gathered together in one place spoke in the languages of all nations.

How we, when we receive the Holy Spirit, still speak in the tongues of all nations

7. So what about now, brothers and sisters? Just because nowadays those who are being baptized in Christ and who believe in Christ do not speak in the languages of all nations, is it to be assumed that they have not received the Holy Spirit? No such lack of faith should tempt our heart. We are certain that everyone receives him; but whatever size vessel of faith you bring to the fountain is filled up.

"Well, since then he is received nowadays too," somebody may say, "why is no one speaking in the languages of all nations?" Because now the Church speaks in the languages of all peoples. Previously the Church was to be found in one people, when it was speaking in the languages of all. By speaking with the languages of all it was signifying what was going to happen, that by growing among peoples, it would speak everyone's language.

Anyone who is not in this Church does not receive the Holy Spirit even now.[13] Cut off, you see, and divided from the Unity of its members, the Unity which speaks the languages of all, let him admit to himself that he does not have the Spirit.[14] If he does have the Spirit, let him give the sign that was given then.

What does it mean, let him give the sign that was given then?

Let him speak in all languages.

He answers me, "What about you? Are you speaking in all languages?"

I certainly am, because every language is mine, spoken, that is, by the body of which I am a member.

The Church spread throughout the nations is speaking with all tongues; the Church is the body of Christ, you are a member in this body; so then,

---

12. See Acts 1:3.9; 2:1-6; *The Trinity* XV, 26, 46; Sermon 265, 8-9.
13. See Sermon 71, 28-30.
14. Following the Maurist's text: *renuntiet sibi: non habet*. Most codices read: *renuntiet si non habet*. Augustine's point, as he goes on to make clear, is that such people (he has the Donatists in mind) do not speak in all languages, but only in their own local language.

since you are a member in his body, which is speaking with all tongues, confidently believe that you are speaking with all languages. The Unity of members, after all, is kept together by charity; and this Unity now speaks in the way one person spoke at that time.[15]

*Charity is the supreme gift of the Spirit, binding the members
of Christ's body together; all share in the gifts of each*

8. We too, then, receive the Holy Spirit, if we love the Church, if we are united by charity, if we rejoice in the Catholic name and faith. Let us believe, brothers and sisters, that to the extent that someone loves the Church of Christ, to that extent he has the Holy Spirit. The Spirit was given, you see, as the apostle says, *for manifestation*. For what sort of manifestation? As he says himself, *That to one is given through the Spirit the word of wisdom, to another the word of knowledge according to the same Spirit,*[16] *to another faith in the same Spirit, to another the performance of acts of power in the same Spirit* (1 Cor 12:7-10). Many things, in fact, are given for manifestation, but you perhaps have none of the sort of things I have mentioned. Yet, if you love, you cannot claim to have nothing; if you love the Unity, you see, whoever has anything of that sort in it has it for you. Get rid of envy, and what I have is yours; get rid of envy, and what you have is mine.[17]

A livid mark[18] sets people apart, health unites them. In the body, only the eye sees; but does the eye only see for itself? It also sees for the hand, it also sees for the foot, it also sees for the other parts of the body; after all, if the foot is in danger of stubbing its toe, the eye does not look away so as to fail to warn the foot. Once again, in the body only the hand does things; but it does not do them only for itself, does it? It also does things for the eye; for, if there is danger of something hitting not the hand but just the face, the hand does not say, does it, "I am not budging, because it is not aimed at

---

15. Augustine understood this account (Acts 3:6) as meaning that each of the 120 Christians on whom the Holy Spirit came then began to speak in each language, and not that each listener heard his own language. See Sermons 175, 3; 265, 12; and the sermons preached at Pentecost (266-270).
16. See *The Trinity* XIII, 19, 24.
17. See Sermons 137, 1; 162A, 4.
18. *Livor*—as contrasted with health—can mean a physical contusion as well as envy or jealousy. Hence, certain sicknesses were evident (leprosy, measles, etc.) and led to quarantine or isolation. *Livor*, therefore, has the overtone of a jealousy that visibly indicates separation, an overtone we cannot reproduce in English.

me"? So too the foot in walking marches for all the members of the body; and while all the other parts keep quiet, the tongue talks for them all.[19]

So then, we have the Holy Spirit, if we love the Church; while we love it if we remain steadily in its unity and in charity. The apostle himself, you see, after saying that different gifts are given to different people, like the tasks assigned to each particular part of the body, went on to say, *I have a still more excellent way to show you* (1 Cor 12:31), and he began to talk about charity. He put it before the tongues of men and of angels, he put it before miracles of faith, he put it before knowledge and prophecy, even before that great work of mercy of distributing what one possesses to the poor; and finally he went so far as to put it before martyrdom;[20] before all such great things as these he put charity. Only have this, and you will have them all, because without it nothing will do you any good, whatever you may manage to have.

The charity we are talking about belongs to the Holy Spirit (it is a question about the Holy Spirit, after all, that is under consideration at the moment in the gospel). Listen to the apostle telling us so: *The charity of God has been poured out in our hearts through the Holy Spirit who has been given to us* (Rom 5:5).

In waiting till he was glorified before sending the Spirit, Christ wished to direct our love and charity to the things that are above

9. So why did the Lord only wish to give the Spirit, whose greatest benefits are in us because through him the charity of God has been poured out in our hearts, after his resurrection? What significance does that have? That our charity should be on fire for our resurrection and set apart from love of the world, that we might, fully dedicated, hasten toward God.[21] Here, after all, we are born and we die; let us not love that. Let us emigrate with charity, dwell up above with charity, that charity with which we love God. Let us reflect on nothing else in the wandering of this life but that we will not always be here, and that by living good lives we shall be preparing a place for ourselves up there, from which we shall never move on. Our Lord

---

19. See Sermons 162A, 6; 267, 4.
20. See 1 Cor 13:1-3.
21. See Sermon 378.

Jesus Christ, after all, after he rose again, *dies no more*; *death*, as the apostle says, *has no further dominion over him* (Rom 6:9).

That is what we should love. If we live, if we believe in the one who rose again, he will give us not what people love here, those who do not love God, and who love the world all the more as they love him less, or even love the world less the more they love him. But let us see what he has promised us: not earthly wealth in this world of time, not honors and power in this world; for you can see that all these things are given to bad people too, so that the good do not have high esteem for them.[22] Finally, he did not even promise health of body, not because he does not give it, but because, as you can see, he also gives it to animals; nor a long life; what is long after all, which at some time or other comes to an end?[23] He never promised longevity to us believers as something great, or a decrepit old age, which everyone looks forward to before it comes, everyone moans about when it does come. He did not promise a beautiful body, which is eliminated either by disease or by that old age you look forward to. You want to be attractive,[24] and you want to be old; these two desires cannot be harmonized; if you become an old man, you will not be attractive; when old age comes, good looks flee; and the bloom of good looks and the groans of old age cannot live together in one person.

So then, he was not promising us any of these things, when he said, *He who believes in me, let him come and drink, and streams of living water shall stream from his belly* (Jn 7:37-38). He was promising eternal life, where we have nothing to fear, where we are not ever disturbed, from where we are not ever deported, where we never die, where there is no mourning for the one who went before us, no hoping for someone to succeed us. So then, because such is the kind of thing he was promising to us, his lovers, to those on fire with the charity of the Holy Spirit, that is why he did not wish to give the Holy Spirit until he had been glorified, when he could demonstrate in his own body the life which we do not now have but which we hope for in the resurrection.

---

22. See Sermon 311, 13.
23. See Sermons 17, 7; 335B, 2.
24. *Pulcher* could be translated "beautiful" or "handsome," but rather than use words whose connotation may suggest feminine or masculine applications, "attractive" (or "good looking") allows for a general understanding.

Homily 33

On John 7:40 - 8:11[1]

Disagreement about Jesus; the failure to arrest him

1. Your Graces will remember that in my last sermon, when the gospel was read, I spoke to you about the Holy Spirit. The Lord had just invited those who believed in him to drink of this Spirit, while he was speaking in the midst of those who wanted to arrest him and were longing to kill him, and could not do so because he was unwilling that they should.[2] So when he said that, a disagreement about him arose in the crowd, with some of them thinking that he was the Christ, others saying that the Christ would not arise from Galilee.[3] But those who had been sent to arrest him returned guiltless of this offence and full of admiration; in fact, they even bore witness to his divine teaching, when those they had been sent by said, *Why did you not bring him in?* For they replied that they had never heard a man speak like that: *No man after all ever speaks like that.* (Jn 7:45-46) He had spoken like that, though, because he was both God and man.

Even so, the Pharisees, rejecting their testimony, said to them, "*Have you too been led astray?* We can see, after all, that you were pleased with his words. *Has any of the authorities believed in him, or any of the Pharisees? But this crowd, which does not know the law, is under a curse.*" (Jn 7:47-49) The ones who did not know the law were the ones who believed in the one who had given the law; and the one who had given the law was spurned by the ones who were teaching the law, to fulfill what the Lord himself had said, *I have come so that those who do not see may see, and those who do see may become blind* (Jn 9:39). For the Pharisee teachers became blind, the peoples,[4] who were ignorant of the law and believed in the author of the law, were enlightened.

---

1. Preached shortly after Homily 32.
2. See Jn 7:37-39.
3. See Jn 7:41.
4. *Populi*, in the plural. Berrouard is right in thinking that Augustine had the gentile nations in mind when using this word. In the plural it is well translated by the English plural "peoples." It hardly ever has the weak sense that "people," a collective treated as a plural, has come to have in English, as in "people say."

Nicodemus speaks, a man lacking in courage, not in faith

2. *Nicodemus, however, one of the Pharisees, who had come to the Lord at night*—indeed he was not lacking in faith, but only in courage, and that, in fact, was why he had come at night to visit the Light, because he wanted to be enlightened and was afraid of being known—responded to the Jews, *Does our law pass judgment on a man without first hearing from him and finding out what he is doing?* (Jn 7:50-51) Perversely, they wanted to pass judgment before finding out the facts. Nicodemus knew, or rather believed, that if only they would patiently listen to Jesus, they might become like those who had been sent to arrest him, and might prefer to believe. They gave him the same answer, from the prejudice of their heart, as they had given the others: *Are you too a Galilean?* (Jn 7:52) Are you not being led astray, that is, by a Galilean? The Lord, you see, was called a Galilean, because his parents were from the city of Nazareth. I said "parents" because of Mary, not because of any real human fatherhood; all he required on earth, after all, was a mother, he that up above already had a Father. Each birth of his, I mean to say, was marvelous; the divine birth without mother, the human birth without father.

So then, what did those so-called teachers of the law say to Nicodemus? *Search the scriptures, and see that a prophet does not arise from Galilee*; no, but the Lord of the prophets arose from there. *They returned*, says the evangelist, *each one to his own home.* (Jn 7:52-53)[5]

The rightness of Jesus' teaching on the Mount of Olives

3. From there *Jesus went up the mount,* up the mount *of Olives* (Jn 8:1), up the fruit-bearing mount, up the mount of ointment, up the mount of chrism. Where else, after all, was it right and proper for Christ to teach but on the Mount of Olives? The name "Christ," after all, comes from "chrism"; unction is called *chrisma* in Greek, "anointing" in Latin. The reason indeed why he has anointed us is that he has made us wrestlers against the devil.[6] *And early in the morning he came again into the temple,*

---

5. The passage from this verse, 7:53, to the end of the story of the woman taken in adultery, 8:11, is missing from nearly all the best Greek manuscripts, and it is agreed by all the scholars that it has no place in John's gospel. A few manuscripts place it in Luke's gospel, after 21:38, where indeed it would fit very well.
6. Athletes in the games, wrestlers in particular, were anointed all over their bodies with olive oil.

and all the people came to him, and sitting down he started teaching them (Jn 8:2). And he was not arrested, because he was not to suffer yet.

Reign in virtue of truth, gentleness and justice

4. Now comes the moment for you to observe where the Lord's gentleness is tested by his enemies. *Now the scribes and Pharisees bring him a woman taken in adultery, and they placed her in the middle and said to him, Master, this woman was just now caught in the act of adultery. Now in the law Moses commanded us to stone such people; you then, what do you say? But they were saying this in order to test him, so that they might be able to accuse him.* (Jn 8:3-6) Accuse him of what? They had not caught him, had they, in any misconduct, they were not suggesting, were they, that this woman had anything to do with him? So what is the meaning then of *to test him, so that they might be able to accuse him*?

Let us understand, brothers and sisters, that a wonderful gentleness was a most prominent characteristic of our Lord. His foes had noticed he was exceedingly kind, excessively gentle; that had, in fact, been foretold about him: *Gird your sword upon your thigh, most mighty one; step out in your finery and beauty, march on successfully, and reign in virtue of truth and gentleness and justice* (Ps 44:3-4). So he brought truth as a teacher, gentleness as a liberator, justice as a guarantor. Because of these qualities a prophet foretold that he was going to reign in the Holy Spirit. When he spoke, truth was recognized; when he did not react against his enemies, gentleness was praised; so when his enemies were convulsed by jealousy and envy by these two things, that is, by his truth and gentleness, a third thing, that is justice, was used to set a trap for him.

Why?

Because the law had decreed that adulterers were to be stoned; and of course the law could not have laid down anything that was unjust; if anyone said anything at variance with what the law had laid down, he would be caught in being unjust.

So they said to one another, "People think him truthful; people see him as gentle; a charge must be sought in relation to justice. Let us present him with a woman caught in the act of adultery, let us tell him what the law has to say about her. If he orders her to be stoned, he will no longer possess gentleness; if he lets her off, that will be the end of his justice." They said then to themselves, "So as not to lose his gentleness, which is what the peoples[7] have already come to love him for, he is undoubtedly going to say that she should be let off. That is where we get the chance to accuse him, and find him guilty as a transgressor of the law, and thus say to him, 'You are an enemy of the law, you are giving an answer contrary to Moses, indeed contrary to the one who gave the law through Moses. You deserve death, you should be stoned together with her.' "

With words and suggestions such as these they could well have inflamed their jealousy, pressed their charges, insisted on his being condemned. But to whom and by whom was all this being said? To the straight by the crooked, to Truth by falsehood, to the upright of heart by the rotten-hearted, to Wisdom by folly.[8] When could they ever set a snare for him, into which they would not thrust their own heads first? Just see how the Lord in giving his answer is going to preserve justice without in any way departing from gentleness. The one the snare was laid for was not caught; instead those who set it were caught, because they still would not believe in the one who could release them from the snare.

Jesus' answer preserves justice and gentleness

5. So what answer then did the Lord Jesus give? What answer did Truth give? What answer did Wisdom give? What did Justice, the one for whom charges were being prepared, respond? He did not say, "She must not be stoned," lest he seem to be speaking against the law. Even less did he say, "She must be stoned!" He came, after all, not to destroy what was found, but *to seek what was lost* (Lk 19:10). So what did he respond, then? Notice how the response is filled with justice, how filled with gentleness and truth. *Let the one among you who is without sin*, he says, *be the first to throw a stone at her* (Jn 8:7).

The response of Wisdom! How it thrust them back into themselves! Outwardly, you see, they were lying; inwardly, they failed to examine themselves; they were looking at the adulteress, they had no eyes for themselves.

---

7. Again the plural, *populi*.
8. See Prov 9:1-6.13-18.

While transgressing the law, they were eager for the law to be carried out, and this by their lying, not as when adulteries are condemned by chastity.

O Jews, you have heard; you have heard, Pharisees; you have heard, teachers of the law; you have heard the Guardian of the law, but you have not yet recognized the Lawmaker. What else does he indicate to you, when he writes with his finger in the earth?[9] God's law, you see, was written by the finger of God, but because of their hard hearts it was written on stone.[10] Now the Lord was finally writing in earth, because he was looking for it to bear fruit.[11] So you have heard then; let the law be carried out, let the adulteress be stoned; but surely in punishing her, the law is not to be carried out by those who themselves deserve its punishment?

"Let each of you examine himself, enter into himself, put himself in the dock before his own conscience, oblige himself to confess. He is the one who knows, after all, who he really is, because *no man knows what is in a man, but the spirit of the man, which is in him* (1 Cor 2:11). As each of you takes a look at himself, he finds himself to be a sinner. Yes, he does. So then, either let this woman go, or else undergo together with her the punishment prescribed by the law."

If he said, "Do not let the adulteress be stoned," he would be convicted of being unjust; if he said, "Let her be stoned," he would not be seen as being gentle; let him say what he has to say, being both gentle and just: *Let the one among you without sin be the first to throw a stone at her.* This is the voice of Justice: let the sinner be punished, but not by sinners; let the law be carried out, but not by transgressors of the law. This is most certainly the voice of Justice; by Justice they were hit as if by a spear as thick as a beam,[12] and so taking a look at themselves and finding themselves guilty, *they all went away, one by one* (Jn 8:9). Two were left, misery and Mercy. When the Lord, in fact, had struck them with that weapon of

---

9. See Jn 8:6.
10. See Ex 31:18.
11. Other explanations Augustine gives of this curious detail are that Jesus was writing the names of his adversaries on earth instead of where he would write the names of his disciples, in heaven (Lk 10:20); and that by bending down to write he was giving a sign of the humility of the Son of God coming down to earth as the Son of Man (see *On the Agreement of the Gospels* IV, 10, 17).
12. See 1 S 17:7 Here the new David is defeating the new Philistines with the enemy's weapon—that of justice! The word Augustine uses here, *trabalis*, is not the word employed by the Vulgate in that passage, which calls the weaver's beam a liciatorium *texentium*; but the noun this adjective comes from, *trabs*, may well have been the word here in the version he was most familiar with.

justice, he did not even bother to watch them falling, but, averting his gaze from them, *again started writing with his finger on the earth* (Jn 8:9).

Christ left alone with the woman, the sinless with the sinner

6. With that woman left there alone as they all went away, he raised his eyes to the woman. We have heard the voice of justice, let us also hear that of gentleness. That woman, after all, was more terrified than ever, I rather think, when she heard the Lord saying, *Let the one among you without sin be the first to throw a stone at her.* So then, when they had all taken a good look at themselves and confessed what they were by their departure, they left the woman with a great sin to the one who was without sin; and because she had heard, *Let the one among you without sin be the first to throw a stone at her*, she was expecting to be punished by the one in whom no sin could be found.

But he who had repulsed her adversaries with the tongue of justice now raised the eyes of gentleness to her, and asked her, *Has no one condemned you?* She answered, *My Lord, no one.* And he said, *"Neither will I condemn you*, by whom perhaps you were afraid of being condemned, because you did not find any sin in me. *Neither will I condemn you."*

What is this, Lord? So are you in favor of sin?

Not at all; pay attention to what comes next:

Go, from now on, sin no more (Jn 8:10-11).

So then, the Lord also condemned—but the sin, not the person. I mean, if he had been in favor of sins, he would have said, "Neither will I condemn you; go, live as you please; be assured of my setting you free; however much you sin, I will also set you free from every punishment of Gehenna and from the torments of hell." That is not what he said.

The Lord is both tender-hearted and true

7. Pay attention then, all who love gentleness in the Lord, and let them fear his truth. Indeed, *agreeable and upright is the Lord* (Ps 24:8). You love him because he is agreeable; fear him because he is upright. In his gentleness he said, *I kept silent*; but as being just, *Shall I keep silent for ever?* (Is 42:14 LXX). *Tender-hearted and full of pity is the Lord.* Most certainly he is. Add to that *longsuffering*; add once more *and very tender-hearted*;

but fear what comes last, *and true* (Ps 85:15). Those, you see, whom he now puts up with for their sins, he is going to pass judgment on for treating him with disdain. *Or do you disdain the riches of his gentleness and forbearance, disregarding the way God's patience is leading you to repentance? You though, with the hardness of your heart, your unrepentant heart, are storing up wrath for yourself on the day of wrath and the revelation of the just judgment of God, who will pay back each one of us according to our works.* (Rom 2:4-6)

The Lord is gentle, the Lord is longsuffering, the Lord is tender-hearted; but the Lord is also just, the Lord is also true. You are being granted time for correction; you, though, love putting it off more than putting it right. You were bad yesterday? Be good today. Even today on this very day have you persisted in bad behavior? At least change it tomorrow. You are always full of great expectations, and promising yourself ever so much from the mercy of God, as though, as well as promising you pardon for repentance, he has also promised you an ever longer lease of life. How do you know what tomorrow is going to bring? You are quite right to say in your heart, "When I start going straight, God will forgive all my sins." There is no denying that God has promised pardon to those who have straightened themselves out and turned back to him. In the prophet, though, where you read to me that God has promised pardon to the one who corrects himself, you will not be able to read to me that God has promised you a long life.

The dangers of both hope and despair

8. So it is that we are all faced with each of these dangers, both with hope and despair, two contrary things, contrary moods. The one is deceived by hope who says, "God is good, God is tender-hearted, let me do what I like, what gives me pleasure; let me loosen the reins on my lusts, let me carry out the desires of my soul."[13]

Why do you say this?

Because God is tender-hearted, God is good, God is gentle.

These people are endangered by hope.

---

13. Of my *anima*, which I have in common with animals, not of my *animus*, my rationality.

Endangered by despair, however, are those who have fallen into grave sins, thinking that they can no longer be forgiven, even if they repent, and see themselves as certainly destined for damnation. They thus say to themselves, "We are already going to be damned; why not do whatever we want?" That is the attitude of gladiators destined to die by the sword. That is why desperate men are such a menace; I mean, they no longer have anything to fear, and so they are all the more to be feared.

Despair kills these, the others are killed by hope. The mind, the spirit,[14] fluctuates between hope and despair. Be on the watch lest hope kill you and, while pinning your hopes on mercy, you come under judgment; be on the watch as well lest despair kill you, and, while assuming you cannot be forgiven for the grave sins you have committed, you refuse to repent and run into the judgment of Wisdom, who says, *I too will laugh at your ruin* (Prov 1:26).

So what does the Lord do, then, for those in danger of either disease? To those endangered by hope he has this to say: *Do not be slow to turn to the Lord, do not put it off from day to day; for suddenly his wrath will come, and will destroy you in the time of vengeance* (Sir 5:8-9). As for those endangered by despair, what does he say to them? *On whatever day the wicked man turns to me, I will forget all his wickedness* (Ez 18:21-22). So then, for the sake of those who are prone to despair he provided the haven of pardon; for the sake of those who are prone to hope and to deluding themselves with putting things off, he made the day of death uncertain. You do not know when your last day will come. Are you not grateful for having this day in which to straighten yourself out? So it was, then, that he said to this woman, *Nor will I condemn you*; but on being assured about the past, take care of the future. *Nor will I condemn you*; I have blotted out what you have committed; keep what I have commanded, in order to find what I have promised.

---

14. *Animus.*

Homily 34

On John 8:12[1]

Those who have understood these words of Jesus are asked to put up with Augustine's explaining them to those who have not

1. What we heard just now when the holy gospel was read, and what we listened to attentively, all of us have also, I am sure, tried to understand, and each of us, according to our capacity, has grasped what we could of the great matter that was read, and, with this bread of the word set before us,[2] no one can complain that he tasted nothing. But again, because it is difficult, I doubt that anyone has understood it all. Yet, even if someone has understood well enough all the words of our Lord Jesus Christ which were now recited from the gospel, let him put up with my ministry until, if I can manage it with his help, I succeed in bringing either all or many to understand what a few are happy to have understood.

Jesus is not identifying himself with the sun

2. I think that what the Lord says, *I am the light of the world* (Jn 8:12), is clear to those who have the eyes which let them share in this Light; but those who only have eyes for the flesh are astonished at what was said by the Lord Jesus Christ, *I am the light of the world*. And someone may be saying to himself, "Is it not possible that the Lord Jesus is this sun, which governs the day by rising and setting?" In fact, there is no dearth of heretics who have held that opinion. The Manichees thought that this sun, visible to the eyes of the flesh, and evident not just to human beings but to animals as well, is Christ the Lord. But the true faith of the Catholic Church rejects such a fiction and recognizes the diabolical quality of this teaching —something that the Church knows not only by believing but also by debating with those it can refute.

And so let us reject this kind of error, which the holy Church has condemned from the beginning. Let us not think that the Lord Jesus Christ

---

1. Preached a few days after Homily 33.
2. See Sermons 56, 10; 58, 5; 59, 6; 95, 1. In the first three of these sermons Augustine is commenting on this phrase from the Lord's Prayer, *Give us this day our daily bread.*

is this sun which we see rising in the east, setting in the west, whose course is followed by night, whose rays are overcast by clouds, and which migrates by a fixed and definite movement from place to place; this is not the Lord Christ. The Lord Christ is not the sun that was made, but the one through whom the sun was made. *For all things were made through him and without him was made nothing* (Jn 1:3).

We now turn to Psalm 35

3. So then, he is the Light which made this light; let us love that light, let us be eager to understand it, let us thirst for it so that, by its lead, we may one day come to it and live in it so as never to die again. This is the light, in fact, about which a prophecy was once sung in the psalm: *Men and beasts you will save, Lord, so has your kindness spread widely, O God* (Ps 35:7-8).[3] These are the words of a holy psalm; pay attention to what the ancient words of the holy men of God foretold about this Light. *Men*, it says, *and beasts you will save, Lord, so has your kindness spread widely, O God.*

After all, since you are God and have expansive mercy, that same expansive mercy has reached both the human beings you created in your own image and the beasts which you subjected to these human beings. From the one who is the salvation of humanity, in fact, comes the salvation of the animal as well. Do not be ashamed of thinking this way about the Lord your God;[4] on the contrary, be confident, presume it, and make sure you do not think otherwise. The one who saves you is the one who saves your horse, who does the same for your sheep, and, to get to the smallest of animals, who does the same for your hen. *Salvation is the Lord's* (Ps 3:8); the Lord saves these beings as well.

Does this bother you? Are you questioning it? I am astonished that you should doubt. Will the one who was prepared to create not also be prepared to save? *Salvation is the Lord's*, the salvation of angels, of human beings, of beasts; *salvation is the Lord's*. Just as nobody and nothing gets being from itself, so nobody and nothing gets salvation from itself. Accordingly,

---
3. See Sermon 23, 10-18 for a similar treatment of this psalm in connection with the same theme as that of this homily; also 213, 1, introducing Augustine's "handing over of the creed" to catechumens.
4. As the Manichees would be.

what the psalm says is fully true and very right: *Men and beasts you will save, Lord.* Why? *So has your kindness spread widely, O God.* After all, you are God; you have created, you save. You have given being, you give health and welfare.[5]

*The key words of the psalm: With you is the fountain of life,
and in your light shall we see light*

4. So then, if God's kindness has been expansive, if human beings and beasts are saved by him, do human beings have nothing granted to them by God the creator which is not granted to animals? Is there no distinction between the being made in God's image and the being subjected to God's image? Of course there is! Besides the salvation which we have in common with mute animals, there is something God bestows on us which he does not bestow on them.

What is that?

The same psalm continues: *But the sons of men shall hope under the cover of your wings* (Ps 35:8). While now having salvation in common with their herds, *the sons of men will hope under the cover of your wings.* They have one salvation in actual fact, another in hope.[6] This salvation in the here and now is common to human beings and the herds; but there is another salvation which human beings hope for, and those who hope for it receive it, while those who despair of it do not receive it. For *the sons of men shall hope*, he says, *under the cover of your wings.* Now those who persevere in hope are protected by you, lest they be driven from hope by the devil; *they will hope under the cover of your wings.*

So if they will be hoping, what will they be hoping for, but something which cattle will not have? *They will get drunk on the abundance of your house, and you will give them to drink of the torrent of your pleasure* (Ps 35:9). What kind of wine is it which is praiseworthy to get drunk on? What kind of wine does not fuddle the mind but guides it? What kind of wine

---

5. The Latin *salus* and *salvus, salvum facere* cover a wide range of meaning. That includes "salvation" at one end of the scale, which for us usually means eternal salvation, and "health" and "welfare" at the other. It would seem, from the qualms Augustine senses in his hearers about God's saving animals, that the religious sense of saving and salvation had come to predominate; they apparently shied away from the notion of God's "saving the souls" of animals.
6. One of Augustine's favorite little rhyming contrasts, *in re... in spe.*

keeps you for ever sane, does not drive you mad when you drink? *They will get drunk.*

What on?

On the abundance of your house, and you will give them to drink of the torrent of your pleasure.

What from?

Since with you is the fountain of life (Ps 35:10). The very fountain of life was walking about on earth, was saying, *Let those who are thirsty come to me* (Jn 7:37). That is the fountain.

But I started to talk about the light and was dealing with the question of light raised by the gospel. For we heard the Lord saying, *I am the light of the world.* A question followed that some people, who were thinking materialistically, might suppose he meant this sun that we can see; then we came to the psalm, and, on taking a look at it, we found meanwhile that the Lord is the fountain of life. Drink and live. *With you*, it said, *is the fountain of life*; that is why the sons of men hope under the shadow of your wings, seeking to drink deeply from this fountain. But we were talking about the Light; so continue, because after the prophet said, *With you is the fountain of life*, he went on to say, *In your light shall we see light* (Ps 35:10); God from God, light from light. Through this light was made the light of the sun; and the Light which made the sun—beneath which we were also made—was itself placed beneath the sun for our sakes. The Light, I repeat, which made the sun was, for our sakes, placed beneath the sun. Do not scorn the cloud of the flesh; the light is clouded, not so as to hide it but to make it tolerable.

This light and this fountain are the same thing

5. So then, speaking through the cloud of the flesh, the Light that never fails, the Light of Wisdom, says to humankind, *I am the light of the world; the one who follows me will not walk in darkness, but will have the light of life* (Jn 8:12). How he withdrew your attention from the eyes of flesh, and called you back to the eyes of the heart! It was not enough, you see, just to say, *The one who follows me will not walk in darkness, but will have the light*; he also added, *of life*; just as it was said in the psalm, *Since with you is the fountain of life*. Observe then, my brothers and sisters, how the words of the Lord are in

agreement with the truth of that psalm, and the psalm also placed the light next to the fountain of life, and the Lord talks about the light of life.

In these material, bodily things we are used to, light is one thing, a fountain another; a fountain is what your mouth and throat go looking for, light is for your eyes. When we are thirsty, we look for a fountain; when we are in the dark, we look for a light; and if we happen to be thirsty at night, we light a lamp so as to get to the fountain. Not so with God; what is light is also fountain; the one who shines for you so that you may see is the very same one as gushes for you so that you may drink.[7]

The folly of literally following the sun

6. You see then, my brothers and sisters, you see what sort of light this is if you see inwardly; about it the Lord says, *The one who follows me will not walk in darkness.* Follow that sun, and we will see whether you will not be walking in the dark. Notice that at its rising it comes toward you; it runs its course to the west; perhaps your journey takes you to the east. Unless you travel in the opposite direction, not the way the sun is moving, by following it you will obviously go wrong, you will be mistaking the west for the east. If you follow it on land, you will go wrong; the sailor following it at sea will go off course.

Finally, you are convinced the sun has to be followed, and so you make your way to the west, the way it is going too; let us see whether you will not be walking in the dark when it sets. Notice how the sun will desert you, finishing the day according to the terms of its service, even if you do not want to forsake it. Our Lord Jesus Christ, however, while he was not seen by all people through the cloud of flesh, embraced all things through the might of his wisdom. Your God is everywhere, whole and entire; if you do not sink below the horizon, away from him, he never sinks below the horizon from you.

Following the Light by desire, by faith

7. *So the one*, he says, *who follows me will not walk in darkness, but will have the light of life.* He stated what he promised in the future tense; he did not say, you see, "have," but he says, *will have the light of life.* Nor,

---

7. See Sermon 225, 4, a sermon preached to the *infantes*, the newly baptized at Easter, where the divine light and fountain are referred to the Holy Spirit.

however, did he say, "who will follow me," but *who follows me*. He put what we ought to do in the present tense, while what he promised to those who act was signified by a verb in the future tense: the one who follows will have. He follows now; he will have later; he now follows by faith; he will have later by sight. For, *as long as we are in the body*, says the apostle, *we are exiled from the Lord; for we walk by faith, not by sight* (2 Cor 5:6-7).

When will it be by sight?

When we have the light of life, when we come to that vision, when this night has passed.

About that day, indeed, that is going to rise, it is said, *In the morning I will stand before you and meditate* (Ps 5:4).

What is the meaning of *in the morning*?

When the night of this world is over, when terrors of temptations are done with, when that lion *who goes round roaring at night, looking for someone to devour* (1 Pt 5:8) has been overcome. *In the morning I will stand before you and meditate*. But right now, brothers and sisters, what do we think is suitable for this time, if not that which is again said in the psalm, *Night after night I will wash my bed, drenching my couch with tears* (Ps 6:7)? Night after night, he says, I shall weep, I shall burn with desire for the light. The Lord sees my longing, since another psalm says to him, *Before you is all that I long for, and my groaning is not hidden from you* (Ps 37:10). Do you long for gold? You can be seen; your seeking for gold, after all, will be obvious to others. Is it corn you want? You ask who stocks it, and you let him know what you are eager to get. Do you long for God? Who sees that other than God? Who is there, after all, from whom you can ask for God, like asking for bread, water, gold, silver, or corn? From whom but God can you ask for God? One asks from the very same one who promises himself.

Let your soul stretch wide its yearning, and seek, by stretching its capacity[8] to grasp *what eye has not seen, nor ear heard, nor has it entered the heart of man* (1 Cor 2:9). That can be desired, can be coveted, that we can sigh for as much as we like; what we cannot do is form fitting thoughts about it, and explain it with words.[9]

---

8. The Latin, *et sinu capaciore quaerat comprehendere*, could also be rendered "to enfold in an ever more capacious lap".
9. See Sermons 21, 2; 52, 6; 117, 5; 308A, 5.

*Those who have followed the Lord on hearing the gospel
compared with the man who heard him in person and went away sorrowful*

8. So then, my brothers and sisters, since our Lord said rather briefly, *I am the light of the world; the one who follows me will not walk in darkness, but will have the light of life*, and commands one thing while promising another, let us do what he commanded so as to avoid yearning for what he promised with cheeky presumptuousness,[10] so that he will not say to us at judgment,

"Did you do what I commanded, so as to demand what I promised?"

"So what did you command, O Lord our God?"

"He says to you, 'That you follow me.'"

You have asked for advice about life; for what kind of life, if not the one about which it is said, *With you is the fountain of life*? Someone once heard, *Go, sell all that you have, and give to the poor, and you shall have treasure in heaven; and come, follow me. He went away sad* (Mk 10:21-22), he did not follow.[11] He sought out *the good master* (Mk 10:17), questioned the teacher, and took no notice of what he taught; *he went away sad*, all tied up by his wants; *he went away sad*, carrying the heavy burden of avarice on his shoulders. He was toiling away, he was sweating, and he decided not to follow but to abandon the one who wanted to relieve him of the burden.

Later on, however, after the Lord cried out through the gospel, *Come to me, all you who labor and are burdened, and I will refresh you; take my yoke upon you, and learn from me, because I am meek and humble of heart* (Mt 11:28-29), how many, on hearing the gospel, have done what that rich man did not do on hearing from the mouth of the Lord himself! So then, let us do it now; let us follow the Lord; let us shake off the shackles which keep us from following. Which of us is capable of loosing such chains without the help of the one to whom it is said, *You have burst my bonds* (Ps 115:16), the one about whom another psalm declares, *The Lord releases those in chains, the Lord raises up those who have been crushed* (Ps 145:7-8)?

---

10. See Sermon 233, 1.
11. See Sermons 38, 7; 86, 2; 299E, 5; 301A, 5.

The way first, then the truth and the life

9. And what else do they follow, those who have been released and lifted up, but the light about which they hear, *I am the light of the world; the one who follows me will not walk in darkness*? For the Lord enlightens the blind. So then, brothers and sisters, we are now being enlightened, since we have the eye-salve of faith. His spittle, with which to anoint the man who had been born blind,[12] was mixed with earth. We too were born blind from Adam,[13] and we need this one to enlighten us. He mixed spittle with earth. *The Word was made flesh, and took up residence among us* (Jn 1:14). He mixed spittle with earth; that is why it was foretold, *Truth has sprung from the earth*[14] (Ps 84:12); while he said, *I am the way, the truth and the life* (Jn 14:6).

We shall enjoy the truth when we see face to face, because this too is promised us. I mean, who would ever dare to hope for what God had not been good enough either to promise or to give? We shall see face to face. The apostle says, *Now I know in part, now in a riddle as in a mirror, but then it will be face to face* (1 Cor 13:12). And John the apostle writes in his letter, *Dearly beloved, we are now children of God, and it has not yet appeared what we shall be; we know that when he appears we shall be like him, because we shall see him as he is* (1 Jn 3:2). There is a promise indeed for you! If you love him, follow.

"I do love," you say, "but what path shall I follow?"

If the Lord your God had said to you, "I am the truth and the life," and you, being eager for the truth, longing for life, were to look around for a way by which you could make sure of reaching these things, and were to say to yourself, "It is a great thing, truth, a great thing, life; if only there were a way my soul could get there!" You are looking for a way? Listen to him saying first of all, *I am the way*; before telling you where, he told you how to go. *I*, he says, *am the way*.

The path to where?

And the truth and the life. First he told you how to go, then he said where you are to go.

---

12. See Jn 9:6.
13. See Sermons 135, 1; 136, 1; 136A, 1.
14. See Sermons 185, 1; 189, 2; 191, 2; 192, 1, 193, 2; each one quotes this psalm verse with reference to Christmas.

I am the way, I am the truth, I am the life. Abiding with the Father, the truth and the life; putting on flesh, he became the way.[15] You are not told, "Work at searching for a way to truth and life." That is not what you are told. Lazybones, get up! The way himself has come to you, and he awakened you from your sleep, if at least he really did wake you up. *Get up and walk* (Jn 5:8). Perhaps you are trying to walk, but cannot, because your feet hurt. What is making your feet hurt? Have they been running over rough ground at the command of avarice? But the Word of God has even healed the lame.[16]

"But look," you say, "I have perfectly sound feet, but I cannot see the way."

He also gave sight to the blind.[17]

The quarrels we are inevitably involved in, not only with others, but inwardly with ourselves

10. All this is happening through faith, *as long as we*, remaining in the body, *roam far from the Lord* (2 Cor 5:6-7), still abiding in the body. But when we have walked the whole way and reached that home country, what will be more joyful for us, what more blessed for us? Because nothing is more at peace. Nothing, after all, will be rebelling against humanity.

Now, on the other hand, brothers and sisters, it is difficult for us to live without quarreling. We have indeed been called to live in harmony, we are ordered to be at peace with each other; this is what we should be striving to do, attempting with all our might, in order to attain perfect peace eventually. As things are now, though, we often find ourselves at odds with the very people we wish to help.

Someone is going astray, you want to lead him to the way; he resists and you quarrel; a pagan resists, you argue against the errors of idols and of demons. The heretic resists, you argue against these other demonic doctrines. A bad Catholic does not want to live a good life, you reprove

---

15. See Sermons 91, 9; 92, 3; 123, 3; 141, 4; 142, 2; 306, 10.
16. See, for example, Mt 15:30.
17. See Mt 9:30; 15:30; Mk 10:46-52; Jn 9:6-7.

even your brother at home;[18] he is staying with you in the house and seeking paths of destruction; you get worked up about how to correct him, so as to give a good account for both of you to the Lord.

From all sides, how many reasons for disputes! Often, when someone is tired of it all, he will say to himself, "What is the point of my putting up with those who contradict, with those who pay back evil for good? I want to help, they want to get lost; I waste my life arguing, I get no peace; what is more, I am making enemies of people I should have as friends, if only they would appreciate the good will in my advice. What is the point of my constantly enduring all this? I will come back to myself, be with myself. I will call upon my God."

Go back to yourself, then; there too you will find quarreling; if you have begun to follow God, there too you will find quarreling.

"What quarreling," you ask, "will I find?"

The flesh lusting against the spirit, and the spirit against the flesh (Gal 5:17). There you are, just you, there you are, all on your own, there you are, all by yourself; there you are, with nobody else to put up with. But you see *another law in your members, fighting against the law of your mind, and taking you prisoner to the law of sin which is in your members* (Rom 7:23). Cry out therefore, and from the quarreling within you cry to God, so that he may make peace between you and yourself, *Wretched fellow that I am, who will deliver me from the body of this death? The grace of God through Jesus Christ our Lord* (Rom 7:24-25). Because, says he, *the one who follows me will not walk in darkness, but will have the light of life*.

Once all your quarreling has ended, immortality will follow, because *death is the last enemy to be destroyed* (1 Cor 15:26). And what sort of peace will there be? *This corruptible must put on incorruption, and this mortal immortality* (1 Cor 15:53). So that the way arrive there, because then we shall be in the reality, let us now follow in faith him who said, *I am the light of the world; the one who follows me will not walk in darkness, but will have the light of life*.

---

18. I am not certain that this is what he means by his curious expression, *interiorem fratrem tuum*, but cannot think what else it could mean.

Homily 35

On John 8:13-14[1]

Introduction; reminder of yesterday's sermon

1. Those of you who were present yesterday will remember that we discussed at some length the words of our Lord Jesus Christ, where he said, *I am the light of the world; the one who follows me will not walk in darkness, but will have the light of life* (Jn 8:12); and if we still wished to continue our discussion of that life, I would be able to go on talking again for a long time, because it cannot be explained in few words. And so, my brothers and sisters, let us follow Christ the light of the world, so as not to walk in darkness. The kinds of darkness that relate to daily living[2] are to be feared, not that which relates to the eyes; but if it were to affect the eyes, it would concern the inner eyes, not those outside; it would concern those which distinguish between the just and the unjust,[3] not those distinguishing between black and white.

*Christ challenges the Jews with the testimony of John the Baptist,
of the lamp bearing witness to the Day*

2. So then, when our Lord Jesus Christ had spoken, the Jews answered, *You are bearing witness to yourself; your testimony is not true* (Jn 8:13). Before our Lord Jesus Christ came, he lit many prophetic lamps and sent them ahead of him. Among them also was John the Baptist, to whom the great Light himself, which is Christ the Lord, bore witness such as to no human being; he said, you remember, *Among those born of women none greater has arisen than John the Baptist* (Mt 11:11).[4] Yet this man—than whom no one was greater among those born of women—says about the Lord Jesus Christ, I indeed baptize you in water; but the one who is coming, whose shoes I am not worthy to undo, is mightier than I am (Lk 3:16). Notice

---

1. Preached the day after Homily 34.
2. *Tenebrae metuendae sunt morum* .. might also be rendered: "The kinds of darkness that are found in lifestyles ...."
3. See Homily 18, 10.
4. See Sermon 288, 2.

how the lamp submits himself to the Day.⁵ The Lord himself testifies that John was a lamp: *He was,* he says, *a lamp, alight and shining, and you were willing to revel in his light for a time* (Jn 5:35).

But when the Jews said to the Lord, *Tell us by what authority you are doing these things,* the Lord knew that they had a high regard for John the Baptist, and that this man for whom they had a high regard had testified to them about the Lord; so he answered them, *I will also ask you one question; tell me where the baptism of John comes from? From heaven or from men?* (Mt 21:23-25) Confused, they thought within themselves: if they said "from men," they ran the risk of being stoned by the mob, which believed that John was a prophet; if they said "from heaven," he would answer them, "The one whose prophecy, you admit, was from heaven bore witness to me; you learned from him about the authority by which I do these things." So they saw that, no matter how they answered his question, they were going to fall into a trap, and they said, *We do not know.* And the Lord replied, *Neither will I tell you by what authority I do these things.* (Mt 21:27) I will not tell you what I know, because you refuse to admit what you know. In any case, they left in confusion, completely rebuffed. Thus was fulfilled what God the Father says in the psalm through the prophet: *I have prepared a lamp for my Christ,* that is, John himself; *I will clothe his enemies with confusion* (Ps 131:17-18).⁶

The point illustrated by the comparison between the eyes in our heads and the eyes of our minds

3. So then, the Lord Jesus Christ had the testimony of the prophets sent ahead of him, like heralds going ahead of a judge; he had the testimony of John; but the testimony that he gave to himself was greater.⁷ Yet they were looking for lamps for their weak eyes, because they could not endure the Day. In fact, this same John, the apostle whose gospel we have in our hands, says about John at the beginning of his gospel, *There was a man sent from God, whose name was John; this man came as a witness, to bear witness to the light, so that all might believe through him. He was not the light, but to*

---

5. See Sermons 67, 9; 128, 2; 289, 5; 290, 1; 293, 4.6; 293D, 2; 342, 2; all of these sermons play on the contrast between the lamp and the Day. See also Homilies 2, 8; 23, 2.
6. See Homily 5, 14.
7. See Homilies 2, 5-7; 7, 16.

bear witness to the light. That was the true light, which enlightens everyone coming into the world. (Jn 1:6-9) If *everyone* was enlightened, then John too. That is why John says, *We have all received from his fullness* (Jn 1:16).[8]

Therefore, you must distinguish between these lights, so that your spirit may progress in the faith of Christ, lest you always be infants seeking the breast and backing away from solid food. You must be nourished and weaned by your holy mother the Church of Christ, and come to more lasting food, not for the body but for the mind. Distinguish therefore; the light which enlightens is one thing and the one that is lit is another. In fact, even our eyes are called lights, and, touching his eyes, each one swears by his lights: "By the life of my lights" is a common oath.[9] If these lights really are lights, open them and let them shine for you when the light in your closed bedroom is out; of course they cannot do so.

So then, these eyes which we have in our faces and call lights still need the help of light from outside, even when they are healthy and are wide open; take that light away or do not bring it in, they still do not see although they are healthy and are wide open. So too with the mind, which is the eye of the soul; unless the light of truth shines on it and is wonderfully illuminated by the one who illuminates and is not himself illuminated, it cannot attain either to wisdom or to justice. Our way, in fact, is to live justly. But how is the one for whom the light does not shine to avoid stumbling on the way? And thus it is necessary to see in that way; it is important to see on a road like that. Tobit, you remember, had the eyes in his face blinded, and his son gave a hand to his father; but the father, with his instructions, showed his son the way.[10]

How Jesus the Light bears witness to himself as validly as any light, once lit, is its own illumination

4. So the Jews then replied, *You are bearing witness to yourself; your testimony is not true.* Let us see what they are hearing; let us listen to it too, but not like them; they listen with scorn, seeking to kill Christ; we listen with faith, longing to live through Christ. Let that difference, for the time

---

8. Augustine always treats this verse as part of the testimony given by John the Baptist himself, not as a further comment by John the evangelist. See Homilies 1, 6; 13, 8; Sermons 66, 1, with note 5; 289, 5; 292, 8; 293, 6.
9. The Latin, *Sic vivant lumina mea*, seems to say, "May my lights live." The translation given, however, is more clearly in the form of an oath. See Sermon 4, 6. The eyes are also called lights in Homilies 2, 6; 14, 1; 19, 11; 22, 10.
10. See Tob 2:10; 4:3-21; Sermons 88, 16; 125A, 5.

being, separate our ears and minds and theirs, and let us listen to the Lord's reply to the Jews: *Jesus answered and said to them, Even if I am bearing witness to myself, my testimony is true, because I know where I came from and where I am going* (Jn 8:14). A light draws attention both to other things and to itself. You light a lamp, for example, to look for a shirt,[11] and the shining lamp helps you find the garment; do you ever light a lamp so as to see another lamp shining? A lighted lamp, of course, is sufficient both to lay bare other things swathed in darkness and to show itself to your eyes.

So too was Christ the Lord distinguishing between his faithful and the hostile Jews just as between light and darkness, as between those within whom he spread the rays of faith and those who, with closed eyes, had light all round them. After all, even that sun sheds its light on the faces both of someone who can see and someone who is blind; both, when they stand up and turn their faces to the sun, receive its light on their bodies, but both do not receive light in their eyes; one of them sees, the other does not see. The sun is present to both of them, but one of them is unaware of the presence of the sun.[12] So too the Wisdom of God, the Word of God, the Lord Jesus Christ is present everywhere, because everywhere there is truth, everywhere wisdom. Someone in the east has an understanding of justice, someone else in the west has an understanding of justice; is the justice which this one understands something other than the justice that one grasps? Separated in body, they are united in the vision of their minds. The justice I see from here, if it really is justice, is the same as that which a just man sees, separated from me by who knows how many days' journey, but united with me in the light of that justice.[13]

So then, the Light bears witness to itself; it opens healthy eyes and is its own witness, that the light be known. But what are we to make of unbelievers? It is present to them too, is it not? Yes, it is present to them; but they do not have the eyes in their hearts to see it with. Listen to the judgment passed on them in this very gospel: *And the light shines in the darkness, and the darkness did not comprehend it* (Jn 1:5). So that is why the Lord says, and he speaks truly, *Even if I am bearing witness to myself, my testimony is true; because I know where I came from and where I am going.* He meant

---

11. *Tunica* was an undergarment. Only soldiers and deacons in liturgical functions wore a tunic over other garments.
12. See Homilies 1, 19; 3, 5.
13. See Sermon 4, 7.

us to understand the Father; the Son was giving glory to the Father. While being his equal, he glorifies the one by whom he has been sent; how much more should a human being glorify the one by whom he was created!

Christ simultaneously up above with the Father and down below with us

5. *I know where I came from and where I am going.* The one who is talking to you in person has something which he did not leave behind, but he still came; for by coming he did not depart from there, nor by going back did he abandon us.[14] Why be surprised? He is God. This cannot be done by a man; this cannot be done by the sun itself. When it proceeds to the west, it leaves the east behind, and until it returns to the east ready to rise again, it is not in the east; our Lord Jesus Christ, however, both comes and is there, goes back and is here.

Listen to the evangelist saying this in another place, and grasp it if you can; if you cannot, then believe. *No one,* he says, *has ever seen God, except the only-begotten Son who is in the Father's lap; he has made him known* (Jn 1:18). He did not say, "Who was in the Father's lap," as though by coming he had left the Father's lap. He was speaking here, and was saying he was there;[15] the very one who, on the point of departing from here, said what? *Behold I am with you even to the end of time* (Mt 28:20).

The Light by its nature bears witness to itself

6. So the evidence given by the Light, then, is true, whether it is pointing to itself or to other things; because without the Light you cannot see the Light, and without the Light you cannot see anything else which is not the Light. If the Light is suited to pointing to things which are not lights, does it lose that capacity with itself? Does the light, without which other things are not revealed, fail to disclose itself? The prophet said something true; but where did he get it from, unless he had drawn it from the fountain of truth? John said something true, but ask him where his speaking came from:[16] *We have all,* he says, *received from his fullness* (Jn 1:16). So then, our Lord Jesus Christ is eminently suited to bearing witness to himself.

---

14. See Homilies 2, 8; 31, 9; Sermons 229K, 2; 263A, 1.
15. See Homilies 12, 8; 27, 4.
16. Compare Homily 5, 1.

But clearly, my brothers and sisters, in the night of this world we must also listen carefully to prophecy; now, in fact, our Lord wanted to come humbly to our frail condition and into the deep, night-like darkness of our hearts. He came as a man to be treated with contempt and with honor, he came to be denied and to be acknowledged; to be treated with contempt and denied by the Jews, to be honored and acknowledged by us; to be judged and to judge; judged unjustly, to judge with justice.[17] Thus did he come in a way that a lamp was needed to bear witness to him. After all, what need would there have been for John—as a lamp—to bear witness to the light of the Day, if the Day itself could have been seen by our weakness? But we were not capable of this; he made himself weak for the weak, healed weakness with weakness; took away the death of the flesh with mortal flesh; made an eye-salve of his body for our lights.[18] So then, because our Lord came, and we are still in the night of this world, it is necessary for us to listen to the prophecies as well.

Refuting the pagans with the aid of the Jews

7. From prophecies, in fact, we refute the pagans who speak against us.
"Who is Christ?" says a pagan.
"The one whom the prophets foretold," we reply.
"Which prophets?" says he.
We quote Isaiah, Daniel, Jeremiah, other holy prophets; we tell him how long they had come before Christ, by how much time they had preceded his coming. So that is our answer, then; the prophets came before him, they foretold he was going to come.
One of them answers, "Which prophets?"
We run through the list of those which are chanted to us every day.[19]
He comes back with, "Who are these prophets?"
We reply, "The ones who also foretold the things we see happening."

---

17. See Homilies 19, 16; 25, 3 for fuller treatment of the theme of Christ coming to judge at the last judgment.
18. For the use of these images in the treatment of this general theme, see Homilies 2, 8, 16; 3, 3; 12, 11; 15, 6; Sermon 233, 4.
19. By referring to daily readings either at Mass or at common prayer, Augustine may be suggesting that there was a reading from the prophets each day or that the reading was an Old Testament reading. Hence, it is possible that Augustine thought of the whole Old Testament as prophecy (see *The City of God* XVII, 1).

"You," says he again, "have made all this up for yourselves; you have seen these things happening, and as though they had been foretold as things to come, you have written them in whatever books you liked."

At this point, against our enemies the pagans, the testimony of other enemies comes to our aid. We present books from the Jews[20] and respond, "Both you and they, for sure, are enemies of our faith. That is why they have been scattered among the nations, so that we may confound our enemies by setting one group against the other. Let the Book of Isaiah be brought forward by the Jews, let us see if I do not read there: *Like a sheep he was led to the slaughter, and just as a lamb before the shearer was without voice, so he did not open his mouth. In humility was his judgment taken away; by his bruising have we been healed; we have all strayed like sheep, and he was handed over for our sins.* (Is 53:7-8.5-6)"[21]

There is one lamp. Bring out another, open the psalter, let the passion of Christ as foretold there be recited: *They have dug my hands and my feet, they have counted all my bones; they, however, looked me over and gazed at me, they divided my garments among them, and over my garment they cast lots. With you is my praise, in the great Church shall I acknowledge you. All the ends of the earth shall be reminded and shall be converted to the Lord; and all the kindreds of the nations shall worship in his presence; because the Lord's is the kingdom, and his shall be the lordship over the nations.* (Ps 21:17-19.26.28-29) Let one enemy blush in shame, because another enemy provides me with a book [with which to put him to shame].

But there you are, with books produced by one enemy I have overcome another; yet the one who provided the books must not be spared; let another book be brought forward by which he too may be overcome. I read another prophet, and there I find the Lord speaking to the Jews: *My pleasure is not in you, says the Lord, nor will I accept a sacrifice from your hands; since from the rising of the sun to its setting a clean sacrifice shall be offered to my name* (Mal 1:10-11). You are not taking part, O Jew, in a clean sacrifice; I convict you of being unclean.

---

20. For this technique of quoting the Jews against the pagans, see Sermons 200, 3; 201, 3; 373, 4.
21. Augustine, quoting from memory, has the verses in the wrong order.

We Christians too have the surer prophetic word
to help us in our apologetics against all scoffers

8. Notice too that the lamps also bear witness to the Day on account of our weakness, because we cannot endure and see the brilliance of the Day. For we Christians too, compared with unbelievers, are already light; that is why the apostle says, *For you were once darkness, now however you are light in the Lord; walk as children of the Light* (Eph 5:8). And elsewhere he said, *The night is far advanced, while the day has drawn near; let us cast aside, then, the works of darkness, and put on the armor of light; let us conduct ourselves, as in the day* (Rom 13:12-13).

Nonetheless, since the day in which we now find ourselves is still night in comparison with that light to which we will come, listen to the apostle Peter; he reports on the voice addressed to Christ the Lord *from the power of majesty*: *You are my beloved Son, in whom I have taken pleasure. This voice*, he says, *we heard resounding from heaven, when we were with him on the holy mountain.* (2 Pt 1:17-18) But because we ourselves were not there and did not hear this voice from heaven at that time, Peter says to us, *And we have a reliable prophetic word.* You did not hear the voice resounding from heaven, but you have *a reliable prophetic word.*

Our Lord Jesus Christ, in fact, foresaw that some impious folk were going to come along, who would misrepresent his miracles, crediting them to magic arts; so he sent the prophets ahead of him. Even if he were a magician, after all, and employed magic arts to ensure that he was worshiped even when he was dead, was he really a magician before he was born? Listen to the prophets, O dead man, you who are a worm-eaten scoffer, listen to the prophets. I will read, you listen to those who came before the Lord: *We have*, says the apostle Peter, *a reliable prophetic word, to which you would do well to pay attention, as to lamps in a dark place, until the day dawns, and the Day Star rises in your hearts* (2 Pt 1:19).

We Christians too need these lamps to light us on our way to the eternal Day

9. So then, when our Lord Jesus Christ comes, and, as the apostle Paul also says, *lights up the things hidden in the dark, and discloses the thoughts of the heart, so that each may receive praise from God* (1 Cor 4:5), then with such a Day present, lamps will not be needed; the prophet will not be read to us, the book of the apostle will not be opened, we shall not require the testimony of

John, we shall not need the gospel itself.[22] Then will all the scriptures—which were lit for us like lamps in the night of this world's age so that we might not remain in darkness—be removed from our midst. With all these taken away, lest they should go on shining as though we needed them, and with the men of God, by whom these things were ministered to us, beholding together with us that true and brilliant Light—with all these aids put aside, then, what shall we see? What will nourish our minds? What will delight our gaze? What will give us *that joy which eye has not seen, nor ear heard, nor has it entered the heart of man* (1 Cor 2:9)? What will we see?

I implore you all, love with me, run with me by believing; let us long for that country up above, let us pant and sigh for that country up above, let us realize that we are strangers here. What will we see then? Let the gospel say it now: *In the beginning was the Word, and the Word was with God, and the Word was God* (Jn 1:1). You will come to the fountain from which you have been sprayed with dew-drops;[23] from where a ray has been sent obliquely by roundabout ways into the darkness of your heart, you will see the naked Light itself; you are being purified so as to see and bear it. *Beloved*, says John himself, as I reminded you yesterday,[24] *we are the children of God, and it has not yet appeared what we shall be; we know that when he appears, we shall be like him, because we shall see him as he is* (1 Jn 3:2). I really do sense your feelings of yearning, of eagerness, being lifted up with me to what is above; but *the body which is perishable is weighing upon the soul, and this earthy dwelling is pressing down the mind filled with many thoughts* (Wis 9:15).[25]

So I too then am going to put aside this book, you are all going to depart as well, each to your own home. It has been good, sharing the Light together, good rejoicing in it, good exulting in it together; but when we depart from each other, let us not depart from him.

---

22. Earlier on in his ministry Augustine thought that Christians, "supported by faith, hope and charity,.. have no need of the scriptures except for instructing others" (*Teaching Christianity*, I, 39, 43). For his more mature view, as we have it here, see Sermons 57, 7; 59, 6.
23. See Homily 5, 1; Sermon 57, 7.
24. See Homily 34, 9.
25. See Homilies 21, 1; 23, 5.

Homily 36

On John 8:15-18[1]

Why John is the eagle among the evangelists

1. In the four gospels, or rather in the four books of the one gospel, Saint John the apostle, who has not undeservedly been compared to an eagle because of his spiritual understanding, raised his preaching up to a much more sublime height than the other three; and, in doing so, he wanted our hearts to be raised up with him as well. The other three evangelists, as if they were walking about with the Lord as a man upon the earth, had little to say about his divine nature. But this one, as if he were bored with walking on earth, raised himself up, as the peal of thunder in the opening words of his work clearly shows, not only above the earth, and above every expanse of air and sky, but also above the whole host of angels, and every establishment of invisible powers, and came right up to the one through whom all things were made,[2] by saying, *In the beginning was the Word, and the Word was with God, and the Word was God; he was in the beginning with God. All things were made through him, and without him was made nothing* (Jn 1:1-3).

The rest of what he went on to proclaim also conformed to the sublime beginning, and he spoke about the Lord's divinity as did no other. He belched out[3] what he had drunk in. Not without reason, after all, is it recounted in this very same gospel that he rested his head on the Lord's breast at the supper. From that breast he drank in secret; but what he drank in secret, he proclaimed openly, so that all nations might learn not only about the incarnation, the passion, death and resurrection of the Son of God, but also about that which was before the incarnation: That he was the only Son of the Father, the Word of the Father, co-eternal with the one who begot him and equal to him by whom he was sent.

---

1. Preached the day after Homily 35, the day before Homily 36.
2. See Homilies 1, 5; 15, 1; 20, 13; Sermons 120, 1; 253, 5.
3. See Introduction, note 69.

Christ is both God and man

2. So then, whatever you hear about the Lord Jesus Christ that is humble,[4] think of it as referring to the ministry of the flesh which he took to himself, to what he was made on our account, not to what he was when he made us; but whatever you hear or read about him in the gospel that is sublime, surpassing all creatures and divine, equal and coeternal with the Father, know that what you are reading belongs to *the form of God*, not to *the form of a slave* (Phil 2:6-7). Because if those of you who can grasp it hold to this rule[5]—not all of you can, I know; but you ought all to believe it—if you hold to this rule, then, you will do battle confidently against the lies of heretical darkness as those who walk in the light.

In fact, there has been no lack of those who, in reading the gospels, only seek and hold on to that which presents Christ's lowliness, and, consequently, have been deaf to those testimonies that speak about his divinity, and because deaf, they are wickedly talkative.[6] Some others, paying attention only to what is said about the Lord's sublime being, have not believed in his mercy, whereby he was made man for our sakes, even though they read about it; they thought it was false and was inserted into the text by men, contending, therefore, that Christ our Lord was God, and not also man. Some go this way, others that way, both are in error.

Catholic faith, however, holding to what is true in each case, and preaching what it believes, has understood Christ to be God and believed him to be man; both have been written and both are true. If you say Christ is only God, you repudiate the remedy by which you have been healed; if you say Christ is only man, you repudiate the power by which you have been created. Hold on to both sides, therefore, O faithful soul and Catholic heart, hold on to both, believe both, faithfully acknowledge both: Christ is God, and Christ is man as well.

How is Christ God?

---

4. *Humiliter* refers to Christ's status as a human being (see Phil 2:6-7), not to the virtue of humility.
5. See Homily 18, 2.
6. A reference to the Photinians, who denied the divinity of Christ—in contrast with the Manichees, who denied the humanity of Christ. See Sermons 37, 17 and note 48; 71, 4 and note 12; 92, 3. Sermon 71, which was probably preached several years later than this homily and the other two sermons, draws a contrast with the Arians.

He is equal to the Father; he is one with the Father.[7]

How is Christ man?

He is born of the Virgin, getting mortality from mankind, not iniquity.

Why Christ's evidence on his own behalf is true

3. So these Jews then saw a man, and they did not understand or believe that he was God, and you have already heard, among other things, how they said to him, *You are bearing witness to yourself; your testimony is not true* (Jn 8:13). You have also heard what he responded, when it was read yesterday and discussed by me to the best of my ability.[8] Today, these words of his were read: *You are judging in terms of the flesh* (Jn 8:15). "That," he is saying, "is why you say to me, *You are bearing witness to yourself; your testimony is not true*; it is because *you are judging in terms of the flesh*; because you fail to comprehend God [in me], and you see the man, and, by persecuting the man, you offend God hidden within. Therefore, *you are judging in terms of the flesh*. Because I bear witness to myself, I therefore appear to be arrogant to you."

In fact, every person who wants to bear witness in praise of himself appears to be arrogant and proud. Thus is it written: *Let not your own mouth praise you, but let the mouth of your neighbor praise you* (Prov 27:2). But that was said to a human being. We, after all, are feeble creatures, and we speak among feeble creatures. We can tell the truth and tell lies; even if we ought to tell the truth, we can still tell lies too when we want to. The Light cannot lie; perish the thought that the darkness of lying should be found in the splendor of the divine Light! He then was speaking as the Light, he was speaking as the Truth; but *the Light was shining in the darkness, and the darkness did not comprehend it* (Jn 1:5); that is why they were judging in terms of the flesh. *You*, he says, *are judging in terms of the flesh*.

Christ's first coming in mercy; mercy such that he chose death on a cross for us

4. *As for me, I do not judge anyone* (Jn 8:15). Is the Lord Jesus Christ not judging anyone? Is he not the one about whom we confess that he rose

---
7. See Jn 10:30.
8. See Homily 35, 4-5.

again on the third day, ascended into heaven, took his seat there at the right hand of the Father, is going to come from there to judge the living and the dead?[9] Is not this our faith, of which the apostle says, *One believes with the heart and so is justified; one confesses with the mouth and so is saved* (Rom 10:10)? So, when we profess these things, are we speaking against the Lord? We are saying that he is going to come as judge of the living and the dead, but he is saying, *I do not judge anyone.*

There are two ways of solving this problem. Either we can understand *I do not judge anyone* as meaning "I am not doing so now"; as he says in another place, *I have not come to judge the world, but to save the world* (Jn 12:47), where he is not repudiating but deferring his sitting in judgment. Or else, because he had said, *You are judging in terms of the flesh*, we should take his now adding, *As for me, I do not judge anyone*, as implying "in terms of the flesh." So let us not allow the slightest shred of doubt to remain in our hearts about the faith which we hold and declare about Christ as judge.

Christ has come, but first of all to save, then to judge. He came to judge those who refused to be saved by passing sentence of punishment, while leading into life those who by believing were careful not to spurn salvation. So the first coming of our Lord Jesus Christ is medicinal, not judicial—if, for instance, he had come in the first place to pass judgment, he would not have found anyone to whom he could render the rewards of justice. So then, because he saw that all of us were sinners, and that nobody at all was immune from the death incurred by sin,[10] his mercy was first distributed all round, and later judgment was exercised, because the psalm had sung about him, *Mercy and judgment will I sing to you, Lord* (Ps 100:1). It does not, you see, say "judgment and mercy," because if judgment came first, there would not be any mercy; but first mercy, afterwards judgment.

What is the mercy that is first? The creator of man agreed to be a man; he was made into what he had made so that what he had made would not

---

9. See Sermons 213, 6; 214, 9; 215, 7; the first two were preached at "the handing over of the creed," the third at "the giving back of the creed." These rites were part of the final stage of the catechumenate. The catechumens were "given" the creed orally and they were to learn it by heart and then to "give it back" or recite it a week or two later.
10. See Homily 12, 13.

perish.[11] What could possibly be added to such mercy? And yet he did add to it. It was too little for him to be made a human being; he also had to be rejected by human beings; too little to be rejected, he had to be disgraced as well; too little to be disgraced, he also had to be killed; even this was too little; it had to be by death on a cross. In fact, when the apostle wanted to acclaim his obedience unto death, it was too little for him to say, *becoming obedient unto death*; for it was not any kind of death,[12] but he added, *but death on a cross* (Phil 2:8). Among all the different kinds of death, nothing was worse than that death. Indeed, the sharpest pains people suffer are called excruciating, from the Latin for cross. Men who were crucified, you see, hanging on a tree by their hands and feet being nailed to the wood, were being killed by a long-drawn-out kind of death. To be crucified, after all, was not just to be put to death, but to linger alive on the cross for a long time; not that a longer life was being chosen for the victim, but that death itself was being stretched out, so that the agony would not end too soon.

He wanted to die for us; that is saying all too little; he agreed to be crucified, becoming obedient to the point of death on a cross. The one who chose the last and worst kind of death was going to do away with death; with the worst kind of death he slew every death.[13] It was the worst kind of death to the uncomprehending Jews; because it was chosen for the Lord. After all, he was going to keep that cross of his as a sign; he was going to place that cross on the foreheads of the faithful as a kind of trophy of victory over the devil, so that the apostle would say, *Far be it from me to boast except in the cross of our Lord Jesus Christ, through whom the world has been crucified to me, and I to the world* (Gal 6:14). Then, nothing was more difficult for the flesh to endure; now, nothing is more glorious on the forehead. What must he still be reserving for his faithful, who gave such honor to the instrument of his execution? Hence, this punishment is no longer used by the Romans on those condemned; where the cross of the Lord is held in honor, after all, it was thought that a criminal would be honored if he were crucified.[14]

---

11. See Homily 31, 5; Sermons 30, 9; 127, 9.
12. See Homily 12, 6; Sermon 264, 3.
13. See Homily 35, 6.
14. This form of execution was abolished by Constantine after he was baptized in 337; see Sozomen, *Ecclesiastical History* I, 8; see also *Exposition of Psalm* 36, 2, 4.

So then, the one who came to be crucified did not pass judgment on anyone, but put up with the wicked. He bore with an unjust judgment, in order to pass one that was just. But his bearing with an unjust judgment was a matter of mercy. In a word, he made himself so low that he came to the cross; he even laid power aside and made mercy manifest. How did he lay power aside? The one who had the power to rise from the tomb refused to come down from the cross.[15] How did he make mercy manifest? He said, as he hung on the cross, *Father, forgive them, because they do not know what they are doing* (Lk 23:34).

Hence, he said, *As for me, I do not judge anyone*, either because he had not come to judge the world but to save the world, or else, as I have been suggesting, because he had said, *You are judging in terms of the flesh*, he added, *As for me, I do not judge anyone*, so that we would understand that Christ does not judge according to the flesh, in the way that men had judgment passed on him.

The representations of the four evangelists; in particular, why John is the eagle among them

5. Well, so that you may recognize that Christ is already judge, listen to what follows: *Even if I for my part do pass judgment, my judgment is true*. There you have him even as judge; but acknowledge him as savior, so as not to experience the judge. But why did he say his judgment was true? *Because*, he said, *I am not alone, but it is I and the Father who sent me.* (Jn 8:16) I have told you, brothers and sisters, that John, this holy evangelist, flies and soars above; it is scarcely possible to understand him with the mind. But I have to remind Your Graces of the mystery of the one who flies higher than the others. Both in the prophet Ezekiel and in the Apocalypse[16] of this same John whose gospel this is, mention is

---

15. See Homilies 3, 3; 12, 6.
16. See Ez 1:5-10; Rev 4:6-7. Ezekiel calls them four animals, each with four faces, and I suppose this is why Augustine begins by talking about one fourfold animal; the Apocalypse, on the other hand makes them four animals with one face each, thus making it easier to distribute them among the four evangelists.

made of a fourfold animal which has four masks:[17] that of a man, a calf, a lion, an eagle. Those who have previously dealt with the mysteries of the holy scriptures have, for the most part, understood the four evangelists in this animal, or rather these animals. The lion represents the king, since the lion seems after a fashion to be the king of wild beasts, because of its power and terrifying courage. This mask has been attributed to Matthew, because in the Lord's genealogy he ran through the series of kings, to show how the Lord was from a royal line, from the seed of the king, David.[18] Since Luke, on the other hand, began with the priesthood of Zechariah the priest,[19] recalling him as the father of John the Baptist, he has been assigned to the calf, because the calf was the main victim in the sacrificial function of a priest. To Mark is Christ the man rightly assigned, because he did not say anything about his royal authority, nor did he begin with his priesthood, but just started off right away with Christ the man.[20]

These three never really departed from earthly matters, that is, from things our Lord Jesus Christ did on earth; they said very little about his divine nature, as if they were walking with him on earth. The eagle remains; that is John, preacher of sublime truths, the one who contemplates the inner and everlasting Light with a steady gaze.[21] This, in fact, is how eagle chicks are said to be tested by their parents, namely, by being suspended from their father's talons, and held facing the rays of the sun; if they gaze at it unflinchingly, they are acknowledged as true sons, while if they so much as blink, they are dropped from his talons as bastard sons. So now then, just see what sublime things he had to speak, because he was compared to an eagle. But I, crawling on the ground, weak and of practically no account among men, dare to discuss these things and to

---

17. Augustine uses the word *persona*, which means the mask worn by an actor to indicate the "person" he was representing. A theater program still indicates the *dramatis personae*. I prefer to render the word by "mask" rather than by "face." Each animal played the part of a different character in the heavenly drama; each has the character of an evangelist.
18. See Mt 1:6-16.
19. See Lk 1:5-25.
20. See Mk 1:1.
21. See Homily 15, 1.

explain them, and I think that either I can grasp them when I ponder them, or that they can be grasped when I am speaking!

His obligation, as a steward of Christ's word,
to refute various heresies about these mysteries

6. Why have I said this? For after those words anyone would have the right to say to me, "So put the book down. Why take in your hands what is beyond you? Why entrust such a task to your tongue?"

I respond to that: many heretics flourish, and God has allowed them to flourish so that we may not always be feeding on milk, thus remaining in a state of mindless infancy. For they never understood how the divinity of Christ was being designated, and so they thought what they wanted to, but not with right understanding. They inflicted the most troublesome questions on faithful Catholics, and the hearts of the faithful began to be shaken and to fluctuate this way and that. Then was there a need for spiritual men, who had not only read about the divinity of our Lord Jesus Christ in the gospel, but also understood it. Thus could they take up arms for Christ against the arms of the devil and fight for the divinity of Christ against false and misleading teachers to the best of their ability in open, public contest, lest, by their keeping silent, others perish.

Many, in fact, have held that our Lord Jesus Christ is either of a different substance from the Father, or that Christ alone was the only one, such that he is the Father, he is the Son, and he is the Holy Spirit. Others also wanted to maintain that he was only a man, not God who became man, or was God in such a way as to be changeable in his divinity, or God in such a way as not to be man as well.[22] All these were shipwrecked in faith and were expelled from the safe haven of the Church so that their restlessness might not wreck the other vessels at anchor there with them. This is what obliges me—however insignificant and unworthy I am, if left to myself, but by his mercy appointed one of his ministers—not to keep silent before you, but to say something to you. Then, if you understand, you may rejoice together with me; but if you do not yet understand, you may remain safely in the port by believing.

---

22. The heretics thus listed were respectively Arians, Sabellians, Photinians, Apollinarists, and Manichees.

The question posed again, how Christ can have been
sent and still not have left the Father

7. So I am going to say, let the one who can, understand; let the one who cannot understand, believe; even so, let me say what the Lord said, *You are judging in terms of the flesh; as for me, I do not judge anyone*—neither now nor in terms of the flesh. *But even if I for my part do judge, my judgment is true.*

Why is your judgment true?

Because I am not alone, he says, *but it is I and the Father who sent me.*

What is this, Lord Jesus? If you were alone your judgment would be false; but the reason the judgment you pass is true is that you are not alone, but it is you and the Father who sent you. What answer am I to give? Let him answer himself: *My judgment is true*, he says.

Why?

Because I am not alone, but it is I and the Father who sent me.

If he is with you, how did he send you? Did he both send you and remain with you? Does that mean that even though sent, you did not leave? Does that mean you both came to us and stayed there? How is one to believe this, how is one to grasp it?

I have two answers to make to this; you are right to ask, "How is one to grasp it?" You are not right to ask, "How is one to believe it?" Indeed, you do well to believe it because it is not understood right away; after all, if it were grasped right away, there would be no need to believe it, because it would be seen. Hence, you believe because you do not grasp it; but by believing you become capable of grasping it; for, if you do not believe you will never understand, because you will remain incapable of understanding.

Let faith cleanse you, then, so that you may be filled with understanding. *My judgment is true*, he says, *because I am not alone, but it is I and the Father who sent me.* Therefore, Lord Jesus Christ, our God, your mission is your being made flesh. Put it that way and I see, put it that way and I understand; finally, when it is put that way I believe so that it may not be arrogant to say, "Put it that way and I understand." Of course, our Lord Jesus Christ is here; or rather he was here in the flesh, he is still here now in his divinity, and he was with the Father, and he did not leave the Father. So then, to say that he was sent and that he came to us is to remember the incarnation itself, since it was not the Father who was made flesh.

The Father never leaves the Son, because as God he is everywhere

8. Indeed, there are some heretics called Sabellians, who are also called Patripassians, because they say that the Father suffered. O Catholic! do not believe that; if the Father did suffer, you will not be sane.[23] So then, know that the incarnation of the Son is also the name of the Son's mission; do not believe that the Father was made flesh, but do not believe either that the Father withdrew from the Son when the Son put on flesh. The Son was burdened with the flesh, the Father was with the Son.

If the Father was in heaven, the Son on earth, how was the Father with the Son?

Because both Father and Son were everywhere; the Father, you see, is not in heaven in such a way that he is not also on earth. Listen to someone who was longing to escape God's judgment, and could not find how to do so: *Where shall I go*, he says, *away from your Spirit, and where shall I flee from your face? If I climb up to heaven you are there.* But the question was about his being on earth; listen to what comes next: *If I go down to hell, there you are.* (Ps 138:7-8) So if he is said to be present in hell, what place can there be where he is not? The the voice of God is speaking through the prophet, after all: *Heaven and earth do I fill* (Jer 23:24).[24]

So then, he is everywhere who is not enclosed in any one space. Do not turn away from him, and he will be with you. If you want to reach him, do not be lazy about loving; you do not run with your feet, after all, but with your affections. While remaining in one place, you came to him, if you believe and love. So then, he is everywhere; if everywhere, how is he not with the Son? Is he not with the Son, the one who, if you believe, is even with you?

Steering between the Scylla of Sabellianism and the Charybdis of Arianism

9. So what ensures then that his judgment is true, other than the fact that he is truly the Son? That, after all, is what he said, *And if I do pass judgment, my judgment is true, because I am not alone, but it is I and the Father who sent me*, as if to say, "My judgment is true, because I am the Son of God."

---

23. In the Latin: *Si enim fueris patripassianus, non eris sanus*. The last word, in this context, primarily means "sane"; but it also carries overtones of its basic meaning, "in good health"; i.e. in good spiritual health.
24. See *The Trinity* II, 5, 7; Sermon 69, 4, for the same combination of texts.

How do you prove that you are the Son of God?

Because I am not alone, but it is I and the Father who sent me.

Blush for shame, Sabellian; you hear "Son," you hear "Father." The Son is Son, the Father is Father. He did not say, "I am the Father, and I am the same as the Son," but *I am not alone* is what he said.

Why are you not alone?

"Because the Father is with me"

It is I and the Father who sent me is what you hear; "it is I and the one who sent me." Do not jettison a person, distinguish persons. Distinguish intelligently; do not separate them perfidiously, lest, after steering clear of Charybdis, you crash on Scylla.[25] The whirlpool of Sabellian impiety, you see, was about to suck you into saying the Father is the same as the Son; just now you have learned that *I am not alone, but it is I and the Father who sent me.* You acknowledge that the Father is Father and the Son is Son. You do well to acknowledge this; but do not go on to say, "The Father is greater, the Son is less." Do not say, "The Father is gold, the Son is silver." There is one substance, one godhead, one coeternity, perfect equality, not the least unlikeness. I mean, if you only believe that Christ is another, and that he is not the Father, yet you still think that he differs in nature, you have indeed avoided Charybdis but have wrecked yourself on Scylla's rocks.

Navigate down the middle, avoid each dangerous shore.[26] The Father is Father, the Son is Son. You are now saying, "The Father is Father, the Son is Son"; you have truly avoided the danger of being sucked into the whirlpool. Why do you want to go to the other side, and say, "The Father is one thing, the Son another"? One person, another person, yes, that is right; one thing and another thing, that is wrong. The Son, after all, is another person, because he is not who the Father is; and the Father is another person, because he is not who the Son is; not, however, another thing, but both Father and Son are the very same. What does that mean, the very same? It is one God. You have heard, *I am not alone, but it is I and the Father who sent me*; now hear what you must believe about Father and Son; listen to the Son: *I and the Father are one* (Jn 10:30). He did not say, "I am the Father," or, "I and the Father are one

---

25. Charybdis a whirlpool on one side if the straits of Messina between the Italian mainland and Sicily, Scylla a reef on the other. An English metaphor speaks about being careful not to jump from the frying-pan into the fire.
26. See Sermon 229G, 4, where however Augustine reverses the roles of the two monsters.

person;" but when he said, *I and the Father are one*, you must hear and listen to both *one* and *we are*,[27] and you will deliver yourself from both Scylla and Charybdis. Of these two words that he used, *one* delivers you from Arius; *we are* delivers you from Sabellius. If *one,* then not different things; if *we are,* then both Father and Son. After all, he would not say *we are* of one person; but neither would he say *one* of different things.

So then, he says in a word, *My judgment is true*, so that you may hear, "I am God's Son." "But I am persuading you," he goes on, "that I am God's Son in such a way that you should understand that the Father is with me; I am not his Son in such a way that I have left him behind; I am not here in such a way that I am not also with him; he is not there in such a way that he is not also with me. I have *taken* on *the form of a slave*, but I have not lost *the form of God* (Phil 2:7)." So then, *I am not alone*, he says, *but it is I and the Father who sent me.*

The problem of two or three witnesses; a clue to the mystery of the Trinity

10. He has spoken about judgment, he wants to say something about testimony. *In your law*, he says, *it is written that the testimony of two persons is true. I bear witness to myself, and the Father who sent me bears witness to me.* (Jn 8:17-18) He would also have explained the law to them, if they had not been ungrateful. In fact, there is an important question here, my brothers and sisters, and that matter seems to me to be thoroughly shrouded in mystery, where God said, *On the word of two or three witnesses shall every charge stand* (Dt 19:15). Is truth to be sought through two witnesses? That is certainly the custom of humankind; but it can still happen that even two witnesses lie. The chaste Susanna was harried by two false witnesses. Does the fact that there were two of them mean that they were not false witnesses?[28] Are we talking just about two, or about three? A whole people gave false evidence against Christ.[29]

So then, if a people consisting of a great number of men and women was found to give false witness, how is this statement, *On the word of two or*

---

27. The plural verb signifying two distinct persons, the singular predicate signifying the one substance. Latin, with its grammatical structure of genders, does this more neatly than English can, with the masculine gender, *alius* ("higher up"), *unus* at this stage signifying person, *aliud* and *unum* in the neuter signifying substance.
28. Susanna 22-41 (Dan 13: 22-41 in the Vulgate).
29. See, e.g., Lk 23:18.

three witnesses shall every charge stand, to be accepted except by seeing it as a mysterious presentation of the Trinity, in which is found the eternal stability of truth? Do you want to have a good case? Have two or three witnesses, Father and Son and Holy Spirit. Thus, to prove the point, when Susanna, a chaste woman and faithful wife, was being harried by two false witnesses, the Trinity sustained her in her conscience, in secret; in secret the Trinity[30] raised up for her one witness, Daniel, and he confounded the two witnesses.

So then, because *in your law it is written that the testimony of two persons is true*, accept our testimony, or you shall experience our judgment. For, he has just said, *I do not judge anyone*, but I bear witness to myself; I defer judgment, I do not put off bearing witness.

The danger of ignoring God the witness

11. Against the human tongues and the baseless suspicions of the human race, let us choose God as our judge, as our witness. For the one who is judge does not disdain the role of witness, nor is it a promotion for him when he becomes a judge, since the one who is a witness is the one who will be judge.

Why is he a witness?

Because he does not need anyone else to tell him who you are.

Why is he a judge?

Because he has the power over dying and over living, of condemning and of forgiving, of hurling into Gehenna and of raising up to heaven, of joining to the devil, and of crowning among the angels.

So then, since he has this power, he is judge. But because he does not need another witness to tell him who you are, the one who will judge you later on is the one who sees you right now; there is no way that you will be able to dupe him, when he begins to judge. After all, you will not be able to bring along false witnesses with you who can get round that judge when he is about to judge. This is what God will say to you then, "When you were contemptuous, I was there watching; and when you were unbelieving, I did not annul my sentence; I delayed it, but did not set it aside. You did not hear what I commanded; you will experience what I foretold. If you do listen to

---

30. Reading *illi Trinitas* instead of the text's *illa Trinitas*.

what I have commanded, you will not experience the evil things I foretold, but you will receive the good things I promised."[31]

Some minor worries eliminated; conclusion

12. There is certainly no reason to be worried by his saying, *My judgment is true, because I am not alone, but it is I and the Father who sent me*, while elsewhere he had said, *The Father does not judge anyone, but has given all judgment to the Son* (Jn 5:22). We have already discussed these very same words of the gospel,[32] and now I will just remind you that this did not mean that when the Son passes judgment the Father will not be with him; but it was said because the Son alone will appear visibly to the good and the bad at the judgment, in the form in which he suffered and rose again and ascended into heaven. In fact, as the disciples watched him ascending on that occasion, the voice of an angel rang out:[33] *He will come again, just as you have seen him going up into heaven* (Acts 1:11); that is, he will judge in the form of a man in which he was judged, so that the prophetic utterance might also to be fulfilled: *They will gaze upon the one whom they have pierced* (Zc 12:10). But when, as the just enter into eternal life, *we shall see him as he is* (1 Jn 3:2), that will not be the judgment of the living and the dead, but only the reward of the living.[34]

13. Again, do not be disturbed by what he said, *In your law it is written that the testimony of two persons is true*, and therefore let no one think that it was not the law of God because he did not say "in God's law." Let them realize that he said *in your law* as if to say "in the law which was given to you." By whom was it given if not by God? Likewise, we say, *our daily bread*, and yet we say, *Give it to us today* (Mt 6:11).

---

31. See the concluding words of Homily 33.
32. See Homily 19, 16.
33. A slight confusion perhaps in Augustine's mind between this episode, in which in fact two men in white garments appeared to the disciples to give them this message, and the episode of Peter's vision at Joppa, in which he heard a voice telling him to kill and eat, etc; see Acts 10:13-15.
34. Who will see him in the form of God, together with the Father.

Homily 37

On John 8:19-20[1]

Recapitulation of yesterday's sermon

1. What is said rather briefly in the holy gospel must not be briefly explained, if what was heard is to be understood. The words of the Lord are few[2] but momentous, to be sized up not by number but by weight; and not to be dismissed because they are few, but to be examined because they are momentous. Those of you who were here yesterday heard me reflecting, as best I could, on some of what the Lord said: *You are judging in terms of the flesh; as for me, I am not judging anyone. But even if I for my part do judge, my judgment is true, because I am not alone, but it is I and the Father who sent me. In your law it is written that the testimony of two persons is true. I bear witness to myself, and the Father who sent me bears witness to me.* (Jn 8:15-18) On some of these words, as I said yesterday, your ears and minds were rightly given a sermon.

When the Lord said this, those who heard *You are judging in terms of the flesh* gave an illustration of what they heard. In fact, they replied to the Lord, who spoke about God as his Father, and they said, *Where is your Father?* (Jn 8:19). They assumed Christ meant his father according to the flesh, because they were judging his words in terms of the flesh. The one however who was speaking was visibly flesh, invisibly he was the Word; a man in appearance; in a hidden way God. They saw the clothing and held the one who wore it in contempt; in contempt because they knew him not; they did not know him because they did not see him; they did not see him because they were blind; they were blind because they did not believe.

You cannot know the Father, unless you first know Jesus as the Son

2. So now let us see what answer the Lord gave to this question too. "Where," they say, "*is your Father?* After all, we have heard you say, *I am not alone, but it is I and the Father who sent me.* But we only see you; we do not see your father with you. How can you say you are not alone, but are with your father? Show us that your father is with you."

---
1. Preached on a Sunday, the day after Homily 36.
2. As Berrouard suggests, it looks as if Augustine only had these two verses of the gospel read.

The Lord replies, "Do you really see me, such that I may show you the Father?" That is, in fact, what follows; that is what he responded in his own words, words which I began to explain beforehand. Notice what he said: *You know neither me nor my Father. If you knew me, perhaps you would know my Father as well.* (Jn 8:19)

"So then, you are saying, *Where is your father?* as if you already knew me, as if the whole of me were only what you see, and therefore, because you do not, in fact, know me, that is why I am not showing you my Father. You are thinking of me, after all, as a man; therefore, you are looking for my father as a man, because you are judging in terms of the flesh. But I am one thing in terms of what you see, and another in terms of what you do not see. I, hidden from you, am speaking of my Father who is hidden from you; the first thing is for you to get to know me, and then can you know my Father."

Perhaps *used to express reproach, not doubt*

3. In fact, *if you knew me, you would perhaps know my Father as well.* When the one who knows everything says *perhaps*, he is not expressing doubt but reproach. Notice how that *perhaps*, a word implying doubt or uncertainty, is used to express reproach. It is a word of doubt when used by someone who, indeed, is in doubt because he does not know; but when God uses a word of doubt, since nothing is hidden from God, it criticizes a lack of faith; divinity does not doubt.

Human beings, after all, on matters they are quite sure about, sometimes express doubt as a reproach; that is, they express doubt, even when they have no doubts in their own heart—for example, if you are cross with your slave and say, "You give me no respect; but I may just be your master." This is also the way in which the apostle talks to some people who gave him no respect when he says, *I rather think that I too have the Spirit of God* (1 Cor 7:40). In saying, *I rather think*, he seems to have his doubts; but in fact he was reproaching them, not expressing doubt.

And Christ the Lord himself, when reproaching the human race for its future lack of faith, says in another place, *When the Son of Man comes, do you think he will find faith on the earth?* (Lk 18:8)

Further comparison of the Word with words

4. You have already, I gather, grasped the way in which *perhaps* is to be taken; so let no weigher of words or scrutinizer of syllables, as if he were well versed in speaking Latin, find fault with the word which was uttered by the Word of God, and thus remain, by finding fault with the Word of God, not eloquent but dumb. Who, after all, speaks in the way which the Word—*which was in the beginning with God* (Jn 1:1)—speaks? Do not just consider these words and presume from these ordinary words to measure the Word which is God. I mean, you hear the Word and belittle it; listen to God then and tremble: *In the beginning was the Word*. You are calling us back to your usual kind of chatter, and you are saying to yourself, "What is in a word? What is so great about a word? It makes a sound and vanishes. It lashes the air, strikes the ear, then ceases to be."[3] Listen to a bit more: *The Word was with God*; it was abiding, not making a sound and then vanishing. Perhaps you are still belittling it: *The Word was God* (Jn 1:1).

Within you, my good man, when a word is in your heart, it is something other than a sound; but for the word which is in you to reach me, it seeks a sound as a vehicle. So it takes a sound, climbs somehow or other onto this vehicle, goes through the air, reaches me, and does not leave you. But for the sound to reach me, it did leave you, and did not remain with me. So then, the word which was in your heart did not go away when the sound went away, did it?

You said what you were thinking, and for what was hidden in you to reach me, you put syllables together in a sound; the sound of the syllables carried your thought to my ears, your thought climbed down through my ears into my heart, the sound which acted as intermediary flew away. But that word, which took on sound, was with you before you uttered it; because you did utter it, it is now with me, and has not left you. Pay attention to that, whoever you are, you scrutinizer of sounds; you belittle the Word of God, you who do not understand the word of a human being!

---

3. See Sermon 237, 4 for Augustine's more usual treatment of this theme.

Comparison of this answer to the Jews with the one given later on to Philip

5. So then, the one *through whom all things were made* (Jn 1:3) knows all things; and yet he reproaches by doubting: *If you knew me, perhaps you would know my Father too.* He is reproaching unbelievers. He did say something similar to the disciples, but the word of doubt is not used on that occasion, because at that time there was no question of reprimanding unbelief. I mean, what he has just now said to the Jews, *If you knew me, perhaps you would know my Father too*, is in substance what he also said to the disciples when Philip asked the question, or rather made the demand, *Lord, show us the Father, and that will satisfy us* (Jn 14:8), as though to say, "We too have already come to know you, you have been plainly visible to us, you have thought fit to choose us, we have followed you, we have seen your miracles, we have heard the words of salvation, we have received your commands, we place all our hopes in your promises; you yourself have been good enough to confer many benefits on us by your presence. But all the same, while we have come to know you, we have not yet come to know the Father, and so we are burning with the desire to see the one we do not yet know. Accordingly, because we know you, but are not satisfied with that until we come to know the Father too, *show us the Father, and that will satisfy us.*[4]

And then, to show them they did not know what they thought they already did know, the Lord said, *I spend all this time with you, and you still do not know me? Philip, whoever has seen me has seen the Father too.* (Jn 14:9) This sentence does not contain the word of doubt, does it? He did not say, did he, "Perhaps whoever has seen me, has seen the Father too"?

Well, why not?

Because a believer was listening to him, not a persecutor of the faith; that is why the Lord was not a critic but a teacher. *Whoever has seen me has seen the Father too*; and here: *If you knew me, you would know my Father too*; let us just remove the word by which the unbelief of the hearers was indicated, and it is exactly the same statement.

---

4. Augustine enlarges on Philip's request in the same kind of way in Homily 14, 12.

Reminder of what he said yesterday on the two contrary heresies, the Sabellian and the Arian

6. In what I said yesterday, I already reminded Your Graces that the words of John the evangelist, in which he describes for us what he learned from the Lord, would never have been discussed—if it were possible —were it not because heretical commentaries made it necessary.[5]

Yesterday, then, I suggested briefly to Your Graces that there are heretics called Patripassians or, from the name of their founder, Sabellians; these say that the Father and the Son are identical; they have different names but are one and the same person. He is the Father when he wants to be, they say, the Son when he wants to be; but he is still one person.

Then there are other heretics called Arians. Indeed, they profess our Lord Jesus Christ as the only Son of the Father; one is the Father of the Son, the other is the Son of the Father. The one who is the Father is not the Son; the one who is the Son is not the Father. They profess that the Son was begotten, but deny his equality. We, that is, the Catholic faith which came from the teaching of the apostles, which was planted in us, which was accepted through a line of succession, and which was to be handed on to posterity as sound and integral—the Catholic faith has stood between them both, that is, has held on to the truth between each of these errors.

In the error of the Sabellians there is just one person, the Father identical with the Son; in the Arians' error, the Father indeed is one person, the Son another; but the Son himself is not only a different person from the Father but also a different thing.

You in the middle, what do you have to say? You have rejected the Sabellian, now reject the Arian as well. The Father is father, the Son is son; he is another person, not another thing, because *I and the Father*, he says, *are one* (Jn 10:30), as I explained yesterday, insofar as I could. Let the Sabellian withdraw in confusion when he hears *we are*; when he hears *one* let the Arian withdraw in confusion also. Let the Catholic steer the boat of his faith between both of them, because shipwreck in each of them is to be avoided. Say, then, what the gospel says: *I and the Father are one*. So not a different thing then, because *one*; not one and the same person, because *we are*.

---

5. See Homily 36, 6-9.

How the Lord's words disqualify both heresies

7. A little earlier on he said, *My judgment is true, because I am not alone, but it is I and the Father who sent me*, as if to say, "The reason my judgment is true is that I am the Son of God, is that I speak the truth, because I am the Truth itself."[6] The Jews, thinking carnally, said, *Where is your Father?* Now listen carefully, O Arian: *You know neither me nor my Father; because if you knew me, you would know my Father as well* (Jn 8:19). What does *if you knew me, you would know my Father as well* mean but *I and the Father are one*?

When you see somebody that is like somebody else—would Your Graces pay attention; this is an everyday manner of talking; what you can see in common should not be difficult for you—so then, when you see somebody just like somebody else, and you know whom he is like, you say, surprised, "How very like that one this person is!" You would not say this, of course, if they were not two people. Then this other one, who does not know the person whom you said this person is just like, says, "Is he really just like him?" And you say to him, "What? Do you not know this one?" "No, I do not," he says. Now you, to help him get to know the one he does not know from the one he can see there in front of him, you answer, "Well, if you have seen this one, you have seen the other."

Of course in saying this you have not been asserting they are one person, and denying they are two; but because of their resemblance you have given that response, "You know this one, then you know the other." In the same way the Lord too: *If you knew me*, he said, *you would know my Father as well*, not because the Father is the Son, but because the Son is like the Father. Let the Arian blush. Thank God that the Arian too has drawn away from the Sabellian error and is not a Patripassian. He does not say the Father was the one who clothed himself in flesh to come to humankind, the one who suffered, the one who rose again, and somehow or other ascended to himself. He does not say that; with me he acknowledges that the Father is father, and the Son is son.

But, dear brother, you have avoided that shipwreck; why do you set your course for the other? The Father is father, the Son is son; why do you say he is unlike the other, why different? Why of a different substance? If

---

6. See Jn 14:6.

he were unlike, would he say to his disciples, *Whoever has seen me has seen the Father*? Would he say to the Jews, *If you knew me, you would know my Father as well*? How could this be true, unless that also were true: *I and the Father are one*?

Against the fatalists, who subjected Christ to fate

8. *Jesus spoke these words in the treasury, teaching in the temple* (Jn 8:20), with great confidence and without fear. After all, the one who would not have been born had he not wished to be, would not suffer anything he did not wish to.[7] What, in fact, comes next? *And no one arrested him, because his hour had not yet come* (Jn 8:20). When some people hear this, they believe that the Lord Christ was subject to fate, and they say, "Look, Christ was in the hands of fate." Oh, if only your heart were not so foolish, you would not believe in fate![8] If fate, as some people have maintained,[9] comes from the Latin *fari*, meaning "to speak," then how can the Word of God be in the hands of fate, when everything that exists here is there in that very Word? For God did not establish anything which he did not know beforehand; what was made was in the Word itself.[10]

The world was made; it was made and it existed there. How was it both made and already there? Because the house which a builder puts up was previously in his idea, in his mind; and there it was something better, never getting old, never falling into ruin; still, in order to realize his idea he constructs the house, and, in some way, a house proceeds from a house; and if that house collapses, the idea remains.[11]

Thus was everything that was created already in the Word of God, because *God has made all things in wisdom* (Ps 103:24), and all he made was known to him; he did not learn about them, after all, because he had made them, but he made them because he knew them. They are known to us, because they have been made; while unless they had been known to him, they would not have been made.

---

7. See Homilies 11, 2; 31, 5; also Sermon 190, 1.
8. See Homily 31, 6; also Sermon 16B, 1.
9. And quite rightly! See, e.g. Varro, *De Lingua Latina* VI, 7, 52; Virgil, *Aeneid*, I, 261-262.
10. See *The Trinity* IV, 1, 3; Sermon 117, 2.
11. See Homily 1, 16-17.

So then, the Word came first. And what was there before the Word of God? Nothing whatsoever. In fact, if there had been anything before, it would not be said, *In the beginning was the Word*, but "In the beginning was made the Word." In any case, what did Moses say about the world? *In the beginning God made heaven and earth* (Gn 1:1). He made what was not yet there; so if he made what was not yet there, what was there before that? *In the beginning was the Word*. And where did heaven and earth come from? *All things were made through him* (Jn 1:3).[12] So are you, then, subjecting Christ to fate? Where are the fates?

"In heaven," you say, "in the arrangement and the revolutions of the stars."

So how then can the one through whom heaven and stars were made be in the hand of fate, seeing that your own will, if you are truly wise, surpasses even the stars? Or is it because you know Christ's flesh to have been under heaven, that you imagine Christ's power also was subject to heaven?[13]

Further proofs of Jesus' power to decide the precise time when he would go to his passion

9. Listen, you fool: *His hour had not yet come*, not because he would be forced to die by fate, but because he would deign to be put to death [at the right time]. He himself knew, after all, when it would be right for him to die; he had in mind all the things that had been foretold about him, and he was waiting for everything to be accomplished that had been foretold as due to happen before his passion, so that when that had all been fulfilled, then would come his passion, not by any necessity of fate, but in the established plan.[14] Finally, listen so as to convince you of the point. Among other things which were prophesied about him, this also was written: *They gave me gall for my food, and in my thirst they offered me vinegar to drink* (Ps 68:22). We know from the gospel how these things happened; first they gave him gall; he received it, tasted, it, and spat it out;[15] then, hanging on the cross, so that all the prophecies might be fulfilled, he said, *I thirst*; they took

---

12. See Homilies 1, 11; 26, 8; also Sermons 1, 2; 118, 1; 119, 2.
13. The meaning of "heaven" in this case might also be rendered "destiny."
14. See Homily 8, 12, for further elaboration of this point.
15. See Mt 27:34.

a sponge full of vinegar, tied it to a cane, and held it up to him as he hung there; he took it, and said, *It is finished*. What does that mean, *It is finished*? "All the things that had been prophesied before my passion have been fulfilled; so what am I still doing here?"[16] Finally, after saying, *It is finished, he bowed his head and yielded up the spirit* (Jn 19:28-30).

Did those thieves, crucified beside him, breathe their last when they wished to? They were held in the bonds of the flesh, because they were not creators of the flesh; fixed there by nails, they endured a long agony, because they had no control over their weakness.[17] The Lord, however, when he so wished, took flesh in the Virgin's womb; when he so wished, came toward humanity; as long as he so wished, lived his life among human beings; when he so wished, took off the flesh; all this was in power, not necessity.[18]

So this then was the hour he was waiting for, not the fated hour but the appropriate hour and the one he chose, so that everything might first be fulfilled which had to be fulfilled before his passion. How, in fact, could he have been placed under the necessity of fate, who said elsewhere, *I have the power to lay down my life, and I have the power to take it up again; no one takes it from me, but I myself lay it down, and again I take it up* (Jn 10:18)? He showed this power when the Jews were looking for him. *Whom are you looking for?* he said. They answered, *Jesus*. Then he in his turn, said, *I am he*. On hearing him say this, *they stepped back and fell down* (Jn 18:4-6).

Why Christ did not come down from the cross;
his divine power and his merciful weakness

10. Someone may say, "If he had such power, why did he not come down, when the Jews were mocking him as he hung there, and saying, *If he is the Son of God, let him come down from the cross* (Mt 27:40)? By coming down, he would have shown them his power."

Because he was teaching patience, he delayed the demonstration of power. After all, if he had come down as though he were moved by their words, it would have been thought that he was overcome by the pain of their

---

16. See Homily 31, 6; Sermons 5, 3; 218, 12.
17. See *The Trinity* IV, 13, 16.
18. See Homilies 8, 10; 11, 12; 29, 1-2; 31, 6.

taunts. Clearly, he did not come down, he remained nailed there; when he wished, he departed. I mean, what would have been so great about coming down from the cross for someone who could rise again from the tomb?[19]

Let us then, who have been served with this nourishment, understand that the power of our Lord Jesus Christ was hidden at that time, to be manifested in due course at the judgment, about which it says, *God will come manifestly, our God, and he will not keep silent* (Ps 49:2-3). What is the meaning of *he will come manifestly*? Because he came secretly, this God of ours—that is, Christ—will come manifestly. *And he will not keep silent.* What is the meaning of *he will not keep silent*? Because he did keep silent the first time.[20] When did he keep silent? When he was being judged, so as to fulfill what the prophet had also foretold, *Like a sheep he was led to be sacrificed, and, like a lamb with no voice before the shearer, he did not open his mouth* (Is 53:7).

So then, if he had not been willing to suffer, he would not have suffered; if he had not suffered, that blood would not have been shed; if that blood had not been shed, the world would not have been redeemed. So let us be grateful both to his divine power and to his compassionate weakness; let us be grateful for his hidden power of which the Jews had no inkling, which is why he now said, *You know neither me nor my Father*, and for the flesh he took on, which the Jews were well aware of, just as they also knew his place of origin; that is why he said to them in another place, *You know both me and where I come from* (Jn 7:28). We, though, know both things about Christ, both what makes him equal to the Father, and what makes the Father greater than him. In the first case, it is the Word; in the second, it is the flesh; in the first case he is God; in the second, he is man; but Christ is one, both God and man.

---

19. See Homilies 3, 3; 12, 6; 36, 4.
20. See Homilies 4, 2; 28, 6.

Homily 38

On John 8:21-25[1]

Reminder of what had been said last time

1. The reading of the holy gospel which preceded today's reading ended like this: *Teaching in the treasury, the Lord spoke* about the things he wished to, and which you heard, *and no one arrested him, because his hour had not yet come* (Jn 8:20). What the Lord was good enough to give on this passage was discussed on Sunday. I suggested to Your Graces why it said that *his hour had not yet come*—so that no one would shamelessly dare to entertain the impious idea that Christ was held by some necessity of fate. For the hour which had not yet come was the time when, in due course and in accordance with what had been foretold about him, he would be ready to be killed—not a death forced on him in spite of himself.

Why the Jews would not be able to go where Christ was going

2. Now, however, he was speaking to the Jews about his passion, which came about not by some necessity but by his power. He said, *I am going away*. For Christ the Lord, in fact, death was a return to the one from whom he had come, to the one he had never left.[2] *I*, he says, *am going away, and you will look for me* (Jn 8:21), not out of longing, but because of hatred. For, after he had withdrawn from human sight, both those who hated and those who loved him kept up the search for him; the former by persecuting, the latter by their longing for him. In the psalm, the Lord himself spoke through a prophet, *Flight has failed me, and no one would seek my soul* (Ps 141:5). And again he spoke in a psalm somewhere else, *May they be confounded and put in dread, those who seek my soul* (Ps 39:15). He found fault with those who would not seek him, he condemned those who did. It is wrong, in fact, not to seek the soul of Christ,[3] but to seek him in the way the disciples did; and it is wrong to seek the soul of Christ, if seeking in the way the Jews did; the former sought him to hold on to him; the latter sought to destroy him.

---

1. Preached during the week following Homily 37.
2. See Homilies 27, 4; 31, 9.
3. "Seeking the soul" is just a Hebrew idiom for seeking the person; "my soul" is a way of saying "myself."

Well, because these were looking for him in a bad way, a perverse way, what did he add? *You will all look for me, and,* lest you should think you are looking for me in a good way, *you will die in your sin* (Jn 8:21). Seeking Christ in a bad way is to die in one's sin; that is hating the one by whom alone you can be saved. For while those whose hope is in God ought not even to pay back evil for evil,[4] these were paying back evil for good. So the Lord told them beforehand, and, in his foreknowledge, he pronounced sentence on them, that they would die in their sin. Then he added, *Where I for my part am going, you cannot come* (Jn 8:21). In another place he said this to his disciples, but he did not say to them, *You will die in your sin*. What did he say to them? The same as to these people: *Where I for my part am going, you cannot come* (Jn 13:33). He did not deprive them of hope, but predicted a delay. For, when the Lord was saying this to the disciples, they could then not go where he was going, but later they were going to go there.[5] But those to whom he said in his foreknowledge, *You will all die in your sin,* would never go there.

The crass misunderstanding of Christ's words

3. But on hearing these words, as those who think in a carnal way and judge in terms of the flesh are accustomed to do, by hearing it and savoring it in a crass literal-minded way, they said, *Would he take his own life?* since he said, *Where I for my part am going, you cannot come* (Jn 8:22). Foolish words, reeking of stupidity! What in fact is this? Would they not be able to go where he went if he did kill himself? Will they not die as well? So what does this all mean, *Would he take his own life?* just because he had said, *Where I for my part am going, you cannot come*? If he were speaking of the death of a human being, what human being does not die? So, by *where I am going,* he did not mean going to his death, but where he was going after death. Thus, failing to understand, they replied in that way.

---

4. See Rom 12:17; 1 Thes 5:15; 1 Pt 3:9.
5. See Homily 31, 9.

The meaning of Christ's words: I am from above

4. And what did the Lord say to those who had a taste for the earth? *You all are from below.* That is why you have a taste for the earth, because, like snakes, you eat earth.[6]

What does "you eat earth" mean?

You feed on earthly affairs, you take pleasure in earthly matters, you pant after earthly things, you do not lift up your hearts. *You are all from below, but I am from above. You are all of this world, but I am not of this world.* (Jn 8:23) How, after all, could the one through whom the world was made be of this world? All those are of the world who come to be after the world, because the world precedes, and thus human beings are of the world. But Christ is first, and then the world, since Christ was before the world, and before Christ nothing was, because *in the beginning was the Word; all things were made through him* (Jn 1:1.3). Thus was he from above.

From how far above? From the air?

Not at all! Even birds fly there.

Then, from the heavens we can see?

Not that either! Stars and the sun and the moon revolve there.

From the angels, then?

Do not understand it that way either; through him, *through whom were made all things*, the angels were also made.

So from what height is Christ? From the Father. Nothing is above that God who begot a Word equal to himself, coeternal with himself, the only-begotten Son; who begot outside time the one through whom he established all times.[7]

So then, accept Christ as from above, so that you may soar in thought beyond everything that has been made, beyond absolutely the whole of creation, every material body, every created spirit, everything which is in any way at all subject to change; yes, soar above it all, just as John did, so that he might reach and touch[8] *In the beginning was the Word, and the Word was with God, and the Word was God* (Jn 1:1).

---

6. An allusion to the curse on the serpent; see Gen 3:14.
7. See Homilies 14, 7; 19, 13; Sermon 127, 4.
8. See Homilies 1, 5; 20, 13; 36, 1; Sermons 120, 1; 253, 4-5.

Not of this world; the difference between the Jews and the apostles

5. So *I*, then, he says, *am from above. You are all from this world; as for me, I am not from this world. Therefore I said to you that you will die in your sins* (Jn 8:23-24). That is how he explained to us, brothers and sisters, what he wished us to understand by *You are from this world.* Therefore he said, *You are from this world*, because they were sinners, because they were wicked, because they were unbelievers, because they had a taste for earthly things.[9]

What do you think about the holy apostles? How great was the difference between the Jews and the apostles? As great as the difference between darkness and light, between faith and unbelief, between godliness and godlessness, between hope and despair, between charity and greed; so the difference was great. So what? Was the difference so great that the apostles were not of the world? If you think about how they were born,[10] and where they came from, because they had all come from Adam, then they were of this world. But what did the Lord himself say to them? *But I have chosen you from the world* (Jn 15:19). So those who had been of the world were turned into not being from the world; and they began to belong to the one through whom the world was made. These others, however, continued to be of the world, the ones who were told, *You will die in your sins.*

We all need to be cleansed from the world, in order not to die in our sins

6. So none of us, then, brothers and sisters, should say, "I am not of this world." If you are a human being, whoever you are, then you are of this world; but the one who made the world has come to you, and has set you free from the world. If you set your heart on the world, that means you want to remain unclean forever; but if you no longer set your heart on this world, you are already clean.[11] However, if through some weakness the world still delights you, let the one who cleanses reside in you, and you will be clean. If you are clean, you will not remain in the world; nor will you hear what the Jews heard, *You will die in your sins.*

---

9. See Homily 2, 11.
10. In original sin is what he means, as the reference to Adam in the next few words makes clear.
11. An important play on words, that he will keep up for the next sentence or two, between *mundus* ("world") and *mundus, immundus* ("clean, unclean"). If you love the *mundus*, it means you are *immundus*; if you stop loving the *mundus*, you become *mundus*. This transformation, though, can only be effected by the one who made the *mundus*; he alone can *mundare*, cleanse you.

In fact, we were all of us born with sin; by living, we have all added to what we were born with, and have become more of the world than we were when we born of our parents. And where would we be if that man, who had no sin, did not come to forgive all sin? Because the Jews did not believe in this man, they deserved to hear, *You will die in your sins*; because in no way could you be without sin, having been born with sin; but he still says, "If you believe in me, even though you have been born with sin, you are not going to die in your sin."

So the entire misfortune of the Jews, then, was not having sin, but dying in sin. That is what every Christian should flee; for this reason a Christian runs to baptism;[12] for this reason those who are in danger because of sickness or for any other cause long for someone to come to their help; for this reason too a sucking child is brought by its mother's loving arms to the church, so that the child may not depart this life without baptism and thus die in the sin it was born with.[13] A most unhappy state, the wretched lot of those who heard from the mouth of Truth, *You will die in your sins*.

There is hope even for the worst of sinners, if many of those who crucified Christ came to believe, and were saved

7. However, he goes on to explain why this may happen to them: *In fact, if you do not believe that I am, you will die in your sins* (Jn 8:24). I believe, brothers and sisters, that in that crowd which was listening to the Lord, there were also people who were going to believe.[14] But that most severe sentence appeared to have been passed on them all, *You will die in your sin*, and, for that reason, appeared to take hope away, even from those who were going to believe. Some were filled with rage, others were fearful; or rather, they were not afraid, but were already in despair. He called them to hope, for, he added, "*If you do not believe that I am, you will die in your sins*. So if you do believe that I am, then, you will not die in your sins." Hope was restored to the desperate, an appeal was addressed to sleepers, in their hearts they were vigilant; thenceforth a great many believed, as the rest of this very gospel testifies.[15]

---

12. See Sermons 174, 7.8; 176, 2; 293, 10; 294, 18.
13. See Sermons 323, 3; 324; 393.
14. See Homilies 30, 1; 31, 9; Sermon 196, 4.
15. See Jn 8:30; 10:40-42.

After all, there were members of Christ there who had not yet attached themselves to the body of Christ, and, among that people by whom he was crucified, by whom he was hanged on the tree, by whom he was jeered at as he hung there, by whom he was wounded with a lance, by whom he was given gall and vinegar to drink, there were members of Christ for whom he said, *Father, forgive them, because they do not know what they are doing* (Lk 23:34). But, if the shedding of Christ's blood is forgiven, what sin could not be forgiven to someone who is converted? If hope was restored even to someone by whom Christ was slain, what murderer should despair?

As a result of that many came to believe; the blood of Christ was given them, so that they should drink that which would save them rather than be held guilty for shedding it; so who could despair? And if a thief was saved on the cross, a murderer not long before that, then accused, convicted, condemned, hanged and set free,[16] do not be surprised. He was condemned when he was convicted; but when he changed, he was set free. So then, among the people to whom the Lord was speaking, some were going to die in their sin; some too would believe in the one who was talking to them and be set free from all sin.

The mystery of I am

8. Pay close attention, however, to what Christ the Lord said, *If you do not believe that I am, you will die in your sins.* What is the meaning of, *If you do not believe that I am?* What is *I am* about? He did not add anything; and because he did not add anything, something great is being suggested. For you are expecting him to say what he was, and yet he did not say.

What were we expecting him to say? Perhaps *Unless you believe that I am* the Christ; *Unless you believe that I am* the Son of God; *Unless you believe that I am* the founder of the world; *Unless you believe that I am* the one who formed and reformed man, his creator and recreator, his maker and remaker. *Unless you believe that I am, you shall die in your sins.*

He says so much with *I am*, because that is also what God said to Moses: *I am who I am* (Ex 3:14). Is anyone capable of giving a fitting explanation of *I am?* Through his angel God was sending his servant Moses to deliver his

---

16. See Sermon 232, 6.

people from Egypt. You have read what you just heard, and you know the story; but still I will remind you of it. He was sending a frightened man, who was full of excuses, but ready to obey. So then, while looking for a way out, he said to God, who he realized was speaking to him through the angel, *If the people ask me, And who is the God that has sent you, what shall I say to them?* And the Lord said to him, *I am who I am*; and he repeated, *You shall say to the children of Israel, He who is has sent me to you.* (Ex 3:13-14) He did not then say, "I am God," or "I am the architect of the world," or "I am the creator of all things," or "I am the one who has multiplied the people to be freed," but only this, *I am who I am; and you shall say to the children of Israel, He who is*; he did not add, who is your God, who is the God of your ancestors, but all he said was this, *He who is has sent me to you.*

It was perhaps a lot for Moses, just as it is a lot for us, and, in fact, much more for us, to understand what was said: *I am who I am*, and, *He who is has sent me to you.* And even if Moses did grasp it, when would those to whom he was being sent grasp it? So then, the Lord put off explaining what humanity could not grasp, and added something that they could grasp; for, he added to it and said, *I am the God of Abraham, and the God of Isaac, and the God of Jacob* (Ex 3:15). This at least you are able to grasp; what mind, after all, could grasp *I am who I am?*

We must question the Lord, not argue with him

9. So what should I do, then? Will I dare to say anything about what was said, *I am who I am*, or rather about what you heard the Lord saying, *Unless you believe that I am, you will die in your sins*? With my abilities, small and almost non-existent, will I dare to explain what Christ the Lord said, *Unless you believe that I am?* Will I dare to question the Lord? Listening to me questioning, not arguing, seeking more than assuming I know the answer, leaning rather than teaching; and, in fact, in me or through me, you too should be raising questions. The Lord, who is everywhere, is also close by; may he listen to the affection of his questioners and give them understanding. After all, even if I may perchance grasp something, with what words can I convey what I grasp to your minds? What sound will suffice? What eloquence will be equal to the task? What intellect can understand, what skill can explain?

The changeable was and will be, never is;
only the Truth that abides unchanging truly is

10. Let me speak then to our Lord Jesus Christ; let me speak, and may he hear me. I believe he is present; I do not doubt it at all, for he said, *Behold, I am with you, until the end of time* (Mt 28:20).

O Lord our God, what is the meaning of your words, *Unless you believe that I am*? After all, of the things you have made, which of them *is* not? The sky, *is* it not? The earth, *is* it not? The things in heaven and on earth, *are* they not? Man himself, to whom you speak, *is* he not? *Is* the angel you send not? If all the things made by you *are*, what is this *being* that you have kept for yourself, and have not given to other things, so that you alone *are*? How, after all, am I to hear *I am who I am*? As if other things *are* not? And how am I to hear *Unless you believe that I am*? Were those, who were listening to you, not [in existence]? Even though they were sinners, they were human beings. So what am I to do then? Let him tell the heart what being *is*, let him say it within, let him speak within; let the inner self listen, let the mind grasp what true being *is*: always being in the same manner.

Anything, in fact, anything at all—I have begun to argue and stopped seeking! But perhaps I want to tell what I have heard; when I speak, may he give my hearing and yours joy[17]—so anything at all, no matter how distinguished or excellent, if it is changeable, truly *is* not. After all, no real, true being is not found where nonbeing is also found.[18] Whatever can change, in fact, once changed, is not what it was; if it is not what it was, a kind of death has taken place; something that what was there has been destroyed, and *is* not. The color black is dead on the grieving head of an old man; good looks are dead in the feeble, bent body of an old man; strength is dead in the body of an invalid; standing still is dead in the body of someone walking; walking is dead in the body of someone standing still; walking and standing still are dead in the body of someone lying down; speech is dead on the tongue of someone keeping quiet. Anything that changes and is what it was not, I see there a kind of life in

---

17. See Sermons 23, 1; 28, 1.
18. See *The Trinity* V, ii, 3; Sermon 6, 4.

what it is, and a kind of death in what it was. Finally when you ask about someone who has died, "Where is so-and-so?" the answer follows, "He has been."[19]

O Truth, who truly *are*! Because in all our acts and movements, and in absolutely every motion of any creature, I find two times, past and future. I look for the present, nothing stands still; what I have just said is no more, what I am about to say is not yet; what I have just done is no more, what I am about to do is not yet; the life I have lived is no more, the one I am going to live is not yet. I find past and future in every motion of things; in the Truth that abides I do not find any past and future, but only present, and imperishably so; something not to be found in anything created. Debate the way things change, you will find "was" and "will be"; think about God, you will find "is," where there can be no "was" and "will be."[20]

So then, in order that you might be, soar above time. But can anyone soar under his own power, on his own wings? Let him lift you up there who said to the Father, *It is my wish that where I am, they too might be with me* (Jn 17:24). And that is why, it seems to me, by promising us that we would not die in our sins, the Lord Jesus Christ said that in these words: *Unless you believe that I am* God, *you will die in your sins.* Well, thank God that he said, *Unless you believe,* and not, "Unless you understand"; who, after all, could ever understand it? Or did you really, because I dared to speak and because you seem to have understood, did you really grasp anything of such an unutterable mystery? So, if you do not grasp it, faith sets you free. That too is why the Lord did not say, "Unless you understand that I am," but said what they were capable of, *Unless you believe that I am, you shall die in your sins.*

Believe that I am the beginning

11. As for those who always have a taste for earthly things, always hearing and answering in carnal ways, what did they say to him? *Who are you?* In fact, when you said, *Unless you believe that I am*, you did not add what you were. Say who you are so that we may believe. He responded, *The*

---
19. *Fuit.* Was this an idiom of everyday Latin, the equivalent of English "He is no more"?
20. See Sermon 293E, 2.

beginning (Jn 8:25). That is what it is *to be*. The beginning cannot change; the beginning abides in itself and renews all things; the beginning is the one to whom it was said, *You though are the same, and your years will not run out* (Ps 101:28). "*The beginning*," he says, "*because I am also speaking to you* (Jn 8:25). Believe me to be the beginning, so as not to die in your sins." It was as though, in saying, "You are who?" they were saying, "What are we to believe you to be?" He answered, *The beginning*, that is, "Believe that I am the beginning."

In Greek, you see, a distinction is made which cannot be made in Latin. With the Greeks, in fact, "beginning" is in the feminine gender,[21] just as with us "law" is feminine, while with them it is masculine, just as "wisdom" is feminine both with us and with them. Thus, the manner of speech in different languages varies the gender of words, because in the things themselves you do not find gender. I mean, wisdom is not really a female, since Christ is the Wisdom of God, and the word "Christ" is masculine in gender, the word "wisdom" feminine.

So, when the Jews said, *Who are you?* he knew that some of them were going to believe, and that was why they said, *Who are you?* so as to know what they ought to believe him to be. Accordingly he answered, *The beginning*, not as if to say, "I am the beginning," but as if to say, "Believe me to be the beginning." As I said, this is quite clear in the Greek, where "beginning" is of the feminine gender.[22] It is as if he wanted to say he was the truth, saying to those who asked, *Who are you?* he would respond, "The truth," while it appears that the proper answer to the question, *Who are you?* would be "The truth," that is, "I am the truth."

---

21. Augustine did not need to say that "beginning" in Latin (*principium*) is neuter (a gender lacking in Greek).
22. Augustine really is tying himself up in knots! The point about the word's being feminine in Greek is that in the Greek text it is quite evident that it is in the accusative case, and that therefore it is, so Augustine wrongly thinks, the object of a verb; whereas in Latin, *principium* being neuter (not masculine, the distinction he brought in earlier purely and simply to muddy the waters!), there is no distinction with it between nominative and accusative. So Christ's saying in reply "The beginning" in the accusative case means he was answering the question (unspoken), "Who are we to believe you to be," not the question, "Who are you," to which the answer would normally be in the nominative case. He goes on to illustrate with the word "truth," feminine in Latin, where the distinction of cases is apparent.

In fact he was wrong about the Greek use of the accusative here, which is being used adverbially, "What I have been telling you from the beginning"; it is, however, a very peculiar phrase.

But his answer went deeper; as it seemed that by their question they really meant, "Since we have heard you say, *Unless you believe that I am*, what ought we to believe?" To this question, he answered, *The beginning*, as if to say, "Believe me to be the beginning." And he added, *because I am also talking to you*; that is, "because I have been made humble on your account, I have come down to these words." After all, if the Beginning as he really is had remained with the Father, and had not *taken the form of a slave* (Phil 2:7) and spoken to men as a man, how would they be able to believe him, seeing that weak human minds would be unable to hear the intelligible Word without the aid of a voice accessible to the senses? "Therefore," he says, "believe that I am the beginning; because, to help you believe, not only is that what I am, but I am also speaking to you."

But on this subject much remains to be spoken to you; and so may it please Your Graces that we keep what is left to give you, with his assistance, tomorrow.

Homily 39

On John 8:26-27[1]

The question of Christ's being the beginning, taken over from the previous sermon

1. The words of our Lord Jesus Christ—which he had with the Jews, read from today's holy gospel, adapting his language so that the blind would not see and believers would open their eyes—were these: *So then the Jews said, Who are you?* (Jn 8:25) They raised the question because the Lord had just said, *Unless you believe that I am, you will die in your sins* (Jn 8:24); hence, they asked him, *Who are you?* as if wanting to know whom they should believe in, to avoid dying in their sin. His answer to those who asked, *Who are you?* was, *The beginning, because I am also speaking to you* (Jn 8:25).

If the Lord called himself the beginning, one can also ask whether the Father too is the beginning. After all, if the Son, who has a Father, is the beginning, how much more readily can God the Father be understood to be the beginning, seeing that he has a Son whose Father he is, but does not have anyone from who he himself is! The Son, after all, is the Son of the Father, and the Father of course is the Father of the Son; but the Son is called God from God, the Son is called Light from Light; the Father is called Light, but he is not from Light, the Father is called God, but he is not from God.[2] So then, if God from God, Light from Light is the beginning, how much more readily is the beginning understood to be the Light from which is Light, God from whom is God! Therefore, it appears absurd, dearest friends, for us to call the Son the beginning and not to call the Father the beginning.

The problem of the three and the one

2. But what are we to do? Will there be two beginnings? We must be on our guard against saying this. Well, what then? If both the Father is the beginning and the Son is the beginning, how are they not two beginnings?

---

1. In all likelihood preached the day after Homily 38.
2. See Homilies 29, 5; 31, 4.

Notice how we call the Father God and the Son God, and yet we do not say two gods.[3] It is, after all, wicked to say two gods, wicked to say three gods; and yet the one that is the Father is not the Son; the one that is the Son is not the Father; while the Holy Spirit, Spirit of the Father and of the Son, is neither the Father nor the Son.

Therefore, even though—as Catholic ears have learned from the bosom of mother Church—the one who is Father is not Son, nor is the one who is Son the Father, nor is the Holy Spirit of the Father and of the Son either Father or Son, we do not say that there are three gods; if, however, questioned about any one of them, we have to profess that, no matter which of them we are asked about, that one is God.

The problem of the Trinity for unbelievers

3. All this appears to be absurd to those who measure the unfamiliar by what they are used to or measure things that cannot be seen by things that can, putting the creature on a par with the creator. For unbelievers do sometimes question us and say, "The one you call the Father, do you say he is God?"

We answer, "He is God."

"The one you call the Son, do you say he is God?"

We answer, "He is God."

"The one you call the Holy Spirit, do you say he is God?"

We answer, "He is God."

"So then," they say, "Father and Son and Holy Spirit are three gods?"

We answer, "No."

They are bewildered, because they have not been enlightened; they have a closed heart, because they do not have the key of faith. As for us then, brothers and sisters, guided by the faith which heals the eye of our heart, let us hold to what we understand without ambiguity; let us believe without hesitation what we do not understand; let us not pull away from the foundation of faith, so as to make sure we attain the fullness of perfection. The Father is God, the Son is God, the Holy Spirit is God; and for all that the Father is not who the Son is, nor is the Son who the Father is, nor is the Holy Spirit of the Father and the Spirit of the Son either the Father or the Son. A

---

3. See *The Trinity* V, 13, 14.

Trinity, one God; a Trinity, one eternity, one authority, one majesty; they are three, but not three gods.

Do not let any carping critic answer me, "Three what, then? I mean, if they are three, you are bound to say three what."

I answer, "Father and Son and Holy Spirit."

"Look," he says, "You have said three; but say clearly three what."

"On the contrary, do the counting yourself; in fact, I complete the number three when I say Father and Son and Holy Spirit. For the Father is God in reference to himself; he is Father in reference to the Son; the Son is God in reference to himself and, in reference to the Father, he is Son."[4]

Again no answer to the question: Three what?

4. You can get some idea of what I am saying by comparison with everyday things. Take a man and another man; if the first is a father, the second his son, he is a man with reference to himself, a father with reference to his son. And the son is a man with reference to himself, while his being a son is with reference to his father. The word "father," you see, is about a relationship, and "son" too is about a relationship; but these are two men. But God the Father is Father in relationship with the Son; and God the Son is Son in relationship with the Father; they are not, however, two gods in the same way as those are two men.

Why is it not the same in this case?

Because that is one case, this is another; because here it is a matter of the divine. In this case there is something inexpressible which cannot be put into words, such that it is about counting and it is not about counting.[5] Just notice, in fact, if it does not look like a matter of counting, Father and Son and Holy Spirit, a trinity. If three, three what? Counting does not work. Thus God neither refuses to be counted, nor submits to being counted.[6]

---

4. Augustine is reluctant to use the word "person." In *The Trinity* VII, 7-11, he discusses the Latin custom of saying three persons, and the Greek of saying three hypostases. He did not favor the use of "person" when speaking about the Trinity. See Berrouard's note in BA 73A, 475.
5. See *The Trinity* VII,4,7.
6. This phrase will be quoted by the Council of Toledo in 675 to counter the Arians who were dominant in the Iberian peninsula since the invasion of the Visigoths: *Haec sancta trinitas, quae unus et verus est Deus, nec recedit a numero, nec capitur numero.* I have translated *numerus* by "counting."

Because they are three, it looks like counting; if you ask three what, counting does not work. That is why it says, *Great is our Lord and great is his strength, and there is no counting his wisdom* (Ps 146:5). When you start thinking about it, you begin counting; when you have counted, you cannot say what you have counted. The Father is the Father, the Son is the Son, the Holy Spirit is the Holy Spirit.

What are these three, Father and Son and Holy Spirit? Three gods?
No.
Three almighties?
No.
Three creators of the world?
No.
So then, is the Father almighty?
Certainly he is almighty.
So then, is the Son also not almighty?
Certainly the Son too is almighty.
So then, is the Holy Spirit not almighty?
He too is almighty.
Three almighties, then?

No, only one almighty. You see, this number three only creeps into their relation to each other, not into what each is to oneself. Because God the Father is God with reference to himself, together with the Son and the Holy Spirit, they are not three gods; because he is almighty with reference to himself, together with the Son and the Holy Spirit, they are not three almighties; but because he is not Father with reference to himself but to the Son, and neither is the Son such with reference to himself but to the Father, and neither is the Holy Spirit such with reference to himself, in that he is called the Spirit of the Father and of the Son, I cannot say what they are three of, but only say Father and Son and Holy Spirit, one God, one almighty. Therefore one Beginning.

An illustration from Acts; so many believers, one soul, one heart in God

5. Accept something from the sacred scriptures, by which you may be able to grasp in some way what is being said. After our Lord Jesus Christ had risen, and had ascended into heaven when he wished, and, ten days

later, had sent from heaven the Holy Spirit, those who were together in one hall, filled with the Holy Spirit, began to speak in the languages of all nations. Terrified at the miracle, the Lord's murderers were goaded into sorrow; in sorrow they changed, and through change they believed; they were added to the body of the Lord, that is, to the number of the faithful, three thousand of them.[7] After another miracle, some five thousand more joined them; thus was formed a single, considerable people, in which all received the Holy Spirit who kindled spiritual love in them and bound them together as one by that charity and fervor of spirit. Thus people began, within the unity of that fellowship, to sell what they had and to lay the money at the feet of the apostles, for distribution to each according to each one's need.[8] And this is what scripture says about them, that *they had one soul and one heart in God* (Acts 4:32).[9]

So take note of this, brothers and sisters, and recognize there the mystery of the Trinity and how we can say that there is the Father, and there is the Son, and there is the Holy Spirit, and yet there is one God. Notice, they were so many thousands, but one heart; notice, they were so many thousands, but only one soul. But where? In God. How much more unity then in God himself! Am I wrong in my words when I say, "Two men two souls," or "Three men three souls," or "Many men many souls"? No, I am speaking correctly. Let them approach God; for all of them, there is one soul. If by approaching God many souls become one soul through charity, and many hearts one heart, what is the very fount of charity doing in the Father and the Son? In that way, is not the Trinity even more one God? After all, charity comes to us from there, from the Holy Spirit, as the apostle says, *The charity of God has been poured out in our hearts through the Holy Spirit who has been given to us* (Rom 5:5). If, therefore, *the charity of God is poured out in our hearts through the Holy Spirit who has been given us*, making many souls into one soul, many hearts into one heart, how much more are Father and Son and Holy Spirit one God, one Light, one Beginning?

---

7. See Acts 2:1-41.
8. See Acts 4:2-4; 32-35.
9. The final *in God* (*in Deum*) is not in any current Greek or Latin text; but Augustine always includes it in his quotation of this verse, most notably in his *Rule*. So it may have been in some local African variant of the text.

Christ not judging now, judging in the future

6. So let us listen then to the Beginning who is speaking to us. *I have many things*, he says, *to say and to judge about you* (Jn 8:26). You remember that he had said, *As for me, I do not judge anyone* (Jn 8:15); now he says, *I have many things to say and to judge about you*. But *I do not judge* is one thing, and *I have things to judge about* is another. *I do not judge* he said with reference to the present; he had come, after all, to save the world, not to judge the world.[10] But when he says, *I have many things to say and to judge about you*, he is referring to the judgment to come. That, you see, is why he ascended, so that he might come again to judge the living and the dead. Nobody will judge more justly than the one who was judged unjustly.

I have many things, he says, *to say and to judge about you; but the one who sent me is truthful* (Jn 8:26). Notice how glory is given to the Father by the co-equal Son. He is giving us an example, you see, and as it were speaking in our hearts: "O faithful man, if you listen to my gospel, the Lord your God is saying to you, 'Where I, the Word in the beginning, God with God, equal to the Father, coeternal with the Father, give glory to him whose Son I am, how is it that you behave so proudly toward him whose slave you are?'"[11]

Truth and truthfulness; which has priority?

7. *I have many things*, he says, *to say and to judge about you; but the one who sent me is truthful*, as though to say, "The reason I pass true judgments is that as Son of the Truthful One I am the Truth." The Father truthful, the Son truth; which do we think is greater? Let us search into, if we can, which one is greater, truthful or truth. Let us enquire about some other cases. Is a pious man worth more, or piety? Piety is worth more; being pious comes from piety, not piety from being pious. There can still be piety, after all, even if the one who was pious has become impious. He has lost piety, he has not deprived piety of anything. Then what about beautiful and beauty? Beauty is worth more than beautiful; it is beauty, after all, that makes you beautiful, not your being beautiful that makes beauty. Chaste and chastity? Chastity is worth more than being chaste. After all, if there were no such

---

10. See Jn 12:47; and Homily 36, 4, where Augustine discusses this text, and also gives an alternative explanation.
11. See Homilies 29, 8; 35, 4 for similar warnings against pride.

thing as chastity, you would not have anything to be chaste with; while if you did not want to be chaste, chastity would still remain undiminished.

So then, if piety is something more than being pious, beauty more than being beautiful, chastity more than being chaste, are we not going to say that truth is something more than being truthful? If we say this, we shall start saying that the Son is something more than the Father. After all, the Lord says as plainly as can be, *I am the way and the truth and the life* (Jn 14:6). So then, if the Son is Truth, what is the Father but what Truth itself says, *The one who sent me is truthful*? The Son Truth, the Father truthful; I am enquiring which is more than which, but what I find is equality. The truthful Father, you see, does not derive being truthful from a truth in which he participates, but from the Truth which he begot as a whole.

Some analogies to pinpoint the uniqueness of God

8. I see that this has to be explained more fully. And so as not to detain you too long, I will only treat the reading up to this point today. When I have finished what I want to say, with the help of God, the sermon will end. I said this to gain your full attention. Every soul, since it is something subject to change, and even though it is a magnificent creature, is still a creature. Even though it is better than the body, still it is something made. So then, every soul is subject to change; that is, in one moment it believes, in the next it does not believe; in one moment it wants something, in the next it does not; in one moment it is adulterous, in the next it is chaste; in one moment it is good, in the next it is bad; the soul is changeable. God however is what he is, which is why he kept as his own name *I am who I am* (Ex 3:14). In line with this, the Son says, *Unless you believe that I am* (Jn 8:14); also related is: *Who are you? The beginning.* (Jn 8:25)[12] God then is beyond change; the soul is changeable.

When the soul receives from God the wherewithal to be good, it becomes good by participation, like your eye sees by participation. Take the light away, in fact, and the eye does not see; by sharing in the light, the eye sees. Since the soul becomes good by sharing, if it changes and begins to be bad, the goodness which made it good through participation remains.

---

12. See Homily 38, 11.

In fact, it was good when it shared in goodness; when it changes for the worse, goodness remains as it was. If the soul draws away from it and becomes bad, the goodness is not diminished; if it returns and becomes good again, the goodness is not increased.

Your eyes become sharers in this light, and you see. Did you close your eyes? You have not diminished this light. Did you open them again? You have not increased this light. With this comparison, brothers and sisters, you understand that if the soul is pious, the piety in which it shares is in God; if the soul is chaste, the chastity in which it shares is in God; if the soul is good, the goodness in which it shares is in God; if the soul is truthful, the truth in which it shares is in God, and if the soul does not have a share in this truth, *everyone is a liar* (Ps 115:11); if *everyone is a liar*, no one is truthful of himself.

The Father, however, is truthful; he is truthful of himself, because he gave birth to Truth. It is one thing to say this man is truthful, because he has already learned the truth; it is quite another to say God is truthful because he gave birth to Truth. That then is how God is truthful: not by sharing in, but by giving birth to Truth. I can see you have understood, and I am delighted. Let that be enough for you today. I will comment on the rest when it pleases the Lord and as he will give.[13]

---

13. *Sicut donaverit* may mean according to the grace (French translation) or according to the light (Italian translation) of God, or it may refer to the interpretation that God will give. In any case, it suggests Augustine's openness to receive what God gives.

Homily 40

On John 8:28-32[1]

Introduction; John the eagle among the evangelists

1. Your Graces have already heard me say a great many things about the holy gospel according to John, which you see me holding in my hands, and which I have discussed as best I could with the help of God. I have most especially pointed out to you how this evangelist chose to talk about the divinity of the Lord, according to which he is equal to the Father as the only-begotten Son of God; for that reason John has been compared to an eagle. No bird, in fact, is said to fly at a greater height.[2] So then, listen with the closest attention to what comes next; I will discuss it according to what the Lord will give.

The implications of When you have lifted up the Son of Man, *etc.*

2. I have spoken to you about the previous reading, suggesting how we are to understand the Father as truthful and the Son as Truth.[3] But when the Lord Jesus had said, *The one who sent me is truthful* (Jn 8:26), the Jews did not realize that he was talking to them about the Father; and he went on to say to them what you have just heard when it was read: *When you have lifted up the Son of Man, then you will realize that I am, and that I do nothing of myself, but as the Father has taught me, that is what I speak* (Jn 8:28). Now what does this mean? All he seems to have said, in fact, is that after his passion they would come to realize who he was. So he undoubtedly saw some people there whom he already knew, whom he had chosen, along with the rest of the saints, before the foundation of the world, and who he knew would believe in him after his passion.

These are the ones whom I constantly bring to your attention and earnestly set before you as examples to imitate. For when the Holy Spirit was sent from above after the Lord's passion, resurrection and ascension, and when miracles were done in the name of the one whom the Jews had

---
1. Preached some days after Homily 39.
2. See Homily 36, 1.5.6.
3. See Homily 39, 7-8.

persecuted and despised as definitively dead, they were cut to the heart. Those who had killed him in their rage were changed and believed in him, and those had shed his blood in their rage drank him in faith. They were three thousand and five thousand[4] whom he saw there when he said, *When you have lifted up the Son of Man, then you will realize that I am*, as if to say, "I am putting off your knowing me so as to accomplish my passion; in your own time you will realize who I am."

Not that all those listening to him were going to believe at that time, that is, after the passion of the Lord; shortly afterwards, in fact, it says, *While he was saying this, many came to believe in him* (Jn 8:30); and the Son of Man had not yet been lifted up. This lifting up, of course, refers to his passion, not to his glorification; it refers to the cross, not to heaven; because he was also lifted up when he hung on the tree. But that lifting up was a humiliation. For he was then made *obedient unto death on a cross* (Phil 2:8). This had to be accomplished at the hands of those who were going to believe later on, to whom he says, *When you have lifted up the Son of Man, then you will realize that I am*. Why is this so, if not so that no one should despair, no matter what dreadful crime he had on his conscience, once he saw that the murder committed by those who killed Christ was forgiven them?[5]

A reminder of Sabellianism, and of how the full text here rules it out

3. So then, to acknowledge such people in that crowd, the Lord said, *When you have lifted up the Son of Man, then you will realize that I am*. You already know what *I am* means; that does not need to be repeated constantly, or this great matter may elicit boredom.[6] Remember the text, *I am who I am*, and *He who is has sent me* (Ex 3:14), and you will recognize the force of *then you will know that I am*. Yet the Father also is, and the Holy Spirit is; the whole Trinity shares in that very *is*.

But because the Lord was speaking as the Son, so as to avoid that his saying, *Then you will realize that I am*, might allow the error of the Sabellians, that is of the Patripassians, to creep in (I explained to you that this error is not to be held but to be avoided, that is, the error of those who

---

4. See Acts 2:41; 4:4.
5. Compare Homily 38, 7.
6. See Homilies 38, 8-10; 39, 8.

have said, "One and the same is the Father and the Son; they are two names for one reality") —so to warn us of this error, lest we should suppose that it referred to the Father, once he said, *Then you will realize that I am*, the Lord immediately added, *And I do nothing of myself, but as the Father has taught me, that is what I speak*. A Sabellian had already begun to rejoice at finding a basis for his error; as soon as he showed himself, as if in the dark, he was thwarted by the light of the next sentence. Did you think that he was the Father because he said, *I am*?[7] Listen to how he is the Son: *And I do nothing of myself*. What does that mean, *I do nothing of myself*? I am not from myself. The Son, after all, is God from the Father. The Father on the other hand is not God from the Son. The Son is God from God, while the Father is God, but not from God. The Son is light from light, while the Father is light, but not from light. The Son is, but there is one from whom he is, while the Father also is, but there is not one from whom he is.[8]

Avoid all mental idolatry in thinking about God

4. As for what he added, then, *As the Father has taught me, that is what I speak*, none of you, brothers and sisters, must let flesh-bound thoughts creep in. Human frailty, in fact, can only think in terms of what it is used to doing or hearing. So do not then put before your eyes, as it were, two men, one a father, the other a son, or see the father talking to the son, in the way you do when you say some words to your son, advising him and instructing him how he should speak, so that he can commit to memory whatever he has heard from you; when he has committed it to memory, may he utter it with his tongue, making distinct sounds in order to bring to other people's ears what he has perceived with his own. Do not think in that sort of way, or you will be fabricating idols in your heart.[9]

A human form, the outlines of a human figure, the shape of human flesh, those senses in full view, the stature and movements of a body, the role of the tongue, distinctions of sounds—do not think of these things in that Trinity, except for that which pertains to *the form of a slave* (Phil 2:7) which the only-begotten Son assumed when *the Word was made flesh*, so

---

7. Saying *I am* was apparently taught by the Sabellians as referring only to the God of the Exodus, to God the Father.
8. See Homilies 19, 13; 29, 5; 31, 4; 39, 1.
9. See Homilies 18, 5; 19, 1; 23, 8.

as *to take up residence among us* (Jn 1:14). There, O human weakness, I do not forbid you to think in terms familiar to you; in fact, I even require you to do so. If the faith in you is true, think that Christ is like that, but think of Christ as he was born of the Virgin Mary, not that he was born in that way of God the Father. He was a baby, he grew as a man, he walked as a man, he was hungry and thirsty as a man, he slept as a man, finally he suffered as a man, he was hanged on the tree, slain, and buried as a man. In the same form he rose again, in the same form he ascended into heaven before the eyes of his disciples, in the same form he will come again in judgment. The voice of angels, after all, asserts in the gospel, *He will return in the same way as you have seen him going into heaven* (Acts 1:11).

So then, whenever you think about the *form of a slave* in Christ, think of the human form, if faith is in you; but when you think, *In the beginning was the Word, and the Word was with God, and the Word was God* (Jn 1:1), let every human shape fade away from your heart; drive from your thoughts everything bounded by bodily limits, everything held in the confines of place, or spread in a mass, however vast; let any such figments vanish from your heart. Think, if you can, about the beauty of wisdom, let the beauty of justice occur to you. Is it a shape, a size, a color? It is none of these, and yet it is; for, if it were not, it would neither be loved nor rightly praised, nor when it is loved and praised would it be held in the heart nor in behavior. As it is, however, people do become wise; how would they become so if there were no such thing as wisdom? But, even more, O man, if you cannot see wisdom with the eyes of flesh, nor think about it with the imagination that thinks in physical ways, will you dare to introduce the shape of a human body to the wisdom of God?

The analogy of God the teacher within our minds;
so the Father teaching the Son is the same as his begetting him

5. So what are we to say then, brothers and sisters? How did the Father speak to the Son, since the Son said, *As the Father has taught me, that is what I speak*? Did he speak to him? When the Father was teaching the Son, did he use words in the way that you use them when you are teaching your son? How does he use words to the Word? What words, however many, are addressed to the unique Word? Did the Word of the Father have ears turned to the mouth of the Father? This is literal thinking; banish such ideas from your hearts.

Look at what I am saying; see whether you have understood what I said. I, of course, have been speaking and my words have been making sounds, and the sounds have struck your ears, and, through your sense of hearing, those sounds have conveyed my meaning to your heart, if you have understood. Suppose a Latin speaker has heard, but only heard, and not understood what I said. As regards the noises issuing from my mouth, the man who has not understood a word has received as big a share of them as all of you have; he has heard the same sounds, the same syllables have struck his ears, but they have not given birth to anything in his heart. Why not? Because he has not understood. But, if you have understood, how did you understand? I made sounds in your ears; am I the one who turned on a light in your heart?

If what I have said is true, and you have not only heard this truth but also understood it, then beyond doubt two things have happened there; distinguish then the hearing and the understanding. I am responsible for your hearing; who is responsible for your understanding? You heard because of me; through whom did you understand? I spoke to your ears so that you would hear; who spoke to your heart so that you would understand? Someone undoubtedly did something to your heart so that, as well as the noise of these words striking your ears, some truth would also enter your heart; someone has also spoken to your heart, but you do not see him; if you did understand, brothers and sisters, something was also spoken to your heart. Understanding is a gift from God;[10] who did this in your heart, if you have understood? The one to whom the psalm says, *Give me understanding, so that I may learn your commandments* (Ps 118:73).

For example, the bishop has been talking.

Someone asks, "What has he been saying?"

You tell him what he has been saying, and you add, "What he said is true."

Then the other person who did not understand says, "Well, what did he say?" or "What is it that you are praising him for?" They both heard me, I spoke to both of them, but God only spoke to one of them—if it is permissible to compare little things with great, because what are we in comparison with him?

Still God does something in us, I do not know what, in a spiritual, non-material way; it is neither a sound to strike the ears, nor a color to be

---

10. For this doctrine of God the teacher within see Sermon 153, 1—and many other passages in Augustine's works.

distinguished by the eyes, nor a smell to be picked up by the nostrils, nor a flavor to be judged by the palate, nor something hard or soft to be perceived by touching it; all the same, it is something that is easy to perceive and impossible to explain. So then, if God, as I started to say, speaks in our hearts without a sound, how does he speak to his Son? This then is the way, brothers and sisters, this is the way you should think, as best you can, if, as I said, it is permissible to compare little things somehow or other with great things; this is how you should think. The Father spoke to the Son in a non-material way, because the Father gave birth to the Son in a non-material way.

Nor did he teach him as if he had begotten him as uneducated; but having taught him is the same as having begotten him as already learnéd; and so *the Father has taught me* means the same as "the Father has begotten me already understanding." If, after all (few people understand this), the nature of truth is simple,[11] being for the Son is the same as knowing. So he receives his knowing from the one from whom he receives his being, and not first his being from him and afterwards his knowing. But just as the Father gave him being by begetting him, so also by begetting him he gave him knowing; because for the simple nature of truth, as it has been said, being and knowing are not different things, but one and the same.

The Father and the Son always together

6. This one, then, taught by the Father, said to the Jews, adding to the previous phrase, *And the one who sent me is with me* (Jn 8:29). He had already said this, but he reminds us insistently of an important truth: *He sent me and is with me.* So if he is with you, O Lord, one of you was not sent by the other, but you both came.

And yet, while they are both together, one was sent, the other did the sending, because the mission is the incarnation, and that incarnation is of the Son alone, not also of the Father.[12] And so the Father sent the Son, but did not separate from the Son. After all, it cannot be said that the Father was

---

11. Not of course in the ordinary sense of simple meaning easy, but in the sense of not complex, not consisting of parts. The absolute simplicity of the divine being may be said to be the foundation of all sound theology.
12. See Homily 23, 13. This is an earlier, less profound interpretation of the mission of the Son by the Father. Later on, when he had a deeper, more accurate understanding of the Arian doctrine, Augustine will identify the Father's mission of the Son with his begetting of the Son—without denying its identity with the Son's incarnation. This more mature view will see the incarnation

not where he sent the Son to; where, in fact, is the one who made all things not found? Where is the one who said, *Do I not fill heaven and earth?* (Jer 23:24) not found? Is it perhaps that the Father is everywhere, and the Son is not everywhere? Listen to the evangelist: *He was in the world, and the world was made through him* (Jn 1:10).

"So then," he says, "*the one who sent me*, on whose paternal authority, as it were, I became flesh, *is with me, he has not abandoned me.* Why has he not abandoned me? *He has not abandoned me to myself alone, because I for my part always do what is pleasing to him.*" (Jn 8:29). This equality exists always, not after some beginning, but without beginning, without ending. The begetting of God, after all, does not have a beginning in time, because all times were made through the begotten one.[13]

Appeal to any Arians present to believe according to orthodox faith

7. *Since he spoke in this way, many came to believe in him* (Jn 8:30). O would that many of those who used to think differently might, by my words, understand and come to believe in him! Perhaps there are, in fact, some Arians in this crowd. I do not dare suspect that some Sabellians may be here, those who say that the Father is who the Son is; that heresy is much too old, and it has gradually been gutted. The heresy of the Arians, however, still seems to have a little life, like the movements of a rotting corpse, or, at least, like the movements of a man giving up the ghost. Those few who are left need to be freed, as indeed many already have been. Indeed, this city used not to have any at all, but after the arrival of many immigrants, some Arians also came here.[14] There you are then, *since the Lord spoke in this way, many came to believe in him*; and here too, may the Arians, by my words, come to believe—not in me, but with me!

---

as the visible "sacrament" of the eternal generation of the Son by the Father; the temporal sending thus reveals the eternal sending.
13. See Homily 38, 4; *The Trinity* XV, 26, 47.
14. Many immigrants went to North Africa after the invasion of Italy by the Visigoths and their sack of Rome under Alaric in 410. Augustine may also be suggesting that some Arians also came, not fleeing from the Goths, who were all Arians, but from a more rigorous enforcement of imperial laws in Italy.

The effects of faith; illustrative comparisons

8. *So then, the Lord was saying to those Jews who had come to believe in him, If you abide in my word* (Jn 8:31). You will abide because you have been initiated, because you have begun to be there. *If you abide*, that is, if you abide in the faith which has begun to be in you who believe, where will you get to? Notice what kind of beginning and where it leads. You loved the foundation,[15] pay attention to the summit, and, on the basis of this humility, seek other heights.[16] Faith, in fact, has a humble quality; knowledge and immortality and eternity have no humble qualities, but have qualities of exaltation: upraising, a lack of defect, eternal stability, no hostile assault by the enemy, no fear of failure.

What begins from faith is great indeed, but it is disdained. Those who have no expertise usually think little of the foundation of a building. A deep hole is dug, stones are randomly thrown in, there is no polishing, no evident beauty, just as there is no evident beauty in the roots of a tree; nonetheless, everything you enjoy about a tree has grown up from its roots.[17] But you see the roots and take no pleasure; you see the tree and are lost in admiration. Fool, what you admire grew from what you take no pleasure in.

The faith of believers seems to be a small thing; you have no scale to weigh it. So listen to where it reaches, and notice how great it is—just as the Lord says in another place, *If you have faith like a grain of mustard seed* (Lk 17:6). What could be more insignificant, what more potent? What is more petty, what is more all-embracing? So then, *You too*, he says, *if you abide in my word*, in which you have come to believe, where will that lead you? *You will really be my disciples.* And what good will that do us? *And you shall know the truth.* (Jn 8:31-32)

The reward of faith, seeing face to face

9. What is he promising to believers, brothers and sisters? *And you shall know the truth.* Well, so what? Did they not know it when the Lord was talking to them? If they did not know it, how did they come to believe? But

---

15. Faith is the *fundamentum* of the Christian life (see Homily 39, 3) and note 69 in BA 73A, 318.
16. Augustine appears to be recommending a kind of examination of conscience as the basis for progress, that is, be honest about the humble quality of your achievements: the summit is still far; then reach further.
17. For these comparisons see Homilies 1, 4; 25, 3; 28, 5; Sermons 69, 2; 362, 8.

they did not believe because they knew, they believed in order to know. We believe, you see, in order to know, we do not know in order to believe.[18] What we are going to know, after all, *eye has not seen, nor has ear heard, nor has it entered into the heart of man* (1 Cor 2:9). What is faith, after all, but believing what you cannot see?

So faith is believing what you cannot see; truth is seeing what you have believed, just as he says somewhere.[19] That is why the Lord first walked around on earth so as to draw out faith. He was a man, he humbled himself. He was seen by everyone, but he was not known by everyone; he was rejected by many, slain by the mob, mourned by a few. But still he was not recognized for what he was even by those who mourned him.[20] All this was, as it were, the beginning of the outlines of faith and of its future structure. The Lord pays attention to this himself, saying in some place or other, *Those who love me keep my commandments; and those who love me will be loved by my Father, and I will love them and show myself to them* (Jn 14:21). Those who were listening to him could already see him, of course; and yet he was promising them the sight of himself, if they loved him.[21]

So here too, *You shall know the truth.*

Well, so what? Is not what you have been saying the truth?

Yes, it is the truth, but still as believed, not yet as seen. If you remain in what you believe, you will attain to what is to be seen. That is why John himself, the holy evangelist, says in his letter, *Beloved*, he says, *we are children of God, and it has not yet appeared what we shall be.* We already are, and there is something we shall be. What more shall we be than what we are? Listen: *It has not yet appeared what we shall be; we know that when he appears, we shall be like him.*

Why?

Because we shall see him as he is. (1 Jn 3:2)

A magnificent promise, but it is the reward of faith. You are asking for the reward; let the work be done first.[22] If you believe, demand the reward of faith; if you do not believe, though, how can you have the cheek to ask

---

18. See Homilies 19, 15; 27, 7.9; 29, 6; 36, 7.
19. An allusion, possibly, to Jn 11:40. See also Sermons 33A, 1; 43, 1; 97A, 2; 126, 1-5; 127, 1; 235, 3-4.
20. See Sermons 232, 2; 234, 2; 236, 2; 237, 1; 244, 3.
21. See Homilies 19, 18; 21, 15.
22. See Homily 25, 12 where Augustine explains that the work which earns this reward is faith working through love (Gal 5:6).

for the reward of faith? So then, *if you abide in my word, you will really be my disciples*, so that you may contemplate the truth as it is; not conveyed by the sound of words, but by the brilliance of light, when God will satisfy us, as we read in the psalm, *The light of your countenance has been imprinted on us, Lord* (Ps 4:6). We are God's coinage, coins that have gone astray from the treasury. What had been stamped on us has worn off because of our straying; someone has come who will do it over, because he had done it in the first place. He too is looking for his money, just as Caesar looks for his. That is why he says, *Pay back to Caesar the things that are Caesar's, and to God the things that are God's* (Mk 12:17). To Caesar money, to God yourselves. So that then is when truth will be stamped on us.

Appeal to us all to love God more than money

10. What am I to say to Your Graces? Oh, if only our heart were sighing in some way for that inexpressible glory! Oh, if only we were groaning at our wandering and were not so in love with this age, and were constantly knocking with a devoted mind at the door of the one who called us! Yearning is the bosom of the heart; we shall understand if we extend our yearning as far as we can. This is what the divine scriptures do for us, what the assembly of the people[23] does for us, what the celebration of the sacraments, holy baptism, hymns in praise of God, and my own preaching do for us; all this yearning is not only sown and grows in us, but it also increases to such a capacity that it is ready to welcome *what eye has not seen, nor has ear heard, nor has it entered the heart of man.*

But love with me. He who loves God does not have much love for money. And I have probed your weakness; I did not dare to say, "He does not love money," but "He does not love money much"—as if money should be loved, but not much. Oh, if only we were to love God worthily, we would not love money at all! Money for you will be a means for this journey, not a stimulus to greed; something to use when needed, not to delight in pleasure. Love God, if what you heard and praise has had an effect on you. Make use of the world, do not be taken in by the world. You

---

23. *Congregatio populorum*: this has overtones which refer to all the gatherings in the Church, all over the world.

entered the world, you are making a journey, you came intending to leave, not to stay; you are a wayfarer; this life is a wayside inn. Use money in the way a traveler at a wayside inn uses the table, the cups, the pitcher, the bed —intending to leave, not to stay.[24]

If you would be like that, lift up your heart, you who are able to do so, and listen to me; if you would be like that, you will attain to his promises. It will not cost you very much, because the hand of the one who called you is generous. He has called, let us call. Let us say to him, "You have called us, we are calling upon you; see, we have listened to you calling us; listen to us calling upon you, lead us to what you have promised, complete what you have begun. Do not abandon your gifts, do not abandon your field, make sure your seedlings enter your barn." Trials abound in the world, but the one who created the world is great; trials abound, but he does not fail who places his hope in that one in whom there is no failing.

Conclusion; real freedom and slavery to be discussed on another day

11. The reason I have been urging all this on you, brothers and sisters, is that the freedom of which our Lord Jesus Christ is speaking is not of this age. Notice what he added: *You will truly be my disciples, and you will know the truth, and the truth will set you free* (Jn 8:31-32). What is the meaning of *will set you free*? Will make you free people.[25] In any case the literal-minded Jews and those who judge according to the flesh—not the ones who had come to believe, but those in that crowd who did not believe—thought they were being insulted because he said to them, *The truth will set you free*. They were indignant at being thought of as slaves. Yet, they truly were slaves. And he explained to them what slavery was and what the future freedom he promised them would be. But to carry on the discussion of this freedom and that slavery today would take too much time.

---

24. See Sermon 177, 2.
25. As opposed to slaves; see Homily 41, 1.

www.ingramcontent.com/pod-product-compliance
Lightning Source LLC
Chambersburg PA
CBHW030102010526
44116CB00005B/58